THE ART OF THE CORPORATE DEAL

FOURTH EDITION

THE **ART** OF THE CORPORATE DEAL

FOURTH EDITION

BARRY D. LIPSON

KC, JD, LLM

UNIVERSITY OF TORONTO PRESS

Toronto Buffalo London

Irwin Law
An imprint of University of Toronto Press
Toronto Buffalo London
utorontopress.com
Printed in Canada

ISBN 978-1-5522-1721-4 (paper)   ISBN 978-1-5522-1722-1 (PDF)

Library and Archives Canada Cataloguing in Publication

Title: The art of the corporate deal / Barry D. Lipson, KC, LLB, LLM.
Names: Lipson, Barry, 1936– author.
Description: Fourth edition. | Includes index.
Identifiers: Canadiana (print) 20230596312 | Canadiana (ebook) 20230596339 |
    ISBN 9781552217214 (softcover) | ISBN 9781552217221 (PDF)
Subjects: LCSH: Business enterprises—Purchasing. | LCSH: Business enterprises—
    Valuation. | LCSH: Negotiation in business.
Classification: LCC HD1393.25 .L56 2024 | DDC 658.1/6—dc23

Cover design: Val Cooke

We wish to acknowledge the land on which the University of Toronto Press operates. This land is the traditional territory of the Wendat, the Anishnaabeg, the Haudenosaunee, the Métis, and the Mississaugas of the Credit First Nation.

University of Toronto Press acknowledges the financial support of the Government of Canada and the Ontario Arts Council, an agency of the Government of Ontario, for its publishing activities.

For Jared, Cole, Benjamin, and Julie.
The dearest things that I know are what they are.

Summary Table of Contents

Detailed Table of Contents

Preface

The first edition of this book, written in 2000, stated that its purpose was to provide a measure of guidance for the lawyer, accountant, or other professional who may be engaged in the small or middle-market company sector of mergers and acquisitions.

Conventional wisdom today is that it is easier and faster to acquire additional sales and profits through merger or acquisition than it is to build those sales or profits from within. Conventional wisdom notwithstanding, the statistical fact remains that the attempt to create additional value by merger or acquisition is more likely to fail than to succeed. The primary reason is that the buyer paid too much for the seller's company. To the extent that the reason may be that simple, Part 1 of this book directs the reader's attention back to the fundamentals by which to value the company that has been targeted for a merger or acquisition.

There may be many reasons why a buyer overpaid for a seller's company. However, for a buyer not to do so, it is necessary that the buyer be aware that he[1] is overpaying. That is the objective of the material contained in Part 1 of this book.

---

[1] Throughout this text the masculine pronoun has been used for consistency in style only and should be interpreted to include all genders.

Part 1 of the text contains frequent references to the "risk-free rate," and to the "market-risk premium rate." The risk-free rate refers to a security for which there is a total absence of risk. Canada government-insured bonds and treasury bills backed by the credit of the Canadian government would be considered risk free and would therefore attract a risk-free rate. In the first edition of this book the risk-free rate was stated to be 6 percent. In the second edition the rate had moved down to about 2 percent. During the writing of this, the most current edition of the book, the rate began a continual decline due to economic conditions and COVID-19 factors and continues to fluctuate at the time of publication. The decision has been made to leave the risk-free rate as stated in the prior edition and caution the reader that when using any template format, the methodology of which is unchanging and valid, they should determine the daily published Canadian government bond rate.

The market-risk premium rate refers to the difference between the risk-free rate and the required rate of return when an element of risk is present. The market-risk premium rate is the reward or inducement for taking the risk that one assumes in any particular transaction. In the first edition of this book, that rate was stated to be 8 percent to 10 percent over the risk-free rate. Polls at the end of the twentieth century indicated that investors expected stocks to gain upwards of 15 percent per year over an extended period. That optimism no longer prevails. The rate often quoted now is around 6 percent to 7 percent return on equity. This rate also fluctuates, and again the decision has been made to leave the rate as stated in the prior edition but again to caution the reader to check the market-risk premium rate with any of the market advisory firms who quote the market-risk premium rate for any and all manner of investments. Again, the methodology shown in the templates is constant and may freely be adopted.

Having determined the value of the seller's company, the methodology by which to acquire that company is the subject of Part 2 of the book. Successful mergers and acquisitions are less a science than a successful process by which the objectives of both the buyer and the seller are identified and addressed in a fair and balanced manner. The process is somewhat akin to an art in that the buyer, as artist, combines financial creativity and negotiating skills to achieve the objectives and goals of both the buyer and the seller.

Finally, the parties, having struggled their way through lengthy and exhausting negotiations, are often tired and lose the ability to concentrate on wordy, complex acquisition agreements. Therefore, Part 3 of the book is my attempt at instructing the reader on the form and content of the agreement that is intended to reflect the deal the parties believe they have made.

Conspicuously absent from the text of Part 1 is a method by which to value new technology companies. I have deliberately avoided doing so because little or no regard is paid to traditional methods of valuation for companies engaged in e-commerce technology. Take, for example, the 2012 purchase for $1 billion by Facebook (an internet creation of recent vintage and a staggering valuation) of Instagram, a company with a dozen employees and no revenue. For that money, Facebook could have bought the New York Times, Office Depot, or Cooper Tire & Rubber, to name a few companies with a similar valuation.

What determines the value of these companies? If the market value seems unreal, it is, in a sense, unreal. Often, tech companies are trading on multiples of 1,000 times nothing. An explanation may lie in the market demand for any e-commerce product. The perception is that everyone today wants to be e-commerce enabled, and since there is a limited supply of e-service offerings in the sector, the demand creates values in the market that are commonly based on multiples of 10 to 20 times projected revenues. The determination of the multiple will to a great extent depend on the quality of the management of the company, the innovation, and the anticipated need for the technology that the company offers, and the projected time frame within which to achieve the revenues that are needed to generate the earnings that are expected.

Today, anywhere from 40 percent to 90 percent of a company's market value comes from its "intangibles," a category that includes everything from patents and copyrights to the way the company is run and the brand premium and "goodwill" it commands among its customers. Not all these intangibles can be easily measured. Hence the wide disparity in determining the market value of a company whose value is based on something other than its net operating income and proven past performance. If the assessment that is made of the risk of failing to achieve the projected earnings is made too low, the rate at which to discount those earnings will be too low, which in turn will generate an unrealistic value for the company. Hence, traditional models used in the valuation of "old economy companies" clearly demonstrate that the current price/earnings ratios of tech companies are manifestly excessive.

Acknowledgements

I have been blessed for most of my life by being able to surround myself with people who were wiser, and far more able and knowledgeable than I am. The presence of my father and my wife has enabled me to be a better son, husband, and father. In the same way, my relationship over the years with law partners as able as Jack Norman, Robert Macaulay, and Richard Shibley has made me a far better lawyer than I would otherwise have been.

To somewhat narrow the focus on those whose unseen contributions to this book have been significant, I must thank my son, the MBA, for his insight and his comments.

Introduction

The purchase of an income-producing asset (which includes the shares or assets of a corporation, commercial realty, an unincorporated business, a lease, or any money market security such as corporate or government bonds and notes) is essentially a trading ("investing") of present dollars ("capital") in the expectation of receiving both the return of the invested dollars ("return *of* capital") and a profit thereon ("return *on* capital").

It is a two-step process known as the income capitalization approach to value that determines the *value* of any income-producing asset. First, determine the projected future cash flow of the asset; second, *capitalize* that cash flow by a factor that includes an appropriate risk premium that the expected cash flow will not be achieved. This method of determining value applies to all assets that produce income.

Although determining the value of a corporation's shares or assets is the most complex of all income-producing assets, the income capitalization method is the method commonly used by professional consultants to determine value in the most complex mergers or acquisitions just as it is to determine the value of any simple money market security.

The contents of this book focus primarily on the corporation, because determining the value of its shares and assets is the most complex of all income-producing assets. Nevertheless, the purpose of the introductory chapter is to inform the reader of the principles or factors that are at play in determining the value of all assets that produce income.

A. DETERMINING AN ASSET'S VALUE BASED ON ITS PROJECTED INCOME

The simple investment premise is as follows: the greater the projected income, the greater the value of the asset. The certainty of receiving that projected income is what makes the investment attractive. To the extent to which there is a degree of uncertainty, the appropriate rate of return must be augmented by a risk premium. To a buyer, risk is the uncertainty of achieving the projected income, in which case a greater reward, in the form of a higher rate of return, is required in exchange for accepting the greater risk.

Once the potential cash flow of the asset is determined, the value of the asset is determined by converting ("capitalizing") that cash flow into a present value by applying an appropriate conversion or capitalization rate to the income figure, and by converting the future cash flow to a present value through *discounting*. These two concepts, capitalizing cash flow and discounting to achieve present value of the cash flow, are the tools by which the value of the asset is determined.

B. CAPITALIZATION: CHOOSING THE PROPER RATE OF RETURN

The rate of return used to convert cash flow into value must be a rate of return that is attractive to the buyer. The rate is influenced by the degree of risk perceived by the buyer, the market's view of future inflation, and the prospective rates of return on alternate investment opportunities.

Because the rates of return used in the capitalization of income are all prospective rates, the market's perception of the risk of change is particularly important, and consequently rate selection requires judgment and knowledge of *prevailing market attitudes and economic indicators*.

The capitalization rate (the "cap rate"), determined by the factors described in the preceding paragraphs, when divided into 100 creates a "factor," and when the cash flow of the asset is multiplied by that factor, the result is the asset's capitalized value (the "cap value"). As the cap rate increases, the asset's cap value reduces.

By way of illustration, if the projected income flow of the asset were $300,000, a cap rate of 7 would create a cap value of $4.29K (100 divided by 7 = a factor of 14.29 x the cash flow). However, if the cap rate were 8, the asset's cap value would be reduced to $3.75K (100 divided by 8 = a factor of 12.25 x the cash flow).

C. DISCOUNTING: THE PRESENT WORTH OF FUTURE INCOME

Since the return is based on the receipt of future dollars (and inasmuch as the prospect of receiving an amount in two years is not as valuable as receiving the same amount in one year), the present worth of a future benefit, a concept known as the time value of money, will affect the return that the buyer expects.

A future benefit (a payment) is discounted to its present value by calculating the amount that it would grow, if invested today, with compound interest, at a satisfactory rate to equal the future payment. The discount theory is based on the economic fact that present money, because of its earning potential, commands a premium over future money.

By way of illustration, $3,312.12 invested today at 8 percent interest will pay an annuity of $1,000 for four years, at the end of which period the said amount will have been exhausted. The difference between the $4,000 in total annual payments and the $3,312.12 is the discount. Obviously, the discount will vary as the assumed interest rate varies.

By way of further illustration, the present value of $115 that is due to be received one year from now is $100 when the discount rate applicable thereto is 15 percent per annum. That is the amount that if invested now will grow to $115 in one year with compound interest at the rate of 15 percent per annum.

D. THE RISK-FREE INVESTMENT

All forms of investment involve striking a balance between risk and the expected returns. Every investment carries some level of risk. However, all other considerations aside, assuming greater risk warrants receiving a greater return, and conversely little or no risk warrants receiving a lower return.

The buyer always needs a benchmark by which to measure the return he may reasonably expect. That benchmark is available to him when he turns to an acknowledged risk-free investment, to wit, Canadian government bonds and treasury notes, which are risk free because the Canadian government has never defaulted on the repayment of its debt. The risk-free rate paid on short-term Canadian debt varies from day to day and is publicly quoted. The maturity dates of government debt will affect the rates paid on each debt because the present worth of future payouts is dependent on the number of days, months, and years prior to maturity for the reasons set forth above in Section C.

Accordingly, the return that a buyer expects on an investment that is not risk free must exceed the return offered by the risk-free marketable bonds and treasury notes of the Canadian government by a percentage increase commensurate with the perceived magnitude of the risk to which the buyer's capital will be exposed. Simply stated, the greater the risk, the greater the expected rate of return.

E. INCOME CAPITALIZATION METHODS

Direct capitalization and *yield capitalization* are both used in the income capitalization approach to value. These two methods are based on different measures of expected earnings and are also based on different assumptions.

1) Direct Capitalization

This method is used to convert an estimate of a single year's income expectancy into an indication of value on just one direct step either by dividing the income estimate by an appropriate cap rate or by multiplying the income estimate by an appropriate factor.

By way of illustration, assume that the single year's income expectation is $100,000 and the appropriate cap rate is 8 percent (.08) and the appropriate factor is 12.5. The value of the asset in either case is $1,250,000.

In direct capitalization, the income expectancy is frequently the anticipated income for the following year, and the rate or the factor selected was derived using money market data rates. To determine the cap rate on the basis of the sale price being asked by the seller, divide the sale price by the asset's current annual net income or pre-tax cash flow.

When the cap rate is applied to the income produced by the asset, the estimated present value must represent a price that would allow the buyer to earn a rate of return on the capital invested (a return on capital) in addition to a recovery of the capital invested (a return of capital). Therefore, the cap rate selected and applied to the value of the asset must reflect the way that the capital is expected to be recovered. But direct capitalization does not explicitly differentiate between the return on and the return of capital, because the buyer's assumptions are not specified. The selected rate is simply assumed to be sufficiently attractive to satisfy the typical buyer. It is only the yield capitalization that deals with both the return of and the return on capital.

2) Yield Capitalization

This method, also known as the "discounted cash flow analysis," differs from direct capitalization in that it attempts to estimate the return to the buyer over the entire projected holding period (not just the first year, as in the case of direct capitalization).

In the application of this method, the buyer seeks a value for the asset that he intends to hold for a predetermined period of time. The buyer prepares a projection of the net operating income for that period. In addition, an estimate is made of what the selling price (the "reversion") will be after the period ends. This is usually done by direct capitalization. Finally, each year's net operating income plus the reversion are discounted to present value by multiplying each figure by an appropriate present value discount rate.

Direct capitalization is the more conservative method of capitalization because it looks only at the asset's current net operating income and ignores potential appreciation and is far less speculative because the longer holding period tends to create uncertainty.

Although discount rates may vary among buyers, one rule does hold true—during inflationary periods, discount rates do move higher to reflect uncertainty about the future buying power of money.

At the time of writing, the current omnipresence of inflation is reflected in the risk-free rate of government bonds, which range from 4.0 percent to 4.5 percent depending on maturity. In the years prior to inflation, the risk-free rate for the same bonds were as low as 1.0 percent to 1.5 percent.

F.   RISK ASSESSMENT: DETERMINING THE RISK PREMIUM

Is the expected event a probability or merely a possibility? The difference may be said to be the degree of uncertainty. Some would say that there is virtually no difference between certainty and a high degree of probability. They would be wrong. Probabilities are derived from assumptions whose relevance and validity are themselves uncertain. Assessing the degree of risk is neither an art nor a science. Forecasting the probability that a foreseen event will occur or that an unforeseen event will not occur is made more difficult depending on the time frame of the projected holding period. The longer the time frame, the greater the risk that the unforeseen may occur or that the foreseen event will not occur.

The cap rate, used to determine value, includes a risk premium that is intended to compensate the buyer for the degree of risk he is assuming. Chapter 6 of this book is entitled "Risk Assessment." It is that chapter wherein I have attempted to offer some guidance on determining the magnitude of the risk that is being undertaken.

VALUING THE SELLER'S COMPANY

Chapter 1: **Basic Thoughts and Principles**

A. DETERMINING HOW MUCH A PRIVATE COMPANY IS WORTH

Part 1 of this work is dedicated to answering the question, "How much is a private company worth?"

There are several ways by which to merely *estimate* the value of a private company. These methods and a detailed critique thereof are set forth in Chapter 2. However, these methods are at best simplistic and frequently misleading. The most common of these methods is based on a multiple of sales. www.bizstats.com provides a rule of thumb page listing various industrial categories, and by selecting the private company category, a percentage of sales is said to represent the private company value. For example, in the case of a supermarket grocery chain, the rule of thumb valuation is 15 percent of annual sales plus inventory. Presumably, if the company had $500 million in annual sales, the company would be worth $75 million, plus the value of the inventory.

Another rule of thumb approach that is commonly used is to review publicly traded companies in the same industry with comparable revenues and numbers of employees. Having determined the company's total market capitalization, it would be discounted in the case of a private company because of its illiquidity and borrowing costs.

Inc. magazine also provides an annually updated business valuation table that purports to determine the estimate of a company's value. However, as stated earlier, since these methods often yield a false valuation, the purpose of Part 1 is to aid in the determination of the company's "intrinsic value" and, upon achieving that determination, a market value may be said to be the premium that a buyer is prepared to pay to acquire the company.

B.   WHAT CONSTITUTES MONETARY VALUE?

Monetary value is created by the buyer's expectation of monetary benefits to be derived in the future. Value may then be defined as the present worth to the buyer of those future benefits.

Because the *need* for those future benefits may vary from buyer to buyer, the *value* of those benefits may also vary from buyer to buyer. For example, if the benefit that will be conferred on a buyer by the purchase of or the merger with the seller's company is the acquisition of a technology that it sorely needs, the value of the seller's company will be far greater to the buyer than if that buyer already possesses that technology. Therefore, as a basic premise, the seller's company will not have the same value to all buyers. If you like, beauty will very much be in the eyes of the beholding buyer. The benefits to be derived by a buyer must be *monetary* in nature. The buyer is essentially trading present dollars in the expectation of receiving future dollars. If those benefits are not initially in the form of future potential earnings, then they must be capable of being converted into earnings. For example, if the benefit is the acquisition of a technology, the use of that technology must be one that will enhance revenue, or generate a cost saving; in either case, it augments the overall earnings of the buyer.

Since the prospect of receiving $1 in two years is less valuable than the $1 that may be received in one year, the *present worth* to the buyer of a future benefit is a factor that cannot be ignored. This concept is known as the time value of money, without regard for which the buyer cannot properly assess the value of a future benefit.

C. WHAT CONSTITUTES INTRINSIC VALUE?

The basic value of a company, its *intrinsic value*, is based primarily on the present worth of its expected future cash flow.[1] It is a value independent of any anticipated benefits that may be derived by a merger or acquisition. It is a value based on the company continuing under the current management with the revenue growth and the projected performance of improvements, if any, that have been validly forecast in its projected cash flow.

When the definition of intrinsic value refers to *cash flow*, a distinction is intended to be drawn between *earnings* and cash flow. Accounting systems rely on a balance sheet and an income statement, both of which emphasize the earnings of the company. Earnings, however, can be calculated in various ways, all of which comply with accounting conventions and financial reporting requirements. For example, the various treatments of depreciation, inventory, goodwill, and research and development will significantly affect the reported earnings of a company. While earnings, to a great extent, may be said to be subjective, the cash flow of a company is not.

When the definition of intrinsic value refers to the *expected future cash flow*, implicit within the word "expected" is the element of uncertainty that anticipated events may not occur or that unforeseen events will occur. Accordingly, the greater the uncertainty, the greater the risk is of not achieving the expected cash flow; and the greater the risk of not achieving the expected cash flow, the greater should be the "reward" for taking that risk. That reward is the *return on investment* that is required in those circumstances. For example, if government-insured bonds are considered "risk free" and are easily being marketed at a rate

---

1   In this chapter and indeed throughout the text, reference is frequently made to the "risk-free" rate and to the "market-risk premium rate." The former refers to Canadian government bond rates; the latter to the market reward required for the risk being assumed. The rates used in the text and in the illustrative tables were not current at the time of publication, which were considerably lower due to economic factors. Although the templates shown are constant, the rates used in the templates are not. The reader is therefore cautioned to use current rates when using any template format.

of return of 1.25 percent per annum, then the reward for (a) purchasing a bond issued by a company without a solid history of earnings and (b) for accepting the uncertainty of receiving any or all of the bond payments should be a rate of return far greater than 1.25 percent per annum. Finally, you will come to learn that as the rate of return rises, the present worth of that expected future cash flow falls.

The capital that is available to a company is derived from two sources, namely, *debt* and *equity*. What a company will have to pay to obtain the capital that it requires, its *cost of capital*, will at all times be a function of the risk of not achieving its future expected cash flow as that risk is perceived by its shareholders (the equity source) and by its lenders (the debt source). Since shareholders require a higher return on equity than debtholders require on debt, the company's overall cost of capital will also be a function of the proportions or ratios of equity and debt in the composition of the company's capital structure. When a company invests the capital that has been made available to it, the rate of return that that company must achieve from its cash flow must be a rate of return that satisfies, at a minimum, that company's cost of capital. If such is not the case, the equity of the shareholders in that company is diminished to the extent of the deficiency. Therefore, expressed in simplistic terms, to determine the intrinsic value of a company, first determine its expected future cash flow and then convert (capitalize) that sum by a rate of return that is commensurate with the uncertainty of achieving the expected future cash flow, which, presumably, is already reflected in the company's cost of capital. For example, if the future expected annual cash flow of the company is $100,000 and if the appropriate rate of return (its cost of capital) is 8 percent over the Canadian government bonds of 1.25 percent per annum, the cash flow would be converted (capitalized) to $1,081,081, thereby yielding 9.25 percent per annum and arguably creating an intrinsic value for the company of $1,081,081.[2]

---

2   The capitalization "factor" in the illustration above is 10.8% (obtained by dividing 100 by the appropriate rate of return [9.25%]). The conversion

D. MARKET VALUE

In the example given above, $1,081,081 is the stated intrinsic value of the company, as an entity independent of any merger or acquisition. It presumes that the company will continue under current management with whatever revenue growth and performance improvements are already reflected in the company's intrinsic value. However, along comes a buyer. It too has an intrinsic value. If these two companies combine and if there are improvements in the overall cash flow of the two companies as a result of revenue growth, cost reductions, or other performance improvements that have occurred because of the acquisition or merger, the present worth of increased cash flow may be said to be the *synergy value* of the acquisition or merger. That is to say, the whole has become greater than the sum of its parts.

The market value of the seller's company is the purchase price that the buyer is willing to pay for the seller's company. The purchase price may consist of two components—the intrinsic value of the seller's company plus the premium that the buyer is prepared to pay to the shareholders of the seller's company, which represents a portion of the synergy value that hopefully will arise when the two companies have been combined.

The extent of the premium that a buyer may be prepared to pay depends on the extent of the anticipated improvement in the expected future cash flow attributable to the improvements created by the synergies. Essentially the premium allocates some of the future benefits of the acquisition or merger to the shareholders of the seller's company. The reason that the premium is being paid is that without it being paid it is unlikely, or at least less likely, that the shareholders of the seller's company would agree to sell.

(capitalization) of income to capital is achieved either by multiplying $100,000 by the capitalization factor of 10.8% or by dividing .925% into $100,000. In either case, the presumed intrinsic value of the company is $1,081,081.

E. COMMENTARY

Studies have repeatedly shown that over the years well over half of all mergers and acquisitions fail to achieve their expected value. To conclude that buyers are merely offering more than they should for the sellers' companies—although that may often be the case—is too simplistic. Studies have shown that the size of the premium and the success of the transaction are not linear. In one study, low premiums were paid by the buyers in half the cases cited, and one year later, in each case, the returns on investment were negative; whereas in other cases cited high premiums were paid by the buyers and their total one-year returns were positive.[3]

What is more often the case is that the value of the seller's company depends on who the buyer is. If value is defined as the present worth *to a buyer* of future benefits that are derivable from the transaction, and if the need for those benefits varies from buyer to buyer, then so does the value of those benefits. The question then is not whether the buyer is paying too high a price for the seller's company, but whether the buyer is paying more than the acquisition is worth to the buyer. In other words, do the future benefits to the buyer warrant that high a premium over the intrinsic value of the seller's company?

To answer that question, one must first determine the intrinsic value of the seller's company and then determine the extent of the expected synergy. If the premium being paid is equal to or greater than the expected synergy value, the shareholders of the seller's company are absorbing all of the value that the transaction may create.

The next two chapters will explore the various methods by which to determine the intrinsic value of the seller's company.

---

3   Robert G. Eccles, Kersten L. Lanes & Thomas C. Wilson, "Are You Paying Too Much for That Acquisition?" *Harvard Business Review* (July–August 1999), online: https://hbr.org/1999/07/are-you-paying-too-much-for-that-acquisition.

Chapter 2: **Methods of Valuation**

Although all methods should, in theory, yield the same results, they rarely do. There are numerous valuation methods, and in most situations, each yields a different result. However, in determining the true value of the transaction to the parties, a formal mathematical valuation should play only one part in the overall pricing of the transaction. That one part is to determine the intrinsic value of the seller's company. It is the first step toward the buyer making the second and more crucial determination—what is the acquisition or merger worth to the buyer's company?

A. EARNINGS PER SHARE METHOD

This method attempts to arrive at a company's value by using the performance and the potential selling prices of comparable publicly and privately held companies that operate in the same or a similar industry or that provide the same or similar products or services. This method of valuation is commonly referred to as the *earnings per share* (EPS) approach, by which the price to be paid for a share of a company is determined by multiplying its projected or actual earnings per share. The "multiple" is the projected price/earnings ratio. The price/earnings ratio that is chosen to value a company is often determined by examining the price/earnings ratios that the market has conferred on companies that are publicly listed and that operate in the same or a similar industry or that provide the same or similar products or services and that have comparable growth, risk, financial leverage, and dividend payouts.

The reason commonly given for the use of this method is that a potential buyer should not pay more for the seller's company than he would pay for a similar company that trades publicly. Actually, studies have shown that potential buyers are not inclined to pay as much for a privately held company as they will for a similar company that is publicly traded.[1] Due in large part to the absence of any liquidity, these buyers require a higher rate of return from the acquisition of a privately held company. Therefore, because the price/earnings ratio is lower, the values attributable to privately held companies tend to be lower.

For a number of valid reasons, the comparable worth method is generally accepted as being unreliable. Market data based on other transactions may be totally misleading. Every business transaction, to a greater or lesser extent, is unique. Market conditions change so quickly that each transaction becomes almost incomparable. Factors that affect value such as risk, competition, inflation, currency fluctuation, interest rates, tax rates, tax policy, management personnel, capital cost and availability, and personal circumstances are continually in a state of flux. Was the transaction made in a so-called sellers' market because the number of buyers in the marketplace increased the liquidity of the business and afforded the seller an opportunity to maximize the difference between the intrinsic value of its business and its market value? Or was it made in a so-called buyers' market because there were very few buyers interested in that particular business at that particular time?

The method is complicated further in that the goals of financial reporting for a publicly held company are quite different from those of a closely held company. In the former, the company's management strives to demonstrate high earnings in its financial reports to attract

---

1   Business Valuation Resources, *Mergerstat Review* (January 1997).

people to buy its stock and therefore to improve its price/earnings ratio. In a closely held company, management may be a sole entrepreneur or small group who wish to minimize the earnings to minimize the tax burden. Although both goals are legitimate, the difference in objectives will cause confusion in trying to compare key financial ratios.

Moreover, the EPS approach does not consider the risk arising from the uncertainty of achieving the prospective earnings, or the cost of capital associated with the seller's company, or the amount of debt in relation to the equity in the capital structure of the seller's company. Also, to the extent that the calculation does not specify the timing and duration before earnings are in hand, insufficient weight will have been given to the time value of money.

B. ASSET VALUATION METHOD

This method is often adopted if the seller's company has a large portion of its value wrapped up in fixed assets. The reason given for the use of this method is that a buyer should pay no more for the seller's company than he would pay to obtain a comparable set of substitute assets. One method of valuing the substitute assets is by determining the cost of *reproducing* them using the same materials as the original at current prices. Another method of valuing is to determine the cost of *replacing* the assets at current prices to modern standards and using modern materials.

When using this method, each asset of the company, tangible and intangible, is examined and assessed. The value of intangible assets, like patents and customer lists, are often then referred to as the company's *goodwill*—being the difference in value between the company's hard assets and the intrinsic value of the company.

To arrive at a fair valuation, an assessment must be made of all machinery and equipment, real estate, vehicles, furniture, fixtures, and inventory. The degree of detail using this method is extraordinary, and consequently the method is often used as collateral rather than as a primary method of valuation.

C. FINANCIAL PERFORMANCE METHODS

In the traditional balance sheet approach to valuation, the focus of the investigation is on the *earnings* of the seller's company. The accounting system relies on two distinct financial statements—the income statement and the balance sheet—both of which reflect the company's earnings. Because accounting systems emphasize earnings, and because earnings can be calculated in different ways that comply with accounting conventions and financial reporting requirements, decisions about inventory, depreciation, goodwill, amortization, research and development, expenditures, and the life of the asset will all significantly affect the reported earnings of the company. However, the accounting system, based as it is on generally accepted accounting principles, was never intended to be used to determine the value of a company. It was designed as a method by which to report on the past performance of the company and to assist creditors in monitoring the liability of the company and establishing the breakup value of its assets. Nevertheless, *return on investment* and *return on equity*, in certain instances, are relied on in evaluating the seller's company. The return on investment (also known as the return on total capital), shown as a percentage, is the after-tax earnings of the company divided by the book value of its total invested capital. In the return on equity approach, the return, again shown as a percentage, is determined by dividing the after-tax earnings of the company by the book value of its equity. However, the value that may be determined from each of these approaches is capable of manipulation and distortion by the acceleration or delay in recording revenues, or by the deferral of expenses, or the rate or policy of amortization. Also, a return on investment may decline during a period of significant upfront investment even though the expenditure will have a positive impact on the creation of long-term value. Furthermore, a company's return on equity will increase if a company earns more on borrowed money than it pays in interest. However, the higher debt will have increased the company's cost of equity and created a greater risk that the company may fail because of its debt load.

One method of valuation that has gained wide acceptance and is the one more commonly used in the acquisition of small and medium companies is known as the *discounted cash flow* approach by which *the value of a company, business, or any asset or security is the future expected cash flow discounted at a rate that reflects the risk of not achieving the projected cash flow.*

This method is an improvement over other financial performance methods because it is the cash flow of a seller's company that is being valued and not its income or earnings, and because matters relating to present worth (the present value of cash flow), cost of capital, and risk must all be considered and assessed to determine the rate at which the cash flow should be discounted (its *discount rate*).

Chapter 3: **The Intrinsic Value of the Seller's Company**

Defining market value as the present worth to a buyer of the future benefits that may be derived from the transaction with the seller's company, a determination of value may emerge from the answer to the question "How great a premium, if any, over the intrinsic value of the seller's company is warranted by the present worth of the future benefits from the acquisition of or merger with the seller's company?"

However, before the magnitude of the premium can be determined, the intrinsic value of the seller's company must first be determined. To determine the intrinsic value, the discounted cash flow method is applied by which the future expected cash flow of the company is converted (capitalized) at a rate (the *discount rate* or the company's *required rate of return*) that reflects the risk of not achieving the projected cash flow (which in turn reflects the *cost of the company's capital*).

The procedure used to determine the present worth of a company's projected cash flow is called *discounting* and its application in determining the value of the seller's company is examined later in this chapter. But first, to determine the *rate that reflects the risk of not achieving its projected cash flow*, two interrelated factors are at play. One factor is that of *risk*; the other is the *cost of capital*.

A company's cost of capital will presumably reflect the nature and the extent of the risk to which that company is exposed. That being the case, a brief study of the economics of risk is warranted.

A. ECONOMICS OF RISK

Risk may be defined as the *probability* that *foreseen events* will not occur or that *unforeseen events* will occur. In each case, it is the element of *uncertainty* that creates the risk. If it were absolutely certain that the foreseen event would occur or that the unforeseen event would not occur, then there would be no risk. If there were an absence of risk, the *risk-free* investment would warrant a risk-free rate. Presumably, government-insured bonds, treasury bills, and other securities that are backed by the credit of the Canadian government are considered to be risk free. The expected rate of return on a risk-free investment is the risk-free rate. However, when an element of risk is present, a reward, in the form of a *risk premium*, is offered as an inducement to warrant the risk being taken.

The capital available to a company is derived from two sources, *debt* and *equity*. When a debtholder lends money to a company, he does so with the expectation that the company will repay the principal together with an appropriate rate of interest. The rate of interest will depend on the debtholders' expectations with respect to other investment opportunities and their expectations with respect to inflation and risk. The rate to be charged to the borrowing company should be commensurate with the magnitude of the risk, the degree of expectation of inflation, or the nature and extent of the other opportunities by which to earn money. Shareholders, who provide the equity capital to the company, also consider other opportunities, inflation, and risk in determining whether to invest. Since returns on equity are of a greater risk than returns on debt, shareholders will want a higher return than debtholders on the capital they provide.

Risk is also measured by a company's vulnerability to changes or swings in the marketplace. (Risk assessment and its effect on the intrinsic and market value of a company are discussed in Chapter 6.) The vulnerability factor is referred to as its *beta*. The tendency of the company's earnings and cash flow to move in parallel with the earnings and cash flows of most companies in the market is what is being measured. A company with a beta of 1 tends to rise and fall to about the same extent as the market. A company with a beta of more than 1 tends to rise and fall by a greater percentage than the market, and the risk premium is therefore greater for such a company to compensate for its volatility. Conversely, companies that have very stable earnings and whose market fluctuation is modest relative to the fluctuations and earnings of most companies in the economy would have a low beta, such as .5.

Leverage is said to be used when a company borrows money to fund part of its capital requirements. However, in periods of economic turmoil, in tight credit periods, or in recessionary times, the highly leveraged company is more likely to fail. Therefore, both the lenders and shareholders are subjected to a greater risk, and the rate of return required to attract the debt and equity funding for a company increases with the company's level of leverage.

B. THE COST OF CAPITAL

The company's capital cost will, at all times, be a function of risk as perceived by its lenders and shareholders.

The rate at which a company can presently borrow funds will be its *cost of debt*. If the company now and in the immediate future will have the tax rate it presently attracts, the rate at which the company borrows should therefore be adjusted to reflect its after-tax cost. However, an unprofitable company that pays no tax would have a cost of debt equal to its pre-tax cost.

Assuming that a company can acquire debt at a cost of 9.25 percent and that it has a marginal tax rate of 45 percent, the cost of its debt may be determined as follows:

$$\text{Cost of debt} = \text{rate at which the company can borrow} \times (1 - \text{its tax rate})$$
$$= 9.25 \times (1.00 - 0.45)$$
$$= 9.25 \times (.55)$$
$$= 5.09\%$$

A company's *cost of equity* is the minimum rate of return that investors expect that company to earn to induce investors to purchase its shares and to thereby advance the equity the company requires. The rate of return must be a rate that the investors *expect* the company to earn on its *equity* after its corporate tax has been paid. However, the rate of return is not the after-tax return to the shareholder but the after-tax return to the corporation. Expressed differently, the rate of return required by the company's shareholders is the pre-tax return to shareholders that a company must earn after it has paid taxes at the corporate level. This rate of return is the company's *cost of equity*.

Assume that a company attracts a market-risk premium at 12 percent (because the company has a beta of 1 and is not highly leveraged) over the risk-free rate of 2 percent. The cost of its equity may be said to be:

$$\text{Cost of equity} = \text{risk-free rate} + \text{market rate premium}$$
$$= 2.0 + 12.0$$
$$= 14.0$$

To complete the calculation of a company's cost of capital, the overall proportionate capital cost, known as a company's *weighted average cost of capital*, must be calculated. This is because the capital cost will also be a function of the ratio or proportion that the equity and debt bear to one another in the composition of the company's capital structure. That is to say, the cost of debt is weighed against the cost of equity to calculate the weighted average.

By way of illustration, assume that a company has a capital structure of $100 million composed of $40 million in debt and $60 million in equity. If the cost of equity, as indicated above, were 14 percent and if the cost of debt, as indicated above, were 5.09 percent, the weighted average cost of capital in that company would be:

$$\text{Debt} = 40\% \times 5.09\% = 2.036\%$$
$$\text{Equity} = 60\% \times 14.00\% = 8.400\%$$
$$\text{Weighted average cost} = 10.436\%$$

As the debt level rises, changing the proportions of equity and debt in the composition of the company's capital structure, presumably both the cost of the equity and the cost of the debt would also rise, reflecting both the shareholders' and the lenders' perception of the additional risks that a debt-heavy company must bear.

C. DISCOUNTING THE PROJECTED CASH FLOW

Having determined that the company's cost of capital is the rate that may properly reflect the risk of achieving its projected cash flow, the intrinsic value of that company may now be determined by calculating the present worth of that projected cash flow. The procedure used to determine its present worth is called *discounting*. To discount a future cash flow is to calculate the present value of a future payment, a series of payments, or a reversion.

A simple example of the discounting procedure is illustrated by the following problem:

What is the value today of $115 that is due to be received in one year discounted at 15 percent per year?

The value today is known as its *present value*. The *required rate of return* or *discount rate* is 15 percent per year.

The solution to the problem is to determine the amount that if invested today would grow to $115 with compound interest at the rate of 15 percent. The standard formula for discounting future value to present value is:

$$\text{Present Value} = \frac{\text{Future Value}}{(1+i)^n}$$

In applying this formula, i is the required rate of return on capital (in this case, assumed to be 15 percent) per period that will satisfy the investor, and n is the number of periods that the payment will be deferred. The illustrated problem is solved as follows:

$$\text{Present Value} = \frac{\$115}{(1.15)^1}$$
$$= \$115 \text{ divided once by } 1.15$$
$$= \$100$$

If the problem were the same but the $115 was due to be received in two years rather than one, the solution would appear as follows:

$$\text{Present Value} = \frac{\$115}{(1.15)^2}$$
$$= \frac{115}{(1.15) \times (1.15)}$$
$$= \$115 \text{ divided once by } 1.3225$$
$$= \$86.96$$

If a series of future payments is expected, each payment is discounted by applying the standard formula, and the present value of the series is the sum of all their present values.

In the problem given above, 1.3225 is known as the *present value factor.* You will be relieved to learn that present value tables provide the present value factor for any number of periods into the future for any given discount rate. These tables show the present value of one dollar ($1) at any given rate for any number of periods.

Therefore, again in the problem given above, the present value factor of 1.3225 would appear in the column under 15 percent, across from period 2 in the table titled "Future Value of $1 at the End of n Periods." Since the amount to be discounted is $115, it is $115 that is divided by the present value factor of 1.3225 to determine that $86.96 is its present value.

D. DETERMINING THE PROJECTED CASH FLOW

To employ the discounted cash flow method to determine value, the last matter to be considered is what amounts are included and what amounts are excluded in determining the projected cash flow.

Since it is cash rather than income that is central to this analysis, only cash receipts (not income recognition) are considered. The reason for that is that only cash can be reinvested or paid out as dividends or declared as management bonuses.

To determine the projected *free* cash flow that is available to the company's stakeholders (the shareholders and debtholders), the cash flow is determined on an after-tax basis. Having determined the estimated after-tax earnings of the company, the amount of capital expenditures, if any, that may be required to produce future earnings is deducted therefrom, as is the incremental working capital—the cash—that will be "tied-up" in items such as accounts receivable. Added back to the figure that remains are all non-cash expenses, such as depreciation, since such expenses do not alter the company's cash position. Also added back are all finance-related expenses, such as interest, since financing expenses are already embodied in the required rate of return and are part of the capital. Finally, if a premium for anticipated inflation was included in the required rate of return, the expected cash flow should also reflect the same degree of inflation.

E.   AN ILLUSTRATIVE CASE IN POINT

The owner of a company wants to know the value of what it is he has created—in other words, he wants to know his company's intrinsic value. For the purpose of determining the company's value assume that:

- the current risk-free market rate is 2 percent
- the market-risk premium for a business in that industry (a high beta) is 16 percent
- the company can borrow funds at 9 percent
- the company's marginal tax rate is 45 percent
- the company has $16 million in liabilities divided equally between long-term debt and shareholders' equity

Given the above information, the rate at which to discount the company's projected cash flow (its required rate of return, its discount rate) is determined as follows:

```
Cost of equity     = 2% + 16%                    = 18%
Cost of debt       = 9% × (1.00 − 0.45)          = 4.95 (say 5%)
Weighted average = (50% × 18%) + (50% × 5%) = 11.5%
```

Assume that in the current year the company's earnings were $4 million, before interest and taxes, and assume that a review of the company's income statements from prior years indicates that this company has enjoyed annual increases in its earnings before interest and taxes (EBIT) of about 10 percent. Assume that that rate of growth is sustainable for one more year and that thereafter a growth rate of 3 percent is more likely. Assume that the company's non-cash expenses of $750,000 per year for the depreciation of the company's fixed and depreciable assets is equal in amount each year to the company's capital expenditures. Finally, assume that the company's working capital of $180,000 (amounts frozen in accounts receivable and cash required for operations) will increase at 10 percent over the base year and at 3 percent per year thereafter to coincide with the presumed increases in sales.

Given the foregoing, the expected cash flow of the company for the next five years would be forecast as follows:

Table 3.1

	Year 1	Year 2	Year 3	Year 4	Year 5
EBIT	4,400,000	4,532,000	4,668,000	4,808,000	4,950,000
EBIT Less Taxes of 45%[1]	2,420,000	2,492,600	2,567,400	2,644,400	2,722,500
Non-cash expenses (+)	750,000	750,000	750,000	750,000	750,000
Capital expenditures (−)	750,000	750,000	750,000	750,000	750,000
Incremental working capital (−)	200,000	206,000	212,180	218,545	225,100
TOTAL	2,220,000	2,286,600	2,355,220	2,425,855	2,497,400

---

1   The reason that taxes are calculated on earnings without any deduction having first been made for the interest payable on the company's long-term debt of $8,000,000 is that the cost of the company's debt is already calculated as an after-tax cost, so doing so again at this stage will be double counting.

	Year 1	Year 2	Year 3	Year 4	Year 5
Present value @ 11.5% (the presumed discount rate)	1,991,031	1,839,581	1,699,293	1,569,117	1,449,448

What is the value today of \$2,220,000 that is due to be received in one year discounted at 11.5 percent per year? What is the present value of the first year's expected cash flow?

$$\text{Present value} = \frac{\text{Future value}}{(1 + i)^n}$$

In our illustration, i is 11.5 percent and n is 1 period.

$$\text{Present value} = \frac{\$2,220,000}{(1.00 + .115)}$$
$$= \$2,220,000 \text{ divided by } 1.115$$
$$= \$1,991,031$$

Continuing, what is the present value of the second year's expected cash flow?

$$\text{Present value} = \frac{\$2,286,600}{(1.115) \times (1.115)}$$
$$= \$2,286,600 \text{ divided by } 1.243$$
$$= \$1,839,581$$

The present value of the expected cash flow in the remaining three years is calculated in a similar manner unless present value tables are available for "Present Value of \$1 at the End of the n Periods."

The aggregate of the present values is \$8,548,470.

One last step remains to be taken. What has not as yet been taken into consideration is the cash flow beyond the five-year forecast period. To do so, the present value of the *residual* or *terminal value* is added to the aggregate of the present values determined above. This terminal value is the present value of the expected cash flow that is expected to be generated presumably one year after the forecast period.

Assuming that the annual growth rate of 3 percent for the company is sustainable beyond year 5, the cash flow in year 6 is 3 percent greater than the expected cash flow in year 5, namely $2,572,322. The terminal value is determined at a capitalization rate equal to the cost of the company's capital (11.5 percent) minus the company's presumed growth rate beyond the forecast period (3 percent). The expected cash flow in year 6 is capitalized at 8.5 percent, which yields a terminal value of $30,262,600. The present value of the terminal value (six years hence at 11.5 percent) determined at a present value factor of 1.922 is $15,745,369.

The present value of the terminal value ($15,745,369) is added to the present value of the expected cash flow in years 1 through 5 ($8,548,470) for a total of $24,293,839. From this aggregate present value is deducted the company's long-term debt of $8 million, resulting in an estimated value of the company at $16,293,839. This may be said to be the company's intrinsic value.

The value of $16.3 million ascribed to the company may now be tested by varying certain facts and by altering the assumptions that were made. To the extent that the assumptions are varied, a range of values is created, which may be described as the best-case through to the worst-case scenario. Chapter 6 on risk assessment deals with the changes in scenarios created by the changes in the assumptions.

F. COMMENTARY

For the purpose of determining the intrinsic value of a company, this chapter has been devoted in large measure to a study of the required rate of return that is required by the suppliers of capital to that company. We have seen that the rate at which to discount the expected future cash flow to determine its present worth is rooted in the lenders' and the shareholders' required rate of return on a security of comparable risk.

Government-insured notes, bills, and bonds, based on the credit of the government, are considered to be risk free. The required rate of return on these securities seemingly sets the benchmark for all other investments. However, to the extent that there is uncertainty in the supply and demand for a currency, and in the inflation rate, and in a country's monetary and fiscal policy, the risk-free required rate of return will vary.

For example, US Treasury bonds purchased in 1988 with a coupon of 9 percent were offered for resale 10 years later to yield less than 6 percent. Why? Because the rate of inflation in 1988 was 4.5 percent and the real yield on 1988 Treasury bonds was therefore 4.5 percent. However, *in 1998*, the inflation rate was 1.5 percent, and so with a 6 percent coupon the same 4.5 percent real yield was available.

In recent years, the yield on 10-year US Treasury notes was about .85 percent, and the average US market-risk premium was about 5.5 percent.

Similarly, when forecasting the market premium of the future, it is interesting to note that over the period from 1928 to 2014, the average annual market-risk premium has been 9.6 percent.[2]

One last interesting thought is that low interest rates have historically preceded excessive risk taking. Easy money does seem to trigger a speculative search for greater returns. In 1998, bond buyers were prepared to price bonds issued by the Russian government at only 3 percent over US Treasury bonds. Similarly, when a single-digit rate is being offered in money market accounts, investors are unable to resist the double-digit returns that are often projected by the stock market.

---

2   *Stocks, Bonds, Bills, and Inflation: 2014 Yearbook: Market Results for 1928–2014* (Chicago, IL: Ibbotson Associates, 2014).

Chapter 4: **The Market Value of the Seller's Company**

The intrinsic value of the seller's company is a value that is independent of any merger with or acquisition by another company. It is a value predicated on the company continuing under the current management with the revenue growth and the performance improvements, if any, that have been validly forecast in its projected cash flow.

The buyer's company also has an intrinsic value, and if the prospect of the two companies combining indicates that there will be improvements in the overall cash flow of the two companies because of the merger or acquisition, the present worth of the increased cash flow is referred to as the *synergy value* of the acquisition or merger and represents a value that a buyer may choose to add to the intrinsic value of the seller's company.

The purchase price that a buyer is willing to pay for the seller's company will represent that buyer's perception of the *market value* of the seller's company and may consist of two components: the intrinsic value of the seller's company and the *premium* that the buyer is prepared to pay to the shareholders of the seller's company for a portion of the synergy value that may be realized when the two companies combine. This premium represents that portion of the synergy value that the buyer is prepared to transfer to the shareholders of the seller's company to make a deal. In doing so, the buyer is essentially allocating to the shareholders of the seller's company a portion of the future benefit of the acquisition or merger. Since the need or the ability to exploit these future benefits may vary from buyer to buyer, the value of those future benefits may also vary from buyer to buyer. Consequently, the synergy value created by a proposed merger or acquisition will not necessarily be the same amount for all buyers, and to the extent that the synergy value may vary, and to the extent that the buyer may be prepared to allocate a greater or a lesser portion of that synergy value to the shareholders of the seller's company, the market value of the seller's company will change depending on the buyer.

A. DETERMINING THE PURCHASE PRICE

The next step in deciding how much to pay the shareholders of the seller's company is to determine the synergy value that may be created by the transaction.

The synergy value of the *acquisition* may be defined as the *present worth* of the difference between the cash flow of the seller's company before and the cash flow of the seller's company after the acquisition. Similarly, the synergy value of the *merger* may be defined as the *present worth* of the difference between the aggregate cash flow of the two companies before the merger and the aggregate cash flow after the merger.

The maximum premium that should be paid for the seller's company should be for an amount that is less than the synergy value that the transaction is expected to generate.

The market value may be defined as the aggregate of the following:

- The present worth of cash flow from the existing operations of the seller's company less the capital expenditures and working capital needed to maintain those operations, plus the present worth of cash flow from any new operations that are planned, less the capital expenditures and working capital required to achieve those new operations, plus the value of the assets not required to maintain the operations that could be liquidated, and

- The present worth of synergies added by the buyer such as cost savings that increase the cash flow (less the cost to achieve them), plus the present worth of revenues (less the cost to achieve them) generated from new products resulting from the acquisition, plus the present worth of the sale of redundant assets on an after-tax basis, plus the present worth of financing benefits from revised credit rating or credit availability

To determine the *present worth* of the synergy value, the rate at which to discount the anticipated future cash flow must reflect the risk of not achieving that projection. The discount rate to be applied will be the buyer's current cost of capital, provided that the intended transaction does not alter the business-risk complexion of the buyer's company as perceived by its suppliers of capital. If the acquisition will indeed have that effect, the discount rate (the rate of return required by the capital suppliers) must be increased to reflect the increased level of risk. For example, if the beta of the seller's company is greater than the beta of the buyer, the required rate of return should more closely reflect the cost of capital of the seller's company. By way of further example, if the acquisition is to be financed primarily with debt, so that the proportions of debt and equity in the buyer's capital structure are altered, the required rate of return should be increased to reflect the increased risk of financial distress.

B. DETERMINING THE TRANSACTION'S SYNERGY VALUE

A distinction should be drawn between two types of acquisition. A *financial acquisition*[1] is an acquisition that is commonly made by a financial promoter whose motivation is to sell off assets, cut costs, and manage that which remains more efficiently than it was managed before. This is done in anticipation of producing an aggregate value that exceeds the

---

1   Although the *financial acquisition* is beyond the intended scope of this book, its functions and characteristics are reviewed in Chapter 7, which deals with leveraged buyouts.

value that was paid for the acquisition. It is undertaken by a financial promoter who believes that the whole is worth less than the sum of its parts. To accomplish an aggregate value that exceeds the price paid for the acquisition, divestitures, liquidations, and selloffs—the opposite of mergers and acquisitions—are employed. However, this type of transaction is rarely concerned, if ever, with the synergy that may be created by blending two companies together. A financial acquisition is rarely ever a part of an overall strategy involving a cost benefit or a revenue enhancement through market share or through an expanding product line as in the case of the other type of acquisition—the *strategic acquisition*.

In determining the synergy value of a strategic acquisition, the projected post-acquisition value of the companies is generally calculated by reference to seven types of synergies.

1)   Cost Savings

This is the most common type of synergy and the easiest to estimate. These savings arise from elimination of jobs, facilities, and related expenses that are no longer needed when functions are consolidated, or they may arise from economies of scale achieved in purchasing. These economies are best realized with a horizontal merger wherein two companies in the same line of business are combined.[2] A vertical merger, wherein a company expands forward toward the consumer or backward

---

2   A natural response to the excess supply created by companies that are in the same business is to merge those companies and turn off some of the supply. The merger of Exxon and Mobil Oil was essentially an attempt to sustain their profit levels. These two giant oil companies were purveyors of a common commodity and, as a result of what was then a diminished demand for oil, the commodity was available in huge supply and the falling prices that resulted from that oversupply were cutting deeply into their profits. Exxon and Mobil Oil hoped that the cost reductions from the merger would sustain their profitability. The cost reductions came from combining their headquarters and back-office operations, the purchase of supplies and services from an enhanced negotiating power, and a reduction in Mobil's cost for finding and developing oil reserves:

toward the source of raw materials, also brings about economies due to the presence of additional controls over its distribution and purchasing. However, combining two companies in unrelated lines of business, the conglomerate merger, will create few, if any, operating economies.

Although cost savings may be the easiest to estimate, there are several problems that are inherent in doing so. When a consolidation seems to indicate that many jobs are destined to be terminated, if the person at the job is very talented, he may simply be shifted elsewhere within the company and therefore, although a position may be terminated, the salary of the individual who occupied that position is not. Second, buyers notoriously underestimate how long it will take to realize cost savings. This may happen because the senior managers in both companies are resistant to change,[3] and of course the longer it takes for a cost saving to be realized, the less value those cost savings create.

2) Revenue Enhancement

Although revenue enhancement may be difficult to predict, it is sometimes possible for the buyer and seller to achieve a higher level of sales growth together than either company could have achieved on its own. For example, the seller may bring a superior or complementary product to the more extensive distribution channel of the buyer, or the seller's

---

What was true of these two companies is equally true of all commodities in a broader sense. In the expectation of many companies that as supplies rise, so will demand, many companies step up production. Yesterday's Asian crisis has undermined that policy and manufacturing companies of all kinds were unable to sell all that they could produce. These companies were forced to cut prices, hurting profits, and forcing lay-offs. Merger to many, through cost-cutting, appeared to be their salvation. The 78 mergers that were announced in the first four days of December 1998 can be explained in this way.

3　In early 1990, AT&T acquired NCR. However, AT&T's unionized employees objected to working in the same building as NCR's non-union staff, and NCR's conservative centralized management was disoriented by AT&T's insistence on calling its supervisors "coaches" and removing the executives' office doors. Those who had made NCR profitable left, so that by 1997 only four of the top thirty NCR managers at the time of the takeover still worked for the company.

distribution channel may be used to escalate the sales of the buyer's product, or it may be that the post-acquisition company will gain sufficient critical mass to attract revenue that neither company would have been able to realize alone.

Nevertheless, revenue enhancements are very hard to estimate because they involve external variables that are beyond the control of management. For example, the customer base of the seller's company may react negatively to different prices and product features or may balk at making too many purchases from a single supplier. Suffice to say that this category is a "soft" synergy and should not be a major factor in calculating the synergy value.

3) Process Improvements

This type of synergy occurs when managers transfer the best practices and competencies from one company to another that result in both cost savings and revenue enhancements. Moreover, if a company is being inefficiently managed and the profitability of that company is lower than it should be, but the buyer can provide better management, the merger may make sense for that reason alone. Conglomerate mergers are commonly viewed as lacking economic justification unless the buyer is able to manage both the assets and the personnel of the seller's company more productively.

4) Tax Benefits

Although the Canada Revenue Agency does not look favourably on mergers that are motivated solely by the tax loss carry forward advantage, if the buyer merges with a profitable firm in the same line of business the tax loss carry forward is often allowed, in which case the company with the tax losses can shelter the positive earnings of the other company with which it is joined. In doing so, the overall tax rate of the combined company is equal to or lower than the blended tax rates of the two companies before the transaction. There are other tax-related synergies, such as the transfer of brands and other intellectual property to a low-tax subsidiary, placing shared services and central purchasing in tax-advantaged locations, or moving debt into high-tax subsidiaries.

5) Financial Engineering

A transaction may permit a company to refinance the seller's debt at the buyer's more favourable borrowing rate without affecting the buyer's credit rating. To do so, the buyer must first determine that the business-risk complexion of its own operation will not be adversely affected by the transaction.

Nevertheless, the paramount rationale for pursuing a merger or an acquisition is to achieve a better competitive position in the market-place—a lower cost structure or a better platform for growth. This should be the primary objective of the transaction. Tax benefits and financial engineering may produce synergies, but they do not by themselves strengthen a company's competitive position.

6) Diversification

By acquiring a company in a different line of business, the buyer may be able to reduce its seasonal or cyclical earning instability. Since capital suppliers are averse to the total risk that a company bears, reduction in a company's exposure to risk through diversification may have a favourable impact on the cost of capital of the combined companies.

Diversification into a related field may convert the market's perception of the buyer's company from one whose shares achieve a price/earnings ratio of only 10 as a manufacturer of cars (as with the Ford Motor Company) into a consumer products and service corporation commanding a multiple of something closer to 30.[4]

---

4   Car makers are lucky to create operating margins of more than 5% from the manufacture of automobiles, while other businesses, such as leasing, renting, insurance, finance, and car repair, can all achieve margins of 10–15%.

7) A Competitor Takeover

If a buyer were to be adversely affected financially by the seller's company being acquired by one of the buyer's competitors, the premium that may be paid by the buyer for the seller's company is a premium equal to the loss in value that the buyer would experience if that event were to occur.

C. COMMENTARY

Notwithstanding the various ways by which it is possible to enhance the value of companies that are combined by a merger or acquisition, the fact remains that the probability of being able to do so is not great. Statistics indicate that the attempt to create additional value by merger or acquisition is more likely to fail than to succeed.[5]

One study,[6] which summarizes the results of merger and acquisition over a period of eleven years, found that in the case of merger the average return to the shareholders of the seller's company was 20 percent while the average return to the buyer was zero; and when the acquisition of the seller's company's shares was made by public offer, the seller's company's shareholders received an average return of 30 percent while the buyer's return was 4 percent. In an analysis made of acquisitions during the same period, it was determined that failures (the acquisition earned less than its cost of equity capital) outnumbered successes by almost three-to-one.

The primary reason given for the failure of so many mergers and acquisitions is that the buyer paid too much for the seller's company. Many reasons are given as to why the buyer may have overpaid. The rate

---

5   Mark L. Sirower, *The Synergy Trap: How Companies Lose the Acquisition Game* (New York: Free Press, 1997), in which Mark Sirower, studying 168 deals among large public companies in the 1980s and an additional 100 combinations valued at more than $500,000,000 a piece in the 1990s, found that roughly two-thirds lost money for its shareholders.

6   T.E. Copeland, T. Roller & J. Murrin, *Evaluation: Measuring and Managing the Value of Companies* (New York, NY: John Wiley & Son, 1994).

at which it discounted the expected cash flow of the seller's company was too low, or it overestimated the expected cash flow, or it underestimated the capital expenditures and working capital needs of the seller's company, or it was overly optimistic with respect to the synergies of the merged company, or there was a poor post-acquisition integration of personnel or of the merged personnel with customers, employers, employees, and suppliers.

Nevertheless, studies have shown that the magnitude of the premium does not doom the transaction to failure if the synergy value has been calculated carefully. Notwithstanding the size of the premium over the intrinsic value of the seller's company, if the premium is warranted by the synergy value and if the synergy value has been subjected to a risk and sensitivity analysis that examines what the least and most favourable outcomes could be, there are many cases of merger or acquisition that enhanced the combined shareholders' value many times over. If commensurate shareholder value is created, the size of the premium does not matter. This is the conclusion reached by a consulting firm that undertook a study of 117 large merger and acquisition deals over two years.[7] The study also concluded that other often-cited predictors of a transaction's success or failure—such as the similarity of the seller and the buyer or the size of the difference between the seller and the buyer—have no bearing on shareholders' value and that generally the marketplace will justify a greater premium if there is a revenue enhancement rather than only a cost saving.

---

7   Booz Allen & Hamilton, "High Deal Premium, Bad Value? Not Necessarily" *Wall Street Journal* (13 August 1999) C-1.

Chapter 5: **Value and the Capital Structure**

A. INTRODUCTION

In Chapter 3, the discounted cash flow method was used to determine the intrinsic value of a company. However, an identical value can be obtained in a more indirect manner.

In Chapter 3, the following sentiment appears in the third paragraph of the chapter:

> To determine the intrinsic value, the discounted cash flow method is applied by which the future expected cash flow of the company is converted (capitalized) at a rate (the *discount rate* or the company's *required rate of return*) that reflects the risk of not achieving the projected cash flow (which in turn reflects the *cost of the company's capital*).

In other words, to determine the value of any security, calculate the present worth of its expected cash flow. The rate by which to discount the expected cash flow to determine its present worth is the bondholders' or the shareholders' required rate of return on a security of comparable risk.[1] The greater the expectation of risk, the greater will

---

[1]   If the price being asked for the security were higher than the price the investor has determined as its value, the investor would not purchase the security because his expected return thereon would be less than the return on other securities that

be the required rate of return. Because returns on equity carry a greater risk than returns on debt, shareholders require a greater rate of return than bondholders do on the capital that each provides to the company.

It may be said that a company is the embodiment of its debt and equity components manifested in the securities that the company has issued to its lenders and shareholders. Since the value of any security can be determined by calculating the present worth of the expected cash flow of each security, *the value of a company, as a whole, is theoretically the sum of the value of its equity and debt components, and since securities that are issued to bondholders have a different value than securities issued to shareholders, by altering the proportions of debt and equity within the company's structure, the value of the company is significantly and clearly affected.*

Each of the foregoing propositions can be validated by examining how the financial picture of a company changes as the proportions of equity and debt within its capital structure are altered.[2]

To highlight how the level of debt affects the value of the company and also the value of the securities that the company has issued, it simplifies matters to assume that the company's earnings, before interest and taxes, remains constant and are paid out to its shareholders as dividends, that the company's capital structure of $500,000 remains constant, and that only the level of debt changes.

---

carry comparable risk. However, if the price being asked for the security were less, the investor would purchase the security since it would offer a return that is higher than other securities at comparable risk. The investor group as a whole would in the course of its collective action force the price of the security higher until its market value equalled its present worth.

2   This section is based in part on material provided by Harvard Business School, distributed by HBS Case Services, Harvard Business School, Boston, Massachusetts © 1979.

B. THE EFFECTS OF LEVERAGE

Table 5.1. The Leverage Effect on Earnings

Table 5.1 illustrates the impact of leverage on the corporation's income.

		10%	20%	30%	40%	50%
1	Debt in the capital structure (%)[3]		(50,000)	(100,000)	(150,000)	(200,000)	(250,000)
2	Earnings before interest & taxes (EBIT)	120,000	120,000	120,000	120,000	120,000	120,000
3	Interest[4]	0	4,125	8,750	14,625	22,000	31,250
4	Pre-tax earnings	120,000	115,875	111,250	105,375	98,000	88,750
5	Tax (@ 50%)	60,000	57,938	55,625	52,688	49,000	44,375
6	After-tax earnings	60,000	57,937	55,625	52,687	49,000	44,375
7	Dividends	60,000	57,937	55,625	52,687	49,000	44,375
8	Total payments to security holders (line 3 + line 7)	**60,000**	**62,062**	**64,375**	**67,312**	**71,000**	**75,625**

Although the earnings of the firm, EBIT, are unaffected by the leverage, the after-tax earnings of the company fall as debt is added to the capital structure. The aggregate payments made to debtholders and shareholders increase with leverage. This increase is attributable entirely to the tax savings resulting from the tax deductibility of the interest paid on the debt.

Table 5.2. The Leverage Effect on Discount Rates

Table 5.2 shows the various rates of return that are intended to induce investors in our illustration to acquire the debt and equity securities of the company. Since the debtholders and the shareholders are subjected to increased risk as the level of debt rises, the investors require

---

3   Debt refers to the percentage or portion of debt within the $500,000 capital structure of the corporation.

4   The rate of interest is not constant. It increases with the percentage of debt (see line 9), e.g., $50,000 x 8.25 = $4,125.

higher returns to compensate for the increased risk. The required rates of return (lines 9 and 10) are only assumptions, but they are the foundations on which the subsequent analysis of the company's capital structure is based. The relationship between risk and return is the basis for these assumptions, and since these returns are necessary to attract the funds required by the company, these rates of return represent the company's capital costs. The discount rates (lines 9 and 10) that are used are intended to reflect the investors' required return on securities of comparable risk.

9	Required return on debt capital (cost of debt capital)	0	8.25%	8.75%	9.75%	11.00%	12.50%
10	Required return on equity capital (cost of equity capital)	12.00%	12.50%	13.00%	13.50%	14.50%	16.00%

Table 5.3. The Leverage Effect on Security Values

Table 5.3 demonstrates the present worth of the debt and the equity securities based on the application of the said discount rates (lines 9 and 10). The resulting present worth is an estimate of the market value of each security. The market value of the company as a whole is simply the sum of the market value of its debt and the market value of its equity. It is noteworthy that the value peaks at $540,274 and then falls to $527,344 as leverage increases. Why this is so is subsequently explained in Table 5.3.

11	Market value of debt (100 + line 9 × line 3)	0	50,000	100,000	150,000	200,000	250,000
12	Market value of equity (100 + line 10 × line 7)	500,000	463,496	427,885	390,274	337,931	277,344
13	Market value of the company (line 11 + line 12)	**500,000**	**513,496**	**527,885**	**540,274**	**537,931**	**527,344**

Table 5.4. The Leverage Effect on Book Versus Market Value

A comparison of Table 5.3 and Table 5.4 demonstrates that the use of leverage increases the market value of the company's equity (line 12) and its total capital (line 13) over the book value of its equity (line 15) and its total capital (line 16). This increase accrues to the shareholders as a one-time gain. Thereafter, the shareholders receive only the required rate of return (line 10).

14	Book value of debt	0	50,000	100,000	150,000	200,000	250,000
15	Book value of equity	500,000	450,000	400,000	350,000	300,000	250,000
16	Book value of the company (total capital)	**500,000**	**500,000**	**500,000**	**500,000**	**500,000**	**500,000**
17	Return on total capital (ROTC) (EBIT $(1-t)$ + line 16)	12.0%	12.0%	12.0%	12.0%	12.0%	12.0%
18	Return on equity (ROE) (line 6 + line 15)	12.0%	12.9%	13.9%	15.1%	16.3%	17.8%

Line 17 indicates that the return on total capital (ROTC) is unaffected by leverage. When there is no debt, the return on equity (ROE) is equal to the return on total capital. However, the addition of debt causes the ROE to rise above the ROTC. It is worth noting that the returns shown on line 18 are not the returns that shareholders receive. The shareholders receive the dividends plus any increase in the value of their shares. Expressed differently, ROE is a measure that should only be used to determine the performance of a company and not its value (see Chapter 2).

Table 5.5. The Leverage Effect on Share Values

Table 5.5 demonstrates the effects of increased debt on the value of a company and on its returns.

19	Number of shares outstanding	5,000	4,513	4,053	3,612	3,141	2,630
20	Price per share (line 12 + line 19)	$100.0	$102.7	$105.6	$108.1	$107.6	$105.5
21	Earnings per share (line 6 + line 19)	$12.00	$12.84	$13.72	$14.59	$15.60	$16.87
22	Price/earnings ratio (line 20 + line 21 + line 12 + line 6)	8.3	8.0	7.7	7.4	6.9	6.3

The earnings per share (line 21) and the price/earnings ratio (line 22) of the company clearly are affected by the addition of debt. The assumption made in line 19 is that the company initially has no debt and that as debt is incurred the proceeds are used to repurchase outstanding treasury shares.

Line 21 demonstrates that the earnings per share (EPS) increases uninterrupted as debt is added. However, line 20 demonstrates that as debt is added the *price per share* rises, peaks, and then falls (see also line 13). Why? With increased leverage, there is increased risk to the EPS due to the debt load that the company must bear. Because there is increased risk, the price/earnings ratio falls (line 22). The price/earnings ratio falls because as debt increases, shareholders will pay a lower price (because of a greater discount rate) for the expected EPS to reflect the increased risk that the higher debt represents. Even though the EPS dollar amount rises as debt is added (line 21), the price/earnings ratio will continue to fall (line 22).

The reason that the price per share rises, peaks, and then falls (line 20) as debt is added is because at low levels of leverage, the increase in the earnings per share dominates the reduction in the price/earnings ratio and the price of the share rises. But when there are high levels of debt, the EPS no longer dominates the reduction in the price/earnings ratio and the price of the share falls (line 20).[5]

Table 5.6. The Leverage Effect on the Company's Value

Table 5.6 presents the weighted average cost of capital (WACC) percentage for each of the designated levels of debt. As previously shown, this percentage is determined in the following manner:

The company's percentage of debt *times* the after-tax cost of the debt.

Plus

The company's percentage of equity *times* the after-tax cost of the equity.[6]

Using a debt level of $100,000 (line 1, column 3) as an illustration:

i) The company's percentage of debt (line 11) is

$$\frac{\$100,000}{\$527,885} \times 100 = 18.9\%$$

ii) The company's after-tax cost of debt (line 9) (assuming the company bears a 50% tax rate) is

$$8.75\% \times (1.00 - .50) = 4.375\%$$

iii) $4.375 \times .189 = .8269\%$

iv) The company's percentage of equity (line 12) is

$$\frac{\$427,885}{\$527,885} \times 100 = 81.1\%$$

v) The after-tax cost of the equity (line 10) is 1

$$3.00 \times .811 = 10.543$$

vi) The sum of (iii) + (v) = 11.3699%.

---

5   For an explanation as to why this occurs, read the Commentary at the end of this chapter.

6   In line 10 of Table 5.2, the stated cost of capital is already after tax.

23	Book value debt ratio (line 14 + line 16)	0%	10%	20%	30%	40%	50%
24	Market value debt ratio (line 11 + line 13)	0%	9.7%	18.9%	27.8%	37.2%	47.7%
25	Weighted average cost capital (a sample calculation follows)	12.0%	11.7%	11.4%	11.1%	11.2%	11.4%
26	Free cash flow (FCF) [(EBIT) (1 = t) + line 2 × .50]	60,000	60,000	60,000	60,000	60,000	60,000
27	Market value of the company (line 26 + line 25)	500,000	513,496	527,885	540,274	537,931	527,344

As stated earlier, the market value of the company as a whole is simply the sum of the market value of its debt (line 11) and the market value of its equity (line 12). In Table 5.3, the market value of the firm was determined (line 13) by doing just that. However, as we have already seen, an identical valuation is achieved in a more direct manner by employing the discounted cash flow method.

The free cash flow (line 26) is the same figure as the after-tax EBIT amount, namely $120,000 (line 2) × .50% (the presumed rate of tax) = $60,000. The value of the company is the present value of the free cash flow discounted at the weighted average cost of the capital invested in the company (WACC). The company's WACC already includes the cost of financing, so these costs are not again deducted in calculating the free cash flow. The discounted cash flow method was applied in Table 5.6 to determine the value of the company (line 27). The identical value of the company was obtained (line 13) by determining the value of the company's debt and equity components (Table 5.3), and in each case the value obtained was altered significantly by the proportion of debt and equity within the capital structure of the company.

C. COMMENTARY

In the attempt made to strike the most favourable balance between debt and equity, three positive consequences ensue. The value of the company is maximized (lines 13 and 27); the price per share is maximized (line 20); and the WACC of the company is minimized (line 25). Why do these consequences occur?

If the assumptions as to the cost of equity and debt are correct (lines 9 and 10), as debt is added the WACC falls. This increases the value of the company, and the value of its common shares rise. When debt reaches about 30 percent of the total capital, that is the level at which the company reaches its highest value. The reason for the WACC falling and for the value of the company and its shares rising to this level is due to the tax savings gained by the deductibility of the interest payments on the debt. The value of the company has increased by the present worth of these tax savings. This is the single major benefit of the leverage created by the company's debt. But as leverage rises so too does the probability of financial distress within a company that is burdened with debt. In periods of economic turmoil, in tight credit periods, or in recessionary times the highly leveraged company is more likely to fail. The potential costs that are related to financial distress are reflected in the costs of capital (lines 9 and 10), and as the level of debt rises, the value of the company is reduced by the present worth of these higher costs. Expressed differently, at lower levels of debt, the value of the company rises because the advantage of leverage outweighs its disadvantage. But at the higher levels of debt, the present worth of the higher costs of capital is greater than the present worth of the tax savings, and consequently the value of the company falls.

Chapter 6: **Risk Assessment**

Is an expected event likely to occur? Is it a probability or merely a possibility? The difference may be said to be its degree of uncertainty. Where there is no uncertainty, there is no risk. Accordingly, a risk-free investment is one in which the expected return is certain to be received. For example, a return on a treasury bill, backed unconditionally by the Canadian government, would be considered a risk-free investment.

But what, essentially, is the difference between a "certainty" and a "high degree of probability"? Most people would perhaps regard them as almost the same thing. Are they? I think not. Probabilities are derived from assumptions based on calculations whose relevance and validity are themselves uncertain. Consequently, it is misleading to speak of a stated return having a high degree of probability.

A capitalization rate is determined by reference to the cost of money, the expectation of inflation, and finally the perception of risk. The first two of these factors are commonly the subject of publicly announced projections. It is only the presumption of risk that is mutable and always unsettled. What is constant about risk is the concept of risk aversion. Risk aversion in a financial market refers to the mental state of a prospective investor.

It is that state of economic anxiety in which the natural aversion to loss becomes a major consideration.

To the extent that people are wired to dislike potential losses, most people are content to sacrifice profit for security, and in that regard, investors will frequently invest in low yielding bonds rather than in stocks, even though stocks typically earn more than seven times as much as bonds.

This concept of loss of aversion was the subject of many studies conducted to determine how decisions are made. The results all indicate that in human decision making, losses loom much bigger than gains. For example, when a subject was offered a gamble on a toss of a coin and was told that losing would cost $20, the subject demanded an average of about $40 for winning. The pain of loss was almost twice the pleasure generated by gain. That may explain why gain must be more than just commensurate with loss—it must be more, much more than commensurate.

A. THE NATURE OF RISK

Theoretically, the difference between a risk-free rate and the required rate of return on invested capital may be thought of as the premium compensating the investor for the risk and, if applicable, the burden of management and the illiquidity of the capital that has been invested. Leaving aside for the moment the risk of management and illiquidity, the reward for assuming a risk is one that must be commensurate with the magnitude of the risk.

When an investment analyst chooses a number as the expected future cash flow, it is, of course, not the only possible number. It is to his mind the most probable number within a range of possible numbers having due regard to the probability that a foreseen event will occur and that an unforeseen event will not occur.

The analyst must be someone who can anticipate or at least identify every possible outcome in a given situation. An *outcome* is the basic unit of possible occurrences. For example, in a coin toss two outcomes are possible. The probability of an outcome is its long-run relative frequency. For example, if a coin is tossed many times, heads come up half the time and tails the other half. The long-run relative frequency of heads may be said to be 0.5. So, probability may be said to be the numerical assessment of the likelihood. It is a number between zero and one wherein zero means the event is impossible and one means it is absolutely certain to happen. Between zero and one is a range of possible values that can be given in percentage form. A probability of 50 percent means that the event will occur half the time as the outcome of the given situation. For example, economists once held a belief that there was a high probability a recession would occur at least once every five to seven years. This belief was based on one of the mathematical principles at work in all predictions of likelihood—namely, that if one observes a number of outcomes, long-run patterns will emerge.

B. AVERSION TO RISK

The concept of utility of risk involves weights that are subjectively assigned to possible investment outcomes to reflect a particular investor's relative preference for each. Accordingly, an investor who believes in taking risks will give a higher ranking of utility to a higher risk investment than would an investor with a low tolerance for risk. However, an investor would do so only because the expectation of the best-case scenario is attractive enough to warrant the risk of experiencing the worst-case scenario.

A discounted cash flow model may be used to identify the best-case, the worst-case, and the probable-case scenarios. A probability factor is assigned to each outcome by a percentage. Each outcome is then multiplied by the "weighted" probability, and the sum of those figures indicates the expected value of that investment.

Table 6.1

	Net Present Value	Probability	Weighted Value
Best Case	$600,000	.30	$180,000
Mid-Case	$500,000	.60	$300,000
Worst Case	$200,000	.10	$20,000
		1.00	$500,000

In the foregoing illustration, it may be said that the "weighted" value of the proposed investment is $500,000 based on a probability factor.

Applying utility factors to the foregoing will permit you to determine a different value if your tolerance for the worst-case scenario is less than your anticipation of the best-case scenario.

Table 6.2

	Net Present Value	Utility Factor	Utility × Possible Outcome
Best Case	$600,000	.15	$90,000
Mid-Case	$500,000	.35	$175,000
Worst Case	$200,000	.50	$100,000
		1.00	$365,000

The two illustrations above demonstrate that the lower tolerance for loss decreased the company's intrinsic value by 27 percent.

C. SIMULATION

Before an investment decision is actually made, you may be able to test the results by using simulation to approximate the expected return. To do so, you construct an analytical model in which all the elements of the investment are assigned probabilities based on the analyst's assessment of the probable outcomes.

A simple discounted cash flow model can be used to identify high, low, and best-case possibilities for each income and expense item, each with an assigned probability. The computer simulates the trial values of each item and then calculates the return on investment based on the values simulated. When the process is repeated often enough, the rate of return can be plotted in a frequency distribution from which the analyst is able to evaluate the expected return and the uncertainty or risk on this expected return—that is, the probability that an investment will provide a return greater or less than a certain amount.

The simulation method enhances the utility of risk analysis because it allows the analyst to see the range of consequences associated with different combinations of possible outcomes and to weigh their expected values. This is especially useful in identifying extreme outcomes so that the extremes of risk may be properly considered. Accordingly, it is a method used frequently in large-scale decision-making situations.

D. ALTERING THE PROPORTIONS OF DEBT AND EQUITY

As stated in Chapter 5, the value of a company, as a whole, is theoretically the sum of the value of its equity and debt components, and, since securities that are issued to bondholders have a different value than securities issued to shareholders, by altering the proportions of debt and equity within the company's structure, the value of the company is significantly affected.

The extent to which a company uses its "leverage" will affect its earnings, its discount rate, its intrinsic value, and its market value. As shown in the illustration in Chapter 5, when the debt reaches about 30 percent of total capital that is the level at which the company reaches its highest value. But as leverage rises, so does the probability of financial distress within a company that is burdened with debt. In periods of economic turmoil, in tight credit periods, or in recessionary times the highly leveraged company is more likely to fail. The weighted average cost of the capital invested in the company rises while the value of the company falls because the value of the company is extremely sensitive to the cost of its capital. It is a factor that potentially causes the greatest change in value and therefore poses the greatest risk to an expected outcome. The anticipation of an adverse financial circumstance arising within the near future or the need to increase the ratio of debt to equity are variables that clearly affect the risk assessment of the company.

E. PAYBACK PERIOD

The payback period can also be used as a simple measurement of risk. In any application the payback period indicates the amount of time that investment money will be exposed to the risks inherent in a given investment. For example, if the economy is moving from recession into a period of anticipated continuous growth, a buyer may be more willing to be exposed to a longer period of risk because the buyer anticipates the longer term will allow him to take advantage of the growth cycle. Conversely, the buyer may desire a shorter payback period to avoid the adverse circumstance of a downward business cycle. Based on the foregoing, the payback period may be used to determine when to enter into and when to exit from a given investment.

F.   RISK-ADJUSTED DISCOUNT RATES

Assume that a buyer requires a return of 18 percent. The buyer would generally reject pro forma that extend beyond five years to avoid the risk of a future downturn in the business cycle. However, if the buyer is attracted to holding an acquisition beyond five years, the risk associated with the extra period could be offset by adjusting upward the discount rate applied to the period following the fifth year.

G.   SENSITIVITY ANALYSIS

A sensitivity analysis is performed by applying one or more variables at a time to an analytical model to determine the model's sensitivity to each change. Those factors that cause the greatest change in the results are considered more sensitive and therefore pose greater risk to the expected outcome.

Sensitivity tests can be applied to virtually any element in the analysis that is subject to change. As shown in Chapter 5 in Tables 5.2 through 5.6, when the proportion of debt to equity changes, each variable is affected in a way that may either increase or decrease the intrinsic value of the company.

Assume that a buyer is investigating a company that has no debt and a current estimated net operating income of $400,000, but that could also be 10 percent less, say, $360,000; then assume that the required rate of return on equity for such a company is 15 percent, but that could range up to 16.5 percent. At $400,000 at 15 percent the company arguably would have an intrinsic value of $2.67 million. However, a buyer may want to know which variable is more sensitive: a 10 percent change in the net operating income or a 10 percent increase in the cap rate from 15 percent to 16.5 percent. If the net operating income were only $360,000 the value would fall to $2.4 million, a loss of $270,000. If the required cap rate was 16.5 percent on $400,000 of net operating income, the value would fall to $2.42 million, a loss of $250,000. The foregoing test indicates that a 10 percent change in the net operating income is more significant than a 10 percent change in the rate of return.

The results of sensitivity analysis will facilitate decisions regarding the need for further data, the ranges and consequences of risk factors, and the steps that should be taken to implement these decisions.

Chapter 7: **Value and the Financial Acquisitions**

A. LEVERAGED BUYOUTS

Financial acquisitions, oftentimes known as *leveraged buyouts*, are acquisitions in which a transfer of ownership is financed largely with the use of debt secured by the assets of the seller's company. The funds generated by the financing of the company's assets are paid to the shareholders of the company in exchange for their shares. Unlike a *strategic acquisition*, in which there is an overall strategy for blending the two companies together, in a financial acquisition there is commonly no such strategy. The motivation is to sell off assets, cut costs, and operate whatever remains more efficiently than before and in doing so produce a value above that which was paid. To achieve an aggregate value that will exceed the price paid for the acquisition, divestitures, liquidations, and selloffs are employed.

A sale made to the management personnel of a company is often in the form of a leveraged buyout. Whenever the owners of a private company have a large portion of their wealth represented by their shareholdings in the company, or whenever a large company has a subsidiary or division that it wishes to divest, a leveraged buyout may enable the senior management personnel to purchase that private company or that particular subsidiary or division. These leveraged buyouts are commonly referred to as *management buyouts*.

The leveraged buyout transaction will generally take one of two basic forms: a sale of the company's assets or a cash merger. In the former, the operating assets become part of the buyer's company, and shareholders of the seller either continue to hold their shares in the seller's company or liquidate the company and cash out. In the latter form, the seller's company disappears upon merger with the buyer, and its shareholders receive cash for their shares.

Candidates for leveraged buyouts have certain common characteristics. The cash flow generated by the operations of the company must be stable and predictable, and generated by an established market position that is neither seasonal nor cyclical. Service companies or turnaround operations are undesirable. In the former, senior employees who provide the service may leave, while in the latter, there is no predictability of the company's expected performance. Since the cash flow of the company must be dedicated to service the debt that has been created to facilitate the acquisition, the company must not be one that relies on heavy capital expenditures. Simply stated, the asset base must be attractive to a lender and the cash flow must be both available and certain to service the debt that the assets secure. In leveraged buyouts, two forms of debt are commonly employed: *senior debt* and *junior debt*, which is subordinated to the senior debt. A bank or other traditional lender provides the senior debt plus a revolving operating credit line, which it secures by a lien against all of the company's assets.

The junior debt, which is often provided by a pension fund or other investor/lender, is sometimes referred to as *mezzanine financing* because it bears characteristics that are not unlike both equity and senior debt. The junior debt would likely be for a term of years that extends beyond the term of the senior debt and commonly bears a fixed rate as opposed to the floating rate that is usually charged on the senior debt. The junior debt is commonly repayable monthly as interest only as opposed to the repayment of blended principal and interest payments for the senior debt. The junior debt is also secured by the company's assets, but the security ranks subordinate to the senior debt and the company's trade creditors. However, as an inducement to the lenders of junior debt to provide a debt that is subordinate, the "mezzanine loan" will usually carry a share warrant coupon that, if exercised, may be converted into a considerable portion of the issued share capital of the company.

The virtue of mezzanine financing is that it fills the void that exists between senior debt and equity that may not otherwise be available. Mezzanine financing is highly leveraged financing and may therefore be rated as speculative or junk bond grade. Consequently, the required rate of return on such financing (which includes the exercise of share warrants or other such equity participation) is in the range of 20 percent to 30 percent per year. Mezzanine lenders will expect the company to produce earnings, before interest and taxes, that bear a ratio to debt of 1.25 to 1.0. Rarely will these lenders consider a 1:1 ratio.

B. COMMENTARY

The heart of each leveraged buyout transaction is that the financing of the acquisition is based solely on the assets of the seller's company.

Large, unused borrowing capacity is the feature that typically enables the buyer to use the seller's assets to borrow the required purchase price. That borrowing capacity is a function of the following considerations:

- A limited amount of current debt
- The demonstrated ability to achieve considerable earnings over a given number of years
- Large amounts of excess cash or cash equivalent
- Assets that are substantially undervalued in that their market value far exceeds the depreciated value shown on the seller's financial statements
- Assets that can be readily liquidated for cash without adversely affecting the ongoing operations
- The potential for tax-sheltered income because of a step-up in the adjusted cost base of property acquired

Part 2

THE ART OF THE NEGOTIATION

Chapter 8: **The Planning Process**

Long before a prospective buyer and seller have met, the groundwork may be laid for the future negotiation.

The decision to sell or merge is a decision that was presumably predicated on certain desires, motives, goals, and objectives. An offering memorandum prepared by a seller should provide the reader with an insight into the seller's thought process. If the memorandum accurately reflects that thought process, a prospective buyer or a merger candidate is able to determine if there is a fit between the two companies that is worth pursuing. In other words, is there a possibility for the creation of a synergy value through acquisition or merger? If the answer is yes, an opportunity may be present that is worth pursuing.

Similarly, the decision to acquire or to merge with another company is a decision that was predicated on certain desires, motives, goals, and objectives. An acquisition plan, prepared by a prospective buyer, may be tantamount to a traditional business plan, but it should provide the reader with an insight into the buyer's thought process. A potential seller of stock or assets or a candidate for merger should be able to determine if his company meets the criteria that the buyer's acquisition plan has described.

Although both these documents precede the commencement of a negotiation process, they create a "first impression" that the parties must ensure is not misleading.

A. THE SELLER'S OFFERING MEMORANDUM

After the seller has chosen its team of advisors (representing legal, accounting, and investment expertise), to whom the seller will impart its motivations, goals, and post-closing objectives, a set of materials known as the offering memorandum is assembled and discreetly distributed to all potential buyers and their advisors. A confidentiality agreement should be prepared and executed by each prospective candidate to whom a copy of the seller's memorandum is being released. (*See Form 3.*)

The offering memorandum will contain the information that will anchor and thereafter channel the negotiations in a desired direction and should therefore include the following:

- An executive summary of the seller's company describing its key products and services.
- A profile of the management team and organizational form of the seller's company.
- A profile of the *ideal* buyer, describing the standards by which a buyer may be pre-qualified based on the goals and pre- and post-closing objectives of the seller.
- A summary of the financial performance of the selling company, together with a recasting of the financial data by which earnings and profits are maximized (rather than the usual minimization that is characteristic of privately owned and closely held companies).
- A schedule of key customer relationships and other intangible assets.
- Hurdles that may exist prior to a successful completion of sale. These may refer to "skeletons in the closet," such as outstanding litigation, or other pre-closing conditions that a reasonable buyer will want resolved.
- Last, but certainly not least, using the discounted cash formula method, a forecast of the expected earnings of the company and working capital requirements over a five-year planning period showing the enhanced value of the business at the end of the fifth

year, thereby demonstrating the discounted value of the company's future cash flow, its intrinsic value, and the basis for the synergy value with the right buyer or merger candidate.

The information that is contained within the offering memorandum must be presented truthfully. The temptation to create an overly attractive situation should be resisted. The negotiation that follows will be based on information contained in the offering memorandum, and that being the case, its content should be forthright, optimistic, confident, but not reckless. The objective is for the buyer to focus on the information that appears in the memorandum that supports the value that the seller considers the company to be worth. That information must be accurate so that the team representing the seller is capable of defending the projections made therein as to the expected earnings and the cost of capital of the company.

B. THE BUYER'S ACQUISITION PLAN

Conventional wisdom is that it is cheaper to buy than to build a business. What with low interest rates and plentiful capital available, it may be true that the achievement of certain corporate goals and objectives may be facilitated by the external acquisition of assets and other resources needed for growth. But what are those goals and objectives? What criteria are to be applied in analyzing potential target companies? The statement of objectives should be a response to the following questions:

- Why are we doing this?
- Is growth by acquisition preferable to other forms of growth strategies, such as joint ventures, franchise, or licensing?
- Do we enhance the value of the company and the company's competitive position in doing so?

The acquisition plan is intended to define the objectives of the buyer, the criteria to be used in evaluating candidates, the price range to be considered, and related issues. The plan should identify the value-added efficiencies and cost savings that a successful acquisition will generate and explain how the acquisition will enhance the performance and the profitability of the seller's company. In fact, the plan is one that a buyer may choose to release to a prospective seller in dealing with a seller's concerns as to the potential for continued growth in the buyer's shares. If the seller understands and respects the buyer's acquisition strategy and growth plans, the plan can be a valuable negotiating tool if the buyer plans to ask the seller to accept shares in the buyer's company for all or part of the purchase price.

C.   THE LETTER OF INTENT

The prospective buyer and seller have met. They have been matched by a broker or by an investment banker that one or the other may have retained, or they may have come together through industry contacts that they shared, or through commercial networking. Whatever the case, if the seller's offering memorandum and the buyer's acquisition plan have been exchanged, each party may already understand the other's perspective and recognize the complementary and overlapping objectives and goals.

To the extent that there is commonality on the more critical features of the screening criteria, and to the extent that each side has had an opportunity to meet one another's key players and are inclined to think that "this may very well work out" or some such optimistic expression, the next step is *the letter of intent* or the *interim agreement* or, metaphorically speaking, an engagement of the parties made in the hope that it will conclude in their marriage. (*See Forms 1, 2, 11, and 12.*)

1)   On Drafting Letters of Intent

The letter of intent is not a term of art. It is primarily intended as a pre-contractual document that is indistinguishable from other pre-contractual documents that go by a number of other names, such "heads of agreement," "memorandum of understanding," "letter of understanding," "memorandum of intent," and "term sheet."

a) The Purpose

Because the agreement of purchase and sale to acquire an asset or shares, or agreements to form partnerships or ventures or leases may contain extensive and detailed provisions, the effort and the legal costs of creating these agreements are unwarranted unless the parties have already agreed on the basic financial and business terms.

Therefore, the purpose of the letter of intent (LOI) essentially is to record the preliminary understandings of its signatories that may form the basis of a future agreement. It is an efficient and cost-effective means by which to settle terms that have been agreed upon by the parties and that establishes a level of trust that may facilitate making the contract and completing the transaction.

The LOI will contain basic terms, including the price, the bargain, the method of acquisition, the financial terms, the due diligence and inspection timetable, and the date by which the agreement to be executed by the parties will be finalized. The LOI may also deal with the risks that are to be assumed by the purchaser and the risks that are to remain with the vendor.

The law of contract in Canada is that a party is not bound to negotiate in good faith unless a binding contract exists between the parties. Accordingly, the LOI is intended to be morally binding on the parties to negotiate in good faith the issues that may arise after the LOI has been signed.

b) The Intention of the Parties

The parties using an LOI should know in advance what they wish to achieve. There are three possible legal effects of an LOI. It may be considered a complete agreement and enforceable as a final expression of agreement on the subject transaction. That result is most likely in the case of an LOI signed by both parties after both preliminary and essential agreements have been settled regarding the contemplated transaction. Second, an LOI can be partially enforced. That result is most likely in the case of an LOI that includes clauses governing aspects of a negotiation as opposed to aspects of a transaction. Finally, an LOI can be without legal effect altogether.

The first possible effect, enforcement of the LOI as a final contract, is hardly ever intended or decided on by the parties. The second possible effect is partial enforcement, and it is the opposite of full enforcement. Provisions such as sharing of expenses, confidentiality, and the exclusivity of negotiation are probably intended to be binding by the parties who include them in the LOI.

Accordingly, parties who use LOIs should know what they wish to achieve. If the purpose of the LOI is to express a complete agreement on the underlying transaction, that purpose is not well served by the LOI. In that case, the parties should proceed directly to contract. The vendor will view the LOI, at best, as a non-binding expression of the purchaser's willingness to pay a certain price. Since it is non-binding and since it is based on certain unexpressed assumptions, it is totally meaningless. It becomes meaningful only if all of the essential terms of the transaction are included and if all of those terms are mutually agreed on by the parties, and if the parties are willing to be bound by those terms it is no longer an LOI but an enforceable agreement.

c)   In Mergers/Acquisitions

Presumably, the prospective purchaser and vendor have already met, having been matched by a broker or by an investment banker that one or the other may have retained. They have determined that there may be a commonality of interest, and to that extent each side has had an opportunity to meet one another's key players and are inclined to think that this may work out or some other such optimistic expression. In any event, the next step would be the LOI or the interim agreement or, metaphorically speaking, an engagement of the parties made in the hope that it will conclude in their marriage.

As stated earlier, most LOIs fall roughly into one of three types: one that is intended to be binding, one that is intended not to be binding, and one that contains some terms that are binding and other terms that the parties agree to settle subsequently.

The parties may agree to make certain provisions within the LOI binding to encourage both the purchaser and the vendor to work toward a successful completion of the transaction. For example, the LOI may contain a clause that allows the purchaser direct access to the vendor's property, books, and records as part of its due diligence review combined with another clause that requires the purchaser to keep confidential all information that it obtains during its investigation of the vendor's business.

The letter may also contain a provision that requires the vendor to reveal any factors that might have an impact on the purchaser's decision to acquire the business, such as a dependence on certain customers or suppliers, regulatory issues, employment issues, and current or pending litigation involving the business. Both parties may also presume to be bound by a provision that requires them to negotiate in good faith toward the execution and delivery of an acquisition agreement.

Assuming that the agreement is not intended to be a binding enforceable agreement, it nevertheless provides a psychological comfort to the purchaser, who is about to incur significant expense in the course of his due diligence. If nothing else, it represents a moral commitment from each party that should at the least discourage the vendor from continuing to actively "shop his company." Perhaps most importantly, it sets down in writing the pre-agreed terms and highlights the matters that are yet to be negotiated. Critical terms—such as, is this a stock or an asset purchase, at what value, to be paid for in what form or forms of compensation?—are issues the parties may choose to subsequently settle.

What can be achieved with the LOI is the agreed-upon method of valuation. If the vendor has a predetermined value that he claims his company is worth based on a so-called industry multiplier, and if the vendor is not prepared to consider any other basis by which to determine the company's value, a purchaser may be embarking on a futile negotiation if he is not prepared to accept a valuation determined on the basis selected by the vendor. If the vendor is unwilling to have the worth of his company determined by a discounted cash flow method because the resulting value may be substantially lower than the method he has chosen, the purchaser is well advised to know this before embarking on his due diligence and incurring major investigative expenses.

d)   Avoiding the Unintended Contract

Carefully scan the LOI to ensure that the word "agree" does not appear. Words or phrases such as "I agree," "this agreement," or "the parties agree" are to be strictly avoided. The phrase "this is to confirm our verbal understandings" has been interpreted by the courts as language supporting the intent to be bound by those verbal undertakings. The phrase "the wording of the future agreement may also vary somewhat" also supports merely a desire to enter into a future agreement and not as a condition to a binding agreement.

The LOI should contain provisions that state the following:

- The LOI is not binding on the parties nor does it create a contract.
- The parties are only to be bound when a formal contract embodying the terms of the LOI and such other matters as the parties consider appropriate is settled and signed by the parties.
- It is a condition of the parties' obligation to complete the transaction that a formal agreement has been signed.
- This intention not to be bound continues notwithstanding any negotiation or settling of all or any of the issues to be resolved and notwithstanding that all issues have been settled between the parties.

A provision that is substantially similar to the following is recommended:

The parties acknowledge that this LOI is not intended to create a binding contract of agreement between the parties with respect to the matters set out herein and notwithstanding any further negotiations or settling of outstanding issues in whole or in part. The parties expressly confirm that no contract exists between them until a formal binding contract of purchase and sale has been executed by both parties.

It is not recommended that a non-binding LOI contain an arbitration clause. This may be construed by the courts as a transfer of power to complete the terms that are essential to an independent third party.

Equally important is the management of the post-LOI conduct by an LOI signatory. This applies to both a real estate deal and a corporate matter. In the former, part performance may be alleged, lifting the LOI out of the Statute of Frauds. In the latter, if a party demonstrates that it suffered a detriment a part-performance claim may be successful. As a vendor, you should not allow a potential purchaser to spend excessive sums on due diligence without emphasizing in some way that he is doing so without the presence of a final and binding agreement. Finally, when speaking to outsiders, be clear by saying that a deal is not firm or not final.

Lastly, when drafting the final agreement, remember to provide therein that it totally replaces the LOI that preceded it and which thereafter is null and void.

D. ADDRESSING THE PURCHASE PRICE

To lay the groundwork for a successful negotiation, the buyer and seller must share a common frame of reference with respect to the method by which the value is to be determined. If the parties can agree on how the intrinsic value of the seller's company is determined, the scope of the subsequent negotiation is narrowed to determining the amount that may be paid in excess of that value. For example, the letter of intent may state that the purchase price will be that amount that represents a premium of 20 percent over the intrinsic value of the seller's company.

If the seller is unwilling to proceed without a firm price commitment, the buyer's choices are to submit a non-binding letter of intent that sets forth the price required by the seller, or to submit a binding letter of intent that is subject to and conditional on the buyer, in its uncontrolled discretion, being totally satisfied with the financial and other results of its investigation. The letter of intent could also provide a price range that will be narrowed by stipulated financial factors that will subsequently be used to fix the price. For example, the letter of intent may state that the purchase price is predicated on certain assumptions and that the purchase price will be increased or decreased by the positive or negative variations in those assumptions as of the closing date.

A variation on all the foregoing is commonly referred to as an *earn-out*. If no agreement can be reached on the value of the assets or the stock that is being sold, or if the parties anticipate the possibility of a serious change in circumstance, a post-acquisition adjustment in the purchase price is often the solution. The adjustment may provide for additional payments based on a periodic reassessment of the value of the assets or the stock sold, or in the net operating income of the seller's company, or the merged entity, on a post-closing basis. Alternatively, the adjustment, known as a *reverse earn-out* may involve the repayment of part of the purchase price that had been lodged in escrow at the time of closing to be held subject to a change in circumstance or expectation.

E.   THE DUE DILIGENCE INVESTIGATION

The main objective of the due diligence investigation (*see Form 10*) is not just to confirm the factual assumptions and preliminary valuations that support the transaction, but rather to determine if the risk of potential liabilities substantially exceeds that which was reasonably anticipated after having studied the seller's offering memorandum.

The due diligence investigation is intended to detect the presence of unfulfilled obligations that are the responsibility of the seller and then to assess the nature and extent of those obligations. If the obligations are not currently in good standing, the investigation is intended to determine the nature and the extent of their default. If the obligation is assumable, a cost and risk assessment is necessary. If the obligation is not assumable, can the buyer be protected by covenant, warranty, holdback, set-off, or indemnity? To ensure the open and frank disclosure of obligations and liabilities, actual or contingent, that a seller might otherwise prefer to suppress until later in the transaction, the seller may be requested to execute an affidavit attesting to his knowledge of outstanding obligations and liabilities.

However, there is a delicate balance that the buyer's due diligence team is required to maintain in the course of its risk investigation and assessment mission. On the one hand, the team must resist the temptation to conduct a perfunctory examination to save costs or to appease the seller, while on the other hand, the team must avoid an investigative overkill bearing in mind that the due diligence cannot be a perfect process and that no matter how deeply the investigation is conducted, information will invariably "slip through the cracks."

If that balance is not maintained, potential acquisitions and mergers have a tendency to die at an early age. For example, if the buyer's team finds fault with the operations of the seller's business, or questions the loyalty of its customers, or the quality of its accounts receivable, or perhaps even the skill of its personnel, sellers have a tendency to become defensive, uncooperative, evasive, and worst of all impatient. When the seller begins to feel that the buyer has become too critical, the seller may very well demand that the investigation be concluded immediately. When negotiations have reached this point, it is perhaps best to end the investigation and either abort the transaction or rely on the presence of representations, warranties, liability holdbacks, and indemnification provisions in the final purchase agreements to provide the buyer with an appropriate measure of protection.

Chapter 9: **Structuring the Deal**

The due diligence investigation is over. The due diligence team has investigated the "closet" and the skeletons that were discovered therein are few and are considered to be manageable. The letter of intent, to a greater or lesser extent, has identified areas of agreement while high-lighting the differences and the matters that need to be negotiated.

The goal now is to structure the transaction so that it fairly reflects the original goals and objectives of both the buyer and the seller. To do so requires creativity, compromise, and strategy—the tools by which parties negotiate.

There is a vast array of corporate, tax, and security law issues that need to be addressed and that very well may influence the structure of a transaction. But in the end, the structure that will be adopted by the parties will be one that satisfies their primary needs and answers the following three basic questions:

- Will the transaction take the form of an asset or a stock purchase?
- What will be the method of payment and on what terms?
- What protections will be required to address the issues that were detected during the due diligence investigation?

A. STOCK VERSUS ASSET PURCHASE

Depending on the facts and the circumstances that surround the transaction, both the stock and the asset purchase have their respective positive and negative features. The weight of some of the following considerations may tip the scale in favour of one form or the other.

The *stock purchase* yields the following advantages to a buyer or to a seller:

- From a tax perspective, the net operating losses of the seller's company carry over to the buyer.
- The buyer enjoys the continuity of the seller's corporate identity, contracts, and structure, including the buyer's retention of rights and assets that may not otherwise be transferable, such as licences and patents.
- The sale of shares may avoid the various restrictions that may exist in loan agreements and mortgages that preclude the sale of assets without the consent of the security holder.
- It relieves the seller of the problem of disposing of the assets that the buyer does not wish to acquire.
- The obligations and liabilities of the seller become the obligations and liabilities of the buyer.

However, the stock purchase creates the following disadvantages:

- The seller is unable to choose those assets that it may wish to retain.
- The net operating losses that are present in the seller's company are not available to the seller to offset the gain on the sale.
- In the absence of adequate protection, the buyer may become liable for undisclosed or contingent liabilities.
- Because the buyer inherits the seller's asset cost base, the buyer is denied any step-up in basis for the assets that it acquired.

The *asset purchase* yields the following advantages to a buyer or a seller:

- The buyer can select the assets it wishes to acquire.
- Unless the buyer agrees to assume a liability, the buyer is not liable for the seller's liabilities and is likely free of any undisclosed or contingent liabilities.
- The buyer acquires a step-up in basis for the assets it acquires equal to the purchase price paid for those assets, thereby allowing a higher depreciation and amortization deduction.
- In addition to maintaining its corporate existence, name, and goodwill, the seller also retains its operating losses, if any, and the ownership of non-transferable assets or rights.

However, the asset purchase yields the following disadvantages:

- The buyer does not acquire non-transferable rights or assets, such as licences or patents.
- In order to assume a liability to which an asset is subject, a lender's consent may be required.
- The transaction is commonly considered to be more complex and costly in that title to each asset must be transferred and recorded.
- The buyer does not inherit the seller's loss carry forwards, and indeed, if the acquisition is made at a bargain price, there is a step-down in the basis of the assets.
- The asset acquisition requires compliance with applicable provincial bulk sales legislation as well as the payment of provincial sales and land transfer taxes.
- The asset sale generates various types of gain or loss to the seller based on the classification of each asset.
- The seller is responsible for the liquidation of the remaining assets and the corporate shell, and in distributing the proceeds of the asset sale to its shareholders it may create a form of double taxation.

1)   The Choice of Structure

There are three basic alternative structures by which corporations may "come together":

- by statutory amalgamation or merger
- by creating a parent–subsidiary relationship resulting from a stock purchase
- by consolidation resulting from an asset purchase

The *statutory amalgamation* or *merger* involves the combination of two or more companies whereby the amalgamating companies thereafter continue as one surviving corporate entity. The surviving company by law possesses the assets, rights, and privileges and is subject to the liabilities and contracts of each of the amalgamating companies. A statutory amalgamation is subject to the provisions of the *Canada Business Corporations Act* or the various provincial *Companies Acts*. These Acts generally stipulate the basic provisions to be included in the amalgamation agreement, provisions relating to the shareholders' approval of the agreement, and provisions relating to the recourse or remedies available to dissenting shareholders.

Another form of combination is created when a buyer acquires a sufficient amount of the common shares of the seller to give it a controlling interest in the seller's company. A parent–subsidiary relationship is thereby created in which both companies continue to exist as separate legal entities with each being responsible for the management of its assets and its liabilities under the administration of their respective boards of directors. Most corporate charters require that the management of the company present any merger or acquisition proposal to its shareholders for final approval.

A third form of combination is created when a buyer acquires all or substantially all of the assets of another company, in exchange for which the selling company receives cash or shares from the buyer and the selling company remains responsible for its liabilities. The seller's company may be liquidated after it has paid its creditors and distributed the remaining funds to its shareholders, or it may continue as a holding company or as an active entity in some other line of business. Various provincial *Companies Acts* require that the shareholders of the seller approve the sale of the assets, usually by a two-thirds majority vote.

2) Tax Considerations

There is a vast array of tax issues that affect each of the foregoing structures. Simply stated, mergers and acquisitions may be completely or partially tax free or entirely taxable to the seller. However, it is beyond the scope of this text to do more than merely touch on the matter of taxation. Suffice to say that if the acquisition is made with cash or with a debt instrument, the transaction is taxable to the seller or to the seller's company at that time. In other words, any capital gain or loss will be recognized on the sale of the assets or the sale of the stock at the time of the sale. However, if payment is made with voting preferred or common shares, the transaction is not taxable at the time of the sale. The capital gain or loss is recognized only when the shares are sold.

In addition to the requirement that the seller obtain voting shares, a merger must have a business purpose to be tax free. Nevertheless, the avoidance of income tax is indeed a factor, and a company with a tax loss carry forward may want to acquire or be acquired by one or more profitable companies to be able to use a loss carry forward that otherwise may expire at the end of seven years.

3) Other Considerations

The buyer who decides to acquire or to merge with another company does so to achieve internal growth. However, there are a number of alternative strategies that may achieve the same objective, such as joint ventures, franchising, licensing, alliances, or distributorships. The primary difference between merger and acquisition and these alternative strategies is the degree of control the buyer may achieve.

The strongest level of control is vested in a buyer who purchases 100 percent of a seller's company. A movement away from the strongest level would be the acquisition of the assets of the seller's company.

The asset purchase may not achieve the control the buyer desires if the assets the buyer covets are largely intangible assets that don't appear on the traditional balance sheet. The seller's ability to train and retain highly skilled, knowledgeable workers; to obtain and keep loyal customers; and the network of strategic relationships and distribution channels are all intangibles that represent powerful assets that are more easily acquired through the acquisition of the seller's company's capital stock.

Fortunately, the shareholders of the seller are usually predisposed, for tax and other reasons, to a sale of their shares rather than a sale of their assets. This may not necessarily be true, however, if the shareholders have their own agenda that involves maintaining their corporate existence, goodwill, and certain non-transferable assets or rights. If such were the case, a broadly based non-compete agreement with the shareholders of the seller and long-term employment and consulting contracts with its key managers become critical.

Nevertheless, the conventional wisdom is that an asset purchase is preferable if the buyer's fear of unknown, undisclosed, or contingent liabilities cannot be reasonably covered by representations, warranties, and indemnities that a seller may insist be limited both in time and amount. For example, in a manufacturing company, the fear that prior product liability claims against the seller may surface creates a strong case for the asset purchase.

B. METHOD OF PAYMENT

In structuring the elements of the purchase price, there is a wide variety of possible forms of payment beyond that of cash. Marketable securities, real estate, the rights to intangible assets such as franchises and licences, secured and unsecured promissory notes, the common and preferred securities of the buyer or its affiliate, earn-outs, consulting agreements, employment agreements, royalty and licence agreements, or even the exchange of another business are all possible forms of payment.

1) Cash

From the seller's perspective, a payment in cash for the assets or the stock being sold is preferable to a seller who is concerned with the buyer's creditworthiness or the buyer's financial and business viability. This need not necessarily create a problem for a buyer. An all-cash transaction may be internally financed or financed through the cash flow of the combined companies or the seller's company, or financed through a lending secured by the assets or the stock acquired.

2) Stock

If the seller does not harbour concerns about the buyer's financial strength or if the seller is reluctant to dispose of his interest entirely, or if the seller wishes to defer tax to a later year, the common shares of the buyer or a buyer's newly formed subsidiary, or even a new class of preferred shares, may be issued to the seller as payment, in whole or in part, for the assets or stock being sold. In accepting this method of payment, the seller is participating as a shareholder in the anticipated growth in value generated by the profits derived from the combined entities.

3) Debt

If the seller does not have concerns about the strength of the buyer, the seller may accept the buyer's promissory note as part of the purchase price. A promissory note may be secured by the assets of either the buyer, the seller, or both, or the note may not be secured at all. Alternatively, the note may be subordinated to a senior commercial lender if the buyer is borrowing money from a bank or other lending institution as part of the capital needed to acquire the seller's assets or stock.

From the buyer's perspective, debt is often preferable to stock because interest paid is tax deductible. However, the magnitude of debt that a company carries may create negative consequences that have an impact on the buyer's cost of capital.

4) Convertible Debt Securities

Debt securities issued by the buyer that are convertible into the common shares of the buyer provide the seller with a fixed return and a "floor" while still providing the seller with the opportunity to enjoy the benefits of growth in the increased value or the profits derived from the combined operations. From a buyer's perspective, convertible debt securities provide the tax advantages of interest deductibility while still enabling the buyer to perhaps avoid the payment due to the seller upon maturity of the debt.

5) Earn-Outs

When the buyer and the seller are not able to agree on the value of the assets or the stock being sold, or when either wishes to revise the terms of the transaction in light of changes in circumstance or expectation, an earn-out provides for additional payment based on periodic adjustments in the value of the assets or the stock sold, or the net operating income of the seller's company or the merged entity, on a post-closing basis. An agreement may also provide for the repayment of part of the purchase price through the use of an escrow or other security arrangement on the occurrence of a change in circumstance or expectation. This is known as a *reverse earn-out*.

6) Cash Versus Stock Versus Equity

As already stated, if the seller has concerns about the buyer's long-term credibility and financial viability, the seller will prefer payment in cash in full for the assets or the stock being sold. The buyer will of course prefer to invest as little as possible of its own retained earnings and internal capital reserves into the transaction. However, if the seller is reluctant to completely dispose of its interest in the business, or if the seller wishes to defer its taxation to a later year, the seller may be willing to accept the buyer's stock as partial payment for the purchase price.

Therefore, the purchase price may have to be satisfied by a combination of cash, debt, and equity.

The proportion that each bears to the total purchase price will be a function of the seller's willingness to provide financing for the buyer by accepting payment for part of its purchase price in the form of the buyer's common or preferred shares (equity) or by accepting the buyer's promissory note in partial satisfaction (debt). The proportions of cash, debt, and equity will be critically affected by the availability of funding from lenders of senior and subordinated debt.

The buyer's preference of debt over equity for the payment of the purchase price may relate not only to the deductibility of interest as a tax deduction, but also to considerations of share ownership percentages and problems related to the matter of control. The buyer will prefer debt to the issue of capital stock because of the issue of control and because interest paid on debt is tax deductible. The buyer's willingness to take on enormous debt may be the wrong impression to give an uncertain seller. As already seen, the proportions of debt and equity may significantly affect the company's value, its earnings per share, its price/earnings ratio, and the cost of its capital. If a company were able to achieve the most favourable balance between debt and equity, we have already seen that three positive consequences ensue: the value of the company and the price per share is maximized and the weighted average cost of capital is minimized.

7)   The Buyer's Shares as a Source of Funding

When an acquisition is made using the stock of the buyer, a determination must be made as to the value of the stock in the two companies so that a ratio of exchange reflects the relative value of the two companies. If both companies are publicly listed, the ratio of exchange may be the market price of the publicly traded stock. If such is not the case, the intrinsic value of each company may be determined and used as a ratio of exchange.

The ratio of exchange that is chosen will affect the *earnings per share* of the two companies if the earnings of the two companies remain the same after acquisition. An increase in the earnings per share of a buyer will occur if the price/earnings ratio paid to the seller for the seller's company is lower than the price/earnings ratio of the buyer. Conversely, a dilution in the earnings per share of a buyer will occur if the price/earnings ratio paid to the seller for the seller's company exceeds the price/earnings ratio of the buyer. For example, assume the price/earnings ratio of a buyer is 10, which is to say, the buyer, valued at $200,000, has earnings of $20,000. If the seller is valued at $300,000 with earnings of $20,000, that is a price/earnings ratio of 15. Therefore, a dilution in the buyer's per share earnings will occur because the seller's ratio of 15 exceeds the buyer's ratio of 10.

The amount of the increase or the decrease in earnings per share is a function of both the differential in the price/earnings ratio and the relative size of each of the two companies measured by their total earnings. The higher the price/earnings ratio of the buyer in relation to that of the seller, and the larger the earnings of the seller in relation to those of the buyer, the greater the increase in earnings per share of the buyer.[1]

However, the use of the foregoing as criteria for judging the value of a merger is questionable since the earnings of the component companies hopefully will not remain the same after the acquisition. In many cases, because of operating economies or increases in demand, the earnings of the surviving company may be greater than the sum of the earnings of the two companies without the merger. Moreover, if the earnings of the seller are expected to grow at a faster rate than those of the buyer, a high rate of exchange for the stock of the seller may be justified despite the fact that there is an initial dilution in earnings per share of the buyer. However, the longer the duration of the dilution, the less desirable will be the acquisition.

---

1   W. Mead, "Instantaneous Merger Profit as a Conglomerate Merger Move" (December 1969) 7 *Western Economics Journal* 295–306.

The ratio of exchange will also affect the *market value* of the shares of the two companies. The ratio of exchange may be stated by the following formula:

$$\frac{\text{Buyer's market price per share}}{\text{Seller's market price per share}} \times \begin{array}{l}\text{The number of shares offered} \\ \text{to the seller by the buyer}\end{array}$$

Assume that the market price of the shares of the two companies have been determined to be $10 per share for the buyer's shares and $3 per share for the seller's shares and that the buyer is offering one of its shares for every three shares of the seller. In that case, the ratio of exchange would be expressed as follows:

$$\frac{10 \times .3}{3} = 1.00$$

Based on the foregoing, the shares of the two companies would be exchanged on a 1:1 market price basis, and assuming that the market price of the surviving company remains stable, the shareholders of each company are about as well off as before.

However, a buyer commonly will have to pay a price greater than the current market price per share of the company it wishes to acquire because otherwise there is little to motivate the seller being acquired on a 1:1 market value ratio of exchange. A buyer may offer the seller a premium over the market value ratio of exchange and still increase its own value *if* the price/earnings ratio of the buyer exceeds the price/earnings ratio of the seller before the merger, and *if* the price/earnings ratio of the buyer remains the same after the merger. Provided that these two conditions are achieved, the benefit to the seller is that it has been paid a premium in having exchanged its stock for stock that has a greater value, while the benefit to the buyer is that it obtained an immediate increase in its earnings per share despite having paid a premium in the market value ratio of exchange. That is to say, the shareholders of both companies have benefited because a company with a high price/earnings ratio is ostensibly able to acquire a company with a lower price/earnings ratio despite having to pay a premium to effect the acquisition. Theoretically, such a buyer could show a steady growth in its earnings per share if it acquired a number of companies over time with a low price/earnings ratio. Nevertheless, without growth potential in other ways, it is unlikely that the marketplace would continue to hold the price/earnings ratio of the buyer at its pre-merger level. For the benefit of the acquisition to be a lasting one, the buyer must be able to demonstrate a synergy value being created to justify the premium paid to the seller. If such were not the case, the price/earnings ratio of the surviving company would likely approach the weighted average of the prior price/earnings ratios of the two companies.

8) The Seller as a Source of Funding

If the seller does not harbour concerns about the financial strength of the buyer and if the seller has no immediate need for cash, or if the seller believes that the company is worth more than the buyer is able or willing to pay, the seller may choose to provide the buyer with a sub-stantial portion of the purchase price.

From the buyer's perspective, the buyer may choose to use the financing provided by the seller to keep the seller motivated in the company's future success or to force the seller to prove that the business has the upside potential that the seller has represented and therefore absorb some of the buyer's risk.

The seller's financing can be fixed financing, such as the acceptance of an unsecured promissory note, or equity financing, such as the acceptance of some of the buyer's common or preferred shares or convertible debt or contingent financing such as warrants (which are options to purchase the buyer's shares at a fixed price at a later point in time), or the seller's financing may be in the form of a conditional payment such as an earn-out.

With earn-out financings, the seller will receive the additional payments only if the acquired business performs above a specified level in the future, or if a specified post-closing condition is met, or if a certain event occurs such as the issuance of a patent. Sellers who agree to accept a portion of the purchase price in this manner should recognize that they may be assuming a substantial post-closing risk. However, from the buyer's perspective, it is a well-structured transaction if the buyer is able to shift a major risk back to the seller.

By way of illustration, assume the buyer has agreed to acquire all the assets of the seller for $10 million and that the purchase price will be funded as follows:

Table 9.1

The buyer's cash funding	$ 2,000,000	
Bank funding (secured by the assets being acquired)	$ 3,000,000	
Assets subject to a debt assumed by the buyer	$ 500,000	$ 5,500,000
Seller accepts a 5-year promissory note subordinated to the senior bank funding	$ 2,000,000	
Seller accepts stock payment	$ 1,000,000	
Contingent earn-out payment in a newly created company	$ 1,300,000	
Consulting agreement fee of $100,000 for 2 consecutive years	$ 200,000	$ 4,500,000
TOTAL		$10,000,000

In structuring the financing as shown, the buyer has managed to shift more than 40 percent of the purchase price risk back to the seller by making the payment contingent or by deferring the payment. The structure is attractive to the buyer in that the buyer is using only 20 percent of its own funds to make the acquisition and has five years within which to repay the funding provided by the bank and the seller. Presumably the shareholders of the seller are convinced that the buyer will be successful, otherwise they would not accept almost 25 percent of the purchase price in the form of fees and earn-out payments. Nevertheless, the sellers are receiving 50 percent of the purchase price in cash on closing and unloading $500,000 of debt to which the seller's company was subject. Lastly, the promissory note may be collaterally secured by a secondary security position against all of the assets sold, in which case the seller, at most, ranks behind only $3.5 million in prior debt.

C. CORPORATE CONTROL

It is a timeless maxim: "Don't tell me who owns the property. I need to know who controls it."

To the extent that a seller acquires a stock position in the buyer or in a newly formed subsidiary, control over management has a considerable value apart from the shares acquired by the seller.

1) In the Absence of a Shareholders' Agreement

In the absence of a shareholders' agreement, control of a corporation with respect to its management of the business and affairs is governed by the provisions of the Ontario *Business Corporations Act* (OBCA), the corporation's articles, and its by-laws. An example of the application of the OBCA is in section 1.02(1), which states "Unless the articles provide otherwise, each share of the corporation entitles the holder thereof to one (1) vote at a meeting of shareholders." With respect to the management of the business and affairs of the corporation, section 115(1) of the OBCA states "Subject to any unanimous shareholders agreement [to be commented on hereafter] the directors shall manage or supervise the management of the business and affairs of the corporation."

However, the authority of the directors is subject to limitations. For instance, the directors may not exercise powers that are expressly reserved for the shareholders, nor may the directors act contrary to the OBCA, or the articles or the by-laws of the corporation, or a unanimous shareholders agreement [to be commented on hereafter]. However, subject to these exceptions, clearly the powers of the directors are very broad and encompass all the authority required to conduct the ordinary, ongoing operations and business of the corporation.

The legal control vested in the board of directors is recognized in law as the prime moving force in managing corporate business and administering corporate affairs and is put in that position by statute, not by corporate constitution. Moreover, the board of directors acts collectively, as their power is given to the board as a unit, not to individual board members.

While the corporate statutes provide instances in which directors may delegate certain of their powers, such as through the appointment from among board members to a managing director [commented on hereafter] or a committee of the board, or the appointment of officers for the corporation, no such appointment will eliminate the supervisory responsibility of the directors.

It is important to remember that corporate statutes do not limit the responsibility of directors when a passive rather than an active approach to management and supervision is taken. There are also instances in which the corporate statutes will impose liabilities of a corporation on its directors without regard to the practical control that they exercise over the corporation.

As stated earlier, in the absence of a written agreement among the shareholders the conduct of the company is governed by the OBCA and the company's by-laws. In the event of a conflict between the provisions of the OBCA and the by-laws of the company, the by-laws will prevail. This is because many of the provisions in the OBCA begin with the words "Subject to the by-laws of the company."

The contents of the usual By-law No. 1 (see attached precedent) relate generally to the transaction of the business and affairs of the company and includes sections that govern the actions of the board of directors and the decision making at any meeting of shareholders, in each case based on a majority of votes cast on the question.

In summary, in the absence of a shareholders' agreement, control is vested in a simple majority vote made by directors and shareholders unless the articles and the by-laws of the company provide otherwise.

2) In the Presence of a Shareholders' Agreement

Given that the directors of the corporation are appointed by its shareholders, it is logical that those same shareholders are statutorily empowered to limit or entirely remove from the directors their authority and duties by entering into a "Unanimous Shareholder Agreement" (USA):

> A shareholder who is a party to a USA has all of the rights, powers, duties and liabilities of a director of a corporation, whether arising under the OBCA or otherwise, including any defences available to the directors to which the agreement relates to the extent that the agreement restricts the discretion or powers of the directors and managers supervise the management of the business and affairs of the corporation and the directors are relieved of their duties and liabilities, including any liabilities under the directors liability to employees for wages (s 108(5) of the OBCA).

An agreement that serves the foregoing purpose is what is referred to in the OBCA as a USA. If the agreement between the shareholders does not relieve directors of any of their rights, the agreement is a shareholders' agreement but is not a USA.

The freedom of the board of directors to act is subject to the presence of a USA by which all the company's shareholders have agreed to restrict, in whole or in part, the powers of the directors to manage or to supervise the management of the company's business and affairs. A further limitation may be imposed on the freedom of the board to act if, subject to the articles or by-laws of the company, the directors of the company have appointed from their number a managing director and have delegated to that managing director any of the powers of the board.

When the rights and obligations of the shareholders as set forth in the OBCA or in the company's articles or in its by-laws conflict with the provisions of the USA, the provisions of the USA prevail (see section 1.02 of By-Law No. 1). This of course represents a reversal of the company's default position as set forth in the Canadian corporate statutes wherein the company is managed entirely by its directors and officers. The use of the USA restricts the power of the directors to manage the company and instead transfers the additional authority to the shareholder (see section 108(1) through (11) of the OBCA).

It is important to note that to the extent that the USA removes powers and responsibilities from the directors and transfers those powers and responsibilities to the shareholders, the shareholders become subject to the liabilities normally assigned to the officers and directors. Since protection from liability for shareholders is one of the prime reasons for incorporating a company, the loss of this protection should be carefully considered.

In the case where one shareholder owns the majority of shares, it is important to consider whether any issues exist that should not be decided by simple majority vote. The USA can set out a class of material decisions that require supra-majority or unanimous shareholder approval to ensure that the majority stakeholder is not able to make unilateral decisions without first obtaining the consent of the other shareholders involved.

3) Negative Control

When a shareholders' agreement does not restrict the power of the directors to manage the company (that is, when a shareholders' agreement is not a USA), every question that comes before the board is decided by a simple majority of votes cast on the question. However, when one shareholder owns the majority of shares and in the absence of cumulative voting provisions in the articles of the company (see OBCA section 120), it is possible that the minority shareholders may not have a representative nominee on the board, in which case the majority shareholder will be in control and will be able to make unilateral decisions disregarding the views of the other shareholders.

To magnify the power and authority of a minority shareholder to elect a director, cumulative voting allows the shareholder to cast all of his votes for a single nominee of the board. In straight voting, consider that there are thirty shares issued, twenty to one shareholder, ten to another, and that there are three directors to be elected. The majority shareholder will elect all three directors because he will cast twenty votes for each director against ten for each director by the minority shareholder. However, with cumulative voting, the shareholder with ten shares may cast all thirty votes for one of the three directors, and accordingly has the potential to elect at least one director to the board. The following formula will be of assistance in determining the number of shares required to elect a desired number of directors:

S multiplied by X divided by the sum of D plus 1

In the foregoing, S represents the number of shares voting in the election of directors (that is, the total number of votes). X represents the number of directors to be elected. D represents the number of directors up for election. That is to say, to elect the desired number of directors the shareholder must have more than the number created by the formula.

Linked to cumulative voting, the shareholders' agreement may set up a class of material decisions that require unanimous directorial approval and thus grant to a minority shareholder what is commonly referred to as negative control.

4) The Managing Director

Section 127(1) of the OBCA provides that:

> Subject to the articles or by-laws, directors of a corporation may appoint from their number a managing director or a committee of directors and delegate to such managing director or committee any of the powers of the directors.

To accomplish the foregoing, the following provision should appear in the company By-Law No. 1:

The board may from time to time also appoint from its number a managing director. If appointed and if no chief executive officer has been appointed, the managing director shall be the chief executive officer and, subject to the authority of the board, shall have the general supervision of the business and affairs of the corporation and such other powers and duties as the board may specify. During the absence or disability of the president or if no president has been appointed, the managing director shall also have the powers and duties of that office.

Notwithstanding the broad powers that may be granted to the managing director, section 127(3) of the OBCA provides as follows:

Limitations on authority

(3) Despite subsection (1), no managing director and no committee of directors has authority to,

   (a) submit to the shareholders any question or matter requiring the approval of the shareholders;

   (b) fill a vacancy among the directors or in the office of auditor or appoint or remove any of the chief executive officers, however designated, the chief financial officer, however designated, the chair or the president of the corporation;

   (c) subject to section 184, issue securities except in the manner and on the terms authorized by the directors;

   (d) declare dividends;

   (e) purchase, redeem or otherwise acquire shares issued by the corporation;

   (f) pay a commission referred to in section 37;

   (g) approve a management information circular referred to in Part VIII;

   (h) approve a take-over bid circular, directors' circular or issuer bid circular referred to in Part XX of the *Securities Act*;

(i) approve any financial statements referred to in clause 154 (1) (b) of the Act and Part XVIII of the *Securities Act*;

(i.1) approve an amalgamation under section 177 or an amendment to the articles under subsection 168 (2) or (4); or

(j) adopt, amend or repeal by-laws.

When the owners of the company (its shareholders) have not executed a USA and the directors of the company have delegated to a director (who may not even be a shareholder) the authority of the entire board to manage the company's business and affairs, the maxim stated at the outset of this section is seen to be true. That is, the owners of the company are its shareholders, but control rests with its managing director.

D. SHIFTING THE FORESEEN AND THE UNFORESEEN RISK

1) Commentary on Risk

I have chosen this section in the text to bring together that which, in my opinion, is the essence of the commercial contract, namely, which party bears the risk of the anticipated foreseeable risk and which party bears the risk of the unanticipated unforeseeable risk.

What is worthy of being repeated here is that monetary value is created by the buyer's expectation of monetary benefits to be derived in the future. Value is then defined as the present worth to the buyer of those future benefits—commonly, its expected future cash flow. Implicit in the word "expected" is the element of "uncertainty" that anticipated events may not occur or that unforeseen events will occur. The greater the uncertainty, the greater the risk of not achieving the expected cash flow and thus the greater the reward should be for having assumed the risk.

The use of the warranty and the indemnity is the buyer's protection against the foreseeable and the unforeseen risk, respectively. The buyer uses the warranty by enumerating in the contract all of the risks that are foreseeable in that particular transaction. The breach of any warranty will create a claim in damages against the seller, the amount of which is intended to restore the buyer to the position he would have been in had the breach not occurred. If there is a breach but no damages are suffered by the buyer, then no damage claim arises.

The buyer's use of the indemnity, if worded appropriately, is capable of protecting the buyer against unforeseen risk. Unlike the warranty, the indemnity does not give rise to a claim in damages. Instead, it is tantamount to a promise by the seller to "reimburse" the buyer with respect to an actual monetary loss or liability.

By way of illustration, let's say that both a warranty and an indemnity state that the company's records are current. The buyer discovers they are not. If the value of the shares of the company have not been adversely affected by the breach, no damage claim may be made for the breach of warranty. But if the cost of bringing the records up to date is a cost to be incurred by the buyer, the buyer is entitled to be reimbursed for that cost. The wording of the indemnity may be as broad in scope as is the uncertainty in the mind of the buyer. It could refer to "all losses incurred by or imposed upon the buyer for any claim, without limitation in nature or kind, based upon any matter related to the company operations that pre-dates the closing of this transaction."

2)   Allocation of Risk: Warranty Versus Indemnity

The allocation of risk to be borne by the buyer and seller after closing is a critical feature in the negotiation process. The buyer will naturally want to be reimbursed for any transaction or occurrence that took place before closing and that after closing gives rise to a claim or liability. On the other hand, the seller will want to be free from the liability to which the assets were subject. The goal of the negotiation process is to allocate risk in a balanced and economically appropriate manner.

The buyer is concerned both with risks created by misrepresentation or breach of covenant and with risks that were created by facts and circumstances that were not necessarily anticipated by either party at the time of negotiation. Buyers will seek full indemnity against any specific liability that has not been assumed by the buyer and any damages or losses that are incurred owing to inaccuracy of representations, warranties, or agreements. However, a seller will be unwilling to provide as broad and comprehensive an indemnity provision as that.

In the alternative, a compromise may be struck wherein a buyer agrees not to demand any indemnity unless its claim for indemnity exceeds a specified amount. The amount will, of course, be vigorously negotiated as well as whether the indemnity is for the amount that exceeds the specified amount or whether the specified amount is only a trigger, which permits the buyer to recover its full claim for indemnity.

In addition to the limitations described in the preceding paragraph, the seller may seek to establish a limitation on its overall liability, a limitation on the types of claims for which the seller can be held liable, a limitation to claims about which the seller had prior actual knowledge, a limitation on the types of assets that would be available to repay the buyer in the event of a claim, and a limitation on the time after closing after which the buyer may no longer proceed on a breach of warranty against the seller.

In addition to indemnifying the buyer, the seller will be expected to provide a wide range of representations and warranties to the effect that the sale is not in breach of any other agreement or obligation of the seller, that the assets are free and clear of any claim or encumbrance, that the assets are in good operating condition, and that all material facts have been disclosed. The buyer will want the representations and warranties to be as broad and comprehensive as possible in that the buyer views post-closing events that reduce the value of an asset or increase its liability as being the seller's responsibility.

In many of the representations and warranties, the buyer may be willing to accept the phrase "to the best of the seller's knowledge" as one kind of limitation. A time or dollar limitation on a particular representation or warranty may be acceptable to a seller, such as a dollar limit attached to environmental or product liability representations and warranties.

Chapter 10: **Negotiating Strategies and Tactics**

A. GAME THEORY

The price paid to purchase a target company invariably is different from the corporate finance valuations (see Part 1 of this text). Psychological pricing factors do exist and are often based on whether the buyer is risk averse or risk taking and whether the seller is pessimistic or optimistic.[1] If the buyer is a risk taker, he will be prepared to offer more for a sale. If a seller is pessimistic, he will be more likely to negotiate with the buyer on a reasonable price. The studies have analyzed what behaviour would be best for these players to adopt in such a game. Four possible combinations can occur in this model:

Buyer: Risk Taking	**Seller:** Optimistic
Buyer: Risk Taking	**Seller:** Pessimistic
Buyer: Risk Averse	**Seller:** Optimistic
Buyer: Risk Averse	**Seller:** Pessimistic

---

1   Nipun Agarwal & Panlop Zeephongsekul, "Psychological Pricing in Mergers and Acquisitions Using Game Theory" (Paper delivered at the Proceedings of the 19th International Congress on Modelling and Simulation, Perth, Australia, 12–16 December 2011), online: https://researchrepository.rmit.edu.au/esploro/ outputs/conferenceProceeding/Psychological-pricing-in-mergers-and-acquisi- tions-using-game-theory/9921858409101341 at 1437.

To obtain the most optimal offer, one that will provide the best result to both the buyer and seller, game models indicate that that result is best achieved when the buyer is a risk taker, and the seller is pessimistic. That would arise since the buyer would be willing to pay more and the seller would be willing to accept less for the sale of his company.

Game theory consists of models from which a negotiating party can derive useful principles. The following page references offer detailed study and application of the following principles:

- All things being equal, a good strategy is to minimize your opponent's maximum payout even if that means guaranteeing him a higher minimum (see Chapter 9, "Structuring the Deal" and this chapter, sections D and G).
- Making the first proposal is always advantageous and allows you to frame the negotiation to your advantage (this chapter, sections B, E, and H).
- Making promises and threats are valuable so long as you are prepared to live with the consequences (this chapter, sections E, H, and I).
- Most buyers have a greater aversion to risk than an appetite for large gains (Chapter 6, Section B and this chapter 10, Section G). Buyers are often prepared to pay a higher price to reduce their exposure to risk.

The tendency that people have to miscalculate probabilities when confronted with simple financial choices was clearly demonstrated in a series of experiments.[2] A sample group was given $250 each. Then they were offered a choice between either (a) a 50 percent chance of winning an additional $250 or (b) a 100 percent chance of winning $125. Eighty-four percent of the group chose (b). Then the same sample was given $500 and a choice between either (c) a 50 percent chance

---

2   D. Kahneman & A. Tversky, "Prospect Theory: An Analysis of Decision Under Risk" (1979) 47:2 *Econometric* 273.

of *losing* $250 or (d) a 100 percent chance of *losing* $125. However, this time 69 percent of the group chose (c). However, viewed in terms of their payoffs, these two problems are actually identical. In both cases the choice was between a 50 percent chance of ending up with $250 and an equal chance of ending up with $500 ((a) and (c)), or the certainty of ending up with $375 ((b) and (d)). The difference therein proves that there is a risk aversion to losing but a risk taking for winning. That is, the contemplation of a loss was two-and-a half times the impact as the contemplation for a gain.

B. ATTITUDE

Without any exaggeration, a tone is set and an atmosphere is created by the attitude that one brings to the negotiation. If the other side senses in your client an inordinate desire to "make a deal," there will be an immediate shift against you in the balance of power. You will be perceived as an easy opponent. To enter the negotiations with an attitude that is appropriate—hopeful but not anxious—there must a background against which the deal is viewed.

The party that thinks it has the least to lose has the most leverage. The standard by which to measure any agreement is to measure that agreement against the next best available alternative. The better your next best available alternative is, the greater is your strength in the ensuing negotiation. In other words, the relative negotiating power of the two sides primarily depends on how unattractive to each is the prospect of not reaching an agreement. That alternative should always be the answer to the unspoken question "What will I do if this deal falls through?" Advise your client to think of himself as someone going into a job interview having already received one or two attractive job offers as opposed to someone walking into an interview having been found unacceptable on the last two interviews. His attitude and yours should be confident, not diffident; aggressive, creative, and compromising, but not anxious, impatient, or yielding.

Psychologists who study human behaviour patterns have stated that at the onset of most relationships, parties will be perceived or will perceive themselves as either dominant or submissive. Why that is so is for others to study. That such is often the case is relevant for our purposes because if one senses that he is a dominant player, he will not want to lose that advantage. He will endeavour to maintain the control he feels he has by being assertive, confident, firm, and assured while avoiding the appearance of being uncompromising and unreasonable. If, on the other hand, you or your client are perceived as submissive or passive, you should endeavour somehow to seize control. Submissiveness is often perceived in one who is unwilling or unable to make eye contact with the person who seems to be in charge. Advise your client to make eye contact, to sit upright, and hold his head erect, and when the opportunity arises to be inventive, resourceful, or original, encourage him to seize the moment and speak assertively.

Presumably, there will be a team of lawyers representing the buyer and a team of lawyers representing the seller. Commonly, there will be a lawyer who emerges in the transaction as the "lead" lawyer who will bear the responsibility for ensuring that his client achieves his objectives. Whether that lawyer will be representing the buyer or the seller in any particular transaction will depend on a number of factors, such as which party has initiated the transaction, which party needs the transaction more, or which party is more assertive in taking the lead.

C. CONFLICTS

When acting for a company, there are always several potential clients. It may be the company itself, or the person with whom you are directly dealing, or a controlling shareholder, or a minority shareholder, or one or more directors. Once that determination is made, be cognizant throughout the transaction of the party to whom you owe your primary duty. Reassess the issue of conflict periodically during the course of the transaction to ensure that you are not in any way compromising the primary objectives of your client.

D. UNDERSTANDING THE NEEDS OF THE PARTIES

Equal to attitude in importance is the lawyer's understanding of his client's needs and concerns, and the extent of the client's desire to make a deal. What are his minimum acceptable terms? What is the price spread within which the client will deal? What are the assumptions made by the client with respect to income, expense, debt service, cash flow, capitalization rate, yield rate, and tax benefits upon which his business decision rests? How does the client, as the buyer, expect to finance the acquisition? How does the client, as seller, expect to receive the proceeds of sale?

Identifying who your client is forces you to consider the business issues that must be addressed and, in doing so, you are better able to identify the preferred legal structure for your client. While you may not be there to provide business advice, you must participate in the business side of the transaction. In doing so, you acquire an understanding of the business issues that affect the legal process. You are well advised to record in the file your client's primary objectives, the original business terms of the transactions, and those verbal representations made to your client upon which he relies. In doing so, you are able to review your memorandum periodically to ensure that the transaction is not straying from what was intended and that the legal documents achieve that result.

It is also imperative that you keep in mind the needs of the other party. Actively listen to every aspect of what the other party is saying. *When* they choose to enter the discussion and *which* subjects they raise will reveal their agenda and what their motivations are. Persuade your client to be flexible. Flexibility makes compromise and concession possible. Remember always that the best compromise is an exchange by which the client gives up something that is less valuable than what he obtains in return. You will be of assistance to your client in identifying potential trade-offs and by pointing out which terms are of vital interest and which terms are not. In doing so, you enter the negotiations with a list of concessions that you grudgingly but carefully surrender in return for those concessions from the other party that are more valuable to your client.

E. SETTING THE AGENDA AND THE TIMETABLE

Having identified your client's business objectives and goals, establish an agenda for the transaction. Often, this is the best way by which to keep the transaction moving forward and perhaps to determine when a transaction is in trouble. If the agenda is to be linked to a timetable, ensure that the time frames are realistically achievable. If there are regulatory approvals and consents from third parties that must be obtained, these must be sought in a timely manner so that they will be available in time for closing. In establishing an agenda linked to a timetable, begin with a date that must be met and then run the timeline backwards to the present date. Then outline the critical path to meeting the deadline. In doing so, you may then determine whether the available time frames are realistic. (*See Forms 8 and 9.*)

F. WHERE TO NEGOTIATE

In certain circumstances who comes to whose office can be important. Generally, it is a sign of strength to be able to require the other side to come to one's office. In fact, the belief generally held is that it is easier to control a meeting that is being held in your office. You can obtain control by simple sitting at the head of the table, sitting next to the only phone in the office, or sitting next to the only door in the room, and although it is not necessary to maintain control at all times, it is important that you understand how to reacquire control at any particular time during the negotiation.

There are times, however, when it is advantageous to accept an offer to meet at the other side's office. It puts the other side at ease, makes them more open to your suggestions, and perhaps most importantly it is easier for you to walk out if necessary.

If the negotiation must take place over the telephone, either be the caller or agree to make contact at an appointed hour. At the inception of a negotiation, you must be in command of the subject matter and in a proper frame of mind. If at the time the telephone call comes in you are already concerned with another matter, decline to take the call.

It is, however, always preferable to negotiate in person. People can and do hang up the telephone without responding. They can and do toss out mail. But people will rarely walk out of a face-to-face meeting. Even if the other side does not like your proposal, you will, nevertheless, have the opportunity to discover their objection and see how far apart you are. You can learn from the other side's facial expressions and body language. These are advantages that are not available to you through a telephone negotiation.

G. OBJECTIVES

When acting for a buyer, the best arrangement is one in which the cash equity required by the buyer is as small as possible. The reason the small cash equity is preferred by a buyer is that as the cash equity diminishes, the yield commonly increases. However, the seller's demand for cash is often a function of the seller's need for a secure sales transaction, in which case the buyer should consider providing the seller with the monetary security he desires in the form of a letter of credit rather than cash.

From the buyer's perspective, it is best that the seller satisfies the balance of the purchase price by providing the buyer with long-term debt financing at a rate that is lower than the buyer's cost of capital, or by accepting part payment in stock, or by agreeing to make a portion of the purchase price payable only on a stipulated income achievement or other type of threshold. In doing so, the structure becomes far more attractive to the buyer, who now has an extended period of time within which to repay the funding provided by the seller and who has shifted a major portion of the purchase price risk back onto the seller in stock and in contingent earn-out payments.

The reason the buyer chooses to defer the payment of purchase price as long as possible is, of course, to provide the buyer with sufficient time to retire the debt created by the unpaid purchase price from the company's own expected future cash flow. Buyers focus on the future and its uncertainty. Sellers focus on the present. A buyer will likely pay a higher price if he can pay the bulk of that price at a much later date. When acting for a seller, the postponement that a buyer requests may often be traded for a higher sale price.

The reason the interest rate preferred by a buyer is one that is lower than its cost of capital is to enable the buyer to generate upside leverage. With upside leverage, the buyer is earning an additional profit on the spread between his required rate of return and the rate he is paying on his debt. Essentially, he is borrowing money at a lower rate and investing it to obtain a higher rate. A seller will often agree to reduce or even waive interest for an interest-free period if the purchase price is enhanced by the concession. There are tax-driven reasons for the seller to do so, but the advice of tax counsel will be required if the concession is so great as to amount to a capitalization of interest in the form of an increased purchase price.

Most buyers have a greater aversion to risk than an appetite for large gain. Risk aversion explains why most people would rather take a $25 gift than toss a coin for a chance at $50—a "bird in the hand is worth two in the bush." Buyers are often prepared to pay a higher price to reduce their exposure to risk. The larger the amount that is subject to an earn-out, the less the exposure to risk in the event that the buyer determines that the company is not worth the price he has agreed to pay. Conversely, when acting for a seller, the risk aversion that a buyer expresses may be traded for a higher sale price.

Aside from price, the seller's primary objective is to obtain an agreement that is binding and enforceable upon the buyer, and if representations and warranties are required, that they be limited in scope, monetary value, and the time period during which they may be effective.

H. ADVANCING YOUR POSITION

Begin by discarding the notion that the two negotiating parties are adversaries. When the parties think of themselves as adversaries, the risk of overt or covert hostility is created. You are not opponents. You would do well to think of the two sides as judges trying to reach agreement on how to decide a case. Your goal is to apply a standard of merit and reason to the positions being taken on each issue.

1)   Before Introducing Your Proposal

Before offering your proposal, first present all the reasons that brought you to the proposal. If the merits or reasons are presented afterwards, they will appear to the other side not as objective criteria but as a mere justification for an arbitrary position. By explaining your reasons first, you show that you are open to persuasion and that you are aware of a need to convince the other side. If you announce your proposal first, the other side will probably busy themselves considering what the objections and counterproposal should be and not even bother to listen to the reasons that follow your proposal.

By basing your proposal on the facts as you understand them, you invite the other side to correct them by establishing a dialogue based on reason. You invite the other side to participate in either agreeing with the facts as presented or setting them right. This process makes you and the opposite side attempt to establish the facts and diffuse the confrontation.

2) Be Unequivocal

Be direct and unequivocal about what you want. Even if you fear that your position will be unpopular, state it and move the discussion on to a less controversial issue to give the other side time to digest your point. In doing so, when the crucial point arises again, the shock effect will have been dissipated. There is a tendency among many to believe that by misleading the other side by means of vague or ambiguous statements you will be able to advance your true position later in the negotiation by clarifying your intentions after the other side has been "caught up in the deal" and hopefully has passed a point of no return. This tactic is an egregious example of bad faith dealing and only serves to destroy the credibility of the person using it.

3) Responding to Counterproposals

If the other side offers a reasonable compromise, you should promptly accept it. The idea that a compromise can be advantageous to both sides rarely occurs to young lawyers whose insecurity is such that they are often afraid that a suggestion made by the other side is a trap that they have not yet recognized. A mature negotiator hears a suggestion that advances the deal and jumps at it. If he is afraid of appearing too eager, he can say, "I believe I can live with that. Let me think about it. But let's assume for the moment that it is okay and move on."

If the other side announces a firm but totally unsupportable proposal, resist the temptation to criticize and reject it. Instead of attacking its proposal, treat it merely as one possible option. Moreover, when the other side critically attacks your proposal, again resist the inclination to defend it. Instead, ask the other side to focus on what it is about your proposal that it finds objectionable. In doing so, you may be able to rework your proposal in light of what you learn.

Always endeavour to keep the dialogue focused on the merits of any issue. Question the other side's position and request reasons for its position. By assuming the other side has a good reason for its position, you cause the other side to search for those reasons even if there are none. Whatever else it may produce, it keeps the negotiation squarely focused on the merits of any position.

A very useful tool, if used sparingly, is silence. If the other side has made an absurd proposal or has engaged in a verbal attack that is wholly unjustified, no response is more telling or profound than simply staring at the other side in apparent disbelief. By not going on to another question or comment, you leave them dangling, so to speak, on the hook created by their last remark.

Whenever you are in doubt as to the next step to take, fall back on the merits of your position. Your position presumably was not arrived at arbitrarily. There is legitimacy to that position. Question the legitimacy of the other side's position. Present an argument that is logical. Force the other side to acknowledge the logic of that argument. No one wants to appear unreasonable, and if you can convince the other side of the reasonableness of your position, eventually the effect will take hold even if not at the moment.

4) Avoid Making Statements

Avoid making statements. Somehow frame your remark as a question. Statements generate resistance while questions engender answers. Questions offer the other side no target at which to strike; no position to attack. Questions allow the other side to respond with information. Listen to information. Evaluate the information and then endeavour to use it to your advantage.

5) Avoid Flat-Out Rejections

If you cannot make any further concession to the issue that is in dispute, you should say so openly and directly. However, a flat refusal to make a concession does carry the risk that the negotiation will promptly end, and therefore you should use it infrequently. But if you are being truthful, and you are willing to risk the deal by taking a stand on that issue, either the goal will be achieved quickly, or the negotiation will promptly end.

Never state an ultimatum unless you truly mean it. Many people find it difficult to deal with ultimatums. To yield to an ultimatum is widely regarded as a surrender. Most people will simply "leave it" and that is the end of the negotiation. If you do issue an ultimatum and the other side calls what has been a bluff, you must either walk away from the deal or otherwise lose all your credibility.

Never resort to threats. There are other ways to express the same information. Warnings are far more legitimate and are not subject to counterthreats.

I.   CONFRONTING NEGATIVE TACTICS

One of the strengths that comes with experience in negotiation is the ability to recognize a negotiating ploy as no more than a ploy or tactic.

1)   The Prior Offer Tactic

If the other side says they already have a better offer than the one you are proposing, if you cannot afford to match it you should simply say so. You might even say "That is a great offer. If I were you, I would take it." In fact, if they have such an offer, then there is no sense in wasting time. However, if they continue to negotiate with you, you instantly know there is no better offer.

2)   When the Other Side Won't Negotiate

When the other side refuses to negotiate altogether "take it or leave it" recognize the tactic as a negotiating ploy. In such a case, talk about the reasons for their refusal to negotiate, but do not attack them for refusing to negotiate—find out their reason for not doing so. Ask what facts they have relied on in reaching their position, and if their facts are manifestly wrong, indicate the facts upon which your position is based and suggest that perhaps there is a need to determine whose facts are correct.

3)   Confronting Confrontation

It is a common strategy to create confrontation as an initial ploy and in doing so seek to take initial control of the meeting. To those who believe that the first impression is everything, a negotiator may believe that a tactic of impasse will obtain the best possible outcome. He may believe that you will be reluctant to spend the time and endure the continuing unpleasantness of a long and difficult negotiation and that you will prefer to look for compromise to find a non-confrontational solution to each problem. It is this element of human relations that the other side may seek to exploit by creating confrontation and prolonging the negotiation.

4) Confronting Rudeness

If the person with whom you are negotiating raises his voice to you either because he is ill-mannered or because he is hoping to intimidate you, your response in either case should be to leave the meeting. Do let him know that you are prepared to resume discussion when he returns to civility. When you sense that you are being subjected to a tactic that you consider to be illegitimate, resist the temptation to reproach the person personally. Question the tactic, not the person. For example, rather than say "You put me in a chair lower than yours and facing the sun," say, "I find that the sun in my eyes is distracting" or "I find this chair uncomfortable." If the tactic continues, as a last resort walk out.

There are many ways for one side to use verbal or non-verbal communication to make you uncomfortable, such as asking you to repeat yourself, appearing not to listen to you, or deliberately refusing to make eye contact with you. In each case, recognizing the tactic helps to negate its effect. As a last resort, you might identify it specifically by saying "Is there a reason why you won't look me in the face when I'm speaking to you?" If you receive a threat from the other side, an appropriate response is to say, "I don't respond well to threats—I negotiate on the basis of merits."

5) Don't Bid Against Yourself

Never feel forced to bid, especially against yourself. If the other side tells you that your proposal is inadequate, find out precisely what modification the other side requires. In fact, require a counterproposal and, until one is presented, stand pat. When a seller refuses to state his price, he may say "Come up with a figure and I'll respond." Whatever you offer, the seller will invariably ask for more. Frequently, a seller will simply say "You will have to come up with something better than that."

6) Don't Respond to an Extreme Position

Negotiators will often start with extreme proposals, the goal of which is to lower your expectations. The theory is that the parties will end up splitting the difference between their respective positions. Bring the tactic to the other side's attention and ask for the reasoning and the merits of that position. Hopefully, it will look ridiculous even to them.

7) Negotiate Only with Your Counterpart

A common tactic is to allow you to believe that the person with whom you are negotiating has full authority to compromise. After he has pressed you as hard as he can, he then announces that he must take it to someone else for approval—a technique commonly known as a "second bite at the apple." Therefore, do not assume that the other side has full authority just because he is the one present. If there is any doubt, no commitment should be made. Adjourn the meeting, perhaps until the other side can produce someone who is able to make a binding decision.

8) "Good Guy/Bad Guy" Tactic

Another common tactic is the so-called good guy/bad guy routine. Sometimes two people on the same side will stage a quarrel. If you recognize it, chances are you won't be taken in. When the good guy then makes his pitch, you might ask the same question you asked the bad guy, namely, "I know you are trying to be reasonable, but I would still like to know why you feel the price you stated is a fair price. What is the basis for your proposal?"

J.   WINNING FRIENDS AND INFLUENCING PEOPLE

The objective of creating a frame of reference within which both sides can share the common goal of determining a price and terms that are fair to each side and independent of the will of either side can best be achieved by using a mix of negotiation and human relations skills. As a tool for persuasion, Dale Carnegie's book *How to Win Friends and Influence People* remains unsurpassed.

Never underestimate the concern of the other side for face-saving and self-image. Often people will hold out not because the proposal is inherently unacceptable but because the other side wants to avoid the feeling, or perhaps the appearance, of having backed down.

It is always best to make the other side feel that it has walked out with a win and has done well regardless of the reality—make the other side feel that it has been as successful as possible under the circumstances.

Always ensure that cogent reasons and rational purposes are offered for the positions you take. Sometimes the argument may be nothing more than the simplistic excuse that "this is corporate policy," but in doing so you remove the sting of what might otherwise be thought of as a harsh exercise of power.

Since a successful negotiation depends on the other side making the decision you want them to make, you should do what you can to make that decision an easy one. There is such a thing as a "yes-inducing proposal"—a proposal to which the other side can respond with a simple "yes."

Always endeavour to be pleasant. It is unwise to antagonize the other side. A negotiation should be a positive event. Hopefully, the deal will give all parties something they want.

Never embarrass or intimidate the other side. Even if the other side has said something stupid, do not be tempted to tell them so. Indeed, when you have won your point, promptly move on. Many people unfortunately like to linger over their victory. When the other side has conceded a point, dwelling on the subject may irritate him enough to cause him to rethink his position. Never condemn the motives of the other side. If it's anger you feel, the anger should not be directed against the other person but against his position. Statements, not personalities, should be attacked. Describe a problem in terms of its impact on you rather than in terms of what the other side did or said. For example, "I feel let down" is preferable to "you broke your word to me."

Always be sure that you are looking directly at the other party. Refusing to make eye contact with someone is often taken as a sign of insincerity.

Never be reluctant to ask the other side for its help. One of the most effective phrases in human relations is "I need your advice on this." This is an effective way to channel criticism constructively by turning the situation around and asking what the other side would do if it were in your position. Give credit generously to the other side for any ideas it advances. By giving personal support to the other side, you are separating the person from the problem.

When presenting a proposal, present it as a fair option that deserves the consideration of the other side. That is to say, don't claim it as the only fair solution but rather as one possibility.

Regardless of how bitter or difficult a negotiation was, it is always appropriate to end the negotiation with some degree of cordiality.

Lastly, it is a wise negotiator who understands that it is foolish to beat up the other side if the resulting rancour and resentment will endure into the future and affect the unfolding of the transaction. Good relationships are critical to moving a deal forward. If the other side does not feel sufficiently content with the agreement reached through negotiation, it is unlikely that it will want to honour the agreement, and in the end, no matter how successful the negotiation was, the other side will always find a way to withdraw from the agreement.

Chapter 11: **Negotiating a Contract in Good Faith**

There is no positive duty to negotiate the terms of a transaction in good faith in Canadian law. Our judicial system emphasizes individual reliance and self-responsibility. Parties negotiating a contract normally expect that each side will act entirely in its own best interests.[1] Naturally, given the bilateral nature of most negotiations, the gains are commonly obtained at the other party's expense. Imposing a positive duty to negotiate in good faith would be incompatible with the activity of negotiating and bargaining.[2] However, once an agreement has been entered into in writing there is a duty to negotiate the documents arising therefrom in good faith. It is an implied duty that requires each party to not act in a way that eviscerates the objectives of the contract and takes into account the legitimate interests of the other side. A party to an executed agreement may believe, disingenuously or otherwise, that the position that he is taking is reasonable.

In Part 3, "The Art of Drafting," the duty to act in good faith when a contract has been executed by the parties is discussed in detail.

---

1   *978011 Ontario Ltd v Cornell Engineering Co* (2001), 53 OR (3d) 783 (CA).

2   *Martel Building Ltd v Canada*, 2000 SCC 60, [2000] 2 SCR 860.

THE ART OF DRAFTING

Chapter 12: **Preliminary Considerations**

A. CONTROL THE DRAFTING

The due diligence has been completed. Price and terms have been negotiated. The financing has been arranged. Now is the time to document all the work that preceded this stage.

Unless the benefits derived from the negotiation are properly drafted, they may not be realized. No matter how successfully the issues were resolved, the party drafting the documents has the ability to put his own "spin" on those resolutions. The only lasting result of the negotiation is the written words that document the negotiation. Therefore, it is critical that you control the drafting.

The drafter will see the issue and the resolution of the issue from his own client's perspective, and in doing so the drafter will word the provisions that relate to issues that were won by the other side in a way that will limit their application.

There are a number of words and expressions that a drafter may employ in an effort to either limit or expand the scope of a provision. If the seller is representing the accuracy of financial statements the following words are often employed to qualify what is otherwise an absolute statement: "materially," "except for," "subject to," "substantially all," "primarily related to." If the seller is required to perform, the use of the following expressions may limit the extent of that effort:

"endeavour to," "commercially reasonable efforts," "to use best efforts." If the seller is representing that there are no outstanding claims or liabilities, the following words will qualify what is otherwise a bald position: "of which the seller is aware," "to the best of the seller's knowledge," "reasonably believes," "have received no written notice of," "would not have a material adverse affect on," "in the ordinary course of business." On the other hand, if the drafter's intention is to expand the scope of a provision, words such as "may" rather than "will" or "could possibly" rather than "do" have a tendency to expand and allocate risk more heavily on the seller.

Moreover, there are usually dozens of issues that the negotiating parties never addressed. However, once the parties have agreed to the basic elements of the deal, the principals become impatient and anxious to sign the papers and call it a day. The drafter of the documents, then, is in a position to control the pace and indeed the frustration of the parties. If, when a drafter refuses to make the appropriate changes, a provision keeps reappearing in a draft in a form that is unacceptable to the other side, sooner or later the other side may decide that the issue is too small and concede the point so that the deal can be concluded.

B. BE PRECISE

If, due to loose or imprecise wording or due to oversight, your client is burdened with a cost that was either unforeseen or the responsibility for which was left unclear, then to that extent the agreement has failed to support and reflect the bargain that was made by your client.

There are some lawyers who believe that there is professional merit in drafting a provision in which the wording is capable of more than one interpretation so long as one of those interpretations benefits the drafter's client. This is usually done with respect to those issues that were "lost" by the drafter's client in the negotiations. However, the lawyer who deliberately does so has ignored the fact that it is not that one issue but rather the entire transaction that is thereby placed in jeopardy. Indeed, if that is the desire of his client, the client should simply not sign the agreement rather than proceed on the basis of probable litigation.

As a matter of professional pride, the drafter must, with deliberation and precision, draft or review the agreement to ensure that it does truly reflect the bargain that was made by the parties.

C. THE AGREEMENT'S SKELETON

Even before the drafting of the agreement begins, a skeletal outline of the agreement should be prepared. The outline will contain a reference to each provision needed to achieve the anticipated result. The steps must build on one another so that there is a logical sequence to a series of promises. At this stage, it is the skeleton outline, not the wording, that is important.

Once the outline is completed, you will be able to draw from the outline a number of words or expressions that may appear therein more than once. If a definition is given to such words or expressions, it not only shortens the agreement but more importantly it avoids the use of different words or expressions that are intended to say the same thing, and which create uncertainty when attempting to interpret the meaning that was originally intended. The more complex the agreement, the greater is the need for two- or three-word expressions that incorporate into the agreement a multi-worded meaning or definition.

Any term, provision, dollar amount, or event that is referred to in the agreement more than once should be defined so that its meaning remains constant. If we assume that a proposed purchase is subject to a number of conditions and that upon the fulfillment of each a payment is due, each condition should be defined, the date by which it is to be fulfilled should be defined, and the payment that is to be made upon its fulfillment should be defined.

D. DRAFTING AND GOOD FAITH

The *contra proferentum*[1] construction of an agreement does not have application to an agreement that is drafted, reviewed, revised, and redrafted even when all of the drafting is done by one side. However, it would serve a drafter well to remember that more judges feel free to alter the apparent meaning of an agreement by implying terms into an agreement that they perceive would otherwise be unfair. The courts would, it seems, assume that the parties intended for the contract to stipulate that which is fair and reasonable since the parties are presumed to be acting in good faith. For example, a commission payable "at the sole discretion of the employer" requires the employer to act reasonably, honestly, and in good faith.

To ensure that the concept of *contra proferentum* is ignored by the courts, I suggest the following provision be part of the general provisions of any commercial contract:

> Seller and buyer acknowledge that each party and its counsel have reviewed and revised this agreement and that the normal rule of construction to the effect that any ambiguities are to be resolved against the drafting party shall not be employed in the interpretation of this agreement (including the exhibits hereto) or any buyer, but shall be given a reasonable interpretation in accordance with the plain meaning of its terms and the intent of the parties.

The drafter of the agreement must remember that the courts, when interpreting a contract, have always given due consideration to factors such as the legitimate expectation of the parties. Therefore, the power to imply terms, as a judicial tool, is more than a mere guide to the interpretation of an agreement. The tool available to the courts is indeed to

---

1   *Contra proferentum* (against the party putting forward) refers to the interpretation of a document in case of ambiguity against the party who drafted it or whose document it is.

create an obligation, if that appears to have been a reasonable expectation of the buyer.

E. REPRESENTATIONS, WARRANTIES, AND CONDITIONS

In contract law, a warranty is basically a written stipulation that a certain fact in relation to the subject matter of the contract is as stated or will be as promised. A warranty differs from a representation in that the warranty must always be given contemporaneously with and as part of the contract, while a representation usually precedes and induces the contract. While that is the difference in nature, the difference in consequence or effect is that upon a breach of a warranty, the contract remains binding and only damages from the breach are recoverable, while with a false representation by the seller the buyer may elect to void the transaction and recover the entire price paid.

The wording that usually appears in the standard term section of an acquisition agreement is that the obligation of the buyer to close the transaction is subject to the fulfillment, at or prior to closing, of each of a number of stipulated conditions precedent, any one or all of which the buyer may choose to waive. This section of the agreement usually contains two types of conditions: one type is the occurrence of events that must occur, or consents that must be obtained, or documents that must be signed and delivered, while the other type refers collectively to the seller's representations and warranties and requires that each be true and correct in all material respects at or as of the closing as if made at or as of such time.

The nature and the scope of these conditions must be carefully considered because the failure to satisfy them will give the buyer the right to "walk away" from the transaction if he chooses to do so. However, after having spent time and money for a financial investigation and legal services rendered with respect to the negotiation and drafting of the agreement, unless the failure of the condition goes to the heart of the transaction and is not monetarily curable, the buyer, more likely, will take the position that the corresponding or related warranty has been breached by the seller and insist on closing the transaction with an appropriate set-off or abatement in the purchase price for the monetary loss in value caused by the breach.

In other words, the essential difference between a condition and a warranty is that the unfulfilled condition entitles the innocent party to treat himself as discharged from further performance under the contract while a breach of warranty does not entitle the party to treat himself as discharged but to claim damages for the loss sustained by a breach of warranty.

On the other hand, the seller will want the agreement to eliminate, or at least monetarily limit, any set-off or abatement that may be made against the purchase price by a buyer who claims that a breach of warranty has occurred. The seller will want to limit the scope of the warranties and restrict the time period during which they may be effective. Lastly, the representations and warranties should not be worded as bald statements of fact but rather as statements made to the best of the seller's knowledge and belief.

The issue is, which party bears the risk of the unforeseen? Neither party wants to bear the risk. Compromise will permit the parties to allocate the risk by limiting the monetary exposure of either the buyer or the seller, depending on which of the two is more forceful.

F.   THE OTHER MATTERS

Having dealt with price, payment terms, conditions, representations, and warranties, the rest, as they say, is "boilerplate." Having ground their way through the bulk of the negotiation, the pace may quicken when the end is in sight and the parties hasten to work through all the remaining issues. It is at this time in the negotiation that many seemingly small points are given away without a struggle by tired parties who have lost their ability to concentrate. It is at this point that the side with the greater resolve and tenacity can cause the other side to compromise. If your client is tired or restless and the other side is focusing on every little point, the best strategy may simply be to adjourn the meeting early. Taking the position that nothing further can be done and postponing the balance of negotiation to another day may very well alter the momentum of a negotiation. If your client's resolve is indeed weakening, end the meeting by saying that the remaining unresolved issues can be worked out by telephone conference. By contrast, the side that has the greater strength as the meeting winds down will try to resist adjournment by reminding everyone how difficult it is to get everyone together, enumerating the problems he has and saying how difficult it will be for the parties to find time in their schedules for another session.

G. THE DOMINANT POSITION OF THE BUYER

When on the eve of closing a seller is informed that the buyer has decided not to close the transaction, the seller in a commercial transaction is far more vulnerable than the buyer would be if the seller had chosen not to close. When perceived from a psychological, economic, legal, or other basis, the seller is in a far weaker position than the buyer. In anticipation of closing, the buyer's role is to deliver a cheque on the closing. However, a seller has a mindset as to where to place the funds arising from the closing. He will have alerted his employees to the prospect of the closing and attended to all the details required to satisfy and deliver the company to the buyer.

The buyer's refusal may either be legitimate or illegitimate. It may be a genuine concern or a disingenuous scheme. In either event, the seller has been given a disarming situation that needs to be addressed.

Two questions arise: Why *can* a buyer do this? Why *might* a buyer do this? For the answer to the first question look to the boilerplate provisions of most agreements and focus on the representations, warranties, and conditions therein. Unless a seller has anticipated a buyer's last-minute refusal to close, he will not address each of these provisions with the same focus and attention that he would if he did anticipate a refusal by the buyer to close. The seller may have allowed provisions similar to the following to remain in the contract to his detriment:

- No Adverse Change. *There shall have been no adverse change since the Financial Statement Date in the business, prospects, financial condition, earnings, or operations of Seller's business.*
- Confirmation of Statements. *The Buyer shall review and confirm the results of Seller's operations as of [ ], which shall be satisfactory to the Buyer in its sole and absolute discretion.*
- Absence of Certain Changes or Events. *Since the Latest Statement Date, the Corporation has not made or incurred any material change in or become aware of any event or condition which is likely to result in a material change in either of the Corporation or its respective assets.*
- No Material Change. *There shall have been no material change in the financial position, value, or assets of the Corporation during the Interim Period.*

The answer to the second question as to why the buyer might do this is probably because the seller has enabled him to easily do so. Every buyer is aware of a seller's vulnerability and may choose to exploit that vulnerability by improving the deal he had made with the seller. The seller, in the ordinary course of events, has only two alternatives, namely, either to extend the closing and renew negotiations or to capitulate to the buyer's demands for monetary concessions. Given the unlevel field that exists between them, the seller is more likely to yield and to make the best of what has become a bad deal.

However, there is a possible third alternative.

H. CONFRONTING THE BUYER'S DOMINANCE

There is no duty to negotiate in good faith prior to a contract being formed.[2] However, when a contract exists, the duty to negotiate in good faith does arise and imposes the following conditions:

---

2   *978011 Ontario Ltd v Cornell Engineering Co* (2001), 53 OR (3d) 783 (CA); *Martel Building Ltd v Canada*, 2000 SCC 60, [2000] 2 SCR 860.

1) A party by its action may not eviscerate or defeat the objectives of the contract into which the parties entered.[3]
2) A party's conduct must meet objective legitimate expectations and community standards of honesty, reasonableness, and fairness.
3) A party may not unilaterally nullify contractual objectives or cause significant harm to the other party contrary to the original expectations of the parties.[4]

However, it is not uncommon for lawyers to use the pretext of acting reasonably when making demands that are in fact unreasonable. Form 17 contained in this text may be useful as a basis upon which the dispute as to the reasonableness and good faith of a party's position may be resolved.

It is a simple arbitration that calls for a mandatory resolution of any dispute with respect to the content of any document or the position taken by a party prior to closing. It serves several purposes. It creates a mechanism to resolve the dispute, to extend the closing date until such time as the dispute is resolved, and to force the parties to be particularly reasonable given that they cannot force a closing or strong arm the other side under threat of declaring breach of contract. The *Resolution of Dispute Provisions* may be incorporated into virtually every major commercial contract to achieve fairness in dealing by each side.

I.   DRAFTING DEFAULT REMEDIES

Another provision (*see Form 19*) that may be used to lessen an uneven balance of power that the buyer may have over the seller is to limit the consequences of a seller's alleged default:

> In the event of the seller's default herein, the buyer shall be entitled as its sole remedy to terminate this agreement and receive a refund of its deposit money and interest thereon.

---

3   *Transamerica Life Canada Inc v ING Canada Inc*, 2003 CanLII 9923 (Ont CA).

4   *Arton Holdings Ltd et al v Gateway Realty Ltd*, 1991 CanLII 2707 (NS SC).

The buyer may object to the provision by claiming that it is tantamount to granting the seller a mere option to sell. However, a satisfactory answer to the buyer may be to provide a mere loss of deposit as the sole remedy for a buyer's alleged default:

> In the event that all conditions of this agreement are satisfied and in the event performance of this agreement is tendered by the seller and the sale is not consummated through default on the part of the buyer, the deposit money paid to the seller shall constitute liquidated damages for the buyer's default. Such amount is agreed upon by and between the seller and the buyer as liquidated damages, due to the difficulty and inconvenience of ascertaining and measuring actual damages, and the uncertainty thereof; and no other damages, rights, or remedies shall in any case be collectible, enforceable, or available to the seller other than in the section defined.

Chapter 13: **Drafting an Asset Purchase Agreement**

A. GENERAL CONSIDERATIONS

The buyer has agreed to pay a price to acquire a future income stream. Any uncertainty in or variation from that which the buyer reasonably expects is an issue that the agreement must address. To ensure that the buyer's expectations as to income and expense are met, the agreement must contain the representations and warranties made by the seller that created that expectation in the buyer. The buyer will want these provisions worded broadly, comprehensively, and unqualifiedly so that the seller will be accountable for any post-closing claim or liability that arises with respect to something that occurred while the seller owned the company or is a claim or liability that arises due to a misrepresentation or material omission by the seller.

The seller, however, wants finality and the comfort of knowing that what he has sold will not come back to "haunt him." The seller's counsel will attempt to limit the scope of the wording required by the buyer's drafter by inserting monetary and time limitations and by detracting from the absolute wording of the warranties by making them subject to provisos and qualifiers.

Neither party wants to bear the risk. Compromise will permit the parties to allocate the risk of the unforeseen by limiting the monetary exposure of either the buyer or the seller, depending on which of the two is more forceful.

B. COMPOSITION OF THE AGREEMENT[1]

1) Description of the Parties

The company that owns the assets will be a party designated in the agreement as the "Seller." However, it is more than just good form to have the holders of all the issued and outstanding shares of the Seller join in the agreement as the "Stockholders" or "Principals." In doing so, the representations and warranties contained within the agreement may be given by both the Seller and by the Principals, both jointly and severally. Indeed, if an employment agreement or a non-competition agreement involving one or more of the Principals is part of the transaction, it is yet another reason for adding these parties to the agreement. (*See forms 15 and 16.*)

2) Definitions

Terms that are defined at the outset of the agreement are those terms and expressions that appear two or more times in the text of the agreement. If a definition is given to such words or expressions, it not only shortens the agreement but avoids the uncertainty that arises from inconsistent wording that is intended to have the same meaning. Terms that are commonly defined include: "Business," "Purchased Assets," "Assumed Liabilities," "Excluded Assets," "Excluded Liabilities," "Closing Financial Statements," "Financial Statement Date," "GAAP," "Stockholder Debt," and "Scheduled Employees." (*See Form 13, Section 1.2.1.*)

---

1   The references hereinafter made to "Forms" are references to the precedent contained in the Part 4, "Forms," entitled "An Asset Purchase Agreement."

3) Description of Assets Purchased

Presumably, it is a "business" that is being acquired. The business is actively engaged in day-to-day customer and employee-related operations. The assets that are being acquired are all of the assets that are used in that operation.

After defining the term "business," the definition of "assets" requires the most particularity. It is defined generally as "all of the properties, assets, and goodwill used in the Business, of whatever in nature or kind, real or personal, tangible or intangible (including all of the rights of the seller arising from its operation of the Business)." Then, without limiting the generality of the foregoing, each "type" of asset is defined. (*See Form 13, Section 1.2.2.*)

When defining "personal property," reference is made to "all of the Seller's machinery, equipment, equipment leases, supplies, vehicles, furniture, fixtures, tools, computers, and all other personal property, wherever located, which are used in the business, including, but not limited to, the items that are listed on Schedule [ ]." A similar approach should be taken when defining real property, inventory, intellectual property, contracts, permits, rights against third parties, accounts receivable, insurance, and books and records. In each case, the general precedes the particular, and the particular is the subject for a separate schedule. When defining "goodwill" a reference should be made to all intangible property including the seller's right to commence or maintain future and existing actions relating to the operation of the Business or the ownership of the Assets for events occurring after the closing date and the right to settle those actions and retain the proceeds therefrom.

The only "assets excluded" are those assets that the seller stipulates as those "retained by the seller and not sold or assigned to the buyer." The excluded assets usually relate to the cash on hand and cash equivalent. (*See Form 13, Section 1.2.5.*)

4) Purchase Price: Payment

Depending on the method of payment, the purchase price for the Assets could be stipulated to be the aggregate of an amount payable in cash, plus an amount evidenced by a promissory note to be delivered on closing, plus an amount equal to the "Assumed Liabilities" by the buyer. (*See Form 13, sections 1.3 and 1.4.*) Alternatively, the purchase price may be a stipulated amount to be satisfied by various forms of payment including cash, debt, obligations assumed, or securities provided to the seller by the buyer.

If the method of payment involves debt in the form of a promissory note, the form of the note should be an exhibit. (*See Form 6.*) If the note is to be secured, a pledge agreement or a form of mortgage should also be incorporated as an exhibit.

A portion of the purchase price is usually withheld on closing to satisfy any claims of third parties relating to the liabilities that have not been assumed by the buyer and any claims to be made by the buyer against the seller pursuant to the terms of the agreement. (*See Form 13, Section 1.5.*) The purchase price may be subject to specific adjustments that are applied to either the cash portion of the purchase price or the deferred portion of the purchase price. These adjustments may be in favour of the buyer or the seller or both and commonly relate to accounts receivable or other cash-related adjustments. (*See Form 13, sections 1.2.4(b) and 1.3(ii).*)

5) Risk Allocation Provisions

A major portion of the agreement will contain provisions by which risk is allocated or channelled to one party or the other. This result is achieved by representations, warranties, and covenants primarily given to the buyer by the seller. Overriding the obligation of either party to close the transaction will be the pre-closing conditions, any one of which may be waived by a party if the condition to be waived is expressed to be for the benefit of that party.

The representations and warranties of the seller commonly fall within an asset-related category, a financial-related category, a business-related category, or an employee-related category.

The seller will warrant that it has clear title to all Assets and that these Assets are not subject to any undisclosed restrictions or claims, that they are in good operating condition, and that it owns its intellectual property subject to no claims or infringement actions pending or threatened. (*See Form 13, sections 2.12 and 2.19.*)

The seller will also warrant that it has fairly presented the *financial condition* of the Business; that it is not subject to any material liability or contingent liability not already noted in the financial statements; that it is not in default on any material contract or loan, nor is it aware of any claims pending or threatened; that its statements are prepared in accordance with generally accepted accounting principles; and that since the date of the statements the seller has not transferred or encumbered any assets. (*See Form 13, sections 2.7–2.11, 2.20, 2.25, 2.30, and 2.31.*)

The seller will warrant that the Business is properly organized under corporate law; is in good standing; is qualified to do business in the locations in which it is currently operating; that it is not in breach of any licence or other agreement; that it is in compliance with all applicable local, provincial, and federal laws and no notice of violations has been received; that licences and other permissions necessary to conduct its business have been obtained; and that the benefits may be transferred thereunder to the buyer. (*See Form 13, sections 2.1–2.6, 2.13–2.17, 2.22–2.24, and 2.26–2.29.*)

The seller will also warrant that pension and employee benefits are clearly disclosed and that there has been full compliance with all labour-related laws and that all scheduled employees are "on-side" with the proposed transactions. (*See Form 13, sections 2.8 and 2.21.*)

The representations and warranties of the buyer commonly relate to corporate matters regarding the acquisition representing that the acquisition will not result in any contravention of or conflict with the buyer's articles of incorporation or any other restrictions to which the buyer may be subject. (*See Form 13, sections 3.1–3.5.*)

The *indemnity* sought by the buyer will be for all claims and liabilities that are the result of any misrepresentation or breach of any warranty by the seller, or that are the result of any non-fulfillment of a covenant or agreement made by the seller, or for a claim or liability arising out of the business, its operations or the assets of the seller prior to the closing date, or the actions or omissions of the seller's directors, officers, shareholders, employees, or agents prior to the closing date— except for any obligations and liabilities assumed by the buyer. The seller will of course seek to moderate the full extent of the foregoing indemnity by subjecting the obligation to indemnify to monetary and time limitations. For example, a buyer may not demand any indemnity unless its claim for indemnity exceeds a specific amount and its claim is made within a given period of time, after which the buyer is no longer entitled to be indemnified for a breach of a warranty by the seller. (*See Form 13, sections 11.1–11.4.*)

The indemnity sought by the seller is with respect to any claim or liability suffered by the seller as a result of the buyer's breach of warranty, or a non-fulfillment of any covenant or agreement made by the buyer, or more importantly arising directly or indirectly from the ownership of the assets being purchased or the operation of the business by the buyer following the closing date. (*See Form 13, Section 9.2(e).*)

6) Covenants

The seller's financial picture is snapped as of the date shown on the seller's most recent unaudited balance sheet and the related unaudited statements of income, shareholders' equity, and cash flow for the year then ended. That date is referred to as the "Financial Statement Date." From the Financial Statement Date until the Closing Date, the seller covenants to continue to operate the business in substantially the same manner as is ordinary and usual. In other words, the seller covenants to maintain the status quo to the best of its ability and to continue to promote the business and to maintain its goodwill and reputation and not permit material deterioration in its relationships with suppliers, customers, or employees. The seller's obligation is to notify the buyer of any change in fact or circumstance that could render any of its representations and warranties to be inaccurate or misleading. The seller agrees to furnish all the information that the buyer reasonably requires concerning the seller's business, assets, operations, properties, or affairs; to notify its customers of the pending sale; and to cooperate with the buyer in the collection of receivables. (*See Form 13, Section 4.1.*)

The Agreement may provide that each of the shareholders of the seller agree that for a period of years from the date of the agreement they will not directly or indirectly engage in competition with the buyer in any manner or capacity. (*See Form 13, Section 6.4.*)

The agreement may provide that the seller support the buyer with reasonable assistance in connection with the transition of the business to the buyer. This will include the seller providing the buyer with all further assurances that may be necessary to enable the buyer to conduct the operation of the business.

The agreement will provide that the seller satisfy and discharge all of the seller's obligations other than the obligations and liabilities assumed by the buyer.

The agreement may provide that so long as any monetary obligation remains outstanding, the seller will be entitled to financial information regarding the buyer's operation and shall have access to financial reports and the books and records of the buyer, or a representative chosen by the seller will be entitled to occupy one seat on the buyer's board of directors. (*See Form 13, Section 5.4.*)

The agreement may also provide that in the event the buyer chooses to sell to an arm's-length third party assets that exceed a certain percentage of the buyer's total assets, the unpaid balance of the purchase price is accelerated.

7) Pre-closing Conditions

The obligation of the buyer to conclude the transaction is commonly made subject to the fulfillment, at or prior to closing, of a number of stipulated conditions precedent, any one or all of which the buyer may choose to waive. This section of the agreement usually contains two types of conditions:

1) One type is the occurrence of events that must occur, or consents that must be obtained, or documents that must be signed and delivered—these may be conditions precedent that are beyond either party's control such as regulatory approval or consent, the existence or non-existence of which may excuse one or both parties from its obligation to close the transaction.

2) The other type refers collectively to the seller's representations and warranties and requires that each be true and correct in all material respects at or as of the closing as if made at or as of such time, and that the seller has delivered or caused to be delivered all of the items stipulated to be delivered at the time of closing. (*See Form 13, sections 7.1–7.13.*)

Similarly, the seller's obligation to complete the transaction is subject to the performance by the buyer of each obligation and covenant required by the agreement to be performed or complied with by the buyer, including the payment or satisfaction of the purchase price and the delivery of all documents incidental thereto. (*See Form 13, sections 8.1–8.6.*)

Chapter 14: **Drafting a Share Purchase Agreement**

A. GENERAL CONSIDERATIONS

One reason why the parties may choose to structure the transaction as a share purchase is that it is generally considered to be more straightforward than an asset purchase since the only "asset" that is being conveyed is the shares of the corporation.

In most instances, the parties to a share purchase transaction will not have to consider the effects of federal goods and services tax, retail sales tax, bulk sales legislation, or labour, employment, and pension statutory requirements as they do on an asset purchase transaction. In a share purchase transaction, it should not be necessary for the purchaser to obtain new permits, licences, and regulatory orders or rulings since the legal entity in whose names such permits, licences, and regulatory orders or rulings were obtained remains the same. Similarly, obtaining consents from third parties to the assignment of contracts or the transfer of assets is unnecessary in connection with a share purchase transaction unless such consents are specifically required. Moreover, a share transaction is the preferred structure when tax losses are to be preserved.

However, when a buyer agrees to purchase the shares rather than the assets of the seller's company, he does so in spite of his fear that the representations, warranties, and indemnities may prove to be insufficient, inadequate, or ineffective in protecting him against unknown, undisclosed, contingent liabilities. The buyer must balance that fear against the realization that a share purchase transaction facilitates, to a greater extent, the acquisition of those intangible assets that the seller's company possesses, and which represent a substantial portion of the purchase price.

Since the buyer is assuming all the assets and all the liabilities of the company in a share purchase transaction, those assets the buyer *expects* the company to possess and those liabilities the buyer *expects* the company to be subject to must be laid out with great particularity. Each category of asset will be described generally, then specifically, with the more important assets being scheduled and annexed to the agreement. The liabilities to which the company will be subject will be identified by reference to financial statements annexed to the agreement and supported by a warranty that the company has "no liabilities or obligations, secured or unsecured, whether accrued, absolute, contingent, unliquidated, disputed, anticipated, or otherwise, in excess of" a specified dollar amount. In addition to the seller's warranty, indemnities provided by the seller and possibly his guarantor, or mechanisms for a holdback or for an escrow of a portion of the purchase price, or rights of set-off against any deferred portion of the purchase price are all supplementary measures intended to allay the very legitimate fears of the buyer.

B. COMPOSITION OF THE AGREEMENT

1) Description of the Parties

If the seller of the shares in the company to be acquired ("Businessco") is a corporation ("Vendco"), the individuals who own the shares of Vendco are commonly added to the agreement as the "Principal Shareholders" or "Principals." To the extent that certain provisions within the agreement are intended to be binding on Businessco, its covenant therein not to do or omit to do any act or thing that would cause or result in a breach of those provisions is required, and it, therefore, becomes a party to the agreement.

If part of the purchase price is to be deferred and taken back in the form of a promissory note, Vendco may insist that the obligations of the buyer to pay the deferred purchase price and to fulfill the obligations of the purchaser as set forth in the agreement be guaranteed by a third party such as the parent company, the beneficial owner, or a guarantor of the buyer, or indeed the obligation to pay may be guaranteed by Businessco.

2) Definitions and Schedules

The terms that are to be defined at the outset of the agreement are those terms and expressions that appear two or more times in the text of the agreement. The key terms to be found in Form 4 include the following: "Purchaser," "Vendors," "Vendco," "Businessco," "Corporations," "Purchase Shares," "Shareholder Tangible Net Equity," "Interim Period," "Financial Statements," "Latest Statement Date," and "Closing Financial Statements." (*See Form 4, Section 1.1.*)

The contents of the schedules annexed to the agreement should be expressed to be incorporated into the agreement by reference and deemed to be a part thereof. The schedules will contain those documents, financial statements, and the detailed particulars of matters that are referred to within the text.

3) Purchase Price: Payment

To provide the maximum protection for the buyer against the unknown, undisclosed, or contingent liabilities of Businessco, the buyer should endeavour to defer the payment of as much of the purchase price as possible. This is commonly done by a promissory note that is expressed to be subject to a full set-off in favour of the buyer to satisfy any purchase price adjustment and to satisfy any claim arising by virtue of a breach of warranty, covenant, or indemnity provision contained in the agreement. As an example of a purchase price adjustment, the agreement may state a stipulated dollar amount as being the *shareholder tangible net equity* in Businessco. Then, if as of a specified date (the "Effective Date"), the shareholder's tangible net equity in Businessco is less than the stipulated dollar amount, the buyer would be entitled to deduct from the payments due under the promissory note, on a dollar-for-dollar basis, the amount by which the shareholder tangible net equity is less than the stipulated dollar amount. As a security for the payment of the promissory note, the buyer may be required to lodge the purchased shares with an escrow agent pursuant to a negotiated pledge agreement. Moreover, when the agreement provides for Businessco to guarantee the payment of the promissory note, as security for Businessco's guarantee, Businessco may be required to give to the seller a general security agreement over all of the assets of Businessco, subordinated of course to Businessco's bank and other lenders. Lastly, if the covenant of the buyer is insubstantial, the sellers may demand that the obligations and performance of the buyer be guaranteed by a more substantial covenantor to support those obligations as a principal debtor. (*See Form 4, sections 2.1–2.6.*)

Alternatively, or in addition to the deductions that are permitted to be made against the payments due under promissory note, the agreement may provide for an amount to be deducted from the cash portion of the purchase price and deposited into an escrow account to be held for a limited period of time for post-closing adjustments.

If the purchased shares are composed of both special shares and common shares, a portion of the purchase price is allocated to the redemption value of the special shares and the balance of the purchase price to the common shares.

4) Risk Allocation Provisions

The purpose of demanding broad and comprehensive representations and warranties from the seller is not only to force the seller to make full disclosure of all matters relating to the business, its operation, and its finances and to ensure that all such information is accurate and complete (*see Form 4, sections 7.1(1)–(26)*) but also to place responsibility on the seller for all liabilities related to the business for a limited period of time after the transaction closes. (*See Form 4, Section 8.1.*)

5) Covenants

After the acquisition agreement has been executed and prior to the closing date, a period of time (the "Interim Period") is usually required for the purchaser to finalize its review of the operations of Businessco and for all pre-closing conditions to be satisfied. To provide the purchaser with some measure of control over the business operations during the interim period, the seller will covenant to allow the buyer access to its premises, property, and personnel for the buyer to conclude its due diligence review. The buyer will covenant to keep confidential any non-public information concerning the seller or the business in the event that the transaction is not completed. The seller will covenant to carry on business in the ordinary course, to consult the buyer regarding any material matters relating to the business, to maintain all insurance in respect of the business, and to notify the buyer of any material changes. The buyer will seek to impose limitations with respect to capital expenditures, borrowing, and the making of any significant commitment by the seller.

6) Pre-closing Conditions

The agreement will contain conditions for the benefit of either the buyer or the seller that, if not satisfied prior to closing, may give the party for whose benefit the condition was expressed certain remedies pursuant to the agreement, including the option not to complete the transaction or to sue for damages.

The buyer's obligation to complete the transaction is commonly made to be conditional on the completion of all formalities regarding the acquisition; on no material changes having occurred to the business, its assets, or its prospects prior to the closing; on certification from the sellers that the representations and warranties contained in the agreement are true and correct in all respects; on all necessary consents required under material contracts and leases; on all permits and licences necessary to carry on the business having been obtained; and on all consents or notices required pursuant to legislation having been received.

The seller will resist the presence of any pre-closing condition that rests totally on the buyer's subjective assessment. The seller will want conditions of that type to be waived or acknowledged, having been met early in the transaction.

Chapter 15: **Drafting a Hybrid Share/Asset Purchase and Sale Agreement**

A. GENERAL CONSIDERATIONS

The preliminary question when considering an acquisition transaction is whether it will be conducted as a share sale or an asset sale. Subject to extraordinary circumstances, for the reasons set forth in chapters 13 and 14, share sales are preferred by a vendor while asset sales are preferred by a purchaser.

This is especially so when the vendor is a qualified small business corporation (QSBC) because it allows the vendor selling the QSBC shares to use their lifetime capital gains exemption (LCGE) which, indexed annually, is now at $971,190 for the year 2023. QSBC is a subset of LCGE in that the LCGE covers both qualified small business corporations and also qualified farm and fishing properties.

On the other hand, purchasers prefer an asset sale because they acquire only the specific assets they want and avoid taking on the obligations and liabilities of the corporation holding the assets. Most importantly for tax reasons, the purchaser can "step-up" the tax base of the assets acquired that are either depreciable property or eligible capital property, which allows for greater deduction of capital cost allowances and therefore lower future income tax.

This hybrid type of transaction helps to bridge the competing interests of the vendor and the purchaser. It typically involves a combination of both a share and an asset sale to achieve some or all of the benefits of both sales. Simply stated, a hybrid structure involves the vendor disposing of shares to the purchaser for the vendor to claim the capital gains exemption, followed by a sale of the assets to the purchaser for the purchaser to obtain his "step-up" in the tax base of the assets he wishes to acquire.

B. COMPOSITION OF THE AGREEMENT

Since both assets and shares are being sold by virtue of this agreement, the text contained in Chapter 13, sections B(1) through (7) dealing with the sale of assets, and the text contained in Chapter 14, sections B(1) through (6) sealing with the sale of shares are applicable and pertinent.

However, what is critically different in the hybrid agreement is its structure. Care must be taken in the proposed structure to avoid the ever-present risk of a Canada Revenue Agency (CRA) tax reassessment challenging the transaction to be in contravention of the anti-avoidance provisions set forth in sections 84(2) and 245 of the ITA (*Income Tax Act*) and declaring the proceeds received by the vendor to be a deemed dividend.

C. STRUCTURE OF THE AGREEMENT

There are many variations of the structure depending on the circumstances. For example, common variations on the share sale may include using an internal freeze, under section 85 of the ITA, thereby crystallizing the capital gains exemption, or incorporating a new corporation and crystallizing the exemption by a section 85 "rollover." A common variation on the sale of assets is that instead of a direct sale of the target assets from the vendor to the purchaser, the target assets can be spun out into a "new corporation," especially if a section 85 rollover was used to crystallize the gain on the shares, following which the new corporation can be acquired by the purchaser. This was the structure used in the *Geransky v The Queen* case, which is described below.

1)   *Geransky v The Queen*, 2001 CanLII 480 (TCC)

This was the only case that successfully defied the application of section 84(2) and section 245 (GAAR (general anti-avoidance rule)) of the ITA. The other case that attempted unsuccessfully to do so, *Foix v The Queen*, 2021 TCC 52, was structured differently and is reviewed in subsection C(3) hereafter.

The structure in the *Geransky* case was one where the taxpayers held shares in the operating company ("Opco") through the use of a holding company ("Holdco"). They incorporated a new corporation ("Newco") and crystallized their capital gains exemptions using section 85 to roll over some of their shares of Holdco into Newco and spun out the target assets into Newco as a dividend. Holdco then repurchased its shares that were held by Newco, after which the taxpayers sold Newco, which now held both the target shares and assets, to the purchaser.

The sequence adopted in *Geransky* was the following:

1)   Opco declares a $1 million dividend in kind to Holdco.
2)   The dividend is satisfied by the transfer by Opco to Holdco of $1 million worth of assets (these being the assets the buyer wants to acquire).
3)   The Holdco shareholders transfer to Newco their shares in Holdco in exchange for shares in Newco (with ACB (adjusted cost base) of $500,000).
4)   Newco now owns shares in Holdco, which holds assets worth $1 million.
5)   Holdco redeems Newco's shares paid by the transfer to Newco of the assets it held.
6)   The original shareholders in Holdco sell their shares in Newco to the purchaser for $1 million (to which the LCGE applies).
7)   By acquiring Newco, the purchaser now has both the shares the vendor wanted to sell and the assets the purchaser wanted to acquire.

8)   The purchaser now merges his original company with Newco.

The CRA's legal position was that both the GAAR section 245 and specific anti-avoidance rules, such as section 84(2), applied to this transaction. Section 84(2) operates to deem a dividend to a taxpayer when funds or property of a corporation are appropriated in any manner whatever on windup, discontinuance, or reorganization of a business. The court disagreed and held that there was no windup, discontinuance, or reorganization, and even if there was no funds or property of the target corporation had made its way into the hands of the taxpayer—the funds that the taxpayer received were funds sourced from the purchaser. Finally, GAAR was not applicable as there was no misuse or abuse of any provision of the ITA.

The CRA filed an appeal but withdrew the appeal before it came to court. The CRA has since released technical interpretations that indicate that hybrid transactions that resemble the *Geransky* structure do not run afoul of section 84(2) or GAAR (see the next subsection).

2)   Round Table 2003 — Technical Interpretation

Two years after the *Geransky* decision was handed down by the Tax Court of Canada, a Round Table on Federal Taxation was held on 10 October 2003, at which the CRA was asked to comment on whether sections 84(2), 84.1, or 245(2) would apply to a series of transactions related to the sale of a business, to wit:

- Opco transfers its assets to Subco.
- Goodwill is transferred on a taxable basis while the other Opco assets are transferred on a rollover basis.
- Subco and Opco are merged, resulting in a year end for tax purposes.
- After the merger, the capital dividend account (CDA) is paid out as a dividend to the vendors.
- The shares of Opco are then sold and the vendors claim the capital gains exemption.

Although the CRA's comments contain a number of caveats, it is their view that where none of Opco's "funds or property are distributed or otherwise appropriated in any manner whatever to or for the benefit of the selling shareholders of Opco in the Given Situation, subsection 84(2) of the ITA would not be applicable."

This would generally be the case where the vendor and the purchaser are dealing at arm's length and the selling shareholder receives a cash payment for the Opco shares from the purchaser's own funds:

> Where the proposed transaction is a business transaction and is supported by a bona fide business purpose (other than obtaining a tax benefit), where a purchaser is interested in the assets of an unrelated person (the "Target Corporation"), and where the purchaser and the shareholders of the Target Corporation are unrelated persons with distinct and different interests, the sole fact that the parties have finally agreed that the purchaser would acquire the Target Corporation's assets by purchasing shares of its capital stock would not be sufficient, in and by itself, to consider that the purchaser and the vendors are not dealing at arm's length, with respect to the disposition of the shares of the Target Corporation.[1]

In the situation described, GAAR (section 274 of the ITA) would not normally apply.

The CRA was then asked to comment on the following principal issue: shareholders of an operating corporation ("Opco") sell their shares in Opco after it transfers all of its assets to a newly created subsidiary ("Subco"). Do sections 84(2), 84.1, or 245 apply in the given fact situation? The CRA's position was as follows:

> Where none of Opco's funds or property are distributed or otherwise appropriated in any manner whatever to or for the benefit of the selling shareholders of Opco in the Given

---

1   From the Tax Court of Canada, Round Table on Federal Taxation (10 October 2003), online: https://taxinterpretations.com/cra/severed-letters/2003-0029955.

Situation, section 84(2) of the ITA would not be applicable. This could be the case where the selling shareholders and the purchaser are dealing at arm's length, the selling shareholders would receive a cash amount from the purchaser's own funds in return for their Opco shares, and Opco's assets would continue to be used in an active business by Opco or by another entity within the Purchaser's corporate group. In such a situation, subsection 245(2) would not normally apply to the selling shareholders to redetermine the tax consequences arising from the sale of their shares. Where the proposed transaction is a business transaction and is supported by bona fide business purposes (other than obtaining a tax benefit), where a purchaser is interested in the assets of an unrelated person (the "Target Corporation"), and where the purchaser and the shareholders of the Target Corporation are unrelated persons with distinct and different interests, the sole fact that the parties have finally agreed that the purchaser would acquire the Target Corporation's assets by purchasing shares of its capital stock would not be sufficient, in and of itself, to consider that the purchaser and the vendors are not dealing at arm's length, with respect to the disposition of the shares of the capital stock of the Target Corporation.[2]

The CRA was then asked to comment on the following situation: The shareholders of an operating corporation ("Opco") would like to sell the business carried on by Opco. The transaction may involve either assets or shares. Discussions with a potential buyer have been initiated. The buyer is interested in Opco's assets. After negotiations, it was agreed that the shareholders would sell their shares in Opco after it transfers all of its assets to a newly created subsidiary ("Subco"). The sale of goodwill to Subco is made on a fully taxable basis, that is, without using the provisions set out in section 85 of the ITA, and the transfer of the other assets is done on a rollover basis. The capital dividend

---

2   *Ibid.*

account is paid to the selling shareholders immediately after a year end created by the merger of Opco and Subco, or by the acquisition of control of Opco. The price of the shares sold is adjusted to take into account the tax payable as a result of the sale of the assets and the disbursement related to the payment of the CDA. The selling shareholders use their capital gains deduction on qualified small business corporation shares.

The result of this transaction should normally be less questionable than the *Geransky* case because the transaction described above involves all the assets, rather than a portion only ("stripping"). Is it therefore the CRA's position that section 84(2) of the ITA, as applied in *Geransky*, and section 84.1 of the ITA, applicable in situations where there is a factual non-arm's-length relationship (see question no. 5 of the 1995 Ontario Tax Conference Round Table) are not applicable in the above situation to prevent sellers from benefiting from their lifetime capital gains deduction? Moreover, taking into account the fact that the taxes resulting from the sale of assets to Subco have been paid, can the CRA confirm that it would not apply section 245 of the ITA? Here is the CRA's response:

> It should first be noted that the text of this question only summarizes very briefly a hypothetical situation (the "Given Situation") and, among other things, does not provide information about the consideration received by the selling shareholders and the use of Opco's assets after the transaction is completed. Without this information, it is impossible to make a definitive statement on the potential application of subsections 84(2) and 245(2) of the ITA as they relate to the Given Situation. We can, however, provide the following general comments.
>
> It is our opinion that where none of Opco's funds or property are distributed or otherwise appropriated in any manner whatever to or for the benefit of the selling shareholders of Opco in the Given Situation, subsection 84(2) of the ITA would not be applicable. This could be the case, particularly, where the selling shareholders and the purchaser are dealing

at arm's length, the selling shareholders would receive a cash amount from the purchaser's own funds in return for their Opco shares, and Opco's assets would continue to be used in an active business by Opco or by another entity within the purchaser's corporate group.

As for the application of subsection 245(2), it is impossible for us to take a definitive position in the Given Situation. The potential application of subsection 245(2) requires a review of all the facts and circumstances surrounding a specific situation, yet the text of this question only summarizes very briefly a hypothetical situation. As a general comment, however, we can confirm that, in a situation such as the one described in the preceding paragraph, subsection 245(2) would not normally apply to the selling shareholders to redetermine the tax consequences arising from the sale of their shares.

It is also difficult for us to take a definitive position on the potential application of section 84.1 in the Given Situation because the text of this question only summarizes very briefly the Given Situation and, among other things, does not provide any information about the consideration the selling shareholders would receive, or if the selling shareholders are not dealing at arm's length or are deemed not to be dealing at arm's length with the purchaser.

It is our opinion, however, that, in general, where the proposed transaction is a business transaction and is supported by bona fide business purposes (other than obtaining a tax benefit), where a purchaser is interested in the assets of an unrelated person (the "Target Corporation"), and where the purchaser and the shareholders of the Target Corporation are unrelated persons with distinct and different interests, the sole fact that the parties have finally agreed that the purchaser would acquire the target Corporation's assets by purchasing shares of its capital stock would not be sufficient, in and of itself, to consider that the purchaser and the vendors are not dealing at arm's length, with respect to the disposition of the shares of the capital stock of the Target Corporation.

In closing, we point out that the application of subsections 84(2) and 245(2) and section 84.1 of ITA generally requires a review of all the facts and circumstances surrounding a specific situation. Where the shareholders intend to carry out transactions to which one of these provisions may apply, we recommend that they obtain an advance income tax ruling beforehand.

It should also be noted that the purpose of the above question is essentially to obtain CRA's opinion on the tax consequences for selling shareholders arising from the disposition of their Opco shares, and that our comments are limited to this aspect of the transaction. Consequentially, and given that the text of this question only summarizes very briefly a hypothetical situation, the above comments must in no way be interpreted as being applicable to other tax consequences that may arise from the Given Situation, such as those that may arise from the transactions carried out by the Target Corporation prior to the sale of the Opco shares. On this point, it should be noted that under the legislative proposals of December 20, 2020, variable "A" in the definition of "cumulative eligible capital" (CEC) in subsection 14(5) of the ITA has been amended in such a way that the non-taxable portion of Opco's gains that would be realized on the transfer of goodwill to Subco would be excluded from Subco's CEC account.[3]

3) *Foix v The Queen*, 2021 TCC 52

This case upheld the application of section 84(2) in a hybrid business sale transaction. The transaction was originally proposed as an asset sale, but it was converted later to a hybrid sale of assets and shares.

---

3   *Ibid.*

There was an ongoing agreement that the excess cash of the corporation could be distributed to its shareholders prior to closing. The Tax Court held that the purchasers were the instruments and the intermediaries through which the distribution of the target corporation's funds or assets for the benefit of its shareholders took place, following a prior reorganization that brought about the hybrid sale.

This case is considered distinguishable from the *Geransky* case in that a hybrid transaction was seen by the court to have been structured to extract excess cash even in the context of a genuine sale of the business or part of a business, and accordingly it attracted section 84(2).

The case seems to highlight the concept that the intention of the parties may be a consideration in determining whether section 84(2) applies where a share sale is implemented as a mechanism to distribute excess cash.

4) Commentary

In the absence of a hybrid transaction that involves the distribution of excess cash it is difficult to ascertain a perceived abuse inherent in hybrid transactions, bearing in mind that more tax revenue is collected on a current basis in a hybrid sale than would be collected under a share sale. Moreover, the courts (in *Evans v The Queen*, 2005 TCC 684; *Gwartz v The Queen*, 2013 TCC 86; and *Collins & Aikman Products Co v The Queen*, 2009 TCC 299) have not found any scheme in the ITA that requires distributions to be taxed as dividends when section 84(2) is not applicable. Perhaps, most importantly, the CRA has not updated their position stated in the Round Table 2003 technical interpretation as set forth above.[4]

The risk of possible CRA reassessment with attendant costs is of course ever present, but the *Geransky* case and the cases that have been

---

4   The type of hybrid involved using section 111(4)(e) to trigger capital gains pre-closing in order to step up the tax cost of the shares being transferred has now been rendered ineffective by the new "substantive CCPC rules" introduced in the 2022 budget.

litigated since *Geransky* seem to suggest the following rules of thumb as to when the hybrid structure may succeed:

- Whenever possible, the seller should continue to operate a "portion" of the business.
- The buyer should pay the purchase price from its own funds without recourse to funds contained within the seller's company.
- Avoid the amalgamation or other form of merger of the target corporation with the buyer's corporation.
- Avoid the distribution of cash from the target corporation. Instead, reduce excess cash held by the target corporation by repaying debt or by paying taxable dividends to the shareholders prior to the hybrid transaction.
- Lastly, and perhaps most importantly, the intention and the separate interests of the parties to the transaction is imperative.

Chapter 16: **Drafting an Earn-Out Arrangement**

A. GENERAL CONSIDERATIONS

When an earn-out is negotiated as part of the acquisition's purchase price, part of the consideration payable to the seller essentially becomes contingent on the ability of the buyer to meet its financial and growth projections. The seller is counting on the ability of the buyer's management team to both manage and operate the assets in a profitable manner. However, if the seller's shareholders become members of the buyer's management team, the earn-out presents these shareholders with an incentive for performance from which both the buyer and the seller benefit.

The earn-out arrangement is also used when no agreement can be reached on the value of the assets or the stock that is being sold, or if the parties anticipate the possibility of a serious change in circumstance. In that case, a post-acquisition adjustment in the purchase price is often the solution.

Alternatively, the earn-out arrangement may provide for a *reverse earn-out*, wherein a penalty is imposed on the seller in the event that performance targets are not met. For example, if the seller accepts a purchase price composed of cash and promissory notes, either the amount of the note or the interest rate charged thereon may be reduced if minimal performance criteria are not met or if representations or warranties by the seller are breached.

The earn-out is intended to achieve one or more objectives:

1) As an incentive payment, it can be used to motivate the founding shareholder to remain with the buyer's management team to help build the business after closing and ensure that the seller's management team remains in place after closing.

2) As a purchase price adjustment, it can be used to resolve differing views over the valuation of the seller's business, particularly when the seller feels that its stock or assets are being sold for less than they may be worth.

3) As a means of managing risk, the earn-out can be used to allocate substantial risk back to the seller in the event that minimal performance criteria are not met, or in the event that warranties are breached, or if the future value of the business is uncertain, which may prevent the buyer from overpaying.

The key provisions that must be addressed to achieve the foregoing are as follows:

1) The financial formula used to determine the contingent payment that may be payable to the seller

2) The minimum and maximum payout that may be realized by the seller

3) The nature and extent of the controls, if any, that the shareholders of the seller will have over budgets and expenditures that are to be made by the buyer to ensure that the financial targets are reached

4) The audit and inspection rights that should be granted to the seller

5) The business plan and financial projections annexed to the agreement as a methodology to be adopted by the parties to achieve their goals

6) The term of the earn-out period

7) The method and frequency of payment

8) The form of consideration itself, such as cash, stocks, notes, and warrants

9) The relationship of the earn-out to other liability and risk allocation sections, such as the impact of the bankruptcy or insolvency of the purchaser, and the rights of set-off arising from the indemnity provisions of the acquisition agreement

10) The tax implications of the transaction

B. VARIOUS FORMS OF EARN-OUT

Whatever form is chosen, a periodic reassessment is made of the value of the assets or the stock that has been sold based on a post-closing performance of the seller's company or the merged entity.

The form may be the pre-tax net operating income, as defined, of the company's operations, in which case in addition to the purchase price an additional amount is paid annually to the seller equal to that percentage of the company's net operating income that exceeds a stipulated earnings threshold. The company's "pre-tax operating earnings" is commonly defined to be the company's operating earnings before deduction for bonuses, salaries, director's fees, or other monetary benefits payable to any director of the company and before deduction is made for any expenses incurred or accrued by the company for charges made by the purchaser or any of its affiliates for management rendered to the company.

A form of reverse earn-out may be adopted if the free cash flow generated by the company's operations are insufficient to achieve a threshold stipulated, in which case the interest, and latterly the principal, secured by a subordinated promissory note is postponed or waived.[1]

C. A FORM OF EARN-OUT

If the formula to be applied is the "pre-tax operating earnings" of the seller's company, a definition is required to determine what amounts are included or excluded.

---

1   Although not strictly a reverse earn-out, it is important to note that an earn-out should always be made subject to the set-off claims of the purchaser pursuant to the indemnification provisions contained within the acquisition agreement.

A hypothetical earn-out based on pre-tax operating earnings might provide that annually, in each of three fiscal years that follow the closing date, an amount will be paid to the seller equal to a designated percentage of the amount by which the corporation's audited pre-tax operating earnings exceed a designated sum. That amount may be said to be payable within forty-five days after the corporation's receipt of its audited financial statements for each of the said three fiscal years, together with interest thereon from the last day of each such fiscal year until the date of payment. The "pre-tax operating earnings" of the corporation may be defined as being the corporation's operating earnings before deduction for income tax and before extraordinary items, in accordance with generally accepted accounting principles consistently applied in the manner indicated on the consolidated financial statements for each of the three prior years and, without limitation, for the purpose of calculating the pre-tax operating earnings it is understood and agreed that:

1) No deduction will be made for any expenses incurred or accrued by the corporation for charges made by the buyer or any of its affiliates (as defined in the Ontario *Business Corporations Act*) for management or other services, rendered to the corporation, except for such services rendered at competitive rates on a per diem basis that have been agreed to in advance by the seller or its representative.

2) No deduction will be made for bonuses, salaries, director's fees, or other monetary benefits payable to any director of the corporation.

The parties agree to rely on the financial statements prepared by the accountants to determine the deferred consideration. The seller should have the right to consult with the corporation's accountants to review all aspects of such calculations before the delivery thereof to the seller. However, such determination should thereafter be final and binding on the parties.

Part 4

FORMS*

---

* Please note that the following forms have been reproduced from their original source and as such may contain typos that existed in the original content.

Form 1: **Letter of Intent**

To: Mr. John S. (the "**Seller**")
 Toronto, Ontario, Canada

Dear Mr. S:

This letter is intended to set forth the terms by which the "**Buyer**" agrees to purchase all of the current issued capital stock of the seller's company on and subject to the terms and conditions set forth herein. The Purchaser and the Seller are hereinafter collectively referred to as the "**Parties**".

Section "**A**" of this letter summarizes the principal terms that have been proposed in earlier meetings and do not represent terms that are binding at this time upon either of the Parties. These principal terms are subject to the execution and delivery by the Parties of the share acquisition agreement, employment agreement and other documents related to these transactions.

Section "**B**" of this letter contains a number of covenants by the Parties, including the Buyer's funding commitment and the execution and delivery of a promissory note in consideration thereof which shall be legally binding upon the execution of this letter by the Parties. The binding terms of Section "**B**" below are enforceable against the Parties regardless of whether the aforementioned agreements are executed or the reasons for non-execution.

SECTION "A": PROPOSED TERMS

1)   Share Purchase

The Parties will execute a share acquisition agreement, pursuant to which Purchaser will purchase all of the issued capital stock of the Seller's company (the "**Shares**") for a total purchase price which is to be determined in the following manner:

> *Employing a method of valuation known as discounted cash flow the average of the free, after-tax cash flow of the Seller's company for the last fiscal year and the expected free after-tax cash flow of the Seller's company for the ensuing fiscal year shall be discounted by a rate mutually agreed upon by the Parties, plus a premium thereon equal to 20% of the average of the said two amounts.*

2)   Employment Agreement

Prior to closing, the Purchaser will enter into an individual employment agreement with the Seller for three-year term at a compensation level set forth in the Seller's company's business plan as previously presented by the Seller to the Purchaser. The employment agreement will contain such other terms and conditions as a reasonable and customary in the type of transaction contemplated herein.

3)   Closing and Documentation

The Parties intend that a closing of the agreement shall occur on or before ●, 20●, at a time and place mutually acceptable to the Parties. The Purchaser or its representatives will prepare and revise the initial and subsequent drafts of the necessary agreements.

SECTION "B": BINDING TERMS

In consideration of the costs to be incurred by the Parties in undertaking the actions toward the negotiation and consummation of the share acquisition agreement and the related agreements, the Parties hereby agree to the following terms (the "**Binding Terms**").

4)   Deposit

The Purchaser will pay a refundable deposit in the amount of $● to the Seller at the time of the execution of this letter and will pay an additional $● no later than sixty (60) days after the execution of this letter. All sums paid hereunder shall be deductible from the purchase price to be paid for the shares as described in paragraph 1. If the Purchaser does not complete the purchase of the shares, the sums payable hereunder shall be deemed an advance and subject to repayment to the Purchaser within six months from the date of the execution of this letter in a lump sum with interest thereon at a rate equal to 1% over the prime commercial lending rate of the Royal Bank from the date of advance to the date of repayment. In the event that the closing is delayed beyond ●, 20●, the Purchaser will advance additional funds of $● on ●, 20●. Each additional advance shall be repaid within six months of the date of advance at the said rate from the date of advance to the date of repayment. The Seller and the Seller's company shall execute and deliver a promissory note in consideration of the advances of funds hereunder.[1]

5) Due Diligence

The directors, officers, shareholders, and other representatives, (the "**Representatives**") of the Seller's company shall grant to the Purchaser and its Representatives:

- full access to the Seller's company's properties, personnel, facilities, books and records, financial and operating data, contracts and other documents, and
- furnish all such books and records, financial and operating data, contracts and other documents or information and as the Purchaser may reasonably request.

6) Covenants of the Seller and the Seller's Company

The Seller and the Seller's company agree that from and after the execution of this letter agreement until the earlier of the termination of the Binding Terms in accordance with paragraph 11 hereof or the execution and delivery of the Agreements described herein:

---

1   In other cases, the seller may request a deposit or option fee, and the Parties must determine to what extent, if any, this deposit will be refundable and under what conditions. For example, the buyer will want the deposit to remain totally refundable if the seller is being uncooperative or at least the buyer has completed the first round of due diligence to ensure that there are no major problems discovered that might cause the buyer to walk away. The seller will want to set a limit on the due diligence and review period at which point the buyer forfeits all or a portion of its deposit. Often the result is a progressive downward scale of refundability as the due diligence and the transaction generally reach various checkpoints toward closing.

- The Seller's company's business and operations will be conducted in the ordinary course in substantially the same manner as such business and operations have been conducted in the past and the Seller will notify the Purchaser of any extraordinary transactions, financing or business involving the Seller.[2]
- The Seller and the Seller's company will not initiate or conclude, through its representatives or otherwise, any negotiations with any corporation, person or other entity regarding the establishment of a line of credit, the sale of substantially all of the assets of or the management of the Seller. The Seller's company will immediately notify the other party regarding any such contact.[3]

7)   Stand-Still Share Agreement

From and after the execution of this letter until the consummation of the transaction as contemplated in Section A, and the execution of the share acquisition and related agreements,[4] or in the event that said agreements are not executed, until the repayment of all amounts advanced pursuant to paragraph 4 hereof, plus accrued interest, without the prior written approval of the Purchaser and subject to any anti-dilution provisions imposed herein, the company agrees that no shares currently issued from the capital stock of the company shall be sold,

---

2   A buyer will want protection that the business he is going to investigate will not materially change during the course of the investigation. The seller will need to ensure that equipment is kept in good repair, new customers are pursued, and bonuses are not magically declared. In fact, any steps that may deplete the value of the company prior to closing should be the subject of negative covenants contained within the stock purchase agreement or a collateral agreement executed by the Seller and the Seller's company. Often, the letter of intent is subject to these collateral agreements which address key matters such as covenants, indemnification, representations, warranties and pre-closing conditions. In fact, both parties will want to articulate conditions for and circumstances under which, they will not be bound to proceed with the transaction. For example, if certain contingencies are not met or events subsequently occur, the Parties may wish to be released from the transaction.

3   The buyer will want a period of exclusivity during which time the buyer has the confidence of knowing the seller is not entertaining other offers. The seller, however, will want to place a limit or outside date on this provision in order to allow it to begin entertaining other offers if the buyer is dragging its feet.

4   In this case, the definitive agreements would include the stock purchase agreement, the employment agreement, and post-closing agreements.

transferred or assigned to any party, that no such shares shall be pledged as security or in any other manner disposed of or encumbered, and the company shall issue no additional shares of capital stock of any class, whether now or hereafter authorized.

8) Confidentiality

Prior to closing, neither Party nor any of their representatives shall make any public statement or issue any press release regarding the agreements, the proposed transaction contemplated herein or this letter without the prior written consent of the other Party, except to the extent that such disclosure may be required by law. Notwithstanding the foregoing, the Parties acknowledge that certain disclosures regarding the agreement, the proposed transaction or this letter may be required to be made to each Party's representatives or certain of them, and to any other party whose consent or approval may be required to complete the agreements and the transactions provided for herein and that such disclosures shall not require prior written consent. The Purchaser and its employees will treat all information received from the Seller and the Seller's company confidentially, shall not disclose such information to third parties without the prior written consent of the Seller's company, except as such disclosure may be required by law, and shall not use such information for any purpose other than the consideration of the matters contemplated by this Letter of Intent, including related due diligence, and shall return to the Seller's company any such information if this matter terminates pursuant to paragraph 11 hereof.[5]

9) Expenses, Finder's and Break-Up Fees

a) The Parties are responsible for and shall bear all of their own costs and expenses incurred at any time in connection with the transactions contemplated herein provided, however, that ● shall be responsible for any finder's fees payable in connection with the transaction contemplated herein.[6]

b) The Seller agrees to pay the Purchaser a break-up fee of $● in the event that the sale and purchase of the shares contemplated in Section A is not

---

5　If an announcement is not made directly to the seller's employees, those employees may get the impression their jobs are unimportant or in jeopardy. Supervisory personnel should be briefed first so that they can inform their subordinates.

6　The letter must specify which party is to bear responsibility for investment bankers' fees, finder's fees, legal expenses and other costs pertaining to the transaction.

accomplished by ●, 20●, as a result of the Seller's company's failure or refusal to close pursuant to the terms set forth above and not due to any refusal or delay on the part of the Purchaser to close by that date.[7]

10) Enforceability of Binding Terms

The foregoing obligations of the Parties under Section B of this letter agreement shall be effective as of the date of execution by the Seller's company and shall terminate upon the completion of the transactions contemplated in Section A, or, if such transactions are not completed, then at such time as all of the obligations under Section B have been satisfied, unless otherwise extended by the Parties or specifically extended by the terms of the foregoing provisions. Such termination, however, shall not relieve the Parties of liability for the breach of any obligation occurring prior to such termination.

Please indicate your agreement to the Binding Terms as set forth in Section B by executing and returning a copy of this letter to the undersigned no later than ●, 20●. Following receipt, we will instruct legal counsel to prepare the agreements contemplated herein. The Binding Terms shall become binding on the Seller's company upon the advance of funds pursuant to paragraph 4 hereof and the execution of the promissory note which is to be given in consideration.

Yours very truly,

Purchaser _______________

Per: _______________

ACKNOWLEDGED and ACCEPTED

By:

Seller _______________

Per: _______________

Dated: _______________ 20●

---

7   The buyer will want to include a provision providing an opportunity to recoup some of its expenses if the seller tries to walk from the transaction owing either to a change in circumstance or a desire to accept a more attractive offer from a different buyer. The seller may want a reciprocal clause to protect against its own expenses if the buyer walks away or defaults on a preliminary obligation or pre-condition to closing.

Form 2: **Letter of Intent [*Alternate Form*]**

[*Date*]

[*Name of Purchaser*]
[*Address*]

PRIVATE AND CONFIDENTIAL

The Shareholders
[*Name of Business*]
[*Alternatively, insert actual names of shareholders*]
[*Address*]

Dear Sirs:

Re: Proposed Acquisition of the shares of ● (the "Company")

This letter outlines the basis upon which ● or its designated affiliate ("**the Purchaser**") will proceed with the acquisition of the Company from the shareholders of the Company. This letter is intended to set forth the general principles pursuant to which the parties will expeditiously proceed with due diligence and the preparation of formal agreements.

1) Nature of Transaction
The Purchaser will acquire all of the issued and outstanding shares (the "**Purchased Shares**") in the capital of the Company, which we understand are owned by ●, ● and ● (collectively, the "**Vendors**").

2) Purchase Price

Subject to the results of the Purchaser's due diligence in accordance with Section 7, the aggregate purchase price (the **"Purchase Price"**) which the Purchaser is prepared to pay to the Vendors for the Purchased Shares will be [●].

The calculation of the Purchase Price is based on and subject to the following:

a)   The Purchaser being satisfied based solely on its own due diligence review of the books, records and operations of the Company and that the Company has earned and collected revenues for the past ● fiscal years of not less than $● per annum;

b)   Execution and delivery of a Formal Agreement (as defined below) and the terms and conditions herein as contemplated in Section 5;

c)   The completion to the Purchaser's sole satisfaction of the Purchaser's evaluation of the assets of the Company (the **"Company Assets"**) and the business of the Company (the **"Company Business"**) as described in Sections 3, 7 and 9;

d)   Delivery of the consents and approvals contemplated in Section 6; and

e)   The aggregate debt and liabilities of the Company will not exceed $● at Closing.

$100,000 of the Purchase Price (the **"Holdback"**) is to be held in escrow in an interest bearing account by Torkin Manes LLP, solicitors for the Purchaser, for a period of ● months from Closing to be used to satisfy any uncollected accounts receivable and indemnity and warranty claims under the Formal Agreement. The Purchase Price less the Holdback will be payable on Closing in cash or certified funds. [*Note: Amend as required based on business deal*]

[*Consider whether a working capital adjustment should be included*]

The Purchase Price will be allocated among the Purchased Shares in such manner as may be mutually determined by the parties in the Formal Agreement.

3) No Encumbrances on Purchased Shares

The Purchased Shares are or will be on Closing, free and clear from any liens or encumbrances.

4) Formal Agreement

The parties will agree to use their reasonable efforts to negotiate, execute and deliver a formal purchase and sale agreement (the **"Formal Agreement"**) by ● or such other date as the parties may agree, such Formal Agreement being based on the understandings recorded in this letter. Upon its execution and delivery, the Formal Agreement will supersede this letter in all respects.

5)   Terms of Formal Agreement

The Formal Agreement will contain terms and conditions, representations, warranties, covenants, indemnities, closing conditions and opinion requirements that are customary in purchase and sale transactions of the nature contemplated herein. The Purchaser's counsel will draft the Formal Agreement. The Purchaser will require ●, ●, and ● as the founders (the **"Founders"**) to provide their personal joint and several guarantee of the obligations of the Vendors under the Formal Agreement. The representations, warranties and covenants of each Vendor will be joint and several and will survive closing for a period of 4 years. The Formal Agreement will be governed by the laws of the Province of Ontario and the parties will irrevocably attorn to the exclusive jurisdiction of the Province of Ontario. The Vendors and Founders will be required to provide a release of the Company on Closing relating to their capacity as shareholder, officer, director or employee and the Vendors and Founders will resign such positions as at Closing.

6)   Consents and Approvals

It is understood that any required consents and approvals for the transfer of the Purchased Shares to the Purchaser including consents required as a result of change of control and for the operation of the Company Business by the Purchaser will be obtained by the Vendors at their cost on or before Closing or otherwise provided for in a mutually agreeable manner.

7)   Due Diligence

It is understood that the Purchase Price proposed by the Purchaser is based on certain assumptions and on certain preliminary data and information received by the Purchaser from the Company, and that such data and information must be confirmed by the Purchaser in its legal and business due diligence process. The Purchaser's evaluation process will include, but not be limited to the following matters:

a)   Confirmation, review and evaluation of the Company Assets, operating costs, revenues, customer contracts, prices and customer information;

b)   Review of tax returns filed by the Company and all working papers of the auditors for the Company;

c)   Detailed review of the Company's organization, wage and salary structure, employee benefit plans and employment arrangements with employees and independent contractors;

d)   Review of all outstanding or pending litigation;

e)   Confirmation that all certificates, permits, licenses and controls necessary for the operation of the Company Business will not be affected by the change of control or that the appropriate consents can be obtained;

f)   Review of the accuracy of the Company's inventory database;

g)   Review of minute book, corporate records, contracts, licenses and permits;

h)   Confirmation, review and evaluation of revenues earned by the Company Business in each of the last 5 fiscal years;

i)   Inspection and assessment of machinery, equipment, buildings and land;

j)   Environmental assessments and investigations;

k)   Title to all the Company Assets; and

l)   Review and confirmation of all lease arrangements with tenants and status of leases.

8)   Closing

The Formal Agreement will provide for a closing date upon which the proposed purchase and sale transaction is to be completed (the **"Closing"**). The parties anticipate the Closing to take place on or before ● or at such other mutually agreeable date.

9)   Conditions of Closing

In addition to the various terms and conditions set-out in this Letter of Intent, the completion of the transactions contemplated in this Letter of Intent are conditional on and subject to the Purchaser being satisfied in its sole discretion at Closing, with the results of its due diligence review of the Company Assets and the Company Business and Purchased Shares, including its due diligence as contemplated in Section 7.

10)   Conduct of The Company's Business, Etc.

From and after the date hereof to the date of Closing (the **"Interim Period"**), it is understood that the Company will and the Vendors will cause the Company to:

a)   Not make changes to the capital structure of the Company or capitalization of the Company, without the prior written consent of the Purchaser;

b)   Use its best efforts to maintain the goodwill of the Company Business;

c)   Not engage in any activities or transactions which are outside the ordinary and usual course of the Company Business, consistent with past practice;

d)   Maintain the Company Assets in good working order and condition and not sell or otherwise dispose of any the Company Assets without the prior written consent of the Purchaser;

e)   Ensure that no legal or professional fees associated with this transaction are charged to or paid by the Company;

f)   Retire all shareholder loans and not incur any other indebtedness with any related party;

g)   Not enter into any material employment or consulting agreement with any employee or make any material change to the terms of any existing employment or contractual arrangement with the Company's employees or consultants, without the prior written approval of the Purchaser; and

h)   Not to amend or alter any lease arrangements with tenants or enter into any new leases with tenants without the prior written approval of the Purchaser.

11) Financial Data and Reports

It is understood that this letter is based on preliminary and limited financial data and reports provided to date by the Company to the Purchaser in its review of the Company Business, the Company Assets and the Purchased Shares. It is further understood that, during the Interim Period, the Company and the Vendors will make available to the Purchaser, its representatives and counsel, all documents, contracts and agreements in its possession or under its control relating to the Company Business, the Company Assets and the Purchased Assets and that the Purchaser and its representatives and advisors shall be permitted to inspect and test the Company Assets and interview and meet with key employees, suppliers and customers, if required by the Purchaser.

12) Non-Disclosure, Non-Competition, Non-Solicitation Agreement

It will be a condition of Closing that the Vendors and, where a Vendor is a corporation, its principals and affiliates (collectively, the **"Covenantors"**) will provide the Purchaser with a five-year non-competition and non-solicitation covenant in respect of the Company Business anywhere [*in the Provinces of Ontario and Quebec.*] The Covenantors will also provide a non-disclosure covenant. The Purchaser will pay in consideration of the foregoing covenants the aggregate sum of $●, which is included in the Purchase Price described in Section 2.

13) Public Announcements

No public announcement or press release concerning the proposed purchase and sale transaction herein contemplated will be made by any party during the Interim Period without the prior written consent of the other party.

14) Confidentiality

No disclosure shall be made to any party to any other person (other than to the parties' respective advisors) with respect to this Letter of Intent or the transaction contemplated herein except as required in respect of the transactions contemplated in this Letter of Intent.

The parties reaffirm the existence and continued effectiveness of the confidentiality agreement (the **"Confidentiality Agreement"**) dated ● executed by the Company and the Purchaser.

15) Exclusivity

The Vendors and the Company jointly and severally covenant and agree that they will not either individually or collectively, from the date of this letter until ●, directly or indirectly enter into or conduct discussions or negotiations with any other party, or entertain any offers, for the purchase of any of the assets of the Company, other than in the ordinary course of business, or any of the shares in the capital of the Company. The parties hereby agree to extend the provisions of section 17 of the Confidentiality Agreement to ●.

16) Expression of Intention

It is understood that this Letter of Intent sets forth the understandings to date of the parties concerning the proposed purchase by the Purchaser of the Purchased Shares and other than Sections 4, 5, 10, 11, 12, 13, 14 and 15 above, is not intended to create enforceable legal rights and obligations between the parties. However, the parties confirm their serious intention to complete the proposed purchase and sale transactions contemplated hereby on the terms and pursuant to the timetable set forth in this Letter of Intent. Unless otherwise agreed, the provisions of Sections 4, 5, 10, 11, 12, 14 and 15 are essential to the proper negotiation of the proposed transaction, and in consideration of the parties' continued participation in these negotiations, the parties have agreed to be bound by these covenants.

* * *

We trust that the above reflects the understandings we have to date. If you are in concurrence with the above, please sign the enclosed copy of this letter and return it to the Purchaser as confirmation of the status of our negotiations, and in the case of Sections 4, 5, 10, 11, 12, 14 and 15 of our agreement.

It is the express wish of the parties that this agreement and any related documents be drawn up and executed in the English language. Les parties conviennent que la présente convention et tous les documents s'y rattachant soient rédigés en anglais.

Yours truly,

[Name of Purchaser]

Agreed and accepted this ● day of ●, 20●.

By: By:
Name: _______________   Name: _______________
Title: _______________   Title: _______________

____
Signature of Witness

____
Signature of Witness

____
Print Name of Witness

____
Print Name of Witness

Form 3: **Confidentiality Agreement**

THIS CONFIDENTIALITY AGREEMENT ("Agreement") is made as of this ● day of ● 20●, by and among Company 1, Inc., a corporation ("**Company1**") and Company2, Inc., a corporation ("**Company2**") and each of the under-signed representatives of each of Company1 and Company2, respectively (the "**Representatives**"). Company1 and Company2 are collectively referred to hereinafter as the "**Parties.**"

WHEREAS, the Representatives executing this Agreement shall include, but are not limited to, the following individuals: On behalf of Company1, ●, and on behalf of Company2, ●; provided, however, that any additional Representatives also shall execute a copy of this Agreement;

WHEREAS, Representatives of the Parties intend to meet on ●, 20● to discuss certain transactions related to the businesses of the Parties, including a potential purchase and sale transaction between the Parties or other possible combinations of Company1 and Company2 (all of which shall be referred to hereinafter as the "**Transaction**");

WHEREAS, each of the Representatives, during meetings and discussions relating to the Transaction, may disclose certain confidential and proprietary information regarding each Party's business plans, financial and operational data, services, products, and product development plans;

WHEREAS, each of the Parties desires to protect its proprietary rights and further desires to prevent unauthorized disclosure of any information regarding its individual business plans, financial and operational data, products and services;

WHEREAS, the Representatives collectively desire to prevent unauthorized disclosure by any one of them of any information regarding the Transaction and the business plans, financial and operational data, products and services associated therewith;

WHEREAS, the Parties intend to have the **"confidential information"** as defined below treated as being confidential and/or proprietary.

NOW, THEREFORE, in consideration of the premises and the mutual covenants contained herein, the parties agree as follows:

1) Definition of Confidential Information

In connection with the Transaction being discussed among the Representatives, each of the Parties and their Representatives may disclose certain information intended to remain as proprietary and confidential, including information regarding business plans, financial data, operational data, product development plans, products and services. The information furnished by either of the Parties or any Representative is hereinafter referred to as **"Confidential Information"** and such Confidential Information shall belong to the Party furnishing the same (through one or more of its Representatives) and shall be treated as Confidential Information as provided herein. Confidential Information shall also include all discussions in connection with, and all information in any medium in any way related to, the Transaction.

The term **"Confidential Information"** shall not include information which was or becomes generally available to the public other than as a result of a disclosure by a Representative or his affiliates, agents or advisors including, without limitation, attorneys, accountants, consultants, bankers and financial advisors (collectively "Affiliates").

2) Use of Confidential Information

The Representatives of a Party shall not use any Confidential Information disclosed by the Representatives of the other Party or pertaining to the Transaction for its own use or for any purpose other than to carry out the discussions between the Parties and to further the evaluation of the Transaction and the business relationship between the Parties.

3) Permitted Disclosure

A Party or its Representatives may disclose Confidential Information if required by a governmental agency or court of competent jurisdiction, or the rules thereof, provided, however, each Party agrees to give to the other prompt notice of the receipt of the subpoena or other process requiring or requesting disclosure of Confidential Information.

4)   Proprietary Rights

All Confidential Information furnished by a Party or its Representatives to the other Party or its Representatives shall remain the property of the Party furnishing the same and shall be promptly returned or destroyed at the request of the Party furnishing the Confidential Information.

5)   No Licence or Right to Reproduce

Nothing contained in this Confidentiality Agreement shall be construed as granting or conferring on any Party or its Representatives, any rights, by licence or otherwise, to reproduce or use in any other matter any Confidential Information disclosed hereunder by the other Party or its Representatives or pertaining to the Transaction, except to further the Transaction and the business relationship between the Parties.

6)   Non-Competition

For a period of one (1) year from the date of this Confidentiality Agreement, no Party nor any of its respective Representatives shall, directly or indirectly, on behalf of itself or himself or any other person, use any Confidential Information disclosed by the other Party or its Representatives or pertaining to the Transaction, except in connection with the furtherance of the Transaction and the business relationship between the Parties.

7)   No Further Obligation

Neither the disclosure nor receipt of Confidential Information shall obligate a Party to undertake any business relationship with the other Party in connection with the Transaction. The Parties and the Representatives understand and acknowledge that neither Party is making any representation or warranty, express, or implied, as to the accuracy or completeness of the Confidential Information, and that only those representations or warranties that are made in a definitive purchase and sale or merger agreement when, as, and if executed, and subject to such limitations and restrictions as may be specified in such definitive agreement, will have any legal effect.

8)   No Waiver

Failure to enforce any provision of this Agreement shall not constitute a waiver of any other term herein and any waiver of any breach shall not be construed as a waiver of any subsequent breach. If any provision of this Agreement is held to be invalid, void or unenforceable, the remaining provisions shall continue in full force and effect without being impaired or invalidated. This Agreement shall be construed and governed in accordance with the laws of the Province of ●.

9) Termination

This Agreement shall terminate on the earlier of the execution of definitive agreement by the Parties, the unanimous agreement of the undersigned parties, or one year from the date hereof.

10) Entire Agreement

This Confidentiality Agreement embodies the entire understanding among the Parties and their respective Representatives with regard to the Transaction, the Confidential Information and all other subject matter described or contained herein. This Agreement may not be amended, changed, altered or modified in any way, except by a writing signed by the Parties. This Agreement may be executed in a number of counterparts which, when taken together, shall constitute one and the same instrument.

IN WITNESS WHEREOF, the parties hereto have executed this Confidentiality Agreement as of the day and year first above written.

COMPANY1, INC.   **COMPANY2, INC.**

By:

_________________, Individually   _________________, Individually

Form 4: **Share Purchase Agreement**

BETWEEN:

      ● (the "**Purchaser**")   OF THE FIRST PART

                  - and -

      ● (the "**Vendors**")   OF THE SECOND PART

WHEREAS:

The Vendors are the registered and beneficial owners of all of the issued and outstanding shares in the capital of [ ] ("**Vendco**") which consists of [ ] Common shares and [ ] Special shares;

Vendco is the registered and beneficial owner of all of the issued and outstanding shares in the capital of [ ] ("**Businessco**"), which consists of [ ] Common shares;

The Purchaser wishes to purchase and the Vendors wish to sell all of the issued and outstanding shares (the "**Purchased Shares**") in the capital stock of Vendco on the terms and conditions herein contained; and

The parties wish to enter into this agreement to give effect to the intention to purchase and sell and to set out the terms and conditions of the purchase and sale.

THEREFORE:

This agreement witnesses that in consideration of the mutual covenants and agreements herein contained and the sum of ONE DOLLAR ($1.00) of lawful money of Canada and other good and valuable consideration paid by each of the parties hereto to each of the other parties hereto (the receipt and sufficiency of which is hereby acknowledged), the parties agree as follows:

1)   INTERPRETATION

1.1)   Defined Terms

In this agreement and in the schedules hereto, unless there is something in the subject matter or context inconsistent therewith, the following terms and expressions will have the following meanings:

"**arm's length**" will have the meaning ascribed to such term as applied pursuant to the *Income Tax Act*, S.C. 1970-71-72, c. 63 (Canada);

"**Business**" means the business carried on by Businessco;

"**business day**" means any day other than a day which is a Saturday, a Sunday or a statutory holiday in the Province of [ ];

"**Vendco**" means [ ];

"**Closing**" means the meeting at which, or event whereupon, the documents and deliveries to complete the transactions by this agreement are delivered and the transactions are completed;

"**Closing Date**" means the date on which the closing is to take place as provided by this agreement;

"**Closing Financial Statements**" means a Financial Statement, as defined herein, for the Corporation as of the Effective Date;

"**Condition**" of the Corporation means the condition of the assets, liabilities, operations, activities, earnings, prospects, affairs or financial position of the Corporation;

"**control**" means, with respect to any corporation, the ownership of more than 50% of the voting shares of that corporation, including any shares which are voting only upon the occurrence of a contingency where such contingency has occurred and is continuing;

"**Corporations**" means Vendco and Businessco;

"**Deposit**" has the meaning set out in section 2.4(1) of this agreement;

"**Encumbrances**" means mortgages, charges, pledges, security interests, liens, encumbrances, actions, claims, demands and equities of any nature whatsoever or howsoever arising and any rights or privileges capable of becoming any of the foregoing;

"**Environmental Laws**" means all applicable laws relating in full or in part to the protection of the environment, product liability or employee and public health, or safety, and includes, without limitation, those environmental laws relating to the storage, generation, use, handling, manufacture, processing, labeling, advertising, sale, display, transportation, treatment, release and disposal of contaminants;

"**Businessco**" means [ ];

"**Financial Statements**" means the unaudited financial statements of the Corporations as at and for the fiscal year ended [ ], 2000, consisting of a balance sheet and an income statement for the corporation, copies of which are attached as Schedule "A" hereto, all prepared in accordance with generally accepted accounting principles, consistently applied;

"**generally accepted accounting principles**" means the accounting principles so described and promulgated by the Canadian Institute of Chartered Accountants which are applicable as at the date on which any calculation made hereunder is to be effective or as at the date of any financial statements referred to herein, as the case may be;

"**Interim Period**" means the period from and including the date of this agreement to and including the Closing Date;

"**Latest Statement Date**" means [ ], 2000;

"**Lease**" means the lease of the premises known municipally as [ ], in the City of [ ], in the Regional Municipality of [ ] (the "**Premises**") , between [ ], as Tenant, and [ ], as Landlord, dated the [ ]day of [ ], 20[ ], a copy of which has been provided to the Purchaser, as amended and extended for a further term of [ ] years, commencing [ ], 20[ ];

"**Licences**" means all of the licences, registrations and qualifications to do business held by the Corporation;

"**person**" means and includes any individual, corporation, partnership, firm, joint venture, syndicate, association, trust, government, governmental agency or board or commission or authority, and any other form of entity or organization;

"**Promissory Note**" means the promissory note delivered by the Purchaser to the Vendor pursuant to the terms of section 2.4 of this Agreement;

"**Purchase Price**" has the meaning set out in section 2.2 of this agreement;

"**Purchased Shares**" has the meaning set out in the recitals to this agreement;

"**shareholder tangible net equity**" means the shareholder equity of Businessco determined in accordance with generally accepted accounting principles and shall include the current book value of fixed assets, accounts receivable net of a reasonable allowance for doubtful accounts and shall not include any amount for goodwill;

"**Vendors**" has the meaning set out in the recitals to this agreement;

1.2) Best of Knowledge

Any reference herein to "**the best of the knowledge**" of the Vendors will be deemed to mean the actual knowledge of the Vendors and the knowledge which they would have had if they had conducted a diligent inquiry into the relevant subject matter.

1.3) Schedules

The schedules which are attached to this agreement are incorporated into this agreement by reference and are deemed to be part hereof. The following are the schedules to this Agreement:

- Schedule "A" — Financial Statements Schedule "B" — Summary of Assets
- Schedule "C" — Employees and Terms of Employment Schedule Schedule "D" — Contracts, Agreement
- Schedule "E" — Tax Matters
- Schedule "F" — Constating Documents Schedule Schedule "G" — Pledge Agreement Schedule Schedule "H" — Guarantee of Businessco Schedule "I" — Guarantee of [ ]. Schedule "J" Employment Agreement Schedule "K" — Major Suppliers Schedule
- Schedule "L" — Customer List Schedule
- Schedule "M" — Intellectual Property Schedule Schedule "N" — Computer Systems Schedule Schedule "O" — Insurance Details Schedule Schedule "P" — Promissory Note
- Schedule "Q" — Non-Competition Agreement Schedule "R" — Accounts Payable
- Schedule "S" — Accounts Receivable Schedule
- Schedule "T" — Indemnity re Warranty Claims

1.4) Currency

All dollar amounts referred to in this agreement are in lawful money of Canada.

1.5)   Choice of Law and Attornment

This agreement shall be governed by and construed in accordance with the laws of the Province of [ ] and the laws of Canada applicable therein.

1.6)   Headings or Party Drafting

The division of this agreement into articles, sections, paragraphs, subsections and clauses and the insertion of headings are for convenience of reference only and shall not affect the construction or interpretation of this agreement. The terms "this agreement", "hereof", "herein", "hereunder" and similar expressions refer to this agreement and the schedules hereto and not to any particular articles, section, paragraph, clause or other portion hereof and include any agreement or instrument supplementary or ancillary hereto. The parties hereto acknowledge that their respective legal counsel have reviewed and participated in settling the terms of this agreement, and the parties hereby agree that any rule of construction to the effect that any ambiguity is to be resolved against the drafting party shall not be applicable in the interpretation of this agreement.

1.7)   Number and Gender

In this agreement, unless there is something in the subject matter or context inconsistent therewith;

a)   words in the singular number include the plural and such words shall be construed as if the plural had been used;

b)   words in the plural include the singular and such words shall be construed as if the singular had been used, and

c)   words importing the use of any gender shall include all genders where the context or party referred to so requires, and the rest of the sentence shall be construed as if the necessary grammatical and terminological changes had been made.

1.8)   Time of Essence

Time shall be of the essence hereof.

2)   PURCHASE OF SHARES

2.1)   Purchased Shares

On the terms and subject to the fulfillment of the conditions hereof, the Vendors will sell, assign and transfer to the Purchaser, and the Purchaser will purchase and accept from the Vendors, the Purchased Shares.

2.2) Purchase Price

The Purchase Price for the Purchased Shares is the sum of $[ ]. In addition thereto the Purchaser shall pay, on Closing, the following:

a)   the sum of $[ ], being the amount of the debt of Vendco to the [ ] (the "**Bank**") as of the Closing Date ("**Vendco's Debt**");

b)   the sum of $[ ] being the net amount of all shareholder advances owing to the Vendors by Vendco as of the Closing Date (the "**Shareholder Advances**");

c)   the sum of $[ ], being the aggregate outstanding indebtedness of Businessco to the Bank as of the Closing Date ("**Businessco's Debt**"); and

d)   the sum of $[ ] to Vendco as a shareholder's advance, and the Purchaser will cause Vendco to pay, on Closing, the sum of $[ ] to [ ], or as he/she may direct, as a retirement allowance (the "**Allowance**").

2.3) Allocation of Purchase Price

The Purchase Price for the Purchased Shares shall be allocated as follows:

Name	Class of Shares	Number of Shares	Allocation of Purchase Price
[ ]	Common	[ ]	$[ ]
	Special	[ ]	$[ ]
[ ]	Common	[ ]	$[ ]
	Special	[ ]	$[ ]
Total			**$[ ]**

2.4) Payment of Purchase Price

On Closing the Purchaser will pay or otherwise advance the aggregate sum of $[ ] (the total of the Purchase Price, Vendco's Debt, the Shareholder Advances, the Businessco Debt and the Allowance), as follows:

a)   pay to the [ ], by certified cheque or bank draft, the sum of $[ ], representing the amount of Vendco's Debt to the [ ] Bank;

b)   pay to the [ ] Bank, by certified cheque or bank draft, the sum of $[ ], representing the amount of Businessco's debt to the [ ] Bank;

c)   pay to [ ], in trust, or as they may direct, by certified cheque or bank draft, the sum of [ ], which represents the sum of $[ ], on account of the amount due on Closing for the Purchased Shares, plus $[ ] on account of Shareholders' Advances and $[ ] on account of the Allowance.

d)   for the balance of the Purchase Price, the Purchaser will give and the Vendors will take back a promissory note (the **"Promissory Note"**) in the principal amount of $[ ] without interest, payable in five equal annual installments of $[ ] each on the [ ]th day of [ ] in each of the years, [ ] and [ ].

2.5) Price Adjustment

The Vendors acknowledge and agree that if the shareholder tangible net equity is less than $[ ] as at [ ] (the **"Effective Date"**), the Purchaser will be entitled to deduct from the payments due under the Promissory Note, on a dollar for dollar basis, the amount by which the shareholder tangible net equity is less than $[ ].

2.6) Security

As security for the payment of the Promissory Note, the Purchaser shall hypothecate the Purchased Shares to the Vendors pursuant to a Pledge Agreement substantially in the form annexed hereto as Schedule "G". In consideration of the sum of ten dollars and other good and valuable consideration, the receipt and sufficiency of which is acknowledged by each of the guarantors, as additional security:

a)   Businessco shall guarantee the payment and performance of the Promissory Note and as security for the guarantee shall give the Vendors a General Security Agreement on all of the Assets of Businessco second in priority only to its bank or other similar lender. The form of the Guarantee and General Security Agreement shall be substantially as annexed in Schedule "H" hereto;

b)   [ ] shall guarantee the payment and performance of the Promissory Note as a principal debtor and not as surety pursuant to a guarantee substantially in the form annexed hereto as Schedule "I".

3) CLOSING

3.1) Time and Place of Closing

The transactions contemplated herein shall be effective as of the Effective Date and shall be closed in escrow on [ ], [ ] (the **"Closing Date"**) at [ ] p.m. at the offices of the Purchaser's solicitors, [ ] or at such other place or places as may be mutually agreed upon by the Vendors and the Purchaser.

3.2) Documents to be Delivered

At or before the Closing, the Vendors shall execute, or cause to be executed, and shall deliver, or cause to be delivered, to the Purchaser all documents, instruments and things which are to be delivered by the Vendors pursuant to the provisions of this agreement, and the Purchaser shall execute, or cause to be executed, and shall deliver, or cause to be delivered, to the Vendors all cheques or bank drafts, the Promissory Note and all documents, instruments and things which the Purchaser is to deliver or to cause to be delivered pursuant to the provisions of this agreement.

3.3) Form of Documents

All documents and instruments shall be in customary form satisfactory to counsel for the receiving party acting reasonably. The parties agree to cause their counsel to exchange draft documents forthwith on execution of this agreement and to agree on the form thereof no less than one day prior to Closing.

4)   INTERIM PERIOD

The provisions in this article shall apply during the Interim Period.

4.1)

During the Interim Period the provisions of this section apply to Vendco and Businessco:

1) **Conduct of Business.** Except as contemplated by this agreement, or with the prior written consent otherwise of the Purchaser, the Vendors will, and will cause Vendco and Businessco to:

    a) operate the Business only in the ordinary course thereof, consistent with past practices;

    b) promptly advise the Purchaser of any facts that come to their attention which cause or would be expected to cause any material change in the Business or the relationships of the Corporations with their bankers, employees, suppliers or customers;

    c) continue to pay the Vendors remuneration and benefits at current levels;

    d) maintain the books, records and accounts in the ordinary course and record all transactions on a basis consistent with past practice;

    e) not terminate any employees, materially alter the terms of employment of any employees or any benefit plan, or engage new employees;

    f) not create, incur or assume any long-term debt (including obligations in respect of leases) or create any Encumbrance upon any of its properties or assets or guarantee or otherwise become liable for the obligations of any other person or make any loans or advances to any person;

g)   ensure that Vendco and Businessco do not sell or otherwise dispose of any of their properties or assets except in the ordinary course of the Business; or except those assets to be transferred pursuant to the provisions of this Agreement;

h)   ensure that Businessco does not terminate or waive any right of substantial value of the Business;

i)   ensure that neither Vendco nor Businessco makes any capital expenditures exceeding $[ ] in the aggregate;

j)   ensure that both Vendco and Businessco perform all obligations falling due during the Interim Period under all agreements to which either Corporation is a party or by which it is bound.

2)   **Investigation of Business and Examination of Documents.** The Vendors will provide and will cause the Corporations to provide access to, and will permit the Purchaser, through its representatives, to make such investigation of the assets and records of the Corporations and the financial and legal condition thereof as the Purchaser deems necessary or advisable to familiarize itself with such assets, records and other matters. The Vendors will make arrangements for the Purchaser, through its representatives, to inspect to the conditions of the lands, premises, buildings and equipment located at the Premises. The Vendors further agree to give the Purchaser and its representatives full access to all key management personnel involved in the operation of the Business. Without limiting the generality of the foregoing, during the Interim Period the Vendors will provide and will cause the Corporations to produce for inspection by the Purchaser:

a)   all agreements and all other documents referred to herein or in any of the schedules attached hereto and all other documents of or in the possession of the Corporations or relating to the Corporations' affairs;

b)   all minute books, share certificate books, registers of security holders, registers of transfers of securities, registers of directors and other corporate documents of the Corporations;

c)   all books, records, accounts, tax returns and financial statements of the Corporations;

d) all other information which, in the reasonable opinion of the Purchaser's representatives, is required in order to make an examination of the Corporations and their affairs;

provided that such investigations and inspections shall not mitigate or affect the representations and warranties of the Vendors hereunder, which shall continue in full force and effect as herein provided.

5) TERMS AND CONDITIONS

5.1) Accounting and Tax Matters Post-Closing

At the Corporations' expense, to be paid prior to closing, the Corporations' Accountants shall prepare the Closing Financial Statements and the income tax returns for the Corporations for the period ended on the Closing Date; provided that at the Purchaser's request, the Corporations' accountants shall consult with the Purchaser's accountant on any matters related thereto, prior to finalizing same. If the Corporations' accounting and legal fees and other professional fees are not paid prior to Closing, they are to be accrued on the Corporations' [ ] financial statements and shareholder tangible net equity will be reduced by the amount thereof.

6) COVENANTS

6.1) Covenants by the Vendors

The Vendors covenant to the Purchaser that they will do or cause to be done the following:

a) **Transfer of Purchased Shares**. At or before the Closing, the Vendors will cause all necessary steps and corporate proceedings to be taken in order to permit the Purchased Shares to be duly and regularly transferred to the Purchaser, subject to the hypothecation thereof pursuant to paragraph 2.5 hereof.

b) **Resignation of Officers and Directors**. At or before the Closing, the Vendors will cause each person who is the nominee of the Vendors as directors or officers of the Corporations to submit his or her written resignation as a director or officer which will be effective at the time of Closing, and to take such reasonable steps as the Purchaser may request to appoint or elect the nominees designated by the Purchaser in writing.

c) **Release by the Vendors. At Closing**, the Vendors will execute and deliver to the Purchaser a release of all claims related to Vendco, save as to matters contained in any document delivered on Closing or that survives Closing.

d) **Undertaking by the Vendors.** At Closing, the Vendors will execute and deliver to Vendco and the Purchaser their undertaking to adjust and reimburse Vendco for any liabilities of the Corporations for income tax or otherwise that are not accrued on the Closing Financial Statements, which undertaking will survive Closing for the warranty period hereafter set forth. Vendco and the Purchaser may set off any such amount which either of them is required to pay against monies otherwise payable to the Vendors for the balance of the Purchase Price or otherwise.

e) **Shareholder Accounts.** At Closing, the Vendors shall repay or settle and release Vendco, and shall cause Vendco to repay or settle and release the Vendors and any person related to or not dealing at arm's length with the Vendors and Vendco, all accounts, loans, amounts, and claims of every nature and kind whatsoever. Without limiting the generality of the foregoing, the Vendors agree that, at Closing, they will pay all amounts owing to either of the Corporations by the Vendors and/or any employees, officers, directors or shareholders of the Corporations or any persons or corporations or other entities who are related to the Vendors or the Corporations, as defined in the *Income Tax Act*, R.S.C. 1985, c. 1 (5th Supp.) or as defined in the [ ] *Business Corporations Act*, or by any persons not dealing at arms' length from any of the foregoing persons.

6.2) Covenants by the Purchaser

The Purchaser covenants to the Vendors, that it will do or cause to be done the following:

1) **Confidential Information**

a) If the transactions contemplated hereby are not completed or are terminated, at all times thereafter the Purchaser will keep confidential all information obtained by it in the course of these transactions relating to the Corporations and the financial affairs of the Vendors, except such information which:

   i)   prior to the date hereof was already in possession of the Purchaser, as demonstrated by written records;

   ii) is generally available to the public, other than as a result of a disclosure by the Purchaser; or

iii) is made available to the Purchaser on a non-confidential basis from a source other than the Vendors or their representatives.

b) The Purchaser further agrees that such information will be disclosed only as confidential information to those of its employees and representatives of its advisors and bank who need to know such information for the purposes of evaluating and implementing the transactions contemplated hereby and who accept these provisions.

c) The obligation to maintain the confidentiality of such information will not apply to the extent that disclosure of such information is required in connection with governmental or other applicable filings or applications relating to the transactions hereunder, provided that, in such case, unless the Vendors otherwise agree, the Purchaser will, if possible, request confidentiality in respect of such governmental or other filings or applications.

d) If the transactions contemplated hereby are not consummated for any reason, the Purchaser will return forthwith, without retaining any copies thereof, all information and documents obtained from the Vendors and the Corporations.

2) **Releases of the Vendors.** At the time of Closing, the Purchaser will cause Vendco to execute and deliver to the Vendors a full and final release of all matters related to Vendco, save as to matters contained in any document delivered on Closing or that survives Closing.

6.3)   Mutual Covenants

Each of the parties agree to take all such actions as are within its or his or her power or control, so as to ensure fulfillment of the conditions of this agreement that are for the benefit of such party, alone or with other parties, ensure compliance with the covenants on the part of such party; and ensure the truth and accuracy of the representations and warranties by such party.

7)   REPRESENTATIONS AND WARRANTIES

7.1)   Representations and Warranties by the Vendors

The Vendors hereby represent and warrant to the Purchaser, and acknowledge that the Purchaser is relying upon the accuracy of each of such representation and warranty in connection with the purchase of the Purchased Shares and the completion of the transactions hereunder:

1) **Binding Obligation**. This agreement is a legal, valid and binding obligation of the Vendors, enforceable against them in accordance with its terms to the extent that adequate consideration has been received by the Vendors from the Purchaser. Each of the Vendors has attained the age of majority and is legally competent to execute this Agreement and take all actions, consummate all transactions and enter into all other agreements required or contemplated pursuant to this Agreement.

2) **No Other Purchase Agreements**. No person has any agreement, option, understanding or commitment, or any right or privilege (whether by law, pre-emptive or contractual) capable of becoming an agreement, option or commitment, including convertible securities, warrants or convertible obligations of any nature, for the purchase, subscription, allotment or issuance of, or conversion into, any of the unissued shares in the capital of either of the Corporations or any securities of the Corporations, or the purchase from the Vendors of any of the Purchased Shares.

3) **Corporate Authority and Binding Obligation**. The Vendors have good right and absolute authority to enter into this agreement and to sell, assign and transfer the Purchased Shares to the Purchaser in the manner contemplated herein and to perform all of the Vendors' obligations under this agreement. Vendco, its shareholders and board of directors have taken all necessary or desirable actions, steps and corporate and other proceedings to approve or authorize, validly and effectively, the entering into, and the execution, delivery and performance of this agreement and the sale and transfer of the Purchased Shares by the Vendors to the Purchaser. Neither Vendor has taken any steps to file personal bankruptcy, nor has either Vendor defaulted on any obligations of such Vendor which would allow any person to take any action against such Vendor for non-payment of an obligation.

4) **Status, Constating Documents and Licences**.

   a) Vendco is a corporation duly amalgamated and validly subsisting in all respects under the laws of the Province of [ ]. Vendco is a "**private company**", as defined in the *Securities Act*, R.S.O. 1990, c. S.5 (Ontario). Vendco has all necessary corporate power to own its properties and to carry on its business as now being conducted.

   b) Businessco is a corporation duly amalgamated and validly subsisting in all respects under the laws of the Province of [ ]. Businessco is a "**private company**", as defined in the *Securities Act*, R.S.O. 1990, c.

S.5 (Ontario). Businessco has all necessary corporate power to own its properties and to carry on its business as now being conducted.

c)   the articles, by-laws and other constating documents of the Corporations, as amended to the date hereof, are listed in Schedule "F" attached hereto, and complete and correct copies of each of those documents have been delivered to the Purchaser.

d)   The Corporations are duly licensed, registered and qualified to do business, are up-to-date in the filing of all required corporate returns and other notices and filings and are otherwise in good standing in all respects in the Province of [ ].

5)   **Compliance with Constating Documents, Agreements and Laws**. The execution, delivery and performance of this agreement and each of the other agreements contemplated or referred to herein by the Vendors and the Corporations, and the completion of the transactions contemplated hereby, will not constitute or result in a violation or breach of or default under, or cause the acceleration of any obligations of either of the Corporations under:

a)   any term or provision of any of the articles, by-laws or other constating document of the Corporations;

b)   the terms of any agreement (written or oral), indenture, instrument or understanding or other obligation or restriction to which the Corporations or the Vendors are a party or by which any of them are bound; or

c)   any term or provision of any order of any court, governmental authority or regulatory body or any law or regulation of any jurisdiction in which the Corporation's business is carried on.

6)   **Corporate Records**. The corporate records and minute books of the Corporations, all of which have been made available to the Purchaser and will be delivered to the Purchaser on Closing, contain complete and accurate minutes of all meetings of the directors and shareholders of the Corporations held since incorporation, and original signed copies of all resolutions and by-laws duly passed or confirmed by the directors or shareholders of the Corporations other than at a meeting. All such meetings were duly called and held. The share certificate books, register of security holders, register of transfers and register of directors and any similar corporate records of the Corporations are complete and accurate.

7) **Authorized and Issued Capital**. The authorized, issued and stated capital of Vendco at Closing will be as follows:

Authorized Share Capital	Issued Share	Stated Capital
Unlimited Common Shares	[ ]	$[ ]
Unlimited Special Shares	[ ]	$[ ]

The shares as set out above have been duly issued and are outstanding as fully paid and non-assessable shares. No shares or other securities of the Corporation have been issued in violation of any laws, the articles of incorporation, by-laws or other constating documents of the Corporation or the terms of any shareholder agreement or any agreement to which the Corporation is a party or by which it is bound.

8) The authorized, issued and stated capital of Businessco at Closing will be as follows:

Authorized Share Capital	Issued Share	Stated Capital
Unlimited Common Shares	[ ]	$[ ]
Unlimited Class "A" Special Shares	[ ]	$[ ]

The shares as set out above have been duly issued and are outstanding as fully paid and non-assessable shares. No shares or other securities of Businessco have been issued in violation of any laws, the articles of incorporation, by-laws or other constating documents of Businessco or the terms of any shareholder agreement or any agreement to which Businessco is a party or by which it is bound.

9) **Ownership of Purchased Shares**. The Vendors own all of the issued and outstanding shares of Vendco as the shareholders of record and as the beneficial owners, with good and marketable title thereto, free and clear of any and all Encumbrances. Vendco owns all of the issued and outstanding shares of Businessco as the shareholders of record and as the beneficial owners, with good and marketable title thereto, free and clear of any and all Encumbrances.

10) **No Shareholder Agreements**. There are no shareholder agreements, polling agreements, voting trusts or other similar agreements with respect to the ownership or voting of any of the shares of Vendco.

11) **Financial Statements**.

a) The Financial Statements have been prepared in accordance with generally accepted accounting principles applied on a basis consistent with that of the previous fiscal year, are true, correct and complete in all material respects, and present fairly the financial condition of the Corporations as of the Latest Statement Date.

b) The Closing Financial Statements will have been prepared in accordance with generally accepted accounting principles applied on a basis consistent with the Financial Statements, and will be true, correct and complete in all material respects and present fairly in all material respects the financial condition of the Corporations as of the Effective Date.

12) **Financial Records.** All material financial transactions of the Corporations have been recorded in the financial books and records of the Corporations in accordance with good business practice, and such financial books and records:

a) accurately reflect, in all material respects, the basis for the financial condition and the revenues, expenses and results of operations of the Corporations shown in the Financial Statements and the Closing Financial Statements, and

b) together with the disclosures made in this agreement or in the Schedules hereto, present fairly in all material respects the financial condition and the revenues, expenses and results of the operations of the Corporations as of and to the date hereof.

13) **Possession and Maintenance of Financial Records.** No information, records or systems pertaining to the operation or administration of the affairs of the Corporations are in the possession, recorded, stored or maintained by anyone other than the Vendors or by the Corporations' accountants or solicitors.

14) **Liabilities of the Corporation.** Other than accounts in the normal course of business which are listed in Schedule "R" attached hereto, there are no liabilities (contingent or otherwise) of the Corporations of any kind whatsoever, and there is no basis for assertion against the Corporations of any liabilities of any kind.

The Vendors agree to indemnify and save harmless the Purchaser and the Corporations from and against all liabilities, claims and demands whatsoever (including liabilities, claims and demands for income, sales, excise or other taxes) of or in connection with the operation of the business with regard to any period prior to the Closing Date and the Vendors agree to enter into an agreement with the Purchaser in form and content satisfactory to counsel for the Purchaser providing such indemnity.

15) **Indebtedness.** The Corporations are not under any obligation to create or issue any bonds, debentures, mortgages, promissory notes or other indebtedness.

16) **Absence of Certain Changes or Events.** Since the Latest Statement Date, the Corporations have not:

a)   incurred any obligation or liability (fixed or contingent) which will not be wholly discharged as of the Closing Date;

b)   created any Encumbrances upon or disposed of any of the Purchased Shares;

c)   purchased, leased or otherwise acquired or sold any properties or assets,

d)   entered into any transaction, contract, agreement or commitment other than such as will be wholly discharged as of the Closing Date;

e)   made any material change with respect to any method of accounting;

f)   suffered any extraordinary loss;

g)   made or incurred any material change in, or become aware of any event or condition which is likely to result in a material change in either of the Corporations or their respective assets;

h)   transferred, assigned, sold or otherwise disposed of any of their respective assets shown or reflected in the Financial Statements or cancelled any debts or entitlements except, in the ordinary and usual course of business;

i)   except as disclosed in any schedule to this Agreement, dismissed any employees. All severance and other payments due to any dismissed employees have been paid in full;

j)   directly or indirectly, declared or paid any dividends or declared or made any other payments or distributions on or in respect of any of its shares or has directly or indirectly, purchased or otherwise acquired any of its shares; or

k)   authorized, agreed or otherwise become committed to do any of the foregoing.

17) **No Purchase Agreements for Assets.** No person has any agreement, option, understanding or commitment, or any right or privilege (whether by law, pre-emptive or contractual) capable of becoming an

agreement, option or commitment, for the purchase or other acquisition from Vendco or Businessco of any of their undertakings, property or assets.

18) **Commitments for Capital Expenditures**. The Corporations are not committed to make any capital expenditure, nor have any capital expenditures been authorized by either of the Corporations at any time since the Latest Statement Date.

19) **Dividends and Distributions**. Since the Latest Statement Date, Vendco has not declared or paid any dividend or made any other distribution on any of its shares of any class, or redeemed or purchased or otherwise acquired any of its shares of any class, or reduced its authorized capital or stated capital, except so as to conform to subsection 7.1(7) or agreed to any of the foregoing, except so as to adjust shareholder equity to conform to subsection 7.1(20) hereof.

20) **Shareholder Equity**. Vendco now has, and at the time of Closing will have, shareholder equity of at least the stated capital of the Purchased Shares. Businessco now has, and at the time of Closing will have, tangible shareholder net equity of at least $[ ]. The Vendors acknowledge and agree that if the shareholder tangible net equity is less than $[ ] as at the Effective Date, the Purchaser will be entitled to deduct from the payments due under the Promissory Note, on a dollar for dollar basis, the amount by which the shareholder tangible net equity is less than $[ ].

21) **Tax Matters**.

   a) For purposes of this provision, the term **"taxes"** means and includes all taxes, customs duties, rates, levies, assessments, reassessments and other charges, together with all penalties, interest and fines with respect thereto, payable to any federal, provincial, municipal, local or other government of governmental agency, authority, board, bureau or commission, domestic or foreign.

   b) The Corporations have duly and on a timely basis prepared and filed all tax returns and other documents required to be filed by it in respect of all taxes and such returns and documents are complete and correct. Complete and correct copies of all such returns and other documents will be provided to the Purchaser, as requested.

   c) The Corporations have paid all taxes which are due and payable on or before the date hereof. An estimate of all taxes payable to the date of Closing will be made and paid by the Corporations prior to Closing. The Corporations have no liability for taxes other than those provided for in the Financial Statements and those arising in the ordinary course of the operation of the Business since the Latest Statement Date.

d)   Canadian federal and provincial income tax assessments have been issued for the Corporations covering all past periods up to and including the fiscal year ended April 30, [ ]. There are no assessments, reassessment, actions, suits, proceedings, investigations, enquiries or claims now pending or made or, to the best of the knowledge of the Vendors, threatened against the Corporations in respect of taxes, nor, to the best knowledge of the Vendors, is there any basis for such.

e)   There are no agreements, waivers or other arrangements providing for any extension of time with respect to the filing of any tax return or other document or the payment of any taxes by the Corporations or the period for any assessment or reassessment of taxes.

f)   The Corporations have withheld from each amount paid or credited to any person the amount of taxes required to be withheld therefrom and has remitted such taxes to the proper tax or other receiving authorities within the time required under applicable legislation.

g)   Schedule E attached hereto accurately sets out, for purposes of the *Income Tax Act*, S.C. 1970-71-72, c. 63 (Canada), the following as of [ ], [ ]; the paid-up capital of all issued and outstanding shares in the capital of the Corporations, by class of shares;

i)   all non-capital losses of the Corporations;

ii)   all net capital losses of the Corporations;

iii)   the amount of all investment tax credits available to the Corporations;

iv)   the adjusted cost base of the Corporations' capital properties;

v)   the cost of the Corporations' depreciable properties, the capital cost allowance taken in respect of each class of such properties and the undepreciated capital cost of each class of such properties;

vi)   the amount (if any) of the Corporations' capital dividend accounts;

vii) the amount (if any) of the Corporations' cumulative eligible capital accounts; and

viii) the amount (if any) of the Corporations' refundable dividend tax on hand.

h) The Corporations are Canadian-controlled private corporations as defined in the *Income Tax Act*, S.C. 1970-71-72, c. 63 (Canada), and have been since the dates of incorporation.

22) **Litigation.** Other than in the normal course of business for the collection of receivables owing to Businessco, there are no actions, suits or proceedings, judicial or administrative (whether or not purportedly on behalf of the Corporations or the Vendors) pending or, to the best of the knowledge of the Vendors, threatened, by or against or affecting the Corporations, at law or in equity, or before or by any court or any federal, provincial, municipal or other governmental department, commission, board, bureau, agency or instrumentality, domestic or foreign. There are no grounds on which any such action, suit or proceeding might be commenced with any reasonable likelihood of success.

23) **Deposit Accounts of the Corporations.** Vendco has bank accounts and Businessco has bank accounts, the details of which will be provided to the Purchaser on closing.

   As of the Closing there will be no overdraft, and no outstanding cheques or orders for payment on such accounts except to the extent that there are funds on deposit in such accounts.

24) **Real Property.** The Corporations do not own or have any right, title or interest in any real property and other than the Lease, and the Corporations are not a party to any other lease, written or oral, under which the Corporations lease or have agreed to lease any real property. The Lease is in good standing, in full force and effect and is unamended. The present business of Businessco may be lawfully carried on at the leased premises without violation or contravention of any by-laws, regulations or statutes.

25) **Subsidiaries and Other Interests.** Businessco is a wholly owned subsidiary of Vendco. As of the Closing Date, neither of the Corporations will own any other securities issued by, or any equity or ownership interest in, any other person. The Corporations are not subject to any obligation to make any investment in or to provide funds by way of loan, capital contribution or otherwise to any person.

26) **Partnerships or Joint Ventures.** Save and except for the profit sharing arrangements with employees disclosed in Schedule "D" hereto, the Corporations are not partners or participants in any partnership, joint venture, profit-sharing arrangement or other association of any kind and are not party to any agreement under which they agree to carry

on any part of the Business or any other activity in such manner or by which either of the Corporations agree to share any revenue or profit with any other person.

27) **Guarantees and Warranties**. The Corporations are not party to or bound by any agreement of guarantee, warranty, indemnification, assumption or endorsement of any other like commitment of the obligations, liabilities (contingent or otherwise) or indebtedness of any person, except as disclosed in the Financial Statements.

28) **Existing Agreements**. Other than those agreements set out in Schedule "D", the Corporations are not parties to or bound by any outstanding or executory agreement, contract or commitment, whether written or oral. All agreements listed in Schedule "D" are in good standing at the date hereof and will be at Closing. Those agreements and contracts which are indicated to be transferred , renewed or held by the Vendors shall be so transferred, renewed or held by the Vendors on or before Closing.

29) **Employees**. The Corporations are not party to any written or oral employment, service or consulting agreement relating to any one or more persons other than as set out in Schedule "C". Schedule "C" accurately sets out the terms of employment for each and every employee of the Corporations and a description of all benefit plans in place for the employees. The agreement with [ ] will be terminated prior to Closing at no cost to the Corporations, a copy of which will be delivered on Closing. The Corporations are not a party, either directly or indirectly, to any collective agreement, letters of understanding, letters of intent or other written communication with any trade union or association which may qualify as a trade union, which would cover any of its employees or any of its dependent contractors. There are no outstanding labour tribunal proceedings of any kind and there are no threatened or apparent union organization activities involving employees of the Corporations. Neither of the Corporations has ever had any serious labour problems that might affect the value of the Corporations or lead to an interruption of its operations at the Premises. Neither of the Corporations has any pension plans.

30) **Non-Arm's Length Matters**. The Corporations are not party to or bound by any agreement with, is not indebted to, and no amount is owing to the Corporations by the Vendors or any officers, former officers, directors, former directors, shareholders, former shareholders,

employees (except for oral employment agreements with employees) or former employees of the Corporations or, any person not dealing at arm's length with any of the foregoing. Since the Latest Statement Date, except so as to adjust shareholder equity to conform to subsection 7.1(20) hereof, the Corporations have not made or authorized any payments to the Vendors or any officers, former officers, directors, former directors, shareholders, former shareholders, employees or former employees of the Corporations or to any person not dealing at arm's length with any of the foregoing, except as contemplated by this agreement.

31) **Compliance with Laws**. The Corporations have no notice that either of them is in violation of any federal, provincial, municipal or other law, regulation or order of any government or governmental or regulatory authority, domestic or foreign, including, without limitation, any law, regulation or order relating to the Business, and to the best knowledge of the Vendors, are not in violation thereof.

32) **Vendors' Residency**. The Vendors are not non-residents of Canada within the meaning of the *Income Tax Act*, R.S.C. 1985, c. 1 (5th Supp.) (Canada).

33) **Copies of Documents**. Complete and correct copies (including all amendments) of all contracts, leases and other documents referred to in this agreement or any schedule hereto or required to be disclosed hereby have been or will be made available to the Purchaser.

34) **Assets**. Businessco is the sole beneficial owner with good and marketable title to its assets free and clear of Encumbrances and all such assets will be located at the Premises at Closing. In particular, without limiting the generality of the foregoing, there has been no assignment, subletting or granting of any licence (of occupation or otherwise) of or in respect of any of Businessco's assets or property or any granting of any agreement or right capable of becoming an agreement or option for the purchase of Businessco assets or property. The sole asset of Vendco is the shares of Businessco.

35) **Disclosure**. No representation or warranty contained in this section 7.1, and no statement contained in any schedule, certificate, list, summary or other disclosure document provided or to be provided to the Purchaser pursuant hereto or in connection with the transactions contemplated hereby contains or will contain any untrue statement of a material fact, or omits or will omit to state any material fact which

is necessary in order to make the statements contained therein not misleading.

36) **No Insolvency.** No proceedings have been or are now being taken by any creditor, shareholder, director or officer of either of the Corporations or by any other person in respect of the bankruptcy, insolvency, winding up, liquidation or dissolution of either of the Corporations.

37) **Major Suppliers.** Schedule "K" is a comprehensive listing of each supplier of goods and services to the Corporations. To the best of the knowledge of the Vendors, no supplier has any intention to change its relationship or terms upon which it conducts business with Businessco as a result of the transfer of the Purchased Shares contemplated by this Agreement.

38) **Major Customers.** Schedule "L" sets forth a comprehensive listing of each customer of the Corporations for the twelve-month period ending April 30, [ ], together with the amount so purchased from the Corporations. To the best of the knowledge of the Vendors, no customer has any intention to change its relationship or the terms upon which such customer conducts business with Businessco as a result of the transfer of the Purchased Shares contemplated by this Agreement.

39) **Accounts Receivable.** The accounts receivable of the Corporations are accurately and correctly recorded in the books and records of the Corporations, are bona fide, have arisen in the ordinary course of business and are not subject to any defence, counterclaim or set off. A listing of the accounts receivable as at [ ], [ ] is attached as Schedule "S".

40) **Inventory.** The level of inventories reflected in the Closing Financial Statements is consistent with that maintained by the Corporations prior to the date of this Agreement in accordance with its normal business practices.

41) **Intellectual Property.** Schedule "M" sets forth a full, complete and true list of all intellectual property of the Corporations.

42) **Computer Systems.** Schedule "N" includes a list of all computer hardware and software owned or leased by the Corporations. All computer hardware is in good condition and repair and in proper working order, is the subject of one or more maintenance agreements (complete and correct copies of which have been delivered to the Purchaser) and has been maintained at all times in accordance with the maintenance instructions recommended by the manufacturers thereof and will continue to be so maintained until Closing. To the best of the knowledge

of the Vendors, all computer hardware and software is free from computer viruses and disabling codes or devices and the Corporations have taken, and will continue to take, all steps and implement all procedures to ensure that such systems remain free of such viruses, codes or devices until the Closing. The computer systems used by the Corporations are sufficient in all respect to perform all functions necessary or desirable in or for the efficient operation of the Business. Except as set out in Schedule "N" the computer systems are year [ ] compliant.

43) Environmental Matters.

a) All operations of the Corporations conducted on the Premises while occupied by the Corporations have been and are now in compliance with all Environmental Laws.

b) The Corporations have no reporting and monitoring requirements under all Environmental Laws.

c) No environmental approvals required to be held by the Corporations.

d) Neither of the Corporations nor their operations or businesses have been or are now the subject of any Environmental Claim, nor, to the best of the knowledge of the Vendors, is any Environmental Claim pending or threatened against either of the Corporations nor have either of the Corporations ever been charged with, prosecuted or convicted of any offence under any Environmental law or been found liable in any proceedings to pay any fine or judgment to any person as a result of any release of any contaminant into the environment or for the breach of any Environmental Law and there is no basis for any such proceeding or claim.

e) There are no contaminants or chemicals located on the Premises other than the inks used in the manufacturing process.

f) Neither of the Corporations has ever conducted or caused to be conducted an environmental assessment or study of the Premises.

44) Insurance. Schedule "O" is a complete list of all policies of insurance which the Corporations maintain and the particulars of such policies. All such policies of insurance are in full force and effect and neither of the Corporations is in default , as to the payment of premiums or otherwise, under the terms of such policy. To the best of the knowledge of the Vendors, such policies of insurance are sufficient to cover all risks associated with or arising out of the Business.

7.2)   Representations and Warranties by the Purchaser

The Purchaser hereby represents and warrants to the Vendors as follows, and acknowledges that the Vendors are relying upon the accuracy of each of such representation and warranty in connection with the sale of the Purchased Shares and the completion of the other transactions hereunder:

1) **Investment Canada Act** — The Purchaser is not a "non-Canadian" for purposes of and within the meaning of the *Investment Canada Act*, R.S.C. 1985, c. 28 (1st Supp.).

2) **Binding Obligation** — This agreement is a legal, valid and binding obligation of the Purchaser, enforceable against him in accordance with its terms subject to bankruptcy, insolvency and other laws relating to or affecting the enforcement of creditors' rights generally, and the fact that equitable remedies, including the remedies of specific performance and injunction, may only be granted in the discretion of a court.

8)   SURVIVAL AND LIMITATIONS OF REPRESENTATIONS AND WARRANTIES

8.1)   Survival of Warranties of the Vendors

1) The representations and warranties made by the Vendors and contained in this agreement, or contained in any documents or certificates given in order to carry out the transactions contemplated hereby, will survive the Closing and, notwithstanding such Closing or any investigation made by or on behalf of the Purchaser or any other person or any knowledge of the Purchaser of any other person, shall continue in full force and effect for the benefit of the Purchaser, subject to the provisions of this Article.

2) The warranty claim period for the Vendors' warranties expires on the latest of the following dates (the **"warranty claim period"**):

   a) two years after the date of Closing;

   b) if the warranty claim is based upon or relates to the tax liability of either of the Corporations for a particular year, 180 days after the date of expiration of the period (if any) during which an assessment, reassessment or other form of recognized document assessing liability for tax, interest or penalties in respect of such taxation year under applicable tax legislation could be issued, assuming that the

Corporation does not file any waiver or similar document extending such period as otherwise determined;

c) if the warranty claim is based upon or relates to the title to the Purchased Shares or is based upon intentional misrepresentation or fraud by the Vendors, no expiration date;

d) the Vendors will be released from all obligations and liabilities in respect of the representations and warranties made by the Vendors and contained in this agreement or in any document or certificate given in order to carry out the transactions contemplated hereby after the expiration of the warranty claim period, except with respect to any warranty claims made by the Purchaser as provided below within the warranty claim period.

8.2) Survival of Warranties of Purchaser

1) The representations and warranties made by the Purchaser and contained in this agreement or contained in any document or certificate given in order to carry out the transactions contemplated hereby will survive the Closing of the purchase and sale of the Purchased Shares provided for herein and, notwithstanding such Closing or any investigation made by or on behalf of the Vendors or any other person or any knowledge of the Vendors or any other person, shall continue in full force and affect for the benefit of the Vendors, subject to the provisions of this Article.

2) The warranty claim period for the Purchaser's warranties expires upon payment of all amounts owing under the Promissory Note.

8.3) Warranty Claims

1) For purposes of these provisions a **"warranty claim"** means a claim made by either the Purchaser or the Vendors based on or with respect to the inaccuracy of non-performance or non-fulfillment or breach of any representation or warranty made by the other party contained in this agreement or contained in any document or certificate given in order to carry out the transactions contemplated hereby.

2) A warranty claim shall be in writing, signed by the party making it, and shall contain full particulars of the nature of the claim, the damages suffered or expected, and the remedy or relief sought. A warranty claim shall be given in the same manner as a notice under this agreement, and must be made before the expiration or the applicable warranty

claim period. A warranty claim properly given or served within the warranty claims period may be clarified subsequent thereto.

9)   CONDITIONS OF CLOSING

9.1)   Purchaser's Closing Conditions

The obligation of the Purchaser to complete the transactions provided for herein will be subject to the fulfillment of the following conditions (the **"Purchaser's Closing Conditions"**) at or prior to the Closing, and the Vendors covenant to use their best efforts to ensure that such conditions are fulfilled.

1) **Accuracy of Representations and Warranties.** The representations and warranties of the Vendors contained in this agreement or in any document delivered in order to carry out the transactions contemplated hereby shall be true and accurate on the date hereof and at the time of Closing with the same force and effect as though such representations and warranties had been made as of the time of Closing (regardless of the date as of which the information in this agreement or in any schedule or other document made pursuant thereto is given). In addition, the Vendors shall have delivered to the Purchaser a certificate in the form prepared by the Purchaser's solicitors confirming that the facts with respect to each of such representations and warranties by the Vendors are as set out herein at the time of Closing.

2) **Performance of Covenants.** The Vendors shall have complied with all covenants and agreements herein agreed to be performed or caused to be performed by them at or prior to the time of Closing. In addition, the Vendors shall deliver to the Purchaser a certificate in the form prepared by the Purchaser's solicitors confirming that the Vendors have performed all covenants required to be performed by them.

3) **No Restraining Proceedings.** No order, decision or ruling of any court, tribunal or regulatory authority having jurisdiction shall have been made, and no action or proceeding shall be pending or threatened which, in the opinion of counsel to the Purchaser, is likely to result in an order, decision or ruling to disallow, enjoin, prohibit or impose any material adverse limitations or conditions on the purchase and sale of the Purchased Shares contemplated hereby or the right of the Purchaser to own the Purchased Shares.

4) **Consents.** All consents required to be obtained in order to carry out the transactions contemplated hereby in compliance with all laws and agreements binding upon the parties hereto shall have been obtained,

including without limitation, any consent that may be required from the landlord of the Premises.

5) **Releases by Directors and Officers**. At the time of Closing, each person who is an officer or director of the Corporations shall have executed and delivered to the Corporations and the Purchaser their resignation and a full and final release in a form satisfactory to the Purchaser.

6) **Opinion of Vendors' Counsel**. At the time of Closing, the Purchaser shall have received an opinion of legal counsel for the Vendors in a form satisfactory to the Purchaser's counsel acting reasonably, which opinion may rely on the certificate of an officer of the Corporations as to factual matters.

7) **Bank Approval**. The Corporations' Bank shall have approved the purchase of the Purchased Shares by the Purchaser on terms satisfactory to the Purchaser or the Purchaser shall have obtained financing from the [ ] Bank in an amount sufficient to repay all amounts owing to the [ ] Bank by Businessco.

8) **Due Diligence**. The Purchaser shall have completed its due diligence in respect of the Corporations and be satisfied in its sole discretion with the results thereof.

9) **Agreements**. All agreements contemplated in this Agreement shall have been executed and delivered, in form and substance satisfactory to the Purchaser.

10) **[ ]**. The profit sharing plan with [ ] will have been terminated at no cost to the Corporations and [ ] will have delivered a release to the Corporations with respect to such termination.

11) **Non-Competition Agreement**. At Closing, the Vendors shall have executed and delivered a non-competition agreement substantially in the form attached as Schedule "Q".

12) **Employment Agreement**. At Closing, [ ] shall have executed and delivered an employment agreement in the form attached as Schedule "J".

13) **Indemnity Agreement**. At Closing, the Vendors shall have executed and delivered an indemnity agreement in the form attached as Schedule "U" with respect to warranty claims, as defined in section 8.2 (3).

14) **Other Agreements**. At Closing, the Vendors shall have executed and delivered such other documents as the Purchaser may reasonably require to give effect to the term of this Agreement.

9.2) Waiver of Termination by Purchaser

1) The Purchaser's Closing Conditions are for the exclusive benefit of the Purchaser and may be waived in whole or in part by the Purchaser in writing at any time.

2) The Vendors acknowledge that the waiver by the Purchaser of any condition or any part of any condition shall be limited thereto, and shall not constitute a waiver of any other condition or any covenant, agreement, representation or warranty made by the Vendors herein that corresponds or is related to such condition or such part of such condition, as the case may be.

3) If any of the Purchaser's Closing Conditions are not fulfilled or complied with as herein provided and cannot be fulfilled or rectified prior to Closing, the Purchaser may at its option at or prior to the time of Closing, by notice in writing to the Vendors, terminate this agreement. Thereupon, the Purchaser shall be released from all obligations hereunder, save as to those stated to survive termination. Unless the condition or conditions which have not been fulfilled are reasonably capable of being fulfilled or caused to be fulfilled by the Vendors or the Corporations, then the Vendors shall also be released from all obligations hereunder, save as to those stated to survive termination.

9.3) Vendors' Closing Conditions

The obligation of the Vendors to complete the transactions provided for herein will be subject to the fulfillment of the following conditions (the **"Vendors' Closing Conditions"**) at or prior to the Closing, and the Purchaser covenants to use its best efforts to ensure that such conditions are fulfilled.

1) **Accuracy of Representations and Warranties.** The representations and warranties of the Purchaser contained in this agreement or in any documents delivered in order to carry out the transactions contemplated hereby shall be true and accurate on the date hereof and at the time of Closing with the same force and effect as though such representations and warranties had been made as of the time of Closing (regardless of the date as of which the information in this agreement or in any schedule or other document made pursuant hereto is given). In addition, the Purchaser shall have delivered to the Vendors a certificate in the form prepared by the Vendors' solicitors confirming that the facts with respect to each of such representations and warranties by the Purchaser are as set out herein at the time of Closing.

2) **Performance of Covenants.** The Purchaser shall have complied with all covenants and agreements herein agreed to be performed or caused to be performed by it at or prior to the time of Closing. In addition, the Purchaser shall have delivered to the Vendors a certificate in the form prepared by the Vendors' solicitors confirming that the Purchaser has performed all covenants required to be performed by it.

3) **No Restraining Proceedings.** No order, decision or ruling of any court, tribunal or regulatory authority having jurisdiction shall have been made, and no action or proceeding shall be pending or threatened which, in the opinion of counsel to the Vendors is likely to result in an order, decision or ruling, to disallow, enjoin or prohibit the purchase and sale of the Purchased Shares contemplated hereby.

4) **Consents.** All consents required to be obtained in order to carry out the transactions contemplated hereby in compliance with all laws and agreements binding upon the parties hereto shall have been obtained.

5) **Release by the Corporation.** The Vendors will have received a release from Vendco in a form of release acceptable to the Vendors releasing the Vendors from all claims, demands covenants and obligations whatsoever based on any matter or thing arising prior to the time of Closing, except for the performance of the Vendors' obligations under this agreement.

6) **Opinion of Purchaser's Counsel.** At the time of Closing, the Vendors shall have received an opinion of the Purchaser's counsel as to legal matters relevant to the obligations of the Purchaser, in a form satisfactory to the Vendors' counsel acting reasonably, which opinion may rely on the certificate of the Purchaser as to factual matters.

7) **Release of Guarantees, Mortgages.** At the time of Closing, the Vendors shall have received full and final releases of all guarantees, indemnities, promissory notes and mortgages from the [ ] Bank in respect of the indebtedness of either of the Corporations and all Charge/Mortgages of Land on property of the Vendors relating to the indebtedness of the Corporations shall be discharged.

8) **No Material Change.** There shall have been no material change in the financial position, value or assets of the Corporations during the Interim Period.

9.4) Waiver of Termination by Vendors

1) The Vendors' Closing Conditions are for the exclusive benefit of the Vendors and may be waived in whole or in part by the Vendors in writing at any time.

2) The Purchaser acknowledges that the waiver by the Vendors of any condition or any part of any condition shall be limited thereto, and shall not constitute a waiver of any other condition or any covenant, agreement, representation or warranty made by the Purchaser herein that corresponds or is related to such condition or such part of such condition, as the case may be.

3) If any of the Vendors' Closing Conditions are not fulfilled or complied with as herein provided and cannot be fulfilled or rectified prior to Closing, the Vendors may at their option at or prior to the time of Closing, by notice in writing to the Purchaser, terminate this agreement. Thereupon the Vendors shall be released from all obligations hereunder, save as to those stated to survive termination. Unless the condition or conditions have not been fulfilled, are reasonably capable of being fulfilled or caused to be fulfilled by the Purchaser then the Purchaser shall also be released from all obligations hereunder, save as to those stated to survive termination.

9.5) Right of Set-Off

The Purchaser shall have the right to satisfy any amount, from time to time, owing by the Purchaser to the Vendors by way of set-off against any amount, from time to time, owing by the Purchaser to the Vendors, including, but not limited to any amount owing pursuant to a warranty claim, or any undisclosed liability. The Vendors shall have the right to satisfy any amount, from time to time, owing by the Purchaser to them, including any amount owing pursuant to a warranty claim, by way of set-off against any amount, from time to time, owing by the Vendors to the Purchaser.

10) GENERAL PROVISIONS

10.1) Further Assurances

Each of the Vendors and the Purchaser hereby covenants and agrees that at any time and from time to time after the Closing Date they will, upon the request and at the expense of the other (including legal or accounting costs to advise thereon), execute, acknowledge and deliver or cause to be executed, acknowledged and delivered all such further deeds, assignments, transfers, conveyances and assurances as may be required for the better carrying out and performance of all the terms of this agreement.

10.2) Remedies Cumulative

The rights and remedies of the parties under this agreement are cumulative and in addition to and not in substitution for any rights to remedies provided by law. Any single or partial exercise by any party hereto of any right or remedy for default or breach of any term, covenant or condition of this agreement does not waive, alter, affect or prejudice any other right or remedy to which such party may be lawfully entitled for the same default or breach.

10.3) Notice

1) Any notice, designation, communication, request, demand or other document, required or permitted to be given or sent or delivered here-under to any party (a **"notice"**) shall be in writing and signed by the party giving the notice.

2) A notice shall be sufficiently delivered if:

    a) served in the manner permitted for service of civil court documents, in which case it will be considered given at the time so served;

    b) delivered to the address of Vendors in a properly addressed envel-ope, in which case it will be considered given at the time so delivered if before 5:00 p.m. on the date delivered, otherwise at 9:00 a.m. on the next business day.

    c) sent to the party entitled to receive it by registered mail mailed in Canada, in which case it will be considered given four (4) business days after mailing, plus such additional number of days during such time as there was an actual discontinuance or interruption of regu-lar postal service for any reason whatsoever.

    d) sent by fax machine, provided a confirmation receipt of the trans-mission is obtained and produced on request, in which case it will be considered given at the time so delivered if before 5:00 p.m. on the day delivered, otherwise at 9:00 a.m. on the next business day.

3) Notices shall be sent to the following addresses or fax numbers

    a) in the case of the Vendors:
        [ ]
        with a copy to: [ ]
        Facsimile: [ ]

b) in the case of the Purchaser:
[ ]
Facsimile: [ ]
with a copy to:
[ ]
Facsimile: [ ]
or to such other address or fax number as the party receiving such notice has stipulated by a notice properly given.

10.4) Expenses of Parties

Each of the parties hereto shall bear all expenses incurred by it in connection with this agreement including, without limitation, the charges of their respective counsel, accountants, financial advisors and finders.

10.5) Announcements and Confidentiality of Agreement

Prior to Closing no announcement with respect to this agreement will be made by any party hereto without the prior approval of the Vendors and the Purchaser. The price and payment terms of this agreement shall be considered confidential and not disclosed by a party to anyone other than in the same manner as the provisions of this agreement dealing with confidential information. The foregoing will not apply to any disclosure required in order to comply with the law or order of any court of competent jurisdiction.

10.6) Assignment

The rights of the Vendors hereunder shall not be assignable without the written consent of the Purchaser. The rights of the Purchaser hereunder shall not be assignable without the written consent of the Vendors.

10.7) Successors and Assigns

This agreement shall be binding upon and enure to the benefit of the parties hereto and their respective successors, heirs, executors, administrators and permitted assigns. Nothing herein, express or implied, is intended to confer upon any person, other than the parties hereto and their respective successors heirs, executors, administrators and assigns, any rights, remedies, obligations or liabilities under or by reason of this agreement.

10.8) Entire Agreement

This agreement and the schedules referred to herein constitute the entire agreement between the parties hereto and supersede all prior agreements, representations, warranties, statements, promises, information, arrangements and understandings, whether oral or written, express or implied, with respect to the subject matter hereof. None of the parties hereto shall be bound or charged with any oral or written agreements, representations, warranties, statements, promises, information, arrangements or understandings not specifically set forth in this agreement or in the schedules, documents and instruments to be delivered on or before the Closing Date pursuant to this agreement. The parties hereto further acknowledge and agree that, in entering into this agreement and in delivering the schedules, documents and instruments to be delivered on or before the Closing Date, they have not in any way relied, and will not in any way rely, upon any oral or written agreements, representations, warranties, statements, promises, information, arrangements or understandings, express or implied, not specifically set forth in this agreement or in such schedules, documents or instruments.

10.9) Waiver

Any party hereto which is entitled to the benefits of this agreement may, and has the right to, waive any term or condition hereof at any time on or prior to the time of Closing provided, however, that such waiver shall be evidenced by written instrument duly executed on behalf of such party.

10.10) Amendments

No modification or amendment to this agreement may be made unless agreed to by the parties hereto in writing.

As Witness, the due execution under seal by the parties this [ ] day of [ ].

Form 5: **Share Purchase Agreement** [*Short Form*]

THIS AGREEMENT made the day of ●, 20●.

AMONG:

> ●, a corporation incorporated pursuant to the laws of ●;
>> (hereinafter called the "**Vendor**")
>> and -
> ●, a corporation incorporated pursuant to the laws of ●;
>> (hereinafter called the "**Purchaser**")
>> and -
> ●, a corporation incorporated pursuant to the laws of ●;
>> (hereinafter called the "**Corporation**")

WHEREAS the Vendor is the owner of ● (●) issued and outstanding [● class] shares (the "**Purchased Shares**") in the capital of the Corporation;

AND WHEREAS the Vendor has agreed to sell and the Purchaser has agreed to purchase the Purchased Shares in accordance with the terms and conditions hereinafter set forth;

NOW THEREFORE THIS AGREEMENT WITNESSETH that in consideration of the mutual covenants and agreements hereinafter set forth, the sum of two ($2.00) dollars now paid by each party to every other party (the receipt and sufficiency whereof is hereby acknowledged), and other good and valuable consideration, the parties agree as follows.

ARTICLE 1: PURCHASE AND SALE

1.01)   The Vendor covenants and agrees to sell and the Purchaser covenants and agrees to purchase the Purchased Shares.

1.02)   The purchase price (the **"Purchase Price"**) for the Purchased Shares shall be the sum of $● Canadian dollars.

1.03)   The Purchase Price shall be paid as follows:

a)   the sum of $● shall be paid by the Purchaser to the Vendor at the time of closing.

b)   the balance of the Purchase Price, being the sum of $●, shall be evidenced by a promissory note (the **"Note"**), of the Purchaser to the Vendor and shall be payable by [*one (1) instalment of principal of the sum of $● on the day of ●, 20● and the balance paid out of future distributions of dividends by the Corporation*] or, in the event the Purchaser disposes of the Purchased Shares, out of the proceeds of such disposition. The Note shall be in the form of promissory note attached hereto as Schedule "A".

c)   Interest at an annual rate of ●% shall be payable annually on the anniversary of the Note.

1.04)   As security for its obligations under the Note, the Purchaser will deliver a pledge of shares agreement (the **"Pledge Agreement"**) whereby it shall pledge the Purchased Shares to the Vendor. The Pledge Agreement shall be in form of Pledge Agreement attached hereto as Schedule "B". [*Consider personal guarantee.*]

ARTICLE 2: COVENANTS, REPRESENTATIONS AND WARRANTIES OF THE VENDOR

2.01)   The Vendor covenants, represents and warrants as follows to the Purchaser and acknowledges that the Purchaser is relying on such covenants, representations and warranties in connection with the purchase by the Purchaser of the Purchased Shares:

a)   the Vendor is the registered, legal and beneficial owner of the Purchased Shares with a good title thereto free and clear of all liens, pledges, charges, mortgages or security interests;

b)   except as disclosed in this Agreement, no person, firm or corporation has any right or option to purchase any of the Purchased Shares from the Vendor;

c)   the Vendor is not **"non-resident"** within the meaning of the *Income Tax Act* (Canada).

ARTICLE 3: SURVIVAL OF COVENANTS, REPRESENTATIONS AND WARRANTIES

3.01)   The covenants, representations and warranties of the Vendor shall survive closing and remain in full force and effect for the benefit of the Purchaser.

ARTICLE 4: CONDITIONS ON CLOSING

4.01)   The purchase and sale of the Purchased Shares contemplated herein is subject to the following conditions for the benefit of the Purchaser or the Vendor, as the case may be. Any party shall be entitled to waive a condition in his or its favour by notice in writing to the other parties:

a)   the Vendor shall execute such corporate documents and share transfers as the Purchaser's solicitors shall require.

b)   the Purchaser shall have delivered the Pledge Agreement and the Note to the Vendor together with delivery of the share certificate(s) for the Purchased Shares to ●.

4.02)   In case any condition has not been fulfilled on or before closing or has not been waived in writing, the party who is entitled to the benefit of such condition shall be entitled to terminate this Agreement by notice in writing to the other party.

ARTICLE 5: INDEMNITY

5.01)   The Vendor covenants and agrees to indemnify and forever save the Purchaser and the Corporation harmless from and against the following:

a)   [●%] of all debts, liabilities, claims, demands and causes of action relating to or against the Corporation for matters arising prior to the time of closing and which are not reflected as liabilities or reserved against in full in the books and records of the Corporation as at the time of closing, including, without limitation, any and all claims, demands and causes of action against the Corporation in respect of federal, provincial, sales, excise, income, corporate or any other taxes until such time as the period of assessment or re-assessment provided in the *Income Tax Act* (Canada) for the Corporation's fiscal period ended on the closing date has expired, notwithstanding investigations made by the Purchaser at any time or any information the Purchaser may have with respect thereto.

5.02)   The indemnity provided for in this Article 5 shall survive closing and remain in full force and effect for the benefit of the Purchaser.

ARTICLE 6: CLOSING

6.01)   Closing of the transaction of purchase and sale of the Purchased Shares shall take place contemporaneously with the execution of this Agreement and the other documentation contemplated herein by the parties.

ARTICLE 7: NOTICES

7.01)   Any notice, request, payment or other communication required or permitted to be given hereunder by either the Vendors, the Corporation or the Purchaser to the other of them, shall be in writing and shall be given, made or communicated by personally delivering the same or by registered or certified mail, first-class postage pre-paid, return receipt requested, addressed as follows:

To the Vendor: ●
With a copy to: ●
To the Purchaser: ●
With a copy to: ●

or at such other address as any party hereto may designate from time to time by giving notice to the other to that effect as herein provided. Any notice, request, payment, or other communication shall be deemed to have been given, made or communicated, as the case may be, at the time that the same is personally delivered, or if by certified or registered mail as aforesaid, on the seventh (7th) business day (excluding Saturdays, Sundays, statutory holidays, and period during which strikes or other occurrences interfere with normal mail service) next following the date when the same is so mailed.

ARTICLE 8: GENERAL CONTRACT PROVISIONS

8.01)   **No Waiver.** The waiver by a party of a breach or default by any of the other of them shall not be deemed to constitute a waiver of any preceding or subsequent breach or default of the same or any other provision of this Agreement.

8.02)   **Entire Agreement.** This Agreement contains the entire understanding of the parties hereto with respect to the matters herein contained. There are no representations, warranties, promises, covenants, or undertakings, other than those expressly stated herein.

8.03)   **No Modification.** No waiver or modification of any of the terms of this Agreement shall be valid unless the same is reduced to writing and signed by the parties hereto.

8.04)   **Headings.** The headings contained in this Agreement are for convenience or reference only and do not form any part hereof and in no manner modify, interpret, or construe the Agreement between the parties hereto.

8.05)   **Enurement.** This Agreement shall enure to the benefit of and be binding on the parties hereto and their respective heirs, executors, administrators, legal personal representatives and successors and may not be assigned by any of the parties hereto.

8.06)   **Recitals.** The parties acknowledge and agree that the recitals to this Agreement are true and correct in substance and in fact and are hereby incorporated into and form an integral part of this Agreement.

8.07)   **Construction.** This Agreement shall be governed, construed, and enforced exclusively in accordance with the laws of the Province of

Ontario. The parties hereto hereby irrevocably attorn to the jurisdiction of the Courts of the said province.

8.08) **Time.** Time shall be of the essence of this Agreement, and of every part hereof.

IN WITNESS WHEREOF the parties hereto have executed this Agreement effective the date set out above.

SIGNED AND DELIVERED
in the presence of

Witness   Witness

_________________________   _________________________

Print Name: _______________   Print Name: _______________

Company Name   Company Name
Per: Per:
Name: _______________   Name: _______________
Title: _______________   Title: _______________
I/We have the authority to bind the   I/We have the authority to bind the
corporation   corporation

Form 6: **Non-Negotiable Subordinated Note**

Date: [ ]

[*Company name*]

[ ], Canada

DUE [*date*]

$[ ]

FOR VALUE RECEIVED, the undersigned, [ ], an unlimited liability company formed under the laws of [ ] (together with its successors, the "**Corporation**"), hereby promises to pay to [ ] (together with its successors and permitted assigns, the "**Holder**"), at the Holder's office at [ ], [ ], the aggregate principal amount of [ ] Dollars ($[ ]) on the installment dates stated in Section 1.2 hereof. Certain capitalized terms are used in this Note as defined in Section 6. Unless otherwise indicated herein, all references to currency shall be to the Canadian dollar.

SECTION 1: PAYMENT

1.1) Interest

Subject to Section 3, the outstanding principal amount of this Note shall bear interest (computed on the basis of a 365 or 366 day year, as the case may be) at a rate equal to eight percent (8%) per annum from (but excluding) the date hereof to (and including) the Maturity Date. Subject to Section 3, such interest shall be payable (i) annually in arrears, with respect to each fiscal year of the Corporation (or portion thereof) on the 120th day following the end of such

Corporation's fiscal year (or portion thereof) ("**Interest Payment Dates**"), commencing with the period ending [ ], and (ii) on the Maturity Date.

1.2)   Principal

Subject to Section 3, the Corporation shall pay within 120 days following the end of the year [ ] a principal payment on this Note equal to $[ ] and shall pay on the Maturity Date the entire then outstanding principal amount of this Note.

1.3)   Business Days

Whenever payment of principal of, or interest on, this Note shall be due on a date that is not a Business Day, the date for payment thereof shall be the next succeeding Business Day and interest due on the unpaid principal and any other Amounts Payable hereunder shall accrue during such extension and shall be payable on such succeeding Business Day.

SECTION 2: PREPAYMENTS; SET-OFF

2.1)   Optional Prepayment

The Corporation shall have the right to prepay the principal amount of this Note in whole or in part at any time, or from time to time, without payment of any premium or penalty whatsoever, together with interest thereon accrued to the date of prepayment, and any such prepayment shall be applied to reduce the Corporation's principal payment obligations under Section 1.2 in the order of maturity of such payment obligations; provided, however, that so long as any Senior Indebtedness remains outstanding and unpaid, any commitment to provide Senior Indebtedness is outstanding, or any other amount is owing to the holders of Senior Indebtedness, this Note may not be prepaid in whole or in part, without the written consent of the holders of Senior Indebtedness.

2.2)   Set-off

The Corporation shall be entitled to set-off and reduce any Amounts Payable hereunder for any obligations or liabilities of the Holder to the Corporation or any claims by the Corporation against the Holder or any party agreeing not to compete under the Purchase Agreement or the Noncompetition Agreements. The Holder, by accepting this Note, hereby acknowledges and agrees to the foregoing provisions and any subsequent transferee or successor shall by becoming such transferee or successor be bound by the foregoing.

SECTION 3: FREE CASH FLOW

3.1) Payment Limitation

Notwithstanding any other provision of this Note, the Corporation shall only be required to pay interest, principal or any other Amounts Payable in respect of this Note if and to the extent the Corporation's Free Cash Flow for the Corporation's fiscal year immediately preceding the required payment date is sufficient and available to make such payment. If the Corporation's Free Cash Flow for such fiscal year is not sufficient to make such payments, then such payments will not be made nor be required to be made under this Note, and the Corporation's payment obligation under this Note will be deferred until the Corporation's Free Cash Flow would permit payment under this Section 3, and such deferral of payment will not be an Event of Default under this Note, provided that the Maturity Date will not be deferred under this Section 3 for more than two years, at which time, all principal of, interest on and other Amounts Payable in respect of this Note will be due and payable.

3.2) Interest Limitation

If, as a result of Section 3.1, the Corporation does not pay interest on an Interest Payment Date, then such interest will be deferred (and not bear interest) and be paid at the Maturity Date.

3.3) Principal and Amounts Payable Deferral

If, as a result of Section 3.1, the Corporation does not pay principal or any other Amounts Payable (other than interest) on any required payment date, then such principal and Amounts Payable will be deferred (and not bear interest) and be paid at the Maturity Date.

3.4) Allocation

If the Corporation's Free Cash Flow for any fiscal year is available to pay some, but not all, of the required payments, then such available Free Cash Flow will be allocated first to required interest payments, second to required principal payments, and then to required payments of any other Amounts Payable.

SECTION 4: DEFAULTS

4.1) Events of Default

If one or more of the following events ("**Events of Default**") shall have occurred and be continuing:

a) the Corporation shall fail to pay within ten Business Days of the due date thereof any principal of this Note or shall fail to pay within five Business Days of the due date thereof any interest or any other Amounts Payable hereunder and the same shall not have been cured within 30 days after written notice thereof has been given by the Holder to the Corporation;

b) the Corporation shall fail to observe or perform any covenant or agreement contained in this Note (other than those covered by clause (a) above) and the same shall not have been cured within 30 days after written notice thereof has been given by the Holder to the Corporation, provided, however, an Event of Default shall not have occurred or be continuing if efforts to cure have commenced within such 30 days and if such efforts to cure continue to be diligently pursued after expiration of such 30-day period;

c) the Corporation shall commence a voluntary case or other proceeding seeking liquidation, reorganization or other relief with respect to itself or its debts under any bankruptcy, insolvency or other similar law now or hereafter in effect or seeking the appointment of a trustee, receiver, liquidator, custodian or other similar official, or shall consent to any such relief or to the appointment of or taking possession by any such official in an involuntary case or other proceeding commenced against it, or shall make a general assignment for the benefit of creditors; or

d) an involuntary case or other proceeding shall be commenced against the Corporation seeking liquidation, reorganization or other relief with respect to it or its debts under any bankruptcy, insolvency or other similar law now or hereafter in effect or seeking the appointment of a trustee, receiver, liquidator, custodian or other similar official, and such involuntary case or other proceeding shall remain undismissed and unstayed for a period of 90 days; or an order for relief shall be entered against the Corporation under the Federal bankruptcy laws as now or hereafter in effect;

then, and in every such event, subject to the provisions of Section 6, the Holder may, by notice to the Corporation and to the holders of Senior Indebtedness, declare the principal amount of this Note together with accrued interest thereon, to be, and such portions of the principal amount of this Note (and accrued interest thereon) shall thereupon become, due and payable on the tenth Business Day following delivery of such notice to the Corporation and to the holders of Senior Indebtedness without presentment, demand, protest or further notice of any kind, all of which are hereby waived by the Corporation; provided, that

(x) the Events of Defaults specified in paragraphs (a) and (b) will be subject to Section 3, and (y) in the case of any of the Events of Default specified in paragraph (c) or (d), such portions of the principal amount of this Note (together with accrued interest thereon) shall immediately (and without notice) become due and payable without presentment, demand, protest or notice of any kind, all of which are hereby waived by the Corporation.

SECTION 5: SUBORDINATION

5.1) Loans Subordinated to Senior Indebtedness

Notwithstanding any provision of this Note to the contrary, the Corporation covenants and agrees, and the Holder by acceptance of this Note likewise covenants and agrees, that subject to the payment rights with respect to the Note set forth herein all Amounts Payable shall be subordinated to the extent set forth in this Section 5 to the prior payment in full, in cash or cash equivalents satisfactory to the holders of Senior Indebtedness, of all Senior Indebtedness. This Section 5 shall constitute a continuing offer to and covenant with all persons who become holders of, or continue to hold, Senior Indebtedness (irrespective of whether such Senior Indebtedness was created or acquired before or after the issuance of this Note). The provisions of this Section 5 are made for the benefit of all present and future holders of Senior Indebtedness (and their successors and assigns), and shall be enforceable by them directly against the Holder.

5.2) Priority and Payment Over of Proceeds in Certain Events.

a)   Upon any payment or distribution of assets of the Corporation, whether in cash, property, securities or otherwise, in the event of any dissolution, winding up or total or partial liquidation, reorganization, arrangement, adjustment, protection, relief or composition, or assignment for the benefit of creditors of the Corporation, whether voluntary or involuntary or in bankruptcy, insolvency, receivership, reorganization, relief or other proceedings or upon an assignment for the benefit of creditors or any other marshaling of all or part of the assets and liabilities of the Corporation (the foregoing events herein collectively referred to as an "**Insolvency Event**"), all Senior Indebtedness shall first be paid in full, in cash, or payment provided for in cash equivalents in a manner satisfactory to the holders of Senior Indebtedness, before the Holder shall be entitled to receive any payment or distribution of assets of the Corporation relating to any Amounts Payable. Upon any Insolvency Event, any payment or distribution of assets of the Corporation, whether in cash, property, securities or otherwise, to which the Holder would be entitled relating to any Amounts Payable, except for the provisions of this Section 5, shall be made by the Corporation or by any receiver, trustee in bankruptcy, liquidating trustee, agent or other person making such payment or distribution, directly to the holders of the Senior Indebtedness or their representatives for application to the payment or prepayment of all such Senior Indebtedness in full after giving effect to any concurrent payment or distribution to the holders of such Senior Indebtedness.

b) If (x) there has occurred and is continuing a default in the payment of all or any portion of any Senior Indebtedness, unless and until such default shall have been cured or waived, the Corporation shall not make any payment on or with respect to any Amounts Payable or acquire this Note (or any portion thereof) for cash, property, securities or otherwise; or (y) an event (not involving the non-payment of any Senior Indebtedness) shall have occurred or, with the giving of notice, or passage of time, or both, would occur, that would allow holders of any Senior Indebtedness to accelerate or otherwise demand the payment thereof, and the holders of the Senior Indebtedness give notice of such event to the Corporation (the date that such notice is received by the Corporation is the **"Notice Date"**), the Corporation shall not make any payment on or with respect to any Amounts Payable or acquire this Note (or any portion hereof) for cash, property, securities or otherwise during the period (the **"Blockage Period"**) commencing on the Notice Date and ending on the earlier of (1) two years after the Notice Date if at the end of such two year period such event is not the subject of judicial proceedings and such Senior Indebtedness shall not have been accelerated, (2) the date such event is cured or waived to the satisfaction of the holders of the Senior Indebtedness, or (3) the date the holders of such Senior Indebtedness shall have given notice to the Corporation of the voluntary termination of the Blockage Period. By virtue of accepting this Note and the benefits hereof, during any time period during which payment of any part of Amounts Payable due under this Note is prohibited by any of the terms of this Note, the Holder shall not be entitled, and will not take any action, including any judicial process, to accelerate, demand payment or enforce any Indebtedness in respect of this Note or any other claim with regard to any Amounts Payable.

c)   If, notwithstanding the foregoing provisions prohibiting payments or distributions, the Holder shall have received any payment of, or on account of, any Amounts Payable that was prohibited by this Section 5, before all Senior Indebtedness shall have been paid in full, then and in such event such payments or distributions shall be received and held in trust for the holders of the Senior Indebtedness and promptly paid over or delivered to the holders of the Senior Indebtedness remaining unpaid thereof to the extent necessary to pay in full, in cash or cash equivalents satisfactory to the holders of the Senior Indebtedness, such Senior Indebtedness in accordance with its terms after giving effect to any concurrent payment or distribution to the holder of such Senior Indebtedness; provided, that any such payment which is, for any reason, not so paid over or delivered shall be held in trust by the Holder for the holders of Senior Indebtedness.

d)   So long as any Senior Indebtedness remains outstanding, or the commitment to make credit extensions of said Senior Indebtedness shall not have been terminated, the Holder will not be entitled to take, demand, or receive, directly or indirectly, by setoff, redemption, purchase or in any manner, any voluntary prepayment or other payment of any Amounts Payable in amounts or in a manner which are in violation of the provisions of this Section 5.

e)   Upon any payment or distribution of assets referred to in Section 5.2(a), the Holder shall be entitled to rely upon any order or decree of a court of competent jurisdiction in which such dissolution, winding up, liquidation or reorganization proceedings are pending, and upon a certificate of the receiver, trustee in bankruptcy, liquidating trustee, agent or other person making any such payment or distribution of assets, delivered to the Holder for the purpose of ascertaining the persons entitled to participate in such distribution of assets, the holders of Senior Indebtedness and other Indebtedness of the Corporation, the amount thereof or payable thereon, the amount or amounts paid or distributed thereon and all other facts pertinent thereto or to this Section 5.

5.3)   Rights of Holders of Senior Indebtedness Not To Be Impaired, etc.

a)   No right of any present or future holder of any Senior Indebtedness to enforce the subordination and other terms and conditions provided herein shall at any time in any way be prejudiced or impaired by any act or failure to act by any such holder, or by any noncompliance by the Corporation, with the terms and provisions and covenants herein regardless of any knowledge thereof that any such holder may have or otherwise be charged with.

b) This Section 5 may not be amended without the written consent of each holder of the Senior Indebtedness and of the Holder, and any purported amendment without such consent shall be void. No holder of Senior Indebtedness shall be prejudiced in such holder's right to enforce the subordination and other terms and conditions of this Note by any act or failure to act by the Corporation or anyone in custody of its assets or property.

5.4) Subrogation

Subject to and upon the payment in full of all Senior Indebtedness, the Holder shall be subrogated, to the extent of payments or distributions made to the holders of Senior Indebtedness pursuant to or by reason of this Section 5, to the rights of the holders of such Senior Indebtedness to receive payments or distributions of assets of the Corporation made on such Senior Indebtedness until all amounts due under this Note shall be paid in full; and for the purposes of such subrogation, no payments or distributions to holders of such Senior Indebtedness of any cash, property or securities to which the Holder would be entitled except for the provisions of this Section 5, and no payment over pursuant to the provisions of this Section 5 to holders of such Senior Indebtedness by the Holder, shall, as among the Corporation, its creditors (other than holders of such Senior Indebtedness) and the Holder be deemed to be a payment by the Corporation to or on account of such Senior Indebtedness, it being understood that the provisions of this Section 5 are solely for the purpose of defining the relative rights of the holders of such Senior Indebtedness, on the one hand, and the Holder, on the other hand.

5.5) Obligations of the Corporation Unconditional

Nothing contained in this Note is intended to or shall impair, as between the Corporation and the Holder, the obligation of the Corporation, which is absolute and unconditional, to pay to the Holder all Amounts Payable, as and when the same shall become due and payable in accordance with their terms, or to affect the relative rights of the Holder and other creditors of the Corporation (other than the holders of Senior Indebtedness), except as provided in Section 5.2(b).

5.6) Section 5 Not To Prevent Events of Default

The failure to make a payment of any Amounts Payable by reason of any provision of this Section 5 shall not be construed as preventing the occurrence of an Event of Default under Section 4.1 hereof, except as provided in Section 5.2(b).

5.7) Additional Rights of Holders of Senior Indebtedness

If the Senior Indebtedness has not been paid in full, in cash or cash equivalents satisfactory to the holders of Senior Indebtedness, at a time in which the Corporation is subject to an Insolvency Event, (a) the holders of the Senior Indebtedness are hereby irrevocably authorized, but shall have no obligation, to demand, sue for, collect and receive every payment or distribution received in respect of any such Insolvency Proceeding and give acquittance therefor and to file claims and proofs of claim, as their interests may appear, and (b) the Holder shall duly and promptly take, for the account of the holders of the Senior Indebtedness, as their interests may appear, such actions as the holders of the Senior Indebtedness may request to collect and receive all Amounts Payable by the Corporation in respect of this Note and to file appropriate claims or proofs of claim in respect of this Note. Upon request by the Corporation, the Holder of this Note shall deliver to the holders of Senior Indebtedness or parties contemplating becoming holders of Senior Indebtedness a written statement confirming that (i) the provisions (including the subordination provisions) of this Note are in full force and effect; and (ii) that such party is or will be entitled to rely upon and enjoy the benefits of the provisions (including the subordination provisions) of this Note as a holder of Senior Indebtedness.

5.8) Senior Indebtedness Changes

By virtue of accepting this Note and the benefits hereof, the Holder hereby waives any and all notice of renewal, extension or accrual of any of the Senior Indebtedness, present or future, and agrees and consents that without notice to or consent of the Holder: (a) the obligations and liabilities of the Corporation or any other party or parties under the Senior Indebtedness may, from time to time, in whole or in part, be renewed, refinanced, replaced, extended, refunded, modified, amended, accelerated, compromised, supplemented, terminated, increased, decreased, sold, exchanged, waived or released; (b) the holders of Senior Indebtedness and their representatives may exercise or refrain from exercising any right, remedy or power granted by any document creating, evidencing or otherwise related to the Senior Indebtedness or at law, in equity, or otherwise, with respect to the Senior Indebtedness or in connection with any collateral security or lien (legal or equitable) held, given or intended to be given therefor (including, without limitation, the right to perfect any lien or security interest created in connection therewith); (c) any and all collateral security and/or liens (legal or equitable) at any time, present or future, held, given or intended to be given for the Senior Indebtedness, and any rights or remedies of the holders of Senior Indebtedness and their representatives in respect thereof, may, from time to time, in whole or in part, be exchanged, sold, surrendered, released, modified, perfected, unperfected, waived or extended by the Holders and their representatives; (d) any balance or balances of funds with any holder of Senior Indebtedness at any time standing to the credit of the Corporation or any guarantor of any of the Senior Indebtedness may, from time to time, in whole or in part, be surrendered or released; all as the holders of Senior Indebtedness, their representatives or any of them may deem advisable and all without impairing, abridging, diminishing, releasing or affecting the subordination to the Senior Indebtedness provided for herein; and (e) the Corporation may incur any amount or type of Senior Indebtedness (including Senior Indebtedness owed to Affiliates), or modify, restate, refinance, replace or amend any Senior Indebtedness from time to time, on terms and conditions acceptable to the Corporation, without notice to or approval by the Holder.

5.9) Waivers

In the event the holders of Senior Indebtedness elect to exercise their remedies to liquidate any collateral given to secure the Senior Indebtedness, the Holder hereby waives any right it may have to contest the validity of or the value obtained as a result of the exercise of remedies by the holders of Senior Indebtedness, including, but not limited to, a foreclosure, a sale pursuant to the *Personal Property Security Act*, R.S.O. 1990, c. P.10 or the acceptance by the holders of Senior Indebtedness in lieu of foreclosure. The Holder further waives any right it may have either in or out of any bankruptcy or similar proceeding to challenge any action taken by the holders of Senior Indebtedness as either a preference or fraudulent conveyance and further agrees not to take any active role in such a proceeding other than the filing of claim in any such proceeding, which claim shall be subordinate (to the extent set forth above) to the claims of the holders of Senior Indebtedness.

SECTION 6: DEFINITIONS

For purposes of this Note, the following terms have the meanings set forth below.

"**Affiliate**" means [ ] and its respective direct and indirect Subsidiaries, and any other person that directly, or indirectly through one or more intermediaries, controls or is controlled by or is under common control with them. For purposes of this definition "**control**" shall mean the power, direct or indirect, to vote or direct the voting of more than 5% of the outstanding shares of voting stock or to direct or cause the direction of management and policies, whether by contract or otherwise.

"**Amounts Payable**" means all principal of, interest on, premium, if any, fees, costs, expenses, indemnities or any other amounts due from the Corporation under this Note, and all claims against or liabilities of the Corporation in respect of this Note.

"**Business Day**" means any day except a Saturday, Sunday or other days on which commercial banks in [ ] are required or authorized by law to close.

"**Capital Expenditures**" means the capital expenditures of the Corporation, determined in accordance with generally accepted accounting principles, consistently applied.

"**Closing Date**" means the date on which the transactions contemplated by the Purchase Agreement are consummated.

"**Default**" means any condition or event that constitutes an Event of Default or that with notice or lapse of time or both would, unless cured or waived, become an Event of Default.

"**Free Cash Flow**" means, for any period, (i) the consolidated net income (or net deficit) of the Corporation and its subsidiaries (excluding, however, all extraordinary and other non-recurring items of income, but not loss, and (B) all interest income as reflected in the Corporation's financial statements); plus (ii) interest (including deferred financing fees and expense) and other expense in respect of the Corporation's Indebtedness (including inter-company Indebtedness or Indebtedness owed to Affiliates) charged, accrued or otherwise allocated against such net income; plus (iii) expenses for amortization charged, accrued or otherwise allocated against such net income; plus (iv) expenses for depreciation (including increased depreciation and increased inventory values resulting from purchase accounting in connection with acquisitions and business combinations) charged, accrued or otherwise allocated against such net income; plus (v) any reductions in Working Capital from the beginning to the end of such period; minus (vi) payments of interest and principal on Indebtedness (other than required interest and principal payments on this Note and other than required interest and principal payments relating directly to Refused Transaction Indebtedness) paid or accrued during such period or otherwise payable on the applicable payment date, provided, however, principal payments on Senior Indebtedness included in this calculation of Free Cash Flow shall equal the amounts set forth in Schedule A attached hereto for the respective years in question unless otherwise agreed by the parties; minus (vii) any increases in Working Capital from the beginning to the end of such period; minus (viii) cash payments for Capital Expenditures during such period. Free Cash Flow will reflect selling, general and administrative expense, management, consulting and service fees, general and overhead, allocated to the Corporation by its Affiliates. Free Cash Flow will be determined by the Corporation's Board of Directors by reference to the Corporation's financial statements, prepared in accordance with generally accepted accounting principles, consistently applied.

"Indebtedness" means any indebtedness (including, without limitation, Senior Indebtedness), whether or not contingent, in respect of borrowed money or evidenced by bonds, notes, guarantees, debentures or similar instruments or letters of credit (or reimbursement agreements in respect thereof) or representing the deferred and unpaid balance of the purchase price of any property (including pursuant to capital leases), and any financial hedging obligations, if and to the extent such indebtedness (other than a financial hedging obligation) would appear as a liability upon a balance sheet of such person prepared on a consolidated basis in accordance with generally accepted accounting principles, other than a trade payable or accrued expense to the extent not otherwise included, the guarantee of items that would be included within this definition. Indebtedness owed to Affiliates will be Indebtedness for purposes of this Note.

"Maturity Date" means [ ] a date later than [ ].

"Non-competition Agreements" means the Non-competition Agreements between the Corporation and each of the other parties to the Purchase Agreement dated as of the Closing Date.

"Note" means this Non-Negotiable Subordinated Note due [ ].

"Purchase Agreement" means the Agreement For Purchase And Sale Of Assets dated as of [ ], among the Corporation and [ ] as the same has been or may be amended from time to time.

"Refused Transaction Indebtedness" means any Indebtedness directly incurred in connection with any acquisition of a business by the Corporation for a purchase price in excess of $[ ] provided Holder designates in writing (by giving a Notice to the Corporation) said acquisition as a refused transaction at least ten days prior to the execution by Corporation of a letter of intent with respect to said acquisition. Corporation shall provide Holder with reasonable financial information regarding said acquisitions at least twenty days prior to the proposed execution date of any such letter of intent.

"Senior Indebtedness" shall mean the principal, interest (including any interest accruing subsequent to an event specified in Sections 4.1(c) and 4.1(d)), premium, if any, fees (including, without limitation, any commitment, agency, facility, structuring, restructuring or other fee), costs, expenses, indemnities, and other amounts due on or in connection with any Indebtedness of the Corporation other than Indebtedness relating to this Note (including, without limitation, any inter-company Indebtedness), now or herewith incurred, or any documents executed under or in connection therewith, and any amendments, modifications, deferrals, renewals or extensions of such Indebtedness, and any amounts owed in respect of any Indebtedness incurred in refinancing, replacing or refunding the foregoing (including any refinancing, replacing or refunding with new lenders). Nothing in this Note shall restrict an affiliate of the Corporation from being a holder of Senior Indebtedness. Indebtedness owed to Affiliates will be Senior Indebtedness for purposes of this Note. Notwithstanding anything herein to the contrary, Senior Indebtedness shall include any payables, accrued expenses, fees or other amounts due to an Affiliate of the Corporation. Notwithstanding anything herein to the contrary, none of the obligations or liabilities of the Corporation to Holder shall be included in Senior Indebtedness.

"Subsidiary" of a person means any corporation or other entity of which securities or other ownership interests having ordinary voting power to elect a majority of the Board of Directors or other persons performing similar functions are at the time directly or indirectly owned by such person.

"Working Capital" means the difference of (a) the sum of the Corporation's net account receivables, inventories (net of reserves), and prepaid expenses, minus (b) the sum of accounts payable and accrued expenses, determined in accordance with generally accepted accounting principles, consistently applied.

SECTION 7: MISCELLANEOUS

7.1)   Notices

ll notices, requests and other communications to any party hereunder ("**Notices**") shall be in writing and shall be delivered personally, sent by facsimile transmission or sent by certified, registered or express mail, postage prepaid, and shall be deemed given when so delivered personally, or sent by facsimile transmission, or if mailed or sent by overnight courier, upon receipt thereof, as follows:

If to the Corporation, to: If to the Corporation, to:

_______________________   _______________________

Telephone:_______________   Telephone:_______________

Telecopier:______________   Telecopier:______________

with a copy to: with a copy to:

_______________________   _______________________

Telephone: ______________   Telephone: ______________

Telecopier: _____________   Telecopier: _____________

Each party may, by notice given in accordance with this Section to the other party, designate another address or person for receipt of notices hereunder.

7.2)   No Waivers

No failure or delay by the Holder in exercising any right, power or privilege hereunder or under this Note shall operate as a waiver thereof nor shall any single or partial exercise thereof preclude any other or further exercise thereof or the exercise of any other right, power or privilege. The rights and remedies herein provided shall be cumulative and not exclusive of any rights or remedies provided by law. No notice to or demand on the Corporation in any case shall entitle the Corporation to any other or further notice or demand in related or similar circumstances requiring such notice.

7.3)   Amendments and Waivers

Any provision of this Note may be amended or waived if, but only if, such amendment or waiver is in writing, signed by the Corporation and the Holder.

7.4)   Successors and Assigns

The provisions of this Note shall be binding upon and inure to the benefit of the Holder and its respective successors and permitted assigns. Without the prior written consent of the Corporation and the holders of Senior Indebtedness, the Holder of this Note agrees that it will not (a) sell, assign, pledge or otherwise transfer, in whole or in part, directly or indirectly, by operation of law or otherwise, this Note or any interest therein or (b) create, incur or suffer to exist any security interest, lien, charge or other encumbrance whatsoever upon this Note. If requested by a holder of Senior Indebtedness as part of any consent, the assignee or transferee of the Holder shall agree in writing to be bound by all of the terms of this Note. The holder hereof hereby waives proof of reliance hereon by the holders of Senior Indebtedness.

7.5)   Replacement Note

Upon receipt of evidence reasonably satisfactory to the Corporation of the loss, theft, destruction or mutilation of this Note and of a letter of indemnity reasonably satisfactory to the Corporation from the Holder and upon reimbursement to the Corporation of all reasonable expenses incident thereto, and upon surrender or cancellation of this Note, if mutilated, the Corporation will make and deliver a new Note of like tenor in lieu of such lost, stolen, destroyed or mutilated Note.

7.6)   Corporation's Obligations

The Holder agrees and acknowledges that this Note and the Corporation's obligations hereunder and for all Amounts Payable are solely obligations and liabilities of the Corporation. None of the Corporation's directors, officers, employees, stockholders, advisors, consultants and affiliates or any other persons shall be obligated or liable in respect of this Note or any Amounts Payable, and Holder hereby releases them from any such obligation of liability.

7.7)   LITIGATION

THIS NOTE SHALL BE GOVERNED BY, CONSTRUED, APPLIED AND ENFORCED IN ACCORDANCE WITH THE INTERNAL LAWS OF THE PROVINCE OF [ ], CANADA, AND NO DOCTRINE OF CHOICE OF LAW SHALL BE USED TO APPLY ANY LAW OTHER THAN THAT OF [ ], AND NO DEFENCE, COUNTERCLAIM OR RIGHT OF SET-OFF GIVEN OR ALLOWED BY THE LAWS OF ANY OTHER STATE OR JURISDICTION, OR ARISING OUT OF THE ENACTMENT, MODIFICATION OR REPEAL OF ANY LAW, REGULATION, ORDINANCE OR DECREE OF ANY FOREIGN JURISDICTION, BE INTERPOSED IN ANY ACTION HEREON.

7.8)   ARBITRATION

THE HOLDER HEREBY WAIVES AND SHALL NOT SEEK TRIAL IN ANY LAWSUIT, PROCEEDING, CLAIM, COUNTERCLAIM, DEFENCE OR OTHER LITIGATION OR DISPUTE UNDER OR IN RESPECT OF THIS NOTE. THE HOLDER AGREES THAT ANY SUCH DISPUTE RELATING TO OR IN RESPECT OF THIS

NOTE, ITS NEGOTIATION, EXECUTION, PERFORMANCE, SUBJECT MATTER, OR ANY COURSE OF CONDUCT OR DEALING OR ACTIONS UNDER OR IN RESPECT OF THIS NOTE, SHALL BE SUBMITTED TO, AND RESOLVED EXCLUSIVELY PURSUANT TO ARBITRATION IN ACCORDANCE WITH THE ARBITRATION ACT ([ ]). SUCH ARBITRATION SHALL BE CONDUCTED BY A MUTUALLY AGREED UPON ARBITRATOR SELECTED FROM THE LIST OF MEMBERS OF THE PRIVATE COURT IN ACCORDANCE WITH THE BINDING DISPUTE RESOLUTION RULES OF THE PRIVATE COURT, SHALL TAKE PLACE IN [ ] AND SHALL BE SUBJECT TO THE SUBSTANTIVE LAW OF THE PROVINCE OF [ ]. DECISIONS PURSUANT TO SUCH ARBITRATION SHALL BE FINAL, CONCLUSIVE AND BINDING ON THE PARTIES.

[ ]

By:

Name: _______________

Title: _______________

SCHEDULE "A": SENIOR INDEBTEDNESS AMORTIZATION SCHEDULE

Year	Payment
	$
	$
	$
	$
	$
	$

Form 7: **Alternate Clauses for Lock-Up/ Exclusivity Arrangements**

Alternate 1

During the period ending the earlier of ● (●) days following the date of execution of this letter by ABC, or the date that we advise ABC that we do not wish to acquire ABC, ABC will not directly or indirectly solicit, encourage or initiate any discussions with or provide any information to, or accept any offers from or enter into any agreement with any other party in connection with the sale of all or a substantially all of the business and assets of ABC or the sale of all or substantially all of the issued and outstanding shares of ABC.

Alternate 2: Exclusive Dealing

The Vendor and ● shall not, directly or indirectly, through any representative or otherwise, solicit or entertain offers from, negotiate with or in any manner encourage, discuss, accept or consider any proposal of any other person relating to the acquisition of the undertaking, property or assets of the Purchased Business, in whole or in part, or of all or any of the shares of the Vendor, whether through direct purchase, merger, consolidation or other business combination (other than sales of inventory in the ordinary course).

Alternate 3: Exclusivity

The Vendor and ● each warrant that the Vendor's principals, shareholders, employees, directors and agents or other persons acting on its behalf:

    a) Do not have any agreement, arrangement or understanding with respect to any other acquisition proposal in respect of the shares or assets of the Vendor ("**Acquisition Proposal**");

b)   Will cease and cause to be terminated any and all discussions with third parties regarding any other Acquisition Proposal; and

c)   Will promptly notify the Purchaser if any Acquisition Proposal or any inquiry or contact with any person or entity with respect thereto is made.

Alternate 4

For a period of six (6) months from the date of this Agreement, the Stipulated Company warrants that it and its principals, shareholders, employees, directors, agents and other persons acting on its behalf:

a)   Do not have any agreement, arrangement or understanding with respect to any other joint manufacturing and production agreement or similar strategic agreement (a **"Third Party Proposal"**);

b)   Will cease and cause to be terminated any and all discussions with third parties regarding any other Third Party Proposal and will not, directly or indirectly pursue or negotiate any Third Party Proposal;

c)   Will promptly notify ● of any Third Party Proposal or any inquiry or contact with any person or entity with respect thereto is made;

d)   Will negotiate and pursue discussions relating to a possible Transaction exclusively with ●.

Form 8: **Draft Project Plan**

Item	Comments	Estimate

1. Structuring the Transaction
• advice relating to the interrelationship between the purchase agreements for each store, including:
  • purchase price and outperform warrants
  • representations and warranties
  • indemnities
  • closing conditions
  • drafting, negotiating and settling Payout Agreement among all shareholders
  • discussions with counsel for Purchaser (we understand that Purchaser's counsel is ●)
	To be handled predominantly by [*name of lawyer*]
	
	Need to consider use of outside counsel to represent individuals (cost would be over and above the estimate)
		$● – $●

2. Competition Act Approval, if required	Not likely applicable – cursory review of issues only	TBD

Item	Comments	Estimate
3. Reviewing and negotiating Template Share Purchase Agreement with Purchaser's counsel (draft disclosure schedules to be prepared by Vendor and TM will assist in finalizing) [*add details*]	To be handled predominantly by [*name of lawyer*]	$● – $●
4. Reviewing and negotiating other Key Agreements with Purchaser's counsel • Template Non-competition Agreement • Template Service/Employment Agreement (negotiating individual employment or non-competition agreements) • Escrow Agreement	To be handled by lawyer [*name of lawyer*]	$● – $●
5. Review of Employee issues • Outperformance Cash Bonus Plan • Staff Share Option Plan	To be handled by one of the [*name of lawyer*]	$● – $●
6. Closing Matters for transactions • reviewing, revising and settling Closing Agenda • assisting with third party consents • assisting with consents from landlords • assisting with issues as they arise during the period between signing and closing • negotiating opinion from Purchaser's counsel • attending to closing .	To be handled by several lawyers and clerks that are members of the Vendor team at TM.	$● – $●
Total		$● – $●

Notes

This project plan and estimate constitutes an estimate only and will vary based on a variety of factors, including:

- protracted negotiation process or several rounds of draft agreements
- changes to the structure of the transaction during the transaction
- level of involvement for third party consents
- transaction taking longer than two months to complete
- unexpected or unusual material issues/complications

The estimate is based on the following assumptions:

- the first draft of all documents (other than the (Payout Agreement) will be prepared by Purchaser's counsel (●) and such draft will constitute a reasonable draft
- TM will not be conducting any due diligence on Vendor, its related entities or Purchaser (limited legal due diligence searches, confirmation of corporate existence and capital structure is included)
- TM will not be involved in any tax planning or provide any advice to individual shareholders
- TM will not be required to update corporate minute books or provide any legal opinions as another firm will be involved in that

This estimate does not include the following:

- Competition Act application fees ($50,000 plus HST, which is usually paid by the Purchaser or split between the Purchaser and the Vendor)
- taxes, disbursements or local counsel fees, if any

Form 9: **Pro Forma Agenda and Timetable**

Timetable	Agenda	Party Responsible
6 Weeks prior to Closing:	i) Board resolution enacted to commence negotiations and to execute letter of intent;	Both Buyer and Seller
	ii) Request for due diligence documentation (detailed schedules).	Buyer's solicitor
5 Weeks prior to Closing:	i) Documentation marshalled and delivered;	Seller's solicitor
	ii) Documentation reviewed;	Buyer's solicitor
	iii) Draft asset (share) acquisition agreement, related schedules and exhibits, and related agreement ("Agreements");	Buyer's solicitor
	iv) Asset title searches undertaken;	Buyer's solicitor
	v) Analysis of Seller's financials.	Buyer's accounting team

Timetable	Agenda	Party Responsible
3–4 Weeks prior to Closing:	i) Negotiate and redraft Agreements;	Solicitors for the Buyer and Seller
	ii) Draft and negotiate opinions of counsel;	Solicitors for the Buyer and Seller
	iii) Documentation analysis and reporting to Buyer;	Buyer's solicitor
	iv) Pre-closing Condition checklist is prepared;	Buyer's solicitor
	v) Regulatory and third party consent or approvals requested (Bank, Landlord, Key Customer)	Seller's solicitor
2 Weeks prior to Closing:	i) Prepare closing agenda and document exchange schedules	Buyer's solicitor
	ii) All Agreements should by this date have been concluded and executed.	
1 Week prior to Closing:	i) Regulatory and third party consents or approvals obtained;	Seller's solicitor
	ii) Review checklist of Pre-closing Conditions to ensure that all have been waived or met;	Buyer's solicitor
	iii) Dry-run closing to identify any "open" issues;	Solicitors for Buyer and Seller
	iv) Closing and exchange of documents as per Closing Agenda.	All parties

Form 10: **Due Diligence Master Checklist**

A. Constating Documents

1) Minute books for ●, and all other predecessor corporations.
2) Certificate of Incorporation (or amalgamation), articles, by-laws, amendments and proposed amendments thereto and minutes of meetings of the board of directors and shareholders of ● not contained in the Minute Books.

   a) Current corporate structure for ●.
   b) List of the shareholders and holders of options or other rights to purchase shares of ● including, without limitation, options, warrants, convertible securities and any other instruments giving rise to a right to acquire securities or assets of ●, including existing and any proposed stock option plans and any debt or equity instruments converting into shares.
   c) Assuming that ● is wholly owned subsidiary of Holdco, copies of any unanimous shareholders' agreements or other agreements in place regarding the shares of ●.
   d) List of names and addresses of the directors and officers of ●, if different from in Minute Book.
   e) List of all jurisdictions in which ● does business and evidence of such qualifications necessary to do such business, such as extra-provincial licenses and registrations.
   f) List of addresses of head office and administrative offices of ●.

3) The above examination should include, but not be limited to, the following:

   a) examination of letters patent and by-laws for unusual provisions, authorized capital, share conditions, preemptive rights, restrictions on transfer of shares, powers of officers, signing authorities, requirement of special majorities for directors' and shareholders' approvals;

   b) examination of the minutes of meetings to determine that all material meetings were properly called, constituted and conducted; major transactions, including enactment of by-laws, election of current directors, appointment of current officers, issuance of shares, were properly approved; all shares have been allotted and issued as fully paid and non-assessable; there are no outstanding options or rights to others to acquire any securities other than as represented; and the existence of any bonus plans, profit sharing plans, stock option and share purchase plans, and other fringes for employees;

   c) examination of the registers of officers and directors; and

   d) review of procedures of compliance department for obtaining and maintaining licences; conduct a random test of major licences by obtaining copies of licences relating to certain material jurisdictions; and if considered appropriate, seeking confirmation from the administrators in such jurisdictions that the licences are in good standing.

4) Confirm from the above, such matters as due incorporation, organization, authorized and issued capital, duly qualified, licenced and registered to carry on business in all appropriate jurisdictions in the manners in which they do business.

5) Obtain and review, for the past three years:

   a) proxy material and other documentation sent to shareholders;

   b) regulatory and enforcement filings in [*province*] *and* Canada; and

   c) press releases and reports.

6) Obtain, with respect to [*material subsidiaries*] opinions of counsel as to

   a) due incorporation,

   b) ability and qualification to carry on business,

   c) issue and outstanding shares, and

    d)   shares owned by the Corporation.

B. Corporate Records [*may be duplicative of parts of A, above*]

  1)   Examination of:

    a)   The constating documents of the Company and all amendments thereto.

    b)   The by-laws of the Company.

    c)   Minutes of meetings of, and signed resolutions of, the board of directors, and committees thereof, of the Company.

    d)   Annual reports and any other communications to shareholders or prospective investors of the Company since incorporation, including information circulars and any other documents.

    e)   Press clippings and releases relating to the Company since incorporation.

    f)   Minutes of all directors and shareholders' meetings of the Company and all signed resolutions from incorporation onwards.

    g)   Copies of any Board Books distributed to new Directors.

    h)   Corporate chart showing the relationship of the Company to its shareholders and Subsidiaries.

  2)   Corporate management organization chart including title, function and responsibility with respect of the Company.

  3)   Shareholders', voting trust and pooling agreements between shareholders of the Company.

  4)   List of Subsidiaries and the Company's percentage of ownership in each Subsidiary.

  5)   List of jurisdictions in which the Company and its Subsidiaries have authority to carry on business.

  6)   Closing books, records or reporting letters relating to all issuances of securities, of the capital of the Company and the Subsidiaries, or any transactions involving the Company or the Subsidiaries since incorporation.

[This section pertains to a private company]

C. Shareholders and Securities Information

  1)   Shareholders transfer registers.

2) Form of share certificate and share certificate books or other evidence of securities authorized, issued and outstanding.

3) Agreements relating to the purchase, sale or issuance of securities including stock options, warrants and/or stock purchase plans.

4) Agreements relating to voting of securities and restrictive share transfers.

5) Agreement relating to pre-emptive or other preferential rights to acquire securities.

6) Other shareholders' agreements.

7) Agreements relating to the qualification of securities.

8) All filings relating to securities with governmental authorities.

[This section below provides a basic non-specific financial review of any company]

D.   Financial Information

1) Auditor name, telephone number and audit manager.

2) Financial information for each of the Companies.

3) All letters from chartered accountants to any of the Companies regarding control systems, methods of accounting, etc.

4) All letters from legal counsel to the chartered accountants regarding litigation in which any of the Companies are or may be involved.

5) Business plans, budgets, strategic planning proposals and financial projections and forecasts on a location by location basis.

6) Particulars of bank accounts, safety deposit boxes and names of authorized signing officers of each of the Companies.

7) List of persons with power of attorney.

8) Recent analyses of the business of the Companies prepared by investment firms, engineers, planners, management consultants, accountants or others, including marketing studies, credit reports and other types of reports, financial or otherwise.

9) Capital spending requirements for the next ● years, with a list of major items/projects.

10) Summary listing of all bank accounts, showing names of the institutions, nature of the account, account number and signing officers.

11) List of investments with both cost and present market value.

12) Summary of accrued liabilities at the last fiscal year end and at the most recent available interim date.

13) Estimate of the value of any assets or potential liabilities not on the books of such Companies.

14) External and internal audit working paper files and reports for the last
    • fiscal years.
15) List of accounts receivable of the Companies.
16) List of all inventory.

[This section is a detailed financial review of any type of company]

E.   Financial Information

1)   Auditors' inquiry letters to attorneys of the Company and replies for
     the last three years •.

   Information about:
   a)   Significant accounting policies and procedures.
   b)   Cost accounting systems.
   c)   Intercompany payables and receivables.
   d)   Allocation methods for overhead and indirect labour.
   e)   Variance reports.
   f)   Operating expenses by significant category.
   g)   Expense budgets.
   h)   Cost allocations from parent, including policies and procedures.

   Information about:

   i)   Price list and recent/expected price changes.
   j)   List of significant customers ranked by sales.
   k)   Customer profitability information.
   l)   Details of agreements with sales agents and distributors.

   Information about accounts receivable, including:

   m)   Accounts receivable aging reports for all financial statement periods.
   n)   Accounts receivable reconciliations to the general ledger for all
        financial statement periods.
   o)   List of all disputed accounts as of most recent balance sheet date.
   p)   Analysis of account receivable write-offs for each income statement
        presented.
   q)   List of any receivables with employees, affiliates or other related
        parties.
   r)   Refunds, returns, credit memo and discounts.
   s)   Schedule of accounts receivable by category.
   t)   Credit policy.

u)   Allowance of uncollectible accounts and past write-offs.

v)   Collection procedures.

Information about inventories, including:

w)   Results of most recent physical inventory observation.

x)   List of inventory on consignment.

y)   Inventory obsolescence reserve for each period presented.

z)   List of any minimum of adverse purchase commitments.

(aa)   Cost of goods sold by product and component.

(bb)   Scrap/rework reports

(cc)   Backlog reports.

(dd)   Inventory balances by location and product line.

(ee) Assigned inventory/consignments.

(ff)   Obsolete or slow-moving inventory.

(gg) Inventory write-offs.

(hh) Book to physical adjustments.

Information about securities and other investments, including:

(ii)   List of all investments showing name, percentage ownership, carrying cost, current market value and method of valuation (cost or equity).

Information about:

(jj)   Prepaid expenses and other assets.

(kk)   Detailed schedule of accounts payable and accrued expenses detail.

(ll)   Accounts payable aging schedule.

(mm) Schedule of roll forward of reserves.

(nn)   Detail of reserves held in subsidiaries and overseas entities.

(oo)   List of other current and non-current liabilities.

(pp)   Approved suppliers of raw materials and purchasing policy.

(qq)   Allowable trade discounts.

(rr)   Schedules of fixed assets, including date acquired, original cost, accumulated depreciation and net book value.

(ss)   General description of office and production facilities.

(tt)   Depreciation methods used for book and tax purposes.

(uu)   Historical, current and planned capital expenditures.

(vv)   Historical maintenance expenses.

Information about notes payable, and long and short-term debt including:

(ww) Bank or other lender, terms, liens, original and current balance, security, compensating balance requirements, interest rates, payment terms, copies of loan documents.

(xx) Any conversion features.

(yy) Any restrictive clauses.

(zz) Restrictions on dividends.

(aaa) Officer and employee loans.

2) All material correspondence with lenders during the last three years, including all compliance reports or certificates submitted by the Company or any Subsidiary or its independents public accountants.

3) Federal and state tax returns of the Company since its inception.

4) Copies of all notices of assessment, proposed assessments or deficiencies from any federal, state or local taxing authority.

5) Copies of any rulings, concessions or the like which have been obtained from any federal, state or foreign taxing authority and which may apply to Company's current or future operations (or to tax years not yet finally audited).

6) A brief description of any disputed tax liability with any federal, state, foreign or other taxing body.

7) List of states in which the Company is doing business or has employees or property.

8) Copies of any tax-sharing agreements, tax provisions or indemnities which apply to the Company as a result of prior acquisitions or divestitures.

9) Most recent year's sales and property tax returns and assessment notices.

10) Tax reconciliations or reserve analysis prepared by the Company's firm.

11) List of acquisitions or dispositions which the Company has made in the last six years.

12) List of open taxable periods.

13) The last three years' financial statements and latest interim financials (balance sheet, income statement, and cash flows), audited if possible.

14) Auditors' letters to management of the Company for the last three years.

15) Financial projections or budgets for the current and the next year. Explanation of key assumptions in the plan and any unusual or

nonrecurring items. Include any recent analysis of budget to actual results.

16) Any recent valuations of the company or any other investment banker reports.

Product and marketing brochures, or a listing of products/services:

a) Market share by product.

b) Sales dollars and units by product line.

c) Cost of goods sold and gross profit by product.

d) Discontinued or obsolete product.

e) Revenues by customer and geographic region.

f) Lost customers/new customers/customer turnover.

g) Description of sales force, including sales offices and facilities.

h) Sales and Marketing plan and budget.

i) Sales agents/distributors ranked by sales.

j) Consignment sales.

k) Customer contracts, proposed and executed.

Information about property, plant and equipment including:

l) Details of fixed assets and depreciation by category such as land, buildings, machinery, etc.

m) Any liens against property.

Information about property, plant and equipment including:

n) Detail listing of significant amounts and a description of the nature of the balances.

o) Description of any potential liabilities which are not recorded on the balance sheet.

p) Description of any EPA, product liability, or other legal claims whether currently active or potentially active in the future.

q) Description of any insurance the company has to cover such matters. Information about equity including:

r) Details of the capital structure.

s) Percent ownership breakdown on primary and on fully diluted shares.

[Sections F, G, H are a detailed financial examination of product industry and retail companies and are drawn from a pharmaceutical retailer's precedent]

F.   Financial Information

1) For last 2 years, ● annual financial statements, including all notes required by generally accepted accounting principles and, if no notes, provide details of all ● significant accounting policies. For all such statements, provide accounting details including detailed trial balances.

2) The current fiscal year's monthly interim financial statements to ●, as well as any monthly or other interim reports prepared concerning financial or operating matters by or for management or the directors of ●.

3) Details of any intangible assets shown on balance sheets in item (a).

4) If not already provided in item (a) above, provide schedule of fixed assets showing cost, accumulated depreciation and net book value for last 2 fiscal year ends and as at ●.

5) Monthly statement of changes in financial position for each of the last 24 months.

6) Breakdown of statement of income for past 2 years and for current fiscal year to ● showing sales and gross profit margin for each of the following categories:

    a) product category
    b) geographic area
    c) retail outlet
    d) retail outlet by product category.

7) For most recently completed fiscal year and for current fiscal year to ●, provide the following information relating to [*prescription*] services:

    a) number of [*prescriptions filled*] by each retail outlet annually
    b) [*usual and customary dispensing fee*] charged by each retail outlet and by geographic region.

8) For last fiscal year and for current fiscal year to ●, ranking of retail stores based on sales and profits.

9) Cost details of top 100 [*prescription*] products for both the most recently completed fiscal year and current fiscal year to ●.

10) For past 2 years, provide applicable annual financial/business plan and for the current fiscal year, provide current financial/business plan broken down by month or by quarter, including financial projections. Provide current business plan, including financial projections for next 3 years.

11) Provide current fiscal year's forecast.

12) For the 4 months ending •, provide actual capital expenditures by programme. For remainder of current fiscal year, provide schedule of planned capital expenditures segregated between committed and not-committed expenditures. For current fiscal year, provide copies of all business case analysis prepared in support of capital expenditures. Provide details of any capital spending programme which is expected to extend beyond the end of the current fiscal year.

13) Provide details of inventory counts completed during last fiscal year and to •, including book value of inventory pre-count, counted value and difference (under/over) by each location counted. Provide details of basis on which inventory is counted (retail method or cost). Where cost method is used, provide details on how cost was determined.

14) Breakdown of expenses relating to head office.

15) Federal and Ontario corporate and income tax returns for last 4 years.

16) Notices of Assessment for last 4 years.

17) Notices of Appeals pending for any fiscal year.

18) All management letters from accountants.

G. Regulatory Matters–drawn from a pharmacy–to be amended based on specific business involved

1) Copies of appropriate accreditation for each store under the • *Act.* (Ontario) or • *Act* as the case may be.

2) Evidence that Company is a corporation exempt (that is, a grand fathered corporation) from the share ownership restrictions contained in the • *Act* (Ontario).

3) Evidence that each store has a designated manager who is duly licensed under the provisions of • *Act* or the • (Ontario) and the name of, copy of the pharmacy licence for and applicable store number for each such designated manager.

4) All letters of opinion and other comments by counsel on the operations of •.

5) Copies of all communications from the Ontario College of • and the • to • and communications by • to •, including details of any past or pending disciplinary matters.

6) Regulatory and enforcement filings in any province or federally, including:

    a)   all filings, reports, correspondence and other items relating to regulatory and licensing agencies, whether domestic or foreign, other than as disclosed above relating to pharmacy licensure.

    b)   a schedule of all governmental and/or regulatory approvals, grants, licenses and permits, together with copies of such approvals, grants, licenses and permits, other than as disclosed above relating to pharmacy licensure.

7)   Undertakings given to any governmental or regulatory authority or courts.

8)   Schedule of governmental approvals, grants, licenses and permits, other than as disclosed above relating to pharmacy licensure, including, without limitation:

    a)   business licenses

    b)   provincial sales tax permits

    c)   goods and services tax registration numbers

    d)   food, drug or health permits

    e)   environmental licenses.

9)   All violation or non-compliance notices from federal, provincial or local regulatory agencies which were sent to ● or to third-party subcontractors with whom ● engages or has engaged in business.

10)   Summary of procedures, rules and regulations in place for control of pharmaceutical products in each retail store.

11)   Details of the type of pharmacy system in place in each retail store. For each applicable pharmacy system, details of whether ● has implemented standards.

12)   Details of third parties who are linked electronically with ● retail stores.

H.   Store Locations and Distribution and Supply Arrangements–*drawn from retail business–amend/revise as needed*

1)   List of each retail store location, store number, municipal address, legal description and name of [*on-site pharmacist(s)*] *and manager, tenure of present* [*on-site pharmacist(s)*] and manager and hours of operation.

2)   List of distribution centres, including municipal address for each distribution centre.

3)   Summary of distribution and inventory arrangements for supplying and shipping inventory to all retail stores, including any arrangements

where [*Holdco*] or its subsidiaries or affiliates are the suppliers, and for all such arrangements, provide details of these supply/inventory arrangements, including financial and pricing arrangements (including, preferential or special pricing, terms or other arrangements), trade terms and conditions of supply, nature of inventory supplied and copies of any written agreements relating to such arrangements.

4) Schematic of distribution process.

5) List of all major suppliers for last 4 fiscal years and summaries of purchases by each such supplier.

L. Financing Documents

1) List of financial institutions with which ● has relations.

2) Documents and agreements evidencing borrowings or available borrowings of ●, including loan and credit agreements, security agreements, debentures, other bank loans, promissory notes and any other evidences of indebtedness together with copies of all loan documentation and list of all covenants, ratios and undertakings to the lenders, whether institutional or non-institutional.

3) Mortgages, pledges, guarantees, other evidence of liens or letters of credit securing the obligations of ●.

4) Schedule of liens or encumbrances on the assets of ●.

5) Any guarantees issued by ●.

6) Any guarantees, comfort letters or other financial support given or issued on behalf of ● by third parties, ● including any comfort letters to suppliers, guarantees on real property or equipment leases, etc.

7) Any loan agreements or security agreements between ● and ● relating to loans or support by ● to ●. Where no written agreement exists, provide a summary of these loan and security arrangements.

8) Documents and agreements relating to credit card arrangements and Interac arrangements for retail stores.

9) Breakdown of fees, if any, charged by ● to ● or by ● to ● for last 4 years and to-date in the current fiscal year and copies of all agreements, documents and contracts evidencing services or arrangements relating to payment of such fees or charges. Where no written agreement exists, provide a summary of the arrangements with respect to such payments, including a breakdown of the nature of the services rendered and the fees attributable to such services.

10) Any letters between ● and its lenders.

11) Notices of any default under provisions of any financing arrangement.

J. Accounting Practices and Policies

1) Revenue recognition policy. Sales return policy.
2) Policy on accruals for vacations, audit expenses, AR reserves, Inventory reserves, other reserves.
3) Policy on inventory valuation.
4) Credit policy.
5) Capitalization of any expenses, particularly [*development of software*].
6) Description of any other deferred revenue or expenses or accrued revenues or expenses.

K. Personal Property

1) List of all material plant, equipment, machinery, rolling stock, trade fixtures and all other chattels used by Holdco in the Company operation indicating location, serial number, general character and condition, other than leasehold improvements in retail locations, supply depots, distribution centres and warehouses;
2) In those cases where Holdco does not own but uses or leases major items of equipment, provide the name of the owners, and terms of usage including copies of the applicable lease or licence agreement and if no written agreement exists, provide details of the major terms governing the usage thereof;
3) Summary of arrangements in respect of point-of-sale terminals, including copies of lease agreements, licence agreements and other agreements, if leased or owned by third parties;
4) Details of all inventory control systems and copies of all documents and agreements relating to such inventory control systems; and
5) Summary of arrangements for store security and distribution and warehouse security, including copies of any contracts or documents relating to such security arrangements.

L. Real Property

1) Copies of all real property leases, offers to lease and a summary of lease arrangements in the case of oral agreements, for real property leased by • on behalf of Company including stores, administrative offices, warehouses, distribution centres, etc. whether • is the head tenant or subtenant;

2)   To the extent they are in your possession, drawings/plans of store sites;

3)   Notices from any landlord regarding any breach of a lease or notice to cancel or terminate a lease;

4)   Summary of details of any proposed store closings or openings for the next twenty-four (24) months; and

5)   All drawings, plans and reports related to store modifications, upgrades or construction, pending or proposed.

[This section is applicable for a detailed review for a small technology company]

M. Intellectual Property

1)   A list of all patents, copyrights, trademarks, service marks, certification marks, industrial designs, domain names (whether registered, pending or otherwise) (collectively, the **"IP"**) held by Holdco for use in Company's business and operations as well as any trade secrets which relate to Company products;

2)   All **"cease and desist"** and other letters or notices or documents received within the past three (3) years asserting claims against Company and/or Diamond for IP infringement, alleged or actual, and copies of replies thereto;

3)   All **"cease and desist"** and other letters or notices or documents forwarded by or on behalf of ● in respect of Company, or Company itself, regarding infringement by third parties of the IP of ● which relate to Company;

4)   Agreements, licensing agreements, agreements relating to technology or software owned, licensed or used by Company or in which Company has any interest, including service agreements. With respect to such rights which have been acquired from third parties, including rights of licence, provide all documents concerning such rights' chain of title, including licence agreement, assignment agreements, settlement agreements, opinions of counsel, etc. and with respect to IP rights created by employees, all documents transferring such rights to Company;

5)   Written descriptions of all inventions and trade secrets material to Company. With respect to rights relating to such inventions and trade secrets which have been acquired from third parties, all documents concerning such rights' chain of title, including assignment agreements, settlement agreements, opinions of counsel, etc., and with respect to inventions and trade secrets created by employees, all documents transferring such rights to Diamond;

6) All registrations, applications, licences or other agreements relating to any technology owned, or used, by Company, including affidavits of continuing use and registration renewals;

7) All documents and files relating to the history and extent of use of IP rights, including those relating to the exercise of quality control over any IP licences or other licences granted by Diamond to third parties which relate to Company; and

8) Details of any private label products manufactured, sold or distributed by, or on behalf of, Company including any reports/analyses of private label programmes, whether past, current or future-oriented. Summary of annual sales of private label products for the past two (2) years and for current fiscal year to date.

N. Research & Development

1) List and description of all R&D programs:

   a) expected completion date
   b) expected product launch date
   c) budget broken down by calendar year
   d) names of project team members
   e) number of full-time employees
   f) future capital expenditure

2) Describe the policies or guidelines for patent application and copyrights vs. proprietary know-how.

3) Identify and describe any instance in which source codes have been disclosed to persons other than company employees.

4) Provide engineering design for specific products, including a list of all the components and the suppliers.

5) Provide data on testing of the various components used in the specific product.

6) Historical information on service, maintenance, and customer complaints of all existing products in the market.

7) Clinical studies, data, and copies of all reports and scientific publications on any.

8) Resumes or summary of background for all R&D employees, including number of years with the company.

9) Description of R&D strategy and facilities.

10) List of products previously developed.

11) Joint development arrangements and in-licensing agreements.

12) What is the regulatory approval strategy and rationale regarding new products? Status of any regulatory approval pending and any plans to obtain regulatory approval. Estimated time and costs in obtaining the approval. What are the competitive advantages?

O. Information Systems

1) Description of key business applications, including vendor name, product name, version number and number of licenses. Key applications vary by business unit, but typically include supply chain, manufacturing, finance, R&D, regulatory, clinical, quality and human resource packages.

2) Describe software applications that are FDA validated or require compliance with other regulations or policies, including ISO 9000, EPA, OSHA and HIPAA. Address implications of electronic records management and electronic signatures. Describe privacy, security, change management and document management policies.

3) Description of IT department including size of the organization and scope of responsibilities.

4) Description of data network infrastructure, including local and wide area network components. Include vendor name and equipment models for hubs, switches and routers, NIC cards, protocols, remote access and cable plant details. Provide address and phone number for all facilities.

5) Description of voice network infrastructure including vendor name and equipment models and software versions for PBX voice switches and voicemail systems. Include information about equipment locations, dialing plans, voice networking, voice-response units and other call-center related technologies.

6) Describe electronic messaging infrastructure including vendor names and hardware and software products and version numbers used for electronic mail, calendaring and collaboration. Include description of mail-enabled applications and interface design supporting Internet-based (SMTP) messaging.

7) Description of all information technology related contracts, including vendor hardware and software purchasing agreements, maintenance contracts and service contracts. Include contracts for long distance

calling, telephone credit cards, audio and video conferencing services, wide-area network services and IT consulting agreements.

8) Description of client and server hardware and software environment and standards including PC workstation models and operating system(s), server models (file, print, database, application) and operating system(s) and system/utility software tools. Include counts of workstations and servers by location.

9) Describe intranet, Intranet and web infrastructure environment including vendor name and hardware and software products and version numbers used for firewalls, web servers, application servers and name servers.

10) Description of software development environment and standards in use including languages, methodologies and development tools.

P. Inventory

1) Schedule of inventory type, stage, amount, condition and location as of a recent date. Is any of the inventory on consignment? Is the inventory pledged as collateral for any obligation? Does the Company receive price protection or obsolescence protection on the inventory?

2) What has the Company's returned goods experience been for the past three years?

3) Description of inventory practices, including:

   a) Costing methods.
   b) Frequency and timing of costing methods.
   c) Standards for obsolescence.
   d) Frequency of physical inventory.
   e) Other inventory practices.

Q. Litigation

1) Description and copies of any outstanding order, injunction, decree, or judgment of any court or any other administrative or regulatory body or any arbitration tribunal binding upon the Company or any of its property.

2) Description and current status of all actions, suits, investigations, or proceeding by or before any courts, arbitration tribunal, or administrative or regulatory body to which the Company is a party.

3) Description and status of any threatened or possible suits based upon the best knowledge of the Company and its officers.

4) Auditors' inquiry letters to attorneys retained by the Company concerning litigation and attorneys' responses thereto since inception.

5) A chronological history of all suits, actions, or threatened actions which have led to settlements either in or out of court with a description of each dispute and the resolution of the same.

R. Material Agreements

1) All distribution, equipment leasing, consumer financing, marketing, servicing, network and advertising agreements, contracts and licenses and any other documents material to the business or affairs of ● or its subsidiaries, if any.

2) All management or consulting agreements.

3) All agreements relating to the products of ● such as agreements with suppliers, distributors.

4) Operating leases or agreements with respect to store security alarms, door control system for shrinkage, telephone system, electricity and any other operating agreements pertaining to equipment normally required to operate the business of ●.

5) All documents relating to recent (3 years) acquisitions or divestitures (of shares or assets).

6) All agreements with agents of ●, outside consultants or other professionals.

7) All agreements between ● and a related party, including its subsidiaries, if any, other affiliates, officers or directors, as well as management and service agreements.

8) All change in ownership agreements, voting agreements or other agreements tied to ●'s direct or indirect ownership of securities or rights thereof of companies that are not wholly owned subsidiaries.

9) All joint ventures or partnership agreements to which ● is a party. All documents establishing or evidencing a partnership relationship between I and any other entity and all documents setting forth the terms of such relationship(s).

10) Any contract containing an unusual restriction, obligation or covenant on "**doing business**" of ●.

11) Any contract the terms of which are altered in the event of a change of control.

12) Forms and standard licensing, distribution or franchise agreements of
●.

13) All material agreements to which ● is a party.

S.   Equipment Leases

1)   Obtain list and copies of all equipment leases including details of the subject equipment.

2)   Summarize major terms of equipment leases (ie. capitalized value, monthly payments, term, maintenance costs, lessee repair obligations, termination rights, etc.).

3)   Determine whether lessee may assign with or without lessor consent, and ascertain whether there are any conditions attaching to a consent (ie. processing fee, rent increases).

4)   Confirm whether lessee has an option to purchase leased equipment and, if so, at what value.

5)   Determine whether lessors have registered leases under applicable personal property security laws.

T.   Employment and Labour Matters

1)   Schedule showing name and age for each executive officer, including the position and office held by each such person, date employment commenced, a brief summary of the responsibilities of each executive officer, salaries/bonuses paid for past 2 years or payable, details of severance/termination arrangements whether written or oral, and details of all previous positions held in ● or [*Holdco*]. Where a written employment contract exists, provide a copy of such contract.

2)   Schedule showing name, age and position held by all key employees who are not executive officers but who make or are expected to make significant contributions to the business of ●, including date employment for each key employee commenced, a brief summary of the responsibilities of each key employee, salaries/bonuses paid for past 2 years or payable, details of severance/termination arrangements whether written or oral and details of all positions previously held in ● or [*Holdco*]. Where a written employment contract exists, provide a copy of such contract.

3)   Schedule of all employees of ● categorized by employee type/function (for example, total number of pharmacists, clerks, distribution centre employees, etc.)

4) Schedule of all employees of • categorized by employment type (for example, total number of salaried and hourly employees and total number of part-time and full-time employees).

5) Resume for each of the directors, executive officers and key employees including each person's principal occupation and employment during past five years.

6) Details of arrangements for remuneration or compensation of directors of •.

7) Schedule of names of all other employees of • not disclosed above, including position held, employment responsibilities, salary and benefits paid to each employee, date employment commenced and, where applicable, copies of all written employment contracts, letters or other documents evidencing terms and conditions of employment.

8) All other employment or consulting agreements or understandings, including any employee bonus arrangements and/or related perks, sales incentive plans, executive financial counselling and senior management incentive plans.

9) Collective agreements and history of grievances or labour problems.

10) Union communication file and current status of any current or pending union negotiations.

11) Pension plan information. Employee benefit plan documents, including trust instruments, plan summaries, stock option plans of employees and officers, financial statements and plan evaluations for the most recent plan year for the pension and benefit plans of •, to the extent available, and the most recent actuarial evaluation report.

12) All communications to employees relating to any of the employee benefits plans, pension plans or summary plan descriptions for past five years.

13) All employee handbooks or personnel policy manuals.

14) All Occupational Health and Safety, Safety committee and any inspection of facilities minutes, notices, citations and/or correspondence.

15) All documentation relating to pay-equity including any governmental compliance filings and/or communications.

16) Documentation relating to any unfair labour practice complaint or claims pending before any Labour Relations Board, pending labour strikes or other material labour troubles, etc.

17) Organizational charts for management and administrative offices showing organization to at least the district manager level.

18) Summary of indebtedness of directors and senior executives to ● which shows amount of indebtedness, terms and conditions of repayment and copies of all documents and agreements evidencing such indebtedness or the terms and conditions of such indebtedness.

19) List of all subsidies and governmental assistance programs in which ● participates including the documentation related thereto.

20) Undertakings given to any governmental or other regulatory authority.

21) Workers' Compensation history of claims, experience ratings, assessments for past four years.

U. Marketing and Advertising Matters

1) Notice of any investigation, complaint or other breaches relating to provincial advertising regulations or *Competition Act* (Canada).

2) Summary of advertising and promotion practices of ●.

3) Copy of advertising black book, if any.

4) Form of advertising approval procedure.

V. Business Practices & Compliance [drawn from medical supplies company]

1) Business Practices/Foreign Corrupt Practices Act Compliance:

   a) All correspondence, minutes of meetings with public officials, internal reports regarding investigations or hearings relating to Company's business practices, relationships with customers, doctors and other medical practitioners, grants, sponsored trips, seminars, clinical trials, entertainment and gifts.

   b) All written opinions received from in-house or outside lawyers relating to Company's business practices, relationships with customers, doctors and other medical practitioners, grants, sponsored trips, seminars, entertainment and gifts.

   c) All internal guidelines or policies relating to rebates or discounts and all written opinions received from in-house or outside lawyers thereto.

   d) All letter agreements/contracts with doctors and other medical practitioners under which doctors or medical practitioners receive monetary or non-monetary compensation for services rendered to Company, or for other reasons.

   e) All letter agreements/contracts with agents, distributors, consultants and other intermediaries under which they receive monetary or non-monetary compensation for directly or indirectly obtaining or retaining business for Company, including but not limited to finder's fees.

f) A list of all Company sponsored seminars/congresses with a copy of the programs of such seminars for the last three years; the budget allocated for such seminars and the details of the payments made to the participants.

g) For the last three years, a list of Company's top ten customers in each country with details of all entertainment, trips, gifts or other monetary or non-monetary compensation granted to these customers or professionals working for such customers.

h) For the last three years, a list of all grants, sponsored trips, seminars, entertainment, and gifts granted to customers, professionals working for such customers, and public officials with a value of more than $1,000.

i) A list of all **"political contributions"** made by Company during the last three years.

2) Export Controls:

a) All internal guidelines or policies relating to the export of products.

b) All correspondence, minutes of meetings with public officials, internal reports, opinions received from in-house or outside lawyers regarding investigations or hearings relating to Company's violation of export control laws.

c) A list of and a copy of all agreements with agents, distributors, consultants and other intermediaries doing business or helping to secure or retain business in Cuba, Libya, North Korea, Iran, Iraq, Syria, Sudan, and Middle East countries.

d) All commercial files relating to bids, offers or contracts of more than $50,000 in Cuba, Libya, North Korea, Iran, Iraq, Syria, Sudan, and Middle East countries.

e) A list of all outside consultants (such as lawyers and auditors) which have written opinions or provided support in establishing or retaining business in Cuba, Libya, North Korea, Iran, Iraq, Syria, Sudan, and Middle East countries, and a copy of the written opinions provided to Company.

f) All reports or studies (including any projections) relating to management, product development, financial, business, operations, or marketing or strategic plans or programs for or with respect to the Company which have been prepared by (a) management consulting or similar firms, (b) independent accountants or (c) the Company's management.

g) Copies of all studies, surveys, analyses and reports which were prepared by or for the Company or any Subsidiary analyzing market shares, competition, markets, potentials for sales growth or expansion into product or geographic markets.

h) Copies of company's ethics policies and related training materials.

i) Determine whether organization has an ethics committee or function, or other process for integrating its ethical standards into the operations of the business.

W. Environmental, Health & Safety

1) Copies of any government inspection reports, citations (including those settled or withdrawn), orders, demands, judgments, or civil or criminal penalties by any foreign, federal, state or local agency or any other damage assessments or claims under applicable environmental, health or safety laws since the Company's inception (or the past five years, whichever is less).

2) A description of the types of (1) wastes generated and how these are disposed and, (2) copies of any logs and reports kept with respect to generation, storage, treatment or disposal of these materials and wastes.

3) Copies of any logs and reports kept with respect to worker health and safety, including but not limited to OSHA logs, risk assessments, or employee complaints, including any ergonomics complaints, and any materials used or stored on site, monitoring results (including noise monitoring), indicating that regulatory threshold levels have been exceeded.

4) Copies of any environmental, health or safety compliance schedule, consent order or administrative order to which any facility is currently subject, and any notice that a facility is not in compliance with applicable environmental, health, or safety laws.

5) All existing environmental, safety or health licenses, permits, or approvals, permits and variances relating to emissions, discharge, hazardous material, waste disposal, noise, etc., which presently exist.

6) Environmental and/or health and safety audits, surveys, investigations, consultant reports, or similar reports or analyses on properties owned, leased, formerly owned or leased, or otherwise utilized by the Company.

7) Any notices of liability or potential liability under state, local, or national cleanup orders, including but not limited to Superfund or any of its state counterparts.

8) Copies of all internal or external environmental, safety, and health assessment findings and reports.

9) Describe the processes or operations at facilities presently or previously operated by the Company (or by others on property presently or previously owned by the Company) which generate, treat, store, transport or dispose any toxic or other hazardous materials or where any of these activities are suspected to have taken place in the past.

10) List any environmental notices, citations, fines, penalties, superfund notices or determinations, or other regulatory citations.

Form 11: **Letter of Intent as an Ongoing Concern**

LETTERHEAD OF PURCHASER

PRIVATE AND CONFIDENTIAL

Date

●

and to:

●

and to:

●

Re: Proposed Acquisition of Business

The purpose of this letter is to set forth certain nonbinding understandings and certain binding agreements among ● ("●", ● ("●", ● ("●" (collectively, the "**Vendor**") and ● ("●" [*consider who should be bound by terms*] with respect to the possible acquisition of the operating assets, undertaking, property and assets of the business conducted by the Vendor, and any other company controlled by, controlling or under common control by any of those companies (the "**Purchased Business**").

PART 1: NONBINDING PROVISIONS

Sections 1 to 8 inclusive of this letter (collectively, the "**Nonbinding Provisions**") reflect the parties mutual understanding of the matters described therein, but each party acknowledges that the Nonbinding Provisions are not intended to create or constitute any legally binding obligations among them, and no party shall have any liability to any other party with respect to the Nonbinding Provisions. The parties intend, subject to the provisions of this letter, to work towards execution of a definitive agreement reflecting their understandings in the proposed purchase and sale of the Purchased Business (the **"Definitive Agreement"**), and other related documents. If the Definitive Agreement is not prepared, authorized, executed or delivered for any reason, no party shall have any liability to any other party based upon, arising from, or relating to the said Nonbinding Provisions.

1.1)   Basic Transaction

● would acquire from ● and ● the Purchased Business as a going concern, save and except only for agreed excluded assets. At closing, ● would assume certain specific agreed operational liabilities relating to the Purchased Business incurred in the ordinary course of business. The parties intend that the closing of the proposed transaction would occur on or before ● ●, ● (the **"Closing Date"**).

1.2)   Proposed Purchase Price

Based on the information known to ● on the date hereof, the total consideration for the Purchased Assets would be ● (Cdn$●) (the **"Purchase Price"**), of which:

a) $● (less any deposit previously paid) would be paid to ● and ● in cash at the Closing; and

b) $● would be delivered to a mutually acceptable escrow agent as security for any undisclosed liabilities and breaches of representations, warranties and covenants, such escrow agreement to be as further provided in section 8.

The Purchase Price is based on the combined equity (as herein defined) of the Vendor being in the aggregate, at least, Cdn$●. The Vendor would support the Purchase Price and combined equity by delivery of audited financial statements of the Purchased Business as at ●, ● on or before ●, ● (see Section 16 below) and the preparation of Closing Date audited financial statements (see Section 16 below). As used herein **"combined equity"** means the sum of the shareholder's equity of the Vendor determined in accordance with generally accepted accounting principles.

The Purchaser understands:

a)   the purchase price will be allocated as follows:

i) $●–●; and

    ii) $●–●;

  b) After the ●, ● audit is completed, the Vendor would be entitled to pay out an amount equal to an amount equal to any amount over and above Cdn$● combined equity amount; and

  c) after the Closing Date audit is completed, the Vendor would be entitled to receive an amount equal to any amount over and above the Cdn$● combined equity amount as at the Closing Date from the Purchaser within fifteen (15) days thereof.

1.3) Due Diligence

The Purchaser has commenced, and intends to continue, its due diligence investigation of the Purchased Business, including financial, commercial, marketing, employee, legal, taxation, systems, regulatory and environmental matters. Such due diligence may continue up to and including Closing Date, however, it is expected that most of the Purchaser's due diligence will be completed by the time the Definitive Agreement is signed.

1.4) Proposed Form of Agreement

The parties intend promptly to begin negotiating [*include specifics*] to reach a written Definitive Agreement containing comprehensive representations, warranties, indemnities, conditions and agreements by ●, ● and ●, on a joint and several basis.

1.5) Conditions to Proposed Transaction

The Definitive Agreement, if successfully negotiated, would provide that the proposed transaction would be subject to terms and conditions including, but not limited to, the following:

  a) combined equity of the Purchased Business shall be, at least, Cdn$●;

  b) receipt of all necessary consents, approvals, exemptions and authorizations of governmental bodies, lenders, lessors and other third parties;

  c) the representations and warranties given by the Vendor and ● in the Definitive Agreement remain true on the Closing Date;

  d) due observance and performance by the Vendor and ● of all their covenants in the Definitive Agreement;

  e) absence of any material adverse change in the business, financial condition, prospects, assets or operations of the Purchased Business since ●, ●;

f)   absence of pending or threatened litigation regarding the Definitive Agreement or the transactions to be contemplated thereby; and

g)   delivery of customary legal opinions, closing certificates and other usual closing documentation.

1.6) Proposed Employment Arrangements

Prior to the execution of the Definitive Agreement, each of • and • would have entered into employment agreements (including, two year non-competition covenants from termination of employment) with the Purchaser, on terms and conditions satisfactory to the Purchaser • and • respectively, each acting reasonably.

Subject to the Purchaser's review of the employment history and wage and salary structure of the Vendor's employees (approximately •), the Purchaser would offer employment to such employees. The mechanics of such hiring (employees resigning at closing and being rehired, etc.) will be agreed to in the Definitive Agreement.

• would execute a consulting agreement with the Purchaser to consult with the Purchaser for an aggregate of • years/months during the first year after the Closing Date, such consulting fees to be based on approximately $• per annum, plus authorized expenses and GST.

1.7) Proposed Non-Competition Agreement

At the Closing, the Vendor and • would enter into a • year non-competition agreement, pursuant to which each such party would agree that such party and such party's affiliates would not compete with the Purchaser or the Purchased Business for three years after the Closing Date in Canada, and containing confidentiality and other customary provisions.

1.8) Proposed Escrow Agreement

At the Closing, the Purchaser, the Vendor and • would enter into an escrow agreement which would contain provisions for an escrow with •, Solicitors for • of Cdn$• of the Purchase Price to secure the Purchaser against undisclosed liabilities, misrepresentations and breaches of warranties, covenants and agreements (including, without limitation, the failure of the Purchased Business to have a combined equity of, at least, Cdn$• by the Vendor and •. The said escrow amount would be held for a period of fifteen days after the Closing Date audited statements (see section 16 below) have been provided to the Purchaser. The escrow funds would be invested (within prudent limits) at the direction of the Vendor and •. Any costs relating to the said escrow of funds would be shared on a 50/50 basis between the Purchaser as to 50% and the Vendor and • as to 50%.

PART 2: BINDING PROVISIONS

Upon execution by the parties of this letter, the following sections • to • of Part II (collectively, the "**Binding Provisions**") will constitute the legally binding and enforceable agreement of the parties hereto (in recognition of the significant costs to be borne by each of the parties in pursuing this proposed transaction and further in consideration of their mutual undertakings as to the matters described herein).

2.1) Definitive Agreement

The Purchaser and its counsel shall be responsible for preparing the initial draft of the Definitive Agreement and required related documents. Subject to the final sentence of section • below, the Purchaser and • shall negotiate in good faith to arrive at a mutually acceptable Definitive Agreement and related documents for approval, execution and delivery on the earliest reasonably practicable date (anticipated to be on or about •, •).

2.2) Deposit

On your acceptance of this letter, the Purchaser will provide to [*Escrow*] a deposit of Cdn$•. The Deposit, with any accrued interest, shall be returned to the Purchaser (i) if the financial statements delivered by the Vendor to the Purchaser at the time of acceptance of this letter (see section • below) do not substantiate, in all material respects, the selected balance sheet information provided by the Vendor (as at •, •) to the Purchaser on •, •; (ii) if the audited financial statements as at •, • (see Section • below) do not materially substantiate the revenue forecast delivered by the Vendor to the Purchaser at the time of acceptance of this letter; (iii) if the combined equity of the Purchased Business is not, at least, Cdn$•, as supported by •, • audited financial statements; or (iv) if the Purchaser does not proceed with the proposed purchase of the Purchased Business because the conditions of closing in its favour in the Definitive Agreement have not been fulfilled or performed prior to closing. On closing, if the Purchaser proceeds with the proposed purchase, the Deposit, and any accrued interest, will be applied against the Purchase Price. Otherwise the Deposit will be forfeited to the Vendor, including if the Purchaser determines not to proceed with the purchase prior to a Definitive Agreement being signed unless its reason for doing so is related to one of the items specified in this Section •.

2.3) Access

The Vendor and • shall provide to the Purchaser complete access to all facilities, books and records of the Purchased Business, and shall cause the directors, employees, accountants, and other agents and representatives of the Vendor to cooperate fully with the Purchaser and its representatives in connection with the Purchaser's due diligence investigation of the Purchased Business and the Purchased Assets and all related contracts, liabilities, operations and records. It is understood and agreed by the Purchaser that it will conduct its due diligence so as not to interfere with the Purchased Business and it will not talk to employees of the Vendor (other than ●) [*consultants under Accountants in Section* ●] without the prior consent of the Vendor, such consent not to be unreasonably withheld. All inspection of the premises and inventory of the Purchased Business shall be done after working hours. The Vendor will make an off-site data room of all relevant Purchased Business materials available to the Purchaser and its representatives. The Purchaser shall be under no obligation to continue with its due diligence investigation or negotiations regarding the Definitive Agreement if, at any time, the results of its due diligence investigation are not satisfactory to it for any reason in its sole discretion of the Purchaser's board decides it is not in its best interests to proceed for any reason at its sole discretion.

2.4) Exclusive Dealing

The Vendor and ● shall not, directly or indirectly, through any representative or otherwise, solicit or entertain offers from, negotiate with or in any manner encourage, discuss, accept or consider any proposal of any other person relating to the acquisition of the undertaking, property or assets of the Purchased Business, in whole or in part, or of all or any of the shares of the Vendor, whether through direct purchase, merger, consolidation or other business combination (other than sales of inventory in the ordinary course).

2.5) Conduct of Business

Until the Definitive Agreement has been duly executed and delivered by all of the parties or the Binding Provisions have been terminated pursuant to Section ●, the Vendor shall conduct the Purchased Business only in the ordinary course, and not engage in any extraordinary transactions with the Purchaser's prior consent, including:

a)   not disposing of any assets of the Purchased Business, except in the ordinary course of business;

b)   not materially increasing the annual level of compensation of any employees of the Purchased Business *and* not granting any unusual or extraordinary bonuses, benefits or other forms of direct or indirect compensation to any employees (save and except any permitted payments from amounts over and above the $• combined equity amount (see Section •) above;

c)   not increasing, terminating, amending or otherwise modifying any plan for the benefit of employees;

d)   not borrowing any funds, under existing credit lines or otherwise, except as reasonably necessary for the ordinary operation of the Purchased Business in a manner, and in amounts, in keeping with historical practices (save and except to accommodate any permitted payments from amounts over and above the $• combined equity amount (see Section • above); and

e)   not enter into any material contractual arrangements for the Purchased Business, other than in the ordinary course of business.

2.6)   Disclosure/Public Announcements

Except as and to the extent required by law or as advised by counsel is required or advisable under Canadian securities laws, without the prior written consent of all parties, no party shall, and each shall direct its representatives not to, directly or indirectly, make any press release, public announcement, public comment, statement or communication with respect to, or otherwise disclose or permit the disclosure of the existence of discussions regarding, a possible transaction between the parties or any of the terms, conditions or other aspects of the transaction proposed in this letter.

2.7)   Confidentiality

Except as and to the extent required by law, the Purchaser shall not disclose or use, and it shall cause its representatives not to disclose or use, any Confidential Information (as defined below) with respect to the Purchased Business furnished, or to be furnished, by either the Vendor, and •, or their respective representatives to the Purchaser or its representatives at any time or in any manner other than in connection with its evaluation of the transaction proposed in this letter. For purposes of this section 15, "**Confidential Information**" means any information about the Purchased Business stamped "confidential" or identified in writing as such to the Purchaser by the Vendor, or •; provided that it does not include information which the Purchaser can demonstrate (i) is generally available to or known by the public other than as a result of improper disclosure by the Purchaser, or (ii) is obtained by the Purchaser from a source other than the Vendor, or •, provided that such source was not bound by a duty of confidentiality to the Vendor or •, with respect to such information. If the Binding Provisions are terminated pursuant to section ● below, the Purchaser shall promptly return to the Vendor any Confidential Information in its possession.

2.8) Financial Statements

The Vendor and ● covenant and agree to provide the Purchaser (i) at the time of acceptance of this letter, with financial statements for the Purchased Business as at their respective ● fiscal year ends and the revenue forecast for the fiscal period ending ●, ●, and (ii) on or before ●, ●. prepared in accordance with generally accepted accounting principles. The Purchaser will also cause to be prepared audited financial statements of the Purchased Business as at the closing date, as soon as reasonably possible after the closing date.

2.9) Costs

Each of the parties hereto shall be responsible for and bear all of its own costs and expenses (including any broker's or finder's fees) incurred in connection with the proposed transaction, including expenses of its representatives incurred at any time in connection with pursuing or consummating the proposed transaction.

2.10) Termination

The Binding Provisions may be terminated:

1)   by mutual written consent of all parties; or
2)   the Purchaser as provided in the last sentence of section ● above; or
3)   by the Purchaser if the ●, audited financial statements are not delivered on or before ●, ●; or
4)   upon written notice by any party to the other parties if the Definitive Agreement has not been executed by ●, ●;

provided, however, that the termination of the Binding Provisions shall not affect the liability of a party for breach of any of the Binding Provisions prior to the termination. Upon termination of the Binding Provisions, the parties shall have no further obligations under this letter, except as stated in Sections ● and ● which shall survive any such termination.

2.11) General

This letter, the Definitive Agreement and all ancillary documents will be interpreted and enforced in accordance with the laws of the Province of Ontario and the federal laws of Canada applicable therein. This letter may be executed in any number of counterparts, and all such counterparts taken together shall be deemed to constitute one and the same instrument.

If this accords with your understanding of our discussions, please so indicate by signing and returning the duplicate copy of this letter on or before (12:00 noon Toronto time) on ●, ●, ●. If your approval and acceptance have not been obtained by such date, the offer contained herein shall be null and void.

Yours truly,

ACCEPTED AND AGREED as to the Binding Provisions this ● day of ●, 20●

Company Name   Company name
Per: Per:
Name: _____________________   Name: _____________________
Title: _____________________   Title: _____________________

Form 12: **Letter of Intent [*Alternate Form*]**

[*Name of Purchaser*]
[*Address*]
[*Date*]

Personal and Confidential

[*Name and Address of Vendor*]

Dear ●:

This Letter of Intent will summarize the terms pursuant to which ● or an affiliate designated by ● (the "**Purchaser**"), proposes to purchase certain assets of ● (the "**Vendor**"), constituting the Subject Business as described in Section 2 below.

A.   Purchased Assets

The Purchaser will purchase certain assets of the Vendor used in the Business including:

1)   All accounts receivable and cash on hand;
2)   All tangible fixed assets;
3)   All operating supplies and inventories;
4)   All rights under all customer contracts and related interests;
5)   All permits, licenses and other approvals or consents necessary to the performance of the Business;
6)   All operational information and data, service contracts, books and records and customer files and records;

7) All equipment, machinery, vehicles and other personal property used in the Business; and

8) All software and related licenses necessary to operate the Purchased Assets as used in the Business.

(collectively, the "**Purchased Assets**").

B. The Subject Business Definition

The "**Subject Business**" means the business operated by the Vendor in connection with ●.

C. Excluded Assets

Excluded from the Purchased Assets will be:

1) Tax refunds;

2) Tax loss carry forwards;

3) Investment tax credits available;

4) Any non-operational facilities and equipment;

5) All leasehold interests in real property, unless the Purchaser elects to assume such leases in accordance with Section 17.

D. Excluded Liabilities

The Purchaser will not assume any debts, obligations or other liabilities of the Vendor or the Subject Business, including without limitation:

1) Trade accounts payable and accrued expenses;

2) Any liabilities pertaining to the employees of the Vendor including without limitation, any liabilities related to any employees the Purchaser offers to hire as contemplated in Section 16 hereof and, in particular, no severance obligations or vacation pay accrued in respect of such employees up to the Closing;

3) City, county, provincial, state, federal or other taxes payable;

4) Bank and other debt together with any interest payable thereon;

5) Any liabilities resulting from the violation of or the application of any applicable environmental protection laws, regulations or common law including any liabilities that might result from the operation of the Subject Business prior to Closing; and

6) Any other liabilities, contingent or otherwise, of the Vendor.

E.   Purchase Price

Subject to the results of the Purchaser's due diligence in accordance with Section 10, the purchase price (the **"Purchase Price"**) which the Purchaser is prepared to pay to the Vendor for the Purchased Assets is estimated to be $●, based on and subject to the following:

[*Note: Modify as appropriate based on business terms*]

1)   The Purchaser being satisfied based solely on its own due diligence review of the books, records and operations of the Subject Business, that the Subject Business currently earns and has earned revenues for the past ● fiscal years of not less than $● per annum;

2)   Execution and delivery of a Formal Agreement (as defined below) and the terms and conditions herein as contemplated in Section 7;

3)   The completion to the Purchaser's sole satisfaction of the Purchaser's evaluation of the Purchased Assets and the Subject Business as described in Sections 6, 10 and 12; and

4)   Delivery of the consents and approvals contemplated in Section 9.

$● of the Purchase Price (the **"Holdback"**) is to be held in escrow in an interest bearing account by Torkin Manes LLP, solicitors for the Purchaser, for a period of 12 months from Closing to be used to satisfy any post-closing adjustments and any indemnity and warranty claims under the Formal Agreement.

One-half of the Purchase Price less the Holdback will be payable on Closing in cash or certified funds and will be subject to the usual closing adjustments. The balance of the Purchase Price will be payable over a period of 3 years, in monthly instalments of principal and interest, with interest to be calculated at a rate per annum (the **"Interest Rate"**) equal to the per annum interest rate announced from time to time by the Bank of Montreal as being the reference rate then in effect for determining interest rates on Canadian dollar denominated commercial loans made in Canada plus ●%. [*Note: Review and revise as required based on business deal*]

The Purchase Price will be allocated among the Purchased Assets in such manner as may be mutually determined by the parties in the Formal Agreement.

F.   No Encumbrances on Purchased Assets

The Purchased Assets are or will be on Closing, free and clear from any liens or encumbrances, with the exception of ● [*consider whether leased equipment used in the Subject Business is to be a permitted encumbrance*], which are to be identified as an appendix to the Formal Agreement and which are to be assumed by the Purchaser.

[*Note: If no leases are to be assumed, but there are leases which need to be bought out so that the Vendor owns the equipment on closing, use the following*]

Leased personal property, if any, utilized in the Business will be acquired by The Vendor prior to Closing and will be transferred to the Purchaser free and clear of all liens or encumbrances.

G.   Formal Agreement

The parties each agree to use their reasonable efforts to negotiate, execute and deliver a formal purchase and sale agreement (the **"Formal Agreement"**) by or such other date as the parties may agree, such Formal Agreement being based on the understandings recorded in this letter. Upon its execution and delivery, the Formal Agreement will supersede this letter in all respects.

H.   Terms of Formal Agreement

The Formal Agreement will contain terms and conditions, representations, warranties, covenants, indemnities, closing conditions and opinion requirements that are customary in purchase and sale transactions of the nature contemplated herein. The Purchaser's counsel will draft the Formal Agreement. ● and ● (the **"Founders"**) have a beneficial interest in the Vendor and shall join personally on a joint and several basis in making certain representations and warranties relating to the Subject Business and the Purchased Assets and to guarantee the obligations of the Vendor contained in the Formal Agreement.

I.   Consents and Approvals

It is understood that any required consents and approvals for the transfer of the Purchased Assets to the Purchaser and for the operation of the Subject Business by the Purchaser will be obtained by the Vendor at its cost on or before Closing or otherwise provided for in a mutually agreeable manner.

J.   Due Diligence

It is understood that the Purchase Price proposed by the Purchaser is based on certain assumptions and on certain preliminary data and information received by the Purchaser from the Vendor, and that such data and information must be confirmed by the Purchaser in its legal and business due diligence process. The Purchaser's evaluation process will include, but not be limited to the following matters:

1) Confirmation, review and evaluation of the Vendor's assets, operating costs, revenues, customer contracts, prices and customer information;

2) Review of tax returns filed by the Vendor;

3) Detailed review of the Vendor's organization, wage and salary structure, employee benefit plans;

4) Review of all outstanding or pending litigation;

5) Confirmation that all certificates, permits, licenses and controls necessary for the operation of the Subject Business are transferable to the Purchaser and that the Purchaser can obtain all consents and approvals necessary to operate the Subject Business;

6) Review of the accuracy of the Vendor's inventory database;

7) Review of corporate records and contracts; and

8) Confirmation, review and evaluation of revenues earned by the Subject Business in each of the last ● fiscal years.

[*Note: Add any specific due diligence concerns or requirements as dictated by the business deal*]

K. Closing

The Formal Agreement will provide for a closing date upon which the proposed purchase and sale transaction is to be completed (the **"Closing"**). The parties anticipate the Closing to take place on or before ● or at such other mutually agreeable date.

L. Conditions of Closing

In addition to the various terms and conditions set-out in this Letter of Intent, the completion of the transactions contemplated in this Letter of Intent are conditional on and subject to the Purchaser (i) obtaining financing in respect of the Purchase Price on such terms and conditions as are satisfactory to the Purchaser in its sole discretion; and (ii) the Purchaser being satisfied in its sole discretion, with the results of its due diligence review of the Subject Business and Purchased Assets, including its due diligence as contemplated in Section 10.

M. Conduct of the Subject Business, Etc.

From and after the date hereof to the date of Closing (the **"Interim Period"**), it is understood that the Vendor will:

1) Not make changes to the capital structure of the Vendor corporation, without the prior written consent of the Purchaser;

2) Use its best efforts to maintain the goodwill of the Subject Business;

3) Not engage in any activities or transactions which are outside the ordinary and usual course of the Subject Business; and

4) Maintain the Purchased Assets in good working order and condition and will not sell or otherwise dispose of any Purchased Assets without the prior written consent of the Purchaser.

N.   Financial Data and Reports

It is understood that this letter is based on preliminary and limited financial data and reports provided to date by the Vendor to the Purchaser in its review of the Subject Business and the Purchased Assets. It is further understood that, during the Interim Period, the Vendor will make available to the Purchaser, its representatives and counsel, all documents, contracts and agreements in its possession or under its control relating to the Subject Business and the Purchased Assets and permit the Purchaser and its representatives with access to the Subject Business and premises on which the Subject Business is operated for the purpose of inspecting the operations, assets and equipment of the Subject Business.

O.   Non-competition Agreement

It will be a condition of Closing that the Vendor, the Founders and ● (collectively, the "**Covenantors**") will provide the Purchaser with a five-year non-competition and non-solicitation covenant in respect of the Subject Business [*in Canada*]. The Purchaser will pay in consideration thereof, the aggregate sum of $● which is included in the Purchase Price described in Section 5.

P.   The Vendor's Employees

Prior to Closing, the Purchaser will interview and may offer employment to some of the current employees of the Vendor who work in the Subject Business (the "**Hired Employees**"), as may be selected by the Purchaser. The Purchaser will provide a comprehensive employment package on substantially the same terms as currently provided to Canadian employees of the Purchaser. The Vendor will terminate the Hired Employees before Closing and will be liable to satisfy all severance and vacation pay owing to the Hired Employees. The Purchaser will not recognize any past service of the Hired Employees except as required by the *Employment Standards Act* (Ontario). The Vendor shall be liable to satisfy all payments required to be made to any employee of the Vendor not hired by the Purchaser or any employee which does not accept the Purchaser's offer of employment including, without limitation, all severance, vacation pay and any amounts owing in respect of wrongful and constructive dismissal claims and the Vendor shall indemnify the Purchaser in respect of such liabilities.

Q. Leased Premises

Prior to Closing, the Purchaser will determine if it requires the real premises (the "**Premises**") leased by the Vendor at ● and, if so, the Vendor shall be responsible to obtain any required consents from the landlord to the assignment of the lease for the Premises in favour of the Purchaser.

R. Public Announcements

No public announcement or press release concerning the proposed purchase and sale transaction herein contemplated will be made by any party during the Interim Period without the prior written consent of the other party.

S. Exclusivity

The Vendor and ● each warrant that the Vendor's principals, shareholders, employees, directors and agents or other persons acting on its behalf:

1) Do not have any agreement, arrangement or understanding with respect to any other acquisition proposal in respect of the shares or assets of the Vendor ("**Acquisition Proposal**");

2) Will cease and cause to be terminated any and all discussions with third parties regarding any other Acquisition Proposal; and

3) Will promptly notify the Purchaser if any Acquisition Proposal or any inquiry or contact with any person or entity with respect thereto is made.

T. Confidentiality

No disclosure shall be made to any party to any other person (other than to the parties' respective advisors) with respect to this letter of intent or the transaction contemplated herein except as required in respect of the transactions contemplated in this Letter of Intent.

U. Expression of Intention

It is understood that this letter sets forth the understandings to date of the parties concerning the proposed purchase by the Purchaser of the Purchased Assets and the Subject Business and other than Sections 8, 13, 14, 19, 20 and 21 above, is not intended to create enforceable legal rights and obligations between the parties. However, the parties confirm their serious intention to complete the proposed purchase and sale transactions contemplated hereby on the terms and pursuant to the timetable set forth in this letter. Unless otherwise agreed, the provisions of Sections 8, 13, 14, 19, 20 and 21 are essential to the proper negotiation of the proposed transaction, and in consideration of the parties' continued participation in these negotiations, the parties have agreed to be bound by these covenants.

* * *

We trust that the above reflects the understandings we have to date. If you are in concurrence with the above, please sign the enclosed copy of this letter and return it to The Purchaser as confirmation of the status of our negotiations, and in the case of Sections 8, 13, 14, 19, 20 and 21 of our agreement.

Yours truly,

Agreed and accepted this ● day of ●, 20●.

Agreed and accepted this ● day of ●, 20●.

By:

By:

____

____

Name: _____________________

Name: _____________________

Title: _____________________

Title: _____________________

Witness:

____

[*insert name of founder*]

Print Name: _____________________

Form 13: **An Asset Purchase Agreement**

THIS AGREEMENT (this "Agreement"), dated as of the bth day of •, 20•, is made by and among [•] ("Seller"), [•] and [•] ("Stockholders") and [•] (the "Buyer").

ARTICLE 1: PURCHASE AND SALE OF ASSETS

1.1) Overview of Purchase and Sale

In consideration of (i) the payment by the Buyer of the Purchase Price (hereinafter defined) and (ii) the assumption by the Buyer of the Assumed Liabilities (hereinafter defined) at the Closing (hereinafter defined): (A) Seller and Stockholders will sell to the Buyer and the Buyer will purchase from Seller and Stockholders all of the Purchased Assets (hereinafter defined) and (B) Seller and the Stockholders will execute and deliver to the Buyer Noncompetition Agreements (as defined and further described in Article VI hereof). Unless otherwise indicated herein, all references to currency shall be to the Canadian dollar.

1.2) Purchased Assets; Definitions.

1.2.1) Definitions

For purposes of this Section 1.2 and other provisions of this Agreement, the following terms have the meanings set forth below:

"Assumed Liabilities" means only the following liabilities of Seller as of the Closing incurred or arising in a manner consistent with and in compliance with the provisions of Article IV hereof and other relevant provisions of this Agreement:

(A) the current portion of trade accounts payable, accrued payroll, accrued payroll taxes, accrued GST (defined below) and PST (defined below) and accrued operating expenses (hereinafter collectively, the **"Part A Assumed Liabilities"**); and (B) payments and obligations due after the Closing under the **"Contracts"** (defined in Section 2.10 hereof).

"Cash Equivalents" means bank certificates of deposit, bank money market accounts or government securities.

"Closing Balance Sheet" means the reviewed statement of financial position of Seller as of the Closing Date (immediately prior to the sale of the Purchased Assets to the Buyer and assumption by the Buyer of the Assumed Liabilities) and reflecting only the Purchased Assets and the Assumed Liabilities and no other assets or liabilities, as prepared by [ ] and reviewed by the Buyer (i) in accordance with GAAP (defined below) and (ii) in a manner consistent with Exhibit 1.2.4.

"Closing Financials and Computations" means the Closing Balance Sheet and calculations prepared by the Buyer of NOA (hereinafter defined) as of the Closing Date based on the Closing Balance Sheet.

"Collective Agreements" means all written communications between Seller and any Union which impose obligations on Seller.

"Employee" means any active or inactive employee, officer or director of Seller whether presently or formerly and all Scheduled Employees.

"Employment Laws" means all Laws relating to employment and labour, including without limitation those relating to employment or labour standards, labour or industrial relations, human rights, pay equity, employment equity, workers' compensation, occupational health and safely, employer health tax, unemployment insurance, income tax with the Buyer and Canada or Quebec Pension Plan.

"Excluded Assets" means the assets, properties and rights of Seller owned or used in the conduct of Seller's business which are not included in the Purchased Assets and which are more particularly described in Section 1.2.5 hereof.

"GAAP" means generally accepted accounting principles as approved from time to time by the Canadian Institute of Chartered Accountants or any successor institute applied on a consistent basis, which are applicable in the circumstances as of the date in question, and the requirement that such principles be applied on a **"consistent basis"** means that accounting principles observed in the current period are comparable in all material respects to those applied in the preceding periods, except as change is required under or pursuant to such accounting principles.

"**Labour Disturbance**" means any strike, cessation of work, refusal to work or to continue to work by employees in combination or in concert or in accordance with a common understanding, or a slow down or other concerted activity on the part of employees designed to restrict or limit output, lockout, closing of place of employment, suspension of work or refusal by Seller to continue to employ any employees or any other disturbance or dispute involving employees.

"**Labour Relations Matters**" means any matter regarding wages, salaries, bonuses, commissions, vacation pay, holiday, severance pay, notice or pay in lieu of notice, termination pay, pension or other employee benefits, worker's compensation, income tax with the Buyer, employment insurance, Canada Pension Plan, Quebec Pension Plan or employer health tax, claims of any kind arising from a collective agreement between the Seller and the unions including accruals in the time bank, human rights complaints, grievances and arbitrations regarding violations of human rights, pay equity, employment equity, collective agreements or Employment Laws provisions.

"**Laws**" means without limitation, all foreign, federal, provincial, state and local laws, statutes, rules, regulations, codes, ordinances, plans, orders, judicial decrees, writs, injunctions, notices, decisions or demand letters issued, entered or promulgated pursuant to any foreign, federal, state, provincial or local law.

"**NOA**" means the value of the Purchased Assets as reflected in the Closing Balance Sheet minus the Part A Assumed Liabilities as calculated in accordance with GAAP. For purposes of the NOA calculation only, all Stockholder Debt, interest-bearing debt, mortgages, shareholder loans, dividends payable, other capital debt, capital lease obligations, and income taxes payable will be excluded from the calculation of NOA. Exhibit 1.2.4 hereof sets forth an example of the NOA calculation as of [ ] (the "**NOA Example**").

"**Reserve Amount**" means $[ ] in cash.

"**Scheduled Employees**" means those employees listed and described in Exhibit 2.21(b) as such Exhibit will be adjusted to the Closing Date to reflect new hires of Seller since the Financial Statement Date and to reflect those employees who leave the employ of Seller since the Financial Statement Date.

"**Stockholder Debt**" means any obligation of Seller for borrowed money, capital leases, or debts of any kind owed to current or former Stockholders or any family members of current or former Stockholders or similar obligations owed to current or former Stockholders or any family members of current or former Stockholders.

"**Union**" means a local or provincial organization or association of employees or a local or provincial branch of a national or international organization or association of employees in a province that has as one of its purposes the regulation in the province of relations between employers and employees through collective bargaining.

1.2.2) Overview of Purchased Assets

The assets to be purchased by the Buyer are all of Seller's assets, properties and rights (real and personal, tangible and intangible) owned or used in the conduct of Seller's business at the Financial Statement Date (as defined in Section 2.7) or acquired after said date and owned or used by Seller on the Closing Date in the conduct of Seller's business, except for (i) assets disposed of in the ordinary course of business consistent with Article IV hereof and other relevant provisions hereof and past practices since the Financial Statement Date, and (ii) the Excluded Assets (as described in 1.2.5). The Purchased Assets are further described in the subsections below of this Section 1.2.2; provided, however, the following subsections shall not be construed as limitations on the breadth or scope of the above definition of Purchased Assets. The intent and purpose of the following subsections is to further illustrate the intent and meaning of the term "**Purchased Assets.**"

    a) **Equipment.** All of Seller's fixed assets, machinery, equipment, furniture, fixtures, telephone numbers (toll-free and others) and other personal property used in the conduct of Seller's business and listed in Exhibit 1.2.2(a).

    b) **Cash and Accounts Receivable.** Except for Excluded Assets, all of Seller's cash and Cash Equivalents (collectively, the "**Purchased Cash**"). Except for the Excluded Assets, all notes receivable (and security therefor), accounts receivable and all other receivables of any other kind including those due from Affiliates (defined below). A schedule of the foregoing assets of Seller as of [ ] is set forth on Exhibit 1.2.2(b). Seller will deliver to the Buyer a schedule of all accounts and notes receivable (and the face amounts thereof) other than Excluded Assets which are outstanding on the Closing Date.

All accounts and notes receivable listed on the schedule delivered at the Closing will constitute valid claims against third parties not affiliated with Seller arising in the ordinary course of business of Seller. The parties hereto agree that the Buyer may assign to Stockholders any accounts and notes receivable which are outstanding on the Closing Date, and which are uncollected as of the date six months after the Closing Date, and concurrently with such assignment Stockholders shall pay to the Buyer in cash an amount equal to the aggregate value of such accounts and notes receivable to the extent the same exceeds the reserve for doubtful accounts on the Balance Sheet. All amounts which are collected from an account or note debtor after the Closing Date shall be first applied to reduce the oldest outstanding balance on such account or with such note debtor.

c) **Records.** Subject to the provisions of Section 9.2(b) hereof, all of Seller's books (other than Seller's corporate minute books and stock-books), financial and business records, insurance policies and any claims and credits thereunder used in the conduct of Seller's business.

d) **Inventory.** All inventories and other supplies pertaining to Seller's operations on hand or at third party premises or in transit including raw materials, work-in-process and finished goods, and including any rights of Seller to warranties received from suppliers.

e) **Intellectual Property.** All of Seller's interests and rights to any and all patents, copyrights, trade names, service marks, trademarks, product designations, trade secrets, formula, processes, know how and any other intellectual property (all of which shall be set forth in Exhibit 2.19), all registrations, applications, assignments, amendments, research, development, updates and modifications pertaining thereto.

f) **Other Intangibles.** All of Seller's right, title and interest in franchises, licences, permits, options and any inventions, developments and ideas relating to Seller's business or business prospects.

g) **Contracts; Prepaids; Materials; etc.** Seller's rights and privileges arising from its unshipped orders, prepaid expenses, customer contracts, customer lists, outstanding offers, sales records, advertising materials, and all agreements for the sale, purchase or lease of goods or services, and all other contracts, agreements, assets and things of value now beneficially owned or acquired by Seller at or before the Closing Date, whether tangible or intangible, real or personal, inchoate, partial or complete, fixed or contingent, of every kind and description and wherever situated relating to Seller's business or business prospects.

1.2.3) Retention of Earnings to Closing

The parties agree that between [ ] and the Closing Date Seller shall retain and not distribute its earnings and profits and shall not make any distributions of its assets to Stockholders other than (i) Excluded Assets, or (ii) distributions made with the prior written consent of the Buyer.

1.2.4) Financial Requirements Regarding Purchased Assets; Post Closing Adjustments.

a) **Financial Requirements.** Notwithstanding anything in this Agreement to the contrary, the following conditions shall exist at Closing (hereinafter defined) with respect to the Purchased Assets: (i) Purchased Cash will be at least $[ ] net of customer deposits; and (ii) NOA at the Closing shall not be less than $[ ]. An example of NOA as of [ ] is attached as Exhibit 1.2.4.

b) **Post-Closing Adjustments.** Immediately after the Closing, at no cost to either Seller or Stockholders, the Buyer will prepare the Closing Financials and Computations. The Closing Financials and Computations will be completed on or before [ ] and delivered to Seller and the Stockholders for review. If the Seller or the Stockholders have any objections to or otherwise dispute the Closing Financials and Computations, the parties agree that the provisions of Section 12.7 hereof will apply in resolving said dispute. Immediately upon the completion of the Closing Financials and Computations, and the review and acceptance of the same by Seller and the Stockholders, or, if applicable the resolution in accordance herewith of any dispute between the parties with respect to the Closing Financials and Computations, the parties agree that the Reserve Amount, or portions thereof, shall be paid over to the Buyer to satisfy any deficiency (the "Aggregate Deficiency") in any of the financial requirements described in Section 1.2.4(a) above. If the NOA and the Purchased Cash are at least equal to the amounts set forth in Section 1.2.4(a), the Buyer shall pay to Seller the Reserve Amount. To the extent that the Aggregate Deficiency at Closing exceeds the Reserve Amount, such deficiency shall not constitute Damages (as defined in Section 11.1), and shall be immediately due and payable to the Buyer in cash by Seller and Stockholders and said obligation to pay shall be joint and several among each of them. If and when required, the Buyer shall pay Seller the Reserve Amount, or portions thereof in accordance with the allocation provisions of Section 1.6 below, by delivery to Seller of a certified or cashier's check or by wire transfer to Seller's account.

c)   Seller and the Buyer will provide for all year-end expense adjustments on a pro-rata basis prior to the preparation of the Closing Financials and Computations and disbursement of the Reserve Amount in accordance with Section 1.2.4(b).

1.2.5)   Confirmation of Assets Excluded From Purchased Assets

The parties hereto acknowledge and agree that the Purchase Price (hereinafter defined) has been calculated, and is being paid, based on the agreement and understanding that the Purchased Assets do not include the Excluded Assets. The Excluded Assets are described in Exhibit 1.2.5 hereof.

1.3)   Payment of Purchase Price for The Purchased Assets and The Noncompetition Agreements

Subject to the terms and conditions of this Agreement and in reliance on the representations and warranties of the Seller and the Stockholders herein contained, and in consideration of the purchase, sale, conveyance, transfer, and delivery of the Purchased Assets, and the execution and delivery of the Noncompetition Agreements (as defined in Article VI), the Buyer agrees to pay Stockholders and Seller (to be allocated among the Stockholders and the Seller in accordance with Section 1.6 below) an aggregate purchase price of $[ ] subject to the remaining provisions hereof and Section 1.2.4(b) plus the assumption by the Buyer of the Assumed Liabilities and payment of Canadian Transfer Taxes (defined below) (the **"Purchase Price"**) as follows:

a)   the Buyer will assume the Assumed Liabilities at the Closing as herein provided;

b) $[ ] minus the amount described in subpart (v) below and minus the Reserve Amount which shall be retained by the Buyer or paid over to Seller in accordance with Section 1.2.4(b) and if so paid to Seller shall constitute a portion of the Purchase Price (the amount payable pursuant to this subpart (ii) shall be payable at Closing by delivery to the Seller of a certified or cashier's check by wire transfer to Seller's account);

c) all provincial sales taxes (**"PST"**) and goods and services taxes (**"GST"**) exigible on the purchase of the Purchased Assets (collectively, **"Canadian Transfer Taxes"**); provided however, the parties covenant and agree that they will sign a joint election respecting goods and services taxes under Section 167(1) of the *Excise Tax Act*, R.S.C. 1985, c. E-15 (Canada), if applicable, in the prescribed form and within the prescribed time for purposes of the *Excise Tax Act*, R.S.C. 1985, c. E-15 (Canada) in connection with the sale of the Purchased Assets hereunder; and provided the Buyer may deliver purchase exemption certificates, where applicable, to the Seller to reduce the amount of GST and PST otherwise exigible; and

d) $[ ] by delivery of an [ ] percent (%) subordinated note (in the form designated as Exhibit 1.3 hereto) in the aggregate principal amount of $[ ] (the **"Subordinated Note"**).

1.4) Assumed Liabilities

Provided the transactions herein contemplated are consummated, and as a precondition of the sale of the Purchased Assets and the execution and delivery of Noncompetition Agreements, the Buyer will assume and discharge, and will indemnify (in a manner consistent with Section 9.2(e)) Seller against the Assumed Liabilities, and no others, except as provided herein.

1.5) Liabilities Not Assumed

The Buyer shall not be responsible for any liability or obligation of Seller or the Stockholders other than those which are specifically defined as Assumed Liabilities hereunder. Without limitation, the Buyer shall not be responsible for:

a) any of Seller's liabilities for borrowed money or capital leases;

b) any products liability, liability, including fines, losses and costs, arising from or relating to Environmental Laws and Regulations (as defined herein) or other environmental matters, or any other liabilities resulting from the violation of Laws by Seller or the Stockholders or associated with the conduct of Seller's business (including acts or omissions) prior to the Closing Date;

c) any liability of Seller insured against to the extent such liability is paid by an insurer;

d)   except as provided in Section 5.3, any liability of Seller to any of the Stockholders or any other employee of Seller for compensation of any type or any liability for Stockholder Debt;

e)   any liabilities or expenses which are incurred by Seller in making or carrying into effect this Agreement or which are incidental thereto;

f)   except for Canadian Transfer Taxes and PST and GST which constitute Part A Assumed Liabilities, any liability for taxes, including any income, sales, transfer, stamp, excise and other taxes, foreign or domestic, Federal, provincial or state, required to be paid in respect to or as a result of Seller's operations up to and including the Closing Date including, without limitation, any tax due on account of recapture of appreciation or tax credit;

g)   any and all costs, expenses or liabilities of Seller that arise in connection with this Agreement or out of the sale herein contemplated, including any liquidation or dissolution of Seller, or that arise after the Closing Date;

h)   any Pre-Closing Taxes;

i)   any customer claims relating to services rendered by Seller prior to the Closing Date, and customer claims relating to, or returns of, products of Seller sold and shipped by Seller prior to the Closing Date or in the finished goods inventory of Seller as of the Closing Date. If a customer makes a claim or seeks a return and, in the judgment of the Buyer the claim or return is proper, the Buyer shall replace or repair, as the case may be, the services rendered or product purchased at the Buyer's then generally prevailing prices and labour rates. Such repairs or returns shall be for the account of Stockholders who shall promptly reimburse the Buyer for the amounts thereof in excess of reserves for such items included in the Balance Sheet.

1.6)   Purchase Price Allocation

The Purchase Price shall be allocated among Seller and the Stockholders and to the Purchased Assets and the Noncompetition Agreements as set forth on Exhibit 1.6.

ARTICLE 2: REPRESENTATIONS AND WARRANTIES
OF SELLER AND STOCKHOLDERS

Seller and Stockholders hereby jointly and severally represent and warrant to the Buyer the following with respect to Seller:

2.1) Corporate Organization, etc.

Seller is a corporation duly organized, validly existing and in good standing under the laws of the Province of [ ] with all requisite corporate power and authority to carry on its business as it is now being conducted and to own, operate and lease its properties and assets. A detailed description of Seller's business as it is now being conducted is attached as Exhibit 2.1.1. The conduct of its business and its ownership or use of property do not require Seller to be qualified or licensed to do business as a foreign corporation in any jurisdiction other than the Province of [ ]. Exhibit 2.1.2 contains complete and correct copies of Seller's (i) Articles of Amalgamation; and (ii) Bylaws, each as amended to date. Seller has all federal, provincial, state, local and foreign licences, permits or other approvals required for the operation of its business as now being conducted.

2.2) Capital Stock; Options

The authorized capital stock of Seller and the shares of capital stock issued and outstanding, of all classes, and the respective holdings of each Stockholder are as set forth in Exhibit 2.2 and Seller has no treasury stock. All issued and outstanding shares of capital stock are validly issued, fully paid and nonassessable and are owned by the Stockholders, free and clear of all encumbrances or claims. There are no issued and outstanding options, warrants, rights, securities, contracts, commitments, understandings or arrangements by which Seller is bound to issue any additional shares of its capital stock or options to purchase shares of its capital stock.

2.3) Subsidiaries and Affiliates

Except as set forth in Exhibit 2.3, Seller has no subsidiaries, Affiliates or investments in any other entity or business operation. The term **"Affiliates"** includes each shareholder, director, officer and employee of Seller, the family members of each Stockholder, and any director, officer or employee of Seller, and any corporation, partnership or other entity in which Seller, any Stockholder, any family member of a Stockholder or director or officer of Seller has any financial interest or is a controlling person, as that term is used in connection with applicable federal or provincial securities laws, if such person or entity has, or in the past had, a contractual relationship with or is transacting, or has in the past transacted, business with Seller. All of the outstanding shares of all classes of capital stock of each subsidiary of Seller are owned by Seller free of any liens, security interests, claims or encumbrances. Seller has no Affiliate whose liabilities or obligations will be assumed by the Buyer.

2.4) Authorization

Seller has full corporate power and authority, and each Stockholder has full power and authority, to enter into this Agreement and to carry out the transactions contemplated hereby. This Agreement and all actions contemplated herein which require the approval of Seller's directors or of the Stockholders have duly received the required approval and Seller shall have delivered a certified copy of its stockholder list and consents to resolutions which shall have been duly adopted by its directors and by the Stockholders, substantially in the form of Exhibit 2.4.

2.5) No Violation

Except as set forth in Exhibit 2.5, Seller is not subject to or obligated under any article or certificate of incorporation, bylaw, Law, or any agreement or instrument, or any licence, franchise or permit, which would be breached or violated by Seller's execution, delivery and performance of this Agreement. Seller and Stockholders will comply with all applicable Laws in connection with their execution, delivery and performance of this Agreement and the transactions contemplated hereby.

2.6) Governmental Authorities

Except as set forth in Exhibit 2.6, neither Seller nor any Stockholder is required to submit any notice, report or other filing with, and no consent, approval or authorization is required, by any governmental or regulatory authority in connection with their execution, delivery, consummation or performance of this Agreement or the consummation of the transactions contemplated hereby.

2.7) Financial Statements

Exhibit 2.7 contains Seller's reviewed statement of financial position as of [ ] and reviewed statement of income and retained earnings for the fiscal year then ended, as prepared by [ ] and audited statements of financial position as of June 30 for each of the years [ ] and [ ] and audited statements of income and retained earnings for the fiscal years then ended, each such audited statement being prepared by [ ]. All such statements of financial position and the notes thereto are complete and accurate and fairly present the financial position of Seller as of the respective dates thereof, and such statements of income and retained earnings and the notes thereto fairly present the results of operations for the periods therein referred to, all in accordance with generally accepted accounting principles consistently applied throughout the periods indicated (except as stated therein or in the notes thereto). The statement of financial position as of [ ] and the notes thereto are referred to as the "**Balance Sheet**". [ ] is referred to as the "**Financial Statement Date.**"

2.8)   No Undisclosed Liabilities, Claims, etc.

Except for (a) liabilities fully reflected or reserved against in the Balance Sheet; and (b) regular and usual liabilities and obligations incurred in the ordinary course of business consistent with past practices after the Financial Statement Date, Seller has no liabilities, obligations or claims (absolute, accrued, fixed or contingent, matured or unmatured, or otherwise), including liabilities, obligations or claims which may become known or which arise only after the Closing and which result from actions, omissions or occurrences of Seller prior to the Closing.

2.9)   Absence of Certain Changes

Since the Financial Statement Date, there has not been (a) any adverse change in the business, prospects, financial condition, earnings or operations of Seller's business; (b) any damage, destruction or loss, whether covered by insurance or not, adversely affecting Seller's properties and business; (c) any declaration, setting aside or payment of any dividend whether in cash, stock or property with respect to Seller's capital stock, or any redemption or other acquisition of such stock by Seller; (d) any increase in the compensation payable or to become payable by Seller to its directors, officers, key employees, Affiliates or any of Stockholders or any adoption of or increase in any bonus, insurance, pension or other employee benefit plan, payment or arrangement made to, for or with any such party; (e) any entry into any commitment or transaction, including, without limitation, any borrowing or capital expenditure other than in accordance with the Schedule of Capital Expenditures (Exhibit 2.25); (f) any change by Seller in accounting methods, practices or principles; (g) any adoption of any statute, rule, regulation or order which adversely affects Seller; (h) any termination or waiver of any rights of value to the business of Seller; (i) any other transaction or event other than in the ordinary course of Seller's business; (j) any transaction or conduct inconsistent with Seller's past business practices; (k) any adoption, alteration, revision or amendment of any collective bargaining, bonus, profit sharing, compensation, stock option, pension, retirement, deferred compensation, or other plan, agreement, trust, fund or arrangement for the benefit of employees; or (l) any agreement or understanding made or entered into to do any of the foregoing.

2.10) Contracts

Exhibit 2.10A contains a schedule of, and copies of, all Contracts to which Seller is a party other than any one Contract which does not involve total obligations in excess of $[ ] and multiple Contracts with a single party which do not involve total obligations in excess of $[ ]. The term "**Contracts**" shall include, but shall not be limited to, all oral (which shall be summarized in Exhibit 2.10A) and written contracts, agreements, agency agreements, loan agreements, mortgages, indentures, deeds of trust, guarantees, commitments, joint venture agreements, purchase and/or sale agreements, collective bargaining, union, consulting and/ or employment contracts, leases of real or personal property, easements, distribution or dealer agreements, service agreements, license agreements and advertising agreements. Seller is not in default or alleged to be in default under any Contract nor is Seller aware of any default by any other party to any Contract, and there exists no event, condition or occurrence which, after notice or lapse of time, or both, would constitute a default under any Contract. All of the Contracts are in full force and effect and constitute legal, valid and binding obligations of the parties thereto in accordance with their terms, and are capable of assignment to the Buyer pursuant to this Agreement without any notice to or consent by any other party.

2.11) True and Complete Copies

Copies of all agreements, contracts and documents delivered and to be delivered hereunder by Seller or Stockholders are and will be true and complete copies of such agreements, contracts and documents. All written summaries of oral agreements will be true and complete.

2.12) Title and Related Matters

Except as set forth in Exhibit 2.12, Seller has good and marketable title to all of the properties and assets reflected in the Balance Sheet or acquired after the date thereof (except properties sold or otherwise disposed of since the date thereof in the ordinary course of business and consistent with past practices) including, without limitation, the specific assets referred to in paragraphs (a), (b) and (c) below, free and clear of all mortgages, security interests, liens, pledges, claims, escrows, options, rights of first refusal, indentures, easements, licences, security agreements or other agreements, arrangements, contracts, commitments, understandings, obligations, charges or encumbrances of any kind or character, except as reflected on the Balance Sheet. Except as set forth in Exhibit

2.12, Seller owns or leases, directly or indirectly, all of the assets and properties, and is a party to all licenses and other agreements, presently used or necessary to carry on the business or operations of Seller as presently conducted.

a) Real Property.

   i) Seller does not own any real property.

   ii) Seller is not a tenant under any lease(s) of real property used by Seller except as described on Exhibit 2.10A. With respect to the leased real property described on Exhibit 2.10A (A) all such leases are in full force and effect and constitute valid and binding obligations of the respective parties thereto; (B) there have not been and there currently are not any defaults thereunder by any party thereto; (C) no event has occurred which (whether with or without notice, lapse of time or the happening or occurrence of any other event) would constitute a default thereunder entitling the lessor to terminate the lease; and (D) the continuation, validity and effectiveness of all such leases under the current rentals and other current terms thereof will in no way be affected by the transactions contemplated by this Agreement or, if any would be affected, Stockholders shall use all necessary means at their disposal to cause an appropriate consent to such transactions to be delivered to the Buyer prior to the Closing Date at no cost or other adverse consequences to the Seller ((A) through (D) are hereinafter collectively referred to as **"Lease Restrictions"**).

   iii) Each parcel of real property, building, structure and improvement, leased or otherwise utilized by Seller (collectively the **"Premises"**) conforms to all applicable Laws, including zoning regulations, none of which will, upon the sale of the Purchased Assets to the Buyer, prohibit the use of such properties, buildings, structures or improvements, for the purposes for which they are now utilized. The Premises are of good quality construction throughout, are in good condition and working order, are adequate for their intended purposes, have no structural or other substantial deficiencies, and are free from deferred maintenance.

   iv) Seller does not currently have, and in the past has not had, any interest (as owner, tenant or otherwise) in any real property.

b) **Personal Property.** Seller holds all right, title and interest in and to the Purchased Assets and has good and marketable title thereto capable of being conveyed to the Buyer. The personal property constituting the Purchased Assets currently being utilized in the aggregate is in good condition and working order, and each individual item of personal property which would cost in excess of $5,000 to replace is in good condition and working order. None of the Purchased Assets is subject to any (i) contracts of sale or lease; (ii) security interests, encumbrances, liens, actual or contingent legal claims, or charges of any kind or character; or (iii) licenses, certificates of approval or permits or other authorization. Except as may otherwise be set forth herein, there are no Lease Restrictions with respect to the personal property leased by Seller.

c) **Inventories.** In addition to subsection (b) of this Section, the inventories of Seller included on the Balance Sheet, to be included on interim balance sheets provided pursuant to Section 4.8 and owned by Seller on the Closing Date: (i) are valued with respect to each category of inventory at the lower of cost (on a FIFO basis) or market; and (ii) do not include any items which are below standard quality, damaged or spoiled, obsolete or of a quality or quantity not usable or saleable in the normal Course of the business of Seller as currently conducted within normal inventory "turn" experience, the value of which has not been fully written down, or with respect to which adequate reserves have not been provided. Seller has the proper amount of inventories to conduct its business consistent with past practices. There has not been since the Financial Statement Date any provision for markdowns or shrinkage with respect to inventories other than in the ordinary and regular course of business consistent with past practices or as otherwise consented to by the Buyer.

d) **No Disposition of Assets.** There has not been since the Financial Statement Date any sale, lease or any other disposition or distribution by Seller of any of its assets or properties and any other assets now or hereafter owned by it, except transactions in the ordinary and regular course of business consistent with past practices or as otherwise consented to by the Buyer.

e) **Purchased Assets.** The Buyer, in completing the transaction contemplated by this Agreement is, within the meaning of the *Excise Tax Act*, R.S.C. 1985, c. E-15 (Canada), acquiring from Seller ownership, possession, or use of all or substantially all of the property that can reasonably be regarded as being necessary for the Buyer to carry on the business carried on by the Seller.

2.13) Litigation

There is no suit, action, investigation or proceeding pending or, to the knowledge of Seller or any of the Stockholders, threatened against Seller or any of Stockholders or which, if adversely determined, would adversely affect the business, prospects, operations, earnings, properties or the condition, financial or otherwise, of Seller nor is there any judgment, decree, injunction, rule or order of any court, governmental department, commission, agency, instrumentality or arbitrator outstanding against Seller having, or which, insofar as can be reasonably foreseen, in the future may have, any such effect.

2.14) Tax Matters

The term **"Taxes"** means all net income, capital gains, gross income, gross receipts, sales, use, transfer, ad valorem, franchise, profits, licences, capital, withholding, payroll, employment, excise, goods and services, severance, stamp, occupation, premium, property, assessments, or other governmental charges of any kind whatsoever, together with any interest, fines and any penalties, additions to tax or additional amounts incurred or accrued under applicable federal, provincial, state, local or foreign tax law or assessed, charged or imposed by any governmental authority, additions to tax or additional amounts that relate to Taxes for such period, regardless of when such items are incurred, accrued, assessed or charged. For the purposes of this Section 2.14 and Section 6.6, Seller shall be deemed to include any predecessor of Seller of any person or entity from which Seller incurs a liability for Taxes as a result of transferee liability.

    a)   Seller has duly and timely filed (and prior to the Closing Date will duly and timely file) true, correct and complete tax returns, reports or estimates, all prepared in accordance with applicable laws, for all years and period (and portions thereof) and for all jurisdictions (whether federal, provincial, state, local or foreign) in which any such returns, reports or estimated were due. All Taxes shown as due and payable on such return, reports and estimates have been paid, and there is no current liability for any Taxes due and payable in connection with any such returns. Any charges, accruals and reserves for Taxes provided for on the financial statements delivered or to be delivered pursuant to Section 2.7 and Section 4.8 are adequate. There are no existing liens for Taxes upon any of the Purchased Assets. Attached hereto as Exhibit 2.14.2 are copies of all federal, provincial, state and foreign tax returns filed by Seller for the past five (5) years. All applicable sales taxes to the extent due, were paid by the Seller when the Purchased Assets were acquired by the Seller.

b) Seller has (i) withheld all required amounts from its employees, agents, contractors and nonresidents and remitted such amounts to the proper agencies; (ii) paid all employer contributions, remittances and premiums; and (iii) filed all federal, provincial, state, local and foreign returns and reports with respect to employee income tax withholding, employment insurance premiums and Canada Pension Plan contributions, and employer health tax, all in compliance with the withholding tax provisions of the *Income Tax Act*, R.S.C. 1985, c. 1 (5th Supp.) of Canada and the regulations thereunder (the "**ITA**"), or any prior provision of the ITA and other applicable laws.

c) Seller has no (and has not previously had any) permanent establishment in any foreign country and Seller does not engage (and has not previously engaged) in a trade or business in any foreign country.

d) Seller is not a non-resident of Canada within the meaning of Section 116 of the ITA.

e) Neither the ITA nor any other provision of law requires the Buyer to withhold any portion of the Purchase Price.

2.15)   Government Contracts

No Contract is subject to the regulations of any governmental agency. None of Seller's expected sales or orders will be lost, and Seller's customer relations will not be damaged, as a result of the Buyer continuing the operations of Seller as an entity that does not qualify as a small business under applicable law.

2.16)   Compliance with Law

a) Seller has not previously failed and is not currently failing to comply with any applicable Laws, including Employment Laws, Environmental Laws and Regulations (as defined herein), relating to the business of Seller or the operation of its assets where such failure or failures would individually or in the aggregate have an adverse effect on the financial condition, business, operations or prospects of Seller. In particular, but without limiting the generality of the foregoing, Seller is in compliance with all applicable Laws, including Environmental Laws and Regulations (as defined herein), relating to anti-competitive practices, price fixing, occupational health and safety, environmental, employment and discrimination matters. There are no proceedings of record and no proceedings are pending or threatened, nor has Seller or any Stockholder received any written notice regarding any violation of any Employment Laws, Environmental Laws and Regulations (as defined herein) including those related to environmental matters of any kind including pollution of or releases of any Hazardous Materials into the environment (including air, surface water, groundwater, the soil or the subsurface).

   b) Exhibit 2.16 contains copies of all reports of inspections by representatives of any federal, state provincial or local governmental entity or agency of the Seller's business and properties from January 1, 1992 through the date hereof under all applicable Employment Laws and under any Environmental Laws and Regulations (as defined herein) as well as any reports or assessments or evaluations conducted of the Seller's business and properties by private consultants or any other non-governmental representative. The deficiencies, if any, noted on such reports or any deficiencies noted by such inspections, reports or assessments through the Closing Date shall be corrected by the Closing Date. Neither Seller nor Stockholders know or have reason to know of any other safety, health, environmental, anti-competitive or discrimination problems relating to the financial condition, business, assets, operations, prospects, earnings or employment practices of Seller.

2.17)   Absence of Certain Business Practices

None of Seller, Stockholders, any person or entity related to or affiliated with any Seller or Stockholder, any officer, employee or agent of Seller or Stockholders, any other person or entity acting on behalf of or associated with Seller or Stockholders, nor any other entity directly or indirectly owned or controlled by Seller or any Stockholder, acting alone or together, has (a) received, directly or indirectly, any rebates, payments, commissions, promotional allowances or any other economic benefit, regardless of its nature or type, from any customer, supplier, trading company, shipping company, governmental employee or other entity or individual with whom Seller has done business directly or indirectly; or (b) directly or indirectly, given or agreed to give any gift or similar benefit to any customer, supplier, trading company, shipping company, governmental employee or other person or entity who is or may be in a position to help or hinder the business of Seller (or assist Seller in connection with any actual or proposed transaction) which (i) might subject Seller to any damage or penalty in any civil, criminal or governmental litigation or proceeding, (ii), if not given in the past, might have had an adverse effect on the assets, business or operations of Seller as reflected in the financial statements set forth as Exhibit 2.7 or (iii), if not continued in the future, might adversely affect the assets, business, operations or prospects of Seller or which might subject Seller to suit or penalty in any private or governmental litigation or proceeding.

2.18)   Pension and Employee Benefit Matters

a) **Plans.** Exhibit 2.18(a) sets out each pension, retirement, profit sharing, supplemental retirement, bonus, deferred compensation, incentive compensation, stock purchase, stock option, severance or termination pay, health or other medical, life, disability or other insurance, supplementary unemployment benefit, and all other employee benefit plans, programs, agreements or arrangements, whether written or oral, formal or informal, legally binding or not, maintained or contributed to or required to be contributed to by the Seller for the benefit of Employees or their dependents or beneficiaries (the **"Plans"**), as well as the compensation practices and policies applicable to Employees, including practices and policies regarding vacations, sick leave, leaves of absence and perquisites of employment. Except as disclosed on Exhibit 2.18(a), there exists no formal plan, agreement or commitment to create any additional Plan, or compensation policy or practice, or to change any existing Plan, or compensation policy or practice, that would affect any Employees or their dependents or beneficiaries.

b) **Pension Plans.** Seller has no Plan which is or is intended to be a registered pension plan as defined in the ITA and/or is a pension plan registered under any federal or provincial pension legislation.

c) **Copies of Plans.** Exhibit 2.18(c) includes true and complete copies of: each of the Plans, or a written description of any unwritten Plan, including all amendments thereto; each trust or other funding or investment management agreement relating to any of the Plans, including all amendments thereto; the most recent financial statements and/or auditor's reports for each of the Plans; the three most recent annual information returns filed with any governmental agency in respect of any of the Plans; the most recent description of each of the Plans which has been provided to Employees, and any and all other descriptive materials provided to Employees, including employee booklets; any advance tax ruling or related professional opinions on the tax status of any of the Plans.

d) **Compliance with Applicable Laws**. Each of the Plans has been established, operated, administered and invested in accordance with the terms of such Plan and any applicable Laws, including without limitation all applicable pension and taxation legislation, regulations, and all rules and policies in relation thereto. Each of the Plans has been duly registered where required by, and is in good standing under, such Laws and no act or event has occurred which would affect the registered or tax-exempt status of any Plan.

e) **No Defaults, etc**. All obligations regarding the Plans have been satisfied, and there are no outstanding defaults, liabilities or violations by Seller or any other party in relation to any of the Plans. There have been no improper withdrawals, applications or transfers of assets from any of the Plans, and no Taxes, penalties or fees are owing or eligible by Seller or any other party under or in relation to any of the Plans. There has been no breach of statutory or fiduciary duty on the part of Seller, the administrator of any of the Plans, any employee or agent of the foregoing, or any other party in relation to any of the Plans.

f) **No Claims**. There are no pending or threatened complaints, actions, suits or claims against any of the Plans, whether by any Employee or beneficiary or any other party (other than routine claims for benefits), and no Plan, nor any related trust or other funding medium thereunder, is subject to any pending investigation, examination or other proceeding, action or claim initiated by any governmental agency or any other party, and there exists no state of facts which could give rise to any such investigation, examination or other proceeding, action or claim.

g) **Full Payment**. All contributions or premiums required to be made by Seller under the terms of each Plan or any applicable Laws have been made in a timely fashion in accordance with applicable Laws and the terms of such Plans.

h) **No Notification**. No notification is required to be given to any governmental agency having jurisdiction over any of the Plans with respect to the consummation of the transactions contemplated by this Agreement in relation to the Plans.

> **i)**   **No Post-Retirement Benefits.** None of the Plans provides benefits, including without limitation retiree health benefits, to Employees beyond their retirement or termination of service, other than (i) coverage mandated by applicable Laws; (ii) death or retirement benefits under any Pension Plan; (iii) deferred compensation benefits which are accrued as liabilities on the books of Seller; or (iv) benefits, the entire cost of which are borne by Employees or their beneficiaries.

2.19)   Intellectual Property

Seller has good and marketable title to, and Exhibit contains a detailed listing of, each copyright, trademark, trade name, service mark, trade dress, patent, franchise, trade secret, product designation, formula, process, know-how, right of publicity, design and other similar rights (collectively "**Intellectual Property Rights**") used in, or necessary for, the operation of its business as currently conducted. Except as otherwise set forth on Exhibit 2.19, all of said Intellectual Property Rights are free and clear of all royalty obligations, security interests, liens and encumbrances. Seller has the exclusive right to use all Intellectual Property Rights used in, or necessary for, the operation of its business as currently conducted. The Stockholders and Seller have taken all action necessary to protect against and defend against, and have no knowledge of, any conflicting use of any such Intellectual Property Rights. Seller does not have nor does Seller utilize any Intellectual Property Rights except those which are set forth in Exhibit 2.19. Except as set forth in Exhibit 2.19, Seller is not a party in any capacity to any franchise, license, royalty or other agreement respecting or restricting any Intellectual Property Rights, and the Intellectual Property Rights used by Seller in the conduct of Seller's business do not conflict with the Intellectual Property Rights of any third party. No product made, sold or distributed by Seller, or service provided by Seller, violates any license or infringes any Intellectual Property Rights of any third party, and there are no pending claims or demands by any third party to the contrary.

2.20)   Warranties

There are no claims existing or threatened under or pursuant to any warranty, whether expressed or implied, on products or services sold by Seller and the Balance Sheet reserves, if any, for anticipated claims are adequate to cover any such claims. Seller has never had any form of written warranties with respect to its goods or services.

2.21) Labour Relations

a) **Employee Agreements**. Exhibit 2.21(a) lists and summarizes each agreement of any kind between Seller and its Employees or group of Employees, including without limitation, employment, collective bargaining, retainer and consulting agreements or contracts. All of the written employment, collective bargaining, retainer and consulting agreements or contracts are enforceable in accordance with their terms and Seller has provided the Buyer with a true and complete copy of such agreements or contracts. There are no oral or written agreements or contracts with any employee which are not terminable by Seller upon providing that period of notice, or at Seller's option, pay in lieu of notice, required by the *Employment Standards Act* of [ ] or by providing reasonable notice under common law.

b) **Scheduled Employees**. Set forth in Exhibit 2.21(b) is a complete list of all employees of Seller currently actively employed together with particulars of their salary, positions held, the amount of vacation pay currently accrued to each such employee, the location of their employment, and length of service with the Seller. Where a written employment agreement or contract exists for a Scheduled Employee, same is indicated on exhibit 2.21(a). **"Actively employed"** includes those employees currently on pregnancy, parental, family responsibility, bereavement, maternity, education and training, or adoption leave, workers' compensation, and short or long-term disability.

c) **Collective Agreements**. Seller is not a party to any Collective Agreements with any Union.

d) **Labour Relations**. Except as disclosed in Exhibit 2.21(d):

i) neither Seller nor any person acting on behalf of or as a bargaining agent for Seller, has received or sent notice to commence collective bargaining for the purposes of bargaining a collective agreement or revision or renewal of same, and has not agreed to conduct collective bargaining with any Union(s) representing its Unionized Employees; and

ii) there are no outstanding applications for certifications or any other proceedings in which a Union is claiming or seeking exclusive authority to bargain collectively for any employees of Seller.

e) **Relations with Employees**. Except as disclosed on Exhibit 2.21(e), since July 1, 1996, no non-officer Employee of Seller and no officers of Seller have resigned, advised Seller of an intention to resign from such employment or refused to continue employment with Seller. Exhibit 2.21(e) lists each former Employee and/or officer of Seller whose aggregate annualized compensation exceeded $75,000 and whose employment by Seller has ceased for any reasons since [ ]. Set forth opposite the name of each such Employee and/or officer are: the positions held, the beginning and ending employment dates, and the reason for the cessation of employment.

f) **Liabilities to Scheduled Employees**. Seller has no liability of any kind to any Scheduled Employee, except for compensation or remuneration and benefits payable to such Scheduled Employee or to which such Scheduled Employee may be entitled, in the ordinary course. There are no outstanding loans or advances made or granted by Seller to any Scheduled Employee, except for normal travel advances or in the ordinary course, all of which, in excess of $50,000 in the aggregate to any individual are set out on Exhibit 2.21(f).

g) **No Labour Disturbances**. Except as set out in Exhibit 2.21(g) Seller has not been involved in any Labour Disturbance. Nor has any Labour Disturbance been threatened in writing and, to the best of Seller's knowledge, none has been threatened verbally, and no complaint, claim, proceeding, question, issue or matter under any Employment Laws currently exists or is pending or has been threatened in writing, and no such complaint, claim, proceeding, question, issue, or matter has been raised or threatened in writing, within the three year period prior to the date of this Agreement. There are no occurrences or events which might reasonably be expected to give rise to any Labour Disturbance.

h) **Compliance with Employment Laws**. Seller is in compliance with all Employment Laws. Seller is not liable for any assessments, penalties or other sums for failure to comply with any Employment Laws. Except as disclosed on Exhibit 2.21(h) there are no outstanding or threatened complaints, claims, proceedings, questions, issues or matters against Seller under any Employment Laws. Exhibit 2.21(h) contains copies of all reports of inspections by representatives of any federal, provincial or local governmental entity or agency of the Seller's business and properties from January 1, 1992 through the date hereof under all Employment Laws. The deficiencies, if any, noted on such reports or any deficiencies noted by such inspections through the Closing Date shall be corrected by the Closing Date. Neither Seller nor Stockholders know or have reason to know of any other safety, health, or discrimination problems relating to the financial condition, business, assets, operations, prospects, earnings or employment practices of Seller. All assessments required to be remitted under any applicable workers' compensation legislation as of the Closing Date and all filings in relation to such assessments have been remitted or filed and there are no circumstances that would permit a penalty reassessment under such legislation.

i) **No Effect of Transaction on Scheduled Employees**. Other than common law and statutory rights arising in the ordinary course, the consummation of the transactions contemplated by this Agreement will not entitle any Scheduled Employee to pay in lieu of notice of termination, termination pay, severance pay, retiring allowance, retirement benefit or any other payment under any written or oral agreement with Seller.

j) **Accounting**. All obligations of Seller, whether arising by operation of law, contract, past custom or otherwise, for wages, salaries, remuneration, compensation bonuses, commissions, vacation and holiday pay, sick pay or leave, or any other form of compensation payable to any Employees in respect of the services rendered by any of them have been paid, including any termination or severance pay or pay in lieu of notice of termination payable to any Employees other than Scheduled Employees.

k) **Employee Safety**. No Employee has suffered any disease, injury or death by reason of his or her handling or becoming exposed to or otherwise having been harmed by any Hazardous Materials which may at any time up to the date hereof have been present at his or her workplace in the course of his or her employment by Seller.

2.22) Insurance

Exhibit 2.22 lists and includes copies of all certificates of coverage regarding all of Seller's existing insurance policies, the premiums therefor and the coverage of each policy. Such policies and the amount of coverage and the risks insured are, in the aggregate, sufficient to protect and insure Seller against perils which good business practice demands be insured against or which are normally insured against by other industry members similarly situated, and will remain in full force and effect after the Closing.

2.23) Customer Claims

There exist no claims, whether known or unknown, against Seller for injury to person or property of its employees or any third parties suffered as a result of the sale of services by Seller including, but not limited to, errors or omissions claims. Seller has full and adequate insurance coverage for any such potential liability claims against it. Said liability insurance maintained by Seller has been on an "**occurrence**" basis during the six (6) year period prior to the Closing Date.

2.24) Environmental.

a) For purposes of this Agreement:

i) "**Hazardous Materials**" means any hazardous, infectious or toxic substance, chemical, pollutant, contaminant, as defined in the *Environmental Protection Act* of [ ] as amended, discharge, release, emission or waste which is or becomes regulated by any local, state, provincial, federal or foreign authority under Environmental Laws and Regulations (as hereinafter defined) and includes, without limitation, petroleum products or by-products, asbestos, polychlorinated biphenyls, radon and UFFI.

ii) "**Environmental Laws and Regulations**" means all limitations, restrictions, conditions, standards, prohibitions, requirements, guidelines, policies obligations, schedules and timetables contained in any Laws relating to pollution, Hazardous Materials, nuisance, or the environment whether by a local, state, provincial, federal or foreign authority and including, without limitation, (i) the *Environmental Protection Act* ([ ]), the [ ] *Water Resources Act* and the Canadian *Environmental Protection Act*, R.S.C. 1985, c. 16 (4th Supp.); (ii) Laws relating in whole or part to emissions, discharges, releases, or threatened releases of any Hazardous Material; and (iii) Laws relating in whole or part to the manufacture, processing, distribution, use, coverage, disposal, transportation, storage or handling of any Hazardous Materials.

b) The operations and activities of Seller comply, and have in the past complied, in all respects, with all Environmental Laws and Regulations. There are no pending or currently proposed changes to any

Environmental Laws and Regulations which, when implemented or effective, may affect the operations of Seller.

c) Seller has obtained and is and has been in full compliance with all requirements, permits, licences, Certificates of Approval and other authorizations which are required with respect to Seller's operations, as well as the transactions contemplated hereby under all Environmental Laws and Regulations. Exhibit 2.24 lists each such permit, licence, Certificate of Approval or other authorization. There are no other such permits, licences, Certificates of Approval or other authorizations which are required by any Environmental Laws and Regulations after the Closing.

d) There is no civil, criminal, quasi-criminal administrative or other action, suit, demand, claim, hearing, notice of violation, proceeding, investigation, notice, order or demand pending, received, or, to the best knowledge of the Seller, threatened against Seller relating in any way to any Environmental Laws and Regulations.

e) Seller has not caused, permitted, allowed or experienced any past or present events, conditions, circumstances, plans or other matters which: (i) are not in compliance with all Environmental Laws and Regulations; (ii) may give rise to any statutory, common law, or other legal liability, or otherwise form the basis of any claim, action, demand, suit, proceeding, hearing, notice of violation, order, requirement or investigation based on or relating to Hazardous Materials including, without limitation, such matters relating to any property owned, leased or utilized by Seller at any time; (iii) arise from inventory of or waste from Hazardous Materials; or (iv) arise from any offsite disposal, release or threatened release of Hazardous Materials.

f) No asbestos, polychlorinated biphenyls, lead-based paints, UFFI or radon are on or in any real property or in any building now or previously owned, operated, leased or utilized by Seller.

g) No employee or former employee of Seller has been exposed to any Hazardous Material owned, produced or utilized by Seller or any former subsidiary.

h) Seller has not received any notice or indication from any governmental agency or private or public entity advising it that it is or may be responsible for any investigation or response costs with respect to a release, threatened release or cleanup of chemicals or materials used by, transported by, stored by, manufactured by or produced by or resulting from any business, commercial or industrial activities, operations or processes, including, without limitation, any Hazardous Materials. Seller is not aware of any facts which might give rise to such notices.

i) No underground tanks, piping or subsurface structures of any type or contamination emanating therefrom exist or have existed on any real property now or previously owned, operated, leased or utilized by Seller.

j) Exhibit 2.24 contains complete copies of all environmental investigations, assessments, audits, studies, tests and related materials in possession of Seller, or known to Seller to exist, which relate to the current or prior operations of Seller or any real property now or previously owned, operated, leased or utilized by Seller.

k) No property owned, leased or otherwise utilized by Seller has ever been used as a waste disposal site.

l) Neither the Seller nor any of its officers or directors or servants have ever been charged with an environmental offense, including the offense of failing to report an incident to the appropriate authorities, which has either proceeded to acquittal, conviction or has been settled short of adjudication or conviction nor are there facts in existence which could give rise to such a charge.

2.25) Capital Expenditures

Seller has outstanding commitments for capital expenditures as set forth in Exhibit 2.25 which includes a schedule of substantially all monies disbursed on account of capital expenditures made by Seller between the Financial Statement Date and the date hereof. After the date hereof, no capital expenditures or commitments in excess of $25,000 in the aggregate will be made by Seller, except as set forth in Exhibit 2.25 or with the Buyer' prior written consent.

2.26) Suppliers

No suppliers of goods or services to Seller that has made sales or provided services representing, individually or in the aggregate, more than $10,000 in payments or commitments by Seller within the last twelve (12) months has (i) ceased, or indicated any intention to cease, doing business with Seller, or (ii) changed or indicated any intention to change any terms or conditions for future supply or sale of products or services from the terms or conditions that existed with respect to the supply or sale of such products or services during the twelve (12) month period ending on the date hereof.

2.27) Dealings with Affiliates

Exhibit 2.27 sets forth a complete list (including the parties) and copies (or a detailed summary in the case of an oral agreement) of all oral or written contracts, arrangements or other agreements to which Seller or any Affiliate is, will be or has been a party at any time from [ ], to the Closing Date, and to which any other Affiliate or Seller was or is also a party.

2.28) Business Generally

Except as disclosed in Exhibit 2.28 since [ ], there have been no events, transactions or information which have come to the attention of Seller or Stockholders (other than matters in the public domain) which could be expected to have an adverse effect on the business and operations of Seller, and Seller is not a party to any agreement, contract or covenant limiting Seller from competing in any line of business or with any person or other entity in any geographic area.

2.29) Bank Accounts

Exhibit 2.29 is a list of all bank accounts, lock boxes, safe deposit boxes and post office boxes maintained in the name of or controlled by Seller and the names of the persons having access thereto.

2.30) Compensation

Except as disclosed on Exhibit 2.30, Seller has not since the Financial Statement Date and will not prior to the Closing Date increase or commit to increase the base compensation, bonus or the rate (or any other component) of total remuneration payable or to become payable by Seller to any employee (including any director or officer), and no extraordinary compensation, commission, or bonus will be paid by Seller.

2.31) Disclosure

No representation or warranty made by Seller or any Stockholder in this Agreement or in any agreement, instrument, document, certificate, statement or letter furnished to the Buyer, by or on behalf of Seller or any Stockholder in connection with any of the transactions contemplated by this Agreement contains any untrue statement of fact or omits to state a fact necessary in order to make the statements herein or therein not misleading in light of the circumstances in which they are made.

ARTICLE 3: REPRESENTATIONS AND WARRANTIES OF THE BUYER

The Buyer hereby represents and warrants to Seller, as follows:

3.1) Corporate Organization

The Buyer is an Unlimited Liability Company duly organized, validly existing and in good standing under the laws of the Province of [ ], Canada and as of the Closing Date will be qualified to do business in [ ].

3.2) Capitalization

As of the date of this Agreement, the Buyer has authorized capital stock consisting of 10,000 shares of common stock.

3.3) Authorization

The Buyer has full corporate power and authority to enter into this Agreement and to carry out the transactions contemplated hereby. The Board of Directors of the Buyer has duly authorized the execution and delivery of this Agreement and the transactions contemplated hereby, and no other corporate proceedings on its part are necessary to authorize this Agreement and the transactions contemplated hereby.

3.4) No Violation

The Buyer is not subject to or obligated under any certificate of incorporation, bylaw, Law, or any agreement or instrument, or any licence, franchise or permit, which would be breached or violated by its execution, delivery or performance of this Agreement. The Buyer will comply with all Laws in connection with its execution, delivery and performance of this Agreement and the transactions contemplated hereby.

3.5) Governmental Authorities

Except for a notice to Investment Canada advising it of the transactions contemplated herein, the Buyer is not required to submit any notice, report or other filing with and no consent, approval or authorization is required by any governmental or regulatory authority in connection with the Buyer' execution or delivery of this Agreement or the consummation of the transactions contemplated hereby.

ARTICLE 4: COVENANTS OF SELLER AND STOCKHOLDERS

Except as otherwise consented to or approved by the Buyer in writing, Seller and the Stockholders jointly and severally covenant and agree (and will cause Seller to act or refrain from acting where required hereinafter) as follows:

4.1) Regular Course of Business

Seller will operate its business in the ordinary course, diligently and in good faith, consistent with past management practices; will maintain all of its properties in customary repair, order and condition, reasonable wear and tear excepted; will maintain (except for expiration due to lapse of time) all leases and contracts described herein in effect without change except as expressly provided herein; will comply with the provisions of all Laws, applicable to the conduct of its business; will not engage in any significant or unusual transaction; will not cancel, release, waive or compromise any debt, claim or right in its favor having a value in excess of $[ ] other than in connection with returns for credit or replacement in the ordinary course of business; will maintain insurance coverage up to the Closing Date in amounts adequate to protect and insure Seller against perils which good business practice demands be insured against or which are normally insured against by other industry members similarly situated.

4.2) Amendments

Except as required for the transactions contemplated in this Agreement, no change or amendment shall be made in Seller's articles or certificate of incorporation or bylaws. Seller will not merge into or consolidate with any other corporation or person, or change the character of its business.

4.3) Capital Changes

Seller will not issue or sell any shares of its capital stock of any class or issue or sell any securities convertible into, or options, warrants to purchase or rights to subscribe to, any shares of its capital stock of any class.

4.4) Dividends; Bonuses

Prior to Closing, Seller will not declare, pay or set aside for payment any dividend or other distribution in respect of its capital stock, nor shall Seller, directly or indirectly, redeem, purchase or otherwise acquire any shares of its capital stock, provided, however, Seller may make distributions of Excluded Assets set forth on Exhibit 1.2.5. Except for the Excluded Assets, Seller will not pay, set aside, accrue, agree to or become liable in any manner for any bonus, of any nature or type, to any Stockholder or to any employee or officer of Seller.

4.5)   Capital and Other Expenditures

Seller will not make any capital expenditures, or commitments with respect thereto, except as set forth in Exhibit 2.25. Except with respect to payments of Assumed Liabilities as required herein, Seller will not prepay any debt or obligation in excess of $[ ] (except for prepaying trade accounts payable in the normal course of business to take advantage of cash discounts).

4.6)   Borrowing

Seller will not incur, assume or guarantee any indebtedness or capital leases. Seller will not create or permit to become effective any mortgage, pledge, lien, encumbrance or charge of any kind upon its assets other than in the ordinary course of business.

4.7)   Other Commitments

Except in the ordinary course of business consistent with past practices, Seller will not enter into any transaction, make any commitment or incur any obligation.

4.8)   Interim Financial Information

Seller will supply the Buyer with unaudited monthly financial statements within twenty days of the end of each month ending between the Financial Statement Date and the Closing Date certified by its President and chief financial officer as having been prepared in accordance with procedures employed by Seller in preparing prior monthly financial statements. All such financial statements shall be accompanied by a certificate of Seller's President and chief financial officer certifying that such financial statements were prepared in accordance with generally accepted accounting principles applied on a basis consistent with the unaudited financial statements for the preceding months and such unaudited statements include all adjustments (all of which were normal recurring adjustments) necessary to fairly present the financial position, results of operations and changes in financial position at and for such period.

4.9)   Full Access and Disclosure

a)   Seller shall afford to the Buyer and its counsel, accountants and their authorized representatives access during business hours to Seller's plants, properties, books and records in order that the Buyer may have full opportunity to make such reasonable investigations as it shall desire to make of the affairs of Seller and Seller will cause its officers and employees to furnish such additional financial and operating data and other information as the Buyer shall from time to time reasonably request.

b)   From time to time prior to the Closing Date, Seller and Stock holders will promptly supplement or amend, in writing, information previously delivered to the Buyer with respect to any matter hereafter arising which, if existing or occurring at the date of this Agreement, would have been required to be set forth or disclosed.

4.10)   Consents

Seller will use all necessary means at its disposal to obtain on or prior to the Closing Date all consents necessary to the consummation of the transactions contemplated hereby.

4.11)   Breach of Agreement

Neither Seller nor any of the Stockholders will take any action which, if taken prior to the Closing Date, would constitute a breach of this Agreement.

4.12)   Further Assurances

Seller, Stockholders and Seller's counsel will furnish the Buyer or their designated assigns with such other and further documents, certificates, opinions, consents and information as either the Buyer or its designated assigns shall reasonably request to enable the Buyer or its designated assigns to borrow funds from a bank or other lending entity or individual(s) to acquire the Purchased Assets and to evidence compliance with the terms and conditions of any credit agreement in existence or to be entered into between the Buyer, or its designated assigns and a bank and/or other lending entities or individuals.

4.13)   Fulfillment of Conditions

Seller and Stockholders will take all commercially reasonable steps necessary or desirable and proceed diligently and in good faith to satisfy each condition to the obligations of the Buyer contained in this Agreement and will not take or fail to take any action that could reasonably be expected to result in the nonfulfillment of any such condition.

4.14)   Employee Liabilities

Seller covenants and agrees that it shall be responsible for all liabilities and obligations in respect of any and all Employees relating to any period up to and including the Closing Date and in respect of all Scheduled Employees who do not commence employment with the Buyer effective upon the Closing, and which relate to Labour Relations Matters, whether such liabilities and obligations are asserted by or after the Closing Date. In addition, Seller covenants and agrees that it shall be solely responsible for all liabilities and obligations arising out of any Labour Disturbances or Labour Relations Matters which arose or accrued up to and including the Closing Date. Without limiting the generality of the foregoing, Seller covenants and agrees that in the event the Buyer is required to pay any damages, costs, fees or assessments of any kind in connection with any Labour Relations Matters regarding Employees of the Seller which are the obligations of the Seller under this Agreement, it shall reimburse the Buyer for all damages, costs and fees of any kind associated with any applications, complaints, claims, grievances, suits or actions of any kind and the resolution of same whether by settlement or adjudication, including those related to the termination of any employee of the Buyer required to be terminated because of the reinstatement of any other employee.

4.15)   Maintain Employment

Seller hereby agrees to use all reasonable efforts to maintain the employment of all Scheduled Employees from and after the date hereof up to and including the Closing Date.

4.16)   If No Closing

In the event that the transactions under this Agreement are not completed in accordance with the terms and conditions hereof, Seller shall remain solely responsible for all Employees and Seller hereby covenants and agrees to indemnify and save the Buyer harmless from any liability in respect thereof, including, without limitation, any and all obligations for pay in lieu of notice, termination pay or severance pay.

ARTICLE 5: COVENANTS OF THE BUYER

The Buyer hereby covenants and agrees with Seller and Stockholders that:

5.1)   Confidentiality

The Buyer will hold in strict confidence and not disclose to any other party (other than its counsel and other advisors), without Seller's prior consent, all information received by the Buyer from Seller, and any of Seller's officers, directors, employees, agents, counsel or auditors in connection with the transactions contemplated hereby except as may be required by applicable law or as otherwise contemplated herein.

5.2) Books and Records

The Buyer shall preserve and keep Seller's books and records delivered hereunder for a period of three (3) years from the date hereof and shall, during such period, make such books and records available to officers and directors of Seller for any reasonable purpose.

5.3) Additional Assumed Liabilities

The Buyer covenants and agrees that, subject to Closing, it shall be responsible for all liabilities and obligations in respect of each Scheduled Employee who commences employment with the Buyer effective upon the Closing, to the extent such liabilities or obligations arise or accrue after the Closing Date and which relate to Labour Relations Matters. Notwithstanding the foregoing, in the event the Buyer terminates the employment of any Scheduled or Unionized Employee after the Closing Date, the Buyer shall be responsible for notice or pay in lieu, termination pay or-severance pay based on such Scheduled Employee's service with both Buyer and Seller and any predecessor, the Buyer further covenants and agrees that it will comply with the obligations of a purchaser pursuant to Section 13 of the *Employment Standards Act* of [ ].

5.4) Board of Directors

[ ] or his designated successor will occupy one seat on the Board of Directors of the Buyer until the Subordinated Note is paid in full.

ARTICLE 6: OTHER AGREEMENTS

The Buyer, each Seller and Stockholders covenant and agree that:

6.1) Agreement to Defend

In the event any action, suit, proceeding or investigation of the nature specified in Section 7.5 or Section 8.2 hereof is commenced, whether before or after the Closing Date, all the parties hereto agree to cooperate and use their best efforts to defend against and respond thereto.

6.2) Consultants, Brokers and Finders

Stockholders, Seller and the Buyer each represent and warrant to the other that they have not retained any consultant, broker or finder in connection with the transactions contemplated by this Agreement. The Buyer hereby agrees to indemnify, defend and hold the Stockholders, Seller and their respective officers, directors, employees and affiliates, harmless from and against any and all claims, liabilities or expenses for any brokerage fees, commissions or finders fees due to any consultant, broker or finder retained by the Buyer. Seller and Stockholders each hereby agree to indemnify, defend and hold the Buyer and its officers, directors, employees and affiliates, harmless from and against any and all claims, liabilities or expenses for any brokerage fees, commissions or finder's fees due to any consultant, broker or finder retained by Seller or any Stockholder.

6.3) Assumption Agreement

At the Closing, the Buyer and Seller will enter into the Assumption Agreement, as contemplated by Section 9.2(e) hereof, in the form set forth in Exhibit 6.3.

6.4) Noncompetition Agreements

At the Closing, the Buyer will enter into Non-competition Agreements ("**Non-competition Agreements**") with Seller and the Stockholders in the form set forth in Exhibits 6.4(a), and 6.4(b).

6.5) Apportionment of Taxes

Seller shall be liable and indemnify the Buyer for all Taxes attributable to the ownership of the Purchased Assets or any operations of the Seller for all taxable periods ending on or before the Closing Date ("**Pre-Closing Taxes**") except with respect to Pre-Closing Taxes which are included in Part A Assumed Liabilities. Taxes which are real property or personal property Taxes shall be allocated to Pre-Closing Taxes based on the number of days in the applicable taxable period during which the Purchased Assets were owned by the Seller. If the Buyer makes a payment of any Pre-Closing Taxes or any Taxes specified in the last sentence of this Section 6.5, it shall be entitled to prompt reimbursement from Seller for such Taxes upon presentation to Seller of evidence of such payment. Seller shall be liable and indemnify the Buyer for any sales, use, documentary, recording, stamp, transfer or similar Taxes arising from the sale of the Purchased Assets and the transactions contemplated by this Agreement.

6.6) Offer of Employment

The Buyer hereby agrees, conditional upon Closing, that it shall employ from and after the Closing date every Scheduled Employee on terms and conditions suitable to the Buyer. Except with respect to the Plans, the Buyer shall accord to such Scheduled Employees all service credits and seniority based on their service with Seller. Seller shall use its reasonable efforts to ensure that all Scheduled Employees accept such offers of employment. All items in respect of those Scheduled Employees who are employed by the Buyer after the Closing Date which require adjustment including, without limiting the generality of the foregoing, premiums for Unemployment or Employment Insurance, applicable hospital or medical plans or employer health tax, Union dues, Canada or Quebec Pension Plan contributions, accrued wages, salaries, commissions, bonuses, vacation pay or other employee benefits shall be adjusted to the Closing Date.

ARTICLE 7: CONDITIONS TO THE OBLIGATIONS OF THE BUYER

Each and every obligation of the Buyer under this Agreement shall be subject to the satisfaction, on or before the Closing Date, of each of the following conditions unless waived in writing by the Buyer:

7.1) Representations and Warranties; Performance

The representations and warranties made by Seller and Stockholders herein shall be true and correct on the date of this Agreement and on the Closing Date with the same effect as though made on such date; Seller and Stockholders shall have performed and complied with all agreements, covenants and conditions required by this Agreement to be performed and complied with by them prior to the Closing Date; Stockholders, Seller, and the Buyer shall execute and deliver at the Closing, if the Closing occurs, Exhibit 7.1 hereto, certifying to the conditions contained in this Article VII.

7.2) Consents and Approvals

All consents from and filings with third parties, regulators and governmental agencies required to consummate the transactions contemplated hereby, or which, either individually or in the aggregate, if not obtained, would cause an adverse effect on Seller's financial condition or business shall have been obtained and delivered to the Buyer.

7.3) Opinion of Counsel to Seller and Stockholders

The Buyer shall have received an opinion of counsel to Seller and Stockholders, dated the Closing Date, substantially in the form attached hereto as Exhibit 7.3.

7.4) No Adverse Change

There shall have been no adverse change since the Financial Statement Date in the business, prospects, financial condition, earnings or operations of Seller's business.

7.5) No Proceeding or Litigation

No action, suit or proceeding before any court or any governmental or regulatory authority shall have been commenced or threatened, and no investigation by any governmental or regulatory authority shall have been commenced or threatened against Seller, Stockholders or the Buyer or any of their respective principals, officers or directors seeking to restrain, prevent or change the transactions contemplated hereby or questioning the validity or legality of any of such transactions or seeking damages in connection with any of such transactions.

7.6) Solvency Certificate

The Buyer shall have received a "**solvency**" certificate from Seller's President and chief financial officer substantially in the forms of Exhibit 7.6, which shall relate to the operations and financial conditions of Seller and the interim financial statements delivered pursuant to Section 4.8 hereof.

7.7) Financial Condition at Closing

Each of the following financial conditions will exist at the Closing:

a) Except for liabilities set forth in the Balance Sheet and accounts payable incurred in the ordinary course of business of Seller consistent with past practices, Seller shall not owe any debt at the Closing Date. The term "**debt**" includes notes payable and the short-term and long-term portions of any and all debt or obligations, including capitalized lease obligations.

b) From [ ] until the Closing, Seller shall: (x) not make any distributions of assets to the Stockholders other than (i) Excluded Assets, and (ii) distributions made with the prior written consent of the Buyer; and (y) not declare or pay any additional dividends, shareholder distributions, bonuses, debt repayments except in the ordinary course of business, or compensation in excess of current compensation levels, except as provided on Exhibit J .2.3 hereof.

c) Seller's NOA at Closing will be equal to or shall exceed $[ ]. Purchased Cash at Closing will be equal to or shall exceed $[ ] net of customer deposits.

d) Seller's net sales for the fiscal year ending [ ] will be on schedule to equal at least $[ ]. Seller's net sales for the year ending [ ] shall equal at least $[ ]. Seller's net sales for the year ended [ ] shall equal at least $[ ]. Seller's net sales for the year ended [ ] shall equal at least $[ ].

e) Seller's earnings before interest, income taxes, depreciation, and amortization calculated in accordance with generally accepted accounting principles, consistently applied ("**EBITDA**") for the year ending [ ] will be on schedule to equal at least $[ ]. Seller's EBITDA for the year ended [ ] shall equal at least $[ ]. Seller's EBITDA for the year ended [ ] shall equal at least $[ ]. Seller's EBITDA for the year ended [ ] shall equal at least $[ ].

f)   The mix and composition of the assets and liabilities of Seller on the Closing Date will not be materially different than those indicated on the Balance Sheet, subject to changes occurring in the ordinary course of business.

g)   Seller's interim statements since [ ] shall be reasonably satisfactory in all respects to the Buyer.

7.8)   Confirmation of Statements

The Buyer shall review and confirm the results of Seller's operations as of [ ], which shall be satisfactory to the Buyer in its sole and absolute discretion.

7.9)   Review

A full due diligence review of Seller's business shall be completed by the Buyer, its legal counsel, its outside consultants, or others appointed by the Buyer. The Buyer shall be satisfied in its sole and absolute discretion with the results of the Buyer' due diligence review of Seller and its business operations, prospects and assets. The Buyer shall bear the costs of this review.

7.10)   Other Documents

Stockholders and Seller will furnish the Buyer with such other and further documents and certificates of Stockholders' and Seller's officers and others as the Buyer shall reasonably request to evidence compliance with the conditions set forth in this Agreement.

7.11)   Other Agreements

The Agreements described in Article VI shall have been entered into and delivered.

7.12)   Board of Directors Approval

The Board of Directors of [ ] shall have approved this Agreement, the transactions contemplated hereby and the Closing.

7.13)   Bulk Sales

The Seller shall fully comply with the provisions of the *Bulk Sales Act* ([ ]) in connection with this Agreement and the transactions contemplated herein, all in form and Substance satisfactory to the Buyer.

ARTICLE 8: CONDITIONS TO THE OBLIGATIONS OF SELLER AND STOCKHOLDERS

Each and every obligation of Seller and Stockholders under this Agreement shall be subject to the satisfaction, on or before the Closing Date, of each of the following conditions unless waived in writing by Seller and Stockholders:

8.1)   Representations and Warranties; Performance

The representations and warranties made by the Buyer herein shall be true and correct on the date of this Agreement and on the Closing Date with the same effect as though made on such date; the Buyer shall have performed and complied with all agreements, covenants and conditions required by this Agreement to be performed and complied with by it prior to the Closing Date; the Buyer shall have delivered to Seller a certificate of its President, dated the Closing Date, certifying to the fulfillment of the conditions set forth herein, in the form designated as Exhibit 8.1 and the other conditions contained in this Article VIII.

8.2)   No Proceeding or Litigation

No action, suit or proceeding before any court or any governmental or regulatory authority shall have been commenced, or threatened, and no investigation by any governmental or regulatory authority shall have been commenced, or threatened, against Seller, any Stockholder, the Buyer, or any of their respective principals, officers or directors, seeking to restrain, prevent or change the transactions contemplated hereby or questioning the validity or legality of any of such transactions or seeking damages in connection with any of such transactions.

8.3)   Opinion of Counsel

Seller shall have received an opinion of counsel to the Buyer dated the Closing Date substantially in the form of Exhibit 8.3.

8.4)   Payment

The payment(s) of the Purchase Price described in Section 1.3 shall have been made.

8.5)   Other Documents

The Buyer will furnish Seller with such other documents and certificates to evidence compliance with the conditions set forth in this Article as may be reasonably requested by Seller.

8.6)   Other Agreements

The agreements described in Article VI shall have been entered into and delivered.

ARTICLE 9: CLOSING

9.1) Closing

Unless this Agreement shall have been terminated or abandoned pursuant to the provisions of Article X hereof, a closing (the **"Closing"**) shall be held on [ ], or on such other date (the **"Closing Date"**) mutually agreed upon at such place or places as the Buyer shall designate. Each party has the right at any time to extend the Closing Date for a period of up to thirty (30) business days from the date stated above, by written notice to the other party or parties.

9.2) Deliveries at Closing.

a) At the Closing, Seller shall transfer and assign to the Buyer all of the Purchased Assets, the Subordinated Note and FPP's and the other agreements, certifications and other documents required to be executed and delivered hereunder at the Closing shall be duly and validly executed and delivered.

b) At and after the Closing, Seller shall have the right to review and obtain copies of any financial records of Seller, in the possession of the Buyer, necessary for the preparation of Seller's tax returns, and the Buyer agrees to retain such records until the statute of limitations pertaining to the final tax returns filed by Seller expires, and the Buyer shall have the right to review and obtain copies of the minute book, stock book and stock register of Seller.

c) At the Closing, Seller shall deliver to the Buyer, in form reasonably satisfactory to counsel for the Buyer, such bills of sale, assignments, deeds or other conveyances and all third party consents as may be appropriate or necessary to effect the transfer to the Buyer of the property and rights as contemplated herein.

d) From time to time after the Closing, at the Buyer' request and without further consideration from the Buyer, Seller shall, and Stockholders shall cause Seller to, execute and deliver such other instruments of conveyance and transfer and take such other action as the Buyer reasonably may require to convey, transfer to and vest in the Buyer and to put the Buyer in possession of any assets or property to be sold, conveyed, transferred and delivered hereunder.

e) The assumption of liabilities and obligations hereunder shall be by assumption agreement (as set forth in Exhibit 6.3). The Buyer and its successors and assigns will forever defend, indemnify and hold Seller and Stockholders harmless from any and all liabilities and obligations of Seller which have been assumed by the Buyer at the Closing, or which shall arise from any acts or omissions of the Buyer after the Closing. The Buyer agrees at Seller's request from time to time (but no earlier than ninety (90) days after the Closing) to supply to Seller proof of or a certificate by its Chief Financial Officer of the payment and satisfaction by the Buyer of liabilities and obligations of Seller due to date and assumed by the Buyer.

f)   Seller shall obtain and provide to the Buyer on Closing a clearance certificate pursuant to section 6 of the *Retail Sales Tax Act* ([ ]).

g)   At the Closing, the Buyer shall deliver to the Seller cheques payable to the order of the relevant taxing authorities in the amount of any applicable Canadian Transfer Taxes payable in connection with the sale of the Purchased Assets.

9.3) Legal Actions

If, prior to the Closing Date, any action or proceeding shall have been instituted by any third party before any court or governmental agency to restrain or prohibit this Agreement or the consummation of the transactions contemplated herein, the Closing shall be adjourned at the option of any party hereto for a period of up to one hundred twenty (120) days. If, at the end of such 120-day period, the action or proceeding shall not have been favorably resolved, any party hereto may, by written notice thereof to the other party or parties, terminate its obligation hereunder.

9.4) Specific Performance

The parties agree that if any party hereto is obligated to, but nevertheless does not, consummate this transaction, then any other party, in addition to all other rights or remedies, shall be entitled to the remedy of specific performance mandating that the other party or parties consummate this transaction. In an action for specific performance by any party against any other party, the other party shall not plead adequacy of damages at law.

9.5) Name Change

Upon the Closing, the Seller shall change its name to another name different from its present name and do such other things as shall be necessary or desirable to permit the Buyer to assume and use all names utilized by Seller in operating its business as an ongoing concern other than "[ ]".

ARTICLE 10: TERMINATION AND ABANDONMENT

10.1) Methods of Termination

This Agreement may be terminated and the transactions herein contemplated may be abandoned at any time (notwithstanding approval by the Board of Directors of the Buyer):

a) by mutual consent of the Buyer and Seller; or

b) by either Seller or the Buyer if (i) such party is not in breach hereunder and the other party is in breach hereunder, and (ii) this Agreement is not consummated on or before the Closing Date, including extensions.

10.2) Procedure Upon Termination

In the event of termination and abandonment pursuant to Section 10.1 hereof, this Agreement shall terminate and shall be abandoned, without further action by any of the parties hereto. If this Agreement is terminated as provided herein:

a) each party will upon request redeliver all documents and other materials of any other party relating to the transactions contemplated hereby, whether so obtained before or after the execution hereof, to the party furnishing the same;

b) no party hereto shall have any liability or further obligation to any other party to this Agreement; and

c) each party shall bear its own expenses.

ARTICLE 11: INDEMNIFICATION

11.1) Indemnification by Seller and Stockholders

The Seller and the Stockholders, jointly and severally, agree to indemnify the Buyer and each of its shareholders, officers and directors against any loss, damage, or expense (including but not limited to reasonable attorneys' fees) ("**Damages**"), incurred or sustained by the Buyer or any of its shareholders, officers or directors as a result of (a) any breach of any term, provision, covenant or agreement contained in this Agreement by Seller or any Stockholder; (b) any inaccuracy in any of the representations or warranties made by Seller or any Stockholder in Article II of this Agreement; (c) any inaccuracy or misrepresentation in any certificate or other document or instrument delivered by Seller or any Stockholder in accordance with any provision of this Agreement; (d) any liability or obligation of Seller or any Stockholder not expressly assumed in writing by the Buyer; or (e) failure of Seller and the Buyer to comply with the provisions of any applicable *Personal Property Security Act*, R.S.O. 1990, c. P. 10 provisions or similar laws and/or regulations relating to bulk sales. The obligations of Seller and Stockholders as set forth in Section 11.1(b) shall be subject to and limited by the following:

a) No claim for Damages shall be made until the cumulative amount of such Damages shall equal or exceed $[ ]; provided, however, that such limitation shall not apply to any Damages resulting from violations under Sections 2.2, 2.4, 2.12, 2.14, 2.18 or 2.24 hereof or from intentional or fraudulent actions, misrepresentations or breaches;

b) The Seller's and Stockholder's obligations under this Section 11.1 shall not exceed the Purchase Price.

c) The Buyer shall give written notice to Seller and Stockholders stating specifically the basis for the claim for Damages, the amount thereof and shall tender defence thereof to Seller and Stockholders as provided in Section 11.2; and

d) In addition to any other remedy, the Buyer shall be entitled, but shall not be obligated, to offset all such claims for Damages against any obligation of the Buyer to Seller or any Stockholder now or hereafter existing.

11.2) Tender of Defence for Damages

Promptly upon receipt by the Buyer of a notice of a claim by a third party which may give rise to a claim for Damages, the Buyer shall give written notice thereof to Seller and the Stockholders. No failure or delay of the Buyer in the performance of the foregoing shall relieve, reduce or otherwise affect the Seller's or Stockholders' obligations and liability to indemnify the Buyer pursuant to this Agreement, except to the extent that such failure or delay shall have adversely affected the Seller's or Stockholders' ability to defend against such claim for Damages. If Seller and the Stockholders give to the Buyer an agreement in writing, in a form reasonably satisfactory to the Buyer's counsel, to defend such claim for Damages, Seller and Stockholders may, at their sole expense, undertake the defence against such claim and may contest or settle such claim on such terms, at such time and in such manner as Seller and Stockholders, in their sole discretion, shall elect and the Buyer shall execute such documents and take such steps as may be reasonably necessary in the opinion of counsel for Seller and Stockholders to enable Seller and Stockholders to conduct the defence of such claim for Damages. If Seller and Stockholders fail or refuse to defend any claim for Damages, Seller and Stockholders may nevertheless, at their own expense, participate in the defence of such claim by the Buyer and in any and all settlement negotiations relating thereto. In any and all events, Seller and Stockholders shall have such access to the records and files of the Buyer relating to any claim for Damages as may be reasonably necessary to effectively defend or participate in the defence thereof.

11.3)　Survival of Warranties

The respective representations and warranties of Seller, Stockholders and the Buyer contained herein or in any certificates or other documents delivered prior to or at the Closing are true, accurate and correct and shall not be deemed waived or otherwise affected by any investigation made by any party hereto or the occurrence of the Closing. Each and every such representation and warranty shall survive for a period of two (2) years from the Closing Date; provided, however, all representations and warranties made pursuant to Section 2.14 shall survive for the applicable statute of limitations for assessment of such taxes. The representations and warranties made pursuant to Sections 2.2, 2.4, 2.12, 2.18 and 2.24 shall never expire; and all claims for Damages based on intentional or fraudulent actions, misrepresentations or breaches shall never expire.

11.4)　Closing Date Damages

The Buyer acknowledges that to the best of its knowledge there are no claims as of the Closing Date which would give rise to a Damage claim by the Buyer.

ARTICLE 12: MISCELLANEOUS PROVISIONS

12.1)　Amendment and Modification

Subject to applicable law, this Agreement may be amended, modified and supplemented only by written agreement of Seller, Stockholders and the Buyer.

12.2)　Waiver of Compliance; Consents

Any failure of Seller or Stockholders on the one hand, or the Buyer on the other hand, to comply with any obligation, covenant, agreement or condition herein may be waived in writing by the Buyer or by Seller and Stockholders, respectively, but such waiver or failure to insist upon strict compliance with such obligation, covenant, agreement or condition shall not operate as a waiver of, or estoppel with respect to, any subsequent or other failure. Whenever this Agreement requires or permits consent by or on behalf of any party hereto, such consent shall be given in writing in a manner consistent with the requirements for a waiver of compliance as set forth in this Section 12 2.

12.3)   Expenses

Each party will pay its own legal, accounting and other expenses incurred by such party or on its behalf in connection with this Agreement and the transactions contemplated herein. If Seller shall at any time pay any expenses incurred in connection with this Agreement or any part thereof or any of the proceedings and transactions contemplated hereunder including, without limitation, any legal, accounting, printing, filing or other costs, then the Purchase Price shall be reduced by an equal amount.

12.4)   Notices

Any notice, request, consent or communication (collectively a **"Notice"**) under this Agreement shall be effective only if it is in writing and personally delivered, (ii) sent by certified or registered mail, return receipt requested, postage pre-paid, (iii) sent by a nationally recognized overnight delivery service, with delivery confirmed, or (iv) telexed or telecopied, with receipt confirmed, addressed as follows:

a)   If to Seller or Stockholders:
[ ]
in each case with a copy to: [ ]
Telecopier: [ ]
Telephone: [ ]

b)   If to the Buyer to: [ ]
Telecopier: [ ]
Telephone: [ ]
with a copy to: [ ]
Telecopier: [ ]
Telephone: [ ]

or such other persons or addresses as shall be furnished in writing by any party to the other party. A Notice shall be deemed to have been given as of the date when (i) personally delivered, (ii) five (5) days after the date when deposited with the Canada mail properly addressed, (iii) when receipt of a Notice sent by an overnight delivery service is confirmed by such overnight delivery service, or (iv) when receipt of the telex or telecopy is confirmed, as the case may be, unless the sending party has actual knowledge that a Notice was not received by the intended recipient.

12.5) Assignment

This Agreement and all of the provisions hereof shall be binding upon and inure to the benefit of the parties hereto and their respective heirs, successors and permitted assigns, but neither this Agreement nor any of the rights, interests or obligations hereunder shall be assigned by Seller or the Stockholders without the prior written consent of the Buyer; provided, however, that without the prior written consent of Sellers and Stockholders, the Buyer may assign its rights and interests under this Agreement without restrictions or limitations to any party including but not limited to an affiliate of the Buyer or to any lender who shall provide financing to the Buyer or [ ] in connection with the Purchased Assets.

12.6) Governing Law

This Agreement shall be governed by the laws of the Province of [ ], Canada (regardless of the laws that might otherwise govern under applicable [ ] principles of conflicts of law of the Province of [ ] as to all matters including, but not limited to, matters of validity, construction, effect, performance and remedies.

12.7) Arbitration

THE PARTIES HERETO AGREE THAT ANY SUCH DISPUTE RELATING TO OR IN RESPECT OF THIS AGREEMENT, ITS NEGOTIATION, EXECUTION, PERFORMANCE, SUBJECT MATTER, OR ANY COURSE OF CONDUCT OR DEALING OR ACTIONS UNDER OR IN RESPECT OF THIS AGREEMENT, SHALL BE SUBMITTED TO, AND RESOLVED EXCLUSIVELY PURSUANT TO ARBITRATION IN ACCORDANCE WITH THE ARBITRATION ACT ([ ]). SUCH ARBITRATION SHALL BE CONDUCTED BY A MUTUALLY AGREED UPON ARBITRATOR SELECTED FROM THE LIST OF MEMBERS OF THE PRIVATE COURT AND SHALL TAKE PLACE IN [ ], [ ]. DECISIONS PURSUANT TO SUCH ARBITRATION SHALL BE FINAL, CONCLUSIVE AND BINDING ON THE PARTIES. UPON THE CONCLUSION OF ARBITRATION, THE PARTIES MAY APPLY TO ANY COURT OF COMPETENT JURISDICTION TO ENFORCE THE DECISION PURSUANT TO SUCH ARBITRATION. THE PARTIES HERETO HEREBY WAIVE AND SHALL NOT SEEK JURY TRIAL IN ANY LAWSUIT, PROCEEDING, CLAIM, COUNTERCLAIM, DEFENCE OR OTHER LITIGATION OR DISPUTE UNDER OR IN RESPECT OF THIS AGREEMENT.

12.8) Counterparts

This Agreement may be executed in two or more counterparts, each of which shall be deemed an original, but all of which together shall constitute one and the same instrument.

12.9)   Neutral Interpretation

This Agreement constitutes the product of the negotiation of the parties hereto and the enforcement hereof shall be interpreted in a neutral manner, and not more strongly for or against any party based upon the source of the draftsmanship hereof.

12.10) Headings

The article and section headings contained in this Agreement are for reference purposes only and shall not affect in any way the meaning or interpretation of this Agreement.

12.11) Entire Agreement

This Agreement, which term as used throughout includes the Exhibits hereto, embodies the entire agreement and understanding of the parties hereto in respect of the subject matter contained herein. There are no restrictions, promises, representations, warranties, covenants or undertakings other than those expressly set forth or referred to herein. This Agreement supersedes all prior agreements and understandings between the parties with respect to such subject matter.

IN WITNESS WHEREOF, the parties hereto have entered into this Agreement as of the date first hereinabove set forth.

By: By:

_______________________   _______________________

Name: _______________________   Name: _______________________

Title: _______________________   Title: _______________________

STOCKHOLDERS

Witness:

____

Print Name: _______________________

SCHEDULE OF EXHIBITS TO
AGREEMENT FOR PURCHASE AND SALE OF ASSETS

Exhibits		Title
S	Exhibit 1.2.2(a)	Machinery, Equipment, Furniture and Fixtures and Other Personal Property and Fixed Assets
S	Exhibit 1.2.2(b)	Cash, Cash Equivalents, Certificates of Deposit, Notes Receivable, Accounts Receivable and All Other Receivables
H	Exhibit 1.2.4	NOA Example
S	Exhibit 1.2.5	Excluded Assets
H	Exhibit 1.3	Subordinated Note
S	Exhibit 1.6	Allocation
S	Exhibit 2.1.1	Description of Business
S	Exhibit 2.1.2	Articles of Amalgamation and Bylaws
S	Exhibit 2.2	Authorized, Issued and Outstanding Capital Stock of Seller
S	Exhibit 2.3	Subsidiaries and Affiliates
S	Exhibit 2.4	Stockholder List and Consents to Resolutions
S	Exhibit 2.5	Restrictions on Ability to Perform
S	Exhibit 2.6	Governmental Consent
S	Exhibit 2.7	Financial Statements
S	Exhibit 2.10A	Contracts
S	Exhibit 2.10B	Contracts requiring Consents
S	Exhibit 2.12	Title and Related Matters
S	Exhibit 2.13	Legal Proceedings and Judgments
S	Exhibit 2.14.1	Certain Tax Matters
S	Exhibit 2.14.2	Tax Returns
S	Exhibit 2.16	Certain Copies of Reports and Inspections
S	Exhibit 2.17	Certain Business Practices
S	Exhibit 2.18(a) and (c)	Pension and Employee Benefit Matters
S	Exhibit 2.19	Intellectual Property Rights

Exhibits		Title
S	Exhibit 2.20	Warranties and Claims Under Warranties
S	Exhibit 2.21(a)	Employee Agreements
S	Exhibit 2.21(b)	Employees of Seller
S	Exhibit 2.21(d)	Labour Relations
S	Exhibit 2.21(e)	Employee Relations
S	Exhibit 2.21(f)	Liability to Employees
S	Exhibit 2.21(g)	Labour Disturbance
S	Exhibit 2.21(h)	Employment Laws
S	Exhibit 2.22	Schedule of Insurance
S	Exhibit 2.24	Environmental Matters
S	Exhibit 2.25	Capital Expenditures
S	Exhibit 2.27	Contracts with Affiliates
S	Exhibit 2.28	Business Generally
S	Exhibit 2.29	Bank Accounts
S	Exhibit 2.30	Compensation Schedule
H	Exhibit 6.3	Assumption Agreement
H	Exhibit 6.4(a)	Non-competition Agreement—Stockholders
H	Exhibit 6.4(b)	Non-competition Agreement—Seller
H	Exhibit 7.1	Certificate of Fulfilment of Conditions by Seller and Stockholders
H	Exhibit 7.3	Opinion of Seller's Counsel
H	Exhibit 7.6	Solvency Certificate
H	Exhibit 8.1	Certificate of Fulfilment of Conditions by the Buyer
H	Exhibit 8.3	Opinion of the Buyer' Counsel
S		To be prepared by counsel for Seller
H		To be prepared by counsel for the Buyer

Form 14: **Asset Purchase Agreement**

THIS AGREEMENT made this day of ●, ●.

BETWEEN:

● of the Province of Ontario;

(hereinafter called the "Vendor")

and -

●, a corporation incorporated under the laws of the Province of Ontario, having its registered office at ●; (hereinafter called the "**Purchaser**")

WHEREAS the Vendor carries on the business of under the name and style ●;

AND WHEREAS the Purchaser desires to purchase and the Vendor agrees to sell the business of the Vendor carried on under the name and style "I" on and subject to the terms of this Asset Purchase Agreement;

NOW THEREFORE THIS Agreement witnesseth that in consideration of ONE DOLLAR ($1.00) and the covenants and agreements herein, the parties agree as follows:

ARTICLE 1: DEFINED TERMS

1.1) Definitions

In this Agreement,

a)   "**Business**" means the ● business presently carried on as a going concern by the Vendor as a sole proprietorship under the name and style "●".

b) **"Closing"** means the closing of the transactions contemplated in this Agreement at the Time of Closing.

c) **"Closing Date"** means ● or such earlier or later date mutually agreed on.

d) **"Lease"** means the lease for the Premises dated ● between the Vendor as lessee and ●, as lessor.

e) **"Premises"** means the premises at ● Ontario.

ARTICLE 2: SCHEDULES

2.1)   Schedules

The following schedules are attached to and incorporated in this Agreement by reference and deemed to be part hereof:

- Schedule 1 – Equipment and Inventory Listing
- Schedule 2 – Transferable Contracts

ARTICLE 3: AGREEMENT TO PURCHASE

3.1)   Assets to be Purchased and Sold

Subject to the terms and conditions hereof and relying on the representations and warranties herein, the Vendor agrees to sell, assign, convey and transfer to the Purchaser and the Purchaser agrees to purchase and accept assignments from the Vendor as a going concern all of the undertaking and all property and assets of the Business, as, at and from the close of business on the Closing Date, of every kind and description and wheresoever situate (except for those Excluded Assets as provided in Section 3.2) (collectively, the **"Assets"**), including without limitation:

a) all right, title and interest in and to the Lease and all plant, structures, erections, improvements, appurtenances and fixtures used in connection with the Business and situate at the Premises (the **"Leasehold Improvements"**);

b) all equipment, machinery, furniture, furnishings and accessories and supplies of all kinds used in connection with the Business, including without limitation the equipment and machinery disclosed in Schedule 1 (the **"Equipment"**);

c)   all inventories of, pertaining to and used in connection with the Business including, without limitation the inventory listed on Schedule 1 all finished goods, work in progress, new and unused production, shipping and packaging supplies used or consumed in the Business but excluding defective goods, goods returned by customers claiming such goods are below required standards, inventories that are no longer usable or saleable due to engineering changes or physical deterioration or in excess of one year's supply based on the prior 12 months of usage or sales, based on current quantities or orders on hand, whichever is higher, all as determined by the Vendor and jointly agreed on by the Vendor and the Purchaser (the **"Inventory"**);

d)   the benefit of all transferable contracts, agreements and commitments in connection with the Business and all transferable licences, quotas, consents, permits and approvals granted in connection with the Business, written or oral, including without limitation the transferable contracts and agreements disclosed in Schedule 2 and the full benefit of all unfilled orders received by the Vendor in connection with the Business and all other contracts, engagements or commitments (except as hereinafter provided) to which the Vendor is entitled in connection with the Business, whether written or oral, including the full benefit and advantage of all forward commitments by the Vendor for supplies or materials entered into in the ordinary course of the Business for use in the Business whether or not there are any contracts with respect thereto, provided that the Purchaser is agreeable to assuming such contracts (the **"Transferable Contracts"**);

e)   all registered and unregistered trademarks, trade or brand names, service marks, copyrights, designs, inventions, patents, pending patent applications, patent rights (including any patents issuing on such applications or rights), licences, sub-licences, franchises, formulae, processes, technology and other industrial and intellectual property of or pertaining to the Business, together with the benefit of all goodwill associated therewith, including without limitation the trade names and trademark for the Business ● and ● and any other variation thereon (the **"Intellectual Property"**);

f)   all copies, both in machine-readable and human-readable form, of all computer programs and software or interests therein or rights thereto used in connection with the Business, together with the media on

> which such software and programs are stored, including all documentation and information relating thereto (the "**Computer Programs**");

g) the rights relating to all amounts prepaid in connection with the Business that may be used by the Purchaser, including without limitation rent, business taxes, insurance premiums and the benefit of any contracts relating thereto (the "**Prepaid Expenses**");

h) the goodwill of the Business, together with the exclusive right of the Purchaser to represent itself as carrying on the Business in continuation of and in succession to the Vendor and the right to use any words indicating that the Business is so carried on, including the exclusive right to use the names ● and ● or any variation thereof as part of the name of or in connection with the Business or any part thereof carried on or to be carried on by the Purchaser, including all restrictive agreements and negative covenant agreements which the Vendor may have with its employees of the Business, past or present (the "**Goodwill**");

i) all contracts with customers, whether written or oral and all quotations, orders or tenders for contracts with existing or prospective customers which remain open for acceptance;

j) all books, records, books of account, sales and purchase records, lists of customers, prospects and suppliers, recipes and formulae, business plans and projections, plans, architectural drawings and blueprints and all other documents, files, records and other data and information relating to the Business, including without limitation all data and information stored on magnetic tape or other computer related media (the "**Books and Records**"); and

k) all other property, assets and rights, real or personal, tangible or intangible, used by the Vendor or to which it is entitled, in connection with the Business.

3.2) Excluded Assets

The following assets and liabilities (collectively, the "**Excluded Assets**") are hereby specifically excluded from the purchase and sale of assets and the definition of Assets herein:

a) cash on hand or in banks or other depositories, life insurance proceeds receivable and income taxes refundable in favour of the Vendor;

b) assets of the Vendor not relating to the Business and such other assets relating to the Business as are specifically excluded by any other term or provision of this Agreement; and

c)   all accounts receivable, trade accounts, notes receivable, book debts, insurance claims recorded as receivable on the Vendor's books of account and unrecorded insurance claims in respect of losses incurred prior to Closing and other debts due or accruing due to the Vendor in connection with the Business as at Closing and the full benefit of all securities for such accounts, notes, debts or claims (the **"Accounts Receivable"**).

ARTICLE 4: LIABILITIES

4.1)   Assumed Liabilities

The Purchaser does not assume and will not be liable for, and the Vendor agrees to indemnify and save the Purchaser harmless from and against, all debts, liabilities, contracts, obligations or commitments of or claims against the Vendor (whether absolute, accrued or contingent) and whether arising out of or in any way connected with the Business or otherwise, except:

a)   liabilities for services, merchandise, materials and supplies contracted for by the Vendor in the ordinary course of the Business but not delivered prior to Closing; and

b)   the Vendor's liability from and after the Closing Date under the Transferable Contracts,

(collectively, the **"Assumed Liabilities"**) which Assumed Liabilities the Purchaser hereby expressly assumes and agrees to indemnify and save the Vendor harmless from and against and all obligations, claims or demands in respect thereof.

4.2)   Bulk Sales Act

The Vendor agrees and hereby covenants to comply with the provisions of the *Bulk Sales Act*, R.S.O. 1990 c.B.14, including, but not limited to providing the Purchaser with a sworn affidavit listing all creditors of the Business as at the Closing Date, and the Vendor agrees to indemnify and save the Purchaser harmless from and against, all claims against the Purchaser (whether absolute, accrued or contingent) and whether arising out of or in any way connected with any breach by the Vendor of any requirement of the *Bulk Sales Act*.

ARTICLE 5: PURCHASE PRICE, SATISFACTION OF PURCHASE PRICE, ALLOCATION, AND TAXES

5.1) Purchase Price

a)   The purchase price payable by the Purchaser to the Vendor for the Assets (the **"Purchase Price"**) shall be $●. The purchase price shall be allocated as follows:

- $● to be paid for equipment, inventory and accounts receivable; and
- $● to be paid for the goodwill of the Business;

   and each party will prepare and file its income tax returns in accordance with such allocation.

b)   The Purchase Price will be paid and satisfied by delivery on Closing by the Purchaser of a certified cheque payable to the Vendor in the amount of $●, subject to usual adjustments.

c)   The Purchaser will be liable for and pay all federal and provincial sales taxes, federal taxes and all other taxes, duties or other like charges properly payable on and in connection with the conveyance and transfer of the Assets by the Vendor to the Purchaser, save and except any income or corporation taxes payable by the Vendor.

d)   The parties shall on the Closing Date, to the extent permitted under the *Excise Tax Act* (**"ETA"**) jointly elect under subsection 167(1) of the ETA, in the form and manner prescribed for purposes of that subsection, in respect of the sale and transfer of the Assets.

ARTICLE 6: LEASES AND TRANSFERABLE CONTRACTS

6.1) Transferable Contract

The parties will use all reasonable efforts to procure assignments of the Transferable Contracts. If any Transferable Contract is not capable of being assigned at Closing or can only be assigned on the basis that the terms of such Transferable Contract be modified in a manner which, in the Purchaser's sole opinion is adverse to the Purchaser, at the Purchaser's option:

a)   Such Transferable Contract will not be assigned to the Purchaser at Closing;

b) The Vendor will hold all rights or entitlements that the Vendor has thereto for the exclusive benefit of the Purchaser; provided that the Purchaser will pay, perform and discharge all obligations arising or accruing with respect thereto; or

c) The Purchaser may terminate this Agreement by written notice to the Vendor.

ARTICLE 7: REPRESENTATIONS

7.1) Representations and Warranties of the Vendor

a) The Vendor represents and warrants to the Purchaser as follows with the knowledge and expectation that the Purchaser is placing complete reliance thereon and, but for such representations and warranties, the Purchaser would not have entered into this Agreement:

b) The Vendor has not committed an act of bankruptcy, is not insolvent, has not proposed a compromise or arrangement to his creditors generally, has not had any petition for a bankruptcy order filed against him, has not taken any proceeding and no proceeding has been taken to have a receiver appointed over any of his assets, has not had an encumbrancer take possession of any of his property and has not had any execution or distress become enforceable or levied against any of his property.

7.2) Sole Proprietorship and GST Registration

The Vendor is the sole proprietor of the Business. The Vendor is a registrant for ETA purposes, with registration number ●.

7.3) Absence of Conflicting Agreements

The Vendor's execution and delivery of this Agreement, the performance of his obligations hereunder and his completion of the transactions will not result in (i) the violation of any term or provision of any agreement, written or oral, to which the Vendor is a party or by which he is bound; (ii) the creation of any security interest, lien or other encumbrance on the Assets; or (iii) the violation of any law or regulation, or any order or decree of any court, tribunal or arbitrator to which the Vendor is subject.

7.4)   Ownership of Assets and Right to Sell

a)   Except for the Assumed Liabilities, the Vendor owns, possesses and has good title to the Assets as absolute beneficial owner thereof, free and clear of any and all mortgages, liens, charges, pledges, security interests, encumbrances, actions, claims or demands of any nature whatsoever or howsoever arising and is exclusively entitled to possess and dispose of the Assets. No person, firm or corporation has any written or oral agreement, option, understanding or commitment, or any right or privilege capable of becoming an agreement, for the purchase from the Vendor of any of the Assets, other than in the ordinary course of the Business.

b)   No assets other than the Assets are required to be transferred to the Purchaser in order that the Purchaser may operate the Business and the Assets represent all of the assets required to operate the Business and which have been used by the Vendor to operate the Business.

7.5)   Effect of Transactions

There are no rights, privileges or advantages presently enjoyed by the Business as a result of the Business being conducted by the Vendor which, to the Vendor's knowledge, might be lost as a result of the consummation of the transactions contemplated in this Agreement.

7.6)   Books and Records

The Vendor's books and records fairly and accurately set out and disclose in all material respects the Vendor's financial position as at the date hereof. All material financial transactions of the Vendor relating to the Business have been accurately recorded in such books and records.

7.7)   Changes Since Date of Financial Statements

Since the Financial Statements shown to the Purchaser and dated ● there has been no change in the terms of any contract, agreement or commitment with respect to the Business (apart from normal price changes) or the affairs, business, liabilities, assets or operations of the Business, financial or otherwise, whether arising as a result of any legislative or regulatory change, revocation of any licence or right to do business, fire, explosion, accident, casualty, labour trouble, flood, drought, riot, storm, condemnation, act of God, or other public force or otherwise except changes occurring in the ordinary course of business, which changes have not affected and will not adversely affect the organization, business, properties or financial condition of the Business.

7.8) Taxes and Assessments

All taxes, assessments and other governmental charges in respect of the Business or any of the Assets which are due and payable have been paid and the charges, accruals and reserves on the Vendor's books in respect of taxes of any kind relating to the Business or Assets for all years to date are adequate.

7.9) Liabilities

a) There are no liabilities of the Vendor relating to the Business of any kind whatsoever, whether or not accrued and whether or not determined or determinable, in respect of which the Purchaser may become liable on or after the consummation of the transaction contemplated by this Agreement other than liabilities incurred in the ordinary course of the Business since ●.

b) The Vendor has no indebtedness to any person, firm, corporation or government or agency thereof which, in the absence of satisfaction thereof by the Vendor, by operation of law or otherwise, now or hereafter might become a liability of the Purchaser or constitute a lien, charge or encumbrance on any of the Assets.

c) The Vendor is not bound by or a party to any written employment or service agreement. There are no employees or independent contractors of the Business except for the Vendor. All salaries, benefits, remuneration, bonuses, commission and other payments and endowments due to the Vendor are in good standing as of the date hereof and no monies are owed to the Vendor on account of wages, salary or benefits. No former employee is subject to re-instatement.

7.10) Compliance with Law

The Vendor is conducting the Business in compliance in all respects with all applicable laws, by-laws, rules and regulations of each jurisdiction in which the Business is carried on. The Vendor has not received any notice alleging breach of any such laws, by-laws, rules and regulations, is duly licensed, registered or qualified in each jurisdiction in which the Vendor owns or leases property or carries on the Business, to enable the Business to be carried on as now conducted and its property and assets to be owned, leased and operated, and all such licences, registrations and qualifications are valid and subsisting and in good standing and none of the same contains any burdensome term, provision, condition or limitation which has or may have an adverse effect on the operation of the Business.

7.11)   Insurance

The Assets and the Business are insured in the Vendor's name against loss or damage by all insurable hazards or risks on a replacement cost basis. Such insurance coverage will be continued in full force and effect until Closing. The Vendor is not in default of any provision of any such insurance policy, the premiums thereon are not delinquent and the Vendor has not failed to give any notice or present any claim under any such insurance policy in a due and timely fashion. The Vendor has not received notification from any insurer denying or disputing any coverage for any claim or the amount of any claim. There are no pending or anticipated claims under any policy and there has been no occurrence of any kind that would give rise to any claim.

7.12)   Lease

The Lease is and will be at Closing in good standing, in full force and effect without amendment thereto and neither the Vendor nor the Landlord pursuant to the Lease is in breach of any covenant, condition or agreement contained in the Lease or in breach of any covenant, condition or agreement contained in any such lease that would give rise to a termination right.

7.13)   Contracts

There are no outstanding agreements, understandings, contracts or commitments, written or oral, of any nature or kind whatsoever relating to the Business, except

    i)   forward commitments by the Vendor for supplies or materials entered into in the ordinary course of the Business for use in the Business,

    ii)   sales commitments entered into in the ordinary course of the Business,

    iii)   the Lease,

    iv)   the insurance policies, and

    v)   the Transferable Contracts.

No such agreement, contract or commitment has been assigned or amended.

The Vendor is not in default or breach of any contract, agreement, written or oral, indenture or other instrument to which it is a party. There exists no state of facts which after notice or lapse of time or both would constitute such a default or breach. All such contracts, agreements, indentures or other instruments are now in good standing and in full force and effect without amendment thereto and the Vendor is and the Purchaser will be entitled to all benefits thereunder.

7.14)   Litigation

There are no actions, suits, proceedings (whether or not purportedly on behalf of the Vendor), investigations, arbitrations, prosecutions, grievances or controversy, commenced or to the best of the Vendor's knowledge pending or threatened, against or affecting the Vendor at law or in equity or before or by any federal, provincial, municipal or other governmental department, commission, board, bureau, agency, instrumentality or arbitrator, domestic or foreign. The Vendor is not aware of any existing ground on which any such action, suit, proceeding, investigation, prosecution or grievance might be commenced with any reasonable likelihood of success.

The Vendor is not subject to or in violation or default of any judgment, order, writ, injunction, decree or rule or any court, administrative agency, governmental authority or arbitrator.

7.15)   Products Liability

No claim has been asserted in the last five years against the Vendor relating to the products of the Business pertaining to breach of warranty or guarantee, misrepresentation, strict liability, negligent manufacturing defects in material or labour, damage to property or injury, except goods returned in the ordinary course of the Business.

7.16)   Trade Names, Trademarks and Patents

The trade-marks (the "**Trademarks**") • and • are validly and beneficially owned by the Vendor with the sole and exclusive right to use the same and the Vendor has the right to assign the Trademarks to the Purchaser. To the best of the Vendor's knowledge, there has been no unauthorized or improper use of the Trademarks likely to affect the distinctiveness thereof, or constitute an infringement thereof. Nothing herein will prevent the Vendor from acquiring or adopting Trademarks between the date hereof and Closing, and, in such event, the representation and warranty made herein will apply with respect to such Trademarks as of Closing.

7.17)   Licences, Quotas, Permits, Etc.

The Vendor has all necessary licences, quotas, consents, permits and approvals required to enable it to carry on the Business as heretofore carried on.

7.18)   Facilities and Equipment

All equipment owned and used by the Vendor in connection with the Business are in good operating condition and in a state of good repair and maintenance, reasonable wear and tear excepted.

7.19)   Not Non-Resident

The Vendor is not a non-resident of Canada within the meaning of the *Income Tax Act* (Canada).

7.20)   Schedules

All lists or other statements, information or documents set forth in or attached to any Schedule delivered or required to be delivered pursuant to this Agreement or otherwise delivered pursuant to this Agreement, will be deemed to be representations and warranties of the Vendor with the same force and effect as if such lists, statements, information or documents were set out herein.

7.21)   Disclosure

The Vendor has no information or knowledge of any fact relating to the Business that, if known to the Purchaser, might reasonably be expected to deter the Purchaser from completing the transaction of purchase and sale.

ARTICLE 8: PURCHASER'S REPRESENTATIONS

8.1)   Representations and Warranties of the Purchaser

The Purchaser represents and warrants to the Vendor as follows with the knowledge and expectation that the Vendor is placing complete reliance thereon and, but for such representations and warranties, the Vendor would not have entered into this Agreement:

8.2)   Due Incorporation

The Purchaser is a corporation duly incorporated and validly subsisting under the laws of the Province of Ontario.

8.3)   Due Authorization

The Purchaser has all necessary corporate power and authority to enter into this Agreement and to carry out its obligations hereunder. The execution and delivery of this Agreement and the consummation of the transactions contemplated herein have been duly authorized by all necessary corporate action on the part of the Purchaser. This Agreement is a valid and binding obligation of the Purchaser enforceable in accordance with its terms.

The Purchaser has not committed an act of bankruptcy, is not insolvent, has not proposed a compromise or arrangement to its creditors generally, has not had any petition for a bankruptcy order filed against it, has not taken any proceeding and no proceeding has been taken to have a receiver appointed over any of its assets, has not had an encumbrancer take possession of any of its property and has not had any execution or distress become enforceable or levied against any of its property.

8.4) Absence of Conflicting Agreements

The Purchaser's execution and delivery of this Agreement, the performance of its obligations hereunder and its completion of the transactions will not result in the violation of (i) any term or provision of any indenture or other agreement, written or oral, to which the Purchaser is a party or by which it is bound; or (ii) any law or regulation, or any order or decree of any court or tribunal to which the Purchaser is subject.

8.5) Investment Canada Act

The Purchaser is not a **"non-Canadian"** within the meaning of the *Investment Canada Act.*

8.6) GST

The Purchaser is a registrant for purposes of the ETA and its registration number is l.

ARTICLE 9: VENDOR'S COVENANTS

9.1) Vendor's Covenants and Conditions to the Purchaser's Obligations

The Vendor covenants and agrees to use its best efforts to satisfy each of the following conditions on or before Closing and the Purchaser will not be obligated to complete the purchase of the Assets and the Business unless at Closing each of the following conditions has been satisfied by the Vendor:

a) All terms, covenants and conditions of this Agreement to be complied with or performed by the Vendor at or before Closing will have been complied with or performed.

b) The Purchaser must be satisfied, in its sole and absolute discretion, with all aspects of the Business, the adequacy of the Assets and any third party approvals required for the completion of the transactions contemplated herein will have been obtained on terms satisfactory to the Purchaser and no action or proceeding shall be pending or threatened to restrict or enjoin the purchase transaction.

c) The Purchaser will have been furnished with evidence satisfactory to it that the purchase and sale of the Assets complies with the *Bulk*

Sales Act (Ontario) and any other applicable bulk sales legislation in any other jurisdiction, or the Vendor will have had the transaction exempted from the provisions of such Acts. The Vendor covenants to hold the Purchaser harmless and agrees to indemnify the Purchaser for all legal costs, including but not limited to the defence and judgment of liability arising out of any misrepresentation on behalf of the Vendor which relates to any contravention of a provision of the *Bulk Sales Act* (Ontario).

d)   The Vendor will deliver to the Purchaser a certificate issued pursuant to the *Retail Sales Tax Act* (Ontario) to the effect that all requisite taxes under such Act relating to the Assets (other than relating to the transfer of the Assets to the Purchaser hereunder) have been paid to Closing and including like certificates where required under the laws of other jurisdictions in which the Business is carried on or in which any of the Assets is located.

e)   The Vendor agrees to deliver to the Purchaser the Books and Records and all other documents, files, records and other data, financial or otherwise relating to the Business, all of which will become the Purchaser's property at Closing. The Purchaser will preserve the documents, books and records so delivered to it for a period of three 3 years from Closing, or for such other period as required by any applicable law, and permit the Vendor or its authorized representative(s) reasonable access thereto in connection with the affairs of the Vendor relating to its tax matters. The Purchaser will not destroy any such records either before or after such period without giving the Vendor an opportunity to take back such records, but the Purchaser will not be responsible or liable to the Vendor for or as a result of any loss or destruction of or damage to any such documents, books or records.

f)   The Vendor will deliver to the Purchaser all necessary deeds, conveyances, bills of sale, assurances, transfers, assignments and consents, including all necessary consents and approvals to the assignment of the Leases and the Transferable Contracts and any other documents necessary or reasonably required to effectively transfer the Assets to the Purchaser with good title thereto, free and clear of all mortgages, liens, charges, pledges, claims, security interests or encumbrances whatsoever except the Assumed Liabilities. To the extent that such deeds and conveyances are registerable in appropriate offices, the Vendor will deliver such deeds and conveyances in registerable form.

The Vendor will deliver actual physical possession of the Assets to the Purchaser.

g)   The Vendor will make all requisite arrangements with insurers so that the Purchaser's insurable interest in the Assets is held covered in respect of any loss.

h)   The Landlord will have provided its written consent to the assignment of the Lease to the Purchaser.

i)   The Vendor will obtain and deliver a discharge of any *Personal Property Security Act* (Ontario) ("**PPSA**") registrations against the Assets including, without limitation, PPSA reference file no. ● by ● and PPSA reference file no. ● by ●, all at the Vendor's sole cost and expense.

j)   The Vendor shall have entered into an Employment Agreement in form and content satisfactory to the Purchaser. [*Note: Consider Scheduling the Agreement*]

If any condition, obligation or covenant of the Vendor to be performed prior to Closing is not performed prior to Closing, the Purchaser may terminate this Agreement by written notice to the Vendor and in such event the Purchaser will be released from all its obligations hereunder. Unless the Purchaser can show that the condition or conditions the non-performance of which the Purchaser has rescinded this Agreement are reasonably capable of being performed or caused to be performed by the Vendor, the Vendor will also be released from all obligations hereunder; provided however, that the Purchaser will be entitled to waive compliance with any of such conditions, obligations or covenants in whole or in part as it sees fit without prejudice to any of its rights of termination in the event of non-performance of any other condition, obligation or covenant in whole or in part.

ARTICLE 10: PURCHASER'S COVENANTS

10.1) Purchaser's Covenants and Conditions to the Vendor's Obligations

The Purchaser covenants and agrees to use its best efforts to satisfy each of the following conditions on or before Closing and the Vendor will not be obligated to complete the purchase of the Assets and the Business unless at Closing each of the following conditions has been satisfied by the Purchaser:

a) All terms, covenants and conditions of this Agreement to be complied with or performed by the Purchaser at or before Closing will have been complied with or performed.

b) The Purchaser will have taken or caused to have been taken all necessary or desirable actions, steps and corporate proceedings to approve or authorize validly and effectively the transfer of the Assets from the Vendor and the execution and delivery of this Agreement and all other agreements and documents contemplated hereby and will cause all necessary meetings of directors of the Purchaser to be held for such purpose.

c) All documents or copies thereof required to be delivered to the Vendor will have been so delivered.

If any condition, obligation or covenant of the Purchaser to be performed prior to Closing is not performed prior to Closing, the Vendor may terminate this Agreement by written notice to the Purchaser and in such event the Vendor will be released from all its obligations hereunder. Unless the Vendor can show that the condition or conditions the non-performance of which the Vendor has rescinded this Agreement are reasonably capable of being performed or caused to be performed by the Purchaser, the Purchaser will also be released from all its obligations hereunder; provided however, that the Vendor will be entitled to waive compliance with any of such conditions, obligations or covenants in whole or in part as it sees fit without prejudice to any of its rights of termination in the event of non-performance of any other condition, obligation or covenant in whole or in part.

ARTICLE 11: NON-COMPETITION AND NON-SOLICITATION COVENANT BY VENDOR

11.1)   Non-Competition and Non-Solicitation

From and after the Closing Date and for so long as the Vendor remains an employee of the Purchaser (or any of its subsidiaries or affiliates) and for a period of ● years thereafter, the Vendor covenants and agrees that he will not (except with the prior written consent of the Purchaser, which consent may be unreasonably withheld):

a) directly or indirectly, solicit for employment, or advise or recommend to any other person, firm, corporation or entity that they employ or solicit for employment any person employed by the Company;

b) directly or indirectly, engage, send any work to, place orders with or in any manner be associated with any contractor, subcontractor or other person, firm, corporation or entity which rendered or renders any services to the Company, if such action would have a material adverse effect on the business activity, assets or financial condition of the Company or its subsidiaries;

c) directly or indirectly, within a mile radius of the Purchaser's head office, engage in any activity in competition with, perform services for or become interested in, whether as an individual, manager, consultant, independent contractor, employee, employer, partner, syndicate member, officer, director, advisor, principal, agent, trustee, lender of money, shareholder (except as a shareholder of a public corporation holding 2% or less of all outstanding voting shares in such public corporation) or in any other manner whatsoever, carry on, advance or lend money to, guarantee the debts or obligations of or permit his name to be used, serve or cater to, in any relation or capacity whatsoever, a similar or competitive business as that conducted by the Company or any other business now or at any time during the period of time that the Vendor is an employee of the Company; or

d) solicit any customer or client that was or is a customer or client of the Company during the period of time that the Vendor was an employee of the Company.

11.2) Relief

The Vendor acknowledges that the Purchaser is relying on the foregoing covenant in connection with its decision to enter into and proceed with the transactions contemplated in this Agreement and acknowledges that his agreement not to compete and his obligations under the term of an Employment Agreement with the Purchaser even dated herewith makes his relationship with the Company special, unique, unusual and extraordinary in character which gives it peculiar value, the loss of which cannot adequately be compensated in damages in an action at law. The Company will be entitled to all equitable and legal remedies, including interlocutory and permanent injunctive relief, relating to any violation or breach of the provisions of this Article.

11.3)   Survival

The covenants in this Article shall survive the Closing and remain in full force and effect for the benefit of the Purchaser.

ARTICLE 12: SURVIVAL OF REPRESENTATIONS, WARRANTIES AND COVENANTS

The Vendor's representations, warranties and covenants in this Agreement and any document or certificate given pursuant hereto will survive Closing and will continue in full force and effect without any time limitation, for the Purchaser's exclusive benefit notwithstanding the Closing and any investigation made by or on behalf of the Purchaser.

The Purchaser's representations, warranties and covenants in this Agreement and any document or certificate given pursuant hereto will survive Closing and will continue in full force and effect without any time limitation, for the Vendor's exclusive benefit notwithstanding the Closing and any investigation made by or on behalf of the Vendor.

ARTICLE 13: INDEMNITY

13.1)   Indemnity

The Vendor will each jointly and severally indemnify and save the Purchaser harmless from and against:

a)   any loss and costs (including legal fees on a solicitor and client basis and disbursements) suffered by the Purchaser as a result of any breach of any representation, warranty or covenant of the Vendor in this Agreement;

b)   all liabilities (whether accrued, actual, contingent or otherwise), claims, demands, damages, losses, costs (including legal fees on a solicitor and client basis and disbursements), expenses, contracts, duties, obligations and liabilities whatsoever (collectively, **"Claims"**) of or in connection with the Business existing or incurred as at the Closing which are not expressly agreed to form part of the Assumed Liabilities (including Claims in respect of income, sales, excise or other taxes); and

c)   all Claims in respect of claims made by a consumer related to a product manufactured or produced or provided or services provided by the Vendor prior to the Closing, whenever such product may be sold and whether such product or services are or is sold by the Vendor or the Purchaser or related to a product or services sold by the Vendor, whether or not manufactured by the Vendor prior to the Closing; provided that the Vendor will not be responsible to the Purchaser if such claim arises as a result of the wilful act or negligence of the Purchaser subsequent to the Closing and notwithstanding any investigation made by or on behalf of the Purchaser.

If the Purchaser suffers any loss for which it is indemnified or if a claim is asserted against the Purchaser for which it is indemnified, the Purchaser will promptly notify the Vendor (the **"Notice"** in this Article) thereof, including all relevant information and the exact or estimated amount lost or claimed, and:

a)   Within ten (10) days of the Vendor's receipt or deemed receipt of the Notice, the Vendor will pay to the Purchaser the full amount set out in the Notice;

b)   The Vendor will be entitled, at its own expense, to participate in the negotiation and defence of such claim;

In addition to and notwithstanding any other remedies or rights available to the Purchaser, in the event of a claim for which an indemnity or right of set-off is available under this Agreement, the Purchaser may set-off and deduct from any amounts otherwise payable to the Vendor, under this Agreement or otherwise, the amount of such claim and any legal costs or other professional fees.

The rights granted to the Purchaser pursuant to this Article are in addition to and not in substitution for any and all other rights or indemnities of which the Purchaser may be entitled to avail itself.

ARTICLE 14: REMEDIES

If the Vendor is unable or unwilling to perform this Agreement in accordance with its terms, the Purchaser will enjoy all rights available at law or in equity, including without limitation the right to rescind this Agreement, the right to specific performance and/or the right to sue for damages. If this Agreement is rescinded at the Purchaser's election, this Agreement will be null and void and of no further force and effect and neither party will be under any obligation or liability to the other.

ARTICLE 15: GENERAL CONTRACT PROVISIONS

15.1)   Place of Closing

Closing will take place at the office of the Purchaser on the Closing Date.

15.2)   Arbitration

Except as otherwise expressly provided herein, any dispute, difference or question arising between the parties concerning the construction, meaning, effect or implementation of this Agreement or any part hereof will be settled by a single arbitrator mutually agreed on by the parties or failing agreement, an arbitrator appointed pursuant to the *Arbitration Act* (Ontario). The decision of such arbitrator appointed pursuant to this Agreement or such Act will be final and binding on the parties and no appeal will lie therefrom.

15.3)   Further Assurances

From time to time after Closing, the Vendor will, at the Purchaser's request and at the Vendor's expense, execute and deliver such additional conveyances, transfers and other assurances as may, in the opinion of the Purchaser's counsel, be reasonably required effectually to carry out the intent of this Agreement and transfer the Assets to the Purchaser. On receipt, the Vendor will deliver to the Purchaser all cheques pertaining to the Business received by the Vendor after Closing.

15.4)   Notice

All notices, requests, demands, waivers, consents, agreements, approvals, communications or other writings required or permitted to be given hereunder or for the purposes hereof (**"Notice"** in this Article) will be in writing and be sufficiently given if personally delivered, sent by prepaid registered mail or transmitted by facsimile, addressed to the party to whom it is given, as follows:

   a)   to the Vendor:

-
-
-

       Attention: •
       Telephone: •
       Facsimile: •

   b)   and to the Purchaser:

-
-
-

Attention: •

Telephone: •

Facsimile: •

or such other address of which Notice has been given. Any Notice mailed as aforesaid will be deemed to have been given and received on the third business day following the date of its mailing. Any Notice personally delivered will be deemed to have been given and received on the day it is personally delivered, provided that if such day is not a business day, the Notice will be deemed to have been given and received on the business day next following such day. Any Notice transmitted by facsimile will be deemed given and received on the first business day after its transmission.

If a Notice is mailed and regular mail service is interrupted by strike or other irregularity on or before the fourth business day after the mailing thereof, such Notice will be deemed to have not been received unless otherwise personally delivered or transmitted by facsimile.

15.5) Tender

Any tender of documents or money may be made on the parties or their respective counsel and money may be tendered by official bank draft drawn on a Canadian chartered bank or by negotiable cheque payable in Canadian funds and certified by a Canadian chartered bank.

15.6) Waiver

No party will be deemed or taken to have waived any provision of this Agreement unless such waiver is in writing and such waiver will be limited to the circumstance set forth in such written waiver.

15.7) Governing Law

This Agreement will be governed by and construed in accordance with the laws of the Province of Ontario and the laws of Canada applicable therein. The parties irrevocably attorn to the jurisdiction of the courts of Ontario.

15.8) Entire Agreement

This Agreement and the Schedules and the Employment Agreement to be entered into concurrently with the completion of the transactions contemplated herein, constitute the entire agreement between the parties and supersede all prior agreements and understandings between the parties. There are not and will not be any verbal statements, representations, warranties, undertakings or agreements between the parties. This Agreement may not be amended or modified in any respect except by written instrument signed by both parties.

15.9)   Time of the Essence

Time will be of the essence, provided that if the parties establish a new time for the performance of an obligation, time will again be of the essence of the new time established.

15.10) Commissions, etc.

No broker, agent or other intermediary acts or has acted for the Vendor in connection with the sale of the Assets and the Vendor agrees to indemnify and save harmless the Purchaser from and against any claims whatsoever for any commission or other remuneration payable or alleged to be payable to any broker, agent or other intermediary who purports to act or have acted for the Vendor.

15.11) Announcements

The Vendor will not make any announcement with respect to this Agreement without the Purchaser's prior written consent.

15.12) Enurement

This Agreement will enure to the benefit of and be binding on the parties and their respective heirs, executors, legal and personal administrators, successors and permitted assigns.

15.13) Statutes

Any reference in this Agreement to a statute includes any amendment thereto, its regulations and applicable successor legislation.

15.14) Gender

The necessary changes in gender required to make this Agreement apply to either corporations or individuals, males or females, will in all instances be assumed as though in each case fully expressed.

15.15) Currency

All dollar amounts referred in this Agreement and the Schedules are in Canadian funds.

15.16) Counterparts

This Agreement may be executed in one or more counterparts, each of which will constitute an original and all of which together will constitute one and the same agreement.

15.17) Index and Headings

The Index to this Agreement and Article and Section headings are included solely for convenience, are not intended to be full or accurate descriptions of the content thereof and will not be considered part of this Agreement.

15.18) Assignment

The Purchaser shall have the right to transfer and assign this Agreement.

15.19) Expenses

All costs and expenses (including, without limitation, the fees and disbursements of legal counsel) incurred in connection with this Agreement and the transactions contemplated hereby shall be paid by the Party incurring such expenses.

15.20) Severability

If any covenant or provision of this Agreement is prohibited in whole or in part in any jurisdiction, such covenant or provision shall, as to such jurisdiction, be ineffective to the extent of such prohibition without invalidating the remaining covenants and provisions hereof and shall, as to such jurisdiction, be deemed to be severed from this Agreement to the extent of such prohibition.

15.21) Legal Advice

The Vendor acknowledges and agrees that Torkin Manes LLP are acting as solicitors for the Purchaser and that the Vendor has been advised to seek and obtain his own legal advice in connection with this Agreement and the transactions contemplated herein and has been given an opportunity to obtain whatever advice he feels is appropriate.

IN WITNESS WHEREOF this Agreement has been executed by the parties.

Per: Per:

___________________   ___________________

Name: ___________________   Name: ___________________

Title: ___________________   Title: ___________________

SCHEDULE 1 – EQUIPMENT AND INVENTORY LISTING

SCHEDULE 2 – TRANSFERABLE CONTRACTS

Form 15: **Non-Competition Agreement**

THIS NON-COMPETITION AGREEMENT (this "**Agreement**"), dated this [ ] day of [ ], by and between [ ], an Unlimited Liability Company formed under the laws of [ ] ("**Holdings**"), and [ ], an individual ("**Stockholder**");

WITNESSETH:

WHEREAS, Stockholder has been actively involved in the business of [ ], a corporation organized under the laws of the Province of [ ] (the "**Company**"), as a substantial stockholder, and as an employee, officer or member of the Board of Directors of the Company; and

WHEREAS, Holdings has agreed to purchase all of the assets of the Company (the "**Assets**") pursuant to an Agreement for Purchase and Sale of Assets dated [ ], by and among the parties hereto and others (the "**Purchase Agreement**"); and

WHEREAS, the continued involvement by Stockholder in a business in competition with the Company would substantially diminish the value of the Assets to be purchased by Holdings; and

WHEREAS, as an inducement to Holdings to consummate its purchase of the Assets, Stockholder has agreed not to compete with Holdings and to refrain from making disclosures to the extent set forth below;

NOW, THEREFORE, in consideration of the premises and the covenants and agreements contained herein, the parties hereto agree as follows:

1)   Restrictive Covenants

Subject to Section 2 below, in consideration of the transactions contemplated in the Purchase Agreement, Stockholder agrees that for a period equal to the greater of (i) three (3) years from the date hereof, or (ii) one (1) year after Stockholder is no longer employed by Holdings, Stockholder shall not:

a) directly or indirectly, either individually or as a principal, partner, agent, employee, employer, consultant, stockholder, joint venturer, or investor, or as a director or officer of any corporation or association, or in any other manner or capacity whatsoever, engage in, assist or have any active interest in a business located anywhere in the Province of [ ] or the greater metropolitan area of the [ ] (**"Geographic Territory"**) that engages in the business of direct mail marketing, database management, or mailing services or that otherwise competes with or is similar in concept, design, format, or otherwise to the business conducted by Holdings on the date hereof or at any time during the term of this covenant; or

b) directly or indirectly, either individually or as a principal, partner, agent, employee, employer, consultant, stockholder, joint venturer, or investor, or as a director or officer of any corporation or association, or in any other manner or capacity whatsoever, engage in, assist or have any active interest in a business located anywhere in the Geographic Territory that sells to, supplies, or provides goods or services to Holdings provided in the previous calendar year said business was one of the top five suppliers of all goods and services to Holdings; or

c) directly or indirectly, either individually or as a principal, partner, agent, employee, employer, consultant, stockholder, joint venturer, or investor, or as a director or officer of any corporation or association, or in any other manner or capacity whatsoever, solicit, contact, advise or perform services for any person, firm, or corporation which was a customer of Holdings in the preceding two (2) years; or

d) directly or indirectly, either individually, or as a principal, partner, agent, employee, employer, consultant, stockholder, joint venturer, or investor, or as a director or officer of any corporation or association, or in any other manner or capacity whatsoever, (i) divert or attempt to divert from Holdings any business with any customer or account which was under the supervision of the Stockholder during Stockholder's employment with Holdings, or (ii) induce any salesperson, distributor, supplier, vendor, manufacturer, representative, agent, jobber or other person transacting business with Holdings to terminate their relationship or association with Holdings, or to represent, distribute or sell services or products in competition with services or products of Holdings, or

(iii) induce or cause any employee of Holdings to leave the employ of Holdings.

2) Exceptions

Notwithstanding the above, Section 1 shall not be construed to prohibit Stockholder from owning less than [ ] percent ([ ]%) of the securities of a corporation which is publicly traded on a securities exchange or over the counter.

3) Non-Disclosure

Stockholder shall not at any time or in any manner, directly or indirectly, use or disclose to any party other than Holdings any trade secrets or other Confidential Information (as defined below) learned or obtained by him while a stockholder, officer or director of Holdings or the Company. As used herein, the term **"Confidential Information"** means information which is not readily available to the general public and which is disclosed to or known by Stockholder as a consequence of his position with Holdings or the Company and not generally known in the industry in which the Company or Holdings is engaged and that in any way relates to Holdings' products, processes, services, inventions (whether patentable or not), formulas, techniques or know-how, including, but not limited to, information relating to distribution systems and methods, research, development, manufacturing, purchasing, accounting, engineering, marketing, merchandising and selling.

4) Affiliate Transactions

For as long as Stockholder or any member of his family is employed by Holdings, neither Stockholder, any member of his family nor any Affiliate (as defined in the Purchase Agreement) of Stockholder shall engage, directly or indirectly, in any business transaction with Holdings or any of its Affiliates.

5) Specific Performance

The parties hereto agree that their rights hereunder are special and unique and that any violation thereof would not be adequately compensated by money damages, and each grants the other the right to specifically enforce (including injunctive relief where appropriate) the terms of this Agreement.

6) Notices

Any notice, request, consent or communication (collectively, a **"Notice"**) under this Agreement shall be effective only if it is in writing and (i) personally delivered, (ii) sent by certified or registered mail, return receipt requested, postage prepaid, (iii) sent by a nationally recognized overnight delivery service, with delivery confirmed, or (iv) telexed or telecopied, with receipt confirmed, addressed as follows:

    a)   If to Stockholder: [ ]
        Telephone: [ ]
        Telecopier: [ ]
        with a copy to: [ ]
        Telephone: [ ]
        Telecopier: [ ]
    b)   If to Holdings to: [ ]
        Telephone: [ ]
        Telecopier: [ ]
        with a copy to: [ ]
        Telephone [ ]
        Telecopier [ ]

or such other persons or addresses as shall be furnished in writing by any party to the other party. A Notice shall be deemed to have been given as of the date when (i) personally delivered, (ii) five (5) days after the date when deposited with the Canada Post mail properly addressed, (iii) when receipt of a Notice sent by an overnight delivery service is confirmed by such overnight delivery service, or (iv) when receipt of the telex or telecopy is confirmed, as the case may be, unless the sending party has actual knowledge that a Notice was not received by the intended recipient.

7) Assignment

This Agreement and all of the provisions hereof shall be binding upon and inure to the benefit of the parties hereto and their respective heirs, successors and permitted assigns, but neither this Agreement nor any of the rights, interests or obligations hereunder shall be assigned by Stockholder.

8) Litigation

THIS AGREEMENT SHALL BE GOVERNED BY, CONSTRUED, APPLIED AND ENFORCED IN ACCORDANCE WITH THE INTERNAL LAWS OF THE PROVINCE OF [ ], CANADA, AND NO DOCTRINE OF CHOICE OF LAW SHALL BE USED TO APPLY ANY LAW OTHER THAN THAT OF [ ], AND NO DEFENCE, COUNTER-CLAIM OR RIGHT OF SET-OFF GIVEN OR ALLOWED BY THE LAWS OF ANY OTHER STATE OR JURISDICTION, OR ARISING OUT OF THE ENACTMENT, MODIFICATION OR REPEAL OF ANY LAW, REGULATION, ORDINANCE OR DECREE OF ANY FOREIGN JURISDICTION, BE INTERPOSED IN ANY ACTION HEREON.

9) Arbitration

THE STOCKHOLDER HEREBY WAIVES AND SHALL NOT SEEK JURY TRIAL IN ANY LAWSUIT, PROCEEDING, CLAIM, COUNTERCLAIM, DEFENCE OR OTHER LITIGATION OR DISPUTE UNDER OR IN RESPECT OF THIS AGREEMENT. THE STOCKHOLDER AGREES THAT ANY SUCH DISPUTE RELATING TO OR IN RESPECT OF THIS AGREEMENT, ITS NEGOTIATION, EXECUTION, PERFORMANCE, SUBJECT MATTER, OR ANY COURSE OF CONDUCT OR DEALING OR ACTIONS UNDER OR IN RESPECT OF THIS AGREEMENT, SHALL BE SUBMITTED TO, AND RESOLVED EXCLUSIVELY PURSUANT TO ARBITRATION IN ACCORDANCE WITH THE PURCHASE AGREEMENT. SUCH ARBITRATION SHALL BE CONDUCTED BY A MUTUALLY AGREED UPON ARBITRATOR SELECTED FROM THE LIST OF MEMBERS OF THE PRIVATE COURT AND SHALL TAKE PLACE IN [ ], AND SHALL BE SUBJECT TO THE SUBSTANTIVE LAW OF THE PROVINCE OF [ ]. DECISIONS PURSUANT TO SUCH ARBITRATION SHALL BE FINAL, CONCLUSIVE AND BINDING ON THE PARTIES. THE PREVAILING PARTY IN ARBITRATION SHALL BE ENTITLED TO RECOVER REASONABLE COSTS AND ATTORNEYS' FEES FROM THE OTHER PARTY. UPON THE CONCLUSION OF ARBITRATION, THE PARTIES MAY APPLY TO ANY APPROPRIATE COURT TO ENFORCE THE DECISION PURSUANT TO SUCH ARBITRATION.

10) Severability

Holdings and Stockholder believe the covenants against competition contained in this Agreement are reasonable and fair in all respects, and are necessary to protect the interests of Holdings. However, in case any one or more of the provisions or parts of a provision contained in this Agreement shall, for any reason, be held to be invalid, illegal or unenforceable in any respect in any jurisdiction, such invalidity, illegality or unenforceability shall not affect any other provision or part of a provision of this Agreement or any other jurisdiction, but this Agreement shall be reformed and construed in any such jurisdiction as if such invalid or illegal or unenforceable provision or part of a provision had never been contained herein and such provision or part shall be reformed so that it would be valid, legal and enforceable to the maximum extent permitted in such jurisdiction. Without limiting the foregoing, the parties intend that the covenants and agreements contained in Sections 1(a), 1(b), 1(c) and 1(d) shall be deemed to be a series of separate covenants and agreements. If, in any judicial proceeding, a court or arbitrator shall refuse to enforce all the separate covenants and agreements deemed to be included in Sections 1 (a), 1(b), 1(c) and 1(d) it is the intention of the parties hereto that the covenants and agreements which, if eliminated, would permit the remaining separate covenants and agreements to be enforced in such proceeding shall, for the purpose of such proceeding, be deemed eliminated from the provisions of Sections 1(a), 1(b), 1(c) and 1(d).

11) Neutral Interpretation

This Agreement constitutes the product of the negotiation of the parties hereto and the enforcement hereof shall be interpreted in a neutral manner, and not more strongly for or against any party based upon the source of the draftsmanship hereof.

12) Miscellaneous

This Agreement may be executed in two or more counterparts, each of which shall be deemed an original, but all of which together shall constitute one and the same instrument. The section headings contained in this Agreement are for reference purposes only and shall not affect in any way the meaning or interpretation of this Agreement. This Agreement embodies the entire agreement and understanding of the parties hereto in respect of the subject matter contained herein and may not be modified orally, but only by a writing subscribed by the party charged therewith. There are no restrictions, promises, representations, warranties, covenants or undertakings, other than those expressly set forth or referred to herein. This Agreement supersedes all prior agreements and understandings (whether oral or written) between the parties with respect to such subject matter.

IN WITNESS WHEREOF, the parties hereto have made and entered into this Agreement the date first hereinabove set forth.

HOLDINGS   HOLDINGS

[ ]:   [ ]:

By: By:

Name: _________________   Name: _________________

Title: _________________   Title: _________________

Form 16: **Non-Competition Agreement** [*Alternate Form*]

THIS NON-COMPETITION AGREEMENT (this "**Agreement**"), dated this [ ] day of [ ], by and between [ ], an Unlimited Liability Company formed under the laws of [ ] ("**Holdings**"), and [ ], a corporation formed under the laws of the Province of [ ] ("**Seller**");

WITNESSETH:

WHEREAS, Seller is in the business of direct mail marketing, data base management and mailing services; and

WHEREAS, Holdings has agreed to purchase all of the assets of the Seller (the "**Assets**") pursuant to an Agreement for Purchase and Sale of Assets dated [ ], by and among the parties hereto and others (the "**Purchase Agreement**"); and

WHEREAS, the continued involvement by Seller in a business in competition with Holdings following the closing of the transactions contemplated in the Purchase Agreement would substantially diminish the value of the Assets to be purchased by Holdings; and

WHEREAS, as an inducement to Holdings to consummate its purchase of the Assets, Seller has agreed not to compete with Holdings and to refrain from making disclosures to the extent set forth below;

NOW, THEREFORE, in consideration of the premises and the covenants and agreements contained herein, the parties hereto agree as follows:

1)   Restrictive Covenants

Subject to Section 2 below, in consideration of the transactions contemplated in the Purchase Agreement, Seller agrees that for three (3) years from the date hereof Seller shall not:

a)   directly or indirectly, either as a principal, partner, agent, employer, consultant, stockholder, joint venturer, or investor, or as a director of any corporation or association, or in any other manner or capacity whatsoever, engage in, assist or have any active interest in a business located anywhere in the Province of [ ] or the greater metropolitan area of the [ ] ("**Geographic Territory**") that engages in the business of direct mail marketing, database management, or mailing services or that otherwise competes with or is similar in concept, design, format, or otherwise to the business conducted by Holdings on the date hereof or at any time during the term of this covenant; or

b)   directly or indirectly, either as a principal, partner, agent, employer, consultant, stockholder, joint venturer, or investor, or as a director of any corporation or association, or in any other manner or capacity whatsoever, engage in, assist or have any active interest in a business located anywhere in the Geographic Territory that sells to, supplies, or provides goods or services to Holdings provided in the previous calendar year said business was one of the top five suppliers of all goods and services to Holdings; or

c)   directly or indirectly, either as a principal, partner, agent, employer, consultant, stockholder, joint venturer, or investor, or as a director of any corporation or association, or in any other manner or capacity whatsoever, solicit, contact, advise or perform services for any person, firm, or corporation which was a customer of Holdings in the preceding two (2) years; or

d)   directly or indirectly, either as a principal, partner, agent, employer, consultant, stockholder, joint venturer, or investor, or as a director of any corporation or association, or in any other manner or capacity whatsoever, (i) divert or attempt to divert from Holdings any business with any customer or account, or (ii) induce any salesperson, distributor, supplier, vendor, manufacturer, representative, agent, jobber or other person transacting business with Holdings to terminate their relationship or association with Holdings, or to represent, distribute or sell services or products in competition with services or products of

Holdings, or (iii) induce or cause any employee of Holdings to leave the employ of Holdings.

2) Exceptions

Notwithstanding the above, Section 1 shall not be construed to prohibit Seller from owning less than [ ] percent ([ ]%) of the securities of a corporation which is publicly traded on a securities exchange or over the counter.

3) Non-Disclosure

Seller shall not at any time or in any manner, directly or indirectly, use or disclose to any party other than Holdings any trade secrets or other Confidential Information (as defined below). As used herein, the term **"Confidential Information"** means information which is not readily available to the general public and which is not generally known in the industry in which Holdings is engaged and that in any way relates to Holdings' products, processes, services, inventions (whether patentable or not), formulas, techniques or know-how, including, but not limited to, information relating to distribution systems and methods, research, development, manufacturing, purchasing, accounting, engineering, marketing, merchandising and selling.

4) Specific Performance

The parties hereto agree that their rights hereunder are special and unique and that any violation thereof would not be adequately compensated by money damages, and each grants the other the right to specifically enforce (including injunctive relief where appropriate) the terms of this Agreement.

5) Notices

Any notice, request, consent or communication (collectively, a **"Notice"**) under this Agreement shall be effective only if it is in writing and (i) personally delivered, (ii) sent by certified or registered mail, return receipt requested, postage prepaid, (iii) sent by a nationally recognized overnight delivery service, with delivery confirmed, or (iv) telexed or telecopied, with receipt confirmed, addressed as follows:

    a)   If to Seller:

       [ ]
       Telephone: [ ]
       Telecopier: [ ]
       with a copy to: [ ]
       Telephone: [ ]
       Telecopier: [ ]

b)   If to Holdings to:

[ ]
Telephone: [ ]
Telecopier: [ ]
with a copy to: [ ]
Telephone [ ]
Telecopier [ ]

or such other persons or addresses as shall be furnished in writing by any party to the other party. A Notice shall be deemed to have been given as of the date when (i) personally delivered, (ii) five (5) days after the date when deposited with the Canada Post mail properly addressed, (iii) when receipt of a Notice sent by an overnight delivery service is confirmed by such overnight delivery service, or (iv) when receipt of the telex or telecopy is confirmed, as the case may be, unless the sending party has actual knowledge that a Notice was not received by the intended recipient.

6)   Assignment

This Agreement and all of the provisions hereof shall be binding upon and inure to the benefit of the parties hereto and their respective heirs, successors and permitted assigns, but neither this Agreement nor any of the rights, interests or obligations hereunder shall be assigned by Seller.

7)   Litigation

THIS AGREEMENT SHALL BE GOVERNED BY, CONSTRUED, APPLIED AND ENFORCED IN ACCORDANCE WITH THE INTERNAL LAWS OF THE PROVINCE OF [ ], CANADA, AND NO DOCTRINE OF CHOICE OF LAW SHALL BE USED TO APPLY ANY LAW OTHER THAN THAT OF [ ], AND NO DEFENCE, COUNTER-CLAIM OR RIGHT OF SET-OFF GIVEN OR ALLOWED BY THE LAWS OF ANY OTHER STATE OR JURISDICTION, OR ARISING OUT OF THE ENACTMENT, MODIFICATION OR REPEAL OF ANY LAW, REGULATION, ORDINANCE OR DECREE OF ANY FOREIGN JURISDICTION, BE INTERPOSED IN ANY ACTION HEREON.

8)   Arbitration

THE SELLER HEREBY WAIVES AND SHALL NOT SEEK JURY TRIAL IN ANY LAWSUIT, PROCEEDING, CLAIM, COUNTERCLAIM, DEFENCE OR OTHER LITIGATION OR DISPUTE UNDER OR IN RESPECT OF THIS AGREEMENT. THE SELLER AGREES THAT ANY SUCH DISPUTE RELATING TO OR IN RESPECT OF THIS AGREEMENT, ITS NEGOTIATION, EXECUTION, PERFORMANCE,

SUBJECT MATTER, OR ANY COURSE OF CONDUCT OR DEALING OR ACTIONS UNDER OR IN RESPECT OF THIS AGREEMENT, SHALL BE SUBMITTED TO, AND RESOLVED EXCLUSIVELY PURSUANT TO ARBITRATION IN ACCORD-ANCE WITH THE PURCHASE AGREEMENT. SUCH ARBITRATION SHALL BE CONDUCTED BY A MUTUALLY AGREED UPON ARBITRATOR SELECTED FROM THE LIST OF MEMBERS OF THE PRIVATE COURT AND SHALL TAKE PLACE IN [ ], AND SHALL BE SUBJECT TO THE SUBSTANTIVE LAW OF THE PROVINCE OF [ ]. DECISIONS PURSUANT TO SUCH ARBITRATION SHALL BE FINAL, CONCLUSIVE AND BINDING ON THE PARTIES. THE PREVAILING PARTY IN ARBITRATION SHALL BE ENTITLED TO RECOVER REASONABLE COSTS AND ATTORNEYS' FEES FROM THE OTHER PARTY. UPON THE CON-CLUSION OF ARBITRATION, THE PARTIES MAY APPLY TO ANY APPROPRIATE COURT TO ENFORCE THE DECISION PURSUANT TO SUCH ARBITRATION.

9) Severability

Holdings and Seller believe the covenants against competition contained in this Agreement are reasonable and fair in all respects, and are necessary to protect the interests of Holdings. However, in case any one or more of the provisions or parts of a provision contained in this Agreement shall, for any reason, be held to be invalid, illegal or unenforceable in any respect in any jurisdiction, such inval-idity, illegality or unenforceability shall not affect any other provision or part of a provision of this Agreement or any other jurisdiction, but this Agreement shall be reformed and construed in any such jurisdiction as if such invalid or illegal or unenforceable provision or part of a provision had never been contained herein and such provision or part shall be reformed so that it would be valid, legal and enforceable to the maximum extent permitted in such jurisdiction. Without limiting the foregoing, the parties intend that the covenants and agreements contained in Sections 1(a), 1(b), 1(c) and 1(d) shall be deemed to be a series of separate covenants and agreements. If, in any judicial proceeding, a court or arbitrator shall refuse to enforce all the separate covenants and agreements deemed to be included in Sections 1(a), 1(b), 1(c) and 1(d) it is the intention of the parties hereto that the covenants and agreements which, if eliminated, would permit the remaining separate covenants and agreements to be enforced in such proceeding shall, for the purpose of such proceeding, be deemed elimin-ated from the provisions of Sections 1(a), 1(b), 1(c) and 1(d).

10) Neutral Interpretation

This Agreement constitutes the product of the negotiation of the parties hereto . and the enforcement hereof shall be interpreted in a neutral manner, and not more strongly for or against any party based upon the source of the draftsmanship hereof.

11) Miscellaneous

This Agreement may be executed in two or more counterparts, each of which shall be deemed an original, but all of which together shall constitute one and the same instrument. The section headings contained in this Agreement are for reference purposes only and shall not affect in any way the meaning or interpretation of this Agreement. This Agreement embodies the entire agreement and understanding of the parties hereto in respect of the subject matter contained herein and may not be modified orally, but only by a writing subscribed by the party charged therewith. There are no restrictions, promises, representations, warranties, covenants or undertakings, other than those expressly set forth or referred to herein. This Agreement supersedes all prior agreements and understandings (whether oral or written) between the parties with respect to such subject matter.

   IN WITNESS WHEREOF, the parties hereto have made and entered into this Agreement the date first hereinabove set forth.

HOLDINGS   SELLER
[ ]:   [ ]:
By: By:
Name: _______________   Name: _______________
Title: _______________   Title: _______________

Form 17: **Hybrid Asset/Share Purchase and Sale Agreement**

ASSET/SHARE PURCHASE AGREEMENT

BY AND AMONG

●

---

1) Asset Purchase Agreement

THIS ASSET PURCHASE AGREEMENT (as amended, modified or supplemented from time to time, this **"Agreement"**) is made and entered into as of ●, ● by and among ●, an Ontario corporation (**"C"**), R (the **"Principal"** or **"R"**, and together with C, **"Sellers"**) and ● (**"Buyer"**) a corporation and wholly-owned subsidiary of Holding.

2) Recitals

WHEREAS, Buyer desires to purchase from Sellers, and Sellers desire to sell to Buyer, as applicable, the Shares and substantially all of the assets of C (including the Equity Interests of the Transferred Subsidiaries) used in the conduct of the Business (as defined below) by C, at Closing, and Buyer desires to assume from C and C desires to assign to Buyer, the obligations and liabilities of C relating to the Business other than the Excluded Liabilities (as defined herein), all upon the terms and subject to the conditions contained herein in exchange for (i) the cash consideration provided herein and (ii) the issuance of Buyer New Shares in Buyer;

AND WHEREAS, immediately following the issuance to C of Buyer New Shares, C will exchange Buyer New Shares for Holding New Shares as further described herein;

AND WHEREAS, Principal and the board of directors of C and Buyer have approved this Agreement and approved the transactions contemplated by this Agreement;

AND WHEREAS, concurrently with Closing, Buyer intends to borrow under a new credit facility and use the proceeds, together with cash in an amount equal to the Debt Payoff Amount, to satisfy and discharge all of C's Debt under the Existing Credit Facility;

AND WHEREAS, concurrently with the execution and delivery of this Agreement, R is entering into an Employment Agreement with Buyer, effective upon the Closing, substantially in the form attached hereto as Exhibit A (the "**R Employment Agreement**");

AND WHEREAS, the parties to this Agreement desire to make certain representations, warranties, covenants and agreements in connection with the Contemplated Transactions.

3)   Agreement

NOW THEREFORE, in consideration of the premises and mutual promises herein made, and in consideration of the representations, warranties and covenants herein contained, and other good and valuable consideration the receipt and sufficiency of which are hereby acknowledged, and intending to be legally bound, the parties to this Agreement hereby agree as follows:

ARTICLE 1: DEFINITIONS; CERTAIN RULES OF CONSTRUCTION

Section 1.01)   Definitions

In addition to the other terms defined throughout this Agreement, the following terms shall have the following meanings when used in this Agreement:

"**20● Audited Financials**" means the audited combined balance sheets of Buyer and its Subsidiaries as of ●, 20●.

"**Action**" means any claim, controversy, action, cause of action, suit, litigation, grievance, examination, arbitration, investigation, opposition, interference, audit, assessment, hearing, complaint, demand or other legal proceeding (whether sounding in contract, tort or otherwise, whether civil or criminal and whether brought at law or in equity) that is commenced, brought, conducted, tried or heard by or before, or otherwise involving, any Governmental Authority.

"Affiliate" means, with respect to any specified Person, any other Person directly or indirectly controlling, controlled by, or under direct or indirect common control with such specified Person. For purposes of the foregoing, a Person shall be deemed to control a specified Person if such Person (or a Family Member of such Person) (a) possesses, directly or indirectly, the power to direct or cause the direction of the management and policies of such specified Person or (b) is at such time a direct or indirect beneficial holder of at least 5% of any class of the Equity Interests of such specified Person.

"Ancillary Agreements" means each of the agreements, certificates, instruments and documents to be executed and delivered by the parties in connection with the Contemplated Transactions including, the Escrow Agreement, the R Employment Agreement, and the Holding Shareholders Agreement, and the Holding New Shares Agreement.

"Assumed Fee Amount" means an amount equal to $● (inclusive of HST).

"Assumed Change of Control Payments" means the following Change of Control Payments: (i) an amount equal to $● that becomes due and payable under the C Participation Plan by C immediately upon the Closing, plus applicable remittances related thereto and (ii) the reasonable fees and expenses of C incurred in connection with obtaining the necessary third-party consents listed in Section 3.04 of the Disclosure Schedules, if any.

"Assumed Liabilities" has the meaning ascribed thereto in Section 2.03.

"Assumed Seller Transaction Expenses" means any of the following Seller Transaction Expenses: (i) the Assumed Fee Amount payable to ●, (ii) any fees or expenses that are reflected or accrued on the Most Recent Balance Sheet and (iii) the reasonable fees and expenses, including those of legal counsel, incurred by C in connection with the Debt Financing.

"Assumed Subsidiary Liabilities" means with respect to each of Ca and any of the Transferred Subsidiaries, any and all Liabilities of such Person (including without limitation Ca's obligations under the Ca Note) that are not an Excluded Liability.

"Bulk Sales Laws" means the Laws of any jurisdiction with respect to **"bulk sales"** or **"bulk transfers"** of assets.

"Business" means the business conducted by C and its Subsidiaries and Ca as at the Closing.

"Business Day" means any day other than a Saturday or a Sunday or a weekday on which banks in Toronto, Ontario are authorized or required to be closed.

"Buyer Class B Common Shares" means the Class B Common Shares in the capital of Buyer.

"Ca" means ●, a corporation incorporated pursuant to the laws of the Province of Ontario.

"Ca Note" means the promissory note of $● due by Ca to C and issued in connection with the Pre-Closing Reorganization.

"Cash" means, with respect to Ca, C and its Subsidiaries, all cash, cash equivalents and marketable securities, in each case determined in accordance with GAAP, and excluding checks that have been issued but have not cleared.

"C" has the meaning set forth in the Preamble.

"C Participation Plan" means the "● Participation Plan" dated as of ●, 20●.

"C Shareholders Agreement" means the Shareholders Agreement dated ● by and among ●.

"C Trading" means ● an Ontario corporation.

"Change of Control Payment" means (a) any bonus, termination, severance, retention or other payment or other form of Compensation that is created, accelerated, accrues or becomes payable by Ca, C or any of their Subsidiaries to any present or former director, shareholder, employee, agent, independent contractor, service provider or consultant thereof, including pursuant to any employment agreement, services agreement, benefit plan or any other Contractual Obligation (including awards under the C Participation Plan), including any Taxes payable on or triggered by any such payment (other than payments in respect of the securities under or as described in Article II of this Agreement) and (b) without duplication of any other amounts included within the definition of Seller Transaction Expenses, any other payment, expense or fee that accrues or becomes payable by Seller or any of their Subsidiaries to any Governmental Authority or other Person under any applicable Legal Requirement or Contractual Obligation, including in connection with the making of any filings, the giving of any notices or the obtaining of any consents, authorizations or approvals, in the case of each of (a) and (b), as a result of, or in connection with, the execution and delivery of this Agreement or any Ancillary Agreement or the consummation of the Contemplated Transactions or the Pre-Closing Reorganization.

"Credit Agreement" means the Credit Agreement between Buyer as Borrower and the Existing Lender, as lender and agent, entered into as of the date hereof.

"Class B Common Shares" means the Class B common shares in the capital of Holding.

"Class B Junior Preferred Shares" means the Class B junior preferred shares in the capital of Holding.

"Class B Senior Preferred Shares" means the Class B senior preferred shares in the capital of Holding.

"Closing Date" means the date hereof.

"Collective Agreements" means the collective agreements binding any of Ca, C or their Subsidiaries in respect of the Business and all related documents including letters of understanding, letters of intent and other written communications with bargaining agents for the Employees which impose any obligations upon Ca, C or their Subsidiaries.

"Company Intellectual Property Rights" means all Intellectual Property Rights owned by Ca, C and its Subsidiaries or used by Ca, C and its Subsidiaries in connection with the Business, including all Intellectual Property Rights in and to Company Technology.

"Company Technology" means any and all Technology used in connection with the Business.

"Company Shares" means each of the issued and outstanding Common Shares and Preferred Shares of C.

"Compensation" means, with respect to any individual, all salaries, compensation, remuneration, commissions, bonuses, incentives or benefits of any kind or character whatsoever (including issuances or grants of Equity Interests), made directly or indirectly by Ca, C and its Subsidiaries to or for the benefit of such Person or any Family Member of such individual.

"Competition Act" mean the *Competition Act* (Canada), as amended.

"**Competitive Business**" means (i) the manufacturing, distribution, marketing and sale of ● and (ii) any other line of business that C conducts or, as reflected in C's business plans or board of director minutes, has specific plans to conduct as of the Closing Date.

"**Contemplated Transactions**" means the transactions contemplated by this Agreement, including the transactions described in the recitals to this Agreement.

"**Contractual Obligation**" means, with respect to any Person, any contract, agreement, deed, mortgage, lease, sublease, license, sublicense or other legally enforceable commitment, promise, undertaking, obligation, arrangement, instrument or understanding, whether written or oral, to which or by which such Person is a party or otherwise subject or bound or to which or by which any property, business, operation or right of such Person is subject or bound.

"**Management Agreement**" means that Management Agreement as defined in the C Shareholders Agreement.

"**Debt**" means, with respect to any Person, and without duplication, all obligations in respect of principal, accrued interest, penalties, fees and premiums, of such Person (a) for borrowed money (including amounts outstanding under overdraft facilities), (b) evidenced by notes, bonds, debentures or other similar Contractual Obligations, (c) in respect of "earn-out" obligations and other obligations for the deferred purchase price of property, goods or services (other than trade payables or accruals incurred in the Ordinary Course of Business), (d) for the capitalized liability under all capital leases of such Person (determined in accordance with GAAP), (e) in respect of letters of credit and bankers' acceptances, (f) for Contractual Obligations relating to interest rate protection, swap agreements, currency forward contracts, collar agreements and any other hedging instruments, in each case, to the extent payable if such Contractual Obligation is terminated at the Closing, and (g) in the nature of Guarantees of the obligations described in clauses (a) through (f) above of any other Person.

"**Debt Payoff Amount**" means the amount in cash equal to the amount necessary to satisfy and discharge all of the Debt of C and its Subsidiaries under the Existing Credit Facility as of the date hereof as set forth in the payoff letter delivered pursuant to Section 2.06(b)(ix).

"**Deductible Amount**" means an amount equal to $●.

"**Disclosure Schedule**" means the disclosure schedule delivered by Seller and their Subsidiaries to Buyer and dated as of the date of this Agreement.

"**Employee**" means those individuals listed on Section 3.21(e) of the Disclosure Schedule who are employed as employees by any of Ca, C or their Subsidiaries in the Business.

"**Employee Plan**" means any plan, program, policy, arrangement or Contractual Obligation, whether or not reduced to writing, and whether covering a single individual or a group of individuals, that is (a) a health, welfare, medical, dental, disability or life insurance plan, (b) a pension benefit plan, (c) a stock bonus, stock purchase, stock option, restricted stock, stock appreciation right or similar equity-based plan or (d) any other deferred-compensation, retirement, savings, severance, supplemental unemployment benefit, reimbursement, bonus, profit-sharing, incentive or fringe-benefit plan, program or arrangement, which Ca, C and its Subsidiaries sponsor or maintain, or to which any of Ca, C and its Subsidiaries contributes or is obligated to contribute, or under which any of Ca, C and its Subsidiaries has or may have any Liability, or which benefits any current or former employee, director, consultant or independent contractor, or agent of Ca, C and its Subsidiaries or the beneficiaries or dependents of any such Person.

"**Employment Contracts**" means each written employment contract between any of Ca, C or their Subsidiaries and an Employee, other than a Collective Agreement,

"**Encumbrance**" or "**Encumbered**" means any charge, claim, equitable or ownership interest, lien, license, option, pledge, security interest, mortgage, hypotheque, deed of trust, right of way, easement, encroachment, servitude, right of first offer or first refusal, buy/sell agreement and any other restriction or covenant with respect to, or condition governing the use, construction, voting (in the case of any security or Equity Interest), transfer, receipt of income or exercise of any other attribute of ownership (other than, in the case of a security, any restriction on the transfer of such security arising solely under applicable securities laws).

"**Enforceable**" means, with respect to any Contractual Obligation stated to be Enforceable by or against any Person, that such Contractual Obligation is a legal, valid and binding obligation of such Person enforceable by or against such Person in accordance with its terms, except to the extent that enforcement of the rights and remedies created thereby is subject to bankruptcy, insolvency, reorganization, moratorium and other similar laws of general application affecting the rights and remedies of creditors and to general principles of equity (regardless of whether enforceability is considered in a proceeding in equity or at law).

"**Environmental Laws**" means any Legal Requirement relating to (a) releases or threatened releases of Hazardous Substances, (b) pollution or protection of public health or the environment or worker safety or health, (c) the manufacture, handling, transport, use, treatment, storage, or disposal of Hazardous Substances, or (d) civil or tort law governing any act or omission relating to the environment.

"**Equity Interest**" means, with respect to any Person, (a) any share, partnership or membership interest, unit of participation or other similar interest (however designated) in such Person and (b) any option, warrant, purchase right, conversion right, exchange right or other Contractual Obligation which would entitle any other Person to acquire any such interest in such Person or otherwise entitle any other Person to share in the equity, profits, earnings, losses or gains of such Person (including stock appreciation, phantom stock, profit participation or other similar rights).

"**Escrow Amount**" means an amount equal to $●.

"**Escrow Agent**" means ●.

"**Escrow Agreement**" means the Escrow Agreement substantially in the form attached hereto as Exhibit C.

"**Existing Credit Facility**" means the credit facilities with the Existing Lender evidenced by the agreement, dated as of ●, as such agreement has been amended from time to time.

"**Existing Lender**" means ●.

"**Facilities**" means any buildings, improvements or structures located on the Leased Real Property.

"**Family Member**" means, with respect to any individual, (a) such Person's spouse, (b) each parent, brother, sister or child of such Person or such Person's spouse, (c) the spouse of any Person described in clause (b) above, (d) each child of any Person described in clauses (a), (b) or (c) above, (e) each trust created for the benefit of one or more of the Persons described in clauses (a) through (d) above and (f) each custodian or guardian of any property of one or more of the Persons described in clauses (a) through (e) above in his or her capacity as such custodian or guardian.

"Fundamental Representations" means, collectively, Section 3.01(a), Section 3.02(a), Section 3.04(b)(iii), Section 3.05(a), Section 3.05(b), Section 3.07, Section 3.08(d) and Section 3.26.

"GAAP" and all references to "generally accepted accounting principles" unless the context otherwise requires, means Canadian generally accepted accounting principles applied on a consistent basis (other than changes to accounting rules related to the implementation of Accounting Standards for Private Enterprises (ASPE)) and which are in accordance with the recommendations made from time to time by the Canadian Institute of Chartered Accountants (as published in the CICA Handbook) on the date on which such generally accepted accounting principles are applied.

"Government Order" means any order, writ, judgment, injunction, decree, stipulation, ruling, decision, verdict, determination or award made, issued or entered by or with any Governmental Authority.

"Governmental Authority" means any Canadian federal, provincial, municipal, local or other governmental or public department, or political subdivision thereof, or any multinational organization or authority, or any other authority, agency or commission entitled to exercise any administrative, executive, judicial, legislative, police, regulatory or taxing authority or power, any court or tribunal (or any department, bureau or division thereof), or any arbitrator or arbitral body.

"Guarantee" means, with respect to any Person, (a) any guarantee of the payment or performance of, or any contingent obligation in respect of, any Debt or other Liability of any other Person, (b) any other arrangement whereby credit is extended to any obligor (other than such Person) on the basis of any promise or undertaking of such Person (i) to pay the Debt or other Liability of such obligor, (ii) to purchase any obligation owed by such obligor, (iii) to purchase or lease assets under circumstances that are designed to enable such obligor to discharge one or more of its obligations or (iv) to maintain the capital, working capital, solvency or general financial condition of such obligor and (c) any liability as a general partner of a partnership or as a venturer in a joint venture in respect of Debt or other Liabilities of such partnership or venture.

"**Hazardous Substance**" means any pollutant, petroleum, or any fraction thereof, contaminant or toxic or hazardous material (including toxic mold and asbestos), substance or waste as defined by Environmental Laws.

"**Holding**" means ●.

"**Holding Class B Common Shares**" means the Class B Common Shares in the capital of Holding.

"**Holding Class B Junior Preferred Shares**" means the Class B Junior Preferred shares in the capital of Holding.

"**Holding Class B Senior Preferred Shares**" means the Class B Senior Preferred shares in the capital of Holding.

"**Holding New Shares**" means, collectively, ● Class B Common Shares, ● Class B Senior Preferred Shares and ● Class B Junior Preferred Shares in Holding.

"**Holding Shareholders Agreement**" means the Shareholders Agreement substantially in the form attached hereto as Exhibit B.

"**Indemnified Person**" means, with respect to any Indemnity Claim, each Buyer Indemnified Person or Seller Indemnified Person asserting the Indemnity Claim (or on whose behalf the Indemnity Claim is asserted) under Section 8.01 or Section 8.02, as the case may be.

"**Indemnifying Party**" means, with respect to any Indemnity Claim, the party or parties against whom such Indemnity Claim may be or has been asserted pursuant to this Agreement.

"**Indemnity Cap**" means $●.

"**Indemnity Claim**" means any claim for indemnification pursuant to ARTICLE VIII.

"**Intellectual Property Rights**" means all rights, title, and interests in and to all proprietary rights of every kind and nature however denominated, throughout the world, in and to all intellectual property, including:

(a) Patents, copyrights, industrial designs, integrated circuit topographies, trade secrets, and all other proprietary rights in Technology;

(b) trademarks, trade names, service marks, service names, brands, trade dress and logos, and the goodwill and activities associated therewith;

(c) domain names and moral rights;

(d)   any and all registrations, applications, recordings, licenses, common-law rights, statutory rights, and contractual rights relating to any of the foregoing; and

(e)   all Actions and rights to sue at law or in equity for any past or future infringement or other impairment of any of the foregoing, including the right to receive all proceeds and damages therefrom, and all rights to obtain renewals, continuations, divisions, or other extensions of legal protections pertaining thereto.

"Inventory" or "Inventories" means all inventories of Ca, C and its Subsidiaries, wherever located, including all finished goods, work in process, raw materials, spare parts and all other materials and supplies to be used or consumed by Ca, C and its Subsidiaries in the production of finished goods.

"Investment Canada Act" means the *Investment Canada Act* (Canada), as amended.

"Knowledge of Seller" and similar formulations mean that one or more of ● should have had knowledge of such fact or other matter assuming the diligent exercise of such individual's duties as a director, officer or employee of Seller and their Subsidiaries.

"Legal Requirement" means any Canadian federal, provincial, municipal or local, or other governmental, or any law, statute, standard, ordinance, code, rule, regulation, resolution, decree or promulgation, or any Governmental Order, or any Permit granted under any of the foregoing, or any similar provision which in each case has the force or effect of law.

"Liability" means, with respect to any Person, any liability or obligation of such Person whether known or unknown, whether asserted or unasserted, whether determined, determinable or otherwise, whether absolute or contingent, whether accrued or unaccrued, whether liquidated or unliquidated, whether directly incurred or consequential, whether due or to become due and whether or not required under GAAP to be accrued on the financial statements of such Person.

"Material Adverse Effect" means any event, change, fact, condition, circumstance or occurrence that, when considered either individually or in the aggregate together with all other adverse events, changes, facts, conditions, circumstances or occurrences with respect to which such phrase is used in this Agreement, has had or would reasonably be expected to have a material adverse effect on (A) the business, operations, results of operations, properties, assets or condition (financial or otherwise) of Ca, C and its Subsidiaries, taken as a whole, or (B) the ability of Seller (and their Subsidiaries) to consummate the Contemplated Transactions, in either case other than the following: (i) events, changes, facts, conditions, circumstances or occurrences generally affecting the ● industry in respect of any market of the Business, but only to the extent that such events, changes, facts, conditions, circumstances or occurrences do not have a disproportionate effect on Ca, C and its Subsidiaries taken as a whole as compared to other industry participants after taking into account Ca, C and its Subsidiaries place of manufacture in such market, (ii) any earthquakes, hurricanes, tsunamis, tornadoes, floods, mudslides, wild fires or other natural disasters, weather conditions and other force majeure events in Canada or any other country or region in the world, sabotage, terrorism, military action or war (whether or not declared), but only to the extent that such events, changes, facts, conditions, circumstances or occurrences do not have a materially disproportionate effect on Ca, C and its Subsidiaries taken as a whole as compared to other participants in the industry referred to in clause (i), (iii) changes in Legal Requirements or GAAP (or interpretations thereof) and (iv) events, changes, facts, conditions, circumstances or occurrences in general economic or political conditions or the financing or capital markets in general in Canada or any country or region in the world, but only to the extent that such events, changes, facts, conditions, circumstances or occurrences do not have a materially disproportionate effect on Ca, C and its Subsidiaries taken as a whole as compared to other participants in the industry and place of industry referred to in clause (i).

"**Ordinary Course of Business**" means with respect to Ca, C and its Subsidiaries an action taken by such Person(s) in the ordinary course of such Person(s)' business that is consistent in all material respects with the present and past customs and practices of such Person(s) (including present and past practice with respect to quantity, amount, magnitude and frequency, standard employment and payroll policies and past practice with respect to management of working capital and the making of capital expenditures) and that is taken in the ordinary course of the normal day-to-day operations of such Person.

"**Organizational Documents**" means, with respect to any Person (other than an individual), (a) the certificate or articles of incorporation or organization and any joint venture, limited liability company, operating or partnership agreement and other similar documents adopted or filed in connection with the creation, formation or organization of such Person and (b) all by-laws, voting agreements and similar documents, instruments or agreements relating to the organization or governance of such Person, in each case, as amended or supplemented.

"**Permits**" means, with respect to any Person, any license, franchise, permit, consent, approval, right, privilege, certificate or other similar authorization issued by, or otherwise granted by, any Governmental Authority to which or by which such Person is subject or bound or to which or by which any property, business, operation or right of such Person is subject or bound.

"**Permitted Encumbrance**" means (a) statutory liens for Taxes not yet due and payable, (b) mechanics', materialmen's, carriers', workers', repairers' and similar statutory liens arising or incurred in the Ordinary Course of Business the existence of which would not constitute an event of default under, or breach of, a Real Property Lease and the Liabilities of Ca, C and its Subsidiaries (c) liens to secure landlords, lessors or renters under leases or rental agreements (to the extent Seller (or any Subsidiary of Seller) or Ca is not in default under such lease or rental agreement) or (d) the liens described in Schedule 2.01.

"**Person**" means any individual or any corporation, association, partnership, limited liability company, unlimited liability company, joint venture, joint stock or other company, business trust, trust, organization, Governmental Authority or other entity of any kind.

"**Post-Reference Date Payments**" means any of the following payments by Ca, C or any of their Subsidiaries (but in each case excluding any inter-corporate payments between and among the foregoing, Assumed Change of Control Payments and Assumed Seller Transaction Expenses), without duplication: (i) all dividends, distributions or other similar payments (whether in cash or in kind) made to any shareholder between the Reference Date and the Closing and any such dividends, distributions or other similar payments declared at any time between the Reference Date and the Closing but unpaid as of the Closing, (ii) all payments made to any shareholder in connection with the purchase, redemption or other acquisition or retirement of any Equity Interests or debt interests between the Reference Date and the Closing and any such payments agreed at any time between the Reference Date and the Closing to be made to the extent the obligation to make any such payment survives after the Closing, (iii) all payments made to any shareholder or any Affiliate thereof in connection with any management, monitoring, consulting, transaction or other similar fees or arrangements between the Reference Date and the Closing and any such payments agreed at any time between the Reference Date and the Closing to be made to the extent the obligation to make any such payment survives after the Closing, (iv) all bonus payments made to any employee of Ca, C or their Subsidiaries between the Reference Date and the Closing and any such payments agreed at any time between the Reference Date and the Closing to be made to the extent the obligation to make any such payment survives after the Closing, but only to the extent not made in the Ordinary Course of Business and to the extent not taken into account in the calculation of the Cash Purchase Price paid at the Closing pursuant to Section 2.04 hereof and excluding any Assumed Change of Control Payments and (v) all Seller Transaction Expenses which are not Assumed Seller Transaction Expenses that are incurred, paid or accrued, as applicable, between the Reference Date and the close of the Closing Date and any such payments agreed at any time between the Reference Date and the Closing to be made to the extent the obligation to make any such payment survives after the Closing.

"**Post-Reference Date Tax Period**" means any Tax period or portion thereof that is not a Pre-Reference Date Tax Period.

"**Pre-Closing Reorganization**" means Seller pre-Closing plan of reorganization set forth on Section 3.27 of the Disclosure Schedule.

"**Pre-Reference Date Tax Period**" means any Tax period ending on or before the Reference Date and the portion through the end of the Reference Date for any Tax period that includes (but does not end on) the Reference Date.

"**Reference Date**" means ●.

"**Representative**" means, with respect to any Person, any director, officer, employee, agent, manager, consultant, advisor, or other representative of such Person, including legal counsel, accountants, and financial advisors.

"**Restricted Area**" means any jurisdiction listed on Exhibit J hereto, or any other jurisdiction within which C or any of its Affiliates conducts business or, as reflected in C's business plans or board of director minutes, has specific plans to conduct business as of the Closing Date.

"**Retained Books and Records**" means all corporate and Tax related books and records of C however stored and in whatever medium.

"**Seller Transaction Expenses**" means the aggregate amount of all out-of-pocket fees and expenses, incurred by or on behalf of, or to be paid by, Seller and their Subsidiaries, relating to the negotiation, preparation or execution of this

Agreement or any documents or agreements contemplated hereby or the performance or consummation of Contemplated Transactions and the Pre-Closing Reorganization hereby (or any alternative transaction), which shall include, but not be limited to (A) any fees and expenses associated with obtaining necessary or appropriate waivers, consents or approvals of any third parties on behalf of Ca, C and its Subsidiaries, (B) any fees or expenses associated with obtaining the release and termination of any Encumbrances, (C) all brokers' or finders' fees, including, but not limited to, all fees and expenses for professional services rendered by ● and (D) fees and expenses of counsel, advisors, consultants, investment bankers, accountants, auditors and experts, including, but no LLP and, in all cases, excluding any Assumed Seller Transaction Expenses and Assumed Change of Control Payments.

"Shareholder Loans" means the shareholder loans made to C by each of ● in each case as evidenced by the C Shareholders Agreement.

"Shares" means all of the issued and outstanding shares of Ca.

"Subsidiary" means, with respect to any specified Person, any other Person of which such specified Person, directly or indirectly through one or more subsidiaries, (a) owns at least 50% of the outstanding Equity Interests entitled to vote generally in the election of the board of directors or similar governing body of such other Person, or (b) has the power to generally direct the business and policies of that other Person, whether by contract or as a general partner, managing member, manager, joint venturer, agent or otherwise. For the avoidance of doubt, immediately prior to Closing, Ca shall be a Subsidiary of Principal.

"Tangible Personal Property" means all machinery, equipment, tools, furniture, office equipment, computer hardware, supplies, materials, vehicles and other items of tangible personal property of every kind owned or leased by Ca, C and its Subsidiaries (wherever located and whether or not carried on the books of Ca, C and its Subsidiaries), together with any express or implied warranty by the manufacturers or sellers or lessors of any item or component part thereof and all maintenance records and other documents relating thereto.

"Tax" or **"Taxes"** means (a) any and all federal, provincial, local, municipal, non-U.S. or other taxes, assessments, governmental fees, escheat or unclaimed property obligations, duties, contributions, premiums or other governmental charges of any kind whatsoever, including gross income, net income, gross receipts, license, payroll, employment, governmental plan premium and contributions, excise, severance, stamp, occupation, recapture, premium, windfall profits, environmental, customs duties, shares, capital, franchise, profits, withholding, social security (or similar), unemployment, disability, real property, personal property, goods and services, harmonized sales, sales, use, surplus lines, transfer, registration, value added, ad valorem, alternative or add-on minimum, estimated, or other tax of any kind, including any interest, penalty, fines or addition thereto, whether disputed or not and (b) any liability for the payment of any amounts of the type described in clause (a) of this definition as a result of being a member of an affiliated, consolidated, combined, unitary or similar group for any period, as a result of any tax sharing or tax allocation agreement, arrangement or understanding, or as a result of being liable for another person's taxes as a transferee or successor, by Contractual Obligation or otherwise.

"Tax Return" means any return, declaration, report, document, election, designation, disclosure, estimate, claim for refund, information return, statement or other information or filing relating to Taxes, including any schedule or attachment thereto, and including any amendment thereof.

"Technology" means all inventions, works, discoveries, innovations, know-how, information (including ideas, research and development, formulas, algorithms, compositions, processes and techniques, data, designs, drawings, specifications), databases, computer software (excluding open source software or freeware), firmware, computer hardware, integrated circuits and integrated circuit masks, and any improvements, modifications, works in process, derivatives, or changes, whether tangible or intangible, embodied in any form and all documents and other materials recording any of the foregoing.

"Transferred Subsidiaries" means ●.

Section 1.02) Certain Matters of Construction

    a)   The parties have participated jointly in the negotiation and drafting of this Agreement. In the event an ambiguity or question of intent or interpretation arises, this Agreement shall be construed as if drafted jointly by the parties and no presumption or burden of proof shall arise favoring or disfavoring any party by virtue of the authorship of any of the provisions of this Agreement.

    b)   Section and subsection headings are not to be considered part of this Agreement, are included solely for convenience, are not intended to be full or accurate descriptions of the content of the Sections or subsections of this Agreement and shall not affect the construction hereof.

c) Except as otherwise explicitly specified to the contrary herein, (i) the words "hereof," "herein," "hereunder" and words of similar import shall refer to this Agreement as a whole and not to any particular Section or subsection of this Agreement and reference to a particular Section of this Agreement shall include all subsections thereof, (ii) references to a Section, Exhibit, Annex or Schedule means a Section of, or Exhibit, Annex or Schedule to this Agreement, unless another agreement is specified, (iii) definitions shall be equally applicable to both the singular and plural forms of the terms defined, and references to the masculine, feminine or neuter gender shall include each other gender, (iv) the word "including" means including without limitation, (v) any reference to "$" or "dollars" means Canadian dollars and (vi) references to a particular statute or regulation include all rules and regulations thereunder and any successor statute, rule or regulation, in each case as amended or otherwise modified from time to time.

d) The parties intend that each representation, warranty and covenant contained herein will have independent significance. If any party has breached or violated, or if there is an inaccuracy in, any representation, warranty or covenant contained herein in any respect, the fact that there exists another representation, warranty or covenant relating to the same subject matter (regardless of the relative levels of specificity) which the party has not breached or violated, or in respect of which there is not an inaccuracy, will not detract from or mitigate the fact that the party has breached or violated, or there is an inaccuracy in, the first representation, warranty or covenant.

e) The term "made available" shall mean provided to the online data room managed by ● and Seller as of 5:00 p.m. (Eastern time) as of the date immediately prior to the date hereof.

f) Time is of the essence with regard to all dates and time periods set forth or referred to in this Agreement.

g) For the convenience of the parties an index of additional terms defined throughout this Agreement has been included at the end of this Agreement but does not form a part of this Agreement.

ARTICLE 2: SALE AND TRANSFER OF ASSETS
AND SHARES; CLOSING

Section 2.01) Purchase and Sale of Assets and Shares

Upon the terms and subject to the conditions set forth in this Agreement, at the Closing, Seller will sell, convey, assign, transfer and deliver to Buyer as applicable, and Buyer will purchase and acquire from Seller, as applicable, (i) the Shares and (ii) all of Seller' rights, titles and interests in and to the Acquired Assets, free and clear of any Encumbrances other than Permitted Encumbrances. **"Acquired Assets"** means, with respect to C, the property, goodwill and assets, real, personal or mixed, tangible and intangible, of every kind and description, wherever located, owned or licensed by C, purported to be owned or licensed by C and/ or used by or on behalf of C in connection with the Business, including, but not limited to, the following (but excluding the Excluded Assets):

a) all of the Equity Interests of the Transferred Subsidiaries;

b) all Tangible Personal Property of C (including all rights with respect to leasehold interests and subleases and rights thereunder relating to the Tangible Personal Property);

c) all Inventories of C;

d) all accounts receivable, notes receivable, Cash and other current assets of C;

e) all Contractual Obligations of C (excluding any Employment Contracts (which, for the avoidance of doubt is addressed in ARTICLE VII) and including all Leased Real Property described in Section 3.12(a) of the Disclosure Schedule) and all outstanding offers or solicitations made by or to C to enter into any Contractual Obligations;

f) all Permits of C and all pending applications thereof or renewals thereof, to the extent transferrable;

g) all data and records related to the Business, including client and customer lists, equipment logs, operating guides and manuals, Tax, financial and accounting records, advertising materials, promotional materials, studies, reports and correspondence;

h) all of the intangible rights and property of C, including Intellectual Property Rights, goodwill associated therewith, licenses and sublicenses granted in respect thereto and rights thereunder, remedies against infringement, and rights to protection of interest therein;

i) all insurance benefits of C, including rights in and with respect to the Liability Policies to the extent transferrable;

j) all claims, causes of action and rights of recovery of C;

k) all rights of C under and with respect to assets associated with the Assumed Employee Plans;

l) all rights of C relating to deposits and prepaid expenses and rights to offset, if any, in respect thereof;

m) the Ca Note; and

n) all other assets of C of every kind and description, tangible or intangible, pertaining to or used in the Business other than the Excluded Assets.

Section 2.02) Excluded Assets

Notwithstanding anything to the contrary contained in Section 2.01 or elsewhere in this Agreement, the following assets of C (collectively, the **"Excluded Assets"**) are not part of the sale and purchase contemplated hereunder, are excluded from the Acquired Assets and shall remain the property of C after the Closing:

a) all rights of C under this Agreement, the Bill of Sale, the Assignment and Assumption Agreement(s) and any of the Ancillary Agreements;

b) the Retained Books and Records;

c) any rights of recovery for income taxes for any Pre-Reference Date Tax Period of C to the extent not reflected as a current asset on the Most Recent Balance Sheet; and

d) all of the assets and undertakings listed or otherwise described in Schedule 2.02;

Notwithstanding anything to the contrary in this Agreement, C shall not sell, assign, transfer, license or convey (collectively, **"Transfer"**) to Buyer any of its rights and obligations in and to any of the Acquired Assets without first obtaining all approvals, consents or waivers necessary to effect such Transfer or the consent and agreement of Buyer. If C is unable to obtain all necessary approvals, consents or waivers, other than approvals, consents or waivers of C, Buyer or their respective Affiliates necessary to Transfer the Acquired Assets to Buyer, including such approvals, consents and waivers for the Contractual Obligations set forth in Section 3.16, until the earlier of such time as approval, consent or waiver can be obtained, C shall, at Buyer's sole cost and expense, use reasonable best efforts to obtain, and Buyer shall use its reasonable best efforts to assist and cooperate with C in connection therewith, all necessary approvals, consents and waivers to the Transfer of the Acquired Assets, it being understood that to the extent the foregoing shall require any action that would, or would continue to, negatively affect the Business after the Closing, such action shall require the written consent of Buyer. Until an Acquired Asset is transferred and assigned to Buyer hereunder, each of C and Buyer agrees to use all reasonable best efforts to perform all acts and execute any and all documents as may be reasonably requested by the other party so that Buyer may realize the benefits of such Acquired Asset (a **"Non-Assigned Asset"**), as Buyer deems reasonably necessary until such time as their formal assignment to Buyer is made or such Non-Assigned Asset is terminated or expires. If any such Non-Assigned Asset cannot be subcontracted or assigned, Buyer and C agree to cooperate with each other and enter into such other commercially reasonable arrangements (including regarding performance of C's duties and obligations under such Non-Assigned Asset) as will enable C to fulfill its remaining obligations thereunder and Buyer to realize the benefits and assume the Liabilities thereof. To the extent that, after the date hereof, C receives any payments in respect of any accounts receivable, C shall promptly, but in any event no later than ten Business Days from the date of receipt, use reasonable best efforts to remit to Buyer such payment.

Section 2.03) Liabilities

a) On the Closing Date, subject to Section 2.03(b), Buyer shall assume and agree to discharge any and all Liabilities of C (**"Assumed Liabilities"**), including:

   i) all Liabilities arising out of the Acquired Assets (except for Excluded Liabilities) and Non-Assigned Assets;

   ii) all Liabilities for any of the Employees whether or not any such Employee accepts Buyer's offer of employment in accordance with ARTICLE VI, including without limitation, any severance obligations and any other Liabilities under or in respect of the Assumed Employee Plans;

   iii) all Assumed Seller Transaction Expenses and Assumed Change of Control Payments; and

   iv) all Liabilities arising out of the C Incentive Plan.

b) Notwithstanding anything else to the contrary contained in this Agreement Buyer will not assume or perform any of the Liabilities listed or described in Schedule 2.03(b) and, for the avoidance of doubt, Seller, as applicable, shall retain, pay for, perform and discharge such Liabilities (the "**Excluded Liabilities**"); and

c)   From and after the Closing, notwithstanding anything else to the contrary contained in this Agreement, Ca and the Transferred Subsidiaries shall each remain liable for such Person's respective Assumed Subsidiary Liabilities.

Section 2.04) Consideration

The aggregate consideration for the purchase and sale of the Acquired Assets and the Shares shall be the assumption, and where applicable, payment of the Assumed Liabilities by Buyer and:

a)   a cash payment to C equal to (A) $●, plus (B) a cash payment to the Existing Lender for and on behalf of C and its Subsidiaries equal to the Debt Payoff Amount and minus (C) the aggregate amount of any Post-Reference Date Payments that are not an Assumed Seller Transaction Expenses or an Assumed Change of Control Payments;

b)   a cash payment to Principal equal to $● in exchange for all of the issued and outstanding shares of Ca (collectively, with the cash payments contemplated by Section 2.04(a), the "**Cash Purchase Price**");

c)   ● Buyer Class B Common Shares, (the "**Buyer New Shares**").

Section 2.05) The Closing

The purchase and sale of the Acquired Assets and the Shares (the "**Closing**") shall take place at 11:00 a.m. (EDT) on the date hereof at the offices of ●.

Section 2.06) Closing Deliveries and Payments

a)   **Buyer Closing Deliveries and Payments.** Upon the terms and subject to the conditions set forth in this Agreement, Buyer shall deliver or cause to be delivered at the Closing the following:

i)   to C (or any other Person designated in writing by C on or prior to the date hereof), the Cash Purchase Price less the Escrow Amount, less the Debt Payoff Amount by wire transfer of immediately available funds to accounts designated in writing by Seller to Buyer not less than two (2) Business Days prior to the Closing Date; provided, that for the avoidance of doubt, if such payment under this Section 2.06(a)(i) is delivered to a Person designated by C, Buyer's obligation to pay C shall be fully satisfied and discharged upon delivery of such payment;

ii) to C (or any other Person designated in writing by C on or prior to the date hereof), an amount necessary to satisfy in full the amounts under the Shareholder Loans that become due and payable by C immediately upon the Closing (but in an aggregate amount not to exceed $●); provided, that for the avoidance of doubt, if such payment under this Section 2.06(a)(ii) is delivered to a Person designated by C, Buyer's obligation to pay C shall be fully satisfied and discharged upon delivery of such payment;

iii) to C, certificates evidencing ownership of Buyer New Shares;

iv) to the Existing Lender for and on behalf of C and its Subsidiaries, an amount equal to the Debt Payoff Amount;

v) to the Escrow Agent, by wire transfer of immediately available funds, the Escrow Amount in accordance with the terms of the Escrow Agreement;

vi) to the recipients specified in Schedule 2.06(a)(vi), each recipient's portion of the Assumed Change of Control Payments as set out in such Schedule; provided, however, that notwithstanding anything to the contrary contained herein, the amounts payable under the C Participation Plan shall be paid by Buyer through Buyer's payroll on the next regular date that payroll occurs and at least 5 Business days after the Closing Date;

vii) to ●, the Assumed Fee Amount;

viii) duly executed assignment and assumption agreement(s) in the form attached hereto as Exhibit D (the **"Assignment and Assumption Agreement(s)"**);

ix) an executed counterpart signature page to the R Employment Agreement and the Escrow Agreement executed by Buyer;

x) the Holding Shareholders Agreement executed by Buyer and each of its shareholders other than Principal and C;

xi) each of the Ancillary Agreements and the R Employment Agreement, as well as, the Management Agreement, Initial Subscription Agreement, the Continuing Investor Subscription Agreement, the Senior Note and Subordinated Notes (each as defined in the Holding Shareholders Agreement), in each case duly executed by each of the parties thereto other than Seller, as applicable;

xii) a certificate of status or equivalent of Buyer issued by the relevant Governmental Authority in the applicable jurisdiction of organization, as of the Closing Date;

xiii) to C, an agreement of purchase and sale pursuant to which Holding shall acquire Buyer New Shares from C (the **"Holding New Shares Agreement"**) duly executed by Holding in exchange for the Holding New Shares on a tax deferred basis pursuant to Section 85(1) of the *Income Tax Act* (Canada);

xiv) to C, immediately following the execution and delivery of the Holding New Shares Agreement, certificates evidencing ownership of the Holding New Shares; and

xv) such other documents and other instruments as may reasonably be requested by Sellers each in form and substance reasonably satisfactory to Buyer and Sellers, acting reasonably, and executed by Buyer.

b) **Seller Closing Deliveries.** Upon the terms and subject to the conditions set forth in this Agreement, Seller shall deliver or cause to be delivered at the Closing to Buyer the following:

i) share certificates representing the Shares duly endorsed for transfer to Buyer by R, together with evidence satisfactory to Buyer that Buyer has been entered upon the books of Ca as the holder of the Shares;

ii) Certificates of good standing with respect to C and each of its Subsidiaries issued by the relevant Governmental Authority in the applicable jurisdiction of organization, as of the Closing Date;

iii) a bill of sale for all of the Acquired Assets substantially in the form attached hereto as Exhibit E (the **"Bill of Sale"**) executed by C;

iv) the Assignment and Assumption Agreement(s) executed by C;

v) for each Real Property Lease, an assignment and assumption of lease substantially in the form attached hereto as Exhibit F;

vi) duly executed separate assignments of all registered marks and copyrights substantially in the form(s) attached hereto as Exhibit G;

vii) the Holding Shareholders Agreement executed by Principal and C;

viii) an executed counterpart signature page to the R Employment Agreement and the Escrow Agreement executed by Principal;

ix) a payoff letter and lien release documentation in form and substance reasonably satisfactory to Buyer relating to the repayment of the Debt Payoff Amount and the termination of all Encumbrances on any Acquired Assets securing such Debt;

    x)   a certificate of status or equivalent, as applicable, of Ca, C and its Subsidiaries issued by the relevant Governmental Authorities in the applicable jurisdiction of organization, each as of the Closing Date;

    xi) Purchase Certificate issued by the Ontario Workplace Safety and Insurance Board as of a recent date in respect of the Business;

    xii) the consents, waivers and approvals listed on Schedule 2.06(b)(xii) in a manner reasonably satisfactory in form and substance to Buyer;

    xiii) the release in the form attached here as Exhibit I;

    xiv) the Holding New Shares Agreement duly executed by C; and

    xv) such other documents and other instruments as may reasonably be requested by Buyer each in form and substance reasonably satisfactory to Buyer and Sellers, acting reasonably, and executed by Seller, as well as their Subsidiaries, if and as necessary.

Section 2.07) Withholding Rights

Buyer, the Escrow Agent and any other applicable withholding agent will be entitled to deduct and withhold from the consideration otherwise payable to or for the benefit of any Person pursuant to or contemplated by this Agreement such amounts as it is required to deduct and withhold with respect to the making of such payment under any provision of federal, provincial, state, local or non-U.S. Tax Legal Requirements. Any amounts withheld in accordance with this Section 2.07 will be treated for all purposes of this Agreement as having been paid to the Person in respect of which such deduction and withholding was made.

Section 2.08) Purchase Price Allocation

Seller and Buyer agree to allocate the Assumed Liabilities, Cash Purchase Price and Buyer New Shares among the Acquired Assets in accordance with the provisions of Schedule 2.08. The Parties agree to execute and file all of their own Tax Returns and prepare all of their own financial statements and other instruments on the basis of this allocation.

ARTICLE 3: REPRESENTATIONS AND WARRANTIES REGARDING SELLER AND THEIR SUBSIDIARIES

In order to induce Buyer to enter into and perform this Agreement and to consummate the Contemplated Transactions, Seller hereby represent and warrant to Buyer that the statements contained in this ARTICLE III are true and correct in all material respects, except as set forth herein or in the Disclosure Schedule.

The Disclosure Schedule shall be arranged in Sections corresponding to the numbered Sections contained in this ARTICLE III and ARTICLE IV, and the disclosure in any Section of the Disclosure Schedule shall qualify (a) the corresponding Section in this ARTICLE III or ARTICLE IV and (b) the other Sections in this ARTICLE III or ARTICLE IV to the extent that it is reasonably apparent on the face of such disclosure that it also qualifies or applies to such other Sections.

Section 3.01) Organization

Each of Ca, C and its Subsidiaries are duly organized, validly existing and in good standing under the laws of its respective jurisdiction of organization. Seller have made available to Buyer accurate and complete copies of (a) the Organizational Documents of Ca and the Transferred Subsidiaries and (b) the minute books of Ca and the Transferred Subsidiaries.

a) Each of Ca, C and its Subsidiaries are duly qualified to do business and is in good standing in each jurisdiction in which it owns or leases real property or conducts business and is required to so qualify except where the failure to so qualify has not had, and would not reasonably be expected to have, a Material Adverse Effect.

Section 3.02) Contemplated Transactions

a) Each of C and its Subsidiaries and Ca has all requisite power and authority necessary for the execution, delivery and performance by it of this Agreement and each Ancillary Agreement to which it is a party. Each of C and Ca has duly authorized by all necessary action on the part of its board of directors and shareholders, the execution, delivery and performance of this Agreement and each such Ancillary Agreement. This Agreement and each Ancillary Agreement to which C is, or will be at Closing, a party (i) have been duly executed and delivered by C and (ii) is a legal, valid and binding obligation of C, enforceable against C in accordance with its terms.

c) **Conduct of Business.** Each of Ca, C and its Subsidiaries has all requisite corporate power and authority necessary to own, lease, operate and use its assets and carry on the Business.

Section 3.03) Authorization of Governmental Authorities

Except as disclosed in Section 3.03 of the Disclosure Schedule, no action by (including any authorization by or consent or approval of), or in respect of, or filing with, any Governmental Authority is required by or on behalf of Seller or in respect of Seller, Ca or any of each of their Subsidiaries, the Business or any assets of Seller and their Subsidiaries for, or in connection with, (a) the valid and lawful authorization, execution, delivery and performance by Seller of this Agreement or any Ancillary Agreement to which it is a party or (b) the consummation of the Contemplated Transactions and the Pre-Closing Reorganization.

Section 3.04) Noncontravention

Except as disclosed in Section 3.04 of the Disclosure Schedule, none of the authorization, execution, delivery or performance by each of Seller (or their Subsidiaries) of this Agreement or any Ancillary Agreement to which it is a party, nor the consummation of the Contemplated Transactions and the Pre-Closing Reorganization, will:

a)   assuming the taking of each action by (including the obtaining of each necessary authorization, consent or approval), or in respect of, and the making of all necessary filings with, Governmental Authorities, in each case, as disclosed on Section 3.03 of the Disclosure Schedule, conflict with or result in a breach or violation of, or constitute a default (or an event which, with notice or lapse of time or both, would constitute a default) under, any Legal Requirement applicable to Ca, C and its Subsidiaries, the Business or any assets of Ca, C or its Subsidiaries, except where such conflict, breach, violation or default would not reasonably be expected to have a Material Adverse Effect; or

b)   conflict with or result in a breach or violation of, or constitute a default (or an event which, with notice or lapse of time or both, would constitute a default) under, or result in termination of, or accelerate the performance required by, or result in a right of termination or acceleration under, or require any action by (including any authorization, consent or approval) or notice to any Person, or require any offer to purchase or prepayment of any Debt or Liability under, or result in the creation of any Encumbrance upon or forfeiture of any of the rights, properties or assets of Ca, C or its Subsidiaries under, any of the terms, conditions or provisions of (i) any material Permit applicable to or otherwise affecting Ca, C and its Subsidiaries, the Business or any assets of Ca, C and its Subsidiaries, except where such breach, violation, default, termination, acceleration or other event would not reasonably be expected to have a Material Adverse Effect, (ii) any Material Company Contract or (iii) the Organizational Documents of Ca, C or its Subsidiaries.

Section 3.05) Capitalization of Seller and their Subsidiaries

a) Authorized and Outstanding Equity Interests

All of the outstanding Equity Interests of Ca and the Transferred Subsidiaries are, immediately prior to the completion of the Contemplated Transactions, legally owned by the Persons in the respective amounts set forth on Section 3.05 of the Disclosure Schedule. None of Ca or the Transferred Subsidiaries currently owns, or will at Closing own, any Equity Interests in any other Person other than as set forth on Section 3.05 of the Disclosure Schedule. Except as set forth on Section 3.05 of the Disclosure Schedule, each of Ca and the Transferred Subsidiaries has no issued or outstanding Equity Interests at the relevant time and holds no shares of its own capital (or other Equity Interests in itself). Seller have made available to Buyer (and, in the case of the C Participation Plan only, to Buyer's counsel) accurate and complete copies of the share ledgers (or equivalent records) of each of Ca and the Transferred Subsidiaries at the date of this Agreement which records reflect all issuances, transfers, repurchases and cancellations of shares of capital share (or other Equity Interests) of each of Ca and the Transferred Subsidiaries prior to the date of this Agreement. All of the outstanding Shares and shares of the Transferred Subsidiaries (or, where applicable, other Equity Interests) have at all times been duly authorized, validly issued and are fully paid and non-assessable. Ca and the Transferred Subsidiaries have not violated (i) securities laws or any other similar applicable Legal Requirement of each of its jurisdictions of organization, respectively, or (ii) any pre-emptive or other similar rights of any Person in connection with the issuance, repurchase or redemption of any of the Equity Interests owned by Seller in Ca and the Transferred Subsidiaries.

b) Encumbrances on Equity Interests, etc.

C is the registered owner of all of the Equity Interests of each of the Transferred Subsidiaries, and R is the record owner of all of the Shares, in each case free and clear of all Encumbrances other than Permitted Encumbrances. Except as disclosed on Section 3.05 of the Disclosure Schedule: (i) there are no outstanding options, warrants, contractual pre-emptive rights or other rights of any Person to acquire any Shares or any other Equity Interests of, or any Equity Interests in, the Transferred Subsidiaries, (ii) there are no Contractual Obligations relating to, the ownership, transfer or voting of any Equity Interests in Ca, C or their Subsidiaries, or otherwise affecting the rights of any holder of the Equity Interests in Ca, C or their Subsidiaries, and (iii) except for the Contemplated Transactions and as contemplated in Section 3.05(b) of the Disclosure Schedule with respect to the Pre-Closing Reorganization, there is no Contractual Obligation, or provision in the Organizational Documents of Ca, C or any of their Subsidiaries which obligates any of Ca, C or any of their Subsidiaries to purchase, redeem or otherwise acquire, or make any payment (including any dividend or distribution) in respect of, any Equity Interest in Ca, C or their Subsidiaries.

c) Additional Capitalization Representation

With respect to any jurisdiction in which the Company conducts its business other than the jurisdictions referenced in clause (i) of Section 3.05(a), to the Knowledge of Seller, Ca and the Transferred Subsidiaries have not violated any securities laws or any other similar Legal Requirement in such jurisdictions.

Section 3.06) Title to Shares

Upon completion of the Contemplated Transactions, Buyer will have good and valid title to Shares, free and clear of any Encumbrance, other than Permitted Encumbrances as set forth in Schedule 2.01 relating to the Shares and Encumbrances granted by Buyer.

Section 3.07) Business of Ca

Except as set forth in Section 3.07 of the Disclosure Schedule and pursuant to, or as a result of, the Pre-Closing Reorganization (including without limitation Ca's obligations under the Ca Note) and as the successor to the business of C Trading, Ca has never had any assets or liabilities and does not and has never conducted any business operations. Ca does not have and has never had any employees

Section 3.08) Financial Matters

a) Financial Statements

Attached as Exhibit H are copies of each of the following:

i) the audited consolidated balance sheets of C and its Subsidiaries as of ● (the **"Audited Balance Sheet"** and the date of the Audited Balance Sheet, the **"Audited Balance Sheet Date"**), the related audited consolidated statements of operations, the assets, liabilities, (whether accrued, absolute, contingent or otherwise), financial position, sales and earnings of C and their Subsidiaries for the fiscal years then ended, accompanied by any notes thereto and the reports of independent accountants of C and their Subsidiaries with respect thereto (collectively, the **"Audited Financials"**); and

ii) the unaudited consolidated balance sheet of C and its Subsidiaries as of ● (the **"Most Recent Balance Sheet"** and the date thereof, the **"Most Recent Balance Sheet Date"**), and the related unaudited consolidated statements of operations, the assets, liabilities, (whether accrued, absolute, contingent or otherwise), financial position, sales and earnings of C and its Subsidiaries for the six (6) months then ended (the **"Interim Financials"** and, together with the Audited Financials, the **"Financials"**).

b) **Compliance with GAAP, etc.**

Except as disclosed on Section 3.08(b) of the Disclosure Schedule, the Financials (including any notes thereto) (i) reflect, in all material respects, the books and records of C and its Subsidiaries as of the respective dates thereof, (ii) have been prepared in accordance with GAAP, consistently applied (subject, in the case of the unaudited Financials, to normal year-end audit adjustments, the effect of which will not, in the aggregate, be materially adverse, and the absence of footnote disclosure that if presented, would not differ materially from those included in the Audited Financials) and (iii) fairly present, in all materials respects, the consolidated financial position of C and its Subsidiaries as of the respective dates thereof and the consolidated results of the operations of C and its Subsidiaries and changes in financial position for the respective periods covered thereby.

c) **Absence of Undisclosed Liabilities**

Except as disclosed in Section 3.08(c) of the Disclosure Schedule, none of Ca, C nor any of its Subsidiaries has any material Liabilities except for (i) Liabilities set forth on the face of the Audited Balance Sheet (ii) Liabilities incurred in the Ordinary Course of Business since the Audited Balance Sheet Date (none of which results from, arises out of, or relates to any breach or violation of, or default under, a Contractual Obligation or applicable Legal Requirement, but other than a breach or violation of, or default under, a Contractual Obligation which arises solely as a result of Ca, C or any of its Subsidiaries not obtaining an authorization, consent or approval that is listed on Section 3.03 or

Section 3.04 of the Disclosure Schedule) and (iii) other Liabilities that do not exceed $● in the aggregate or which would not be reasonably expected to result in a Material Adverse Effect.

d)   Post-Reference Date Payments

Except as disclosed in Section 3.08(d) of the Disclosure Schedule, Seller and their Subsidiaries have not made or incurred any Post-Reference Date Payments other than those taken into account in the calculation of the Cash Purchase Price paid at the Closing pursuant to Section 2.04 hereof.

e)   Banking Facilities

Section 3.08(e) of the Disclosure Schedule sets forth an accurate and complete list of (i) each bank, savings and loan or similar financial institution with which each of Ca, C and its Subsidiaries has an account or safety deposit box or other similar arrangement, and any numbers or other identifying codes of such accounts, safety deposit boxes or such other arrangements maintained by Ca, C and its Subsidiaries thereat, and (ii) the names of all Persons authorized to draw on any such account or to have access to any such safety deposit box facility or such other arrangement.

Section 3.09) Absence of Certain Developments

Except as disclosed in Section 3.09 of the Disclosure Schedule:

a)   since the Audited Balance Sheet Date (i) no Material Adverse Effect has occurred with respect to the Business; and (ii) each of Ca, C and its Subsidiaries has not:

   i)   made or agreed to make any dividends or distributions to any party or any other payment or transfer of any kind to or on behalf of any Affiliate or engaged in any transaction with an Affiliate (other than as contemplated in the Pre-Closing Reorganization, as disclosed on Section 3.08(d), or reimbursement for expenses incurred by, and Compensation provided to, officer and directors (or equivalent) in the Ordinary Course of Business); or

   ii) settled, agreed to settle, waived or otherwise compromised any pending or threatened Actions (A) involving potential payments by or to Seller (or any of their Subsidiaries) of more than $● in the aggregate, (B) that admit liability or consent to non-monetary relief, or (C) that otherwise are or would reasonably be expected to be material to Seller and their Subsidiaries or the Business; and

b) since the Most Recent Balance Sheet Date, each of Ca, C and its Subsidiaries has not:

    i) made any payment to any Person outside of the Ordinary Course of Business;

    ii) made any payment in respect of any fees or expenses incurred by Principal in connection with the Contemplated Transactions and the Pre-Closing Reorganization, including but not limited to, any Seller Transaction Expenses;

    iii) other than as contemplated by the Pre-Closing Reorganization, amended its Organizational Documents, effected any split, combination, reclassification or similar action with respect to its shares or other Equity Interests or adopted or carried out any plan of complete or partial liquidation or dissolution;

    iv) other than as contemplated by the Pre-Closing Reorganization, issued, sold, granted or otherwise disposed of any of its Equity Interests or other securities, repurchased, redeemed, or otherwise acquired or canceled any of its Equity Interests or other securities or amended any term of any of its outstanding Equity Interests or other securities;

    v) become liable in respect of any Guarantee or incurred, assumed or otherwise become liable in respect of any Debt (except for borrowings in the Ordinary Course of Business under the Existing Credit Facility);

    vi) (A) other than as contemplated by the Pre Closing Reorganization, merged or consolidated with any Person; (B) acquired any material assets; or (C) made any loan, advance or capital contribution to, acquired any Equity Interests in, or otherwise made any investment in, any Person (other than loans and advances to employees in the Ordinary Course of Business in an aggregate amount at any one time outstanding of not more than $●, and other than loans or advances to, or investments in, wholly-owned Subsidiaries of Seller existing on the date of this Agreement that were made in the Ordinary Course of Business);

    vii) made any capital expenditures that were in the aggregate in excess of $●;

viii) increased any benefits under any Employee Plan or increased the Compensation payable or paid, whether conditionally or otherwise, to any employee, officer, independent contractor or director, consultant, agent or service provider of Ca, C and its Subsidiaries (other than (A) any increase adopted in the Ordinary Course of Business in respect of the Compensation of any employee whose annual base Compensation does not exceed $● after giving effect to such increase or (B) any increase in benefits or Compensation required by applicable Legal Requirements or required pursuant to the terms of an existing Employee Plan or an existing employment, consulting, indemnification, change of control, termination, severance or similar agreement with any current or former director, officer, employee, independent contractor, consultant, or agent of the Business so long as such Employee Plan or agreement has been disclosed in the Disclosure Schedule or any other Schedule to this Agreement);

ix) made any material change in its methods of accounting or accounting practices (including with respect to reserves) or its pricing policies, payment or credit practices, failed to pay any creditor any undisputed material amount owed to such creditor when due or granted any extensions of credit other than in the Ordinary Course of Business;

x) made (other than in the Ordinary Course of Business or as contemplated by the Pre-Closing Reorganization), changed or revoked any election in respect of Taxes; adopted (other than in the Ordinary Course of Business) or changed any method of accounting in respect of Taxes; amended any Tax Return; agreed to or settled any Action, in each case in respect of Taxes; entered into any Contractual Obligation in respect of Taxes; took any action in respect of Taxes outside of the Ordinary Course of Business; surrendered any right to, or filed any claim for, a Tax refund or failed to (A) timely pay Taxes when due or (B) timely file all required Tax Returns;

xi) terminated or amended in any material respect (including by accelerating material rights or benefits under) any Material Company Contract or Employee Plan;

xii) other than in the Ordinary Course of Business, licensed or otherwise disposed of the rights to use any material patent, trademark or other Intellectual Property Rights or disclosed material trade secrets to a third party.

Section 3.10) Debt; Guarantees

Section 3.10 of the Disclosure Schedule sets forth all Contractual Obligations with respect to Debt of Ca, C and its Subsidiaries and, with respect to each such Contractual Obligation, correctly sets forth the debtor, the Contractual Obligations governing the Debt, Principal amount of the Debt as at the date of this Agreement (other than the operating line maintained by the Business with ● which fluctuates on a daily basis and the balance is therefore as of the close of business on the Business Day immediately prior to the date hereof without contemplation of any outstanding or non-negotiated cheques of the Business), the creditor, the maturity date, and the collateral, if any, securing the Debt (and all Contractual Obligations governing all related Encumbrances). Except as set forth on Section 3.10 of the Disclosure Schedule, each of Ca, C and its Subsidiaries has no Liability in respect of a Guarantee of any Debt or other Liability of any other Person.

Section 3.11) Assets

    a) Ownership of Assets

        C has sole and exclusive, good and marketable title to, or, in the case of property held under a lease or other Contractual Obligation, a sole and exclusive, Enforceable leasehold interest in, or rights to use, (whether directly or through its Subsidiaries) all of the Acquired Assets. None of the Acquired Assets is subject to any Encumbrance other than a Permitted Encumbrance.

    b) Sufficiency of Assets

        The Acquired Assets (together with the assets and property of C's Subsidiaries and those assets and property that are owned by Ca following the completion of the Pre-Closing Reorganization) comprise all of the assets, properties and rights of every type and description, whether real or personal, tangible or intangible, that are used to conduct the Business substantially in the manner in which it is currently operated by C.

    c) Condition of Tangible Assets

        All of the material fixtures and other material improvements to the Leased Real Property included in the Acquired Assets and all of the material Tangible Personal Property other than Inventory included in the Acquired Assets are in good operating condition (ordinary wear and tear excepted).

d)   Investments

Except as set forth in Section 3.11(d) of the Disclosure Schedule, C neither (i) controls, directly or indirectly, or owns any direct or indirect Equity Interest in any Person that is not a Subsidiary of C nor (ii) is subject to any obligation to make any investment (in the form of a loan, capital contribution or otherwise) in any Person.

Section 3.12)   Real Property

a)   None of Ca, C or its Subsidiaries owns, nor has any of Ca, C or its Subsidiaries previously owned, within ten (10) years prior to the date hereof, any real property. Section 3.12(a) of the Disclosure Schedule sets forth a list of the addresses of all real property currently leased, subleased or licensed by, or for which a right to use or occupy has been granted to, any of Ca, C and its Subsidiaries (the "**Leased Real Property**"). Section 3.12(a) of the Disclosure Schedule identifies with respect to each Leased Real Property, each lease, sublease, license or other Contractual Obligation under which such Leased Real Property is occupied or used including the date of and legal name of each of the parties to such lease, sublease, license or other Contractual Obligation, and each amendment, modification or supplement thereto (the "**Real Property Leases**").

b)   Except as set forth in Section 3.12(b) of the Disclosure Schedule, there are no written or oral leases, subleases, licenses, concessions, occupancy agreements or other Contractual Obligations granting to any other Person the right of use or occupancy of any of the Leased Real Property and there is no Person (other than Ca, C and its Subsidiaries) in possession of any of the Leased Real Property. With respect to each Real Property Lease that is a sublease, to the Knowledge of Seller, the representations and warranties in this Section 3.12(b) and Section 3.18(b) and Section 3.18(c) are true and correct with respect to the underlying lease.

c)   Seller have made available to Buyer accurate and complete copies of the Real Property Leases, in each case as amended or otherwise modified and in effect, together with extension notices, estoppel certificates and subordination, non-disturbance and attornment agreements related thereto.

Section 3.13) Intellectual Property

a) Company IP

Ca, C and its Subsidiaries own or have the right to use all Company Technology and the Company Intellectual Property Rights (the **"Acquired Intellectual Property"**) without, to the Knowledge of Seller, any conflict with the Intellectual Property Rights of others. Except, with respect to the Technology and Intellectual Property Rights (i) licensed to Ca, C and its Subsidiaries under the Inbound IP Contracts identified on Section 3.13(d) of the Disclosure Schedule, to the extent provided in such Inbound IP Contracts or (ii) licensed by Ca, C and its Subsidiaries under the Outbound IP Contracts identified on Section 3.13(d) of the Disclosure Schedule, to the extent provided in such Outbound IP Contracts, to the Knowledge of Seller, none of the Acquired Intellectual Property is in the possession, custody, or control of any Person other than Seller and their Subsidiaries.

b) Infringement

Except as disclosed in Section 3.13(b) of the Disclosure Schedule, none of Ca, C and its Subsidiaries, in the three (3) years prior to the date hereof: (i) have received any written charge, complaint, claim, demand, or notice alleging interference, infringement, dilution, misappropriation, or violation of the Intellectual Property Rights of any Person (including any invitation to license or request or demand to refrain from using any Intellectual Property Rights of any Person in connection with the conduct of the Business or the use of the Company Technology), and (ii) other than pursuant to the Material Company Contracts, have agreed to, or have, a Contractual Obligation to indemnify any Person for or against any interference, infringement, dilution, misappropriation, or violation with respect to any Intellectual Property Rights. Except as disclosed on Section 3.13(b) of the Disclosure Schedule, to the Knowledge of Seller, no Person has interfered with, infringed upon, diluted, misappropriated, or violated any Company Intellectual Property Rights.

c) Scheduled Intellectual Property Rights

Section 3.13(c) of the Disclosure Schedule and identifies all patents, patent applications, registered trademarks and copyrights, applications for trademark and copyright registrations, domain names, registered design rights, registered industrial design rights and other forms of registered Intellectual Property Rights and applications therefor, that, owned by or exclusively licensed to Ca, C or any of its Subsidiaries (collectively, the **"Company Registrations"**). Section 3.13(c) of the Disclosure Schedule also identifies each trade name and material unregistered trademark and copyright owned or exclusively licensed by Ca, C or its Subsidiaries that, in each case, is material to the Business. For purposes of this Agreement, all items listed on Section 3.13(c) of the Disclosure Schedule shall be called "Scheduled Intellectual Property Rights". Section 3.13(c) of the Disclosure Schedule specifically identifies those items of Scheduled Intellectual Property Rights that are exclusively licensed to Ca, C or any of its Subsidiaries, including the identification of the Contractual Obligation pursuant to which each such Intellectual Property Right is licensed. For each of the Company Registrations, Section 3.13(c) of the Disclosure Schedule includes the following information: (i) for each registered trademark and trademark application, the mark, application serial number or registration number, jurisdiction, filing date, registration date (if applicable), class of goods or services covered, description of goods or services, owner of record, and present status thereof; (iii) for each domain name, the registration date, any renewal date, owner of record, and name of the registrar and (iv) for each copyright registration and copyright application, the title of the work, number and date of such registration or application, owner of record, and jurisdiction. Each of the Company Registrations is valid, subsisting and enforceable.

d) IP Contracts

Section 3.13(d) of the Disclosure Schedule identifies under separate headings each Contractual Obligation (i) under which Ca, C or its Subsidiaries uses or licenses a material item of Acquired Intellectual Property that any Person besides Ca, C or its Subsidiaries owns (except where such Contractual Obligation for use or license of Acquired Intellectual Property is incidental to the subject matter of the Contractual Obligation) (the **"Inbound IP Contracts"**), (ii) under which Ca, C and its Subsidiaries has granted any Person any right or interest in any material Company Intellectual Property Rights including any right to use any material item of Company Technology (the **"Outbound IP Contracts"**) (except where such Contractual Obligation for use or license of Acquired Intellectual Property is incidental to the subject matter of the Contractual Obligation (e.g. a grant of limited and non-exclusive license to a supplier in connection with the manufacture of products for the Business), and (iii) that otherwise materially affects C's, Ca's and their Subsidiaries' use of or rights in any material Acquired Intellectual Property (including settlement agreements and covenants not to sue) (such Contractual Obligations, together with the Inbound IP Contracts and Outbound IP Contracts, the **"IP Contracts"**). Except as set forth in Section 3.13(d) of the Disclosure Schedule, none of Ca, C and its Subsidiaries owes any royalties or other payments to any Person for the use of any Acquired Intellectual Property. Ca, C and its Subsidiaries have made available to Buyer accurate and complete copies of each of the written IP Contracts (or, where an IP Contract is an oral agreement, an accurate written description of such IP Contract), in each case, as amended or otherwise modified and in effect.

e)   **Title to Company Technology and Company Intellectual Property Rights**

   i)   The right, title, and interest in and to each material item of Acquired Intellectual Property that is owned (not licensed) by each of Ca, C and its Subsidiaries pursuant to an Inbound IP Contract, is owned free and clear of any Encumbrance other than Permitted Encumbrances and licenses granted in the Outbound IP Contracts; and

   ii)   With respect to (A) each material item of Acquired Intellectual Property that is not licensed to Ca, C and its Subsidiaries pursuant to an Inbound IP Contract, and (B) to the Knowledge of Seller, all material Acquired Intellectual Property licensed to Ca, C and its Subsidiaries on an exclusive basis, such item or right is not subject to any outstanding Government Order, and, except as disclosed on Section 3.13(b) of the Disclosure Schedule, and no Action (including any opposition, interference, or re-examination) is pending or, to the Knowledge of Seller, threatened, which challenges the legality, validity, enforceability, use, or ownership of such right or item.

f)   **Confidentiality and Invention Assignments**

(i) Ca, C and its Subsidiaries have maintained commercially reasonable practices to protect the confidentiality of their confidential information and trade secrets and, in the Ordinary Course of Business, have required all Employees and other Persons with access to confidential information of Ca, C or its Subsidiaries to execute or abide by Contractual Obligations requiring them to maintain the confidentiality of such information and use such information only for the benefit of Ca, C and its Subsidiaries. Except as set forth in Section 3.13(f) of the Disclosure

Schedule, all current and former employees whose employment terminated within (2) years prior to the date hereof, consultant and contractors of Ca, C and its Subsidiaries who contributed to the Company Technology that is incorporated in any product of Ca, C and its Subsidiaries have executed enforceable Contractual Obligations that (i) assign to Ca, C and its Subsidiaries all of such Person's respective rights, including Intellectual Property Rights, relating to such product, and (ii) irrevocably waive any common law rights including moral rights such current and former employees, consultants and contractors may possess in such product.

g)   Privacy and Data Security

Except as set out in Section 3.13(g) of the Disclosure Schedule, each of C's, Ca's (and their Subsidiaries') use and disclosure of personal information concerning individuals is in compliance in all material respects with all applicable Legal Requirements in Canada, and material Contractual Obligations applicable to Seller and their Subsidiaries or to which Seller and their Subsidiaries are bound. Except as set out in Section 3.13(g) of the Disclosure Schedule, Ca, C and its Subsidiaries maintain policies and procedures regarding data security and privacy and maintain reasonable administrative, technical, and physical safeguards that are required by applicable Legal Requirements in Canada applicable to Ca, C and its Subsidiaries. To the Knowledge of Seller, there have been no material security breaches relating to, or material violations of any security policy regarding, or any unauthorized access of, any personal information used by Ca, C and its Subsidiaries. Except as set out in Section 3.13(g) of the Disclosure Schedule, the Contemplated Transactions and the Pre-Closing Reorganization will not, as of the Closing, violate in any material respect any privacy policy, applicable Legal Requirements in Canada, the United States or Sweden (or, to the Knowledge of Seller, any other jurisdiction in which C conducts its Business) or Contractual Obligations relating to the use, dissemination, or transfer of personal information previously collected by C, Ca and their Subsidiaries prior to the Closing Date.

Section 3.14) Permits

Seller and their Subsidiaries have been duly granted all material Permits necessary for the conduct of the Business by it and the ownership use and operation of any Acquired Assets, which material Permits are listed in Section 3.14 of the

Disclosure Schedule, except as would not reasonably be expected to result in a Material Adverse Effect. Except as disclosed on Section 3.14 of the Disclosure Schedule (i) the Permits listed or required to be listed thereon are, to the Knowledge of Seller, valid and in full force and effect and may be transferred or modified, as the case may be, in favor of Buyer or its designee, (ii) none of Ca, C nor any of its Subsidiaries is, in any material respect, in breach or violation of, or default under, any such material Permit and (iii) to the Knowledge of Seller, no fact, situation, circumstance, condition or other basis exists which, with notice or lapse of time or both, would constitute a material breach, violation or default under such Permit or give any Governmental Authority grounds to suspend, revoke or terminate any such Permit.

Section 3.15) Tax Matters

a) Other than as set out in Section 3.15(a) of the Disclosure Schedule, each of Ca, C, C Trading and the Transferred Subsidiaries has timely filed, or has caused to be timely filed on its behalf, all income and other material Tax Returns required to be filed by it in accordance with all applicable Legal Requirements. All income and all material Tax Returns filed by each of Ca, C, C Trading and the Transferred Subsidiaries were true, correct and complete in all material respects. All Taxes owed by Ca, C, C Trading and the Transferred Subsidiaries (whether or not shown on any Tax Return) have been timely paid in full. None of Ca, C, C Trading or either of the Transferred Subsidiaries has asked for any extension of time in order to file any Tax Return, which extension is still in effect. No claim has ever been made by a Governmental Authority in a jurisdiction where any of Ca, C, C Trading or either of the Transferred Subsidiaries do not file Tax Returns that such Person is or may be subject to taxation by that jurisdiction, and to the Knowledge of Seller there is no basis for any such claim to be made. There are no Encumbrances with respect to Taxes upon any Acquired Asset (including, for clarity, the assets of Ca, C, C Trading and the Transferred Subsidiaries) other than Encumbrances for current Taxes not yet due and payable.

b) Other than as set out in Section 3.15(b) of the Disclosure Schedule Ca, C, C Trading and the Transferred Subsidiaries have deducted, withheld and timely paid to the appropriate Governmental Authority all Taxes required to be deducted, withheld or paid in connection with amounts paid or owing to any employee, independent contractor, creditor, shareholder or other third party, and Ca, C, C Trading and the

Transferred Subsidiaries have complied with all reporting and record-keeping requirements in all material respects.

c) Each of Ca and the Transferred Subsidiaries have collected from each receipt from any of the past and present customers (or other Persons paying amounts to Ca or the Transferred Subsidiaries) the amount of all Taxes required to be collected and has paid and remitted such Taxes when due in the form required under applicable Laws or made adequate provision in its Financials for the payment and remittance of such amounts to the proper Governmental Authority.

d) Other than as set out in Section 3.15(d), there is no pending, or to the Knowledge of Seller, threatened, claim or Action concerning any Tax Liability of Ca or the Transferred Subsidiaries.

e) Other than as set out in Section 3.15(e) of the Disclosure Schedule, none of Ca, C, C Trading or either of the Transferred Subsidiaries has waived any statute of limitations in respect of Taxes or agreed to any extension of time with respect to a Tax assessment or deficiency, which waiver or extension is still in effect. None of Ca, C, C Trading or either of the Transferred Subsidiaries has executed any power of attorney with respect to any Tax, other than powers of attorney that are no longer in force. No closing agreements, private letter rulings, technical advice memoranda or similar agreements or rulings relating to Taxes have been entered into or issued by any Governmental Authority with or in respect of Ca, C, C Trading or either of the Transferred Subsidiaries.

f) None of Ca, C or their Subsidiaries owns property of a character, the indirect transfer of which, pursuant to this Agreement, would give rise to any documentary, stamp, or other transfer Tax.

g) All unpaid Taxes of Ca, C, C Trading and the Transferred Subsidiaries did not as of the Most Recent Balance Sheet Date exceed the reserve for Taxes (excluding any reserve for deferred Taxes established to reflect timing differences between book and Tax income) set forth on the face of the Most Recent Balance Sheet and all unpaid Taxes of Ca, C, C Trading and the Transferred Subsidiaries for all Tax periods (or portions thereof) commencing after the Most Recent Balance Sheet Date arose in the Ordinary Course of Business.

h) None of Ca, C, C Trading or the Transferred Subsidiaries is a party to any Contractual Obligation relating to Tax sharing or Tax allocation.

i) Since the Audited Balance Sheet Date, none of Ca, C, C Trading or the Transferred Subsidiaries has (i) made, changed or revoked any election in respect of Taxes, (ii) adopted or changed any accounting method in respect of Taxes, (iii) amended any Tax Return, (iv) agreed to or settled any Action in respect of Taxes, (v) entered into any Contractual Obligation in respect of Taxes, (vi) taken any action in respect of Taxes outside of the Ordinary Course of Business, (vii) surrendered any right to, or filed any claim for, a Tax refund or (viii) failed to (A) timely pay Taxes when due or (B) timely file all required Tax Returns.

j)   C is not a non-resident of Canada within the meaning of the *Income Tax Act* (Canada).

k)   C is registered for GST/HST purposes under the *Excise Tax Act* (Canada) and its registration number is ●. C is not registered for QST purposes under *An Act Respecting the Quebec Sales Tax*.

l)   None of the Acquired Assets (excluding any assets owned by a Subsidiary of C classified as a corporation for US federal income tax purposes) is a **"United States real property interest"** within the meaning of (and for purposes of) Code Sections 897 and 1445.

m)   Ca, C, C Trading and the Transferred Subsidiaries have complied with the requirements of Code Section 482 and Section 247 of the *Income Tax Act (Canada)* (and any corresponding or similar state, local or non-U.S. Legal Requirements).

n)   None of Ca, C, C Trading or the Transferred Subsidiaries has participated in any **"reportable transaction"** within the meaning of Treasury Regulations Section 1.6011-4.

o)   None of Ca, C, C Trading or the Transferred Subsidiaries has been a **"distributing corporation"** or a **"controlled corporation"** within the meaning of Code Section 355(a)(1)(A).

Section 3.16) Employee Benefit Plans

a)   Section 3.16 of the Disclosure Schedule lists all Employee Plans. With respect to each such Employee Plan, Seller and their Subsidiaries have made available to Buyer accurate and complete copies of each of the following: (i) if the plan has been reduced to writing, the plan document together with all amendments thereto, (ii) if the plan has not been reduced to writing, a written summary of all material plan terms, (iii) if applicable, any trust agreements, custodial agreements, insurance policies or contracts, administrative agreements and similar agreements, and investment management or investment advisory agreements and (iv) any summary plan descriptions, employee hand-books, policies or similar employee communications.

b) No Employee Plan is or is intended to be a "registered pension plan", "deferred profit-sharing plan", a "retirement compensation arrange-ment", a "tax free savings account" or, except pursuant to the Collect-ive Agreements of C, a "registered retirement savings plan" as each such term is defined in the *Income Tax Act* (Canada).

c) Except as would not reasonably be expected to have a Material Adverse Effect, each Employee Plan, including any associated trust or fund, has been administered in accordance with its terms and any applicable col-lective bargaining agreements and with applicable Legal Requirements, and nothing has occurred with respect to any Employee Plan that has subjected or could subject Ca, C and its Subsidiaries to an excise tax.

d) All required contributions to, and premium payments on account of, each Employee Plan have been made on a timely basis.

e) Except as would not reasonably be expected to have a Material Adverse Effect, there is no pending or, to the Knowledge of Seller, threatened Action relating to an Employee Plan, other than routine claims in the Ordinary Course of Business for benefits provided for by the Employee Plans. Except as would not reasonably be expected to have a Material Adverse Effect, no Employee Plan is or, within the last six (6) years, has been the subject of an examination or audit by a Governmental Author-ity, is the subject of an application or filing under, or is a participant in, a government-sponsored amnesty, voluntary compliance, self-correc-tion or similar program.

f) Except as would not reasonably be expected to have a Material Adverse Effect, no Employee Plan provides benefits or coverage in the nature of health, life or disability insurance following retirement or other termin-ation of employment.

g) Section 3.16(h) of the Disclosure Schedule sets forth the Change of Control payments and the amount of each such payment.

Section 3.17) Environmental Matters

Except as set forth in Section 3.17 of the Disclosure Schedule and only in respect of the locations described in Section 3.17 of the Disclosure Schedule: (a) each of Ca, C and its Subsidiaries is in compliance in all material respects with all applicable Environmental Laws, (b) there has been no release by Seller, or, to the Knowledge of Seller, by any other Person, or threatened release of any material amount of any Hazardous Substance on, upon, into or from any premises currently leased or otherwise operated by each of Ca, C and its Subsidiaries, (c) to the Knowledge of Seller, there are no underground storage tanks located on, no PCBs (polychlorinated biphenyls) or PCB-containing equipment used or stored on, nor any Hazardous Substance present on, in, under or upon, any site currently leased or otherwise operated by each of Ca, C and its Subsidiaries, except for the storage of hazardous waste in compliance with Environmental Laws and (d) each of Ca, C and its Subsidiaries has made available to Buyer accurate and complete copies of all material environmental records, reports, notifications, certificates of need, permits, pending permit applications, correspondence, engineering studies, and environmental studies or assessments for Ca, C and its Subsidiaries, in each case as amended and in effect in its possession or control relating to any premises currently leased or otherwise operated by each of Ca, C and its Subsidiaries.

Section 3.18) Contracts

a) Contracts

Except as disclosed in Section 3.18 of the Disclosure Schedule, none of Ca, C or any of their Subsidiaries is bound by or a party to:

i) any Contractual Obligation (or group of related Contractual Obligations) for the purchase, sale, construction, repair or maintenance of supplies, goods, products, equipment or other property, or for the furnishing or receipt of services, in each case, the performance of which will extend over a period of more than one (1) year and which provides for (or would be reasonably expected to involve) annual payments to or by Ca, C and its Subsidiaries in excess of $●;

ii) any Contractual Obligation relating to the acquisition or disposition by any of Ca, C and its Subsidiaries of any business (whether by merger, consolidation or other business combination, sale of securities, sale of assets or otherwise), in each case with respect to which any of Ca, C or its Subsidiaries has any ongoing obligations or liabilities;

iii) any Contractual Obligation concerning or consisting of a partnership, limited liability company, joint venture or similar agreement;

iv) any Contractual Obligation under which Ca, C or its Subsidiaries have permitted any Acquired Asset to become Encumbered (other than by a Permitted Encumbrance);

v) any Contractual Obligation (A) under which Ca, C or its Subsidiaries have created, incurred, assumed or guaranteed any Debt in excess of $● or (B) under which any other Person has guaranteed any Debt of Ca, C and its Subsidiaries;

vi) any Contractual Obligation containing covenants that in any way purport to (A) restrict any business activity of Ca, C and its Subsidiaries or any Affiliate thereof (including a restriction on the solicitation, hiring or engagement of any Person or the solicitation of any customer of such Person) or (B) limit the freedom of Ca, C or its Subsidiaries or any Affiliate thereof to engage in any line of business or compete with any Person;

vii) any Contractual Obligation under which any of Ca, C or its Subsidiaries is, or may become, obligated to incur any termination, severance or retention pay or Compensation obligations that would become payable by reason of this Agreement, the Contemplated Transactions or the Pre-Closing Reorganization;

viii) any Contractual Obligation under which any of Ca, C or its Subsidiaries is, or may, have any Liability to any investment bank, broker, financial advisor, finder or other similar Person (including an obligation to pay any legal, accounting, brokerage, finder's, or similar fees or expenses) in connection with this Agreement, the Contemplated Transactions or the Pre-Closing Reorganization;

ix) any Contractual Obligation providing for the employment or consultancy or services of any Person on a full-time, part-time, independent contractor, consulting or other basis whose annual Compensation is in excess of $● per annum;

x) any Contractual Obligation relating to any agent, dealer, distributor, sales representative, marketing or other similar arrangement in excess of $● per annum;

xi) any outstanding general or special powers of attorney which to the Knowledge of Seller are executed by or on behalf of any of Ca, C or its Subsidiaries;

xii) any Contractual Obligation, other than Real Property Leases, relating to the lease or license of any Acquired Asset, including Technology and Intellectual Property Rights (and including all customer license and maintenance agreements) that is not included on Section 3.13(d) of the Disclosure Schedule for which Ca, C or its Subsidiaries will be liable for, or entitled to, in excess of $● per annum;

xiii) any Contractual Obligation under which any of Ca, C or its Subsidiaries has advanced or loaned an amount to any of its Affiliates (other than the Subsidiaries of C) or employees other than in the Ordinary Course of Business; and

xiv) any other Contractual Obligation between Ca, C or its Subsidiaries, on the one hand, and Principal (or Affiliate or Family Member thereof), on the other hand, that will continue in effect after the Closing and will be an Assumed Liability.

Seller and their Subsidiaries have made available to Buyer accurate and complete copies of each written Contractual Obligation listed on Section 3.18 of the Disclosure Schedule, in each case, as amended or otherwise modified and in effect. Seller and their Subsidiaries have made available to Buyer a written summary setting forth the material terms and conditions of each oral Contractual Obligation listed on Section 3.18 of the Disclosure Schedule.

b) Enforceability, *etc.*

To the Knowledge of Seller, each Contractual Obligation required to be disclosed on Sections 3.12(a), 3.13(d), Section 3.16 or 3.18 of the Disclosure Schedule (each, a **"Material Company Contract"**) are each Enforceable against each party to such Material Company Contract, and is in full force and effect, and, subject to obtaining any necessary consents disclosed in Sections 3.03 and 3.04 of the Disclosure Schedule, and, unless terminated prior to the Closing in accordance with its terms, will continue to be so Enforceable and in full force and effect on identical terms following the consummation of the Contemplated Transactions.

c) Breach, *etc.*

None of Ca, C its Subsidiaries nor, to the Knowledge of Seller, any other party to any Material Company Contract is in material breach or violation of, or default under, any material provision of, any Material Company Contract.

Section 3.19)   Related Party Transactions

Except for the matters disclosed on Section 3.19 of the Disclosure Schedule (the **"Related Party Contracts"**), neither Principal nor any Affiliate of Principal and no officer or director (or equivalent) of Ca, C or any of their Subsidiaries (or, to the Knowledge of Seller, any Family Member of any such Person who is an individual or any entity in which any such Person or any such Family Member thereof owns a material interest): (a) has any material interest in any material asset owned or leased by Ca, C and its Subsidiaries or used in connection with the Business other than the Excluded Assets; or (b) is engaged in any material transaction, arrangement or understanding with Ca, C or its Subsidiaries (other than payments made to, and other Compensation provided to, officers, directors or Employees in the Ordinary Course of Business).

Section 3.20) Customers, Manufacturers, and Suppliers

Section 3.20 of the Disclosure Schedule sets forth a complete and accurate list of (a) each customer of Ca, C and its Subsidiaries from whom Ca, C and its Subsidiaries generated not less than $● in aggregate revenue during the fiscal year ended on the Audited Balance Sheet Date, (b) each supplier for which services and products purchased exceeded $● per such supplier during the fiscal year ended on the Audited Balance Sheet Date, and (c) each third-party manufacturer for which services and products purchased exceeded $● per such third-party manufacturer during the fiscal year ended on the Audited Balance Sheet Date. Except as disclosed on Section 3.20 of the Disclosure Schedule, none of such customers, suppliers or third-party manufacturers has, within the past twelve (12) months, cancelled, terminated or otherwise materially altered (including any reduction in the rate or amount of sales or purchases or material increase in the prices charged or paid, as the case may be which would have a Material Adverse Effect) its relationship with Ca, C and its Subsidiaries or notified Ca, C and its Subsidiaries, in writing, of any intention to do any of the foregoing or otherwise threatened, in writing, to cancel, terminate or materially alter (including, in the case of customers, any material reduction in the rate or amount of sales or purchase other than as a result of any price increase resulting from the increased price of raw materials, which is consistent with past practice of such party) its relationship with Ca, C and its Subsidiaries which would have a Material Adverse Effect.

Section 3.21) Labour Matters

a)   Except as disclosed in Section 3.21(a) of the Disclosure Schedule, there is no unfair labour practice, complaint, grievance or arbitration proceeding pending or, to the Knowledge of Seller, threatened against C or its Subsidiaries.

b)   Except as disclosed in Section 3.21(b) of the Disclosure Schedule, to the Knowledge of Seller: (a) there are no labour disputes (including any work slowdown, lockout, stoppage, picketing or strike) pending or threatened between any of C or its Subsidiaries, on the one hand, and Employees, on the other hand, (b) except in respect to the Collective

Agreements, no Employee is represented by a labour union or other employee association, (c) no Collective Agreement is currently being negotiated by any of C or its Subsidiaries or any other Person in respect of the Business or the Employees, and the only collective agreements in force with respect to the Employees are the Collective Agreements, true, correct and complete copies of which have been provided to Buyer, (d) there are no grievances or arbitration proceedings pending under the Collective Agreements (e) no petition has been filed or proceedings instituted by an Employee or group of Employees with any labour relations board seeking recognition of a bargaining representative since ●, 20●, (f) there is no organizational effort currently being made or threatened by, or on behalf of, any labour union or other employee association, (g) no demand for recognition of Employees has been made by, or on behalf of, any labour union or other employee association since ●, 20●, and (h) no trade union has applied to have any of C or its Subsidiaries declared a common or related employer pursuant to the *Labour Relations Act* (Ontario) since ●, 20●.

c) To the Knowledge of Seller, each independent contractor, sales agent or consultant has been properly classified as such by C and its Subsidiaries and none of C and its Subsidiaries has received any notice from any Governmental Authority disputing such classification.

d) All amounts due or accrued due to the Most Recent Balance Sheet Date for all salary, wages, bonuses, commissions, vacation with pay, sick days and benefits under the Employee Plans have either been paid or are accurately reflected in C's or its Subsidiaries' books and records, in all material respects.

e) Section 3.21(e) of the Disclosure Schedule contains: (i) a correct and complete list of each Employee employed or retained in connection with the Business conducted by C and its Subsidiaries, whether actively at work or not, showing without names or employee numbers and in respect of C's 20● fiscal year, their salaries, wage rates, commission rates, entitlement to equity (or equivalent) based compensation, bonus and retention arrangements, benefits, positions, status as full-time or part-time employees, location of employment, cumulative length of service with the Business, their annual vacation entitlement in days, their accrued and unused vacation days, any other annual paid time off entitlement in days and their accrued and unused days or such other paid time off and whether they are subject to a written Employment

Contract, and (ii) a correct and complete list, in respect of C's 20● fiscal year, of each consultant, independent contractor, and sales agent and their fees, commissions, length of service with the Business, location of services, and whether they are subject to a written Contractual Obligation.

f) Except as disclosed on Section 3.21(f) of the Disclosure Schedule, no Employee of C is employed pursuant to a work permit issued by Canada Immigration and Section 3.21(f) of the Disclosure Schedule discloses in respect of each Employee of C who is employed pursuant to a work permit the expiry date of such work permit and whether C has made any attempts to renew such work permit.

g) Except as disclosed on Section 3.21(g) of the Disclosure Schedule, there are no material outstanding assessments, penalties, fines, liens, charges, surcharges, or other amounts due or owing pursuant to any workplace safety and insurance legislation in respect of the Business and none of C or its Subsidiaries has been assessed or reassessed in any material respect under such legislation during the past three (3) years and, to the Knowledge of Seller, no audit of the Business is currently being performed pursuant to any applicable workplace safety and insurance legislation. There are no material charges pending under applicable occupational health and safety legislation ("**OHSA**"). Each of Ca, C and its Subsidiaries has complied in all material respects with any orders issued under applicable OHSA in respect of the Business and there are no appeals of any orders under OHSA currently outstanding.

Section 3.22) Litigation; Governmental Orders; Compliance with Laws

a) **Litigation**

Except as disclosed on Section 3.22(a) of the Disclosure Schedule, there is no Action to which any of Ca, C and its Subsidiaries is a party (either as plaintiff or defendant) or to which its assets are or may be subject that is pending, or to the Knowledge of Seller, threatened, except as would not reasonably be expected to result in a Material Adverse Effect. Except as disclosed on Section 3.22(a) of the Disclosure Schedule, there is no Action which any of Ca, C and its Subsidiaries presently intends to initiate.

b) **Governmental Orders**

Except as disclosed in Section 3.22(b) of the Disclosure Schedule, to the Knowledge of Seller, no Governmental Order has been issued that is applicable to Ca, C and its Subsidiaries or their assets or the Business.

c)   Compliance with Laws

Except as disclosed in Section 3.22(c) of the Disclosure Schedule: (i) the Business is conducted in compliance with all applicable Legal Requirements in Canada (and, to the Knowledge of Seller, any other jurisdiction in which C conducts its Business), other than acts of non-compliance which individually or in the aggregate are not material; and (ii) in the last five (5) years, none of the Ca, C and its Subsidiaries have been in material violation of any applicable Legal Requirement in Canada (and, to the Knowledge of Seller, any other jurisdiction in which C conducts its Business).

Section 3.23) Insurance

Section 3.23 of the Disclosure Schedule sets forth an accurate and complete list of all insurance policies by which Ca, C and its Subsidiaries, any of the Acquired Assets, or any employees, officers or directors (or equivalent) or the Business are currently insured (the **"Liability Policies"**) and their respective expiration dates. The list includes for each Liability Policy the type of policy, policy number and name of insurer. Ca, C and its Subsidiaries have made available to Buyer accurate and complete copies of all Liability Policies, in each case, as amended or otherwise modified and in effect. Section 3.23 of the Disclosure Schedule describes any self-insurance arrangements affecting Ca, C and its Subsidiaries. C and its Subsidiaries maintain insurance with respect to the Acquired Assets, including (but not limited to) employees, officers and directors (or equivalent) and the Business, in such amounts as is required by applicable Legal Requirements or Contractual Obligations. No insurer (a) has, for claims made in the three (3) year period prior to the date hereof, denied or disputed coverage in writing of any claim pending under any Liability Policy, (b) has threatened in writing, or, to the Knowledge of the Company, orally to cancel any Liability Policy, or (c) to the Knowledge of Seller, plans to materially increase the premiums for, or materially alter the coverage under, any Liability Policy.

Section 3.24) Competition Act

Ca, C and its Subsidiaries, on a consolidated basis, have assets in Canada with an aggregate value of less than $●, and annual gross revenues from sales in, from or into Canada with an aggregate value of less than $● as determined in accordance with the *Competition Act*.

Section 3.25) Investment Canada Act

a)   The value of the assets of Ca, C and its Subsidiaries, on a consolidated basis, calculated in accordance with the Investment Canada Act, was less than $● at the end of their most recently completed fiscal year.

b)   None of Ca, C or any of their Subsidiaries provide any of the services, or engage in any of the activities, of a "cultural business" within the meaning of the *Investment Canada Act.*

Section 3.26) No Brokers

Ca, C and its Subsidiaries have no Liability of any kind to, or is subject to any claim of, any broker, finder or agent in connection with the Contemplated Transactions or the Pre-Closing Reorganization except for those which will be borne by Principal as set forth in Section 3.26 of the Disclosure Schedule.

Section 3.27) Pre-Closing Reorganization

The Pre-Closing Reorganization has been implemented in the manner described in Section 3.27 of the Disclosure Schedule.

ARTICLE 4: INDIVIDUAL REPRESENTATIONS AND WARRANTIES OF PRINCIPAL

In order to induce Buyer to enter into and perform this Agreement and to consummate the Contemplated Transactions, Principal hereby represents and warrants to Buyer that the following statements are true and correct:

Section 4.01) Capacity

Principal has the full legal capacity to execute and deliver this Agreement and the other agreements contemplated hereby, to perform his obligations hereunder and thereunder and to consummate the transactions contemplated hereby.

Section 4.02) Power and Authorization

This Agreement and each Ancillary Agreement to which Principal is a party (a) have been duly executed and delivered by Principal and (b) is a legal, valid and binding obligation of Principal, enforceable against Principal in accordance with its terms.

Section 4.03) Authorization of Governmental Authorities

No action by (including any authorization, consent or approval), or in respect of, or filing with, any Governmental Authority is required for, or in connection with, the valid and lawful (a) execution, delivery and performance by Principal of this Agreement and each Ancillary Agreement to which Principal is a party or (b) consummation of the Contemplated Transactions or the Pre-Closing Reorganization by Principal.

Section 4.04) Noncontravention

Except as described in Section 4.04 of the Disclosure Schedule, neither the execution, delivery and performance by Principal of this Agreement or any Ancillary Agreement to which Principal is a party nor the consummation of the Contemplated Transactions or the Pre-Closing Reorganization by Principal will:

a) assuming the taking of all necessary action by (including the obtaining of each necessary authorization, consent or approval) or in respect of, and the making of all filings with, Governmental Authorities, violate any provision of any Legal Requirement applicable to Principal; or

b) conflict with or result in a breach or violation of, or constitute a default (or an event which, with notice or lapse of time or both, would constitute a default) under, or result in termination of, or accelerate the performance required by, or result in a right of termination or acceleration under, or require any action by (including any authorization, consent or approval) or notice to any Person, or result in the creation of any Encumbrance upon any Equity Interests transferred pursuant to this Agreement.

Section 4.05) Title

Principal is the registered and beneficial owner (whether directly or indirectly through a corporation wholly owned by Principal) of all of the outstanding Equity Interests in C and Principal has good and marketable title to such Equity Interests, free and clear of all Encumbrances other than Permitted Encumbrances. Principal is not a party to, and the Equity Interests in C are not subject to, any shareholders agreement, voting agreement, voting trusts, proxy or other Contractual Obligation relating to the transfer or voting of the C Equity Interests (other than the C Shareholders Agreement).

Section 4.06) No Brokers

Except as disclosed in Section 4.06 of the Disclosure Schedule, Principal has no Liability of any kind to any broker, finder or agent with respect to the Contemplated Transactions or the Pre-Closing Reorganization, and Principal agrees to satisfy in full any Liability required to be disclosed on Section 4.06 of the Disclosure Schedule.

Section 4.07) Residence of Principal

Principal is not a non-resident of Canada within the meaning of the *Income Tax Act* (Canada).

ARTICLE 5: INDIVIDUAL REPRESENTATIONS AND WARRANTIES OF BUYER

In order to induce Seller to enter into and perform this Agreement and to consummate the Contemplated Transactions, Buyer hereby represents and warrants to Seller that the following statements contained in this ARTICLE V are true and correct:

Section 5.01) Organization

Buyer is duly organized, validly existing and in good standing under the laws of the jurisdiction of its organization.

Section 5.02) Power and Authorization

The execution, delivery and performance by Buyer of this Agreement and each Ancillary Agreement to which Buyer is a party and the consummation of the Contemplated Transactions by Buyer are within the power and authority of Buyer and have been duly authorized by all necessary action on the part of Buyer. This Agreement and each Ancillary Agreement to which Buyer is a party (a) have been duly executed and delivered by Buyer and (b) is a legal, valid and binding obligation of Buyer, enforceable against Buyer in accordance with its terms.

Section 5.03) Authorization of Governmental Authorities

No action by (including any authorization, consent or approval), or in respect of, or filing with, any Governmental Authority is required for, or in connection with, the valid and lawful (a) authorization, execution, delivery and performance by Buyer of this Agreement and each Ancillary Agreement to which it is a party or (b) consummation of the Contemplated Transactions by Buyer.

Section 5.04) Noncontravention

Neither the execution, delivery and performance by Buyer of this Agreement or any Ancillary Agreement to which either of them is a party nor the consummation of the Contemplated Transactions will:

a)   assuming the taking of any action by (including the obtaining of each necessary authorization, consent or approval) or in respect of, and the making of all filings with, Governmental Authorities, if any, violate any provision of any Legal Requirement applicable to Buyer; or

b) conflict with or result in a breach or violation of, or constitute a default (or an event which, with notice or lapse of time or both, would constitute a default) under, or result in termination of, or accelerate the performance required by, or result in a right of termination or acceleration under, or require any action by (including any authorization, consent or approval) or notice to any Person under, any of the terms, conditions or provisions of (i) any Governmental Order applicable to or otherwise affecting either Buyer or its assets or properties, (ii) any material Contractual Obligation of Buyer or (iii) the Organizational Documents of Buyer.

Section 5.05) Required Consents

There is no requirement for Buyer to obtain any consent, approval or waiver of any Person under any Contractual Obligation of Buyer, or by which Buyer is bound, to any of the transactions contemplated by this Agreement or any other Ancillary Agreement to which it is a party.

Section 5.06) Capitalization

Immediately prior to the issuance by Buyer to C of Buyer New Shares, the authorized capital of Buyer will consist of an unlimited number of Class A Common Shares and Class B Common Shares, of which ● Class A Common Shares will have been issued to Holding and no more.

a) Immediately following the issuance by Buyer of Buyer New Shares: (i) the authorized capital of Buyer will consist of ● Shares, of which ● Class A Common Shares will have been issued to Holding and ● Class B Common Shares will have been issued to C and no more.

b) Immediately prior to the issuance to C of Holding New Shares pursuant to Holding New Share Agreement, the authorized capital of Holding will consist of an unlimited number of Class A Senior Preferred Shares, Class B Senior Preferred Shares, Class A Junior Preferred Shares, Class B Junior Preferred Shares, Class C Junior Preferred Shares, Class A Common Shares, and Class B Common Shares of which ● Class A Common Shares and ● Class A Senior Preferred Shares will have been issued to the Investors (as defined in the Holding Shareholders Agreement) and no more.

c) Immediately following the issuance to C of the Holding New Shares: (i) the authorized capital of Holding will consist of Class A Senior

Preferred Shares, Class B Senior Preferred Shares, Class A Junior Preferred Shares, Class B Junior Preferred Shares, Class C Junior Preferred Shares, Class A Common Shares, and Class B Common Shares of which ● Class A Senior Preferred Shares and ● Class A Common Shares will have been issued to Investors (as defined in the Holding Shareholders Agreement) and ● Class B Senior Preferred Shares, ● Class B Junior Preferred Shares and ● Class B Common Shares will have been issued to C and no more; and (ii) Holding will hold all of the Equity Interests of Buyer.

d)   No options, warrants or other rights to purchase shares or other securities of Buyer and/or Holding, and no securities or obligations convertible into or exchangeable for shares or other securities of Buyer and/or Holding are as at the date hereof have been authorized or agreed to be, or are issued or outstanding.

e)   Immediately prior to the Closing, Buyer (through Holding) will receive from the Investors (as defined in the Holding Shareholders Agreement) a capital contribution in respect of the Class A Common Shares, which shall be used for purposes of paying certain fees and expenses incurred by or on behalf of, or to be paid by, Buyer and its Affiliates, relating to the negotiation, preparation or execution of this Agreement or the performance or consummation of Contemplated Transactions; such fees and expenses shall not exceed, in the aggregate, an amount equal to $●.

Section 5.07) Issuance of Buyer New Shares

The offering, issuance, sale and delivery by: (i) Buyer of Buyer New Shares to C; and (ii) Holding of the Holding New Shares to C; is or will be, as the case may be, in each case, exempt from the prospectus requirements of Ontario Securities Laws and no prospectus is required nor are other documents required to be filed, no proceedings taken and no approvals, permits, consents, orders or authorizations are required to be obtained pursuant to Ontario Securities Laws to permit such offering, issuance, sale and delivery of Buyer New Shares or Holding New Shares to C; however Buyer is required to file, within ten days from the date of such issue and sale, a report of the sale prepared and executed in accordance with Ontario Securities Laws and accompanied by the requisite filing fee. For the purposes of this Section 5.07, **"Ontario Securities Laws"** means the securities act, rules and the regulations of the province of Ontario and the rules, instruments, orders, published policy statements and notices of the securities regulatory authorities of such jurisdiction.

Section 5.08) No Assets or Liabilities

Since its date of formation and prior to Closing, neither Buyer nor Holding has carried on any business, acquired any asset (or entered into any agreement, written or oral, to do so), incurred any liability or entered into any Contractual Obligation, other than as contemplated in this Agreement as described in Section 5.09 and in respect of the Debt Financing. Neither Buyer nor Holding has and has ever had any employees.

Section 5.09) Financing

Buyer has: (i) received equity financing in the aggregate amount of $● from the Investors (as defined in the Holding Shareholders Agreement) and (ii) completed financing arrangements with the Existing Lender (the **"Debt Financing"**) pursuant to which the Existing Lender will provide the financing to Buyer as described in the Credit Agreement and upon the terms and subject to the conditions set forth therein. An accurate and complete copy of the Credit Agreement has been furnished to Seller, which has not been amended, modified, terminated or withdrawn as of the date hereof and is in full force and effect as of the date hereof. Notwithstanding anything to the contrary contained herein, Buyer agrees to be responsible for its fees and expenses, including those of legal counsel, incurred in connection with the Debt Financing.

Section 5.10) Competition Act

Assuming the accuracy of Seller' representation contained in Section 3.24, Buyer, its Affiliates and its Subsidiaries on a consolidated basis, when combined with Ca, C and its Subsidiaries, have assets in Canada and annual gross revenues from sales in, from or into Canada with an aggregate value of less than $●, as determined in accordance with the *Competition Act*.

Section 5.11) No Brokers

Buyer has no Liability of any kind to any broker, finder or agent with respect to the Contemplated Transactions for which Principal could be liable.

Section 5.12) HST Registration

Buyer is registered for GST/HST purposes under the *Excise Tax Act* (Canada) and its registration number is ●.

ARTICLE 6: EMPLOYEES

Section 6.01) Transfer of Employees

Subject to the terms of this Section 6.01, Buyer covenants and agrees that it has (i) offered employment effective as of the Closing Date on the same terms to those existing as of the Closing Date to all non-unionized Employees of C (including any Employees of C on leave as at the Closing Date) as at the Closing Date, and (ii) employ all unionized Employees of C (including any Employees of C on leave as at the Closing Date) commencing on the Closing Date in accordance with the obligations contained in the Collective Agreements (together, the **"Designated Employees"**); provided, however, that it is acknowledged and agreed by the parties that Holding will be adopting the ESOP following the Closing (and Buyer shall use its reasonable best efforts to cause such plan to be adopted no later than ●, 20●), and that Principal's terms of employment with Buyer will be governed by the terms of the R Employment Agreement.

Section 6.02) Assumed Employee Plans

C shall assign to Buyer and Buyer shall assume and be liable for the Liabilities of the Employee Plans listed in on Schedule 7.01 (the **"Assumed Employee Plans"**) as of, and from, the Closing Date. The Designated Employees shall, as of the Closing Date, cease to accrue further benefits under the Employee Plans other than the Assumed Employee Plans.

ARTICLE 7: COVENANTS OF BUYER, PRINCIPAL AND SELLER

Section 7.01) Filings and Authorizations

The parties hereto waive compliance with Bulk Sales Laws.

Section 7.02) Tax Matters

    a)   At the Closing:

        i)   Buyer and C shall jointly execute an election under section 167(1) of the *Excise Tax Act* (Canada) and the corresponding sections of any applicable provincial statute in the forms prescribed for such purposes, such that the sale of the Acquired Assets hereunder will take place without payment of any goods and services tax or harmonized sales tax. Buyer will file the elections with the appropriate Governmental Authorities within the time permitted under the *Excise Tax*

Act (Canada). Buyer shall be responsible for any other share transfer Taxes, real property transfer or mortgage Taxes, sales Taxes, value-added Taxes, documentary stamp Taxes, recording charges and other similar Taxes, if any, arising from the Contemplated Transactions other than from the Pre-Closing Reorganization (**"Transfer Taxes"**).

ii) Buyer and C agree to file an election with respect to the Accounts Receivable under Section 22 of the *Income Tax Act* (Canada) and the corresponding sections of any provincial statute and any regulations under such statutes in a manner consistent with the allocation under Section 2.08.

iii) Buyer and C agree to jointly execute an election pursuant to subsection 85(1) of the *Income Tax Act* (Canada) and the corresponding sections of any applicable provincial statute and any regulations under such statutes with respect to the disposition by C of the Acquired Assets to Buyer. The amount elected as the proceeds of disposition to C and the cost of acquisition to Buyer of the Acquired Assets for purposes of the joint election under subsection 85(1) shall be determined by C. Buyer agrees to file, within the prescribed time, the prescribed election forms and any other documents required to give effect to the foregoing.

iv) Buyer agrees to cause Holding to, and C agrees to, jointly execute with Holding an election pursuant to subsection 85(1) of the *Income Tax Act* (Canada) and the corresponding sections of any applicable provincial statute and any regulations under such statutes with respect to the disposition by C of Buyer New Shares to Holding. The amount elected as the proceeds of disposition to C and the cost of acquisition to Holding of Buyer New Shares for purposes of the joint election under subsection 85(1) shall be determined by C. Holding agrees to file, within the prescribed time, the prescribed election forms and any other documents required to give effect to the foregoing.

v) C and Buyer agree to jointly elect in the prescribed manner under subsection 20(24) and 20(25) of the *Income Tax Act* (Canada) to have the provisions of subsection 20(24) of the *Income Tax Act* (Canada) and the corresponding sections of any provincial statute and any regulations under such statutes apply to such amount paid by C to Buyer for assuming the obligations of C in respect of undertakings to which paragraph 12(1)(a) of the *Income Tax Act* (Canada) applies and which relate to any Post-Reference Date Tax Period or which appeared as a current liability on the Most Recent Balance Sheet. Buyer agrees to file the joint election within the time prescribed under subsection 20(25) of the *Income Tax Act* (Canada).

vi) In accordance with the requirements of the *Income Tax Act* (Canada), the regulations thereunder, the administrative practice and policy of the Canada Revenue Agency, and any applicable equivalent or corresponding provincial legislative, regulatory and administrative requirements, Principal and Buyer agree to jointly elect pursuant to subsection 56.4(7) of the *Income Tax Act* (Canada), and any equivalent or corresponding provision under applicable provincial tax legislation, in respect of the covenants contained in Section 7.04 to file the joint election in the prescribed form and within the prescribed time under the *Income Tax Act* (Canada).

b) Following the Closing:

i) Each of the parties hereto shall prepare and file, and shall fully cooperate with the other party with respect to the preparation and filing of, any Tax Returns relating to Transfer Taxes and other filings relating to any such Taxes or charges as may be required and shall provide draft copies of such Tax Returns to Buyer prior to filing for Buyer's review and approval (not to be unreasonably withheld, conditioned or delayed) in accordance with this Section 7.02

ii) Buyer shall prepare or cause to be prepared all Tax Returns for Ca for any Pre-Closing Tax Period that are due after the Closing Date. Buyer shall file or cause to be filed such Tax Returns. Not less than thirty (30) days prior to the due date for filing any such Tax Returns, Buyer shall provide draft copies of such Tax Returns to Principal for Principal's review and approval (such approval not to be unreasonably withheld, conditioned or delayed). Buyer shall pay or cause to be paid the Taxes shown as due on any such Tax Return as prepared by Buyer, unless such Taxes are Excluded Liabilities (and determined in accordance with Section 7.02(c)).

iii) Principal shall prepare or cause to be prepared all Tax Returns for C and C Trading for any Pre-Closing Tax Period that are due after the Closing Date. Not less than thirty (30) days prior to the due date for filing any such Tax Returns, Principal shall provide draft copies of such Tax Returns to Buyer for Buyer's review and approval (such approval not to be unreasonably withheld, conditioned or delayed). Principal shall file or cause to be filed such Tax Returns. Buyer shall pay or cause to be paid the Taxes shown as due on any such Tax Return as prepared by Principal to the extent such Taxes are Assumed Liabilities and, for clarity, are not Excluded Liabilities (all as determined in accordance with Section 7.02(c). A **"Pre-Closing Tax Period"** is any tax period or portion thereof ending on or before the Closing Date, and a **"Post-Closing Tax Period"** is any tax period or portion thereof that is not a Pre-Closing Tax Period.

c) Straddle Period

  i) In the case of any Tax period that includes but does not end on the Reference Date (a **"Reference Date Straddle Period"**), the amount of any Taxes of or with respect to C, C Trading, and the Acquired Assets for the Pre-Reference Date Tax Period or the Post-Reference Date Period that are not (i) based upon or measured by income, activities, events, the level of any item, gain, receipts, proceeds, profits or similar items, (ii) transfer or transaction-based taxes, (iii) employment taxes or (iv) withholding taxes shall be deemed to be the amount of such Taxes for the Reference Date Straddle Period multiplied by a fraction, the numerator of which is the number of days in the Tax period ending on the Reference Date in the case of a Pre-Reference Date Period or the number of days in the Tax period following the Reference Date in the case of a Post-Reference Date Period and the denominator of which is the number of days in such Reference Date Straddle Period.

  (ii) The amount of any other Taxes of or with respect to C, C Trading, and the Acquired Assets for a Reference Date Straddle Period that relate to the Pre-Reference Date Tax Period will be determined based on an interim closing of the books as of the close of business on the Reference Date; provided, however, that any item determined on an annual or periodic basis (such as deductions for depreciation or real estate Taxes) shall be apportioned on a daily basis.

  (iii) In the case of any Tax Period that includes but does not end on the Closing Date (a **"Closing Date Straddle Period"**), the amount of any Taxes of or with respect to C, C Trading, and the Acquired Assets for the Pre-Closing Tax Period that are not (i) based upon or measured by income, activities, events, the level of any item, gain, receipts, proceeds, profits or similar items, (ii) transfer or transaction-based taxes, (iii) employment taxes or (iv) withholding taxes shall be deemed to be the amount of such Taxes for the Closing Date Straddle Period multiplied by a fraction, the numerator of which is the number of days in the Post-Reference Date Tax Period ending on the Closing Date and the denominator of which is the number of days in such Closing Date Straddle Period.

(iv)   The amount of any other Taxes of or with respect to C, C Trading, and the Acquired Assets for a Closing Date Straddle Period that relate to the Post-Reference Date Tax Period will be determined based on a closing of the books as of the close of business on the day before the Closing Date; provided, however, that any item determined on an annual or periodic basis (such as deductions for depreciation) shall be apportioned on a daily basis.

d)   Buyer, Sellers and Principal will, and will cause their respective Affiliates to, provide each other with such cooperation and information as any of them reasonably may request in connection with any Tax matters relating to Sellers and their Subsidiaries. Any information obtained under this Section 7.02(d) will be kept confidential except as may be otherwise necessary in connection with the filing of Tax Returns or claims for refund or in conducting an audit or other proceeding.

e)   Without the written consent of Buyer, all Tax sharing agreements or similar agreements and all powers of attorney with respect to or involving the Acquired Assets shall be terminated prior to the Closing Date, and, after the Closing, none of Buyer or any of its Affiliates shall be bound thereby or have any liability thereunder.

f)   C and C Trading shall promptly remit to Buyer any refund of Taxes or an amount equal to credits against Taxes (net of Tax and other costs) of C and C Trading other than any refund (or credit) of Taxes (A) for any tax period or portion thereof beginning after the Closing Date (to the extent arising from an item of loss or deduction realized in a Post-Closing Tax Period and excluding any Tax attribute carried forward from a Pre-Closing Tax Period (including without limitation a net operating loss, net capital loss, foreign tax credit, or research and development credit)), (B) (i) for any Pre-Reference Date Tax Period to the extent that such refund was not reflected as a current asset on the Most Recent Balance Sheet, or (ii) for any Pre-Closing Tax Period to the extent such refund is attributable to the carryback of a Tax attribute (including without limitation a net operating loss, net capital loss, foreign tax credit, or research and development credit) arising in a Post-Closing Tax Period, and the carryback of such Tax attribute does not reduce the amount of any refund that would otherwise be received by Buyer or (C) relating to all Taxes, if any, associated with and resulting from the Pre-Closing Reorganization. Any refund (or credit amount) of Taxes with respect to a Straddle Period shall be apportioned between a Pre-Reference Date Tax Period and Post-Reference Date Tax Period (and a Pre-Closing Tax Period and Post-Closing Tax Period in accordance with clause (c) of this Section 7.02 (Straddle Periods). All other refunds (or credit amounts of Taxes) of C, C Trading and Ca shall be for the account of such Person.

Section 7.03) Books and Records

Buyer shall preserve the books and records of the Business so delivered to it accordance with Section 2.01(g) (the **"Assigned Books and Records"**) for a period of 7 years from Closing, or for such other longer period if required by any Legal Requirement, and permit Sellers or their authorized representative(s) reasonable access thereto in connection with the affairs of Ca, C and its Subsidiaries relating to its Tax matters for the periods up to and including the Closing Date. Sellers shall preserve the Retained Books and Records for a period of 7 years from Closing, or for such other longer period if required by any Legal Requirement, and permit Buyer with access thereto in connection with the affairs of C and C Trading to its Tax matters for the periods up to and the Closing Date. Seller shall not destroy any such Retained Books and Records before or after such period without giving Buyer an opportunity to take back such records. Seller shall be entitled to make and keep a copy of any Assigned Books and Records as it may from time to time determine both before, and after, Closing. Buyer covenants and agrees to permit Seller to have reasonable access to, and use, during normal business hours, the Employees after Closing (at no cost to Seller) for the purposes of completing its tax returns for its current fiscal year end(s) and to properly facilitate the proper operation and transition of the Business to Buyer and its Subsidiaries after Closing; provided that such access shall not unreasonably interfere with the normal business operations of Buyer and its Subsidiaries.

Section 7.04) Noncompetition and Nonsolicitation

a) For a period of five (5) years from and after the Closing, Principal shall not, directly or indirectly, whether as owner, partner, investor, consultant, agent, employee, co-venturer or otherwise, carry on or be engaged in or have any financial or other interest in or be otherwise commercially involved in any endeavour, activity or business that is a Competitive Business, or undertake any planning for any Competitive Business, in the Restricted Area (provided that ownership of less than 5% of the outstanding stock of any publicly traded corporation will not be deemed to be so engaged in the Competitive Business solely by reason thereof). For the avoidance of doubt, the foregoing shall not prohibit Principal from complying with his obligations under the R Employment Agreement, holding his direct or indirect shareholder interest in Holding and its Subsidiaries, or otherwise acting as a director or officer of Holding or any of its Subsidiaries.

b) For a period of three (3) years from and after the Closing (the **"Non-Solicitation Period"**), Principal shall not directly or indirectly (i) solicit for hire, employ, engage, lure or entice away, or in any other manner persuade or attempt to persuade, as applicable, any employee or independent contractor of Buyer (or any Subsidiary of Buyer) to leave the employ of, or relationship with, Buyer (or any Subsidiary of Buyer) or (ii) solicit or encourage any customer or prospective customer of Buyer (or any Subsidiary of Buyer) to terminate or diminish its relationship with Buyer (or any Subsidiary of Buyer). Provided, however, that the terms of this Section 7.04(b) shall apply during the Non-Solicitation Period only if Principal has performed work for such customer or prospective customer of Buyer (or any Subsidiary of Buyer) during the term of Principal's employment with Buyer (or one of its Affiliates) or has been introduced to, or otherwise had contact with, such customer or prospective customer as a result of Principal's employment or other associations with Buyer (or one of its Affiliates). Provided, further, that the terms of this Section 7.04(b), shall apply only to employees and independent contractors who have provided services to Buyer at any time within the two (2) years preceding the date of termination of Principal's employment with Buyer and shall not apply as it relates to Principal's executive assistant.

c) If the final judgment of a court of competent jurisdiction declares that any term or provision of this Section 7.04 is invalid or unenforceable, the parties hereto agree that the court making the determination of invalidity or unenforceability will have the power to reduce the scope, duration, or area of the term or provision, to delete specific words or phrases, or to replace any invalid or unenforceable term or provision with a term or provision that is valid and enforceable and that comes closest to expressing the intention of the invalid or unenforceable term or provision, and this Agreement will be enforceable as so modified after the expiration of the time within which the judgment may be appealed.

e) Principal and Buyer agree that the covenants in this Section 7.04 may reasonably be regarded as being granted to maintain or preserve the fair market value of the benefit of the expenditure derived from the **"goodwill amount"** (as defined in subsection 56.4(1) of the *Income Tax Act* (Canada)) in respect of the Business. For greater certainty, Principal and Buyer confirm that no proceeds are received or receivable by Principal for the covenants in this Section 7.04.

Section 7.05) Expenses

Buyer will pay all financial, advisory, legal, accounting and other expenses of the BCP Investors (as such term is defined in the Holding Shareholders Agreement) that are incurred by such Persons or for their benefit prior to the Closing in connection with the preparation and execution of this Agreement and the Ancillary Agreements, the compliance therewith and the Contemplated Transactions and, other than the Assumed Seller Transaction Expenses, Seller shall pay all of their financial, advisory, legal, accounting and other expenses incurred by them or for their benefit in connection with the preparation and execution of this Agreement and the Ancillary Agreements, the compliance therewith and the Contemplated Transactions and the Pre-Closing Reorganization. The legal and placement fees and expenses related to the financing contemplated by the CIBC Credit Agreement shall be borne by Buyer.

Section 7.06) Further Assurances

From and after the Closing Date, upon the request of either Principal, Buyer or Seller, each of the parties hereto shall do, execute, acknowledge and deliver all such further acts, assurances, deeds, assignments, transfers, conveyances and other instruments and papers as may be reasonably required or appropriate to carry out the Contemplated Transactions, which for greater certainty in the case of Buyer will mean Buyer obtaining such Permits and other registrations as are necessary for the continued operation of the Business in the Ordinary Course of Business (as conducted by Ca, C and its Subsidiaries immediately prior to Closing).

Section 7.07) Rights to the Name

Immediately following the Closing, (i) C will change its name to a name that does not include ● or any derivative thereof; (ii) C will consent to, and will provide reasonably cooperation to permit, Buyer's use of the name "●" thereafter; (iii) C will consent to, and to provide reasonable cooperation to permit, Buyer's use of the name "●" thereafter; (iv) Buyer will change its name to "●"; and (v) Buyer will cause Ca to change its name to "●".

Section 7.08) Rollover Election

C covenants and agrees that, immediately following and in connection with the Closing, it will take any and all actions necessary to exchange the New Buyer Shares received at Closing for the following classes and amounts of securities in Holding: ● Class B Common Shares, ● Class B Senior Preferred Shares and ● Class B Junior Preferred Shares (collectively, the **"Holding New Shares"**). Buyer covenants and agrees to cause Holding to take any and all actions necessary to give effect to the transactions described in this Section 7.08.

Section 7.09) Employee Stock Option Plan

Following the Closing, Buyer shall cause Holding to take any actions as may be reasonably necessary to adopt and implement an employee stock option plan for eligible Buyer employees (the **"ESOP"**). The aggregate number of securities initially eligible for issuance shall not exceed ten percent (10%) of the common shares of Holding (on an as-converted or as-exercised basis to or exchangeable into common shares of Holding).

ARTICLE 8: INDEMNIFICATION

Section 8.01) Indemnification

a) **Indemnification by Seller**

Subject to the limitations set forth in this ARTICLE VIII, from and after the Closing, Seller on a joint and several basis shall indemnify and hold harmless each of Buyer and its Affiliates and each of their respective directors, officers, and employees and each of the successors and permitted assigns of each of the foregoing Persons (each, a **"Buyer Indemnified Person"**), from, against and in respect of any and all losses, damages, Liabilities, assessments, fines, penalties, Taxes, fees, costs (including costs of investigation, defence and enforcement of this Agreement), expenses or amounts paid in settlement (in each case, including reasonable attorneys' and experts' fees and expenses), whether or not involving a Third Party Claim (collectively, **"Losses"**) incurred or suffered by any Buyer Indemnified Persons or any of them as a result of, arising out of or relating to, directly or indirectly:

i) any breach of, or inaccuracy in, any representation, warranty or statement by or on behalf of Sellers (or on behalf of their Subsidiaries) in this Agreement or in any Schedule or certificate delivered by or on behalf of Sellers or any of their Subsidiaries pursuant to this Agreement (in each case (other than in Section 3.09(i)), assuming that all qualifications contained in this Agreement and each such Schedule or certificate as to materiality, including each qualifying reference to the defined term **"Material Adverse Effect"**, the phrase "substantial compliance", the words "material" and "materially" and all similar phrases and words were deleted therefrom);

ii) any breach or non-performance by Sellers of any of their covenants contained in this Agreement;

iii) any Excluded Liability;

iv) non-compliance with, or breach of, Section 6 of the *Retail Sales Tax Act (Ontario)*, in respect of the Contemplated Transactions in as much as the liability arising therefrom relates to any periods or portions thereof ending on or prior to ●, 20●, which are not otherwise accrued for on the Most Recent Balance Sheet or any Taxes of C or its Subsidiaries for any periods or portions thereof ending on or prior to ●, 20● which are not otherwise accrued for on the Most Recent Balance Sheet;

v) the Pre-Closing Reorganization (excluding for greater clarity, the acceleration of otherwise existing income tax Liabilities of C and C Trading which acceleration was triggered by the amalgamation of C and C Trading on ●, 20● and the resulting ●, 20● fiscal year end of C and C Trading as part of said Pre-Closing Reorganization, it being agreed and understood that such otherwise existing income tax Liabilities form part of the Assumed Liabilities; and

vi) the income taxes of C Trading arising from the sale of its assets to Ca pursuant to the Pre-Closing Reorganization and the income taxes of C arising from the sale of the Acquired Assets to Buyer.

With respect to indemnification by Seller pursuant to Section 8.01(a)(i) (other than claims for indemnification for breach of those representations and warranties contained in the Fundamental Representations), Buyer Indemnified Persons will not be entitled to make any claim for Losses unless the aggregate amount of Losses arising out of such claims exceeds the Deductible Amount (at which point Seller will indemnify Buyer Indemnified Persons for all such Losses in excess of the Deductible Amount). With respect to indemnification by Seller pursuant to Section 8.01(a)(i) (other than with respect to claims for indemnification for breach of those representations and warranties contained in the Fundamental Representations or Section 3.15), Seller' maximum liability will not exceed the Indemnity Cap. Notwithstanding anything to the contrary contained in this Agreement, in no event will Seller be liable in the aggregate for more than $●.

b)   Indemnification by Buyer

From and after the Closing, Buyer hereby indemnifies and holds harmless each of Seller and each of their respective Affiliates, and the respective directors, officers, and employees and each of the successors and permitted assigns of each of the foregoing Persons, (each, a **"Seller Indemnified Person"**), from, against and in respect of any and all Losses incurred, or suffered by any Seller Indemnified Person or any of them as a result of, arising out of or relating to, directly or indirectly:

i)   any breach of any representation and warranty made by Buyer in this Agreement or in any Schedule or a certificate delivered by or on behalf of Buyer pursuant to this Agreement (in each case, assuming that all qualifications contained in this Agreement and each such Schedule or certificate as to materiality, including each qualifying reference to the defined term **"Material Adverse Effect"**, the phrase "substantial compliance", the words "material" and "materially" and all similar phrases and words were deleted therefrom);

ii)   any breach or non-performance by Buyer of any of its covenants contained in this Agreement; and

iii)   the Assumed Liabilities and Assumed Subsidiary Liabilities.

c)   Time for Claims

The representations and warranties of each of the parties hereto contained in this Agreement or in any certificate or other writing delivered pursuant hereto or in connection herewith, will survive the Closing until thirty (30) days following the earlier of: (i) delivery to Buyer of the ● Audited Financials; and (ii) ●, 20●, after which no claim may be made or suit instituted seeking indemnification pursuant to this

ARTICLE VIII, for any breach of any such representation or warranty (and, for the avoidance of doubt, the covenants, agreements and obligations in this Agreement shall survive in accordance with their terms until the latest date permitted by Legal Requirements). Subject to any Legal Requirement, any breach of representation, warranty, covenant or agreement in respect of which indemnity may be sought under this Agreement will survive the time at which its survival would otherwise terminate pursuant to this Section 8.01(c), if notice delivered in accordance with this Agreement of the inaccuracy or breach thereof giving rise to such right to seek indemnity, stating in reasonable detail the nature of the inaccuracy or breach (including identification of the provisions of this Agreement alleged to be inaccurate or to have been breached), will have been given to the party against whom such indemnity may be sought prior to such time. Notwithstanding the foregoing: (A) the representations and warranties of Seller set out in the Fundamental Representations and in Section 3.15 (solely to the extent that such representations and warranties in Section 3.15 relate to the remittance of Taxes of C and the Subsidiaries for the period ended as at the Audit Balance Sheet Date where such Taxes are not otherwise accrued for on the Most Recent Balance Sheet) shall survive until sixty (60) days following the expiration of the relevant statute of limitations and (B) the representations and warranties of Buyer set out in Section 5.01 (Organization), Section 5.02 (Power and Authority), Section 5.04(b) (Non-Contravention), Section 5.06 (Capitalization of Buyer and Holding), and Section 5.07 (issuance of Buyer New Shares and Holding New Shares) shall survive until sixty (60) days following the expiration of the relevant statute of limitations. For the avoidance of doubt, the covenants and agreements of the parties hereto to the extent they, by their terms, contemplate or provide for performance after the Closing shall survive the Closing in accordance with their terms.

d) Written Notice of Indemnification Claims

In the event that any Indemnified Person wishes to make a claim for indemnification under this ARTICLE VIII, the Indemnified Person shall promptly give written notice of such claim to each Indemnifying Party within the applicable time limitations contained in Section 8.01(c). Any such notice shall describe the breach or inaccuracy and other material facts and circumstances upon which such claim is based and the estimated amount of Losses involved, in each case, in reasonable detail in light of the facts then known to the Indemnified Person; provided that no defect in the information contained in such notice, from the Indemnified Person to any Indemnifying Party will relieve such Indemnifying Party from any obligation under this ARTICLE VIII, except to the extent such failure to include information actually and materially prejudices such Indemnifying Party.

Section 8.02)   Third Party Claims

a)   Notice of Third Party Claims

Promptly (but in no case later than 30 days), after receipt by an Indemnified Person of written notice of the assertion of a claim by any Person who is not a party to this Agreement (a **"Third Party Claim"**) that may give rise to an Indemnity Claim against an Indemnifying Party under this ARTICLE VIII, the Indemnified Person shall give written notice thereof to the Indemnifying Party; provided, that no delay on the part of the Indemnified Person in notifying the Indemnifying Party will relieve the Indemnifying Party from any obligation under this ARTICLE VIII, except to the extent such delay actually and materially prejudices the Indemnifying Party.

b)   Assumption of Defence, *etc.*

The Indemnifying Party may participate in or assume the defence of any Third Party Claim by giving written notice to the Indemnified Party not later than 15 days after receiving notice of that Third Party Claim pursuant to Section 8.02(a) (the **"Notice Period"**) stating that the Indemnifying Party will, and thereby covenants to, indemnify, defend and hold harmless the Indemnified Person from and against the entirety of any and all Losses the Indemnified Person may suffer resulting from, arising out of, relating to, in the nature of, or caused by the Third Party Claim. In addition, the Indemnifying Party will have the right to defend the Indemnified Person against the Third Party Claim with counsel of its choice reasonably satisfactory to the Indemnified Person so long as (i) the Indemnifying Party provides the Indemnified Person with evidence reasonably acceptable to the Indemnified Person that the Indemnifying Party will have adequate financial resources to defend against the Third Party Claim and fulfill its indemnification obligations hereunder, (ii) the Third Party Claim involves only money damages and does not seek an injunction or other equitable relief against the Indemnified Person, (iii) the Indemnified Person has not been advised by counsel that an actual or potential conflict exists between the Indemnified Person and the Indemnifying Party in connection with the defence of the Third Party Claim, (iv) the Third Party Claim does not relate to or otherwise arise in connection with Taxes or any criminal or regulatory enforcement Action, (v) settlement of an adverse judgment with respect to, or conduct of the defence of the Third Party Claim by the Indemnifying Party is not, in the good faith judgment of the Indemnified Person, likely to be materially adverse to the Indemnified Person's reputation or continuing business interests (including its relationships with current or potential customers, carriers or other parties material to the conduct of its business) and (vi) the Indemnifying Party conducts the defence of the Third Party Claim actively and diligently. The Indemnifying Party agrees to pay all of its own expenses of participating in or assuming such defence. The Indemnified Party shall co-operate in good faith in the defence of each Third Party Claim, even if the defence has been assumed by the Indemnifying Party and may participate in such defence assisted by counsel of its own choice at its own expense. The Indemnifying Party shall not consent to the entry of any judgment or enter into any compromise or settlement of any Third Party Claim without obtaining the prior written consent of the Indemnified Party unless such judgment, compromise or settlement (A) provides for the payment by the Indemnifying Party of money as sole relief for the claimant, (B) results in the full and general release of all Indemnified Persons from all liabilities arising or relating to, or in connection with, the Third Party Claim and (C) involves no finding or admission of any violation of Legal Requirements or the rights of any Person and no effect on any other claims that may be made against the Indemnified Person.

c)   If the Indemnified Party has not received notice within the Notice Period that the Indemnifying Party has elected to assume the defence of such Third Party Claim or the evidence contemplated by clause (i) of Section 8.02(b), or if the Indemnifying Party at any time fails to conduct the defence of the Third Party Claim actively and diligently (or is not permitted to conduct the defence pursuant to Section 8.02(b)) the Indemnified Party may, at its option, consent to the entry of any judgment or settle or compromise the Third Party Claim or assume such defence, and the Indemnifying Party shall be liable for all reasonable costs and expenses paid or incurred in connection therewith and, subject to the provisions of this Article, any and all other Losses that the Indemnified

Person may incur or suffer resulting from, arising out of, relating to, in the nature of or caused by the Third Party Claim to the fullest extent of the indemnity provided in this ARTICLE VIII. If such notice and evidence is given on a timely basis and if the Indemnifying Party conducts the defence of the Third Party Claim actively and diligently but any of the other conditions in Section 8.02(b) is or becomes unsatisfied, the Indemnified Person may defend, and may consent to the entry of any judgment or enter into any compromise or settlement with respect to, the Third Party Claim; provided, that the Indemnifying Party will not be bound by the entry of any such judgment consented to, or any such compromise or settlement effected, without its prior written consent (which consent will not be unreasonably withheld or delayed). In the event that the Indemnified Person conducts the defence of the Third Party Claim pursuant to this Section 8.02(b), the Indemnifying Party will remain responsible for any and all other Losses that the Indemnified Person may incur or suffer resulting from, arising out of, relating to, in the nature of or caused by the Third Party Claim to the fullest extent provided in this ARTICLE VIII.

d) The Indemnifying Party and the Indemnified Party will use all reasonable efforts to make available to the Party which is undertaking and controlling the defence of any Third Party Claim (the "**Defending Party**"),

i) those employees whose assistance, testimony or presence is necessary to assist the Defending Party in evaluating and in defending any Third Party Claim; and

ii) all documents, records and other materials in the possession of such Party reasonably required by the Defending Party for its use in defending any Third Party Claim, and shall otherwise co-operate with the Defending Party.

e) If an Indemnifying Party elects to assume the defence of any Third Party Claim as provided in Section 8.02(c), and, at any time thereafter, the Indemnified Party is no longer eligible to conduct the defence of an indemnity claim because a condition in Section 8.02(b) is or becomes unsatisfied, Indemnifying Party shall not be liable for any legal expenses subsequently incurred by the Indemnified Party in connection with the defence of such Third Party Claim unless such expenses form part of the Losses for which the Indemnified Party is otherwise entitled to indemnity in accordance with this Article.

f) Consent to Jurisdiction Regarding Third Party Claim

Buyer and each of Seller hereby consents to the non-exclusive jurisdiction of any court in which any Third Party Claim may be brought against any Indemnified Person for purposes of any claim which such Indemnified Person may have against any such Indemnifying Party pursuant to this Agreement in connection with such Third Party Claim, and in furtherance thereof, the provisions of Section 9.10 are incorporated herein by reference, *mutatis mutandis.*

Section 8.03) No Circular Recovery

Principal hereby agrees that it will not make any claim for indemnification against either Buyer, Ca or their Subsidiaries by reason of the fact that Principal was a controlling person, director, employee or Representative of Buyer, Ca or one of their Subsidiaries or was serving as such for another Person at the request of Buyer, Ca or one of their Subsidiaries (whether such claim is for Losses of any kind or otherwise and whether such claim is pursuant to any Organizational Document, Contractual Obligation or otherwise) with respect to any claim brought by Buyer Indemnified Person against Principal under this Agreement or otherwise relating to this Agreement, any Ancillary Agreement or any of the Contemplated Transactions. With respect to any claim brought by Buyer Indemnified Person against Principal under this Agreement or otherwise relating to this Agreement, any Ancillary Agreement or any of the Contemplated Transactions or the Pre-Closing Reorganization, Principal expressly waives any right of subrogation, contribution, advancement, indemnification or other claim against Seller and their Subsidiaries with respect to any amounts owed by Principal pursuant to this ARTICLE VIII or otherwise.

Section 8.04) Knowledge and Investigation

The right of any Buyer Indemnified Person or Seller Indemnified Person to indemnification pursuant to this ARTICLE VIII will not be affected by any investigation conducted or knowledge acquired (or capable of being acquired) at any time, whether before or after the execution and delivery of this Agreement or the Closing, with respect to the accuracy of any representation or warranty, or performance of or compliance with any covenant or agreement, referred to in Section 8.01. The waiver of any condition contained in this Agreement or in any Ancillary Agreement based on the breach of any such representation or warranty, or on the performance of or compliance with any such covenant or agreement, will not affect the right of any Buyer Indemnified Person or Seller Indemnified Person to indemnification pursuant to this ARTICLE VIII based on such representation, warranty, covenant or agreement.

Section 8.05) Remedies Cumulative

The rights of each Buyer Indemnified Person and Seller Indemnified Person under this ARTICLE VIII are cumulative, and each Buyer Indemnified Person and Seller Indemnified Person will have the right in any particular circumstance, in its sole discretion, to enforce any provision of this ARTICLE VIII without regard to the availability of a remedy under any other provision of this ARTICLE VIII.

Section 8.06) Exclusive Remedy

From and after the Closing, this Article will provide the exclusive remedy for Losses for any misrepresentation, breach of warranty, covenant or other agreement or other claim arising out of this Agreement or the Contemplated Transactions, except in the case of remedies for fraud or any claim for specific performance or injunctive relief which may be pursued against the applicable Person alleged to have engaged in such fraud or other prohibited activity without regard to the provisions of this Agreement.

Section 8.07) Certain Matters Relating to the Calculation of Losses

a) The amount of Losses recoverable by an Indemnified Person under this ARTICLE XI with respect to an indemnity claim shall be reduced by the amount of any insurance payment received by such Indemnified Person (or an Affiliate thereof) with respect to such indemnity claim. An Indemnified Person shall use reasonable best efforts to pursue, and to cause its Affiliates to pursue, all insurance claims to which it is entitled, the proceeds of which would provide compensation with respect to the Losses that are the subject of such indemnity claim. If an Indemnified Person (or an Affiliate thereof) receives any insurance payment in connection with any claim for Losses for which it has already been paid under this ARTICLE VIII by the Indemnifying Party, the Indemnifying Party shall be reimbursed within 30 days after the Indemnified Person (or its Affiliate) received such insurance payment by an amount equal to the lesser of (i) the amount previously received by the Indemnified Person under this ARTICLE VIII with respect to such claim or (ii) the amount of such insurance payment.

b) The amount which the Indemnifying Party is required to pay to, for, or on behalf of the Indemnified Party pursuant to this Article XI with respect to any Loss shall be reduced by any Tax benefit arising from any such Loss actually realized by the Indemnified Party solely for the taxable year of the incurrence, accrual or payment of such Loss.

c) An Indemnified Party shall take reasonable steps to mitigate Losses to the extent required by applicable Legal Requirements.

d) In the event an Indemnified Person is entitled to recover the same Losses under more than one provision of this Agreement, such Indemnified Person shall only be permitted to recover such Losses one time, and without duplication.

e) No indemnification shall be owed to any indemnified party hereunder to the extent such Loss results from any change in any Legal Requirement after the date hereof.

f) For the avoidance of doubt, the terms of this ARTICLE VIII shall not apply to any breaches of any representations, warranties or covenants contained in the R Employment Agreement, the Holding Shareholders Agreement or the Escrow Agreement and any such remedies for any breaches of any representations, warranties or covenants contained in the R Employment Agreement, the Holding Shareholders Agreement or the Escrow Agreement shall be determined in accordance with the respective relevant provisions contained therein.

Section 8.08) Treatment of Indemnity Payments

Any payments made to an Indemnified Party pursuant to this ARTICLE VIII shall be treated as an adjustment to the purchase price for tax purposes paid for the applicable Acquired Assets to the extent permitted by applicable Legal Requirements.

ARTICLE 9: MISCELLANEOUS

Section 9.01) Notices

Any notice, request, demand, claim or other communication required or permitted to be delivered, given or otherwise provided under this Agreement must be in writing and must be delivered personally, delivered by nationally recognized overnight courier service, sent by certified or registered mail, postage prepaid, or (if a facsimile number or e-mail address is provided below) sent by facsimile (subject to electronic confirmation of good facsimile transmission) or e-mail. Any such notice, request, demand, claim or other communication shall be deemed to have been delivered and given (a) when delivered, if delivered personally, (b) the Business Day after it is deposited with such nationally recognized overnight courier service, if sent for overnight delivery by a nationally recognized overnight courier service, (c) the day of sending, if sent by facsimile or e-mail prior to 5:00 p.m. (Eastern time) on any Business Day or the next succeeding Business Day if sent by facsimile or e-mail after 5:00 p.m. (Eastern time) on any Business Day or on any day other than a Business Day or (d) five (5) Business Days after the date of mailing, if mailed by certified or registered mail, postage prepaid, in each case, to the following address or, if applicable, facsimile number or e-mail address, or to such other address or addresses, facsimile number or numbers or e-mail address or addresses as such party may subsequently designate to the other parties by notice given hereunder:

If to Seller, to:

●

with a copy to:

●

If to Buyer, to:

●

with a copy to:

●

Each of the parties to this Agreement may specify a different address or addresses, facsimile number or facsimile numbers or e-mail address or addresses by giving notice in accordance with this Section 9.01 to each of the other parties hereto.

Section 9.02) Succession and Assignment; No Third-Party Beneficiaries
Subject to the immediately following sentence, this Agreement will be binding upon and inure to the benefit of the parties hereto and their respective heirs, successors and permitted assigns, as applicable, each of which such heirs, successors and permitted assigns will be deemed to be a party hereto for all purposes hereof. No party may assign, delegate or otherwise transfer either this Agreement or any of its rights, interests or obligations hereunder (including by way of granting a direct or indirect security or similar interest in the assets and undertakings of such Person) without the prior written approval of the other parties, and any attempt to do so will be null and void *ab initio*; provided, that (a) Buyer may assign this Agreement and any or all of its rights and interests (but not its obligations) hereunder to one or more of its Affiliates or designate one or more of its Affiliates to perform its obligations hereunder and (b) Buyer may assign this Agreement and any or all of its rights and interests (but not its obligations) hereunder to any purchaser of all or substantially all its assets or designate such

purchaser to perform its obligations hereunder. Except as expressly provided herein, this Agreement is for the sole benefit of the parties hereto and their successors and permitted assignees and nothing herein expressed or implied will give or be construed to give any Person, other than the parties hereto and such heirs, successors and permitted assignees, any other right, benefit or remedy of any nature whatsoever under or by reason of this Agreement. For the avoidance of doubt, it is hereby acknowledged and agreed by the parties hereto that an Indemnified Person that is not party hereto is intended to be an express third party beneficiary of this Agreement.

Section 9.03) Amendments and Waivers

No amendment or waiver of any provision of this Agreement will be valid and binding unless it is in writing and signed, in the case of an amendment, by Buyer and Seller, or in the case of a waiver, by the party against whom the waiver is to be effective. No waiver by any party of any breach or violation of, default under or inaccuracy in any representation, warranty or covenant hereunder, whether intentional or not, will be deemed to extend to any prior or subsequent breach or violation of, default under, or inaccuracy in, any such representation, warranty or covenant hereunder or affect in any way any rights arising by virtue of any prior or subsequent such occurrence. No delay or omission on the part of any party in exercising any right, power or remedy under this Agreement will operate as a waiver thereof.

Section 9.04) Entire Agreement

This Agreement, together with the other Ancillary Agreements and any documents, instruments and certificates explicitly referred to herein, constitutes the entire agreement among the parties hereto with respect to the subject matter hereof and supersedes any and all prior discussions, negotiations, proposals, undertakings, understandings and agreements, whether written or oral, with respect thereto. There are no restrictions, promises, warranties, covenants, or undertakings, other than those expressly provided for herein and therein.

Section 9.05) Schedules

a) The Schedules (including the Disclosure Schedule) shall be deemed to be attached hereto and made a part hereof. All references herein to this Agreement shall include the Schedules.

b) Nothing in the Disclosure Schedule is intended to broaden the scope of any representation or warranty contained in the Agreement. The Disclosure Schedule and the information and disclosures contained therein are intended only to qualify and limit the representations, warranties and covenants of Seller, as the case may be, contained in the Agreement and shall not be deemed to expand in any way the scope or effect of any of such representations, warranties or covenants.

c)   No reference to or disclosure of any item or other matter in any Disclosure Schedule (or any section thereof) shall be construed as an admission or indication that such item is required to be referred to or disclosed in any Disclosure Schedule (or any section thereof). Inclusion of any item in the Disclosure Schedule (or any section thereof) does not constitute a determination by Seller that such item is material and shall not be deemed to establish a standard of materiality. No disclosure in the Disclosure Schedule (or any section thereof) relating to any possible breach or violation of any agreement, law or regulation or any potential adverse contingency shall be construed as an admission or indication that any such breach or violation exists or has actually occurred or that such adverse contingency will actually occur.

Section 9.06) Disclaimer of Other Representations or Projections etc.

Each of the parties hereto agrees that except for the representations and warranties set forth in Article III, Article IV and Article V hereof, none of Buyer, Sellers, Principal, Ca, C or any of its Subsidiaries, or any of the foregoing Person's respective Representatives, have made any representation, warranty, projection or forecast nor shall any of the foregoing be construed as having made to any other party hereto or to any Representative thereof.

Section 9.07) Counterparts; Facsimile Signature

This Agreement may be executed in any number of counterparts, each of which will be deemed an original, but all of which together will constitute but one and the same instrument. This Agreement will become effective when duly executed and delivered by each party hereto. Counterpart signature pages to this Agreement may be delivered by facsimile or electronic delivery (*i.e.*, by email of a PDF signature page) and each such counterpart signature page will constitute an original for all purposes.

Section 9.08) Severability

Any term or provision of this Agreement that is invalid or unenforceable in any situation in any jurisdiction will not affect the validity or enforceability of the remaining terms and provisions hereof or the validity or enforceability of the offending term or provision in any other situation or in any other jurisdiction. In the event that any provision hereof would, under applicable Legal Requirements, be invalid or unenforceable in any respect, each party hereto intends that such provision will be construed by modifying or limiting it so as to be valid and enforceable to the maximum extent compatible with, and possible under, applicable Legal Requirements.

Section 9.09) Governing Law

This Agreement, the rights of the parties hereunder and all Actions arising in whole or in part under or in connection herewith, will be governed by and construed and enforced in accordance with the domestic substantive laws of the Province of Ontario and the Laws of Canada applicable therein, without giving effect to any choice or conflict of law provision or rule that would cause the application of the laws of any other jurisdiction.

Section 9.10) Jurisdiction; Venue; Service of Process

a) Jurisdiction

Subject to the provisions of Section 8.02(d)(ii), each of the parties to this Agreement, by its execution hereof, (i) hereby irrevocably submits to the exclusive jurisdiction of the Province of Ontario and the courts of the Province of Ontario for the purpose of any Action among any of the parties relating to or arising in whole or in part under or in connection with this Agreement, any Ancillary Agreement or the Contemplated Transactions, (ii) hereby waives to the extent not prohibited by applicable Legal Requirements, and agrees not to assert, by way of motion, as a defence or otherwise, in any such Action, any claim that it is not subject personally to the jurisdiction of the above-named courts, that its property is exempt or immune from attachment or execution, that any such Action brought in one of the above-named courts should be dismissed on grounds of *forum non conveniens*, should be transferred or removed to any court other than one of the above-named courts, or should be stayed by reason of the pendency of some other Action in any other court other than one of the above-named courts or that this Agreement, any Ancillary Agreement or the subject matter hereof or thereof may not be enforced in or by such court and (iii) hereby agrees not to commence any such Action other than before one of the above-named courts. Notwithstanding the previous sentence a party may commence any Action in a court other than the above-named courts solely for the purpose of enforcing an order or judgment issued by one of the above-named courts.

b)   Venue

Each of the parties to this Agreement agrees that for any Action among any of the parties relating to or arising in whole or in part under or in connection with this Agreement, any Ancillary Agreement or the Contemplated Transactions, such party shall bring such Action only in the Province of Ontario. Notwithstanding the previous sentence a party may commence any Action in a court other than the above-named courts solely for the purpose of enforcing an order or judgment issued by one of the above-named courts. Each party hereto further waives any claim and will not assert that venue should properly lie in any other location within the selected jurisdiction.

c)   Service of Process

Each of the parties to this Agreement hereby (i) consents to service of process in any Action among any of the parties hereto relating to or arising in whole or in part under or in connection with this Agreement, any Ancillary Agreement or the Contemplated Transactions in any manner permitted by Ontario law, (ii) agrees that service of process made in accordance with clause (i) or made by registered or certified mail, return receipt requested, at its address specified pursuant to Section 9.01, will constitute good and valid service of process in any such Action and (iii) waives and agrees not to assert (by way of motion, as a defence, or otherwise) in any such Action any claim that service of process made in accordance with clause (i) or (ii) does not constitute good and valid service of process.

Section 9.11)   Specific Performance

Each of the parties acknowledges and agrees that the other party would be damaged irreparably in the event any of the provisions of this Agreement are not performed in accordance with their specific terms or otherwise are breached or violated. Accordingly, each of the parties agrees that, without posting a bond or other undertaking, the other parties will be entitled to an injunction or injunctions to prevent breaches or violations of the provisions of this Agreement and to enforce specifically this Agreement and the terms and provisions hereof in any Action instituted in any court having jurisdiction over the parties in the matter, in addition to any other remedy to which they are entitled at law or in equity. Each of the parties further agrees that, in the event of any action for specific performance in respect of such breach or violation, it will not assert the defence that a remedy at law would be adequate.

[Remainder of page intentionally left blank; signature page follows.]

IN WITNESS WHEREOF, each of the undersigned has executed this Asset Purchase Agreement as of the date first above written.

BUYER
[ ]:
By:
Name: _______________________
Title: _______________________

SELLER   SELLER
[ ]:   [ ]:
By: By:
Name: _______________________   Name: _______________________
Title: _______________________   Title: _______________________

INDEX TO DEFINED TERMS

*THIS INDEX IS INCLUDED FOR CONVENIENCE ONLY AND
DOES NOT CONSTITUTE A PART OF THE AGREEMENT*

Term	Section
Interim Financials	Section 3.08(a)(ii)
IP Contracts	Section 3.13(d)
Leased Real Property	Section 3.12(a)
Liability Policies	Section 3.23
Losses	Section 8.01(a)
Material Company Contract	Section 3.18(b)
Most Recent Balance Sheet	Section 3.08(a)(ii)
Most Recent Balance Sheet Date	Section 3.08(a)(ii)
Non-Assigned Asset	Section 2.02
Notice Period	Section 8.02(b)
OHSA	Section 3.21(g)
Outbound IP Contracts	Section 3.13(d)
Post-Closing Tax Period	Section 7.02(f)
Principal	Preamble
Real Property Leases	Section 3.12(a)
R Employment Agreement	Recitals
Related Party Contract	Section 3.19
Scheduled Intellectual Property Rights	Section 3.13(c)
Seller Indemnified Person	Section 8.01(b)
Sponsor	Section 5.09
Shareholders	Preamble
Reference Date Straddle Period	Section 7.02(c)
Third Party Claim	Section 8.02(a)
Transfer	Section 2.02
Transfer Taxes	Section 7.02(a)

SCHEDULE 2.01 – PERMITTED ENCUMBRANCES

SCHEDULE 2.02 – EXCLUDED ASSETS

SCHEDULE 2.03(B) – EXCLUDED LIABILITIES

i)   Any Seller Transaction Expense that is not an Assumed Seller Transaction Expense;

ii)   Any Change of Control Payment that is not an Assumed Change of Control Payment;

iii)   Any Liability of C or any other Seller arising out of this Agreement, subject to Buyer's compliance with its payment obligations set forth in Section 2.06(a);

iv)   Any Liability arising out of a Post-Reference Date Payment;

v)   Any Liability arising out of the Shareholder Loans, the Management Agreement (including any payment obligations arising out of the termination thereof) or any other Related Party Contracts;

vi)   Any Liability arising out of any Employee Plan that is not an Assumed Employee Plan;

vii)   Liabilities arising out of the Excluded Assets;

viii)   Any Liabilities arising out of the Existing Credit Facility (other than the obligation to pay the Debt Payoff Amount) or any other continuing Liabilities otherwise contemplated by the pay-out letter referenced in Section 2.06(b)(ix) or otherwise being assumed as part of the Credit Agreement and the credit facility contemplated thereby.

SCHEDULE 2.06(A)(VI) – EMPLOYEE CHANGE OF CONTROL PAYMENT RECEIPTS

SCHEDULE 2.06(B)(XIII) – REQUIRED CONSENTS

SCHEDULE 2.08 – PURCHASE PRICE ALLOCATION

SCHEDULE 7.01 – ASSUMED EMPLOYEE PLAN

Form 18: **Resolution of Dispute Provisions**

The parties agree that, during the performance of their respective obligations under this Agreement, each of them will make good faith efforts to resolve any disputes, controversies, questions or claims arising out of or relating to this Agreement, including the obligations of any Party, the content, nature, reasonableness or necessity of any document to be provided herein or any other issue in dispute in relation to or arising out of this Agreement (all of which are referred to as a **"Dispute"**) by negotiation. Notwithstanding, either party may initiate arbitration as provided for herein in order to resolve a Dispute. Any Dispute not resolved by negotiation shall be referred to and be finally resolved by arbitration in accordance with the following provision.

Whenever any arbitration is permitted or required hereunder to resolve a Dispute between the parties, arbitration proceedings shall be commenced by the Party desiring arbitration (the **"Initiating Party"**) giving notice to the other Party (the **"Responding Party"**) specifying the matter to be arbitrated. The arbitration shall be conducted by a single arbitrator. If the Initiating Party and the Responding Party are unable to agree upon an arbitrator within five (5) days after delivery of such notice, then either Party shall be entitled to make application to the Superior Court of Ontario pursuant to the Arbitration Act (Ontario), as amended from time to time, for selection of the arbitrator, and the provisions of such Act shall govern such selection. In the event of the failure, refusal or inability of the arbitrator to act, or continue to act, a new arbitrator shall be appointed in his or her stead, which appointment shall be made in the same manner as hereinbefore provided. The Parties shall act in good faith to expedite the arbitration process. Subject to agreement by the Parties, the arbitrator shall thereupon determine the process and procedure of the arbitration, subject to considering submissions made by the Parties in that regard, proceed to hear the evidence and submissions of the parties, and shall render a decision within five (5) days after completion of submissions. The decision of the arbitrator shall be final and binding upon the Parties and not subject to appeal except with respect to a matter of law alone. The arbitrator shall have the authority to assess the costs of the arbitration against any one or more of the Parties. If the arbitrator does not render a decision within the time limits aforesaid, any Party to the arbitration may cancel the appointment of the arbitrator so appointed and initiate new arbitration proceedings pursuant hereto. In the event that any Dispute is unresolved by the Closing Date, the Closing Date shall be automatically extended to that date which is seven (7) Business Days following the decision of the said arbitrator determining such Dispute.

Form 19: **Drafting Default Remedies**

In the event of the seller's default herein, the buyer shall be entitled as its sole remedy to terminate this agreement and receive a refund of its deposit money and interest thereon.

In the event that all conditions of this agreement are satisfied and in the event performance of this agreement is tendered by the seller and the sale is not consummated through default on the part of the buyer the deposit money paid to the seller shall constitute liquidated damages for the buyer's default. Such amount is agreed upon by and between the seller and the buyer as liquidated damages, due to the difficulty and inconvenience of ascertaining and measuring actual damages, and the uncertainty thereof; and no other damages, rights or remedies shall in any case, be collectible, enforceable or available to the seller other than in the section defined.

Form 20: **Letters of Intent—Memorandum of Agreement (Formation of Corporation)**

This Agreement made this [*day*] day of [*month, year*] by the undersigned.

NOW THIS AGREEMENT WITNESSETH for good and valuable consideration, the sufficiency whereof is hereby acknowledged.

1) For the purpose of this memorandum, the terms or expressions set forth in Schedule "A" shall have the meanings therein set forth and shall be incorporated herein by reference.

2) The Shareholders shall cause meetings to be held, votes cast, resolutions and by-laws enacted, and documents executed to ensure the following functions of the Newcooperation:

    a) each of the two Principals shall at all times be represented by a minimum of two Directors;

    b) documents to be executed by Newco shall require the signature of both Principals;

    c) the Newco Project shall be strictly as defined unless there is a unanimous approval of a change therein by the Principals; and

    d) the Share Capital issued by Newco shall at all times be equal in number, allotment and type to both Principals.

3) __________ agrees to fund the anticipated shortfall between Receipts and Disbursements, as currently shown on the Budget, attached hereto as Schedule B, for each of years 1 and 2 as shown thereon. If the actual shortfall, at any time, exceeds the anticipated shortfall amount shown on the Budget, Director-Approved cost cutting measures shall be implemented.

4)   ___________ recognizes that there is a value-added contribution to Newco through ___________ that is attributable to ___________ and that is agreed to be $[*dollar amount*] (the "___________ **Factor**"). In the most tax efficient manner possible, ___________ agrees to allocate to ___________ $[*dollar amount*] from the ___________ Financing described in paragraph 3, which sum is to be applied against the Edwards Factor, with a balance thereof payable post-closing in three equal, annual, consecutive instalments, provided however that no annual payment on account of the Edwards Factor shall exceed 30% of Newco's after-tax net profit, in which case the excess thereof shall be deferred.

5)   If the combination of ___________ Financing and Debt Financing shall at any time and from time to time be insufficient to satisfy a Budget-Approved Project Financing, the deficiency thereof shall be funded by Equity Financing. If one of the Principals is unable or unwilling to advance its share of the Equity Financing (the **"Non-Funding Principal"**), the other Principal (the **"Funding Principal"**) may advance the full amount of the Equity Financing which sum shall bear an imputed rate of interest which is at all times equal to the ___________/Equity Financing Costs. The Equity Financing shall be repaid to the Funding Principal out of cash surplus in Newco in priority to any payment to a party who is not at arm's length to Newco.

6)   For managing and supervising the Newco Project on a full day-to-day operational basis, the Directors shall engage the ___________ Principal and the ___________ Principals and, subject to paragraph 8, shall be entitled to the ___________ Principal Fees and ___________ Principal Fees. A monthly management reporting system shall be established, which is intended to monitor the time and activities of the ___________ team. In order to ensure a seamless transition within two years of all Current Business and Future Business from ___________ to Newco, all employees of ___________ will be placed under contract.

7)   In addition to the services of the ___________ Principal, ___________ and other existing employees of ___________ shall provide, on an *ad hoc* basis, services to the Newco Project on a cost shared basis. Schedule C, attached hereto, contains job profiles of those employees of ___________ whose costs are included in the budget set forth in Schedule B.

8)   The Principals of ___________ and ___________ agree to a covenant of non-competition. Newco shall be entitled to the non-exclusive use of the ___________ trademark and branding benefits.

9) The __________ Principal shall be entitled to a carried-interest equal to 20% of the __________ ownership interest in any property developed or acquired by __________ by virtue of the Newco Project.

10) Services currently being rendered by __________ to existing clients on work currently in progress and the income derived therefrom (**"Current Business"**) shall belong to __________ for and during the ensuing two years. Services not currently being rendered by __________ to future or to current clients and the income derived therefrom (**"Future Business"**) will belong to Newco. Notwithstanding the foregoing, within two years, all Current and Future Business shall be transferred by __________ and belong to Newco.

11) The foregoing provisions shall be embodied within a shareholders agreement which shall govern the business and affairs of Newco and upon the execution thereof, this Memorandum shall be superseded and shall no longer bind the parties.

IN WITNESS WHEREOF the parties have hereunto set their hands and seals and agree to be bound by the provisions herein set forth.

Per:

Name: ____________________

Title: ____________________

I have the authority to bind the corporation

SCHEDULE A

The following words, terms and expressions shall have the following meanings and be incorporated by reference into the Memorandum to which the schedule is attached.

(a) **"Budget"** refers to the projected receipts and disbursements set forth in Schedule B, next hereto;

(b) **"Budget-Approved"** refers to a Director-Approved expenditures (capital, operating and other) of the Newco Project for the period covered by the Budget;

(c) "__________" refers to __________;

(d) "__________/Equity Financing Costs" refers to a rate of return on the outstanding aggregate of __________ Financing and Equity Financing which at all times 5% over the prime commercial lending rate charged by the Royal Bank of Canada, compounded monthly;

(e) "__________ Financing" refers to the Director-Approved funding required from time to time to satisfy the Newco Project by the __________ Principals;

(f) "__________ Principals" refers to those persons designated from time to time by __________;

(g) "__________ Principal Fees" refers to the Director-Approved market-driven competitive fees for services to be rendered by the __________ Principals;

(h) **"Debt Financing"** refers to the Director-Approved funding of the Newco Project by lenders chosen and upon terms subject at all times to Director-Approval;

(i) **"Director-Approved"** refers to a decision made by a majority of Directors;

(j) **"Directors"** refers to the nominees designated by the Principals;

(k) **"Equity Financing"** refers to the funding of the Newco Project by the Principals pursuant to paragraph 5 hereof;

(l) "__________" refers to __________ and the corporations, affiliates and companies related thereto directly or indirectly;

Form 21: **Shareholders' Agreement— Shareholder Agreement—Checklist**

ISSUES TO BE CONSIDERED IN CONNECTION WITH A SHAREHOLDERS' AGREEMENT

Issue	Explanation
Principles of Interpretation	
Currency	What currency will be designated for monetary amounts in the Agreement? E.g. Canadian
Jurisdiction	What will be the governing law of the Agreement? E.g. Ontario
Purpose and Scope	
Business of the Corporation	Describe the business of your corporation:
Unanimous Shareholders Agreement	Is this Agreement meant to be a unanimous shareholders agreement? (i.e. will all shareholders at all times be signing this agreement?)
Guarantee by Principals	Will the Principals (the controlling shareholders of the corporate shareholders) guarantee compliance by the corporate shareholders to the Agreement?

Participation in the Corporation

Shareholders and Principals

Please fill out the chart, below:

Shareholder Name	Principal, if applicable	Number and Class of Shares	Percentage of shares of corporate shareholder owned by Principal, if applicable	Address of Shareholder

Issue	Explanation
Indemnities	Are the Shareholders and Principals to indemnify the Corporation and each other in event of a breach?
Shareholder Loans	Will there be an obligation of the shareholders to advance funds to the Corporation as shareholder loans if insufficient funds are obtained from a lender? What Interest rate shall be charged?
Deficit Contributions	If there are Deficit Contributions by a shareholder, what will the interest rate be? Deficit Contributions includes any funds owed, from time to time, by a shareholder to the Corporation or to another shareholder. What Interest rate shall be charged?
Payment of Indebtedness to Shareholders	How will repayment of Shareholder Loans work? E.g. Repayment in proportion to the amount outstanding, or retirement of oldest Shareholder Loan first?
Grant of Security Interest by Shareholders	Will shareholders grant the corporation a security interest in their personal property as security for deficit contributions?
Grant of Security Interest by Corporation	Will the Corporation grant security to the shareholders in its personal property regarding repayment of Shareholder Loans?

Issue	Explanation
Guarantees by Subsidiaries of Shareholder Loans	Are subsidiaries of shareholders to guarantee Shareholder Loans?
Grant of Security Interest by Subsidiaries	Will subsidiaries of corporate shareholders grant a security interest in their personal property to the Corporation with regard to indebtedness owed by subsidiaries?
Additional Shares in Corporate Shareholders	Should the agreement restrict corporate shareholders from issuing additional securities in such shareholder, except to its Principal?
Payments and Distributions	Confirm the standard order of payments and distributions from the corporation (i.e. first to pay third-party loans, second to pay Shareholder Loans, third to pay dividends)

Management of Corporation

Directors

Please list directors, their home addresses, and fax numbers, if applicable:

Director Name	Address	Fax Number

Officers

Please list officers, their titles, addresses and fax numbers, if applicable:

Officer Name	Office	Address	Fax Number

Issue	Explanation
Quorum	What number of directors needs to be present to constitute a valid meeting? E.g. a majority or such larger percentage? Does a certain director need to be present for all votes?

Issue	**Explanation**
Auditors/ Accountants	Which Accountants will the corporation use? Will the corporation be exempt from audits?

Approval of Matters

Please indicate below which matters shall require shareholder approval:

☐ Material change in business of the Corporation

☐ the issuance or sale by the Corporation of any of its share capital or any rights, warrants or securities con- vertible into or exercisable or ex- changeable for shares in the capital of the Corporation or any Subsidiary of the Corporation

☐ the winding up, dissolution or liquidation of the Corporation or a Subsidiary

☐ the amalgamation, merger or con- solidation of the Corporation with one or more other corporations

☐ the continuance of the Corporation under the laws of another jurisdiction

☐ the sale, lease, exchange or other disposition of all or substantially all of the property of the Corporation or of any Subsidiary

☐ the borrowing of money by the Corporation

☐ any amendment to the Articles or by-laws of the Corporation and the enact- ment of new by-laws

☐ a statutory arrangement

☐ the declaration of dividends

☐ the payment of any salaries, bonuses, retiring allowances or other remuner- ation for officers, directors, Shareholders and Principals of the Corporation or any Subsidiary or any Associates or Affiliates of such officers, directors, Shareholders or Principals

☐ except pursuant to contracts to which the Corporation is a party at the date hereof, the payment of management or consulting fees or bonuses or the making of a contract between the Corporation and a Shareholder or Principals or any person, firm, corporation or entity not dealing at arm's length with a Shareholder

☐ the increase or decrease in the number of directors

☐ make any loan or advance, give guarantees for, invest in or give security for or guarantee the debts of any other corporation, person or entity

☐ hypothecate, mortgage, pledge or otherwise encumber its assets, or any of them, except as may be required by its bankers in connection with its normal banking activities and arranged lines of credit

☐ the employment or termination of any Person at an annual level of compensa- tion in excess of $[dollar amount]

☐ the giving of shareholder approval, as shareholder of a Subsidiary, in respect of any matter which shareholder approval for a Subsidiary is required

☐ the delegation by the Board, or the board of any Subsidiary, of any of its powers

☐ ____
  ____

☐ ____
  ____

Issue	Explanation
Shareholder Approval	What percentage is necessary for these decisions to be approved (i.e. 50%, 66-2/3% or 75%)?
Telephone Meetings	Can the Board of Directors meet by telephone or other electronic communication?
Shareholder Quorum	What number of shareholders needs to be present to constitute a valid meeting? E.g. a majority or such larger percentage?
Books and Records	Where will books and records be retained (i.e. office address)?
Bank Accounts	With which bank will the corporation open accounts? Who has the right to open bank accounts and who has signing authority? Is there an amount above which more than one director or officer will have to authorize/sign cheques?

Dealing with Shares	
Restrictions	Will the transfers or pledging of shares require approval of the board of directors and/or shareholders?
Issue of Additional Shares (Preemptive Rights)	Will each shareholder have the right to the first opportunity to purchase any new securities (*pro rata*) before new securities can be offered to outsiders or to any particular existing shareholder?
Permitted Transfers	Will non-arm's length transactions or other types of transfers be permitted? If so, who will be the permitted transferees? (E.g. a holding corporation or family trust)
Right of First Refusal	When an offer by a third party to purchase shares from a specific shareholder at a specific price is received, will the other shareholders have the right to purchase these shares, at the specific price, first?
Tag-Along/Piggyback Rights	When an offer by a third party to purchase shares from a specific shareholder or a group of shareholders is received, will the other shareholders have the right to sell their shares at a specific price, too? If so, provide parameters:

Third Party Offer Drag-along	When an offer by a third party to purchase shares from a specific shareholder or group of shareholders is received, will the other shareholders be required to sell their shares at the same price?
Issue	**Explanation**
Buy-Sell or Shotgun Clause	Will the agreement include a buyout provision whereby one shareholder states a price and the other shareholder must then choose between selling his shares at that price or purchasing the first shareholder's shares at the selected price?
Put	Will certain triggering events allow the Corporation or the other shareholders to require the shareholder experiencing the triggering event to sell his shares? If so, which events:
Call	Will certain triggering events allow a shareholder experiencing a triggering event to require the Corporation or the other shareholders to buy his shares? If so, which events:

Events of Default

Defaulting Shareholders

What constitutes an event of default that causes the forced sale of shares? Please select all that apply:

☐ If the representations and warranties of a Shareholder and/or its Principal contained in the Agreement become untrue and incorrect in each and every respect, or if a Shareholder fails to perform or observe any covenant, term or condition of the Agreement

☐ If any Shareholder or its Principal makes an assignment for the benefit of creditors or is the subject of any proceedings under any bankruptcy or insolvency law, or avails itself of the benefit of any other legislation for the benefit of debtors, or if any corporate Shareholder takes steps to wind-up or terminate its corporate existence

☐ If a trustee in bankruptcy, receiver, receiver and manager, liquidator or other officer with similar powers is appointed for a Shareholder or its Principal over all or any material part of its/his/her respective property (and which material part includes part or all of a Shareholder's Securities)

☐ If an encumbrancer takes possession of any Shares beneficially owned by a Shareholder or a Principal, or if a distress or execution or any similar process is levied or enforced upon or against any Shares beneficially owned by a Shareholder or a Principal and remains unsatisfied for the shorter of a period of 2 Business Days or such period as permits the Shares to be sold

☐ If a Shareholder ceases to Control such Shareholder's Securities

☐ If a Shareholder's nominee on the Corporation's board of directors fails on [three (3)] consecutive occasions to attend a meeting of the board of directors for which proper notice is given and a quorum is not present

☐ If a Shareholder fails on [three (3)] consecutive occasions to attend or be represented by proxy at a meeting of the shareholders for which proper notice is given and a quorum is not present

☐ Upon the termination of employment with the Corporation of any Shareholder or its Principal, for any reason (including termination for cause) other than death, Disability, termination with cause or voluntary resignation

☐ If an order is made by a court of competent jurisdiction pursuant to Applicable Family Law Legislation restraining the depletion of a Shareholder's or its Principal's property or for the possession, delivering up, safekeeping or preservation of a Shareholder's or its Principal's property and such property includes any of such Shareholder's or Principal's Securities

☐ If any Shareholder who is an individual or if any Principal becomes Permanently Disabled

☐ If any Shareholder who is an individual or any Principal, dies

☐ ____

☐ ____

Issue	Explanation
Rights on Default	Will the Corporation or other shareholders have rights upon the default of a shareholder, such as the right to bring proceedings, to receive an equitable remedy, (e.g. specific performance) or damages?
Option to Purchase Shares of Defaulting Shareholder	Will the shareholders or the Corporation have the option to purchase the shares of a defaulting shareholder should such purchase be necessary?
Purchase Price for Shares	What will be the purchase price for shares of a defaulting shareholder? E.g. Fair Market Value or less than Fair Market Value?
Suspension of Provisions	Will a Defaulting Shareholder's ability to deal with his shares be suspended?
Remuneration while disabled	Will the corporation provide remuneration to a disabled shareholder? If so, how much, for how long?

Issue	Explanation
Insurance and Purchase on Death and/or Disability	Will the Corporation or shareholders purchase Life and Disability Insurance (term or whole life) for shareholders, to fund buyouts in the event of death or disability of said shareholder? Who is responsible for the payment of premiums? What happens on default in premium payment? How are insurance proceeds to be utilized by the Corporation? Who owns the insurance policy after the shareholder is no longer a party to the agreement? What happens upon incapacity of the insured, or if incapacity lasts beyond two years?

Intellectual Property

Issue	Explanation
Non-Competition	Should agreement contain a requirement that shareholders not compete with the Corporation?
	Time period:
	Geographical restriction:
Non-Solicitation	Should agreement contain a requirement that shareholders not solicit customers, suppliers, or employees of the Corporation to leave the Corporation?
	Time period:
	Geographical restriction:

General Provisions

Issue	Explanation
Arbitration/ Attornment	Are disputes to be settled by: ☐ arbitration with a binding decision; or ☐ by the courts of the Province of Ontario?

Form 22: **Shareholders' Agreement— Two-Party Shareholder Agreement**

CONSIDER WHETHER NOMINEE DIRECTORS SHOULD ALSO EXECUTE TO ACKNOWLEDGE TERMS & AGREE TO BE BOUND IF NOT ALREADY A PARTY

SHAREHOLDERS AGREEMENT

THIS AGREEMENT made this [*day*] day of [*month, year*].

AMONG:

____

____________, of the Province of Ontario; (hereinafter called "**Shrl1**")

- and -

____________, of the Province of Ontario; (hereinafter called "**Shrl2**")

- and -

____________, a corporation incorporated under the laws of the Province of Ontario; (hereinafter called the "**Corporation**")

- and -

____________, of the Province of Ontario (hereinafter called "**Prin1**")

- and -

____________, of the Province of Ontario (hereinafter called "**Prin2**")

WHEREAS the Corporation is incorporated under the laws of the Province of Ontario by Articles of [Incorporation/Amalgamation/Continuance] dated the [day] day of [month, year];

AND WHEREAS the issued and outstanding shares in the capital of the Corporation consists of ____________ [common] shares, issued as follows:

- Shrl1: _____________ [common] shares;
- Shrl2: _____________ [common] shares;

[*AND WHEREAS, Shrl1 is wholly owned by Prin1 and Shrl2 is wholly owned by Prin2;*]

AND WHEREAS Shrl1 and **Shrl2** wish to enter into certain arrangements regarding the organization and affairs of the Corporation and the purchase and sale of their shares in the capital of the Corporation under certain circumstances;

THEREFORE in consideration of the covenants and agreements herein and $1.00 now paid by each party to each of the others (the receipt and sufficiency whereof are hereby acknowledged), the parties agree as follows:

ARTICLE 1: DEFINITIONS AND SCHEDULES

1.1)

The recitals set out above are true, both in substance and in fact.

1.2)

No person, firm or corporation has any agreement, option or right capable of becoming an agreement for the purchase, subscription or issuance of any unissued shares of the Corporation.

1.3)

The Shares owned by each Shareholder are owned by such Shareholder as registered [*OPTIONAL: and beneficial*] owner, free and clear of all liens and encumbrances whatsoever and no person, firm or corporation has any agreement option or right capable of becoming an agreement for the purchase of such Shareholder's Shares.

1.4)

Each Shareholder represents and warrants that such Shareholder is not a **"non-Canadian"** within the meaning of the *Investment Canada Act* (Canada).

1.5)   Definitions

Wherever used in this Agreement, the following terms will have the following meanings respectively, unless the context indicates otherwise:

a)   **"Act"** means the [*Business Corporations Act (Ontario)/Canada Business Corporations Act (Canada)*];

b)   **"Affiliated Corporation"** has the meaning attributed to such term in the Act;

c) **"Business Day"** means every day except Saturdays, Sundays and holidays (as that term is defined in the *Interpretation Act* (Canada)) in Ontario;

d) **"Closing Date"** means the date on which a Shareholder sells his Shares to another Shareholder or the Corporation pursuant to this Agreement;

e) **"Control"** means control in fact, whether direct or indirect. Shares are controlled if the voting rights which attach to those shares are controlled. [*For the purposes of this Agreement, Prin1 Controls Shrl1 and Prin2 Controls Shrl2*];

f) **"Deficit Contribution"** means an amount, including accrued interest thereon, owing by one Shareholder to another Shareholder or the Corporation pursuant to this Agreement;

g) **"Disability"** means such suffering from a state of mental or physical disability, illness or disease (excluding pregnancy) as prevents a [*Shareholder/Principal*] from carrying out his normal duties as a [*full time employee*] of the Corporation, as certified by 2 medical doctors and "Disabled" has a corresponding meaning;

h) **"Disability Date"** means that date on which a [*Shareholder/Principal*] first became Disabled; provided that vacation and if applicable, the maximum maternity leave available to a [*Shareholder/Principal*] guaranteed by law, will not be included in such calculation. Unless and until a Disabled person will have returned to his employment on a [*full time*] basis for 20 consecutive Business Days, the period of Disability will be deemed to have continued without interruption;

i) **"Event of Default"** has the meaning attributed to such term in ARTICLE 12;

j) **"Fair Value"** means:

    i) with respect to participating Shares, the rateable fair market value (with no discount for minority interests) of the applicable Shares agreed to in writing by the Shareholders after consultation with the Corporation's [*accountants/auditors*], or failing such agreement, as determined in accordance with ARTICLE 18. No additional value will be attributed to voting rights that may be attached to any participating Shares; and

    ii) with respect to non-participating Shares (meaning Shares that have a redemption price), the redemption price thereof. No additional value will be attributed to voting rights that may be attached to any non-participating Shares.

    Fair Value will be calculated on a per Share basis, and the Fair Value of a Shareholder's Shares will be such per Share amount multiplied by the number of Shares owned by that Shareholder;

k) **"Personal Corporation"** has the meaning attributed to such term in ARTICLE 7;

l) **"Prime Rate"** means the per annum interest rate announced from time to time by _____________ as being the reference rate then in effect for determining interest rates on Canadian dollar denominated commercial loans made in Canada. The Prime Rate will be compounded and recalculated on the first banking day of each calendar month and the rate so determined will apply throughout such calendar month and both before and after demand, default, judgment and maturity;

m) [*OPTIONAL: "Principal", in the case of Shrl1 means Prin1 and in the case of Shrl2 means Prin2 and Principal's Corporation has a corresponding meaning*];

n) **"Promissory Note"** means a promissory note given and received in accordance with the terms of this Agreement, which will include the following terms and conditions:

   i)   Such promissory note will be fully open as to additional payments of principal at any time or times without notice or bonus; and

   ii) On any default in payment, which default continues for 10 days after receipt of notice thereof, the entire balance then outstanding, together with interest thereon, will be immediately due and payable.

   [*Note throughout this Agreement that if the promissory note is for a term of 5 years or less, the vendor can take a reserve for the amount not yet due. Confirm with a tax lawyer that this has not been changed.*]

o) **"Proportionate Share"** means that percentage of all of the Shares which is from time to time owned by a Shareholder. The Proportionate Share of each Shareholder at the date hereof is:

   - Shrl1: ___________%
   - Shrl2: ___________%

p) **"Share"** means an issued and outstanding share in the capital of the Corporation;

q) **"Shareholder"** means the owner of any Shares;

r) **"Shareholder Guarantee"** means any indemnity or guarantee given by a Shareholder with the consent of the other Shareholder whereby such Shareholder guarantees the payment of any debt or liability of the Corporation or the performance of any obligation of the Corporation;

s) **"Shareholder Loan"** means an outstanding amount loaned or advanced by a Shareholder to the Corporation and accrued interest thereon;

t) **"Special Resolution"** [*has the meaning attributed to such term in the Act / means a resolution approved by Shareholders who hold not less than __________% of the Shares*];

u) **"Third Party Offer"** means a bona fide offer received by a Shareholder from a person who deals at arm's length (within the meaning of the *Income Tax Act* (Canada)) with such Shareholder for the purchase of all the issued and outstanding Shares of the Corporation, or all the Shares owned by such Shareholder, and pursuant to which:

   i)   no property other than such Shares is to be sold, transferred or otherwise disposed of;

   ii) the sole consideration for such Shares is a stated dollar amount payable either at closing or in instalments or both and/or publicly traded securities; provided that if the proposed consideration is publicly traded securities, the other Shareholder will be permitted to pay cash equal to the aggregate fair market value of such securities, which will be deemed to be the last bid price for such securities at the close of business on the Business Day immediately preceding the date of the Third Party Offer;

   iii) the sole security, if any, for the payment of any instalments of the purchase price is a purchase money security interest in the Shares to be purchased; and

   iv) such offer contains no terms or conditions that would constitute a breach of or require an amendment to this Agreement.

   v)   "Transfer" means to sell, assign, surrender, gift, transfer, pledge, mortgage, charge, create a security interest in, hypothecate or otherwise encumber or deal with any of the Shares or any interest, whether legal or beneficial, in the Shares.

1.6) Schedules

The following are the Schedules to this Agreement:

[*Use "A", "B" and "C" only if there is a buy-sell. Use "D" only if there is life insurance.*]

- Schedule "A"—Buy-Sell Offer
- Schedule "B"—Acceptance of Offer to Purchase
- Schedule "C"—Acceptance of Offer to Sell
- Schedule "D"—Annual Valuation of Fair Value and Details of Insurance

ARTICLE 2: PURPOSE AND INTENTION

2.1)

The parties will cause the Corporation to carry on the business of ____________ and to generally carry on all ancillary and related activities which in the opinion of the directors will enhance the Corporation's income and profit.

2.2)

The parties declare that this Agreement is a unanimous shareholders agreement as defined in the Act and the powers of the directors to manage or supervise the management of the business and affairs of the Corporation are restricted accordingly.

ARTICLE 3: ORGANIZATION AND ADMINISTRATION

3.1)   Voting

Each Shareholder agrees to vote, or cause to be voted, all the Shares which such Shareholder beneficially owns or Controls from time to time in order to give effect to the terms of this Agreement. All decisions, approvals, consents and other determinations required to be made or given by the Shareholders under the terms of this Agreement will be made or given exclusively by the Shareholders and will bind the Corporation.

3.2)   Appointment of Directors

The Corporation will at all times have a board of directors composed of ____________ (________) directors. Each Shareholder will have the right to designate ____________ director[s] and the Shareholders will vote their Shares to ensure that each such designee will be and remain a director until otherwise required by this Agreement. [*Prin1 and Prin2 will be the directors. / Each Shareholder may, from time to time, designate a replacement for the director previously designated by such Shareholder and the Shareholders will vote their Shares to ensure that the previous designee is removed as a director and the designated replacement is appointed in his stead, except that Prin1 shall be a nominee of Shrl1 and Prin2 shall be a nominee of Shrl2.*]

[*OPTIONAL: Except as required by law or except as otherwise provided in this Agreement, the powers of the directors will not be delegated to any committee of directors or a managing director.*]

3.3) Meetings of Directors

a) _________ (________) directors will form a quorum for the transaction of business at any meeting of the board of directors.

b) Except as otherwise provided herein, no resolution will be passed at a meeting of the board of directors without the approval of _________ (________) directors. The chairman of a meeting of directors will [OPTIONAL: *not*] have a second or casting vote.

3.4) Officers

The officers of the Corporation will be:

- President: _________
- Secretary: _________

and such additional officers as the board of directors may determine from time to time.

3.5) Meetings of Shareholders

a) A quorum of a meeting of the Shareholders will consist of that number of Shareholders present in person or by proxy representing [*100%*] of the Shares.

b) Except as otherwise provided herein, at all meetings of Shareholders, no resolution will be passed unless it is approved by [*100%*] of the votes cast by the Shareholders. The chairman of a meeting of Shareholders will [OPTIONAL: *not*] have a second or casting vote.

3.6) Books of Account

Proper books of account and records will be kept by the Corporation at its head office and entries will be made therein in accordance with generally accepted accounting principles. Each Shareholder or his nominee will have free access at all times to examine and copy such books of account and records, provided that any confidential information which is obtained will not be disclosed to others or used for any improper purpose. Each Shareholder will at all times, without any concealment or suppression, furnish correct information, accounts and statements to the Shareholders and the Corporation in respect of all transactions pertaining to the Corporation.

3.7) [*Auditors/Accountants/Auditors and Accountants*]

[*The Corporation's auditors will be _________, chartered accountants, or such other auditors as the Shareholders may determine unanimously. The auditors will be instructed to audit the Corporation's books and accounts at each fiscal year end. For such purpose, they will have access to all books, accounts, records, vouchers, cheques, papers and documents which relate to the Corporation, including those of the Shareholders, if necessary.]*

[The Corporation's accountants will be __________ or such other accountants as the Shareholders may determine unanimously. The Shareholders will not appoint an auditor of the Corporation until required by law or until the Shareholders otherwise determine. The accountants will be instructed to prepare annual financial statements of the Corporation. For such purpose, they will have access to all books of account, records and all vouchers, cheques, papers and documents which relate to the Corporation, including those of the Shareholders, if necessary.]

3.8) Shareholder's Audit

A Shareholder may at any time during normal business hours, at his own expense, cause an audit to be made of the Corporation's books and accounts by a chartered accountant appointed by such Shareholder. Such appointee will, for the purpose of performing the audit, have access to all books, accounts, records, vouchers, cheques, papers and documents of or which relate to the Corporation's business and will be entitled to require from the Shareholders, directors, officers and employees of the Corporation, such information and explanations as in his opinion are necessary to enable him to make such an audit. The results of such audit will be disclosed to the Corporation and the Shareholders. If such audit discloses material irregularities in the books and accounts of the Corporation, then the Shareholder who has caused such audit to be performed will be reimbursed by the Corporation for all costs and expenses reasonably incurred by such Shareholder in connection therewith.

3.9) Bank Account

The Corporation will maintain a bank account or accounts with __________ or such other bank or trust company as the directors may determine. All bank accounts of the Corporation will be kept in the name of the Corporation. All monies received for the account of the Corporation will be paid immediately into a bank account of the Corporation in the same drafts, cheques, bills or cash in which they are received.

3.10) Signing Officers—Cheques, etc.

All banking documents, cheques and negotiable instruments entered into by or on behalf of the Corporation will be in writing and for amounts less than $[dollar amount], will require the signature of any [number] of the __________, the __________ and the __________, and for amounts of $[dollar amount] or more, will require the signature of any [*number*] of the __________, the __________ and __________ of the Corporation, unless otherwise agreed by the Shareholders.

3.11) Signing Officers—Contracts and Documents

All deeds, transfers, contracts, agreements and other documents not expressly referred to in Section 3.10 entered into by or on behalf of the Corporation will be in writing and, with respect to the commitment by the Corporation of an aggregate amount of less than $[*dollar amount*] will require the signature of any [*number*] of the __________, the __________ and the __________, and with respect to the commitment by the Corporation of an aggregate amount of $[*dollar amount*] or more, will require the signature of any [*number*] of the __________, the __________ and the __________, unless otherwise agreed by the Shareholders.

3.12) Share Certificates

All share certificates issued or to be issued by the Corporation will be endorsed with a memorandum as follows: This certificate is subject to a Shareholders Agreement and the shares represented by this certificate cannot be sold, transferred, assigned or otherwise disposed of or mortgaged, pledged, hypothecated, charged or otherwise encumbered except pursuant to the terms of the said Shareholders Agreement.

ARTICLE 4: MATTERS REQUIRING APPROVAL OF SHAREHOLDERS

4.1)

The Corporation will not take any of the following actions unless approved in writing by Shareholders holding or representing [_________%] of the Shares:

a) any material change in the business of the Corporation stated in Section 2.1;

b) the issuance or sale by the Corporation of any of its share capital or any rights, warrants or securities convertible into or exercisable or exchangeable for shares in the capital of the Corporation;

c) the acquisition by the Corporation of any of its Shares, except pursuant to the exercise of any redemption rights attached to such Shares or this Agreement;

d) the winding up, dissolution or liquidation of the Corporation;

e) the amalgamation, merger or consolidation of the Corporation with one or more other corporations;

f)   the continuance of the Corporation under the laws of another jurisdiction;

g)   the sale, lease, exchange or other disposition of all or substantially all of the property of the Corporation;

h)   any amendment to the Articles or by-laws of the Corporation and the enactment of new by-laws;

i)   a statutory arrangement;

j)   the declaration of dividends, provided that such declaration will be in accordance with Sections 5.7 and 5.8;

k)   except pursuant to contracts to which the Corporation is a party at the date hereof, the payment of management or consulting fees or bonuses or the making of a contract between the Corporation and a Shareholder or any person, firm, corporation or entity not dealing at arm's length (within the meaning of the *Income Tax Act* (Canada)) with a Shareholder;

l)   the increase or decrease in the number of directors;

m)   make any loan or advance, give guarantees for, invest in or give security for or guarantee the debts of any other corporation, person or entity; and

n)   hypothecate, mortgage, pledge or otherwise encumber its assets, or any of them, except as may be required by its bankers in connection with its normal banking activities and arranged lines of credit.

ARTICLE 5: FINANCING AND DISTRIBUTIONS

5.1)   Funding

The Shareholders agree that they will actively pursue and work towards attaining satisfactory bank credit and financing for the Corporation (the "**Required Funds**"), it being the intention that such financing be sought in the highest amount possible so that a minimum equity investment is required of the Shareholders. If the Shareholders determine that the Corporation is unable to obtain all the Required Funds on commercially reasonable terms:

a)   The Corporation will give [*number of days*] Business Days' notice (the "**Funding Notice**") to all Shareholders stating the estimated amount of the deficiency, the dates on which the Corporation requires additional financing and the amount of funds required on each such date;

b)   On each date set out in the Funding Notice, each Shareholder will contribute his Proportionate Share of the amount stated in the Funding Notice and such contribution will be a Shareholder Loan;

c)   If a Shareholder (the **"Defaulting Shareholder"**) fails to make any contribution required by this Section, the deficiency will be a Deficit Contribution owing by that Shareholder to the Corporation and:

  (i)   The other Shareholder (the **"Contributing Shareholder"**) may contribute all or part of the deficiency on behalf of the Defaulting Shareholder and the amount of such contribution will be included as a Deficit Contribution owing by the Defaulting Shareholder to the Contributing Shareholder and the Deficit Contribution owing by the Defaulting Shareholder to the Corporation will be reduced *pro tanto*; and thereupon

CHOOSE (right to purchase all shares)

  (ii)   The Contributing Shareholder will have the right to acquire the Defaulting Shareholder's Shares for a purchase price of [*percentage*]% of the Fair Value of the Defaulting Shareholder's Shares determined as at the date of the default (the cost of such determination to be borne by the Defaulting Shareholder which may be set off against the purchase price) on the following terms and conditions:

  a) $1.00 will be paid on the Closing Date; and

  b)   The balance of the purchase price, together with interest thereon at the Prime Rate [*OPTIONAL: plus* ___________% *per annum*] will be evidenced by a Promissory Note of the payor and will be repayable in __________ consecutive equal [*monthly*] instalments of principal, plus interest on the principal balance then outstanding. The first instalment will be due and payable __________ month after the Closing Date.

  c)   The Closing Date will be the 20th Business Day after delivery of notice by the Contributing Shareholder to the Defaulting Shareholder and the Corporation that the Contributing Shareholder has paid the amount of the Defaulting Shareholder's Deficit Contribution to the Corporation and that the Contributing Shareholder intends to exercise his right contained in this Section to purchase the Defaulting Shareholder's Shares.

OR CHOOSE (acquire enough shares to eliminate Deficit Contribution)

  (iii)   The Contributing Shareholder will have the right to acquire that number of the Defaulting Shareholder's Shares, the Fair Value of which is equal to the aggregate of the Defaulting Shareholder's Deficit Contribution plus the cost of determining Fair Value. Fair Value will be determined as at the date of the default. The Closing Date will be the 20th Business Day after delivery of notice by the Contributing Shareholder to the Defaulting Shareholder and the Corporation that the Contributing Shareholder has paid the amount of the Defaulting Shareholder's Deficit Contribution to the Corporation and that the Contributing Shareholder intends to exercise his right contained in this Section to purchase Shares of the Defaulting Shareholder. On completion of such purchase and sale, the Defaulting Shareholder's Deficit Contribution owing to the Contributing Shareholder will be reduced pro tanto. ARTICLE 11 and Subsections 19.1(f), (g), (j) and (l) will not apply to such purchase and sale of Shares unless, pursuant to this Section, the Contributing Shareholder acquires all of the Defaulting Shareholder's Shares.

5.2) Guarantees

If a Shareholder (the **"Payor"**) receives notice from anyone demanding the payment of money or the performance of any obligation pursuant to a Shareholder Guarantee:

(a)   The Payor will give [*number*] Business Days' notice to the other Shareholder (i) describing the Shareholder Guarantee and the demand made thereunder, (ii) stating the amount required to be paid pursuant to such demand or the costs incurred (or likely to be incurred) in complying with such demand, and (iii) stating the date or dates on which such amounts will be paid or costs incurred (if not then already paid or incurred);

b)   The other Shareholder (the **"Indemnifier"** in this Section) will pay his Proportionate Share of the amount set out in such notice when and as directed in the notice (subject to the Payor delivering reasonable proof that he has paid such amounts or incurred such costs);

c)   The Indemnifier will make such payment notwithstanding any dispute as to the Payor's obligation to make payment pursuant to the Shareholder Guarantee or the notice received by the Payor under the Shareholder Guarantee; and

d)   If the Indemnifier fails to make all or any part of such payment, the Indemnifier will be deemed to be a Defaulting Shareholder and the Payor will be deemed to be a Contributing Shareholder and have the rights and remedies of a Contributing Shareholder pursuant to Section 5.1, such provisions to apply *mutatis mutandis*.

5.3) Deficit Contributions/Shareholder Loans

Deficit Contributions will bear interest at the greater of Prime Rate [*OPTIONAL: plus* ________*% per annum*] or, if Payor borrows the amount of the Indemnifier's Deficit Contribution, the rate of interest charged to the Payor on the amount so borrowed, and, together with such accrued interest, be payable on demand. Shareholder Loans will bear interest at the Prime Rate [*OPTIONAL: plus* ________*% per annum*] and be payable out of the funds available for such purpose.

5.4) Grant of Security Interest by Shareholders

As security for the repayment of a Shareholder's present and future Deficit Contributions, each Shareholder (the **"Charging Shareholder"** in this Section) grants to the Corporation and the other Shareholder (the **"Secured Party"** in this Section) a mortgage, charge and security interest (a **"Charge"** in this Section) in the following property (the **"Collateral"** in this Section):

a) all Shares now and in the future beneficially owned by the Charging Shareholder;

b) all debts, accounts and monies now and in the future owing to the Charging Shareholder by the Corporation (including, without limitation, declared and unpaid dividends and all Shareholder Loans); and

c) the proceeds of the Collateral.

It is the intention of this Section that each Secured Party will have the rights and remedies of a secured party under the *Personal Property Security Act* (Ontario) in connection with all Deficit Contributions from time to time owing to the Secured Party by the Charging Shareholder. The security interest created pursuant to this Section will attach upon execution of this Agreement. A Charge becomes enforceable if the Charging Shareholder fails to pay any indebtedness secured by that Charge within 15 days following demand for payment or on the occurrence of an Event of Default. Each Charging Shareholder irrevocably directs that, after any Charge becomes enforceable against him, all amounts otherwise payable to him by the Corporation are to be paid in accordance with Section 5.9. Every security interest granted by a Charging Shareholder under this Section will rank *pari passu* and share *pro rata* in the Collateral.

5.5) Power of Attorney

Each Charging Shareholder hereby irrevocably nominates, constitutes and appoints the Secured Party as his true and lawful attorney-in-fact and agent for, in the name of and on behalf of the Charging Shareholder to execute and deliver in the name of the Charging Shareholder all assignments, transfers, deeds or instruments as may be necessary to effectively transfer and assign the Collateral to the Secured Party on a Charge becoming enforceable. Such appointment and power of attorney, being coupled with an interest, will not be revoked by the death, incapacity (whether mental or physical), dissolution, winding up, bankruptcy or insolvency of the Charging Shareholder. The Charging Shareholder hereby ratifies and confirms, and agrees to ratify and confirm, all that a Secured Party may lawfully do or cause to be done by virtue of such appointment and power of attorney.

5.6)   Grant of Security Interest by the Corporation

As security for the repayment of all Shareholder Loans, the Corporation hereby grants to each Shareholder a mortgage, charge and security interest in all of the Corporation's property and assets, both present and future, real and personal, and the proceeds thereof. It is the intention of this Section that each Shareholder will have the rights and remedies of a secured party under the *Personal Property Security Act* (Ontario) in connection with all Shareholder Loans from time to time owing to such Shareholder by the Corporation. The security interest created pursuant to this Section will attach on execution of this Agreement. All Shareholder Loans will become due and payable and the security hereby constituted will become enforceable if the Corporation makes an assignment for the benefit of creditors, a proposal is filed under the *Bankruptcy and Insolvency Act*, the Corporation is declared bankrupt or becomes insolvent or a trustee in bankruptcy, receiver, receiver and manager, liquidator or other officer with similar powers is appointed for the Corporation or all or any material part of its property. Every security interest granted by the Corporation under this Section will rank *pari passu* and share *pro rata* in the property and assets subject to this mortgage, charge and security interest. The security hereby constituted will be subordinate to any security granted by the Corporation in favour of a chartered bank, trust company or other institutional lender and to any security authorized by all of the Shareholders. Each Shareholder agrees to execute such subordination agreements and acknowledgments as are reasonably requested in order to evidence or better give effect to such subordination. The Corporation will execute general security agreements over all its assets and undertakings, both present and future, in favour of each Shareholder at the request of either Shareholder and, notwithstanding the order of registration of such general security agreements, the security granted by the Corporation to the Shareholders will rank *pari passu*.

5.7) Payments and Distributions

All funds from time to time available to the Corporation not otherwise required for its purposes will be paid, applied and distributed as follows:

a) first, to the repayment of interest owing on Shareholder Loans, such payments to be made *pro rata* in accordance with the interest owing to each Shareholder;

b) next, to the repayment of the principal amount of Shareholder Loans, such payments to be made *pro rata* in accordance with the principal amount owing to each Shareholder; and

c) last, the balance, if any, will be distributed to the Shareholders by way of dividends.

No distribution will be made in any of the above categories unless and until the preceding category has been satisfied.

5.8)

Notwithstanding ARTICLE 4 and Section 5.7, in respect of a single payment of funds by the Corporation to the Shareholders, the Shareholders may by Special Resolution declare that the order of priority set out in Section 5.7 will be amended; provided that the effect of such payment in accordance with such Special Resolution will not be detrimental, prejudicial or oppressive to any Shareholder who either does not vote on or votes against such Special Resolution.

5.9)

Notwithstanding any other provision of this Agreement, all amounts payable by the Corporation to a Defaulting Shareholder will be paid to his Contributing Shareholder first, in reduction of accrued interest outstanding on the Defaulting Shareholder's Deficit Contribution owing to such Contributing Shareholder and thereafter to his Contributing Shareholder in reduction of the principal portion outstanding on the Defaulting Shareholder's Deficit Contribution owing to such Contributing Shareholder. Each Defaulting Shareholder hereby irrevocably authorizes and directs the Corporation to pay to the Defaulting Shareholder's Contributing Shareholder all or such portion of any distribution to which such Defaulting Shareholder is entitled pursuant to Sections 5.7 and 5.8 as may be required on account of such Defaulting Shareholder's liability to his Contributing Shareholder.

5.10) Performance of this Agreement by Principal's Corporation [*delete if there are no Principals*]

Each Principal agrees to do everything in his power to ensure that such Principal's Corporation observes and performs all its obligations under this Agreement.

ARTICLE 6: PRE-EMPTIVE RIGHTS

6.1)

No shares in the capital of the Corporation will be issued unless such shares have first been offered to the Shareholders at such price and on such terms as those shares are to be offered to others. Such shares will be offered to each Shareholder as nearly as may be in proportion with each Shareholder's Proportionate Share.

6.2)

Notice of such offer will be sent to each Shareholder specifying:

a)   the series, class, attributes and total number of shares then being offered for allotment and issue;

b)   the issue price for each share;

c)   the number of shares being offered to the Shareholder to whom the notice is addressed;

d)   that the offer, if not accepted within 10 Business Days from the date the notice is given by the Corporation, will be deemed to have been declined;

e)   that a Shareholder who wishes to subscribe for shares which are less than his entitlement shall, in his acceptance, specify the number of shares that he wishes to subscribe for; and

f)   that a Shareholder who wishes to subscribe for shares in excess of his entitlement shall, in his acceptance, specify the number of shares in excess of his entitlement that he wishes to subscribe for.

6.3)

Each Shareholder who chooses to accept the offer shall, within the 10 Business Day period, send an acceptance to the Corporation indicating whether he accepts part or all of the shares offered to him.

6.4)

If a Shareholder fails to subscribe for his full entitlement, the unsubscribed for shares will be used to satisfy the subscription of the other Shareholder for shares in excess of his entitlement, if any. If the subscriptions in excess are for a number of shares greater than the number of unsubscribed shares, the unsubscribed shares will be divided among the Shareholders desiring shares in excess of their entitlement as nearly as may be in proportion to their Proportionate Share (provided that no Shareholder will be bound to take up any shares in excess of the number specified in his acceptance).

6.5)

On expiration of the 10 Business Day period for acceptance or on receipt of notice from a Shareholder that he declines to accept the shares offered to him, with respect to those shares not subscribed for by any other Shareholder pursuant to Section 6.4, the Corporation will have the next 40 Business Days within which it may issue those shares not accepted to any person, firm or corporation. If the Corporation does not issue such shares within that 40 Business Day period, the foregoing pre-emptive right will again apply in respect of the unissued shares.

6.6)

This Article will not apply to shares issued as a share dividend or pursuant to the exercise of conversion privileges, options or rights previously granted by the Corporation.

ARTICLE 7: RESTRICTIONS ON SHARE TRANSFERS

7.1) Prohibition on Unauthorized Transfers

Except as otherwise expressly provided in this Agreement or unless the consent of all Shareholders is first obtained, no Shareholder will Transfer any Shares (by operation of law, contract or otherwise). If a Shareholder is a corporation, a change in Control of such corporate Shareholder will be deemed to be a Transfer by such Shareholder of its Shares and will be prohibited unless the consent of the other Shareholder is first obtained.

7.2) New Shareholders

Each Shareholder (the **"Transferor"** in this Article) agrees that he will not Transfer his Shares to anyone who is not then a Shareholder unless such transferee (and if such transferee is a corporation, such transferee's principal) first executes under seal a counterpart of this Agreement pursuant to which the transferee (and principal, if applicable) agrees to be bound by all the terms, covenants and conditions of this Agreement in the place and stead of the Transferor. On so doing, the transferee will be entitled to the benefit of this Agreement as if he had originally executed this Agreement.

7.3)   Transfers to Personal Corporations

A Shareholder will be entitled to transfer any or all of his Shares to a corporation (the "**Personal Corporation**") Controlled by the Transferor; provided that the Transferor will first have delivered to the Corporation all of the following:

a)   The Transferor's statutory declaration and warranty stating that the Personal Corporation is Controlled by the Transferor;

b)   A certificate of the Secretary of the Personal Corporation setting out the names and addresses of all shareholders of the Personal Corporation together with their respective shareholdings in the Personal Corporation;

c)   A counterpart of this Agreement executed by the Personal Corporation under seal in accordance with Section 7.2; and

d)   An agreement executed by the Transferor under seal in favour of the Corporation and the other Shareholder (the "**Remaining Shareholder**" in this Article) pursuant to which the Transferor:

    i)   agrees to Control the Shares owned by the Personal Corporation for so long as the Personal Corporation owns any Shares; and

    ii)   guarantees the observance and performance of all obligations of the Personal Corporation under this Agreement.

7.4)   Transfers to Affiliated Corporations

A Transferor will be entitled to transfer any or all of his Shares to an Affiliated Corporation (the "**Transferee**" in this Section) provided that the Transferor will first have delivered all of the following to the Corporation:

a)   The Transferor's statutory declaration and warranty stating that the Transferee is an Affiliated Corporation;

b)   A certificate of the secretary of the Transferee setting out the names and addresses of all of its shareholders together with their respective shareholdings;

c)   A counterpart of this Agreement executed by the Transferee under seal in accordance with Section 7.2; and

d)   An agreement executed by the Transferor under seal in favour of the Corporation and the Remaining Shareholder pursuant to which the Transferor:

    i)   agrees to Control the Shares owned by the Transferee for so long as the Transferee owns any Shares; and

ii)   guarantees the observance and performance of all obligations of the Transferee under this Agreement.

ARTICLE 8: RIGHT OF FIRST REFUSAL

8.1)

If a Shareholder (the **"Selling Shareholder"** in this Article) receives a Third Party Offer for the purchase of the Selling Shareholder's Shares (the **"Subject Shares"**) which the Selling Shareholder wishes to accept, then the other Shareholder (the **"Responding Shareholder"**) will have an option to purchase the Subject Shares on the terms and conditions contained in the Third Party Offer and the following terms and conditions will apply:

a)   The Selling Shareholder will give notice within 3 Business Days of his receipt of the Third Party Offer to the Responding Shareholder referring to this Article, accompanied by a true copy of the Third Party Offer;

b)   The Responding Shareholder will be entitled to exercise his option to purchase the Subject Shares by giving notice to the Selling Shareholder on or before 10 Business Days following receipt of the Selling Shareholder's notice pursuant to Subsection (a) above (the **"Final Acceptance Date"**);

c)   The Closing Date will be 10 Business Days following the Final Acceptance Date; and

d)   The terms and conditions contained in the Third Party Offer will be deemed amended so that the amount of any commission, brokerage, finder's or similar fee that would otherwise have been payable to a broker, agent or other intermediary by the Selling Shareholder in connection with the Third Party Offer will be deducted from the Purchase Price payable to the Selling Shareholder.

8.2)

If the Responding Shareholder fails to exercise his option to purchase the Subject Shares, the Selling Shareholder may sell the Subject Shares in accordance with the Third Party Offer, provided that the sale is completed prior to a date not later than 60 Business Days after the Final Acceptance Date.

[OPTIONAL: Piggy back

8.3)

*The Responding Shareholder may elect, as a condition of the sale of the Subject Shares, that the Selling Shareholder sell the Responding Shareholder's Shares (the "**Responding Shares**") on the same terms and conditions as contained in the Third Party Offer. Such election may be exercised only by notice given to the Selling Shareholder on or before the Final Acceptance Date. If the Responding Shareholder requires the sale of the Responding Shares pursuant to this Section, the Selling Shareholder will not be entitled to sell the Subject Shares pursuant to the Third Party Offer unless, contemporaneously with the sale of the Subject Shares, the Responding Shares are also sold on the same terms and conditions contained in the Third Party Offer.]*

ARTICLE 9: THIRD PARTY OFFER FOR ALL SHARES

9.1)

If a Shareholder (the "**Initiating Shareholder**" in this Article) receives a Third Party Offer for the purchase of all the issued and outstanding Shares (the "**Outstanding Shares**") which the Initiating Shareholder wishes to accept, then:

a)   The Initiating Shareholder will give notice within 3 Business Days of his receipt of the Third Party Offer to the other Shareholder (the "**Electing Shareholder**") referring to this Article, accompanied by a true copy of the Third Party Offer;

b)   Within 15 Business Days (the "**Final Acceptance Date**") following receipt of the Initiating Shareholder's notice, the Electing Shareholder will give notice to the Initiating Shareholder electing either to sell his Shares, or to purchase the Initiating Shareholder's Shares, at the price per Share and on the terms and conditions contained in the Third Party Offer;

c)   If the Electing Shareholder fails to make the election required by Subsection (b), he will be deemed to have elected to sell his Shares in accordance with the Third Party Offer;

d)   If the Electing Shareholder elects to purchase Shares, he will purchase and pay for the Initiating Shareholder's Shares at the price per Share and on the terms and conditions contained in the Third Party Offer and the Closing Date of a transaction of purchase and sale between the Initiating Shareholder and the Electing Shareholder will be the 10th Business Day following the Final Acceptance Date. Provided that the terms and conditions contained in the Third Party Offer will be deemed amended so that the amount of any commission, brokerage, finder's or similar fee that would otherwise have been payable to a broker, agent or other intermediary by the Initiating Shareholder in connection with the Third Party Offer will be deducted from the Purchase Price payable to the Selling Shareholder; and

e) If the Electing Shareholder elects or is deemed to have elected to sell his Shares in accordance with the Third Party Offer, the Initiating Shareholder will accept the Third Party Offer on behalf of the Initiating Shareholder and the Electing Shareholder (as attorney for the Electing Shareholder) and all Shareholders will be bound by such Third Party Offer; provided that if the transaction contemplated by the Third Party Offer is not completed within 30 Business Days of the Final Acceptance Date, the Initiating Shareholder will not thereafter sell any Shares unless and until he again complies with the provisions of this Article.

ARTICLE 10: CHOOSE ONE
[*BUY-SELL PROVISIONS*]/[*PUT-CALL PROVISIONS*]

10.1) Buy-Sell Provisions

a) [*OPTIONAL: At any time after* __________,] a Shareholder (the **"Offeror"** in this Section) will be entitled to give notice in the form attached as Schedule A (the **"Buy-Sell Offer"** in this Section) to the other Shareholder (the **"Offeree"** in this Section), pursuant to which the Offeror offers to purchase all the Shares beneficially owned by the Offeree, or to sell to the Offeree all the Shares beneficially owned by the Offeror, for a stated price per Share;

b) The Buy-Sell Offer will be accompanied by:

   i)   A certified cheque by way of deposit payable to the Corporation's solicitors in trust equal to [*percentage*]% of the total purchase price of the Offeree's Shares, computed on the basis of the stated price per Share set out in the Buy-Sell Offer; and

   ii) A statement setting out in reasonable detail full reference to any information relating [*OPTIONAL: directly*] to the financial affairs of the Corporation or its business which, to the best of the knowledge of the Offeror, is not known to the Offeree.

c) On or before the 20th Business Day following receipt of the Buy-Sell Offer, the Offeree must accept the Buy-Sell Offer and elect either to purchase the Offeror's Shares (which acceptance will be in the form attached as Schedule

B), or to sell the Offeree's Shares to the Offeror (which acceptance will be in the form attached as Schedule C), for the price per Share set out in the Buy-Sell Offer. If the Offeree fails to make such acceptance and election, he will be deemed to have agreed to sell his Shares to the Offeror in accordance with the Buy-Sell Offer;

d)   The Closing Date will be the 30th Business Day after the Offeree's receipt of the Buy-Sell Offer.

10.2)   Payment of Purchase Price

The purchase price will be payable as set out in Schedule A.

10.3)   Subsequent Sale [*delete if not applicable*]

If a Shareholder (the "**Purchaser**" in this Section) who purchases Shares pursuant to this Article receives an offer for the purchase of all of his Shares at any time within [*number*] months of the Closing Date and the price per Share payable to the Purchaser pursuant to such offer is greater than the price per Share paid by the Purchaser to the selling Shareholder (the "**Vendor**" in this Section) then, if such transaction subsequently closes, the Purchaser will pay to the Vendor an amount equal to the difference between the price per Share received by the Purchaser and the price per Share received by the Vendor pursuant to this Article, provided that any payment to be made by the Purchaser to the Vendor pursuant to this Section will be made on a proportionate basis as and when the Purchaser receives the purchase price from the third party purchaser. In this Section, the term "**Purchaser**" includes an amalgamated corporation of which the Purchaser is an amalgamating corporation.

OR

10.4)   Put Option

Each Shareholder (a "**Departing Shareholder**" in this Article) is granted the right to require the other Shareholder to purchase from the Departing Shareholder all the Departing Shareholder's Shares on the terms and conditions herein set out. The Departing Shareholder will exercise such right by giving 20 Business Days' notice ("**Notice**" in this Article) to the other Shareholder of the Departing Shareholder's intention to exercise the right hereby granted.

10.5)

The purchase price payable for the Departing Shareholder's Shares pursuant to Section 10.1 will be _______% of the Fair Value of the Departing Shareholder's Shares determined as at the date of the Notice; the costs of such determination to be at the expense of the Departing Shareholder, which may be set off against the purchase price.

OR

10.6) Put to the Corporation

Each Shareholder (a "**Departing Shareholder**" in this Article) is granted the right to require the Corporation to purchase from the Departing Shareholder all the Departing Shareholder's Shares on the terms and conditions herein set out. The Departing Shareholder will exercise such right by giving 20 Business Days' notice ("**Notice**" in this Article) to the Corporation and the other Shareholder of the Departing Shareholder's intention to exercise the right hereby granted. The Corporation's obligation hereby created is conditional on the Corporation meeting any solvency tests under any applicable legislation on the Closing Date.

10.7)

The purchase price payable for the Departing Shareholder's Shares will be _________% of the Fair Value of such Shares determined as at the date of the Notice; the costs of such determination to be at the expense of the Departing Shareholder, which may be set off against the purchase price.

10.8) Call Option

Each Shareholder (a "**Remaining Shareholder**" in this Article) is granted the right to require the other Shareholder to sell to the Remaining Shareholder all the other Shareholder's Shares on the terms and conditions herein set out. The Remaining Shareholder will exercise such right by giving 20 Business Days' Notice to the other Shareholder of the Remaining Shareholder's intention to exercise the right hereby granted.

10.9)

The purchase price payable for the other Shareholder's Shares will be the Fair Value of such Shares determined as at the date of the Notice; the costs of such determination to be at the expense of the Remaining Shareholder.

[*Note—no set off against purchase price*]

10.10) Payment of Purchase Price

The purchase price for any Shares purchased and sold pursuant to this Article will be payable as follows:

CHOOSE [*Cash on closing OR structured payments*]

10.11) Payment of Purchase Price

The purchase price will be payable in full by cash or certified cheque on the Closing Date.

OR

The purchase price for any Shares purchased and sold pursuant to this Article will be payable as follows:

a)   [*percentage%*] of the purchase price payable by each purchaser will be paid by cash or certified cheque on the Closing Date; and

b)   The balance of the purchase price payable by each purchaser, together with interest thereon at the Prime Rate [*OPTIONAL: plus* ___________% *per annum*] will be evidenced by a Promissory Note of such purchaser and will be repayable in ___________ consecutive equal [*monthly*] instalments of principal, plus interest on the principal balance then outstanding. The first instalment will be due and payable [*number*] month after the Closing Date.

10.12) Closing

The Closing Date will be the 20th Business Day after delivery of the Notice.

10.13) Subsequent Sale [*delete if not applicable*]

If a Remaining Shareholder (the **"Purchaser"** in this Section) who purchases Shares pursuant to Section 10.3 receives an offer for the purchase of all of his Shares at any time within [*number*] months of the Closing Date and the price per Share payable to the Purchaser pursuant to such offer is greater than the price per Share paid by the Purchaser to the selling Shareholder (the **"Vendor"**in this Section) then, if such transaction subsequently closes, the Purchaser will pay to the Vendor an amount equal to the difference between the price per Share received by the Purchaser and the price per Share received by the Vendor pursuant to this Article, provided that any payment to be made by the Purchaser to the Vendor pursuant to this Section will be made on a proportionate basis as and when the Purchaser receives the purchase price from the third party purchaser. In this Section, the term **"Purchaser"** includes an amalgamated corporation of which the Purchaser is an amalgamating corporation.

10.14) Contemporaneous Arrangements [*delete if not applicable*]

The Remaining Shareholder will not exercise the call option referred to in Section 10.3 unless arrangements satisfactory to the Shareholders are also made for the contemporaneous withdrawal of the Departing Shareholder as ___________. [*For example, as a partner of a partnership*]

ARTICLE 11: DEFICIT CONTRIBUTIONS AND PURCHASE OF SHAREHOLDER LOANS ON TRANSFER OF SHARES

11.1) Deficit Contributions

Contemporaneous with a purchase and sale of Shares pursuant to this Agreement, all Deficit Contributions will be paid and satisfied on or before the Closing Date as follows:

a)   Deficit Contributions owing by the vendor of Shares to a Shareholder who is not the purchaser of the Shares and/or to the Corporation will be paid by the purchaser of the Shares out of the amount otherwise payable to the vendor on the Closing Date and any deficiency remaining thereafter will be paid by the vendor on the Closing Date. Such payments will be a condition precedent (for such Shareholder's and/or the Corporation's benefit, as the case may be) to the closing of such purchase and sale, which condition may be waived by such Shareholder and/or the Corporation, as the case may be. The vendor irrevocably authorizes and directs the purchaser to make such payment;

b)   Deficit Contributions owing by the vendor to the purchaser will be set off against the purchase price payable on the Closing Date and any deficiency will be paid by the vendor on the Closing Date. The payment of such deficiency will be a condition precedent (for the purchaser's benefit) to the closing of such purchase and sale, which condition may be waived by the purchaser; and

c)   Deficit Contributions owing by the purchaser to the vendor will be paid on the Closing Date. Such payment will be a condition precedent (for the vendor's benefit) to the closing of such purchase and sale, which condition may be waived by the vendor.

11.2) Shareholder Loans

Contemporaneous with a purchase and sale of Shares pursuant to this Agreement, the purchaser will purchase from the vendor all Shareholder Loans owing to the vendor for an amount equal to the outstanding principal amount of such Shareholder Loans, together with accrued interest thereon to the Closing Date, payable as follows:

a)   The balance of any insurance proceeds remaining after utilizing the amount required to complete the purchase of the Deceased's Shares pursuant to ARTICLE 14 will be fully utilized towards the purchase of the vendor's Shareholder Loans;

b)   [*number*]% of the then remaining balance will be paid in cash or certified cheque on the Closing Date;

c)   The balance, together with interest thereon at the Prime Rate [*OPTIONAL: plus* _____% *per annum*] will be evidenced by a Promissory Note of the payor and will be repayable in consecutive equal [*monthly*] instalments of principal, plus interest on the principal balance then outstanding. The first instalment will be due and payable [*number*] month after the Closing Date.

ARTICLE 12: DEFAULT PROVISIONS

12.1)   Events of Default

An "Event of Default" will occur with respect to a Shareholder (the "Defaulting Shareholder"):

a)   If pursuant to the *Bankruptcy and Insolvency Act*, [*a Shareholder/a Principal*] makes an assignment or a proposal, is declared bankrupt or becomes insolvent;

b)   If a corporate Shareholder is wound up, dissolved or liquidated, becomes subject to the provisions of the *Winding Up Act* or has its existence terminated, or has any resolution passed therefor;

c)   If a trustee in bankruptcy, receiver, receiver and manager, liquidator or other officer with similar powers is appointed for [*a Shareholder/a Principal*] or over all or any material part of [*its/his*] property (and which material part includes part or all of the Defaulting Shareholder's Shares);

d)   If an encumbrancer takes possession of any Shares beneficially owned by [*a Shareholder/a Principal*], or if a distress or execution or any similar process is levied or enforced upon or against the Shares beneficially owned by [*a Shareholder/a Principal*] and remains unsatisfied for the shorter of a period of 2 Business Days or such period as permits the Shares to be sold;

e)   If an order is made by a court of competent jurisdiction pursuant to family law legislation restraining the depletion of [*a Shareholder's/a Principal's*] property or for the possession, delivering up, safekeeping or preservation of [*a Shareholder's/a Principal's*] property and such property includes any of such [*Shareholder's/Principal's*] Shares;

f) [*If a Shareholder ceases to Control such Shareholder's Shares/If a Principal ceases to Control such Principal's Corporation*];

g) If a Shareholder's nominee on the Corporation's board of directors fails on [*number*] consecutive occasions to attend a meeting of the board of directors for which proper notice is given and as a result a quorum is not present;

h) If a Shareholder fails on [*number*] consecutive occasions to attend or be represented by proxy at a meeting of the shareholders for which proper notice is given and as a result a quorum is not present; or

i) If a Shareholder fails to perform or observe any other term or condition of this Agreement except ARTICLE 5 and such failure continues for a period of 10 Business Days following notice thereof from the other Shareholder.

12.2) Rights on Default

If an Event of Default occurs, the Shareholder other than the Defaulting Shareholder (the "**Non-Defaulting Shareholder**") will have the right to:

a) do such acts and things and make such payments as are reasonably necessary in order to remedy the Event of Default, and which monies expended in attempting to remedy such Event of Default (including legal fees on a solicitor and his own client basis) will constitute a Deficit Contribution owing by the Defaulting Shareholder to the Non-Defaulting Shareholder;

b) borrow on behalf of the Defaulting Shareholder on such terms and conditions and at such rate of interest as may be agreed on between the Non-Defaulting Shareholder and a lender acting in good faith, an amount equal to the amount required to be advanced by the Defaulting Shareholder to the Corporation to cure the default and to advance such amount to the Corporation on behalf of the Defaulting Shareholder and to charge the Defaulting Shareholder with all reasonable costs and expenses (including legal fees on a solicitor and his own client basis) incurred by the Non-Defaulting Shareholder in connection with the amount borrowed and interest on the amount borrowed and advanced at the same rate as charged by such lender on the amount outstanding from time to time. The Defaulting Shareholder hereby irrevocably nominates, constitutes and appoints the Non-Defaulting Shareholder as his true and lawful attorney-in-fact and agent for, in the name of and on behalf of the Defaulting Shareholder to execute and deliver in the name of the Defaulting Shareholder all documents or instruments as may be necessary in connection with this Subsection. Such appointment and power of attorney, being coupled with an interest, will not be revoked by the death, incapacity (whether mental or physical), dissolution, winding up, bankruptcy or insolvency of the Defaulting Shareholder. The Defaulting Shareholder hereby ratifies and confirms, and agrees to ratify and confirm, all that a Non-Defaulting Shareholder may lawfully do or cause to be done by virtue of such appointment and power of attorney;

c)   purchase the Shares beneficially owned by the Defaulting Shareholder pursuant to Section 12.3; and/or

d)   exercise any other right or remedy available to the Non-Defaulting Shareholder, whether at law, in equity or pursuant to the terms of this Agreement.

12.3)   Option to Purchase Defaulting Shareholder's Shares

[If option is not assigned, Non-Defaulting Shareholder's a.c.b. is changed. Capital gain or loss to Defaulting Shareholder whether or not option is assigned]

Each Shareholder (the **"Defaulting Shareholder"**) hereby grants to the other Shareholder (the **"Non-Defaulting Shareholder"**) an option to purchase all, but not less than all, the Defaulting Shareholder's Shares, which option is exercisable on the happening of an Event of Default that has not been remedied by the Defaulting Shareholder, by sending notice (the **"Purchase Notice"** in this Article) to the Defaulting Shareholder of the Non-Defaulting Shareholder's intention to exercise the right hereby granted, specifying the Event of Default. The following terms and conditions will apply:

a)   The option may be assigned by the Non-Defaulting Shareholder at his sole discretion;

b)   Forthwith after giving the Purchase Notice, the Fair Value of the Defaulting Shareholder's Shares will be determined at the sole cost and expense of the Defaulting Shareholder;

c)   The purchase price will be *[percentage]*% of the Fair Value of such Shares as at the date of receipt of the Purchase Notice;

d)   The Closing Date will be the 10th Business Day following the the date on which the Defaulting Shareholder receives the Purchase Notice.

12.4)   Payment of Purchase Price

The purchase price will be paid as follows:

a)   *[10]*% will be paid in cash or by a certified cheque to the Defaulting Shareholder on the Closing Date; and

b)   The balance of the purchase price, together with interest thereon at the Prime Rate [*OPTIONAL: plus* __________% *per annum*] will be evidenced by a Promissory Note of the payor and will be repayable in __________ consecutive equal [*monthly*] instalments of principal, plus interest on the principal balance then outstanding. The first instalment will be due and payable [*number*] month after the Closing Date.

12.5) Loss of Participation

Upon a Non-Defaulting Shareholder giving the Purchase Notice:

a) The Defaulting Shareholder and his nominee(s) will resign and the Non-Defaulting Shareholder will remove the Defaulting Shareholder and his nominee(s) from the board of directors and as officers of the Corporation, if any, and the vacancies thereby created will be filled as the Non-Defaulting Shareholder sees fit; and

b) The Defaulting Shareholder will and does hereby, irrevocably nominate, constitute and appoint, the Non-Defaulting Shareholder as the Defaulting Shareholder's proxy to vote his Shares as such proxy will see fit after the delivery of the Purchase Notice.

ARTICLE 13: FAMILY LAW

13.1) Option to Purchase

[*If option is assigned, result is capital gain to vendor and adjusted a.c.b. to remaining shareholder. If option is not assigned, result is deemed dividend to vendor.*]

Each Shareholder (the "**Optionor**" in this Article) hereby grants to the Corporation an option (the "**Option**" in this Article) to purchase Shares of the Optionor, which Option will be assignable at the discretion of the other Shareholder to any other person, firm or corporation, which Option is not exercisable unless and until, by an order of a court of competent jurisdiction pursuant to family law legislation:

a) 1 or more of the Optionor's Shares has been acquired by the Optionor's spouse and the Option is then exercisable only in respect of such Shares as are so acquired by such spouse; or

b) the Optionor's Principal's spouse has acquired shares in the capital of that Principal's Personal Corporation or Affiliated Corporation to which attaches more than 50% of the voting rights of such Personal Corporation or Affiliated Corporation, as the case may be, and the Option is then exercisable in respect of all Shares owned by such Personal Corporation or Affiliated Corporation.

13.2)

Each Shareholder agrees to marshall all other resources available to him to satisfy a Spouse's claim under family law legislation to preclude such an order being made.

13.3)

The Option will be exercised by the Corporation or its assignee delivering notice (the "**Notice**" in this Article) to the Optionor specifying the number of Shares to be purchased and the Closing Date, which will be 7 Business Days from the date that Fair Value is determined, but in no event will it be later 40 Business Days following receipt of the Notice.

13.4)   Purchase Price

The purchase price will be the Fair Value of such Shares determined as at the date that the Notice is received. The cost of such determination will be at the sole expense of the Corporation or its assignee, as the case may be.

13.5)   Payment of the Purchase Price

The purchase price will be payable as follows:

a)   [*percentage*]% will be paid by cash or certified cheque on the Closing Date; and

b)   The balance of the purchase price, together with interest thereon at the Prime Rate [*OPTIONAL: plus* __________% *per annum*] will be evidenced by a Promissory Note of the payor and will be repayable in __________ consecutive equal [*monthly*] instalments of principal, plus interest on the principal balance then outstanding. The first instalment will be due and payable [*number*] month after the Closing Date.

ARTICLE 14: DEATH OF [*A SHAREHOLDER/A PRINCIPAL*]

14.1)   Annual Valuation

The Shareholders will determine Fair Value on execution of this Agreement and within 10 Business Days following receipt of [*OPTIONAL: audited*] financial statements for each fiscal year of the Corporation and will record such determination on Schedule D attached or on an original duplicate thereof. If the Shareholders do not determine Fair Value, upon the expiry of such 10 Business Days and within 10 Business Days thereafter, the Corporation's [*auditors/accountants*] will determine Fair Value for life insurance purposes only and ARTICLE 18 will not apply to this Section.

[*Choose one of*:
1.   *Cross insurance;*
2.   *Corporation-owned insurance to purchase shares for cancellation;*
3.   *Corporation-owned insurance paid out of capital dividend account to surviving shareholder*]

14.2)   Obligation to Insure [*Cross Insurance*]

Subject to Section 14.6, **Shrl1** agrees to place and maintain in good standing a policy of term insurance on the life of [*Shrl2 /Prin2*] in the amount of $[*dollar amount*]. **Shrl1** will be the owner and beneficiary of such policy. **Shrl1** agrees to pay all premiums and other charges on the said policy during the term of this Agreement as they become due and on request will provide **Shrl2** with satisfactory proof that the coverage is in good standing.

14.3)

Subject to Section 14.6, **Shrl2** agrees to place and maintain in good standing a policy of term insurance on the life of [*Shrl1/Prin1*] in the amount of $[*dollar amount*]. **Shrl2** will be the owner and beneficiary of such policy. **Shrl2** agrees to pay all premiums and other charges on the said policy during the term of this Agreement as they become due and on request will provide **Shrl1** with satisfactory proof that the coverage is in good standing.

14.4)

The Shareholders agree that without the prior written consent of the other, neither of them will exercise any right of ownership in such policies (except to collect the death benefits provided for therein) or modify or impair any rights or values of such policies.

14.5)

The Shareholders [*OPTIONAL: and the Principals*] will use their best efforts to permit the Shareholders to obtain and maintain such life insurance, including without limitation attending for physical examinations, answering such questions as may be reasonably necessary and executing consents to the placing of such insurance coverage.

14.6)

The Shareholders agree that:

a)   The amounts of the insurance policies referred to in Sections 14.2 and 14.3 will be reviewed and adjusted annually to reflect the Shareholders' or the [*auditors'/accountants'*] annual determination of Fair Value of the respective Shareholder's Shares [*OPTIONAL: plus the amount of all outstanding Shareholder Loans of such Shareholder to the Corporation*];

[*OPTIONAL: (b) The policy premiums will be added together and adjustments made so that ultimately each Shareholder will have paid one-half (1/ 2) of the aggregate premium payments;*] and

b)   On any default in payment of the premium or other charges on the due date thereof, the Shareholder whose [*Principal's*] life is insured under such policy may pay the same on behalf of the other Shareholder for as long as such default continues, which amount will constitute a Deficit Contribution. Such default will be an Event of Default.

14.7)   Death of [*a Shareholder/a Principal*]

On the death of a [*Shareholder/Principal*] (the "**Deceased**"), the [*estate of the Deceased/Deceased's Personal Corporation*] will sell, and the other Shareholder (the "**Survivor**") will purchase, all of the Shares beneficially owned by the [*Deceased/Deceased's Personal Corporation*] as follows:

a)   The purchase price will be the Fair Value of the Shares as at the moment immediately before the death of the Deceased;

b)   The Closing Date will be the 10th Business Day following the latest of (i) if applicable, receipt of necessary governmental releases required to effect a valid transfer of the Deceased's Shares (and the parties agree to use their best efforts to obtain such releases); (ii) determination of the Fair Value; and (iii) receipt of the insurance proceeds on the Deceased's life, but in no event will the Closing Date be later than 40 Business Days after the Deceased's date of death;

c)   The purchase price will be paid and satisfied as follows:

    i)   On the Closing Date, the Survivor will pay by cash or certified cheque an amount equal to the lesser of (A) the insurance proceeds received after first deducting all reasonable costs and expenses incurred in connection with collecting such insurance proceeds; and (B) the purchase price;

    ii)   The balance of the purchase price, together with interest thereon at the Prime Rate [*OPTIONAL: plus ___________% per annum*] will be evidenced by a Promissory Note of the payor and will be repayable in ___________ consecutive equal [*monthly*] instalments of principal, plus interest on the principal balance then outstanding. The first instalment will be due and payable [*number*] month after the Closing Date.

14.8) Personal Corporations and Affiliated Corporations

If a Shareholder will have disposed of his Shares to a Personal Corporation or an Affiliated Corporation, the Personal Corporation or Affiliated Corporation, as the case may be, will be obligated to sell and the Survivor will purchase the Shares owned by the Personal Corporation or the Affiliated Corporation on the death of such [*Shareholder/Shareholder's Principal*] in accordance with this Article as though such Personal Corporation or Affiliated Corporation were the personal representatives of such [*Shareholder/Shareholder's Principal*].

14.9) Obligation to Insure

[*Corporation owned insurance to purchase Shares for cancellation. Result is deemed dividend to vendor and no change in survivor's a.c.b.*]

a) Subject to Section 14.5, the Corporation will insure the life of [*Shrl1 /Prin1*] in the amount of $________ and the life of [*Shrl2/Prin2*] in the amount of $________.

b) The Corporation will be the owner and beneficiary of each policy and will, at all times, keep such insurance policies in good standing and pay all premiums and other charges when the same become due and payable. Details of each policy will be recorded in Schedule D attached or an original duplicate thereof and initialled by each Shareholder for identification.

14.10)

The Corporation will not exercise any right of ownership in such policies (except to collect the death benefits provided for therein) or modify or impair any rights or values of such policies, except in accordance with Section 14.5.

14.11)

The Shareholders [*OPTIONAL: and the Principals*] will use their best efforts to permit the Corporation to obtain and maintain such life insurance, including but not limited to attending for physical examinations, answering such questions as may be reasonably necessary and executing consents to the placing of such insurance coverage.

14.12)

The amounts of the policies will be reviewed and adjusted annually to reflect the Shareholders' or the [*auditors'/accountants'*] annual determination of Fair

Value of the respective Shareholder's Shares [*OPTIONAL: plus the amount of all outstanding Shareholder Loans of such Shareholder*].

14.13)

On any default in payment of the premium or other charges on the due date thereof, the Shareholder whose [*Principal's*] life is insured under such policy may pay the same on behalf of the Corporation for as long as such default continues, which amount will constitute a Shareholder Loan by such Shareholder.

14.14) Death of [*a Shareholder/a Principal*]

On the death of a [*Shareholder/Principal*] (the "**Deceased**"), the [*estate of the Deceased/Deceased's Personal Corporation*] will sell, and the Corporation will purchase for cancellation, all Shares beneficially owned by the [*Deceased/ Deceased's Personal Corporation*] as follows:

a) The purchase price will be the Fair Value of the Shares as at the moment immediately before the death of the Deceased;

b) The Closing Date will be the latest of the 10th Business Day following (i) if applicable, receipt of necessary governmental releases required to effect a valid transfer of the Deceased's Shares (and the parties agree to use their best efforts to obtain such releases); (ii) determination of Fair Value; and iii) receipt of the insurance proceeds on the life of the Deceased, but in no event will the Closing Date be later than 40 Business Days after the Deceased's date of death;

c) The purchase price will be paid and satisfied as follows:

  i) On the Closing Date, the Corporation will pay by cash or certified cheque an amount equal to the lesser of (A) the insurance proceeds received after first deducting all reasonable costs and expenses incurred in con-nection with collecting such insurance proceeds; and (B) the purchase price;

  (ii) The balance of the purchase price, together with interest thereon at the Prime Rate [*OPTIONAL: plus* _________*% per annum*] will be evidenced by a Promissory Note of the payor and will be repayable in __________ consecutive equal [*monthly*] instalments of principal, plus interest on the principal balance then outstanding. The first instalment will be due and payable [*number*] month after the Closing Date.

14.15) Personal Corporations and Affiliated Corporations

If a Shareholder will have disposed of his Shares to a Personal Corporation or an Affiliated Corporation, the Personal Corporation or Affiliated Corporation, as the case may be, will be obligated to sell and the Corporation will purchase the Shares owned by the Personal Corporation or the Affiliated Corporation on the death of such [*Shareholder/Shareholder's Principal*] in accordance with this Article as though such Personal Corporation or Affiliated Corporation were the personal representatives of such [*Shareholder/Shareholder's Principal*].

14.16) Obligation to Insure [*Corporation owned insurance for Survivor to purchase Shares out of capital dividend account. Result is capital gain to Estate and tax free capital dividend to Survivor.*]

a)   Subject to Section 14.5, the Corporation will insure the life of [*Shrl1/ Prin1*] in the amount of $[*dollar amount*] and the life of [*Shrl2/Prin2*] in the amount of $[*dollar amount*].

b)   The Corporation will be the owner and beneficiary of each policy and will, at all times, keep such policies in good standing and pay all premiums and other charges when the same become due and payable. Details of each policy will be recorded in Schedule D or an original duplicate thereof and initialled by each Shareholder for identification.

14.17)

The Corporation will not exercise any right of ownership in such policies (except to collect the death benefits provided for therein) or modify or impair any rights or values of such policies except in accordance with Section 14.5.

14.18)

The [*Shareholders/Principals*] will use their best efforts to permit the Corporation to obtain and maintain such life insurance, including without limitation attending for physical examinations, answering such questions as may be reasonably necessary and executing consents to the placing of such insurance coverage.

14.19)

The amounts of the insurance policies will be reviewed and adjusted annually to reflect the Shareholders' or [*auditors'/accountants'*] annual determination of Fair Value of the respective Shareholder's Shares [*OPTIONAL: plus the amount of all outstanding Shareholder Loans of such Shareholder*].

14.20)

On any default in payment of the premium or other charges on the due date thereof, the Shareholder whose [*Principal's*] life is insured under such policy may pay the same on behalf of the Corporation for as long as such default continues, which amount will constitute a Shareholder Loan by such Shareholder.

14.21) Death of [*a Shareholder/a Principal*]

On the death of a [*Shareholder/Principal*] (the "**Deceased**"), the [*estate of the Deceased/the Deceased's Personal Corporation*] will sell, and the other Shareholder (the "**Survivor**") will purchase, all Shares beneficially owned by the [*Deceased/Deceased's Personal Corporation*] as follows:

a)   The purchase price will be the Fair Value of such Shares as at the moment immediately before the death of the Deceased;

b)   The Closing Date will be the latest of the 10th Business Day following (i) if applicable, receipt of necessary governmental releases required to effect a valid transfer of the Deceased's Shares (and the parties agree to use their best efforts to obtain such releases); (ii) determination of Fair Value; and iii) receipt of the insurance proceeds on the life of the Deceased, but in no event will the Closing Date be later than 40 Business Days after the Deceased's date of death;

(c)   The purchase price will be paid and satisfied on the Closing Date as follows:

  i)   A Promissory Note ("**Note No. 1**") of the Survivor due on demand in an amount, together with interest thereon at the Prime Rate [*OPTIONAL: plus __________per cent (__________%) per annum*] equal to the lesser of (A) the insurance proceeds received by the Corporation after first deducting all reasonable costs and expenses incurred in connection with collecting such proceeds; and (B) the purchase price;

  ii)   A Promissory Note ("**Note No. 2**") of the Survivor (and/or the Corporation in accordance with Section 14.8) in an amount equal to the balance of the purchase price, if any, together with interest thereon at the Prime Rate [*OPTIONAL: plus __________% per annum*] repayable in __________ consecutive [*monthly*] instalments of principal, plus interest on the principal balance then outstanding. The first instalment will be due and payable [*number*] month after the Closing Date.

14.22)

If the amount of Note No. 1 is insufficient to purchase all Shares beneficially owned by the [*Deceased/Deceased's Personal Corporation*], that number of Shares not purchaseable by means of Note No. 1 may, at the sole option of the Survivor, be purchased for cancellation by the Corporation.

14.23) Capital Dividend Account

The purchase price payable by the Survivor will, to the greatest extent possible, be payable out of the Corporation's capital dividend account immediately on completion of his purchase of the [*Deceased's/Deceased's Personal Corporation's*] Shares in accordance with this Article and the Survivor hereby irrevocably authorizes and directs the Corporation to pay such capital dividend to the [*Deceased's Estate/Deceased's Personal Corporation*] to the extent required to satisfy repayment of Note No. 1. The Corporation will take all corporate actions and effect all prescribed elections and filings as may be required to give effect to the provisions of this Section.

14.24) Personal Corporations and Affiliated Corporations

If a Shareholder will have disposed of his Shares to a Personal Corporation or an Affiliated Corporation, the Personal Corporation or Affiliated Corporation, as the case may be, will be obligated to sell and the Survivor and/or the Corporation, as the case may be, will purchase the Shares owned by the Personal Corporation or the Affiliated Corporation on the death of such [*Shareholder/Shareholder's Principal*] in accordance with this Article as though such Personal Corporation or Affiliated Corporation were the personal representatives of such [*Shareholder/ Shareholder's Principal*].

ARTICLE 15: DISABILITY OF [*A SHAREHOLDER/A PRINCIPAL*]

15.1)   Payment of Remuneration on Disability

On Disability of a [*Shareholder/Principal*] who is [*a full time employee*] of the Corporation (the "**Disabled Party**"), the Disabled Party will nonetheless be entitled to receive his normal remuneration as an employee [*OPTIONAL: including directors fee, if any*] [*OPTIONAL: excluding bonuses and commissions*] for __________ months following the Disability Date. If the Disabled Party remains Disabled for an additional __________ months or any part thereof, he will be paid [*one-half*] of such [*remuneration*] for such period of time. If the Disabled Party remains unable to fulfil his duties as a [*full time employee*] of the Corporation for any time beyond the __________ month period commencing on the Disability Date, he will receive no remuneration from the Corporation in his capacity as [*an employee*] of the Corporation. It is expressly agreed that the Corporation will be responsible for only the amount of remuneration not otherwise received by the Disabled Party pursuant to any disability insurance policy, Worker's Compensation benefits or from any other third party.

[CHOOSE mandatory sale or option to purchase]

15.2)   Mandatory Sale

On that date (the "**Purchase Date**" in this Section) that is [number] months and 1 day after a Disabled Party's Disability Date, the Disabled Party will sell and the other Shareholder (the "**Purchaser**" in this Section), will purchase all (but not less than all) the Shares then owned (legally or beneficially) by the Disabled Party (including Shares owned by his Personal Corporation or Affiliated Corporation) on the following terms:

a)   The purchase price will be the Fair Value on the Purchase Date;

b)   The Closing Date will be the 10th Business Day following the Purchase Date;

c)   *[percentage]*% of the purchase price will be paid in cash or by certified cheque on the Closing Date; and

d)   The balance of the purchase price, together with interest thereon at the Prime Rate [*OPTIONAL: plus* __________*% per annum*] will be evidenced by a Promissory Note of the payor and will be repayable in __________ consecutive equal [*monthly*] instalments of principal, plus interest on the principal balance then outstanding. The first instalment will be due and payable [*number*] month after the Closing Date.

15.3)   Option to Purchase

Each Shareholder (the "**Remaining Shareholder**" in this Section) is granted the right to purchase from the Disabled Party all (but not less than all) Shares then owned (legally or beneficially) by the Disabled Party (including Shares owned by his Personal Corporation or Affiliated Corporation). The Remaining Shareholder will exercise such right by sending notice (the "**Purchase Notice**") at any time after [*number*] months after the Disabled Party's Disability Date and before the Disabled Party has recommenced his [*full time employment*]. The purchase will be completed on the following terms and conditions:

a)   The purchase price will be the Fair Value on the date of the Purchase Notice;

b)   The Closing Date will be the 10th Business Day following the Disabled Party's receipt of the Purchase Notice;

c)   *[percentage]*% of the purchase price will be paid in cash or by certified cheque on the Closing Date; and

d)   The balance of the purchase price, together with interest thereon at the Prime Rate [*OPTIONAL: plus* __________*% per annum*] will be evidenced by a Promissory Note of the payor and will be repayable in __________ consecutive equal [*monthly*] instalments of principal, plus interest on the principal balance then outstanding. The first instalment will be due and payable [*number*] month after the Closing Date.

ARTICLE 16: TERMINATION OF EMPLOYMENT

[*Choose Deemed Offer to Sell or Option to Purchase*]

16.1) Deemed Offer to Sell

If the full time employment of a [*Shareholder/Principal*] (the "**Employee**" in this Article) with the Corporation is terminated for any reason (excluding death or Disability), on the happening of such event (the "**Termination Date**") the Employee (or his Personal Corporation or Affiliated Corporation, as the case may be) will be deemed to have offered his Shares for sale to the [*Corporation/ other Shareholder (the "Remaining Shareholder")*] and the [*Corporation/Remaining Shareholder*] will purchase all (but not less than all) the Employee's Shares on the following terms and conditions:

a)   The purchase price will be [*percentage*]% of the Fair Value on the Termination Date;

b)   If the Employee terminated his employment, he or his Personal Corporation or Affiliated Corporation, as the case may be, will be responsible for all reasonable costs associated with the determination of the Fair Value and such amount may be set-off against the purchase price payable by the [*Corporation/Remaining Shareholder*];

c)   The Closing Date will be the 30th Business Day following the Termination Date;

d)   The purchase price will be paid and satisfied as follows:

 i)   [*percentage*]% will be paid on the Closing Date;

 ii)   The balance of the purchase price, together with interest thereon at the Prime Rate [*OPTIONAL: plus _________% per annum*] will be evidenced by a Promissory Note of the payor and will be repayable in _________ consecutive equal [*monthly*] instalments of principal, plus interest on the principal balance then outstanding. The first instalment will be due and payable [*number*] month after the Closing Date.

16.2) Option to Purchase

If the full time employment of a [*Shareholder/Principal*] (the "**Employee**" in this Article) with the Corporation is terminated for any reason (excluding death or Disability), on the happening of such event (the "**Termination Date**") the

[*Corporation/other Shareholder (the "Remaining Shareholder")*] will have an option to purchase [*all* [*OPTIONAL: but not less than all*]/*any part (at the discretion of the Remaining Shareholder)*] of the Employee's Shares (including the Shares of his Personal Corporation or Affiliated Corporation, as the case may be) (collectively, the **"Employee's Shares"**), exercisable by notice within [*number of days*] Business Days of the Termination Date on the following terms and conditions:

a)   The purchase price will be [*percentage*]% of the Fair Value of the Employee's Shares on the Termination Date;

b)   If the Employee terminated his employment, he or his Personal Corporation or Affiliated Corporation, as the case may be, will be responsible for all reasonable costs associated with the determination of the Fair Value and such amount may be set-off against the purchase price payable by the [*Corporation/Remaining Shareholder*];

c)   The Closing Date will be the 30th Business Day following the date on which such notice was received by the Employee;

d)   The purchase price will be paid and satisfied as follows:

   i)   [*percentage*] % will be paid on the Closing Date;

   ii)   The balance of the purchase price, together with interest thereon at the Prime Rate [*OPTIONAL: plus* __________% *per annum*] will be evidenced by a Promissory Note of the payor and will be repayable in __________ consecutive equal [*monthly*] instalments of principal, plus interest on the principal balance then outstanding. The first instalment will be due and payable [*number*] month after the Closing Date.

ARTICLE 17: RESTRICTION ON INITIATION
OF SALE/PURCHASE PROVISIONS

17.1)

If any purchase or sale provision of this Agreement has been initiated, no other purchase or sale provision will be initiated under this Agreement until such time as the purchase or sale provision first initiated has ceased to be effective, provided that if the purchase and sale provision first initiated is not completed, the necessary extension of time will be made to all other purchase and sale provisions herein and all other rights of the parties will be so preserved.

ARTICLE 18: FAIR VALUE

18.1)   Failure to Reach Agreement

If the Shareholders fail to reach written agreement as to the Fair Value within 10 Business Days following request given by either of them, the Shareholders will jointly appoint a business valuator (the "**Valuator**") to act as arbitrator and determine Fair Value within 20 Business Days following his appointment.

18.2)   Failure to Jointly Appoint a Valuator

If the Shareholders fail to jointly appoint a Valuator on or before the 10th Business Day following request by a Shareholder for a determination of Fair Value, any Shareholder may apply to a court of law pursuant to the *Arbitrations Act* (Ontario) for the appointment of a Valuator and the decision of such court will be final and binding on the parties.

18.3)   Valuator's Determination Binding

The Valuator's determination of Fair Value will be final and binding on the parties and there will be no right of appeal therefrom.

18.4)   Valuator's Fees and Disbursements

Unless otherwise expressly herein to the contrary, all fees and disbursements charged by the Valuator will be determined and paid in accordance with the *Arbitrations Act* (Ontario).

18.5)   Access to Books and Records

The Valuator will have access to the books, accounts, records, vouchers, cheques, papers and documents of, or which may relate to, the Corporation. The Shareholders will cooperate with the Valuator and provide all information and documents reasonably requested by the Valuator.

ARTICLE 19: CLOSING

19.1)   Closing

Whenever Shares are sold by a Shareholder (the "**Vendor**" in this Article) and purchased by a Shareholder or the Corporation, as the case may be (the "Purchaser" in this Article), the terms and conditions of this Article will apply. Closing will be held at the Corporation's head office at 10:00 o'clock in the morning (local time) on the date stipulated in this Agreement as being the Closing Date and, unless otherwise expressly provided herein to the contrary, the following terms and conditions will apply:

a)   If Fair Value is to be determined, the Closing Date will be [*number of days*] Business Days following such determination, but in any event, not be later than [*number of days*] Business Days after an agreement has been reached for the sale or transfer of Shares or any option to acquire Shares has been exercised. The parties agree to proceed expeditiously towards determining Fair Value so as to permit the closing to be completed in accordance with this Agreement.

b)   At closing, the Vendor will deliver certificates representing the Shares being sold duly endorsed for transfer to the Purchaser.

c)   At closing, the Vendor will deliver to the Purchaser good title to the Shares being sold, free from all mortgages, charges, security interests, claims, encumbrances and restrictions whatsoever (except restrictions created under this Agreement). If, at closing, the Vendor's Shares are subject to any mortgage, charge, security interest, claim, encumbrance or restriction, the Purchaser will be entitled to do such acts and things and make such payments as seem necessary to the Purchaser in order to discharge such mortgage, charge, security interest, claim, encumbrance or restriction and the Purchaser may deduct from the purchase price for the Shares for all costs, outlays and expenses made or incurred in so doing.

d)   So long as any part of the purchase price remains unpaid (unless the purchase is made pursuant to Article 12), the Purchaser will execute and deliver a pledge of the Shares so purchased in favour of the Vendor in form and substance acceptable to the Purchaser's counsel, acting reasonably. Such pledge agreement will provide that the Purchaser may exercise all voting rights attached to the Shares so purchased so long as the Purchaser is not in default thereunder.

e)   If the Purchaser is a Personal Corporation or an Affiliated Corporation of a Principal, such Principal will execute and deliver at closing his personal guarantee of payment of the unpaid purchase price in form and substance acceptable to the Purchaser's counsel, acting reasonably.

f)   If the Vendor is bound by a Shareholder Guarantee, the Purchaser will use all reasonable efforts to cause such Shareholder Guarantee to be delivered up and cancelled at the closing, failing which the Purchaser [*OPTIONAL: and its Principal*] will agree to indemnify and save the Vendor harmless from all claims, costs, demands and actions suffered or incurred by the Vendor after the Closing Date as a result of such Shareholder Guarantee.

OR CHOOSE

g) If the Vendor is bound by a Shareholder Guarantee in favour of the Corporation's bank, the Purchaser will cause such Shareholder Guarantee to be delivered up and cancelled at the closing, failing which the Vendor may, at his option, extend the Closing Date to such date as such Shareholder Guarantee is delivered up and cancelled or accept the Purchaser's [*OPTIONAL: and its Principal's*] agreement to indemnify and save the Vendor harmless from all claims, costs, demands and actions suffered or incurred by the Vendor after the Closing Date as a result of such Shareholder Guarantee. If the Vendor is bound by any Shareholder Guarantees not in favour of the Corporation's bank, the Purchaser will use all reasonable efforts to cause such Shareholder Guarantees to be delivered up and cancelled at the closing, failing which the Purchaser [*OPTIONAL: and its Principal*] will agree to indemnify and save the Vendor harmless from all claims, costs, demands and actions suffered or incurred by the Vendor after the Closing Date as a result of such Shareholder Guarantees.

h) The Vendor will be entitled to purchase the policy on [*his/its Principal's*] life owned by the [*other Shareholder/the Corporation*] on payment of the greater of $[*dollar amount*] or the cash surrender value of such policy at the Closing Date.

i) If the purchase is made pursuant to Article 14, the life insurance policy on the life of the [*Remaining Shareholder/surviving Principal*] will be transferred and assigned to the Remaining Shareholder or as he may direct on payment of the greater of $[*dollar amount*] or the cash surrender value of such policy on the Closing Date.

j) All direct taxes arising out the sale of the Shares will be paid by the Vendor and may be deducted from the purchase price by the Purchaser, provided that the Purchaser promptly remits such amount to the appropriate taxing authority.

k) The Vendor will receive from the Purchaser (and the Corporation if the Corporation is not the Purchaser) a release of any and all claims which the Purchaser and the Corporation may have against the Vendor relating to the Corporation, and the Vendor will deliver to the Purchaser (and the Corporation if the Corporation is not the Purchaser) a release of any and all claims which the Vendor may have against the Purchaser (and the Corporation if the Corporation is not the Purchaser), relating to the Corporation, save and except for:

i)   any claims arising out of a portion of the purchase price remaining unpaid;

ii)   the terms, provisions, representations, warranties and covenants of any purchase and sale documentation relating to the Shares;

iii)   any guarantees or obligations for which a release was not obtained pursuant to Paragraph 19.1(f); and

iv)   the provisions of Article 20.

l)   The Corporation's costs and expenses (excluding the Valuator's fee and disbursements incurred to determine Fair Value of the Shares) relating to the sale of the Shares will be paid equally by the Vendor and Purchaser.

m)   The Vendor and his nominees will resign from the board of directors and from any office or employment with the Corporation.

n)   At closing, the Vendor will execute and deliver to the Purchaser and the Corporation if the Corporation is not the Purchaser, all notices, documents and other materials reasonably necessary to complete the transaction.

o)   At closing, the Vendor will execute and deliver to the Purchaser a statutory declaration if the Vendor is an individual (or a certificate of an officer of the Vendor, if the Vendor is a corporation) stating that on the Closing Date:

i)   the Vendor is not a "non-resident" within the meaning of the *Income Tax Act* (Canada) and will supply satisfactory evidence to the Purchaser of such, or in the alternative with evidence of compliance with Section 116 of such Act;

ii)   the Shares to be purchased are free and clear of all liens, pledges, demands and encumbrances whatsoever; and

iii)   no person, firm or corporation has or will have any agreement, option or any right capable of becoming an agreement or option for the purchase from the Vendor of any of his Shares.

p)   If the Corporation is required to complete any transaction of purchase and sale contemplated in this Agreement and on the Closing Date, such purchase would render the Corporation insolvent, at the option of the other Shareholder, such other Shareholder may purchase the Vendor's Shares in the place and stead of the Corporation.

19.2)   Refusal to Close

If the Vendor is obligated to sell Shares to another Shareholder or the Corporation pursuant to this Agreement and the Vendor fails to complete the transaction of purchase and sale, the amount which the Purchaser would otherwise be required to pay to the Vendor at closing may be deposited by the Purchaser into a trust account in the name of the Vendor at the bank branch used by the

Corporation. On making such deposit and giving the Vendor notice thereof, the purchase of the Vendor's Shares by the Purchaser will be deemed to have been fully completed and all right, title, benefit and interest, both at law and in equity, in and to the Shares to which the Purchaser is entitled, will be conclusively deemed to have been transferred and assigned to and vested in the Purchaser. The Vendor will be entitled to receive the amount deposited in the trust account on satisfying the Vendor's obligations pursuant to this Article.

19.3) Power of Attorney

In connection with the sale of Shares pursuant to this Agreement, the Vendor hereby irrevocably nominates, constitutes and appoints the Purchaser as his true and lawful attorney-infact and agent for, in the name of and on behalf of the Vendor to execute and deliver in the name of the Vendor all such assignments, transfers, deeds or instruments as may be necessary to effectively transfer and assign the Shares being sold to the Purchaser. Such appointment and power of attorney, being coupled with an interest, will not be revoked by the death, incapacity (whether mental or physical), dissolution, winding up, bankruptcy or insolvency of the Vendor. The Vendor hereby ratifies and confirms, and agrees to ratify and confirm, all that a Purchaser may lawfully do or cause to be done by virtue of such appointment and power of attorney.

19.4) Restrictions While Purchase Price Remains Unpaid

Until the balance of the purchase price owing by a Purchaser to a Vendor is paid and satisfied in full and unless proceeds derived from the following are used to repay the indebtedness of the Purchaser to the Vendor, the Purchaser and the Corporation will not:

a)   take any steps or do any act provided in Section 4.1 (excluding Subsections 4.01(h), (i) and (k));

b)   declare any dividends;

c)   Transfer (as such term is defined in this Agreement) any Shares except the transfer of Shares by a Shareholder to a Personal Corporation or an Affiliated Corporation of a Shareholder on the terms and conditions of this Agreement;

d)   repay the principal amount of or interest on any Shareholder Loan;

e)   except for increases to compensate for reasonable cost of living, increase the salary or other remuneration payable to [*the remaining Shareholder/its Principal*] or to officers or directors of the Corporation not dealing at arm's length (within the meaning of the *Income Tax Act* (Canada)) with the remaining Shareholder or any other person or persons not dealing at arm's length (within the meaning of the *Income Tax Act* (Canada)) with the remaining Shareholder, other than bona fide full time active employees of the Corporation except the remaining Shareholder [*OPTIONAL: and its Principal*], nor will the Corporation increase in any amount the benefits and compensation of any director, officer or Shareholder of the Corporation by means of any directors' fees, new bonus or pension plan and/or new contract or commitment;

f)   carry on the business of the Corporation, other than diligently and substantially in the same manner as prior to such sale;

g)   make any commitment for capital expenditures, other than in the ordinary course of business;

h)   amend the Articles or by-laws of the Corporation or enact new by-laws, if such amendment or enactment has a material effect on the sold Shares;

i)   fail to keep insured all property, real and personal, owned, leased or used by the Corporation as it was insured prior to such sale against all risks of loss or fail to use, operate, maintain and repair such property as it was used prior to such sale; or

j)   fail to provide the Vendor with annual financial statements of the Corporation within 180 days of the Corporation's fiscal year end.

19.5)   Rights on Default

On default of any provision of Section 19.4, the Vendor will have the right to require the rectification thereof and if such default is not rectified within 10 Business Days of a request for rectification, the full unpaid balance of the purchase price, together with interest thereon, will be due and payable immediately.

19.6)   Survival

The provisions of this Article will survive termination of this Agreement notwithstanding anything in this Agreement to the contrary.

ARTICLE 20: NON-COMPETITION, NON-SOLICITATION, CONFIDENTIALITY AND INVENTIONS

20.1)   Non-Competition and Non-Solicitation

For so long as:

a)   a Shareholder is a Shareholder and for ____________ years after such Shareholder ceases to be a Shareholder;

b) a Principal is a Principal of a Shareholder and for ___________ years after the later of that Principal ceasing to be a shareholder of that Shareholder or that Shareholder ceasing to be a Shareholder;

c) a Shareholder is a [*full time employee/director*] of the Corporation and for ___________ years thereafter;

d) a Principal is a [*full time employee/director*] of the Corporation and for ___________ years thereafter, that [*Shareholder/Principal*] will not (except with the prior written consent of the Corporation, which consent may be unreasonably withheld):

e) directly or indirectly, solicit for employment, or advise or recommend to any other person, firm, corporation or entity that they employ or solicit for employment any person employed by the Corporation;

f) directly or indirectly, engage, send any work to, place orders with or in any manner be associated with any contractor, subcontractor or other person, firm, corporation or entity which rendered or renders any services to the Corporation, if such action would have a material adverse effect on the business activity, assets or financial condition of the Corporation or its subsidiaries;

g) directly or indirectly, within [*geographic area*], engage in any activity in competition with, perform services for or become interested in, whether as an individual, manager, consultant, independent contractor, employee, employer, partner, syndicate member, officer, director, advisor, principal, agent, trustee, lender of money, shareholder (except as a shareholder of a public corporation holding [2%] or less of all outstanding voting shares in such public corporation) or in any other manner whatsoever, carry on, advance or lend money to, guarantee the debts or obligations of or permit his name to be used, serve or cater to, in any relation or capacity whatsoever, a similar or competitive business as that conducted by the Corporation or any other business now or at any time during the period of time that such [*Shareholder/Principal*] was a Shareholder, director, officer or employee of the Corporation;

h) solicit any customer or client that was or is a customer or client of the Corporation during the period of time that such [*Shareholder/Principal*] was a Shareholder, director, officer or employee of the Corporation.

20.2) Confidentiality

Each Shareholder [*OPTIONAL: and Principal*] acknowledges to the Corporation that in the course of carrying out, performing and fulfilling his responsibilities to the Corporation, whether as a Shareholder, director, officer or employee, he will have access to and be entrusted with detailed confidential information and trade secrets relating to present or contemplated customers or clients and other persons, firms, corporations and entities with which the Corporation may deal, services, marketing techniques, modes of operation and inventions of the Corporation and confidential information concerning the customers or clients of the Corporation. Each Shareholder [*OPTIONAL: and Principal*] further acknowledges that the disclosure of such confidential information or trade secrets to competitors of the Corporation or of the Corporation's subsidiaries, to third parties or to the general public would be highly detrimental to the best interests of the Corporation. Each Shareholder [*OPTIONAL: and Principal*] acknowledges and agrees that the right to maintain the confidentiality of such confidential information and trade secrets constitutes a proprietary right which the Corporation is entitled to protect. Accordingly, each Shareholder [*OPTIONAL: and Principal*] agrees with the Corporation that he will not (either during the term of this Agreement or at any time thereafter) directly or indirectly use for his benefit or disclose, except to the extent required for the performance by him of his duties as a Shareholder, director, officer or employee of the Corporation, any such detailed confidential information or trade secrets to anyone, nor will he use the same for any purpose other than the purposes of the Corporation or upon ceasing to be a Shareholder, director, officer or employee of the Corporation, take with him any document or paper relating to any of the foregoing or any physical property of the Corporation or any of its subsidiaries or affiliates. Nothing herein will prevent the disclosure of information which is public knowledge.

20.3) Inventions

Any and all inventions, products, equipment, devices, discoveries, improvements, processes, methods or techniques, designs or applications thereof (collectively the "**Inventions**") made, developed or created by a [*Shareholder/ Principal/Shareholder and Principal*] (whether at the request or suggestion of the Corporation or otherwise, whether alone or in conjunction with others and whether during regular hours of work or otherwise) during the period of his being a Shareholder, director, officer or employee of the Corporation, and for a period of [*number of years*] year thereafter, or during the period of his being a Shareholder, director, officer or employee of the Corporation prior to the date of this Agreement, which may be directly or indirectly useful in, or relate to, the business of or tests being carried out by, the Corporation or any of its subsidiaries or affiliates, will be the Corporation's exclusive property as against each Shareholder [*OPTIONAL: and Principal*].

20.4)

Each Shareholder [*OPTIONAL: and Principal*] covenants and agrees that he will, at the Corporation's request and without any payment therefor, execute any documents necessary or advisable in the reasonable opinion of the Corporation's counsel to direct issuance of patents to the Corporation with respect to such Inventions as are to be the Corporation's exclusive property as against the [*Shareholder/Principal/Shareholder and Principal*] under Section 20.3 or to vest in the Corporation title to such Inventions as against the [*Shareholder/Principal/ Shareholder and Principal*].

20.5) Relief

Each [*Shareholder/Principal/Shareholder and Principal*] acknowledges that his relationship with the Corporation is of a special, unique, unusual and extraordinary character which gives it peculiar value, the loss of which cannot adequately be compensated in damages in an action at law. The Corporation will be entitled to all equitable and legal remedies, including interlocutory and permanent injunctive relief, relating to any violation or breach of the provisions of this Article.

20.6) No Defences [*amend if no independent counsel*]

Each Shareholder [*OPTIONAL: and Principal*] irrevocably acknowledges that he has reviewed the provisions of this Article with his legal counsel and that the provisions of this Article are reasonable, appropriate and in the interest of the Corporation. Each Shareholder [*OPTIONAL: and Principal*] irrevocably waives and renounces any right to claim or plead in any respect whatsoever that the provisions of this Article are not reasonable or in the interest of the Corporation. The covenants contained in this Article will be construed as independent of any other agreements between or among the parties and the existence of any claim or cause of action of a [*Shareholder/Principal*] against any other party hereto, whether predicated on this Article or otherwise will not constitute a defence to the enforcement by the Corporation of the provisions of this Article.

20.7) Severability

Except as expressly provided to the contrary in this Article, each Section, Subsection, part, term and/or provision of this Article will be considered severable and if, for any reason, any Section, Subsection, part term and/or provision thereof is determined to be invalid and contrary to, or in conflict with, any existing or future law, ruling or regulation by a court or agency having valid jurisdiction, such will not impair the operation of, or have any other effect on such other Section, Subsection, part, term and/or provision of this Article as may remain otherwise intelligible and the latter will continue to be given full force and effect and bind the parties; and such invalid Section, Subsection, part, term and/or provision will be deemed to not be a part of this Article. If a period of time or geographic area specified in this Article is adjudged to be unreasonable in any proceeding, then the period of time will be reduced by such number of months and/or the area will be reduced by the elimination of such portion thereof, so that such restrictions may be enforced in such area and for such time as is adjudged reasonable.

20.8) Survival

Except as provided in Section 22.3, the provisions of this Article will survive termination of this Agreement notwithstanding anything in this Agreement to the contrary.

ARTICLE 21: SUBSIDIARY

21.1)

The parties agree that Article 3 (except Sections __________), Article 20 and __________ will apply *mutatis mutandis* to the Corporation's subsidiary __________, a corporation incorporated under the laws of __________.

ARTICLE 22: GENERAL CONTRACT PROVISIONS

22.1) Term and Termination

This Agreement will take effect on the date hereof and remain in full force and effect until the earliest of that date on which:

(a) If pursuant to the *Bankruptcy and Insolvency Act*, the Corporation makes an assignment or a proposal, or is declared bankrupt or becomes insolvent;

(b) The Corporation is wound up, dissolved or liquidated or becomes subject to the provisions of the *Winding Up Act* or has its existence terminated or has any resolution passed therefor;

(c) A trustee in bankruptcy, receiver, receiver and manager, liquidator or other officer with similar powers is appointed for the Corporation or over all or a material part of its property;

(d) the [*day*] day of [*month, year*];

or as otherwise agreed by the Shareholders.

22.2)

On termination of this Agreement, the ownership of each insurance policy will be transferred to the person whose life is insured thereby or his nominee on payment of the greater of $[*dollar amount*] or the cash surrender value of such policy at the date of transfer.

22.3)

On the termination of this Agreement pursuant to Subsection 22.1(a), (b) or (c), the provisions of Article 20 will contemporaneously be terminated without any further action on the part of the parties.

22.4)   Arbitration

Except as otherwise expressly provided herein, any dispute, difference or question arising among any of the parties concerning the construction, meaning, effect or implementation of this Agreement or any part hereof will be settled by a single arbitrator mutually agreed upon by the Shareholders, or failing agreement, an arbitrator appointed pursuant to the *Arbitration Act* (Ontario) or similar legislation. The decision of such arbitrator appointed pursuant to this Agreement or such Act will be final and binding on the parties and no appeal will lie therefrom.

22.5)   Implementation of this Agreement

The parties will sign such further and other documents, cause such meetings to be held, such resolutions to be passed and such by-laws to be enacted, exercise their vote and influence and do and perform (and cause to be done and performed) such further and other acts or things as may be necessary or desirable in order to give full effect to this Agreement and every part hereof. If conflict will appear between the Corporation's articles, by-laws or resolutions and the provisions of this Agreement, the provisions of this Agreement will govern and supersede the provisions of such articles, by-laws and resolutions. If there is any such conflict, the Shareholders [*OPTIONAL: and the Principals*] will amend the Corporation's articles, by-laws and resolutions so as to ensure conformity with the terms of this Agreement.

22.6)   Notices

All notices, requests, demands, acceptances, consents, communications or other writings required or permitted to be given hereunder or for the purposes hereof ("**Notice**" in this Section) will be in writing and be sufficiently given if personally delivered, sent by prepaid registered mail or transmitted by telex, telecopier or other form of recorded communication tested prior to transmission, addressed to the party to whom it is given, as follows:

(a)   If to **Shrl1**—

Attention: __________

Telex No. __________

Telecopier No. __________

(b)   If to **Shrl2**—

Attention: __________

Telex No. __________

Telecopier No. __________

(c)   If to the Corporation—

Attention: __________

Telex No. __________

Telecopier No. __________

with a copy to: __________ [*the Corporation's solicitors*]

Attention: __________

Telex No. __________

Telecopier No. __________

(d)   If to **Prin1**—

Telex No. __________

Telecopier No. __________

(e)   If to **Prin2**—

Telex No. __________

Telecopier No. __________

or such other address of which Notice has been given. Any Notice mailed as aforesaid will be deemed to have been given and received on the third Business Day following the date of its mailing. Any Notice personally delivered will be deemed to have been given and received on the day it is personally delivered, provided that if such day is not a Business Day, the Notice will be deemed to have been given and received on the Business Day next following such day. Any Notice transmitted by telex, telecopier or other form of recorded communication will be deemed given and received on the first Business Day after its transmission.

If a Notice is mailed and regular mail service is interrupted by strike or other irregularity on or before the fourth Business Day after the mailing thereof, such Notice will be deemed to have not been received unless personally delivered or transmitted by telex, telecopier or other form of recorded communication.

22.7) Time of the Essence

Time will be of the essence of this Agreement and every part hereof, provided that if the parties establish a new time for the performance of an obligation, time will again be of the essence of the new time established.

22.8) Waiver

No party to this Agreement will be deemed or taken to have waived any provision of this Agreement unless such waiver is in writing, and such waiver will be limited to the circumstances set forth in such written waiver.

22.9) Severability

If any Article, Section or portion thereof is determined to be unenforceable or invalid, such unenforceability or invalidity will not affect the remaining Articles, Sections or portions thereof, as the case may be, of this Agreement and such unenforceable or invalid Article, Section or portion thereof will be deemed to be severed from the remainder of this Agreement. No covenant or provision, or part or parts thereof, will be deemed dependent on any other covenant or provision unless so expressed herein.

22.10) Governing Law

This Agreement will be governed by and construed in accordance with the laws of the Province of Ontario and the laws of Canada applicable therein. Each party attorns to the jurisdiction of the courts of the Province of Ontario.

22.11) Statutes

Any reference in this Agreement to a statute includes any amendment thereto, its regulations and applicable successor legislation.

22.12) Entire Agreement

This Agreement constitutes the entire agreement among the parties with respect to the matters herein and its execution has not been induced by, nor do any of the parties rely upon or regard as material, any representation, promise, agreement or statement whatsoever not incorporated herein and made a part hereof. This Agreement will not be amended, altered or qualified except by a memorandum in writing signed by the parties.

22.13) Counterparts

This Agreement may be executed in one or more counterparts, each of which will be deemed an original, but all of which together will constitute one and the same agreement.

22.14) Enurement

This Agreement will enure to the benefit of the parties and their respective heirs, executors, administrators, successors and permitted assigns and will be binding upon the parties and their respective heirs, executors, administrators, successors and assigns.

22.15) Gender

The necessary changes in gender required to make this Agreement apply to either corporations or individuals, males or females, will in all instances be assumed as though in each case fully expressed.

22.16) Headings

Headings in this Agreement are inserted for convenience only and do not constitute part of this Agreement.

ARTICLE 23: TERMINATION OF PRIOR AGREEMENTS

23.1)

The agreement dated ___________ among ___________, ___________, ___________ and ___________ and any other agreements, whether written or oral, between some or all of the parties hereto regarding the organization and affairs of the Corporation and the sale by the Shareholders of their respective Shares, are hereby terminated.

ARTICLE 24: ACKNOWLEDGEMENT

24.1)

Each party acknowledges that he has requested [*name of solicitor*], [*address of solicitor*] to act only for the Corporation in the preparation of this Agreement. The parties further acknowledge that [*counsel*] have advised them that they have conflicting interests with respect to the finalization of this Agreement, and accordingly have recommended to each Shareholder [*OPTIONAL: and Principal*] that it and he obtain independent legal advice concerning the advisability of entering into this Agreement before executing it.

WHEREOF the parties have hereunto set their hands and seals.

SIGNED, SEALED AND DELIVERED

in the presence of

As to the signature of Shrl1   Shrl1
As to the signature of Shrl2   Shrl2
As to the signature of Prin1   Prin1
As to the signature of Prin2   Prin2

    [the Corporation]
Per: Per:
Title   Title

SCHEDULE A: OFFER TO PURCHASE OR SELL

TO: __________

RE: Shareholders Agreement dated the [*day*] day of [*month, year*] among _________, _________ and _________ (the "**Corporation**") (the "**Shareholders Agreement**")

RE: _________ Shares owned by the undersigned and _________ Shares owned by you

I hereby offer to purchase from you all your Shares or to sell to you all my Shares on the following terms and conditions:

1. The purchase price will be $[*dollar amount*] per Share.

2. The Closing Date for the purchase of Shares will be the [*day*] day of [*month, year*] [*30th Business Day after your receipt of this Offer*].

CHOOSE [*cash on closing or structured payment*]

3. The purchase price will be payable in full by cash or certified cheque on the Closing Date.

OR

4. The purchase price will be payable as follows:

    (a) [*percentage*] % will be paid by cash or certified cheque on the Closing Date; and

    (b) The balance of the purchase price, together with interest thereon at the Prime Rate [*OPTIONAL: plus* _________*% per annum*] will be evidenced by a Promissory Note of the payor and will be repayable in _________ consecutive equal [*monthly*] instalments of principal, plus interest on the principal balance then outstanding. The first instalment will be due and payable [*number*] month after the Closing Date.

5. Time will be of the essence of this Agreement.

6.   This Agreement will enure to the benefit of and be binding on the parties hereto and their respective heirs, executors, successors and assigns.

7.   This Agreement will be governed by and construed in accordance with the laws of the Province of Ontario and the laws of Canada applicable therein.

The following are attached:

(a)   a certified cheque payable to the Corporation's solicitors in trust in the amount of $[*dollar amount*] representing [*percentage*] % of the total purchase price of your Shares; and

(b)   a statement setting out in reasonable detail full reference to any information relating directly to the financial affairs of the Corporation or its business which, to my best knowledge, is not known to you.

You have 20 Business Days within which to elect either to sell your Shares or to purchase my Shares at the above price per Share. If you fail to make such acceptance and election within such period, you will be deemed to have agreed to sell your Shares to me at the above price per Share.

The terms and conditions of the agreement formed as a result of your acceptance of this Offer will be the terms and conditions set out herein together with and subject to such other terms and conditions which are applicable pursuant to the Shareholders Agreement.

IN WITNESS WHEREOF the undersigned has executed this Offer [*as of*] the [*day*] day of [*month, year*].

SCHEDULE B: ACCEPTANCE OF AN OFFER TO PURCHASE

TO: __________

RE: Shareholders Agreement dated the [*day*] day of [*month, year*] among __________, __________ and __________ (the "**Corporation**") (the "**Shareholders Agreement**")

RE: __________ Shares owned by you and __________ Shares owned by the undersigned

I acknowledge receipt of your Offer dated the [*day*] day of [*month, year*] to sell to me your Shares and your certified cheque in the amount of $[*dollar amount*].

I accept your Offer and agree to purchase your Shares from you at the price per Share and on the terms and conditions set out in your Offer. I return herewith your certified cheque and deliver to you herewith a certified cheque payable to the Corporation's solicitors in trust representing [*percentage*]% of the total purchase price of your Shares.

This acceptance constitutes a binding contract between us to complete the purchase and sale transaction in accordance with the terms and conditions set out in your Offer.

DATED this [*day*] day of [*month, year*]

SCHEDULE C: ACCEPTANCE OF AN OFFER TO SELL

TO: ___________

RE: Shareholders Agreement dated the [*day*] day of [*month, year*] among ___________, ___________ and ___________ (the "Corporation") (the "**Shareholders Agreement**")

RE: ___________ Shares owned by you and ___________ Shares owned by the undersigned

I acknowledge receipt of your Offer dated the [*day*] day of [*month, year*] to purchase all my Shares and your certified cheque in the amount of $[*dollar amount*]. In accordance with the Shareholders Agreement, I accept your offer and agree to sell to you all my Shares at the price per Share set out in the Offer.

This acceptance constitutes a binding contract between us to complete the purchase and sale transaction in accordance with the terms and conditions set out in your Offer.

DATED this [*day*] day of [*month, year*]

SCHEDULE D: ANNUAL VALUATION OF FAIR VALUE AND DETAILS OF INSURANCE

Date of Valuation	Fair Value of Shares (per Share)	Initials of Each Shareholder
[*Date of Agreement*]	$[*dollar amount*]	
[*Date of Agreement*]	$[*dollar amount*]	
[*Date of Agreement*]	$[*dollar amount*]	
[*Date of Agreement*]	$[*dollar amount*]	
[*Date of Agreement*]	$[*dollar amount*]	

Policy #	Issuer	Life Insured	Amount of Insurance	Initials of Each Shareholder

Form 23: **Shareholders' Agreement— Multiple-Party Shareholder Agreement**

SHAREHOLDERS' AGREEMENT

THIS AGREEMENT is made __________

AMONG:

__________, of the __________ of __________ in the Province of Ontario ("**S1**"),

- and -

__________, a corporation governed by the laws of __________ ("**S2**"),

- and -

__________, a corporation governed by the laws of __________ ("**S3**"),

- and -

__________, of the __________ of __________,
in the Province of Ontario ("**S4**"),

- and -

__________, a corporation governed by the laws of __________
(the "**Corporation**"),

- and -

__________, of the __________ of __________,
in the Province of Ontario ("**P1**"),

- and -

__________, of the __________ of __________,
in the Province of Ontario ("**P2**").

Recitals:

A. The Shareholders together own, directly or indirectly, all the issued and out-standing shares in the capital of the Corporation.

B. The Shareholders wish to record that the following general principles shall apply to the operations of the Corporation:

C. The Shareholders have entered into this Agreement to record their agreement with respect to certain arrangements regarding the organization and affairs of the Corporation and the purchase and sales of their shares in the capital of the Corporation under certain circumstances.

THEREFORE, the parties hereto agree as follows:

ARTICLE 1: DEFINITIONS AND PRINCIPLES OF INTERPRETATION

1.1) Definitions

Whenever used in this Agreement, the following words and terms shall have the meanings set out below:

"**Accountant**" means the auditor or accountant, as the case may be, of the Corporation appointed from time to time;

"**Act**" means the [*Business Corporations Act* (Ontario)/*Canada Business Corporations Act* (Canada)];

"**Affiliate**" and "**Affiliated**" means any Person who, directly or indirectly, Controls, is Controlled by or is under common Control with any other Person. In addition, any partner, limited partner, shareholder or member, as the case may be, of a Shareholder or an Affiliate of a Shareholder shall be deemed to be an Affiliate of such Person;

"**Agreement**" means this agreement and all attached schedules and all instruments supplemental to, or in amendment or confirmation of, this agreement; references to Articles, Sections or subsections are to the specified Articles, Sections or subsections of this Agreement;

"**Applicable Family Law Legislation**" includes the *Family Law Act* (Ontario), the *Succession Law Reform Act* (Ontario), the *Divorce Act* (Canada) and any other law of the Province of Ontario or of any other applicable jurisdiction which will in any way interfere with, encumber, or effect the Corporation or a Party's interest in any Shares and which include all amendments and replacements to any such legislation;

"**Approved List of Valuators**" means __________;

"**Arm's Length**" has the meaning that it has for purposes of section 251(1) the Tax Act;

"**Associate**" has the meaning set out in the Act;

"**Board**" means the board of directors of the Corporation;

"**Business Day**" means a day, other than a Saturday or Sunday, on which the principal commercial banks located at [*insert city where head office of corporation is located*] are open for business during normal banking hours;

"**Children**" mean the lineal descendants to the remotest degree of a shareholder or Principal, as applicable;

"**Closing Date**" means the date on which a Shareholder completes the purchase and sale of his Shares to another Shareholder, the other Shareholders or the Corporation pursuant to this Agreement;

"**Control**":
    (a) when applied to the relationship between a Person and a corporation, means the beneficial ownership by that Person at the relevant time of shares of that corporation carrying more than the greater of: (A) a majority of the voting rights ordinarily exercisable at meetings of shareholders of that corporation and (B) the percentage of voting rights ordinarily exercisable at meetings of shareholders of that corporation that are sufficient to elect a majority of the directors; and
    (b) when applied to the relationship between a Person and a trust, it means the Family Trust of a Principal, and any Shares held by a Family Trust are deemed to be controlled by its Principal; and the words "**Controlled by**", "**Controlling**" and similar words have corresponding meanings;

"**Deficit Contribution**" means an amount, including accrued interest thereon, owing by one Shareholder to another Shareholder or to the Corporation pursuant to this Agreement;

"**Disability**" means such suffering from a state of mental or physical disability, illness or disease as prevents an individual Shareholder or Principal, as applicable, from carrying out his/her normal duties to the Corporation and/ or any Subsidiary in the manner conducted by such Shareholder or Principal, as applicable, in the opinion of both the primary medical doctor treating the applicable Shareholder or Principal with respect to such disability, illness or disease, and such other medical doctor as chosen by the Corporation (or the Corporation's Long Term Disability insurer), and "**Disabled**" has a corresponding meaning

"**Disability Date**" means the date upon which an individual Shareholder or a Principal becomes Disabled pursuant to the terms set out herein;

"**Encumbrance**" means any mortgage, deed of trust, charge, pledge, hypothecation, assignment, encumbrance, lien (statutory or other) or preference, priority, adverse claim, right or other security interest or preferential arrangement of any kind or nature whatsoever;

"**ESOP**" means the employee stock option plan of the Corporation, as same may be amended, restated and/or replaced from time to time;

"**Fair Market Value**" means the purchase price for the Shares, as determined in accordance with Schedule 8.1 hereto;

"**Family Trust**" means a trust, all of the beneficiaries of which are members of the Immediate Family of a Shareholder or Principal, as applicable, and provided that:

    (a) the sole trustee of such Family Trust is the Shareholder or Principal, as applicable;

    (b) the sole trustee of such Family Trust is a corporation that is at all times Controlled by the Shareholder or Principal, as applicable; or

    (c) one of the trustees of such Family Trust is a Shareholder or Principal and such Family Trust provides that such Shareholder has full authority to make all decisions of such Family Trust in connection with voting the Shares and Controlling any rights or entitlements granted with respect to any other Securities;

"**Holding Company**" means a corporation which is Controlled by an individual Party to this Agreement;

"**Immediate Family**" means the current parents, Spouse, Children or siblings of the relevant Shareholder or Principal thereof, as applicable;

"**Permanently Disabled**" means, a Shareholder or Principal who has been Disabled for a period of [*number*] consecutive months or for a cumulative period of [*number*] months in any [*number*] month period;

"**Permitted Transferee**" means, in respect of any Shareholder: [*NOTE TO DRAFT: Customize as needed*]

   (a) if the Shareholder is an individual:

      (i)   its Holding Company, so long as such corporation is not a non-resident of Canada within the meaning of the Tax Act;

      (ii) a Family Trust, provided that such trust is not a non-resident of Canada within the meaning of the Tax Act; or

      (iii) where the context permits, upon the death of the Shareholder, the beneficiary or beneficiaries of the estate of such Shareholder; and

   (b) if the Shareholder is a corporation:

      (i)   an Affiliate of the Shareholder, so long as such corporation is not a nonresident of Canada within the meaning of the Tax Act; or

      (ii) a Family Trust of such Shareholder's Principal, provided that such trust is not a non-resident of Canada within the meaning of the Tax Act; or

      (iii) where the context permits, upon the death of a Principal of such Shareholder the Personal Representative of such Principal; and

   (c) if the Shareholder is a trust:

      (i)   a Holding Company of the Principal of the Shareholder, so long as such corporation is not a non-resident of Canada within the meaning of the Tax Act; or

      (ii) a Family Trust of the Principal of the Shareholder, provided that such trust is not a non-resident of Canada within the meaning of the Tax Act; and

   (d) a corporation that is Controlled by the Transferor (as defined in Section 5.4).

"Person" includes any individual, sole proprietorship, partnership, unincorporated association, unincorporated syndicate, unincorporated organization, trust, body corporate, and a natural person in his capacity as trustee, executor, administrator, or other legal representative;

"Personal Representative" means the executor of a deceased individual named in the last will and testament of the deceased (and provided if the deceased individual had more than one last will and testament naming different persons as executors, then the executor appointed under and acting pursuant to the will and testament that refers to the Shares) or, failing the naming of such Person or the refusal or inability of such Person to act, the administrator of a deceased individual duly appointed by a court or public authority having jurisdiction to do so or, if no such administrator has been appointed, the heirs at law of the deceased;

"Pledged Shares" has the meaning set out in Appendix 5.4;

"Prime Rate" means, at any time, the rate of interest expressed as an annual rate, established by [*insert named bank*] from time to time as its reference rate of interest to determine the interest rates it will charge for loans in Canadian dollars to Canadian customers;

"Principal" means, with respect to a Shareholder who is not an individual, the Person set out adjacent to each Shareholder's name as set out in Schedule 3.1, provided however that such referenced Principal(s) shall be amended from time to time to reflect the purchase and sale of a Shareholder's Shares pursuant to the terms set out herein;

"Promissory Note" means a promissory note given and received in accordance with the terms of this Agreement, which will include the following terms and conditions:

    (a) Such promissory note will be fully open as to additional payments of principal at any time or times without notice or bonus;

    (b) On any default in payment, which default continues for 10 days after receipt of notice thereof, the entire balance then outstanding, together with any accrued but unpaid interest thereon, will be immediately due and payable; and

    (c) Such promissory note will be non-negotiable and non-assignable by the holder thereof;

"Proportionate Share" means that proportion of voting securities of the Corporation owned by a Shareholder as among that Shareholder and certain other Shareholders;

"Securities" means, collectively, Shareholders Loans, the Shares and any other shares or securities of the Corporation outstanding from time to time;

"Shares" means collectively: (i) the authorized shares in the Corporation at the date hereof; (ii) any additional shares in the Corporation which may be created after the date hereof; (iii) any shares in the Corporation into which then-authorized and issued shares may be converted, reclassified, redesigned, subdivided, consolidated or otherwise changed; and (iv) any shares in the Corporation or any successor or other body corporate which may be received by the holders of shares in the Corporation upon an amalgamation, merger or other reorganization of (or including) the Corporation;

"**Shares**" or "**Securities**" means all shares, options, warrants, interests, participations or other equivalents (regardless of how designated) of or in a corporation, unlimited liability company, partnership, limited partnership or equivalent entity, whether voting or non-voting or participating or nonparticipating, or any securities, bonds, notes, debentures or other evidences of indebtedness that are convertible into or exchangeable for any of the foregoing;

"**Shareholders**" means, collectively, the owners of any Shares, and

"**Shareholder**" means any one of such Persons individually;

"**Shareholder Loan**" means any debt obligation of the Corporation to a Shareholder or Principal, or any other amount which may be owing by the Corporation to a Shareholder or Principal, whether currently or in the future and whether or not evidenced by a promissory note, debenture or other evidence of indebtedness issued or which may be issued by the Corporation to a Shareholder or Principal, or on open account;

"**Shareholder Guarantee**" means any indemnity or guarantee given by a Shareholder or a Principal with the consent of the other Shareholders whereby such Shareholder guarantees the payment of any debt or liability of the Corporation or the performance of any obligation of the Corporation; [*NOTE TO DRAFT: Confirm with client if there are any pre-existing shareholder guarantees, and, if so, if they have been approved by all shareholders both at the time and subsequently*]

"**Spouse**" means an individual at a particular time who is legally married to a Shareholder, or Principal, as applicable;

"**Subsidiary**" has, with respect to the Corporation, the meaning set out in the Act;

"**Subsidiary Entities**" means, collectively, — and each individually a "**Subsidiary Entity**"; [*NOTE TO DRAFT: List subsidiaries of the Corporation, or if no subsidiaries of the Corporation, delete this definition as well as sections 3.9 & 3.10*]

"**Tax Act**" means the *Income Tax Act* (Canada) and the regulations thereunder, as each may be amended from time to time and including such applicable successor legislation or regulations, as the case may be;

"**Third Party**" means a Person who deals at arm's length with all of the Shareholders and Principals;

"Third Party Offer" means a *bona fide* offer received by a Shareholder from a Third Party for the purchase of some or all the issued and outstanding Shares of the Corporation and pursuant to which:

    (a) no property other than such Shares is to be sold, transferred or otherwise disposed of, provided however that the Third Party Offer may contemplate the repayment, transfer, assignment, or set-off, as applicable, of any outstanding Shareholder Loans;

    (b) [*the sole consideration for such Shares is a stated dollar amount payable at closing*];

    (c) [*the sole security, if any, for the payment of any instalments of the purchase price is a purchase money security interest in the Shares to be purchased*]; and

    (d) such offer contains no terms or conditions that would constitute a breach of, or require an amendment to, this Agreement;

"Transfer" means to sell, assign, surrender, gift, transfer, pledge, mortgage, charge, create a security interest in, hypothecate or otherwise encumber or deal with any shares or any interest, whether legal or beneficial, in shares;

"Triggering Event" has the meaning set out in Section 7.1;

"Valuation Date" has the meaning set out in Section 8.1; and .

"Voting Securities" manes securities, other than debt securities, carrying a voting right to elect directors generally either under all circumstances or under stated circumstances that have occurred and are continuing.

1.2) Additional Definitions

Unless there is something inconsistent in the subject matter or context, or unless otherwise provided in this Agreement, all other words and terms used in this Agreement which are defined in the Act shall have the meanings set out in the Act.

1.3) Certain Rules of Interpretation

In this Agreement,

    (a) **Recitals**—The recitals set out above are true, both in substance and in fact and form part of this Agreement;

    (b) **Business Day**—Whenever any payment to be made or action to be taken under this Agreement is required to be made or taken on a day other than a Business Day, such payment shall be made or action taken on the next Business Day following;

(c) **Calculation of Time**—Unless otherwise specified, time periods within or following which any payment is to be made or act is to be done shall be calculated by excluding the day on which the period commences and including the day which ends the period and by extending the period to the next Business Day following if the last day of the period is not a Business Day;

(d) **Consent**—Whenever a provision of this Agreement requires an approval or consent by a Party and notification of such approval or consent is not delivered within the applicable time limit, then, unless otherwise specified, the Party whose consent or approval is required shall be conclusively deemed to have withheld its consent or approval;

(e) **Currency**—Unless otherwise specified, all references to money amounts are to Canadian currency;

(f) **Headings**—The descriptive headings of Articles and Sections are inserted solely for convenience of reference and are not intended as complete or accurate descriptions of content and shall not be used to interpret the provisions of this Agreement;

(g) **Including**—Where the word "including" or the word "includes" is used in this Agreement, it means "including (or includes) without limitation";

(h) **Number and Gender**—Unless the context otherwise requires, words importing the singular include the plural and vice versa and words importing gender include all genders; and

(i) **Time**—Time is of the essence in the performance of each party's respective obligations hereunder.

1.4) Accounting Principles

Wherever in this Agreement reference is made to generally accepted accounting principles or GAAP, such reference shall be deemed to be generally accepted accounting principles from time to time approved by the Canadian Institute of Chartered Accountants, or any successor institute, applicable as at the date on which such calculation is made or required to be made in accordance with such generally accepted accounting principles.

1.5) Jurisdiction

This Agreement shall be governed by and construed in accordance with the laws of the Province of Ontario and the laws of Canada applicable therein and shall be treated in all respects as an Ontario contract.

1.6)   Schedules

The Schedules annexed to this Agreement, as listed below, are an integral part of this Agreement:

- Schedule 3.1: List of Shareholders, Principals and Addresses
- Schedule 4.1: List of Directors
- Schedule 4.2: List of Officers
- Schedule 5.1(c): Adherence Agreement
- Schedule 8.1: Principles of Valuation
- [Schedule 10.2 Arbitration Procedure]

ARTICLE 2: PURPOSE AND SCOPE

2.1)   Business of the Corporation

The Shareholders will cause the Corporation to carry on the business of [*describe business*] and to generally carry on all ancillary and related activities which in the opinion of the directors will enhance the Corporation's income and profit.

2.2)   Unanimous Shareholder Agreement

(a)   This Agreement shall be deemed to be a unanimous shareholders' agreement within the meaning of the Act and the power of the directors to manage or supervise the management of the business and affairs of the Corporation is restricted in accordance with the terms of this Agreement. [*NOTE TO DRAFT: Drafter to confirm that this agreement is intended to be a USA*]

(b)   The Shareholders shall have all the rights, powers, duties and liabilities of a director of the Corporation, whether arising under this Act or otherwise, including any defences available to the directors, to which this Agreement relates to the extent that this Agreement restricts the discretion or powers of the directors to manage or supervise the management of the business and affairs of the corporation and the directors are relieved of their duties and liabilities in regard thereto, including any liabilities under section 131 of the Act, to the same extent.

(c)   No amendment to this Agreement which will affect the rights, powers and duties of any of the directors shall become effective until the directors have been given written notice of the proposed amendment and an opportunity to resign.

2.3) Compliance with Agreement

Each Shareholder agrees to vote and act as a shareholder of the Corporation to fulfil the provisions of this Agreement and each party hereto agrees to comply with, and use all reasonable efforts to cause the Corporation to comply with, this Agreement, and to the extent, if any, which may be permitted by law, shall cause its respective nominee(s) who serve as directors of the Corporation, if any, to act in accordance with this Agreement.

2.4) Compliance by Corporation

The Corporation undertakes to carry out and be bound by the provisions of this Agreement to the full extent that it has the capacity and power at law to do so.

2.5) Guarantee by Principals

Each Principal hereby severally, but not jointly, covenants with each other Principal and each of the other parties to this Agreement to take such actions as may be necessary to cause the Shareholder which it Controls to at all times fully and faithfully perform and discharge its obligations under this Agreement and to comply with the laws and conditions of this Agreement. The foregoing covenant and obligation of the Principals are absolute, unconditional, present and continuing and are in no way conditional or contingent upon any event or circumstance, action or omission which might in any way discharge a guarantor or surety.

ARTICLE 3: PARTICIPATION IN THE CORPORATION

3.1) Representations, Warranties and Covenants of Shareholders

Each of the Shareholders, jointly with its respective Principal, if applicable, represent, warrant and covenant to the other parties hereto that:

(a) such Shareholder, at the date hereof, (i) owns legally, and, if not a trust, beneficially, and of record the number of Shares set forth opposite such Shareholder's name on Schedule 3.1 attached hereto, as applicable; (ii) that other than as set out herein, such Shares are not subject to any Encumbrance; and (iii) that no Person has any rights to become a holder or possessor of any of the Shares or of the certificates representing the same;

(b) such Shareholder's Principal, at the date hereof:

    (i) if such Shareholder is not a trust, Controls the Shareholder set forth opposite such Principal's name on Schedule 3.1 attached hereto, and owns beneficially and of record the number of shares of its respective Shareholder set forth adjacent to such Principal's name, and that such shares are not subject to any Encumbrance and that no Person has any rights to become a holder or possessor of any of such shares or of the certificates representing the same; and

(ii) if such Shareholder is a trust, hereby represents and warrants that the trust is a Family Trust of the Principal;

(c) if the Shareholder is an individual, such Shareholder has the capacity to enter into and give full effect to this Agreement in accordance with the terms hereof;

(d) if the Shareholder is a corporation, (i) such Shareholder is duly incorporated and validly existing under the laws of its jurisdiction of incorporation and it has the corporate power and capacity to own its assets and to enter into and perform its obligations under this Agreement in accordance with the terms hereof; and (ii) such Shareholder's Principal has the capacity to enter into and give full effect to this Agreement in accordance with the terms hereof;

(e) if the Shareholder is a trust, it is duly constituted under the laws that govern it and it has the power to enter into and perform its obligations under this Agreement;

(f) if the Shareholder is a limited partnership, (i) such Shareholder is a limited partnership validly existing and in good standing under the laws of the jurisdiction of it registration (as indicated on the first page of this Agreement) and is qualified to do business and is in good standing in each jurisdiction in which it carries on business; and (ii) the general partner of such limited partnership is a corporation duly incorporated, validly existing and in good standing under the laws of the jurisdiction of its incorporation and is qualified to do business and is in good standing in each jurisdiction in which it carries on business [*NOTE TO DRAFT: To be confirmed*];

(g) this Agreement has been duly authorized by such Shareholder, as applicable, and duly executed and delivered by such Shareholder and its Principal, and constitutes a valid and binding obligation enforceable against such Shareholder and its Principal in accordance with its terms, subject to the usual exceptions as to bankruptcy and the availability of equitable remedies;

(h) the execution, delivery and performance of this Agreement does not and shall not contravene the provisions of its articles, by-laws, constating documents or other organizational documents or the documents by which such Shareholder was created or established or the provisions of any indenture, agreement or other instrument to which such Shareholder or its Principal is a party or by which such Shareholder, may be bound;

(i) the Shareholder is not a non-resident of Canada within the meaning of the Tax Act;

(j) the Principal is not a non-resident of Canada within the meaning of the Tax Act; and

(k) subject to the terms of this Agreement, all of the foregoing representations and warranties shall continue to be true and correct during the continuance of this Agreement.

3.2) Indemnities

Each Shareholder [*OPTIONAL: and its Principal*] (collectively, the "**Indemnifiers**") jointly and severally covenant and agree to indemnify and save harmless the Corporation and each of the other parties hereto in respect of any and all costs, charges and expenses which may be suffered or incurred by any of them as a direct or indirect result of a material breach or inaccuracy of any representation, warranty or covenant of any of the Indemnifiers under this Agreement or in any agreement, certificate or other document delivered by any of the Indemnifiers pursuant hereto.

3.3) Additional Capital

Except as provided in this Agreement or as otherwise unanimously agreed, none of the Shareholders shall be obligated to acquire additional Shares or to make loans to the Corporation or guarantee its indebtedness. It is the intention of the Shareholders that further funds required by the Corporation from time to time will be obtained, to the extent possible, by borrowing from a Canadian chartered bank or other lender acceptable to the [*Shareholders/Board*], by way of operating line of credit without guarantee by the Shareholders or Principals. [*NOTE TO DRAFT: Appendix 3.3 CONTAINS ALTERNATIVE PROVISIONS REQUIRING ADDITIONAL CAPITAL.*]

3.4 Shareholder Loans

Unless as otherwise agreed in writing by the Shareholders and the Principals, any and all Shareholder Loans to the Corporation by its Shareholders or Principals shall bear interest at the Prime Rate, plus _________%, both before and after maturity, default and judgement, calculated and payable [*annually*].

3.5) Deficit Contributions

Unless as otherwise agreed in writing by the Shareholders and the Principals, any and all Deficit Contributions by a Shareholder to other Shareholders or to the Corporation shall bear interest at the Prime Rate, plus _________%, both before and after maturity, default and judgement, calculated and payable [*annually*].

3.6) Shareholder Guarantees

If a Shareholder or Principal (the **"Payor"**) receives notice from anyone demanding the payment of money or the performance of any obligation pursuant to a Shareholder Guarantee:

(a) The Payor will give three (3) Business Days' notice to the other Shareholders:

    (i) Describing the Shareholder Guarantee and the demand made thereunder;

    (ii) Stating the amount required to be paid pursuant to such demand or the costs incurred (or likely to be incurred) in complying with such demand; and

    (iii) Stating the date or dates on which such amounts will be paid or costs incurred (if not then already paid or incurred);

(b) Each of the other Shareholders (the **"Indemnifiers"** in this Section) will pay its Proportionate Share of the amount set out in such notice when and as directed in the notice (subject to the Payor delivering reasonable proof that he has paid such amounts or incurred such costs);

(c) The Indemnifiers will make such payment notwithstanding any dispute as to the Payor's obligation to make payment pursuant to the Shareholder Guarantee or the notice received by the Payor under the Shareholder Guarantee; and

(d) If an Indemnifier fails to make all or any part of such payment, such Indemnifier will be deemed to be a Defaulting Shareholder for the purposes of Section 7.1 and the Payor shall be the sole Non-Defaulting Shareholder for the purposes of Section 7.1 and will have the rights and remedies pursuant thereto.

3.7) Payment of Indebtedness to Shareholders

At any time when the Corporation or a Subsidiary of the Corporation makes a payment to a Shareholder (the **"Initial Shareholder"**) on account of Shareholder

Loans, it shall at the same time make payment to each other Shareholder (the "**Secondary Shareholders**") so that the payment received by each Secondary Shareholder from the Corporation is proportional to the amount paid to the Initial Shareholder as the total indebtedness of the Corporation to the Secondary Shareholders is to the indebtedness of the Corporation to the Initial Shareholders.

OR

At any time when the Corporation or a Subsidiary of the Corporation makes a payment to a Shareholder (the "**Initial Shareholder**") on account of Shareholder Loans, it shall ensure that it pays all such amounts on the basis or retiring the oldest Shareholder Loans first. For greater certainty, Shareholder Loans will be repaid in the order of first loaned, first repaid.

3.8) Grant of Security Interest by Shareholders

As security for the repayment of a Shareholder's present and future Deficit Contributions, each Shareholder (a "**Charging Shareholder**" in this Section) grants to the Corporation and each of the other Shareholders (the "**Secured Party**" in this Section) a mortgage, charge and security interest (a "**Charge**" in this Section) in the following property (the "**Collateral**" in this Section):

(a) all Shares now and in the future beneficially owned by the Charging Shareholder;

(b) all debts, accounts and monies now and in the future owing to the Charging Shareholder by the Corporation (including, without limitation, declared and unpaid dividends and all Shareholder Loans); and

(c) the proceeds of the Collateral.

It is the intention of this Section that each Secured Party will have the rights and remedies of a secured party under the *Personal Property Security Act* (Ontario) in connection with all Deficit Contributions from time to time owing to the Secured Party by the Charging Shareholder. The security interest created pursuant to this Section will attach upon execution of this Agreement. A Charge becomes enforceable if the Charging Shareholder fails to pay any indebtedness secured by that Charge within [*number of days*] days following demand for payment or on the occurrence of a Triggering Event. Each Charging Shareholder irrevocably directs that, after any Charge becomes enforceable against him, all amounts otherwise payable to him by the Corporation are to be paid in accordance with Section 3.14. Every security interest granted by a Charging Shareholder under this Section will rank *pari passu* and share pro rata in the Collateral.

3.9)   Grant of Security Interest by the Corporation

As security for the repayment of all Shareholder Loans, the Corporation hereby grants to each Shareholder a mortgage, charge and security interest in all of the Corporation's property and assets, both present and future, real and personal, and the proceeds thereof. It is the intention of this Section that each Shareholder will have the rights and remedies of a secured party under the *Personal Property Security Act* (Ontario) in connection with all Shareholder Loans from time to time owing to such Shareholder by the Corporation. The security interest created pursuant to this Section will attach on execution of this Agreement. Every security interest granted by the Corporation under this Section will rank *pari passu* and share *pro rata* in the property and assets subject to this mortgage, charge and security interest. The security hereby constituted will be subordinate to any security granted by the Corporation in favour of a chartered bank, trust company or other institutional lender and to any other security authorized by all of the Shareholders pursuant to Section 3.3 above. Each Shareholder agrees to execute such subordination agreements and acknowledgments as are reasonably requested in order to evidence or better give effect to such subordination. The Corporation will execute general security agreements over all its assets and undertaking, both present and future, in favour of each Shareholder at the request of any Shareholder and, notwithstanding the order of registration of such general security agreements, the security granted by the Corporation to the Shareholders will rank *pari passu*.

All Shareholder Loans will become due and payable and the security hereby constituted will become enforceable if the Corporation makes an assignment for the benefit of creditors, a proposal is filed under the *Bankruptcy and Insolvency Act* (Canada), the Corporation is declared bankrupt or becomes insolvent or a trustee in bankruptcy, receiver, receiver and manager, liquidator or other officer with similar powers is appointed for the Corporation or all or any material part of its property.

3.10)   Guarantee by Subsidiary Entities of Shareholder Loans

Each Subsidiary Entity hereby unconditionally and irrevocably guarantees the repayment of all Shareholder Loans to the Shareholders and Principals. Each Subsidiary Entity covenants with the Shareholders and Principals that it is jointly and severally bound with the Corporation for the fulfillment of all obligations of the Corporation to repay Shareholder Loans. In the enforcement of its rights hereunder, the Shareholders and Principals may proceed against a Subsidiary Entity as if such Subsidiary Entity was named as the Corporation under this Agreement. Each Subsidiary Entity waives any rights to require the Shareholders and Principals to proceed against the Corporation or to pursue any other remedy whatsoever which may be available to the Shareholders and Principals before proceeding against such Subsidiary Entity.

3.11) Grant of Security Interest by the Subsidiary Entity

As security for the repayment of all indebtedness and other obligations owed by the Subsidiary Entities to the Corporation and/or to the Shareholders and/or Principals from time to time (**"Subsidiary Entity Obligations"**), each Subsidiary Entity hereby grants to the Corporation, the Shareholders and the Principals a mortgage, charge and security interest in all of the Subsidiary Entity's property and assets, both present and future, real and personal, and the proceeds thereof. It is the intention of this Section that the Corporation, the Shareholders and the Principals will have the rights and remedies of a secured party under the *Personal Property Security Act* (Ontario) in connection with all Subsidiary Entity Obligations from time to time owing to the Corporation, the Shareholders and/ or the Principals by the Subsidiary Entities. The security interest created pursuant to this Section will attach on execution of this Agreement. Every security interest granted by a Subsidiary Entity under this Section will rank *pari passu* and share *pro rata* in the property and assets subject to this mortgage, charge and security interest. The security hereby constituted will be subordinate to any security granted by a Subsidiary Entity in favour of a chartered bank, trust company or other institutional lender and to any other security authorized by all of the Shareholders pursuant to Section 3.3 above. The Corporation and each Shareholder and Principal agree to execute such subordination agreements and acknowledgments as are reasonably requested in order to evidence or better give effect to such subordination. Each Subsidiary Entity will execute general security agreements over all its assets and undertaking, both present and future, in favour of the Corporation, each Shareholder and Principal at the request of the Corporation, any Shareholder and/or Principal, and, notwithstanding the order of registration of such general security agreements, the security granted by a Subsidiary Entity to the Corporation, the Shareholders and Principals will rank *pari passu*.

All Subsidiary Entity Obligations of a Subsidiary Entity will become due and payable and the security hereby constituted will become enforceable if such Subsidiary Entity makes an assignment for the benefit of creditors, a proposal is filed under the *Bankruptcy and Insolvency Act* (Canada), such Subsidiary Entity is declared bankrupt or becomes insolvent or a trustee in bankruptcy, receiver, receiver and manager, liquidator or other officer with similar powers is appointed for such Subsidiary Entity or all or any material part of its property.

Each Subsidiary Entity will execute general security agreements over all its assets and undertaking, both present and future, in favour of the Corporation, the Shareholders and/or the Principals at the request of the Corporation, the Shareholders and/or the Principals.

3.12)   Additional Shares in Corporate Shareholders

No Shareholder which is a corporation shall issue any additional securities except to the Principal which Controls it, if after the issuance of such securities or the conversion into voting securities of any convertible securities, such Shareholder would no longer be Controlled by such Principal. [*NOTE TO DRAFT: Parties may want to restrict the right absolutely*]

3.13)   Deficit Contributions

Contemporaneous with a purchase and sale of Shares pursuant to this Agreement, all Deficit Contributions will be paid and satisfied on or before the Closing Date as follows:

(a)   Deficit Contributions owing by a transferor of Shares to a Shareholder who is not the purchaser of the Shares and/or to the Corporation will be paid by such purchaser of the Shares out of the amount otherwise payable to such vendor on the Closing Date and any deficiency remaining thereafter will be paid by such transferor on the Closing Date. Such payments will be a condition precedent (for such Shareholder's and/ or the Corporation's benefit, as the case may be) to the closing of such purchase and sale, which condition may be waived by such Shareholder and/or the Corporation, as the case may be. Such transferor irrevocably authorizes and directs such purchaser to make such payment;

(b)   Deficit Contributions owing by a transferor to a transferee will be set off against the purchase price payable by such purchaser on the Closing Date and any deficiency will be paid by such transferor on the Closing Date. The payment of such deficiency will be a condition precedent (for such transferee's benefit) to the closing of such purchase and sale, which condition may be waived by such transferee; and

(c)   Deficit Contributions owing by a transferee to a transferor will be paid on the Closing Date. Such payment will be a condition precedent (for such transferor's benefit) to the closing of the purchase and sale of Shares, which condition may be waived by such transferor.

3.14)   Payments and Distributions

All funds from time to time available to the Corporation not otherwise required for its purposes will be paid, applied and distributed as follows:

(a)   first, to the repayment of interest owing on Shareholder Loans, [*such payments to be made pro rata in accordance with the interest owing to each Shareholder/in the order as set out in section 3.7 above*];

(b)   next, to the repayment of the principal amount of Shareholder Loans, such payments to be made [*OPTIONAL: pro rata*] [*in accordance with the principal amount owing to each Shareholder/the order as set out in section 3.7 above*]; and

(c)   last, the balance, if any, will be distributed to the Shareholders by way of dividends.

Unless as otherwise agreed in writing by the Shareholders, no distribution will be made in any of the above categories unless and until the preceding category has been satisfied.

Notwithstanding any other provision of this Agreement, all amounts payable by the Corporation to a Defaulting Shareholder (as defined in Section 7.1) will be paid first, in reduction of accrued interest outstanding on the Defaulting Shareholder's Deficit Contribution owing to such a Shareholder and thereafter to a Shareholder in reduction of the principal portion outstanding on the Defaulting Shareholder's Deficit Contribution owing to such Shareholder. Each Defaulting Shareholder hereby irrevocably authorizes and directs the Corporation to pay to such Shareholder all or such portion of any distribution to which such Defaulting Shareholder is entitled pursuant to this Section 3.14 as may be required on account of such Defaulting Shareholder's liability to such Shareholder.

ARTICLE 4: MANAGEMENT OF THE COMPANY

4.1)   Board of Directors

The Board shall be comprised of _________ directors. Each Shareholder, provided that it holds at least _________% of the Shares, shall be entitled to nominate _________ Persons to the Board and shall be entitled to remove and replace its respective nominees from time to time as provided in Section 4.3. Each Shareholder shall vote its Shares to elect the directors nominated in accordance with this Agreement. Except as set out in this Agreement, the Board shall have no authority and that all matters which are generally within the power and control of the Board of Directors shall be restricted accordingly and shall be determined by the Shareholders in accordance with Section 4.6 below. The initial Directors are set out in Schedule 4.1 hereto. [NOTE TO DRAFT: See Appendix 4.1 for alternative mechanism of selecting directors]

4.2) Officers

The officers of the Corporation are set out in Schedule 4.2 hereto.

4.3) Removal and Replacement of Nominees

Any Shareholder entitled to nominate and elect a director shall be entitled to remove any such director by notice to such director, the other Shareholders and to the Corporation. Any vacancy occurring on the Board by reason of the death, disqualification, inability to act, resignation or removal of any director shall be filled only by a further nominee of the Shareholder whose nominee was so affected so as to maintain a Board consisting of the numbers of nominees specified in Schedule 4.1.

4.4) Quorum

A quorum for a meeting of the Board shall consist of a majority of the members of the Board, with at least [*one nominee of each Shareholder/*___________] being present. In the event that a quorum is not obtained at any meeting, the meeting shall be adjourned and may be reconvened upon ___________ hours notice to the directors, at which reconvened meeting the quorum shall be [___________ *directors/a majority of directors*].

4.5) Accountant

___________ shall be appointed the Accountant of the Corporation unless, prior to the appointment of any other Person as Accountant of the Corporation, all of the Shareholders have consented in writing to such other Person being appointed and a copy of such consent has been filed with the Corporation.

Audit Exemption [if no auditor is appointed]

[*In each financial year of the Corporation the Shareholders shall consent to exempt the Corporation from the requirement to appoint an auditor pursuant to the provisions of the Act.*]

4.6) Approval of Matters

Subject to applicable law, including the Act, unless specifically authorized by this Agreement, no obligation of the Corporation or any Subsidiary will be entered into, no decision will be made, and no action taken by or with respect to the Corporation or any Subsidiary with respect to the following matters without the written approval of [*insert names of particular shareholder or directors nominated by them or specify a high level of approval, i.e. 90-100%*]:

    (a) any material change in the business of the Corporation stated in Section 2.1;

(b) the issuance or sale by the Corporation of any of its share capital or any rights, warrants or securities convertible into or exercisable or exchangeable for shares in the capital of the Corporation or any Subsidiary of the Corporation;

(c) the acquisition by the Corporation or a Subsidiary of any of its Shares, except pursuant to the exercise of any redemption rights attached to such Shares or this Agreement;

(d) the winding up, dissolution or liquidation of the Corporation or a Subsidiary;

(e) the amalgamation, merger or consolidation of the Corporation with one or more other corporations;

(f) the continuance of the Corporation under the laws of another jurisdiction;

(g) the sale, lease, exchange or other disposition of all or substantially all of the property of the Corporation or of any Subsidiary;

(h) the borrowing of money by the Corporation;

(i) any amendment to the Articles or by-laws of the Corporation and the enactment of new by-laws;

(j) a statutory arrangement;

(k) the declaration of dividends;

(l) the payment of any salaries, bonuses, retiring allowances or other remuneration for officers, directors, Shareholders and Principals of the Corporation or any Subsidiary or any Associates or Affiliates of such officers, directors, Shareholders or Principals;

(m) except pursuant to contracts to which the Corporation is a party at the date hereof, the payment of management or consulting fees or bonuses or the making of a contract between the Corporation and a Shareholder or Principals or any person, firm, corporation or entity not dealing at arm's length with a Shareholder;

(n) the increase or decrease in the number of directors;

(o) make any loan or advance, give guarantees for, invest in or give security for or guarantee the debts of any other corporation, person or entity;

(p) hypothecate, mortgage, pledge or otherwise encumber its assets, or any of them, except as may be required by its bankers in connection with its normal banking activities and arranged lines of credit;

(q) the employment or termination of any Person at an annual level of compensation in excess of $[*dollar amount*];

(r)   the giving of shareholder approval, as shareholder of a Subsidiary, in respect of any matter which shareholder approval for a Subsidiary is required;

(s)   the delegation by the Board, or the board of any Subsidiary, of any of its powers; and

(t)   any commitment or agreement to do any of the foregoing.

4.7) Shareholder Approval

(a)   With respect to any matters that relate to the operations of a Subsidiary, the Corporation agrees to vote and act as a shareholder of such Subsidiary so as to carry out the intention of the Board.

(b)   Any resolution in writing signed by all of the members of the Board nominated and elected by a particular Shareholder shall be deemed to constitute the consent to such resolution of that Shareholder, and any matter recorded in the minutes of a meeting of directors or shareholders as having been approved or agreed upon, by resolution or otherwise, shall, subject to any contrary intention being indicated in the minutes, be deemed to have been consented to by a particular Shareholder if the minutes are signed by that Shareholder or, in the case of a meeting of directors, by one or more of the directors nominated and elected by that Shareholder.

(c)   Except as otherwise provided herein and subject to the requirements of the Act, at all meetings of Shareholders, no resolution will be passed unless it is approved by [___________*% of the votes cast by the Shareholders/Shareholders who hold* ___________*% of the Shares*]. The chairman of a meeting of Shareholders will [*OPTIONAL: not*] have a second or casting vote.

4.8) Telephone Meetings

Any or all directors may participate in a meeting of the Board by means of such telephone, electronic or other communication facilities as permit all Persons participating in the meeting to hear and communicate with each other simultaneously and a director participating in such a meeting by such means is deemed to be present at the meeting.

4.9) Transactions with Affiliates

A director who is a party to a material contract or transaction, or a proposed material contract or transaction, with the Corporation, or who has a material interest in any Person who is a party to any such contract or transaction, shall disclose in writing to the Corporation or request to have entered in the minutes of the meeting of the Board the nature and extent of his interest and shall otherwise comply with the applicable provisions of the Act.

4.10) Shareholder Quorum

A quorum for a meeting of Shareholders shall consist of [*each Shareholder/ Shareholders who in the aggregate hold at least _________% of the issued and outstanding Shares*] [*OPTIONAL: entitled to vote on the matters being put to the Shareholders at such meeting*] being present by representative or by proxy. In the event that a quorum is not obtained at any meeting, the meeting shall be adjourned and reconvened five (5) Business Days later, at the same time and in the same location, at which reconvened meeting the quorum shall be the Shareholders present.

4.11) Books and Records

The Corporation shall maintain books of account at its registered office which shall contain accurate and complete records of all transactions, receipts, expenses, assets and liabilities of the Corporation. Any Shareholder may, at any time during business hours and without causing unreasonable disruption of the operations of the Corporation, cause such Shareholder's employees, agents, professional advisors or other authorized representatives to review any of the books and records of the Corporation and, at the expense of such Shareholder, take copies thereof. Each Shareholder shall also be entitled from time to time, during usual business hours on reasonable notice to the Corporation, to examine (or cause its representatives to examine) (i) the Articles and the By-laws, and (ii) the minute books of the Corporation.

4.12) Bankers, Banking and other Documents

    (a)   Until changed by a resolution of the [*Board/Shareholders*], [*enter bank name*] located at [*enter bank address*], shall be the bankers of the Corporation (the "**Bank**"). The Corporation shall maintain such bank accounts as the Corporation may from time to time require, at the Bank or at such other bank or trust company as the Directors may from time to time determine.

    (b)   All banking documents, cheques and negotiable instruments entered into by or on behalf of the Corporation will be in writing and for amounts less than $[*dollar amount*], will require the signature of any one of __________ or __________ and for amounts of $[*dollar amount*] or more, will require the signature of both __________ and __________, unless otherwise agreed by the Shareholders.

(c)   All deeds, transfers, contracts, agreements and other documents not expressly referred to in Section 4.12(b) entered into by or on behalf of the Corporation will be in writing and, with respect to the commitment by the Corporation of an aggregate amount of less than $[*dollar amount*], will require the signature of any one of _________ or _________, and with respect to the commitment by the Corporation of an aggregate amount of $[*dollar amount*] or more, will require the signature of both _________ and _________, unless otherwise agreed by the Shareholders.

ARTICLE 5: DEALING WITH SHARES

5.1)   Restrictions on Transfer of Shares

(a)   Except as expressly provided in this Agreement, or as may otherwise be unanimously agreed [*OPTIONAL: in writing*] by the Shareholders, no Shareholder shall, directly or indirectly, Transfer any Securities or shares of a Shareholder which is a corporation, held by it, or any of its rights or obligations under this Agreement, to any Person, except as specifically permitted by this Agreement and only in accordance with the terms of this Agreement.

(b)   Any attempted Transfer of Shares made in violation of this Agreement shall be null and void. Neither the Board nor the Shareholders shall approve or ratify any Transfer of Shares made in contravention of this Agreement and the Corporation shall not permit any such Transfer to be recorded on the share register of the Corporation maintained for the Shares.

(c)   If the requisite approval to transfer the Shares is obtained pursuant to Section 5.1(a) above, or in accordance with any other provisions of this Agreement, each Shareholder agrees that it will not Transfer its Shares to anyone who is not then a Shareholder unless such transferee (and if such transferee is a corporation, such transferee's principal) first executes and delivers to the Corporation the Adherence Agreement in the form attached hereto as Schedule 5.1(c). The transferring Shareholder shall guarantee the obligations of the Transferee under this Agreement.

(d)   Section 5.1(a) shall not in any way limit or prohibit the right of a Shareholder to bequest the shares of its Corporation pursuant to his last will and testament provided that the person(s) to whom the Shareholder bequeaths the said shares executes and delivers to all other parties hereto a copy of the Adherence Agreement in the form attached hereto as Schedule 5.1(c).

5.2) Endorsement on Certificates

Along with such other endorsements required by applicable law, share certificates of the Corporation shall bear the following language either as an endorsement or on the face of such share certificate:

> The shares represented by this certificate are subject to all the terms and conditions of an agreement made ____________ as it may be amended and/ or restated, which agreement contains, among other things, restrictions on the right of the holder hereof to transfer or sell the shares. A copy of such agreement is on file at the registered office of the Corporation.

5.3) Issue of Additional Shares

(a) No shares in the capital of the Corporation will be issued unless such shares have first been offered to the Shareholders (in this section, collectively the "**Pre-Emptive Shareholders**" and each a "**Pre-Emptive Shareholder**") at such price and on such terms as those shares are to be offered to others. Such shares will be offered to such Pre-Emptive Shareholder as nearly as may be in each such Pre-Emptive Shareholder's Proportionate Share of all issued and outstanding Shares.

(b) Notice of such offer will be sent to the Pre-Emptive Shareholders specifying: (i) the series, class, attributes and total number of shares then being offered for allotment and issue; (ii) the issue price for each share; (iii) the number of shares being offered to the Pre-Emptive Shareholder to whom the notice is addressed; (iv) that the offer, if not accepted within ten (10) Business Days from the date the notice is given by the Corporation, will be deemed to have been declined; (v) that a Pre-Emptive Shareholder who wishes to subscribe for shares which are less than his/her/its entitlement will, in his acceptance, specify the number of shares that he/ she/it wishes to subscribe for; and (vi) that a Pre-Emptive Shareholder who wishes to subscribe for shares in excess of his/her/its entitlement will, in his acceptance, specify the number of shares in excess of his/her/its entitlement that he/she/it wishes to subscribe for.

(c) Each Pre-Emptive Shareholder who chooses to accept the offer will, within the ten (10) Business Day period, send an acceptance to the

Corporation indicating whether he accepts part or all of the shares offered to him.

(d) If a Pre-Emptive Shareholder fails to subscribe for his/her/its full entitlement, the unsubscribed for shares will be used to satisfy the subscription of the other Pre-Emptive Shareholders for shares in excess of their entitlement, if any. If the subscriptions in excess are for a number of shares greater than the number of unsubscribed shares, the unsubscribed shares will be divided among those Pre-Emptive Shareholders desiring shares in excess of their entitlement as nearly as may be in the Proportionate Share of such Pre-Emptive Shareholders (provided that no Pre-Emptive Shareholder will be bound to take up any shares in excess of the number specified in his acceptance).

(e) On expiration of the ten (10) Business Day period for acceptance or on receipt of notice from a Pre-Emptive Shareholder that he/she/it declines to accept the shares offered to him/her/it, with respect to those shares not subscribed for by any other Pre-Emptive Shareholder pursuant to subsection 5.3(d) above, the Corporation will have the next forty (40) Business Days within which it may issue those shares not accepted to any person, firm or corporation. If the Corporation does not issue such shares within that forty (40) Business Day period, the foregoing pre-emptive right will again apply in respect of the unissued shares.

(f) This Section 5.3 will not apply to Shares issued or to be issued:

    (i) pursuant to an initial public offering of any Shares;

    (ii) as compensation to employees, officers, or directors of the Corporation or pursuant to an ESOP or phantom equity plan of the Corporation whether or not currently in effect; or

    (iii) pursuant to the exercise of conversion privileges, options or rights previously granted by the Corporation in accordance with this Agreement.

(g) If the Corporation issues any additional shares or securities in the capital of the Corporation which are not Shares, the parties hereto shall, prior to such issuance, give due consideration to any changes which they may wish to make to this Agreement, in particular, the provisions relating to the rights and obligations that relate to such shares or securities.

See Appendix 5.4 for optional language permitting a Shareholder to pledge its shares as part of bank financing.

5.4) Transfers To Permitted Transferees

Any Shareholder (the "**Transferor**") shall be entitled at any time to Transfer [*any/ all (but not less than all)*] of the Securities held by such Shareholder to a Permitted Transferee, provided that the Transferor will first have delivered to the Corporation all of the following:

(a) The Transferor's (and its Principal, if the Transferor is not an individual) statutory declaration and warranty stating that the Permitted Transferee is a Permitted Transferee of such Transferor;

(b) If the Permitted Transferee is a corporation, a certificate of the Secretary of the Permitted Transferee setting out the names and addresses of all shareholders of the Permitted Transferee together with their respective shareholdings in the Permitted Transferee [*NTD: remove if the Permitted Transferee is an individual*];

(c) If the Permitted Transferee is a Family Trust, a certificate of the Trustees of the Permitted Transferee setting out the names and addresses of all trustees and beneficiaries of the Permitted Transferee;

(d) The Permitted Transferee executes and delivers to the Corporation the Adherence Agreement in the form attached hereto as Schedule 5.1(c); and

(e) An agreement executed by the Transferor (and its Principal, if the Transferor is not an individual) in favour of the Corporation and the other Shareholders (the "**Remaining Shareholders**" in this Section) pursuant to which the Transferor (and its Principal, if the Transferor is not an individual):

  (i) if the Permitted Transferee is not a trust, agrees to Control the Permitted Transferee for so long as the Permitted Transferee owns any Securities;

  (ii) if the Permitted Transferee is a trust, agrees to cause the Permitted Transferee to remain a Family Trust for so long as the Permitted Transferee holds any Securities; and

  (iii) guarantees the observance and performance of all obligations of the Permitted Transferee under this Agreement.

Any Holding Company may, at any time, and shall forthwith, if such Holding Company ceases to be under the direct Control of an individual party to this Agreement, other than by reason of the death of the individual party which Controls it, transfer back to the applicable individual all (but not less than all) such Securities held by the Holding Company.

5.5)   Right of First Refusal

[*NOTE: This ROFR allows a shareholder to offer to sell his shares to existing share-holders only once he has procured a Third Party Offer from a third party. See Appendix 5.7 for an offer to sell his shares to existing shareholders when he does not yet have a Third Party Offer on the table and/or he does not yet even have a potential third party purchaser*]

(a)   If, [*OPTIONAL: , at any time after [insert some initial period]*,] a Share-holder (the "**Offeror**") receives a Third Party Offer to purchase such Shares offered for purchase [*OPTIONAL: all, but not less than all,*] of the Shares then held by the Offeror (the "**Offered Shares**") [*OPTIONAL: together with the Shareholder Loans held by the Offeror,*] which Third Party Offer the Offeror has accepted (subject to compliance with the provisions of this Section), the Offeror shall deliver a notice in writing (the "**Notice of Sale**") to the other Shareholders (the "**Other Share-holders**") offering to sell to the Other Shareholders the Offered Shares at the same price and in all other respects on the same terms and conditions as provided in the Third Party Offer (except that the Notice of Sale shall be deemed to contain the provisions of Section 8.2). The Offeror shall deliver with the Notice of Sale, a true copy of the Third Party Offer and if the Third Party is a corporation, the names of the principal shareholders (if available), officers and directors of the Third Party and any other information with respect to the financial capacity of the Third Party in the possession of the Offeror. The offer contained in the Notice of Sale shall be irrevocable except with the consent of the Other Shareholders and shall be open for acceptance for a per-iod of [*number of days*] Business Days after the date upon the which the Notice of Sale was last received by the Other Shareholders, (the "**Acceptance Period**").

(b)   Upon the Notice of Sale being given, the Other Shareholders shall have the right to purchase all, but not less than all, of the Offered Shares, rateably based on the each of the Other Shareholder's Proportionate Share among all of the Other Shareholders as of the date the Notice of Sale or to purchase in such other proportion as the Other Shareholders may agree in writing.

(c)   Within the Acceptance Period, each of the Other Shareholders may give to the Offeror a notice in writing (an "**Acceptance Notice**") accepting the offer contained in the Notice of Sale and specifying the maximum number of the Offered Shares it wishes to acquire (which number may be greater than or less than its pro rata entitlement). If any Other Shareholder does not give an Acceptance Notice or specifies in its Acceptance Notice a number of Shares less than its pro rata entitlement, the resulting unaccepted Offered Shares shall be deemed to have been offered, by the Offeror, to such of the Other Shareholders who specified in their Acceptance Notice a desire to acquire a number of the Offered Shares greater than their pro rata entitlement, and each such Other Shareholder is, subject to the maximum number of the Offered Shares specified in its Acceptance Notice, entitled to acquire its pro rata entitlement of the unaccepted Offered Shares based upon the number of Shares beneficially owned by such Other Shareholders, as between themselves, or in such other proportion as such Other Shareholders may agree in writing. If the Other Shareholders, or any of them, give Acceptance Notices within the Acceptance Period, confirming their agreement to purchase all of the Offered Shares, the sale of the Offered Shares to such Other Shareholders shall be completed within [*number of days*] Business Days of the expiry of the Acceptance Period.

(d) If the Offeror does not receive Acceptance Notices from the Other Shareholders, or any of them, within the Acceptance Period confirming their agreement to purchase all of the Offered Shares, the rights of the Other Shareholders to purchase the Offered Shares shall cease and the Offeror may sell the Offered Shares to the Third Party at the price and upon the terms and conditions specified in the Third Party Offer.

(e) Any transfer to the Third Party pursuant to subsection 5.6(d) above must be completed within [*number of days*] days following the expiry of the Acceptance Period, failing which the provisions of this Agreement shall again apply to any proposed transfer of Shares, and so on from time to time. Notwithstanding the foregoing, before consenting to any transfer of Shares to the Third Party pursuant to the provisions of this Section, the Board shall be entitled to require proof that such transfer was completed at the price and upon the other terms and conditions contained in the Third Party Offer, and the Board shall refuse to permit the recording of the transfer of the Offeror's Shares if they may have been sold otherwise than in accordance with the provisions of the Third Party Offer.

(f) All Acceptance Notices or other notices under this Section shall be given concurrently to all Shareholders and to the Corporation.

5.6) Piggyback Rights

(a) If a Shareholder or group of Shareholders who, in the aggregate, hold at least 75% of the issued and outstanding voting securities of the Corporation (collectively, the **"Offeror"** in this Section), receive(s) a Third Party Offer to purchase all, but not less than all, of its Shares (such Shares offered for purchase the **"Majority Shareholders' Shares"**), which Third Party Offer the Offeror has accepted (subject to compliance with the provisions of this Section), the Offeror shall deliver a notice in writing (the **"Notice of Sale"**) to the other Shareholders (collectively, the **"Other Shareholders"** and each an **"Other Shareholder"**) stating the terms and conditions as provided in the Third Party Offer (except that the Notice of Sale shall be deemed to contain the provisions of Section 8.2). The Offeror shall deliver with the Notice of Sale a true copy of the Third Party Offer.

(b) Each of the Other Shareholders shall have the right, exercisable within 10 days of receipt of the Notice of Sale, upon notice in writing to the Offeror and the Third Party (the **"Piggy-back Notice"**), to require the Third Party to purchase all, but not less than all, of the Shares held by such Other Shareholder, at the time of completion of, and upon the same terms and conditions as those contained in, the Third Party Offer.

(c) If any Other Shareholder gives a Piggy-back Notice to the Offeror and the Third Party within such period, then the Offeror shall be entitled to sell the Majority Shareholders' Shares to the Third Party pursuant to the Third Party Offer only if such Third Party also offers to purchase from such Other Shareholder all of the Shares held by such Other Shareholder, conditional upon the completion of the transaction of purchase and sale contemplated in the Third Party Offer.

(d) If any Other Shareholder does not give a Piggy-back Notice to the Offeror and the Third Party within such period within the Offer Period, such Other Shareholder shall be deemed to have waived their rights under this Section 5.7.

(e) It is a condition precedent of such Third Party Offer that the Third Party (and its Principal, if applicable) must execute and deliver to the Corporation the Adherence Agreement in the form attached hereto as Schedule 5.1(c).

5.7 Third Party Offer for All Shares and Drag-Along Requirement

(a) If a Shareholder or group of Shareholders who, in the aggregate, hold at least 75% of the issued and outstanding voting securities of the

Corporation (collectively, the "**Offeror**" in this Section), receive a Third Party Offer from a Third Party (such potential Third Party purchaser the "**Bidder**") for all Shares of the Corporation (a "**Take-Over Bid**") which it wishes to accept, the Offeror shall give notice of the Third Party Offer to the other Shareholders within three (3) Business Days of the Offeror receiving the Third Party Offer. The Offeror shall have the right to require all Shareholders on 10 days' notice in writing (a "**Compulsory Sale Notice**") to sell all of the Shares held by them to Bidder pursuant to the terms of the Third Party Offer.

(b) Once the Offeror gives a Compulsory Sale Notice to all Shareholders, each Shareholder shall be obligated to sell all of the Shares beneficially held by it, upon the terms specified in the Third Party Offer, to the Bidder, conditional upon the completion of the transaction of purchase and sale contemplated in the Third Party Offer. The Offeror shall accept the Third Party Offer on behalf of the Offeror and all of the other Shareholders and all Shareholders will be bound by the Third Party Offer; provided that if the transaction contemplated by the Third Party Offer is not completed within twelve (12) months of the delivery of the Compulsory Sale Notice, the Offeror will not thereafter sell any Shares unless and until it again complies with the provisions of this Article. All of the Shareholders (other than the Offeror) hereby irrevocably appoint the Offeror as its attorney in that behalf. Such appointment and power of attorney, being coupled with an interest, shall not be revoked by the death, dissolution, winding up, bankruptcy, insolvency or other termination of the existence of the transferor and the transferor hereby ratifies and confirms and agrees to ratify and confirm all that the transferee may lawfully do or cause to be done by virtue of such appointment and power.

5.8) Buy-Sell

[*Note: The following "shotgun" version is applicable where there are more than 3 shareholders. See Appendix 5.7 for buy-sells involving 2 or 3 shareholders.*]

(a) At any time after [*insert some initial period, if any*], any Shareholder (referred to in this Section as the "**Offeror**") shall have the right to give notice (referred to in this Section as the "**Notice**") to the other Shareholders (collectively the "**Offerees**" and individually an "**Offeree**") and to the Corporation, containing the following:

   (i) an offer by the Offeror to purchase all of the Shares beneficially owned by the Offerees (an "**Offer to Purchase**");

     (ii)   an offer by the Offeror to sell all of the Shares beneficially owned by the Offeror to the Offerees [*OPTIONAL: pro rata based upon the number of Shares beneficially owned by the Offerees*] (an "**Offer to Sell**");

     (iii) the price to be paid for each Share pursuant to the Offer to Purchase and the Offer to Sell, which shall be the same for both Offers (the "**Purchase Price**"), and all other terms and conditions of the Offers, which terms and conditions shall be the same for both Offers;

       (A) a certified cheque, bank draft or other form of immediately available funds by way of deposit payable to the Corporation's solicitors in trust equal to [*percentage*]% of the total purchase price of the Offerees' Shares, computed on the basis of the stated price per Share set out in the Offer; and

       (B) A statement setting out in reasonable detail full reference to any information relating to the financial affairs of the Corporation or its business which, to the best of the knowledge of the Offeror(s), is not known to the Offerees or any one thereof.

(b) Within [*number of days*] Business Days of the Notice being given (the "**Offer Period**"), each Offeree shall be entitled to accept either the Offer to Purchase or the Offer to Sell by giving written notice of such acceptance to the Offeror, to the other Offerees and to the Corporation.

(c) If all of the Offerees accept the Offer to Purchase, the Offerees shall sell and Offeror shall purchase all of the Shares beneficially owned by each Offeree at the Purchase Price and the transaction of purchase and sale shall be completed within [*number of days*] Business Days of the expiry of the Offer Period.

(d) If all of the Offerees accept the Offer to Sell, the Offerees shall:

     (i)   Together with the written notice of acceptance of the Offer to sell, deliver to the Offeror a certified cheque, bank draft or other form of immediately available funds by way of deposit payable to the Corporation's solicitors in trust equal to [*percentage*] % of the total purchase price of the Offeror's Shares, computed on the basis of the stated price per Share set out in the Offer; and

     (ii) purchase, rateably based on each Offeree's Proportionate Share of the total number of Shares held by all Offerees, or in such other proportion as such Offerees agree in writing, and the Offeror shall sell all of the Shares beneficially owned by the Offeror at the

Purchase Price and the transaction of Purchase and Sale shall be completed within [*number of days*] Business Days of the expiry of the Offer Period. The Shareholders shall, immediately upon giving the notice under (b) above, instruct the Corporation's solicitors to forthwith return to the Offeror the deposit paid pursuant to subsection 5.8(a)(iii).

(e) If any Offeree does not accept either the Offer to Purchase or the Offer to Sell within the Offer Period, such Offeree shall be deemed to have accepted the Offer to Purchase and to have given notice of such acceptance pursuant to the provisions of subsection (b) on the last Business Day upon which such notice may have been given.

(f) If one or more of the Offerees accept or are deemed to have accepted the Offer to Purchase (the "**Selling Offerees**") and one or more of the Offerees accept the Offer to Sell (the "**Purchasing Offerees**"), the Purchasing Offerees shall be entitled to purchase the Shares beneficially owned by the Offeror and the Shares beneficially owned by the Selling Offerees by giving notice of the exercise of such right to the Offeror, to the Selling Offerees and to the Corporation within 10 Business Days of the expiry of the Offer Period and, if each of the Purchasing Offerees gives notice pursuant to the provisions of this subsection, the Offeror and the Selling Offerees shall sell the Shares beneficially owned by them to the Purchasing Offerees and such transaction of purchase and sale shall be completed within [*number of days*] Business Days of the date upon which the Corporation was given the last of such notices by the Purchasing Offerees. If there is more than one Purchasing Offeree, the Purchasing Offerees shall purchase the Shares of the Offeror and the Selling Offerees rateably based on each Purchasing Offeree's Proportionate Share of the total number of Shares held by all Purchasing Offerees, or in such other proportions as the Purchasing Offerees agree in writing. If any Purchasing Offeree fails to give notice pursuant to the provisions of this subsection within the [*number of days*] Business Day period specified in this subsection, all of the Purchasing Offerees, including those that may have given notice pursuant to the provisions of this subsection, shall be deemed not to have accepted the Offer to Sell but, rather, to have accepted the Offer to Purchase and the provisions of subsection (c) shall apply, mutatis mutandis, to all of the Offerees except that the transaction of purchase and sale shall be completed within [*number of days*] Business Days of the expiry of the [*number of days*] Business Day period specified in this subsection.

(g) Two or more of the Shareholders (collectively, the "**Joint Shareholders**") may jointly give a Notice to the other Shareholders pursuant to the provisions of subsection (a) and, in such event, the further provisions of this Section 5.8 shall apply, mutatis mutandis, except that any Shares purchased by them shall be purchased rateably based on each Joint Shareholder's Proportionate Share of the total number of Shares held by all Joint Shareholders, or in such other proportions as such Joint Shareholders agree in writing.

(h) Two or more of the Shareholders may jointly accept the Offer to Sell pursuant to the provisions of subsection (b) and, in such event, the further provisions of this Section shall apply, *mutatis mutandis*, except that the number of Shares to be purchased by each of them may be set out in the notice given by them provided that the aggregate of such numbers equals the number of Shares beneficially owned by the Offeror.

(i) [*Subsequent Transfer clause—remove if not desired by client*] If the Purchasing Offerees receive an offer for the purchase of all of their Shares at any time within [number of months] months of the Closing Date and the price per Share payable pursuant to such offer is greater than the price per Share paid to the Selling Offerees then, if such transaction subsequently closes, the Purchasing Offerees will pay to the Selling Offerees an amount equal to the difference between the price per Share received by the [*Selling Offerees/Corporation*] and the price per Share received by the Selling Offerees pursuant to this Article, provided that any payment to be made to the Selling Offerees pursuant to this Section will be made on a proportionate basis as between the Selling Offerees and the Purchasing Offerees as and when the purchase price is received from the third party purchaser. In this Section, the term "Purchasing Offeree" includes an amalgamated corporation of which the Purchasing Offeree is an amalgamating corporation.

5.9) Put-Call

[*Note: See Appendix 5.9 PUT-CALL for optional Put-Call clauses.*]

ARTICLE 6: PURCHASE OF SHAREHOLDER LOANS ON TRANSFER OF SHARES

6.1) Shareholder Loans

Contemporaneous with the purchase and sale of the Shares pursuant to this Agreement, and as a condition thereof, the purchaser will purchase from the vendor all Shareholder Loans owing to the vendor of the Shares for an amount equal to the outstanding principal amount of such Shareholder Loans, together with accrued interest thereon to the Closing Date (or if there is more than one purchaser, in proportion that each purchaser is obligated to purchase the vendor's Shares). The full amount shall be paid on closing to the vendor by certified cheque or bank draft.

ARTICLE 7: EVENTS OF DEFAULT

7.1) Defaulting Shareholders

(a) A Shareholder shall be deemed to be a Defaulting Shareholder immediately following the occurrence of any of the following events (each a "**Triggering Event**"):

[NOTE: Delete any of the following that are not applicable or are to be dealt with separately, e.g. death, disability]

(i) If the representations and warranties of a Shareholder and/or its Principal contained in this Agreement become untrue and incorrect in each and every respect, including, but not limited to, subsection 3.1(j) or if a Shareholder fails to perform or observe any covenant, term or condition of this Agreement including, but not limited to sections 9.1 and 9.3 and such failure continues for ten (10) Business Days following notice thereof from any other Shareholder, excluding such representations and warranties which have become untrue and incorrect solely and exclusively as a result of a Transfer of Shares which is otherwise permitted under this Agreement;

(ii) If any Shareholder or its Principal makes an assignment for the benefit of creditors or is the subject of any proceedings under any bankruptcy or insolvency law or, avails itself of the benefit of any other legislation for the benefit of debtors or, if any corporate

Shareholder takes steps to wind-up or terminate its corporate existence;

(iii) If a trustee in bankruptcy, receiver, receiver and manager, liquidator or other officer with similar powers is appointed for a Shareholder or its Principal over all or any material part of its/his/her respective property (and which material part includes part or all of a Shareholder's Securities);

(iv) If an encumbrancer takes possession of any Shares beneficially owned by a Shareholder or a Principal, or if a distress or execution or any similar process is levied or enforced upon or against any Shares beneficially owned by a Shareholder or a Principal and remains unsatisfied for the shorter of a period of 2 Business Days or such period as permits the Shares to be sold;

(v) If a Shareholder ceases to Control such Shareholder's Securities (other than in accordance with this Agreement);

(vi) If a Shareholder's nominee on the Corporation's board of directors fails on [*number*] consecutive occasions to attend a meeting of the board of directors for which proper notice is given and a quorum is not present;

(vii) If a Shareholder fails on [*number*] consecutive occasions to attend or be represented by proxy at a meeting of the shareholders for which proper notice is given and a quorum is not present

(viii) Upon the termination of employment with the Corporation of any Shareholder or its Principal, for any reason (including termination for cause) other than death, Disability, termination with cause or voluntary resignation;

(ix) If an order is made by a court of competent jurisdiction pursuant to Applicable Family Law Legislation restraining the depletion of [*a Shareholder's/its Principal's*] property or for the possession, delivering up, safekeeping or preservation of [*a Shareholder's/its Principal's*] property and such property includes any of [*such Shareholder's/such Principal's*] Securities;

(x) If a Shareholder or its Principal fails to perform or observe any other term or condition of this Agreement and such failure continues for ten (10) Business Days following notice thereof from any other Shareholder or its Principal;

(xi) If any Shareholder who is an individual or if any Principal becomes Permanently Disabled; and/or

(xii) If any Shareholder who is an individual or any Principal, dies.

(b) Each Shareholder or Principal, or its administrator, or other legal or Personal Representative, as the case may be, (each being a "**Representative**"), shall give notice in writing to the Corporation promptly following the occurrence of a Triggering Event.

7.2) Rights on Default

If a Triggering Event occurs, any Shareholder other than the Defaulting Shareholder (a "**Non-Defaulting Shareholder**") will have the right to:

(a) do such acts and things and make such payments as are reasonably necessary in order to remedy the Triggering Event, and which monies expended in attempting to remedy such Triggering Event (including legal fees on a solicitor and his own client basis) will constitute a Deficit Contribution owing by the Defaulting Shareholder to such Non-Defaulting Shareholder;

(b) borrow on behalf of the Defaulting Shareholder on such terms and conditions and at such rate of interest as may be agreed on between such Non-Defaulting Shareholder and a lender acting in good faith, an amount equal to the amount required to be advanced by the Defaulting Shareholder to the Corporation to cure the default and to advance such amount to the Corporation on behalf of the Defaulting Shareholder and to charge the Defaulting Shareholder with all reasonable costs and expenses (including legal fees on a solicitor and his own client basis) incurred by such Non-Defaulting Shareholder in connection with the amount borrowed and interest on the amount borrowed and advanced at the same rate as charged by such lender on the amount outstanding from time to time. The Defaulting Shareholder hereby irrevocably nominates, constitutes and appoints such Non-Defaulting Shareholder as his true and lawful attorney-in-fact and agent for, in the name of and on behalf of the Defaulting Shareholder to execute and deliver in the name of the Defaulting Shareholder all documents or instruments as may be necessary in connection with this Subsection. Such appointment and power of attorney, being coupled with an interest, shall not be revoked by the death, incapacity (whether mental or physical), dissolution, winding up, bankruptcy or insolvency of the Defaulting Shareholder. The Defaulting Shareholder hereby ratifies and confirms, and agrees to ratify and confirm, all that a Non-Defaulting Shareholder may lawfully do or cause to be done by virtue of such appointment and power of attorney;

(c)   purchase the Shares beneficially owned by the Defaulting Shareholder pursuant to Section 7.3; and/or

(d)   exercise any other right or remedy available to a Non-Defaulting Shareholder, whether at law, in equity or pursuant to the terms of this Agreement.

7.3)   Irrevocable Option to Purchase Shares of Defaulting Shareholder

(a)   Each Shareholder grants to the other Shareholders an irrevocable option (which option shall not be revoked by the death, incapacity (whether mental or physical), dissolution, winding up, bankruptcy, insolvency or other termination of the existence of the Shareholder or its Principal) (the "**Purchase Option**"), exercisable in the event that it becomes a Defaulting Shareholder, to purchase all but not less than all of the Shares held by it (the "**Purchased Shares**"), [*OPTIONAL: provided that such Purchase Option shall not apply to any Shares of a deceased Shareholder or any securities of a corporate Shareholder follow- ing the death of its Principal that are bequeathed by such Shareholder or Principal upon his or her death to, or otherwise devolve absolutely upon, a Permitted Transferee which has complied with the provisions of Section 5.4, as the case may be, within [number of days] days following the death of the Shareholder or Principal.*]

(b)   The Corporation shall deliver a written notice to each Shareholder other than the Defaulting Shareholder (the "**Other Shareholders**") immedi- ately following the receipt of notice of, or otherwise becoming aware of, a Triggering Event. The Purchase Option shall be exercisable by the Other Shareholders at any time within [*number of days*] days following receipt of notice of the Triggering Event (the "**Exercise Period**") upon notice in writing (the "**Exercise Notice**") to the Defaulting Shareholder or its Representative and the Corporation.

(c)   If the Other Shareholders elect to exercise the Purchase Option:

(i)   each Other Shareholder shall be entitled to purchase its Propor- tionate Share (as among the Other Shareholders) of the Purchased Shares or in such other proportions as the Other Shareholders may mutually agree in writing and such purchase may be made by one or more Other Shareholders jointly or by any one of them alone;

(ii)   the purchase price for the Purchased Shares shall be determined in accordance with Section 7.4 below;

(iii)   the Closing Date will be the 10th Business Day following determin- ation of the Fair Market Value; and

(iv) the purchase price will be paid and satisfied on the Closing Date as follows:

    (A) *[percentage]* percent (__________%) of the purchase price will be paid by each Other Shareholder by way of certified cheque, bank draft or other form of immediately available funds on the Closing Date; and

    (B) the balance of the purchase price payable by each purchasing Shareholder, together with interest thereon at the Prime Rate *[OPTIONAL: plus __________%]* will be evidenced by a Promissory Note of each purchasing Shareholder and will be repayable in *[number]* equal and consecutive *[annual/monthly]* instalments of principal, plus interest on the principal balance then outstanding. The first instalment will be due and payable on the *[first anniversary of the Closing Date]*.

7.4) Purchase Price for Shares

The purchase price for the Purchased Shares (the **"Purchase Price"**) of the Defaulting Shareholder (the **"Vendor"**) shall be the product obtained by multiplying the number of Purchased Shares and the Fair Market Value of the Shares determined at the moment immediately before the date of the Triggering Event and in accordance with the provisions of Section 8.1. *[NOTE: If different discounts or increases to FMV will apply to differing Triggering Events, then subsections may be added to the above section identifying said discounts or increases]*

7.5) Compulsory Purchase by Corporation

[NOTE: The following section provides the Defaulting Shareholder with the right to put his or her shares if the option has not been exercised by the other shareholders. Delete if not applicable]

If a Shareholder becomes a Defaulting Shareholder pursuant to subsection 7.1(xi) or 7.1(xii) and the Other Shareholders do not exercise the Purchase Option or require the Corporation to purchase the Purchased Shares pursuant to Section 7.2, the Defaulting Shareholder or its Representative shall have the right, upon notice to the Corporation (the **"Compulsory Purchase Notice"**) within *[number of days]* days following the expiry of the Exercise Period (the **"Compulsory Purchase Period"**), to require the Corporation to purchase the Purchased Shares.

7.6) Suspension of Certain Provisions

Following a Triggering Event pursuant to 7.1(a) above:

a)   a Defaulting Shareholder shall only be entitled to Transfer its Shares in accordance with this Article and the provisions of any other buy-sell provisions of this Agreement shall be suspended and inoperative with respect to such Defaulting Shareholder;

b)   such Defaulting Shareholder's nominee to the Board shall resign and the Other Shareholders will remove the Defaulting Shareholder's nominee from the Board and as officers of the Corporation, if any, and the vacancies thereby created will be filled as the Other Shareholders see fit; and

c)   the Defaulting Shareholder will and does hereby, irrevocably nominate, constitute, and appoint, the Other Shareholders as the Defaulting Shareholder's proxy to vote its Shares as such proxy or proxies see fit.

7.7)   Remuneration while Disabled

Upon Disability of a Shareholder or Principal, as applicable (in this Article, the "**Disabled Party**"), the Disabled Party will be entitled to receive his/her normal remuneration, including directors fees, if any, but in each case excluding any commissions whether fixed, discretionary, accrued or contingent, up until the date upon which the Disabled Party becomes Permanently Disabled and in any event only as long as the Disabled Party remains Disabled. Upon the Disabled Party becoming Permanently Disabled, he/she will no longer be entitled to receive further remuneration in his/her capacity as an employee, officer or director of the Corporation. It is expressly agreed that the Corporation will only be responsible for the amount of remuneration not otherwise received by the Disabled Party pursuant to any disability insurance policy owned by the Corporation, Worker's Compensation benefits or from any other third party, in each case adjusted on an after tax basis; provided however, that the Shareholders and Principals acknowledge and agree that any insurance proceeds received by the Disabled Party from any disability or health insurance policy paid for by a person other than the Corporation shall not be deducted from such remuneration entitlement.

7.8)   Insurance and Purchase on Death

[NOTE: If the Corporation is to purchase life insurance for its shareholders or the Shareholders to purchase cross-insurance policies on other Shareholders, add the appropriate article or clauses found in Appendix __________ and remove death as a triggering event.]

ARTICLE 8: ARRANGEMENTS REGARDING DISPOSITIONS

8.1) Valuation

To the extent that the purchase price payable for any Shares to be transferred pursuant to this Agreement is based on the Fair Market Value of such Shares, the Fair Market Value of such Shares shall be determined as at the date of the event which gives rise to the right of purchase or sale (the **"Valuation Date"**), in accordance with the principles of valuation set forth in Schedule 8.1.

8.2) Closing

The following provisions shall apply to any transfer of Securities between Shareholders or between Shareholder(s) and the Corporation pursuant to the terms of this Agreement:

(a) The transaction shall be completed at the Corporation's registered office, subject to subsection 8.2(f), on the date specified for closing at 10:00 o'clock in the morning (local time). At such time the transferor(s) shall transfer to the transferee(s) good title to the Securities being Transferred free and clear of all Encumbrances and deliver to the transferee(s) certificates and other documents of title evidencing ownership of the Securities being Transferred, duly endorsed in blank for transfer by the holders of record. If, at closing, the transferor(s) Shares are subject to any Encumbrance, then the transferee(s) will be entitled to do such acts and things and make such payments as are necessary in order to discharge such Encumbrance and the transferee(s) may deduct from the purchase price for the Securities for all costs, outlays and expenses made or incurred in so doing.

(b) So long as any part of the purchase price remains unpaid (unless the purchase is made pursuant to ARTICLE 7), the transferee(s) will execute and deliver a pledge of the Shares so purchased in favour of the transferor(s) in form and substance acceptable to the transferee(s)' counsel, acting reasonably. Such pledge agreement will provide that the transferee(s) may exercise all voting rights attached to the Shares so purchased so long as the transferee(s) is not in default thereunder.

(c) If the transferee(s) is a Holding Company or an Affiliate of a Principal, such Principal will execute and deliver at closing his personal guarantee of payment of the unpaid purchase price in form and substance acceptable to the transferee(s)' counsel, acting reasonably.

(d)   If the transferor(s) will no longer be Shareholders, they shall deliver to the Corporation all records, accounts and other documents in their possession belonging to the Corporation and the resignations and releases of its nominees on the Board (including the resignation of such Persons as officers of the Corporation), all such resignations to be effective no later than the time of delivery. The transferee(s) shall deliver to the transferor(s) certified cheques in full payment of the purchase price payable for the Securities being transferred.

(i)   At closing, the transferor(s) will execute and deliver to the transferee(s)

(ii)   if the transferor is an individual, a statutory declaration;

(iii)   if a transferor is a corporation, a certificate of an officer of the transferor;

(iv)   if the transferor is a trust, a certificate of all the trustees of the transferor;

stating that on closing:

(v)   the respective transferor(s) is not a "non-resident" of Canada within the meaning of the Tax Act and will supply satisfactory evidence to the transferee(s) of such, or in the alternative with evidence of compliance with Section 116 of the Tax Act;

(vi)   any Shares to be purchased are free and clear of all Encumbrances whatsoever; and

(vii)   no person, firm or corporation has or will have any agreement, option or any right capable of becoming an agreement or option for the purchase from the transferor(s) of any of his/her/its Shares.

(e)   The Principal of any transferee, will execute and deliver at closing his/her personal guarantee of payment of the unpaid purchase price payable by such transferee in form and substance acceptable to both the transferor's counsel and transferee's counsel, acting reasonably.

(f)   If, at the time of closing, a transferor fails to complete the subject transaction of purchase and sale, the transferee shall have the right, if not in default under this Agreement, without prejudice to any other rights which it may have, upon payment of that part of the purchase price payable to the transferor at the time of closing to the credit of the transferor in the main branch of the Corporation's bank, to execute and deliver, on behalf of and in the name of the transferor, such deeds, transfers, share certificates, resignations or other documents that may be necessary to complete the subject transaction and the transferor hereby irrevocably appoints the transferee its attorney in that behalf. Such appointment and power of attorney, being coupled with an interest, shall not be revoked by the death, incapacity (whether mental or physical), dissolution, winding up, bankruptcy, insolvency or other termination of the existence of the transferor and the transferor hereby ratifies and confirms and agrees to ratify and confirm all that the transferee may lawfully do or cause to be done by virtue of such appointment and power.

(g) The transferor(s) will be entitled to purchase the policy on [*his/its Principal's*] life (if any) on payment to the Corporation of the greater of $[*dollar amount*] or the cash surrender value of such policy at the Closing Date. The transferor(s) shall be liable for, and shall pay, to the appropriate taxation authority all taxes and other like charges including interest and penalties related thereto properly payable by him/her/it in connection with the sale of Securities.

(h) At closing, if the transferor(s) will no longer be shareholders, the transferor(s) will receive from the transferee(s) and from the Corporation a release of any and all claims which the transferee(s) and the Corporation may have against the transferor(s) relating to the Corporation, and the transferor(s) will deliver to the transferee(s) and to the Corporation a release of any and all claims which the transferor(s) may have against the transferee(s) and the Corporation relating to the Corporation, save and except for:

(i) any claims arising out of a portion of the purchase price remaining unpaid;

(ii) the terms, provisions, representations, warranties and covenants of any purchase and sale documentation relating to the Shares;

(iii) any guarantees or obligations for which a release was not obtained pursuant to Section 8.3 hereof; and

(iv) the provisions of ARTICLE 9.

(i) At closing, the Corporation's costs and expenses (excluding a Valuator's fee and disbursements incurred to determine Fair Market Value) relating to the sale of the Shares will be paid by the transferor(s) and the transferee(s) in their respective Proportionate Share.

(j) If any transfer is subject to review under the provisions of the *Investment Canada Act* (Canada) or the *Competition Act* (Canada), then the closing of such transfer shall be conditional upon the approval or deemed approval of the appropriate governmental or regulatory authorities, on terms and conditions satisfactory to the transferee and the closing of such transfer shall be delayed until the receipt of such approvals or deemed approvals.

[*Note: Consider what happens if allowance is not obtained.*]

(k) Any Shareholder which agrees to purchase, or is bound by the terms of this Agreement to purchase, any Shares held by any other Shareholder, shall also acquire, and the other Shareholder shall sell, a proportionate interest in the Shareholder Loans held by the other Shareholder for a purchase price equal to the outstanding principal amount of such Shareholder Loans plus all accrued and unpaid interest thereon to the date of payment.

(l) Upon the Transfer of any Shareholder Loans in accordance with the terms of this Agreement, the Corporation shall, upon the notes, debentures or other evidence of indebtedness held by the transferor being delivered to the Corporation for cancellation, issue replacement notes, debentures or other evidence of indebtedness, on the same terms and in the same form as held by the transferor, to the transferee, in the principal amount of such Shareholder Loans Transferred to the transferee.

(m) If the Corporation is required to complete any transaction of purchase and sale contemplated in this Agreement and on the Closing Date, such purchase would render the Corporation insolvent, at the option of the other Shareholders, the other Shareholder(s) may purchase the transferor(s)' Shares in the place and stead of the Corporation, provided that the Shareholders holding [*percentage*]% of the Shares (excluding the transferor(s)) vote in favour of doing so.

(n) If there are two or more transferee(s), the obligations of each transferee in connection with its purchase of Shares will be independent of the obligation of every other transferee in that regard, and the failure of any transferee to pay for a portion of the transferor(s)' Shares will not affect the right of any other transferee to receive a transfer of the Shares purchased by that other transferee.

8.3) Arrangements Regarding Guarantees

If, at the time a transfer of Shares is to be made pursuant to the provisions of this Agreement which will result in the transferor no longer being a Shareholder, the transferor, or, if applicable, a Principal of such transferor, is a guarantor of all or part of any indebtedness or obligations of the Corporation, then any transferee who or which is bound by this Agreement hereby agrees to obtain, at the time of completion of such transfer, a release of any such guarantee from the holders of such guarantee, provided that if, after using reasonable efforts, such transferee is unable to obtain such release, the transferee and, if applicable, its Principal, as a condition precedent to the completion of the transfer of Shares, shall deliver in lieu of such release, an indemnity or other security of a Canadian chartered bank indemnifying and saving fully harmless the transferor and its Principal, if applicable, from any liability or loss which may be suffered or incurred by one or more of them in respect of any such guarantee.

8.4) Restrictions While Purchase Price Remains Unpaid

Until the balance of the purchase price owing by a transferee to a transferor in respect of the transferee's purchase of the transferor's Shares and Shareholder Loans is paid and satisfied in full and unless proceeds derived from the following are used to repay such indebtedness of the transferee to the transferor, the transferee and the Corporation will not:

[Tailor these provisions to the particular situation, keeping in mind that: (i) the promissory note for the unpaid purchase price is fully open, i.e. if the transferee is not willing to live with these restrictions, he can pay off the note; and (2) if all Shareholders do not participate in the purchase, these restrictions will also affect them.]

(a) take any steps or do any act provided in Section 4.6 *[excluding Subsections 4.6(h), 4.6(j) and 4.6(m)]*;

(b) pay any dividends;

(c) Transfer or consent to the Transfer by any other Shareholder of any Shares except the transfer of Shares by a Shareholder to a Permitted Transferee on the terms and conditions of this Agreement;

(d) repay the principal amount of or interest on any Shareholder Loan (other than a Shareholder Loan held by the transferor);

(e) except for increases to compensate for reasonable cost of living, increase the salary or other remuneration payable to *[the remaining Shareholders/ their Principals]* or to officers or directors of the Corporation not dealing at arm's length (within the meaning of the *Tax Act* with the remaining Shareholders or any other person or persons not dealing at arm's length with any of the remaining Shareholders, other than bona fide full time active employees of the Corporation except the remaining Shareholders *[and their Principals]*, nor will the Corporation increase in any amount the benefits and compensation of any director, officer or Shareholder of the Corporation by means of any directors' fees, new bonus or pension plan and/or new contract or commitment;

(f)   carry on the business of the Corporation, other than diligently and substantially in the same manner as prior to such sale; (g) make any commitment for capital expenditures, other than in the ordinary course of business;

(h)   amend the Articles or by-laws of the Corporation or enact new by-laws, if such amendment or enactment has a material effect on the sold Shares;

(i)   fail to keep insured all property, real and personal, owned, leased or used by the Corporation as it was insured prior to such sale against all risks of loss or fail to use, operate, maintain and repair such property as it was used prior to such sale; or

(j)   fail to provide the transferor with annual financial statements of the Corporation within [*number of days*] days of the Corporation's fiscal year end.

ARTICLE 9: INTELLECTUAL PROPERTY

9.1)   Confidentiality

(a)   Each of the parties hereto agrees that it shall not, at any time or under any circumstances, without the unanimous written consent of the Shareholders and the Corporation, directly or indirectly communicate or disclose to any Person (other than the other parties hereto and their employees, agents, advisors and representatives) or make use of (except in connection with its interest in the Corporation) any confidential knowledge or information howsoever acquired by such party relating to or concerning the customers, products, technology, trade secrets, systems or operations, or other confidential information regarding the property, business and affairs, of the Corporation or any of its Subsidiaries, except:

(i)   information which is or becomes generally available to the public (other than by disclosure by such party or its employees, agents, advisors or representatives contrary to this Section);

(ii)   information which is reasonably required to be disclosed by a party to protect its interests in connection with any valuation or legal proceeding under this Agreement;

    (iii) information which is required to be disclosed by law or by the applicable regulations or policies of any regulatory agency of competent jurisdiction or any stock exchange; and/or

    (iv) by a Shareholder in connection with a proposed Transfer of any Shares provided such Shareholder obtains a prior written covenant of confidentiality from the Person to whom it proposes to disclose such information.

(b) Each of the parties hereto acknowledges that disclosure of any confidential information regarding the Corporation in contravention of this Section may cause significant harm to the Corporation and its Subsidiaries and that remedies at law may be inadequate to protect against a breach of this Section. Accordingly, each of the parties hereto agrees that the Corporation shall be entitled, in addition to any other relief available to it, to the granting of injunctive relief without proof of actual damages or the requirement to establish the inadequacy of any of the other remedies available to it. Each of the parties hereto covenants not to assert any defence in proceedings regarding the granting of an injunction or specific performance based on the availability to the Corporation of any other remedy.

9.2) Non-Competition and Non-Solicitation

For so long as:

(a) a Shareholder is a Shareholder and for __________ years after such Shareholder ceases to be a Shareholder;

(b) a Principal is a Principal of a Shareholder and for __________ years after the later of that Principal ceasing to be a Principal of that Shareholder or that Shareholder ceasing to be a Shareholder;

(c) a Shareholder is a [*full time employee/director*] of the Corporation and for __________ years thereafter;

(d) a Principal is a [*full time employee/director*] of the Corporation and for __________ years thereafter,

that Shareholder or Principal will not, as the case may be, (except with the prior written consent of the Corporation, evidenced by [*insert requite approval*], excluding such Shareholder):

(a) directly or indirectly, solicit for employment, or advise or recommend to any other person, firm, corporation or entity that they employ or solicit for employment any person employed by the Corporation;

(b) directly or indirectly, engage, send any work to, place orders with or in any manner be associated with any contractor, subcontractor or other person, firm, corporation or entity which rendered or renders any services to the Corporation, if such action would have a material adverse affect on the business activity, assets or financial condition of the Corporation or its subsidiaries;

(c) directly or indirectly, within [[*geographic area*]/*the respective territories in which such business are carried out*], engage in any activity in competition with, perform services for or become interested in, whether as an individual, manager, consultant, independent contractor, employee, employer, partner, syndicate member, officer, director, advisor, principal, agent, trustee, lender of money, shareholder (except as a shareholder of a public corporation holding [*percentage*]% or less of all outstanding voting shares in such public corporation) or in any other manner whatsoever, carry on, advance or lend money to, guarantee the debts or obligations of or permit his name to be used, serve or cater to, in any relation or capacity whatsoever, a similar or competitive business as that conducted by the Corporation or any other business now or at any time during the period of time that such Shareholder or Principal was a Shareholder, director, officer or employee of the Corporation;

solicit any customer or client that was or is a customer or client of the Corporation during the period of time that such Shareholder or Principal was a Shareholder, director, officer or employee of the Corporation.

9.3) Non-Disparagement

In the event that:

(a) a Shareholder is a Shareholder and ceases to be a Shareholder;

(b) a Principal is a Principal of a Shareholder and ceases to be a Principal of that Shareholder or that Shareholder ceases to be a Shareholder; or

(c) a Principal or a Shareholder is an officer, director or employee of, or a consultant to, the Corporation and ceases to be an officer, director or employee of, or consultant to, the Corporation,

that Shareholder and its Principal and the Corporation shall not, directly or indirectly, communicate, or otherwise distribute information to any third party (written or otherwise) which is disparaging, negative or otherwise harmful in any way to any of that Shareholder and its Principal and the Corporation.

9.4) Inventions

Any and all inventions, products, equipment, devices, discoveries, improvements, processes, methods or techniques, designs or applications thereof (collectively the "**Inventions**") made, developed or created by a party hereto (whether at the request or suggestion of the Corporation or otherwise, whether alone or in conjunction with others and whether during regular hours of work or otherwise) during the period of his/her/it being a Shareholder, director, officer or employee of the Corporation, and for a period of [*number*] year thereafter, or during the period of his/her/it being a Shareholder, director, officer or employee of the Corporation prior to the date of this Agreement, which may be directly or indirectly useful in, or relate to, the business of or tests being carried out by, the Corporation or any of its subsidiaries or affiliates, will be the Corporation's exclusive property as against such party.

9.5) Additional Steps

Each party hereto will, at the Corporation's request and without any payment therefor, execute any documents necessary or advisable in the reasonable opinion of the Corporation's counsel to direct issuance of patents to the Corporation with respect to such Inventions as are to be the Corporation's exclusive property as against such party under Section 9.4 or to vest in the Corporation title to such Inventions as against such party.

9.6) Relief

Each party hereto acknowledges that his/her/its relationship with the Corporation is of a special, unique, unusual and extraordinary character which gives it peculiar value, the loss of which cannot adequately be compensated in damages in an action at law. The Corporation will be entitled to all equitable and legal remedies, including interlocutory and permanent injunctive relief, relating to any violation or breach of the provisions of this Article.

9.7) No Defences

Each party hereto irrevocably acknowledges that he/she/it has reviewed the provisions of this Article with his legal counsel and that the provisions of this Article are reasonable, appropriate and in the interest of the Corporation. Each party hereto irrevocably waives and renounces any right to claim or plead in any respect whatsoever that the provisions of this Article are not reasonable or in the interest of the Corporation. The covenants contained in this Article will be construed as independent of any other agreements between or among the parties and the existence of any claim or cause of action of a party hereto against any other party hereto, whether predicated on this Article or otherwise will not constitute a defence to the enforcement by the Corporation of the provisions of this Article.

9.8) Severability

Except as expressly provided to the contrary in this Article, each Section, Subsection, part, term and/or provision of this Article will be considered severable and if, for any reason, any Section, Subsection, part term and/or provision thereof is determined to be invalid and contrary to, or in conflict with, any existing or future law, ruling or regulation by a court or agency having valid jurisdiction, such will not impair the operation of, or have any other effect on such other Section, Subsection, part, term and/or provision of this Article as may remain otherwise intelligible and the latter will continue to be given full force and effect and bind the parties; and such invalid Section, Subsection, part, term and/or provision will be deemed to not be a part of this Article. If a period of time or geographic area specified in this Article is adjudged to be unreasonable in any proceeding, then the period of time will be reduced by such number of months and/or the area will be reduced by the elimination of such portion thereof, so that such restrictions may be enforced in such area and for such time as is adjudged reasonable.

9.9) Survival

Except as provided in Section 10.1, the provisions of this ARTICLE 9 will survive termination of this Agreement notwithstanding anything in this Agreement to the contrary.

ARTICLE 10: GENERAL

10.1) Bankruptcy or Winding Up of the Corporation

(a) If pursuant to the *Bankruptcy and Insolvency Act* (Canada), the Corporation makes an assignment or a proposal, is declared bankrupt or becomes insolvent;

(b) If the Corporation is wound up, dissolved or liquidated or becomes subject to the provisions of the *Winding-Up and Restructuring Act* (Canada) or has its existence terminated or has any resolution passed therefor; or

(c) If a trustee in bankruptcy, receiver, receiver and manager, liquidator or other officer with similar powers is appointed for the Corporation or over all or a material part of its property;

then,

(d) The provisions of ARTICLE 9 will contemporaneously be terminated without any further action on the part of the parties; and

(e)   The named beneficiary of each insurance policy will be changed forthwith to the person whose life is insured thereby or his nominee with no consideration therefor.

10.2)   Arbitration

[*NOTE: Lawyer to discuss with client the pros and cons of using an arbitration clause. Using an arbitration clause may deny shareholders access to the oppression remedy. Consideration should be given to allowing all disputes to go to court, or alternatively, to specify in which limited circumstances the arbitration provision is to apply*]

[*EITHER:*]

Any controversy or dispute which shall arise between the parties to this Agreement concerning the construction or application of this Agreement, or the rights, duties or obligations of any party to this Agreement, shall be referred to an arbitration subject to the procedures set out in Schedule 10.2 to this Agreement.

[*OR:*]

Attornment

Each party attorns to the non-exclusive jurisdiction of the courts of the Province of Ontario.

10.3)   Restriction on Initiation of Sale/Purchase Provisions

If any purchase or sale provision of this Agreement has been initiated, no other purchase or sale provision will be initiated under this Agreement until the purchase or sale provision first initiated has ceased to be effective, provided that if the purchase and sale provision first initiated is not completed, the necessary extension of time will be made to all other purchase and sale provisions herein and all other rights of the parties will be so preserved.

10.4)   Application of this Agreement

The terms of this Agreement shall apply, *mutatis mutandis*, to any shares:

(a)   resulting from the conversion, reclassification, redesignation, subdivision or consolidation [*OPTIONAL: or* [*other change*]] of the Shares; and

(b)   of the Corporation or any successor body corporate which may be received by the Shareholders on a merger, amalgamation, arrangement or other reorganization of or including the Corporation; and prior to any such action being taken, the parties hereto shall give due consideration to any changes which may be required to this Agreement in order to give effect to the intent of this Section.

10.5)   Benefit of the Agreement

This Agreement shall enure to the benefit of and be binding upon the respective Personal Representatives, heirs, executors, administrators, successors and permitted assigns of the parties hereto.

10.6)   Statutes

Any reference in this Agreement to a statute or any Section thereof includes any amendment thereto, its regulations and applicable successor legislation. [*NOTE TO DRAFTER: Query whether this is in the best interest of the client*]

10.7) Entire Agreement

This Agreement constitutes the entire agreement between the parties to this Agreement with respect to the subject matter of this Agreement and cancels and supersedes any prior understandings and agreements between the parties with respect to such subject matter. There are no representations, warranties, terms, conditions, undertakings or collateral agreements, express, implied or statutory, between the parties with respect to the subject matter of this Agreement other than those expressly set forth in this Agreement.

10.8)   Amendments and Waivers

No amendment to this Agreement shall be valid or binding unless set forth in writing and duly executed by all of the parties to this Agreement. No waiver of any breach of any provision of this Agreement shall be effective or binding unless made in writing and signed by the party purporting to give such waiver and, unless otherwise provided in the written waiver, shall be limited to the specific breach waived.

10.9)   Assignment

Except as may be expressly provided in this Agreement, none of the parties to this Agreement may assign its rights or obligations under this Agreement without the prior written consent of all of the other parties.

10.10) Termination

This Agreement shall terminate upon the earlier of:

    (a)   the written agreement of all of the Shareholders;

    (b)   the dissolution or bankruptcy of the Corporation or the making by the Corporation of an assignment under the provisions of the *Bankruptcy and Insolvency Act* (Canada); or

(c) one Person Controlling all of the Shares; except that the provisions of Sections 9.1 and 9.2 shall continue in the event of a termination under subsection 10.9 and 10.10(c).

10.11) Severability

If any provision of this Agreement is determined to be invalid or unenforceable in whole or in part, such invalidity or unenforceability shall attach only to such provision or part of such provision and the remaining part of such provision and all other provisions of this Agreement shall continue in full force and effect.

10.12) Notices

Any notice or other writing required or permitted to be given under this Agreement or for the purposes of this Agreement (referred to in this Section as a "notice") to any party shall be sufficiently given if delivered personally, or if sent by prepaid registered mail or if transmitted by fax or other form of recorded communication tested prior to transmission to such party to the address and/or fax number as listed in Schedule 3.1 hereto or at such other address as the party to whom such writing is to be given shall have last notified to the party giving the same in the manner provided in this Section. Any notice personally delivered to the party to whom it is addressed as provided in this Section shall be deemed to have been given and received on the day it is so delivered at such address, provided that if such day is not a Business Day then the notice shall be deemed to have been given and received on the Business Day next following such day. Any notice mailed to the address and in the manner provided for in this Section shall be deemed to have been given and received on the [*fifth*] Business Day next following the date of its mailing. Any notice transmitted by fax or other form of recorded communication shall be deemed given and received on the first Business Day after its transmission.

10.13) Further Assurances

The parties hereto shall sign such further and other documents, cause such meetings to be held, resolutions passed and by-laws enacted, exercise their vote and influence, do and perform and cause to be done and performed such further and other acts and things as may be necessary or desirable in order to give full effect to this Agreement and every part hereof.

10.14) Conflict

If a conflict arises between the Corporation's articles, by-laws or resolutions and the provisions of this Agreement, the provisions of this Agreement will govern and supersede the provisions of such articles, by-laws and resolutions and such articles and by-laws shall be amended, and the necessary resolutions passed so as to ensure conformity with the terms of this Agreement.

10.15) Counterparts and Facsimile

This Agreement may be executed in counterparts and may be executed and delivered by facsimile or PDF, and each such facsimile or PDF, or counterpart shall constitute an original and all of which taken together shall constitute one and the same instrument.

10.16) Survival

All of the representations and warranties made in this Agreement shall survive the execution of this Agreement and shall be deemed to be continuing until the termination of this Agreement. The provisions of ARTICLE 9 shall survive the termination of this Agreement.

ARTICLE 11: ACKNOWLEDGEMENT
RE: INDEPENDENT LEGAL ADVICE

11.1)   Acknowledgement re ILA

Each party hereto acknowledges [*name of solicitors*], [*address of solicitors*], acts only for the Corporation in the preparation of this Agreement. Each of the parties hereto further acknowledge that [*solicitors*] has advised such party that it has a conflicting interest with respect to the finalization of this Agreement, and accordingly have recommended to each party hereto (other than the Corporation) that he/she/it obtain independent legal advice concerning the advisability of entering into this Agreement before executing it.

IN WITNESS OF WHICH the parties have duly executed this Agreement.

Company name	Company name
Per:	Per:
Name: ___________________	Name: ___________________
Title: ___________________	Title: ___________________
I/We have the authority to bind the corporation	I/We have the authority to bind the corporation

Company name

Per:

Name: ___________________

Title: ___________________

I/We have the authority to bind the corporation

Company name

Per:

Name: ___________________

Title: ___________________

I/We have the authority to bind the corporation

Witness: ___________________

Witness: ___________________

SCHEDULE 3.1 : SHAREHOLDERS

SHAREHOLDERS

Shareholder	Shares	Address	Fax

PRINCIPALS

Shareholder	Principal	Shares of Shareholder held by Principal (and % of voting shares)	Address of Principal	Fax of Principal

OTHER PARTIES

Name	Address	Fax

SCHEDULE 4.1: DIRECTORS

Director	Address	Fax

SCHEDULE 4.2: OFFICERS

Officer	Address	Fax

SCHEDULE 5.1(C): ADHERENCE AGREEMENT

TO: _____________ (the "Corporation")

AND TO: ITS SHAREHOLDERS

AND TO: THE PRINCIPALS

AND TO: EACH SIGNATORY TO THE UNANIMOUS SHAREHOLDERS AGREE-
MENT OF THE CORPORATION DATED AS _____________ (the "USA")

WHEREAS the Corporation, its shareholders (the **"Shareholders"**) and principals (as listed in Schedule _____________ of the USA, as amended from time to

time) (the "**Principals**") have entered into the USA, as same may be amended, supplemented or restated from time to time, to establish their rights and obligations in respect of the shares of the Corporation, the management and conduct of the business of the Corporation and various other matters;

AND WHEREAS all capitalized terms used in this Adherence Agreement which are not otherwise defined herein, shall have the meanings ascribed thereto in the USA;

NOW THEREFORE, in consideration of the mutual covenants and conditions hereinafter contained and for other good and valuable consideration (the receipt and sufficiency of which are hereby acknowledged) the undersigned hereby agrees that:

The undersigned acknowledges having received a copy of the USA and having read the USA in its entirety.

The undersigned acknowledges having received the opportunity to obtain independent legal advice in respect of this Adherence Agreement.

The undersigned [*is/are*] not a non-resident of Canada within the meaning of the *Income Tax Act* (Canada);

The terms and conditions of the USA shall be binding upon the undersigned as a Shareholder, or Principal, as the case may be, and such terms and conditions shall enure to the benefit of and be binding upon the undersigned's heirs, executors, administrators, legal and personal representatives, successors and permitted assigns. This Adherence Agreement forms part of the USA and by signing below, the undersigned agrees to be a party to the USA in the same manner as if the undersigned was an original signatory to the USA.

For the purpose of giving notice pursuant to the USA, the address of the undersigned is:

Address: _______________________

Telephone: _______________________

Facsimile: _______________________

E-mail: _______________________

The undersigned agrees to sign such further and other documents, and do and perform and cause to be done and performed such further and other acts and things as may be necessary or desirable in order to give full effect to this Adherence Agreement and the USA.

This Adherence Agreement shall be construed in accordance with the laws of the Province of Ontario and the laws of Canada applicable therein.

IN WITNESS WHEREOF the undersigned has executed this Adherence Agreement as of the [*day*] day of [*month, year*].

If Individual:

SIGNED, SEALED AND DELIVERED

in the presence of

Witness: _________________   Print name: _________________

If Corporation:

Print name of Corporation: _________________
Per:
Name: _________________
Title: _________________
I/we have the authority to bind the Corporation

SCHEDULE 8.1: PRINCIPLES OF VALUATION

[*Note: Parties may simplify the procedure by substituting the Corporation's auditor for the independent valuator. If there is more than 1 class of shares the following will need to be amended to specify that it is the shares of a particular class that is being determined.*]

1)   **Determination of Fair Market Value of Securities**

(a)   Upon the occurrence of an event giving rise to a transaction of purchase and sale requiring the determination of the Fair Market Value of Shares (hereinafter in this Schedule called a **"Valuation Event"**), the affected parties shall, within twenty (20) days following the occurrence of the Valuation Event meet to attempt to, agree as to the Fair Market Value of each class and type of Share as at the last day of the month immediately preceding the date on which the Valuation Event occurred. If the affected parties and the Corporation are unable to reach an agreement with respect to any class or type of Share within such aforementioned period, then a certified business valuator (the **"Valuator"**) [*OPTIONAL: chosen from the Approved List of Valuators,*] shall determine the Fair Market Value of each class or type of Share (the **"Subject Securities"**) as at such date within sixty (60) days following his or her appointment or, if the affected parties fail to choose a Valuator within a further fifteen days, then a valuator [*OPTIONAL: from the Approved List of Valuators*] shall be appointed as Valuator by a judge of the Ontario Superior Court of Justice upon application of any of the Shareholders. The determination of the Fair Market Value of the Subject Securities made by the Valuator shall, for all purposes of this Agreement, be binding and effective upon each of the Shareholders and the Corporation as if originally agreed to by them and shall, in the absence of fraud or manifest error, not be subject to appeal, arbitration, judicial process or any other legal proceeding.

(b) In arriving at its valuation, the Valuator shall value the Corporation and the Subject Securities consistent with usual practice concerning a like business and like securities, shall take into account and apply generally accepted accounting and valuation principles as they pertain to this particular type of business and such securities and have regard to Section 2 of this Schedule 8.1.

(c) All fees, disbursements and other costs and expenses associated with the determination of Fair Market Value in accordance with the provisions of this Schedule 8.1 shall be borne by the Corporation.

2) Valuation Principles

In arriving at its valuation, the Valuator shall value the Corporation consistent with usual practice concerning a like business and shall take into account and apply generally accepted accounting and valuation principles as they pertain to this particular type of business.

For the purposes of this Schedule 8.1, **"Fair Market Value"** shall mean the highest price for the Subject Securities available in an open and unrestricted market between informed and prudent parties, knowledgeable with respect to market conditions, industry trends and business synergies, acting at arm's length and under no compulsion to act, expressed in terms of cash, and by applying the following principles:

(a) that there shall be no discount for minority interest;

(b) that all agreements with persons who are not Arm's Length Persons are no longer in place and that the purchaser would not have to assume any obligations under this Agreement;

(c) that there are no restrictions on transfer and that there are no costs associated with determining the Fair Market Value;

(d) the Valuator shall determine Fair Market Value of each class and type of the Subject Securities;

  (e) any non-participating Shares (meaning Shares that have a redemption price), shall have a Fair Market Value which cannot exceed the redemption price thereof as set out in the Articles of the Corporation; and

  (f) Fair Market Value shall be calculated on a per Share basis, and Fair Market Value of a Shareholder's Shares will be such per Share amount multiplied by the number of Shares being acquired from a Shareholder pursuant to the terms hereof;

3) Co-operation with Valuation

Each of the Shareholders, the Corporation, and the Principals shall in all respects co-operate with the Valuator in the determination of Fair Market Value of the Subject Securities. In particular, each of the Corporation, the Shareholders and the Principals shall make available to the Valuator all such documents and information with respect to the affairs of the Corporation as the Valuator may reasonably require to make its determination of such Fair Market Value.

SCHEDULE 10.2: ARBITRATION PROCEDURE

[NOTE: Delete this Schedule if Section 8.3 is Deleted]
Any dispute arising out of or in connection with this Agreement, including any question regarding its existence, validity or termination shall be submitted to and finally resolved by arbitration as follows:

  (a) any party may serve notice upon the others to submit such dispute to expedited arbitration;

  (b) a single arbitrator shall be appointed by agreement between the parties as soon as possible after the date of notice requiring arbitration has been delivered, and if the parties are unable to agree, either party may apply to a court of competent jurisdiction for the appointment of a single arbitrator;

  (c) counsel for the parties shall meet with such arbitrator to determine the schedule and procedure for the arbitration;

  (d) the arbitration shall take place in the [*City of Toronto*] and the arbitrator shall fix the time and place in the [*City of Toronto*] for the purpose of hearing such evidence and representations as the parties may present and, subject to the provisions of this Agreement, the decisions of the arbitrator in writing shall be binding upon the parties;

(e) the arbitrator shall, after hearing any evidence and representations that the parties may submit, make his or her decision and reduce the same to writing and deliver one copy thereof to each of the parties;

(f) the arbitrator may determine any matters of procedure for the arbitration not addressed by counsel pursuant to subsection (c) above. Insofar as they do not conflict with the provisions of this Article, the provisions of the *Arbitrations Act, 1991* (Ontario) shall be applicable to an arbitration held under this Article and the arbitrator shall have jurisdiction to do all acts and make such orders as provided in such act. The arbitrator shall [*OPTIONAL: not*] have the power to award costs of the arbitration [*OPTIONAL: which shall be shared equally by the parties to the arbitration*];

(g) the arbitrator shall have the power to proceed with the arbitration and to deliver his or her award notwithstanding the default by any party in respect of any procedural order made by the arbitrator; and

(h) the decision arrived at by the arbitrator shall be final and binding upon the parties and no appeal shall lie therefrom.

APPENDIX 3.3: ADDITIONAL CAPITAL DEFINITIONS

Definitions

"Reasonable Commercial Terms" means terms of loan (including security) bearing such rate of interest which does not exceed the highest rate of interest payable by the Corporation on its other indebtedness to banks, trust companies and other commercial lenders;

3.3) Additional Capital

(i) Notwithstanding any other provision contained in this Agreement, if, the Board, in the exercise of good faith and in its reasonable judgement, determines that the Corporation requires additional funds and such funds cannot be obtained from a Canadian chartered bank or trust company on Reasonable Commercial Terms and without guarantees of, or recourse to, the Shareholders or Principals or any Person not dealing at arm's length with any Shareholder or Principal, the Board may request, by issuance of a notice (a **"Funding Notice"**) to the Shareholders, that the Shareholders each contribute, within [*number of days*] Business Days after the issuance of the Funding Notice (the **"Funding**

Period"), additional capital to the Corporation, pro rata based upon the number of Shares beneficially owned by the Shareholders, by way of subscription for shares or loan, as determined by the Board and set forth in the Funding Notice.

(j)   If additional capital is to be contributed, pursuant to subsection (a), by way of subscription for Shares, the subscription price for each such Share shall be the Fair Market Value of a Share as of the time of the Funding Notice, as determined [*by the Board and set out in the Funding Notice/in accordance with Section 6.1*]. [*OPTIONAL: Forthwith upon the determination of the subscription price in accordance with Section 6.1,*] the Corporation shall issue to each Shareholder making a contribution of capital pursuant to the Funding Notice, out of its treasury, such number of Shares as shall be equal to the number (rounded, if necessary, to the nearest lower whole number) obtained by dividing the amount of the contribution to be made by such Shareholder by the per Share subscription price, upon receipt by the Corporation of such contribution.

[*Note: If these provisions are used the Parties may want to amend the valuation provisions in Schedule 6.1 so that the cost of the valuation is paid by the Corporation.*]

(a)   If additional capital is to be advanced, pursuant to subsection (a), by way of loan, each such loan shall be made on Reasonable Commercial Terms and shall be upon the security and at the rate of interest (which shall not exceed the rate payable on Reasonable Commercial Terms) and repayable by the Corporation all as determined by the Board, provided that, the terms of all such loans made pursuant to the same Funding Notice (other than the principal amounts) shall be the same for all Shareholders.

(b)   If any Shareholder (a **"Defaulting Shareholder"**) fails to contribute its pro rata portion of the funding required as set forth in the Funding Notice, the deficiency will be a Deficit Contribution owing by the Defaulting Shareholder to the Corporation, and then any other Shareholder (an **"Excess Subscribing Shareholder"**) may, but shall not be obligated to, within [*number of days*] Business Days after the expiry of the Funding Period, advance to the Corporation all or any portion of the amount which the Defaulting Shareholder failed to advance (such additional amount advanced by the Excess Subscribing

Shareholder being referred to as the "**Excess Advance**"). The Excess Advance shall be included as a Deficit Contribution owing by the Defaulting Shareholder to the Excess Subscribing Shareholder and the Deficit Contribution owing by the Defaulting Shareholder to the Corporation will be reduced *pro tanto*; and thereupon.

(k)   At the option of the Excess Subscribing Shareholder making the Excess Advance, exercisable by written notice to the Corporation at the time such Excess Advance is made:

(i)   the amount of the Excess Advance shall be treated as a Shareholder Loan which is repayable upon demand and, until repaid the amount outstanding from time to time shall bear interest at a rate per annum equal to [*percentage*]% above the Prime Rate, compounded monthly, and shall be payable at the same time as the payment of principal. Forthwith upon the Excess Advance being made to the Corporation, the Corporation shall issue an instrument to the Excess Subscribing Shareholder evidencing the indebtedness of the Corporation to the Excess Subscribing Shareholder for the Excess Advance on the terms provided for in this Section; or

(ii)   the amount of the Excess Advance shall be used by the Excess Subscribing Shareholder (and applied by the Corporation) in respect of the subscription, by such Shareholder, for additional Shares, at a subscription price for each Share equal to [*percentage*]% of the price to be determined in accordance with Section 6.1 (as at the day the Board issued the Funding Notice). Forthwith upon such determination of the subscription price, the Corporation shall issue to such Shareholder, out of its treasury, such number of Shares as shall be equal to the number (rounded, if necessary, to the nearest lower whole number) obtained by dividing the amount of the Excess Advance made by such Shareholder, by the subscription price.

(l)   [*OPTIONAL: For greater certainty, under no circumstances shall any Defaulting Shareholder who has failed to provide funds to the Corporation in response to a Funding Notice be considered to be in default under this Agreement or be in any way personally liable for the payment of such funds or repayment of any Excess Advance to an Excess Subscribing Shareholder.*]

[Note: May want to consider providing that a shareholder who does not contribute is in material breach of the Agreement and give the other shareholders who make his contribution, a call on all of his shares or a call on enough shares to eliminate the Deficit Contribution]

(m) If the Board, in the exercise of good faith and in its reasonable judgement, determines that the Corporation requires additional funds and such funds can be obtained from Canadian chartered banks or trust companies on Reasonable Commercial Terms except that guarantees of, or recourse to, the Shareholders or Principals is required by the lender preferred by the Board then, to the extent acceptable to such lender such guarantees or other assurance shall be provided on a several, and not joint, basis by each Shareholder or Principal pro rata based upon the number of Shares beneficially owned, directly or indirectly, by each Shareholder or Principal. If funds can only be obtained upon the joint and several guarantees or other assurances of any or all of the Shareholders or Principals, then the Shareholders or the Principals will execute and deliver such guarantees or other assurances but to the extent that any Shareholder or Principal is required to pay more than its proportionate share of liabilities under any such guarantee or other assurances based upon the number of Shares beneficially owned, directly or indirectly by such Shareholder or Principal, then the other Shareholders shall indemnify and pay to such Shareholder or Principal, on demand, the amount of such excess in such proportions as each such Shareholder should have, but did not, contribute.

OR

3.3) Funding

(a) The Shareholders agree that they will actively pursue and work towards attaining satisfactory bank credit and financing for the Corporation (the **"Required Funds"**), it being the intention that such financing be sought in the highest amount possible so that a minimum equity investment is required of the Shareholders. If the Shareholders determine by [_________ *number of Shareholders voting in its favour* /_________% *of the votes cast*] that the Corporation is unable to obtain all the Required Funds on commercially reasonable terms:

(i) The Corporation will give [*number of days*] Business Days' notice (the **"Funding Notice"**) to all Shareholders stating the estimated amount of the deficiency, the dates on which the Corporation requires additional funds and the amount of funds required on each such date;

(ii) On each date set out in the Funding Notice, each Shareholder will contribute his Percentage of the amount stated in the Funding Notice and such contribution will be a Shareholder Loan;

(iii) If a Shareholder (the **"Defaulting Shareholder"**) fails to make any contribution required by this Section, the deficiency will be a Deficit Contribution owing by that Shareholder to the Corporation and:

(iv) Any other Shareholder (the "**Excess Subscribing Shareholder**") may contribute all or part of the deficiency on behalf of the Defaulting Shareholder and the amount of such contribution will be included as a Deficit Contribution owing by the Defaulting Shareholder to the Excess Subscribing Shareholder and the Deficit Contribution owing by the Defaulting Shareholder to the Corporation will be reduced *pro tanto*; and thereupon

(b) The Excess Subscribing Shareholder will have the right to acquire the Defaulting Shareholder's Shares by sending notice (the "**Excess Subscribing Shareholder's Notice**") to the Defaulting Shareholder and the other Shareholders (the "**Non-Defaulting Shareholders**") that the Excess Subscribing Shareholder has paid the amount of the Defaulting Shareholder's Deficit Contribution to the Corporation and that the Excess Subscribing Shareholder intends to exercise his right contained in this Section to purchase Shares of the Defaulting Shareholder.

(c) Any Non-Defaulting Shareholder will be entitled to participate in the purchase of the Defaulting Shareholder's Shares by giving notice to all other Shareholders on or before the [*10th*] Business Day following receipt of the Excess Subscribing Shareholder's Notice, whereupon such Non-Defaulting Shareholder will become a purchasing Shareholder. If there is more than one purchasing Shareholder, each purchasing Shareholder will purchase and pay for the Defaulting Shareholder's Shares as nearly as may be in his Proportionate Share as among the purchasing Shareholders and on the Closing Date will pay to the Excess Subscribing Shareholder his Proportionate Share, as among all purchasing Shareholders, of the Excess Subscribing Shareholder's payment to the Corporation on behalf of the Defaulting Shareholder, together with accrued interest thereon to the Closing Date.

(d) The purchase price will be [*percentage*]% of the Fair Market Value of the Defaulting Shareholder's Shares determined as at the date of the default (the cost of such determination to be borne by the Defaulting Shareholder which may be set off against the purchase price), payable as follows:

(i)   One Dollar ($1.00) will be paid by each purchasing Shareholder on the Closing Date; and

(ii) The balance of the purchase price payable by each purchasing Shareholder, together with interest thereon at the Prime Rate [*OPTIONAL: plus* ___________*% per annum*] will be evidenced by a Promissory Note of such purchasing Shareholder and will be repayable in ___________ consecutive equal [*monthly*] instalments of principal, plus interest on the principal balance then outstanding. The first instalment will be due and payable [*number*] month after the Closing Date.

(e) The Closing Date will be the [*20th*] Business Day after delivery of the Excess Subscribing Shareholder's Notice.

(a) The Excess Subscribing Shareholder will have the right to acquire that number of the Defaulting Shareholder's Shares, the Fair Market Value of which is equal to the aggregate of the Defaulting Shareholder's Deficit Contribution plus the cost of determining Fair Market Value. Fair Market Value will be determined as at the date of the default. The Excess Subscribing Shareholder will give notice (the **"Excess Subscribing Shareholder's Notice"**) to the Defaulting Shareholder and other Shareholders (the **"Non-Defaulting Shareholders"**) that the Excess Subscribing Shareholder has paid the amount of the Defaulting Shareholder's Deficit Contribution pursuant to this Subsection to the Corporation and that the Excess Subscribing Shareholder intends to exercise his right contained in this Subsection to purchase Shares of the Defaulting Shareholder.

(b) Any Non-Defaulting Shareholder will be entitled to participate in the purchase of the Defaulting Shareholder's Shares by giving notice to all other Shareholders on or before the [*10th*] Business Day following receipt of the Excess Subscribing Shareholder's Notice, whereupon such Non-Defaulting Shareholder will become a purchasing Shareholder. If there is more than one purchasing Shareholder, each purchasing Shareholder (except the Excess Subscribing Shareholder) will purchase and pay for the Defaulting Shareholder's Shares as nearly as may be in his Proportionate Share as among the purchasing Shareholders by paying to the Excess Subscribing Shareholder his Proportionate

Share, as among all purchasing Shareholders, of the Excess Subscribing Shareholder's payment to the Corporation on behalf of the Defaulting Shareholder, together with accrued interest thereon to the Closing Date.

(c) The purchase price will be deemed to have been paid by satisfaction of the Defaulting Shareholder's Deficit Contribution.

(d) The Closing Date will be the [*20th*] Business Day after delivery of the Excess Subscribing Shareholder's Notice.

(e) On completion of such purchase and sale, the Defaulting Shareholder's Deficit Contribution owing to the Excess Subscribing Shareholder will be reduced *pro tanto*.

(f) Subsections 3.12(f) 7.2(______)(______)(______) will not apply to such purchase and sale of Shares unless, pursuant to this Section, the purchasing Shareholders acquire all the Defaulting Shareholder's Shares.

OR

ADDITIONAL CAPITAL

Except as provided in this Agreement or as otherwise unanimously agreed, none of the Shareholders or Principals shall be obligated to make loans to the Corporation or guarantee any of its indebtedness.

APPENDIX 4.1: ELECTION OF DIRECTORS

4.1) Number and Nomination of Directors

The Board shall consist of a minimum of [______] and a maximum of [______] Directors. Initially, the number of Directors shall be set at [______]. The Board shall be empowered by a special resolution of the Shareholders (as defined in the Act) to set the number of Directors from time to time in accordance with the provisions of this Agreement. Each of: (i) [______], (ii) [______] and (iii) [______] shall be entitled to nominate [______] Director(s) to the Board during such time as they beneficially own at least [______]% of the Shares outstanding at such time (calculated without regard to any Shares issued after the date of this Agreement) (the "**Minimum Percentage**") provided, however, if at any time any of (i) [______], (ii) [______] or (iii) [______] beneficially owns less than the Minimum Percentage of the Shares outstanding at such time, they, acting jointly with any other Shareholder, may be entitled to nominate [___________] Director(s) to the Board if he or she or it, together with such other Shareholder, (i) collectively beneficially own at least the Minimum Percentage of the Shares outstanding at such time, and (ii) execute and deliver to the Board a voting trust agreement in respect of such Shares in form and substance satisfactory to the Board, acting reasonably.

APPENDIX 5.4: PLEDGING OF SHARES

5.4)   Pledge of Shares

Notwithstanding the provisions of Section 5.1, any Shareholder may pledge, charge, mortgage or otherwise encumber any of its Shares (the "**Pledged Shares**") to a bank or other financial institution for the purpose of securing any borrowings by such Shareholder, provided that such bank or financial institution acknowledges to the Shareholders in writing that:

(a)   the Encumbrance of such Shares shall at all times be subject to all the terms and conditions of this Agreement, including the prohibition against transferring, pledging, charging or mortgaging or otherwise encumbering such Shares contained in Section 5.1, except as permitted pursuant to this Article, and

(b)   the security interest in respect of the Pledged Shares shall be discharged as against the interest of the pledgor Shareholder upon the sale by the pledgor Shareholder of any of the Pledged Shares to one or more of the other Shareholders pursuant to this Agreement (but such discharge shall apply only to the number of Pledged Shares subject to such sale), if the proceeds due on closing to the pledgor Shareholder are paid to the bank or other financial institution and any other secured Shareholders having a security interest in the Pledged Shares in order of their respective priorities, and the balance, if any, shall be paid to the pledg or Shareholder.

APPENDIX 5.6: ALTERNATIVE RIGHT OF
FIRST REFUSAL/RIGHT OF FIRST OFFER

[NOTE: This ROFR allows a shareholder to offer to sell his shares to existing shareholders when he does not yet have a Third Party Offer on the table and/or he does not yet even have a potential third party purchaser. The Offeror offers to sell his

shares at a certain price per share that he has selected. If all the shares are not purchased internally, he may go out and sell the shares to any third party on the same terms.]

5.6) Right of First Refusal

(a) Any Shareholder (referred to in this Section as the "**Offeror**") who desires to sell all or any of its Shares shall first offer to sell such Shares to the other Shareholders. Notice of the offer (referred to in this Section as the "**Notice**") shall be sent to each of the other Shareholders (referred to in this Section as the "**Other Shareholders**") and shall set out the number of Shares that the Offeror desires to sell (the "**Offeror's Shares**") and shall irrevocably offer to sell the Offeror's Shares, for cash, to the Other Shareholders at the price and on terms set forth in the Notice.

(b) Upon the Notice being given, the Other Shareholders shall have the right to purchase all, but not less than all, of the Offeror's Shares. The Other Shareholders shall be entitled to purchase its respective Proportionate Interest (based upon the number of Shares beneficially owned by the Other Shareholders as of the date the Notice is given) of the Offeror's Shares or to purchase in such other proportion as the Other Shareholders may agree in writing.

(c) Within [*10*] Business Days of having been given the Notice (referred to in this Section as the "**Offer Period**") each Other Shareholder may give to the Offeror a notice in writing (referred to in this Section as an "**Acceptance Notice**") accepting the offer contained in the Notice and specifying the maximum number of the Offeror's Shares it wishes to acquire (which number may be greater than or less than its *pro rata* entitlement). If any Other Shareholder does not give an Acceptance Notice or specifies in its Acceptance Notice a number of shares less than its *pro rata* entitlement, the resulting unaccepted Offeror's Shares shall be deemed to have been offered by the Offeror to such of the Other Shareholders who specified in their Acceptance Notices a desire to acquire a number of the Offeror's Shares greater than their *pro rata* entitlement, and each such Other Shareholder shall be, subject to the maximum number of the Offeror's Shares specified in its Acceptance Notice, entitled to acquire its Proportionate Interest (based upon the number of Shares beneficially owned by such Other Shareholders) entitlement of the unaccepted Offeror's Shares, as between themselves, or in such other proportion as such Other Shareholders may agree in writing. If the Other Shareholders, or any of them, give an Acceptance Notice within the Acceptance Period confirming their agreement to purchase all of the Offeror's Shares, the sale of the Offeror's Shares to such Other Shareholders shall be completed within [*number of days*] Business Days of the expiry of the Offer Period.

(d) If the Offeror does not receive Acceptance Notices from the Other Shareholders, or any of them, within the Acceptance Period, confirming their agreement to purchase all of the Offeror's Shares, the rights of the Other Shareholders, subject to the provisions of this subsection, to purchase the Offeror's Shares shall cease and the Offeror may, subject to subsection (e) below, sell the Offeror's Shares to any bona fide arm's length third party or Parties within [*number of months*] months after the expiry of the Offer Period, for a price and on other terms no more favourable to such Persons than those set out in the Notice. If the Offeror's Shares are not sold within such __________ month period on such terms, the rights of the Other Shareholders pursuant to this Section shall again take effect with respect to any sale of Shares of the Offeror, and so on from time to time.

Notwithstanding the provisions of subsection (d) above, before consenting to any transfer of the Offeror's Shares to any other Person pursuant to the provisions of this Section, the Board shall be entitled to require proof that the transfer was completed at a price and on other terms no more favourable to such Person than those that would have been applicable had the Other Shareholders agreed to purchase the Offeror's Shares, and the Board shall refuse to permit the recording of the transfer of the Offeror's Shares if they may have been sold otherwise than in accordance with the provisions of the Third Party Offer.

(e) All Acceptance Notices or other notices given under this Section shall be given concurrently to all Shareholders and to the Corporation.

APPENDIX 5.7: BUY-SELL

[*Note: The following version is applicable between 2 shareholders.*]

5.7) Sale of Shares

(a) Each of [*S1*] and [*S2*] has the right at any time after [*insert some initial period*] to give notice (such notice being referred to in this Section as the "**Notice**" and any Shareholder giving the Notice being referred to as the "**Offeror**") to the other Shareholder (referred to in this Section as the "**Offeree**") and to the Corporation, containing the following:

(i) an offer by the Offeror to purchase all of the Shares beneficially owned by the Offeree (an "**Offer to Purchase**"); and

(ii) an offer by the Offeror to sell all of the Shares beneficially owned by the Offeror to the Offeree (an "**Offer to Sell**"); and

(iii) the price to be paid for each Share pursuant to the Offer to Purchase and the Offer to Sell, which shall be the same for both Offers (the "**Purchase Price**"), and all other terms and conditions of the Offers, which terms and conditions shall be the same for both Offers.

(b) Within [*number of days*] Business Days of the Notice being given (referred to in this Section as the "**Offer Period**"), the Offeree shall be entitled to accept either the Offer to Purchase or the Offer to Sell by giving notice of such acceptance to the Offeror and to the Corporation.

(c) If the Offeree accepts the Offer to Purchase, the Offeree shall sell and Offeror shall purchase all of the Shares beneficially owned by the Offeree at the Purchase Price and the transaction of purchase and sale shall be completed within [*number of days*] Business Days of the expiry of the Offer Period.

(d) If the Offeree accepts the Offer to Sell, the Offeree shall purchase and the Offeror shall sell all of the Shares beneficially owned by the Offeror at the Purchase Price and the transaction of purchase and sale shall be completed within [*number of days*] Business Days of the expiry of the Offer Period.

(e) If the Offeree does not accept either the Offer to Purchase or the Offer to Sell within the Offer Period, the Offeree shall be deemed to have accepted the Offer to Purchase and to have given notice of such acceptance pursuant to the provisions of subsection (b) on the last Business Day upon which such notice may have been given.

OR

[*Note: The following version is applicable between 3 shareholders.*]

(a) At any time after [*insert some initial period*] any Shareholder (referred to in this Section as the "**Offeror**") shall have the right to give notice (referred to in this Section as the "**Notice**") to the other Shareholders (collectively the "**Offerees**" and individually an "**Offeree**") and to the Corporation, containing the following:

(i)   an offer by the Offeror to purchase all of the Shares beneficially owned by the Offerees (an "**Offer to Purchase**"); and

(ii)   an offer by the Offeror to sell all of the Shares beneficially owned by the Offeror to the Offerees pro rata based upon the number of Shares beneficially owned by the Offerees (an "**Offer to Sell**"); and

(iii)   the price to be paid for each Share pursuant to the Offer to Purchase and the Offer to Sell, which shall be the same for both Offers (the "**Purchase Price**"), and all other terms and conditions of the Offers, which terms and conditions shall be the same for both Offers.

(b)   Within [*number of days*] Business Days of the Notice being given (the "**Offer Period**"), each Offeree shall be entitled to accept either the Offer to Purchase or the Offer to Sell by giving notice of such acceptance to the Offeror, to the other Offeree and to the Corporation.

(c)   If the Offerees both accept the Offer to Purchase, the Offerees shall sell and the Offeror shall purchase all of the Shares beneficially owned by each Offeree at the Purchase Price and the transaction of purchase and sale shall be completed within 20 Business Days of the expiry of the Offer Period.

(d)   If the Offerees both accept the Offer to Sell, the Offerees shall purchase, pro rata based upon the number of Shares beneficially owned by the Offerees, or in such other proportions as the Offerees agree, and the Offeror shall sell all of the Shares beneficially owned by the Offeror at the Purchase Price and the transaction of purchase and sale shall be completed within 20 Business Days of the expiry of the Offer Period.

(e)   If any Offeree does not accept either the Offer to Purchase or the Offer to Sell within the Offer Period, such Offeree shall be deemed to have accepted the Offer to Purchase of the Offeror and to have given notice of such acceptance pursuant to the provisions of subsection (b) above on the last Business Day upon which such notice may have been given.

(f)   If one Offeree accepts or is deemed to have accepted the Offer to Purchase, (the "**Selling Offeree**") and the other Offeree accepts the Offer to Sell pursuant to the provisions of subsection (b) above (the "**Purchasing Offeree**"), the Purchasing Offeree shall be entitled to purchase the Shares beneficially owned by the Offeror and the Shares beneficially owned by the Selling Offeree by giving notice of the exercise of such right to the Offeror, to the Selling Offeree and to the Corporation within 10 Business Days of the expiry of the Offer Period and, if the Purchasing

Offeree gives notice pursuant to the provisions of this subsection, the Offeror and the Selling Offeree shall sell the Shares beneficially owned by them to the Purchasing Offeree and such transaction of purchase and sale shall be completed within [*number of days*] Business Days of the date upon which the Corporation was given such notice by the Purchasing Offeree. If the Purchasing Offeree fails to give notice pursuant to the provisions of this subsection within the 10 Business Day period specified in this subsection, it shall be deemed not to have accepted the Offer to Sell but, rather, to have accepted the Offer to Purchase and the provisions of subsection (c) above shall apply, mutatis mutandis, to both Offerees except that the transaction of purchase and sale shall be completed within [*number of days*] Business Days of the expiry of the Offer Period.

(g) Two of the Shareholders may jointly give a Notice to another Shareholder pursuant to the provisions of subsection (b) above and, in such event, the further provisions of this Section shall apply, mutatis mutandis, except that any Shares purchased by them shall be purchased pro rata based upon the number of Shares beneficially owned by the Shareholders who gave the Notice or in such other proportion as such Shareholders giving the Notice agree.

(h) Two of the Shareholders may jointly accept the Offer to Sell pursuant to the provisions of subsection (b) above and, in such event, the further provisions of this Section shall apply, mutatis mutandis, except that the number of Shares to be purchased by each of them may be set out in the notice given by them, provided that the aggregate of such numbers equals the number of Shares beneficially owned by the Offeror.

APPENDIX 5.9: PUT-CALL

[*Put to all Shareholders*]

(a) Each Shareholder (a **"Departing Shareholder"** in this Section) is granted the right to require the other Shareholders (the **"Remaining Shareholders"**) to purchase, as nearly as may be in the Proportionate Share as among the Remaining Shareholders, all the Departing Shareholder's Shares on the terms and conditions herein set out. The Departing Shareholder will exercise such right by giving twenty (20) Business Days' notice (**"Notice"** in this Article) to all the Responding

Shareholders of the Departing Shareholder's intention to exercise the right hereby granted.

(b)   The purchase price payable for the Departing Shareholder's Shares will be [*percentage*] % of the Fair Market Value of the Departing Shareholder's Shares determined as at the date of the Notice; the costs of such determination to be at the expense of the Departing Shareholder, which may be set off against the purchase price.

OR

[Put to the Corporation]

(c)   Each Shareholder (a "**Departing Shareholder**" in this Section) is granted the right to require the Corporation to purchase from the Departing Shareholder all the Departing Shareholder's Shares on the terms and conditions herein set out. The Departing Shareholder will exercise such right by giving twenty (20) Business Days' notice ("**Notice**" in this Article) to the Corporation and the other Shareholders of the Departing Shareholder's intention to exercise the right hereby granted.

(d)   The purchase price payable for the Departing Shareholder's Shares will be [__________%] of the Fair Market Value of such Shares determined as at the date of the Notice; the costs of such determination to be at the expense of the Departing Shareholder, which may be set off against the purchase price.

OR

[Call by Shareholders]

(a)   Each Shareholder (a "**Remaining Shareholder**" in this Article) is granted the right to require [*any/all*] other [*Shareholder/Shareholders*] (the "**Other Shareholder[s]**") to sell to the Remaining Shareholder all the Other [*Shareholder's/Shareholders'*] Shares on the terms and conditions herein set out. The Remaining Shareholder will exercise such right by giving twenty (20) Business Days' Notice to the Other Shareholder[s] of the Remaining Shareholder's intention to exercise the right hereby granted.

(b)   The purchase price payable for the Other [*Shareholder's/Shareholders'*] Shares will be the Fair Market Value of such Shares determined as at the date of the Notice; the costs of such determination to be at the expense of the Remaining Shareholder.

OR

[*Call by the Corporation*]

(a) The Corporation is granted the right to require any Shareholder (the "**Vendor**") to sell to the Corporation for cancellation all the Vendor's Shares on the terms and conditions herein set out. Such right will be exercisable only if the Shareholders [*including/excluding*] the Vendor holding [*percentage*]% of the Shares vote in favour of directing the Corporation to purchase the Vendor's Shares (the "**Resolution**"). The Corporation will give twenty (20) Business Days' Notice to the Vendor of the Corporation's intention to exercise the right hereby granted, accompanied by a certified copy of the Resolution. Notice will be given within five (5) Business Days of the date of the Resolution.

(b) The purchase price payable for the Vendor's Shares will be the Fair Market Value of such Shares determined as at the date of the Notice (excluding the costs of such determination) and the costs of such determination will be at the expense of the Corporation.

THEN CHOOSE [*Cash on closing OR structured payments*]

(a) The purchase price payable by each purchaser will be paid in full by cash or certified cheque on the Closing Date.

OR

(b) The purchase price for any Shares purchased and sold pursuant to this Article will be payable as follows:
  (i) [*percentage*]% of the purchase price payable by each purchaser will be paid by cash or certified cheque on the Closing Date; and
  (ii) The balance of the purchase price payable by each purchaser, together with interest thereon at the Prime Rate [*OPTIONAL: plus* __________% *per annum*] will be evidenced by a Promissory Note of such purchaser and will be repayable in _________ consecutive equal [*monthly*] instalments of principal, plus interest on the principal balance then outstanding. The first instalment will be due and payable [*number*] month after the Closing Date.

THEN

(a) The Closing Date will be the twentieth (20th) Business Day after delivery of the Notice.

(b) [*Subsequent transfer clause—delete if not desired by client*] [*If a Remaining Shareholder who purchases Shares (the "Purchaser" in this Section) pursuant to this Section receives an offer for the purchase of all of his Shares/If a Third Party Offer is received for all the issued and outstanding Shares of the Corporation,*] at any time within [*number*] months of the Closing Date and the price per Share payable pursuant to such offer is greater than the price per Share paid to the selling Shareholder (the **"Vendor"** in this Section) then, if such transaction subsequently closes, [*the Purchaser/the Corporation*] will pay to the Vendor an amount equal to the difference between the price per Share received by the [*Purchaser/Corporation*] and the price per Share received by the Vendor pursuant to this Article, provided that any payment to be made to the Vendor pursuant to this Section will be made on a proportionate basis as between the Vendor and the [*Purchaser/the Corporation*] as and when the purchase price is received from the third party purchaser. In this Section, the term **"Purchaser"** includes an amalgamated corporation of which the Purchaser or the Corporation, as the case may be, is an amalgamating corporation.

(c) [*delete if not applicable*] The [*Remaining Shareholder/Corporation*] will not exercise the call option referred to in this Section unless mutually satisfactory arrangements are also made for the contemporaneous withdrawal of the Departing Shareholder as [_________. *For example, as a partner of a partnership*]

APPENDIX 7.8: DEATH AND INSURANCE PROVISIONS

[*NOTE: This Precedent Agreement provides for 3 options for an insurance funded buyout of the Deceased's shares*]:

1. Corporate-Owned Insurance that is used by the Corporation to purchase for cancellation the shares of the Deceased;

2. Corporate-Owned Insurance that is distributed by the Corporation to the surviving shareholders and the surviving shareholders purchase the shares of the deceased; and

3. Each shareholder purchases life insurance on the other shareholders and uses the proceeds to purchase the shares of the deceased.

Option 1: Corporate-Owned Insurance that is used by the Corporation to purchase for cancellation the shares of the Deceased

11.1) **Insurance**

(a) The Corporation shall, to the extent that it is reasonably obtainable, acquire and maintain insurance on the life of each of [*S1, S4, P1 and P2*] in amounts of not less than $[*dollar amount*] and, upon such insurance being acquired, the particulars of such insurance shall be inserted in Schedule __________ and shall be initialled by [*S1, S4, P1 and P2*].

[*NOTE: Due to the possibility of the increasing cash surrender value of the insurance policy, the Corporation being the owner of the policy may taint the capital gains exemption that may have otherwise been available due to the "90/ 10" rule (will no longer be a "qualified small business corporation"). In addition, if insurance policy is attributed an "ACB" within the meaning of the Tax Act in relation to insurance policies, then the CDA may be ground down, and the distribution of the insurance proceeds would not be tax free. Tax advisor for the Corporation to determine if insurance policy should be owned by related corporation with the Corporation as beneficiary*].

(b) The Corporation will be the owner and beneficiary of each policy and will, at all times, keep such insurance policies in good standing and pay all premiums and other charges when the same become due and payable. The Corporation shall not deal in any manner with such policies and, without limiting the generality of the foregoing, shall not assign, transfer, modify, impair any rights or values of, dispose of, surrender, borrow upon or in any way encumber such policies, except in accordance with a written agreement among [*all of the Parties hereto/Shareholders who in the aggregate hold at least* __________*% of the issued and outstanding Shares*].

(c) The Shareholders and the Principals will use their best efforts to permit the Corporation to obtain and maintain such life insurance, including without limitation attending for physical examinations, answering such questions as may be reasonably necessary and executing consents to the placing of such insurance coverage.

(d) On any default in payment of the premium or other charges on the due date thereof, the individual Shareholder and/or corporate Shareholder whose Principal's life is insured under such policy may pay the same on behalf of the Corporation for as long as such default continues, which amount will constitute a Shareholder Loan by such Shareholder.

(e) The Shareholders will determine Fair Market Value of each insurance policy on execution of this Agreement and within [*number of days*]

Business Days following receipt of [*OPTIONAL: audited*] financial statements for each fiscal year of the Corporation and will record such determination on Schedule __________ or an original duplicate thereof. If the Shareholders do not determine Fair Market Value upon the expiry of such [*number of days*] Business Days and within [*number of days*] Business Days thereafter, the Corporation's [*auditors/accountants*] will determine Fair Market Value for life insurance purposes only and Section 8.1 will not apply to this Section.

11.2)   Death of a Shareholder or Principal

[*NOTE: Ensure that death is deleted from the list of Defaulting Shareholder triggering events*]

(a)   Upon the death of [*any individual Shareholder/Principal/any individual Shareholder and Principal/[names of particular shareholder(s) and or principal(s)]*] (hereinafter, the "**Deceased**"), such Shareholder and/or any Shareholder for which the Deceased was a Principal (the "**Deceased's Other Entities**"), will in each case sell, and the Corporation and the other Shareholders (the "**Survivors**"), if applicable, will purchase all Shares beneficially owned by the Deceased and the Deceased's Other Entities (collectively, the "**Deceased's Shares**") as follows:

(i)   The purchase price for the Deceased's Shares shall be the greater of: (i) the Fair Market Value of the Deceased's Shares as at the moment immediately before the death of the Deceased; and (ii) the insurance proceeds received by the Corporation in relation to the insurance policy on the life of the Deceased in each case after deducting an amount equal to the Shareholder's Loan which must be repaid by the Corporation and/or purchased by the Survivors, as applicable, in accordance with Section 11.2(a) above (the "**Remaining Insurance Proceeds**").

(ii)   The Closing Date will be the 10th Business Day following the latest of: (i) if applicable, receipt of necessary governmental releases required to effect a valid transfer of the Deceased's Shares (and the Parties agree to use their best efforts to obtain such releases); (ii) determination of the Fair Market Value; and (iii) the Corporation's receipt of the insurance proceeds on the life of the Deceased;

(iii)   The Corporation shall purchase for cancellation, at the purchase price determined in accordance with subsection 11.2(ii) above, such of the Deceased's Shares as are equal to the Remaining Insurance

Proceeds received by the Corporation, with the remainder of the Deceased's Shares to be acquired by the Survivors in accordance with their respective Proportionate Share. The purchase price will be paid and satisfied on the Closing Date as follows:

(iv) A certified cheque, bank draft or other form of immediately available funds of the Corporation of an amount equal to the Remaining Insurance Proceeds after first deducting the amount of all reasonable costs and expenses incurred in connection with collecting such insurance proceeds; and

(v) If and as applicable, a Promissory Note of each of the Survivors for its Proportionate Share of the balance of the purchase price payable for the Deceased's Shares not otherwise acquired by the Corporation under this subsection 11.2(v), together with interest thereon at the Prime Rate [*OPTIONAL: plus* _________%] per annum repayable in [*number*] consecutive monthly instalments of principal, plus interest on the principal balance then outstanding. The first instalment will be due and payable [*number*] month after the Closing Date.

11.3) Capital Dividend Account

(a) The Corporation and the Survivors shall do all things and execute all documents and elections so that the purchase price payable by the Corporation in accordance with subsection 11.2(b), to the greatest extent possible, be payable out of the Corporation's capital dividend account (as defined in the Tax Act) (the "**CDA**"), including without limitation, making, executing and filing with the appropriate taxation authority the election(s) required under subsection 83(2) of the Tax Act, and the applicable provisions of any similar legislation, in prescribed form and within the prescribed time to give effect to the provisions of this Section. Each Survivor hereby irrevocably authorizes and directs the Corporation to pay such capital dividend to the Deceased and/or the Deceased's Other Entities, as applicable, to the extent required to satisfy the payment of such amount.

OR

Option 2: Corporate-Owned Insurance that is distributed by the Corporation to the surviving shareholders and the surviving shareholders purchase the shares of the deceased

11.4)   Insurance

(a)   The Corporation shall, to the extent that it is reasonably obtainable, acquire and maintain insurance on the life of each of [*S1, S4, P1 and P2*] in amounts of not less than $[*dollar amount*] and, upon such insurance being acquired, the particulars of such insurance shall be inserted in Schedule __________ and shall be initialled by [*S1, S4, P1 and P2*].

[*NOTE: Due to the possibility of the increasing cash surrender value of the insurance policy, the Corporation being the owner of the policy may taint the capital gains exemption that may have otherwise been available due to the "90/ 10" rule (will no longer be a "qualified small business corporation"). In addition, if insurance policy is attributed an "ACB" within the meaning of the Tax Act in relation to insurance policies, then the CDA may be ground down, and the distribution of the insurance proceeds would not be tax free. Tax advisor for the Corporation to determine if insurance policy should be owned by related corporation with the Corporation as beneficiary*].

(b)   The Corporation will be the owner and beneficiary of each policy and will, at all times, keep such insurance policies in good standing and pay all premiums and other charges when the same become due and payable. The Corporation shall not deal in any manner with such policies and, without limiting the generality of the foregoing, shall not assign, transfer, modify, impair any rights or values of, dispose of, surrender, borrow upon or in any way encumber such policies, except in accordance with a written agreement among [*all of the Parties hereto/Shareholders who in the aggregate hold at least* __________ *% of the issued and outstanding Shares*].

(c)   The Shareholders and the Principals will use their best efforts to permit the Corporation to obtain and maintain such life insurance, including without limitation attending for physical examinations, answering such questions as may be reasonable necessary and executing consents to the placing of such insurance coverage.

(d)   On any default in payment of the premium or other charges on the due date thereof, the individual Shareholder and/or corporate Shareholder whose Principal's life is insured under such policy may pay the same on behalf of the Corporation for as long as such default continues, which amount will constitute a Shareholder Loan by such Shareholder.

(e)   The Shareholders will determine Fair Market Value of each insurance policy on execution of this Agreement and within [*number of days*] Business Days following receipt of [*OPTIONAL: audited*] financial statements for each fiscal year of the Corporation and will record such determination on Schedule __________ or an original duplicate thereof. If the Shareholders do not determine Fair Market Value upon the expiry of such [*number of days*] Business Days and within [*number of days*] Business Days thereafter, the Corporation's [*auditors accountants*] will determine Fair Market Value for life insurance purposes only and Section 7.1 will not apply to this Section.

11.5) **Death of a Shareholder or Principal**

(a) Upon the death of [any individual Shareholder/Principal/any individual Shareholder and Principal]/[input names of particular shareholder(s) and or principal(s)] (the "**Deceased**"), such Shareholder and/or any Shareholder for which the Deceased was a Principal (the "**Deceased's Other Entities**") will sell, and the other Shareholders (the "**Survivors**") will purchase, as nearly as may be in the Proportionate Share as among the Survivors, all Shares owned and/or Controlled by the Deceased and the Deceased's Other Entities (collectively, the "Deceased's Shares").

(b) The purchase price for the Deceased's Shares shall be the greater of: (i) the Fair Market Value of the Deceased's Shares as at the moment immediately before the death of the Deceased; and (ii) the insurance proceeds received by the Corporation in relation to the insurance policy on the life of the Deceased after deducting an amount equal to the Shareholder's Loan which must be repaid by the Corporation and purchased by the Survivors, as applicable, in accordance with Section __________ above (the "**Remaining Insurance Proceeds**").

(c) The Closing Date will be the 10th Business Day following the latest of: (i) if applicable, receipt of necessary governmental releases required to effect a valid transfer of the Deceased's Shares (and the Parties agree to use their best efforts to obtain such releases); (ii) determination of the Fair Market Value; and (iii) the Corporation's receipt of the insurance proceeds on the life of the Deceased.

(d) The purchase price will be paid and satisfied on the Closing Date as follows:

(i) A promissory note ("**Note No. 1**") of each Survivor due on demand in an amount (plus interest thereon at the Prime Rate [*OPTIONAL: plus __________% per annum*]), equal to the lesser of:

(A) each Survivor's Proportionate Share as among the Survivors of the Remaining Insurance Proceeds after first deducting the amount of all reasonable costs and expenses incurred in connection with collecting such insurance proceeds; and

(B) the purchase price payable by each Survivor; and

(ii) A Promissory Note ("**Note No. 2**") of each Survivor (and/or the Corporation in accordance with Section _________ in an amount equal to the balance of the purchase price payable by each Survivor, if any, together with interest thereon at the Prime Rate [*OPTIONAL: plus* _________%
per annum] repayable in _________ consecutive [*monthly*] instalments of principal, plus interest on the principal balance then outstanding. The first instalment will be due and payable [*number*] month after the Closing Date.

(e) If the aggregate amount of Notes No. 1 is insufficient to purchase all the Deceased's Shares, that number of Shares not purchasable by means of Notes No. 1 may, at the option of the Survivors evidenced by [*a Special/an Ordinary*] resolution (excluding the Deceased and/or the Deceased's Other Entities) be purchased for cancellation by the Corporation.

11.6)   Capital Dividend Account

(a) The Corporation and the Survivors shall do all things and execute all documents and elections so that the purchase price payable by the Survivors in accordance with subsection _________, to the greatest extent possible, be payable out of the Corporation's capital dividend account (as defined in the Tax Act) (the "**CDA**"), including without limitation, making, executing and filing with the appropriate taxation authority the election(s) required under subsection 83(2) of the Tax Act, and the applicable provisions of any similar legislation, in prescribed form and within the prescribed time to give effect to the provisions of this Section. Each Survivor hereby irrevocably authorizes and directs the Corporation to pay such capital dividend to the Deceased and/or the Deceased's Other Entities, as applicable, to the extent required to satisfy the payment of such amount.

OR

Option 3: Each Shareholder Purchases Life Insurance On The Other Shareholders And Uses The Proceeds To Purchase The Shares Of The Deceased

11.7) **Insurance**

(a) In order to ensure that sufficient funds will be available for the purposes of each of the Shareholders acknowledges that they have obtained insurance on the life of each of [*the other individual Shareholders and each of the Principals (other than on the life of the Principal which controls such Shareholder)*] from a certain insurance company or companies and in certain amounts of not less than $[*dollar amount*], all as more particularly set out in Schedule ___________.

(b) Each of the Shareholders shall maintain in good standing at all times the insurance policy or policies on the life of the others of which it is the owner and shall not deal in any manner with such policy or policies and, without limiting the generality of the foregoing, shall not assign, transfer, dispose of, surrender, borrow upon or in any way encumber such policy or policies.

11.8) **Death of a Shareholder or Principal**

(a) Upon the death of [any individual Shareholder/Principal/any individual Shareholder and Principal/[input names of particular shareholder(s) and or principal(s)] (the "**Deceased**"), such Shareholder and/or any Shareholder for which the Deceased was a Principal (the "**Deceased's Other Entities**") will sell, and the other Shareholders (the "**Survivors**") will purchase, as nearly as may be in the Proportionate Share as among the Survivors, all Shares owned and/or Controlled by the Deceased and the Deceased's Other Entities (collectively, the "**Deceased's Shares**").

(b) The purchase price for the Deceased's Shares shall be the Fair Market Value of the Deceased's Shares as at the moment immediately before the death of the Deceased.

(c) The Closing Date will be the 10th Business Day following the latest of: (i) if applicable, receipt of necessary governmental releases required to effect a valid transfer of the Deceased's Shares (and the Parties agree to use their best efforts to obtain such releases); and (ii) determination of the Fair Market Value.

(d) The purchase price will be paid and satisfied on the Closing Date by a Promissory Note of each Survivor (and/or the Corporation in accordance with Section ___________ in an amount equal to purchase price payable by each Survivor, together with interest thereon at the Prime Rate [*OPTIONAL: plus ___________% per annum*] repayable in ___________ consecutive [*monthly*] instalments of principal, plus interest on the principal balance then outstanding. The first instalment will be due and payable [*number*] month after the Closing Date.

(e) If the aggregate amount of the Promissory Notes is insufficient to purchase all the Deceased's Shares, that number of Shares not purchasable by means of such Promissory Notes may, at the option of the Survivors evidenced by [*a Special/an Ordinary*] Resolution (excluding the Deceased and/or the Deceased's Other Entities), be purchased for cancellation by the Corporation.

Index

About the Author

As a practising lawyer for over sixty years, Barry Lipson has represented companies of varying sizes in corporate, trust, and real estate matters in both Canada and the United States and has acted as the lead lawyer on a number of the country's major transactions.

He is widely published in both corporate and real estate-related subjects. He is the author of *The Art of the Real Estate Deal*, now in its fourth edition, and *The Art of Drafting the Commercial Contract*, which was published in 2017 and is updated annually. He is the editor of *The Controlling Mind — Exercising Legal Control*.

His writings and his lectures have been well-received by lawyers, accountants, and other professionals engaged in the small- and medium-market sector of mergers and acquisitions.